W9-CLI-375

AMERICAN SOCIAL WELFARE POLICY

◆ ◆ ◆ ◆ ◆ ◆ ◆ ◆

A PLURALIST APPROACH

THIRD EDITION

Howard Jacob Karger
University of Houston

David Stoesz
Virginia Commonwealth University

◆ ◆ ◆

With a Chapter on the American Welfare State
in International Perspective

by James Midgley

An imprint of Addison Wesley Longman, Inc.

New York • Reading, Massachusetts • Menlo Park, California • Harlow, England
Don Mills, Ontario • Sydney • Mexico City • Madrid • Amsterdam

For Marc, Darcy and Tim

Editor-in-Chief: Priscilla McGeehon
Acquistions Editor: Janice E. Wiggins
Marketing Manager: Wendy Albert
Supplements Editor: Tom Kulesa
Project Coordination and Text Design: Electronic Publishing Services Inc.
Cover Designer: Kay Petronio
Art Studio: Electronic Publishing Services Inc.
Full Service Production Manager: Valerie Zaborski
Manufacturing Manager: Hilda Koparanian
Electronic Page Makeup: Electronic Publishing Services Inc.
Printer and Binder: **R. R. Donnelley & Sons Company**
Cover Printer: Coral Graphics

Library of Congress Cataloging-in-Publication Data

Karger, Howard Jacob, 1948–
American social welfare policy : a pluralistic approach / Howard Jacob Karger, David Stoesz. — [3rd ed.]
p. cm.
"With a chapter on the American welfare state in international perspective by James Midgley."
Includes bibliographical references and index.
ISBN 0-8013-1702-9
1. Public welfare—United States. 2. United States—Social policy. 3. Welfare state. I. Stoesz, David. II. Title.
HV95.K354 1997
361.973—dc21 97-13471
CIP

ISBN 0-8013-1702-9
5678910—RRD—00

CONTENTS

PREFACE

As we finish the third edition of *American Social Welfare Policy*, we realize that in each edition we have faced vastly different challenges. In the first edition, the challenge was to chronicle and analyze the patchwork quilt of American social welfare policies and programs, while at the same time trying to make sense of them. In effect, we were challenged with organizing the American welfare state into a coherent framework that made it understandable. In the second edition, we were challenged with analyzing the welfare state after 12 consecutive years of Republican control of the White House. The verdict: America's welfare state remained standing, if a little bruised and battered.

This final challenge is perhaps the most difficult. In this edition we have had to confront a very different welfare state. Long the whipping boy for Republicans and conservative Democrats, the public assistance portion of the welfare state was no longer being battered but was being systematically deconstructed at its roots. Because of the importance of the elderly vote and the supposedly inviolate nature of the social insurances (e.g., Social Security and Medicare), they have emerged from the last four years relatively unscathed. Arguably, public assistance programs have been sacrificed in order to protect the social insurances. But since the social insurances account for the majority of welfare state expenditures, it remains to be seen whether they, too, will be "reformed" under a conservative One-hundred-fifth Congress and the second term of the Clinton presidency. Nevertheless, this is a welfare state that Ronald Reagan and the conservative think tanks had only dreamed about. They dreamed of a welfare state that devolved virtually all responsibility for public assistance from the federal to the state level through block grants, a welfare state that overturned more than 30 years of precedent and disentitled the nation's poor from its claim to public assistance. Remarkably, it took a centrist Democrat to bring to fruition the "Reagan Revolution." In the midst of the euphoria surrounding the election of the first Democratic president in 12 years, we could not have guessed in late 1992 that the welfare state would change more in the past 4 years than in the preceding 60 years.

In 1994, America elected the Republican One-hundred-fourth Congress. Far to the right of any Congress in recent memory, this body proceeded to craft a social agenda that would have been unimaginable even in the halcyon days of the Reagan administration. Affirmative action and other race- and gender-based policies were under attack. Gay and lesbian rights received a serious blow when Congress passed the Defense of Marriage Act, effectively outlawing homosexual marriages. The rapid and unbridled growth of for-profit human-service corporations was nothing short of stunning. The Aid to Families to Dependent Children (AFDC) program was replaced by the Temporary Assistance to Needy Families (TANF), a program that rescinded the legal entitlement to public assistance received by the poor since the 1935 Social Security Act. TANF also used capped funding and block grants to devolve the responsibility for administering public welfare to the states. This occurred despite the fact that the 1935 Social Security Act federalized public welfare precisely because the states were unable to mount a viable public welfare system. Despite evidence to the contrary, the American public was led to believe that today the states are capable of running innovative and fair public welfare systems.

Privatization and block grants were everywhere by 1996. At the time of this writing, the state of Texas was actively recruiting bids from private companies to run its public welfare system. Even the Department of Housing and Urban Development had plans to devolve federal responsibility for public housing to the states through block grants All of these bills and policies were either signed, endorsed, or condoned by the first Democratic president in 12 years. Not surprisingly, by 1996 traditional welfare liberals stood in stunned silence, too numbed by the events of the past two years to even mount a counteroffensive.

When institutional practices are so out of line with human requirements, momentum builds to change social programs. This seems to have taken two forms in relation to social welfare in the United States. On the one hand, many human-service professionals are leaving the traditional settings of welfare practice—the voluntary and governmental sectors—in favor of new settings—the corporate sector and private practice. On the other hand, recent welfare reform measures have penalized disenfranchised populations—women, racial minorities, the aged, children, the handicapped, and immigrants—who have been a traditional concern of welfare professionals. As a result, much of what we understand to be social welfare in America is in flux; yet welfare professionals are exerting little influence in redefining this important social institution.

The failure of welfare professionals to act effectively in the area of social welfare policy is troubling. It is difficult to imagine changes in health policy or legal policy that did not involve the collaboration of physicians or attorneys. Yet, social workers were not consulted in the crafting of the Personal Responsibility and Work Act of 1996, the most comprehensive welfare reform bill in 35 years. Social workers have not played a prominent role in welfare policy for some time. Such was not always the case. Mary Richmond proved instrumental in the Charity Organization Society movement; Jane Addams became a heroine through her work in the settlement movement; and Harry Hopkins championed programs pioneered by the New Deal. More recently, Wilbur Cohen engineered important parts of the programs that comprised the War on Poverty. But few social workers of national prominence have emerged since the Great Society programs of the 1960s.

Fortunately, this omission is being addressed, albeit in a somewhat haphazard fashion. The National Association of Social Workers (NASW) has mobilized a political action committee. In 1984, Barbara Mikulski, a social worker from Maryland, was elected to the United States Senate joining Ron Dellums, a representative from California, and "Ed" Towns, a representative from New York, as the only members of Congress who are social workers. It remains to be seen whether the large mass of welfare professionals will become accustomed to thinking about social welfare policy. We hope so. This book reflects our belief that social welfare policy has an immediate and profound effect on the work of welfare professionals, and our conviction is that welfare programs could be made more humane and better respond to the needs of the people they serve if these professionals were more actively engaged in setting social policy.

OUR APPROACH

In trying to bridge this gap, we have adopted a "pluralist approach" to social welfare policy. In doing so, we have organized the book around the primary sectors that have evolved in American social welfare: the **voluntary sector,** the **governmental sector,** and, more recently, both the **corporate sector** and **private practice.** These sectors have addressed the problems that presented themselves at different periods in our national life. Today, these sectors of American social welfare coexist, reflecting a diversity that is as characteristic of American pluralism as they are sometimes maddening to the student of welfare policy analysis.

The rationale for our approach is straightforward. First, social welfare encompasses, in the American experience, a complicated arrangement of policies and programs. A pluralist approach helps sort out the major institutional actors and introduces a measure of order to what might otherwise appear to be institutional anarchy. Second, many welfare professionals (and, for that matter, nonprofessionals) begin their careers in agencies of the voluntary sector. Unfortunately, these agencies are not always given the credit they deserve. In our judgment, the voluntary sector is an integral component of social welfare in the United States, even if it relates to policy with a small *p*. Our emphasis on the voluntary sector is based on the belief that as public policy shifts, more of the welfare burden will be transferred from the government to the private sector. Third, a proprietary, corporate sector has rapidly emerged during the last two decades, providing a substantial volume of services and a corresponding number of employment opportunities for human-service professionals. Failure to recognize the importance of this sector is tantamount to ignoring what is probably the most important development in social welfare since the War on Poverty and possibly even since the New Deal. Finally, many social workers have found private practice, independent of the organizational restraints associated with the voluntary, governmental, and corporate sectors, an attractive method of service delivery. The popularity of private practice among human-service professionals justifies its inclusion in any discussion of social welfare policy. Through an examination of these sectors we hope to acquaint students with the central structures and processes now shaping American social welfare.

ORGANIZATION

To facilitate the comprehension of material, we have used **Part One** to focus on the basic concepts underlying social policy analysis. This segment also includes a historical survey of social welfare in the United States and a discussion of the values, social forces, and theoretical assumptions that affect the creation, operation, and implementation of social policies. In much of this we have borrowed heavily from economics as well as from political and social theory. Because of the disparity between the intentions of policymakers and the program realities facing welfare professionals, we have examined in a critical manner the legislative, judicial, and administrative processes that influence the design and implementation of social welfare policy. A special focus is placed on the interactional effects of social policies and programs on such vulnerable groups as the aged, minorities, women, homosexuals, and the poor, as well as on children and families. This segment of the book also provides students with a framework for understanding the complex nature of American social welfare. Throughout the book, essential social policy terms are referenced to a **glossary** located at the end of the book. With the basic conceptual tools at hand, students will find the descriptive material of **Parts Two** and **Three,** dealing with voluntary, governmental, corporate, and private practice, less overwhelming. Familiarity with these analytic concepts will also help students to better understand the preliminary welfare reform proposals we make in Chapter 19. Finally, we have included a chapter on the American welfare state in international perspective. Written by James Midgley, a well-known authority in the field of international social policy and the dean of the University of California-Berkeley's School of Social Work, this chapter was added in the recognition that the American welfare state exists within a continuum of other welfare states. Moreover, this chapter is an acknowledgment that we can learn from the experiences, successes, and mistakes of other nations. We wish to thank Dean Midgley for taking his valuable time to write a chapter for this book.

NEW EDITION FEATURES

Features of the third edition include:

- A thorough update of material to reflect the newest welfare reforms passed by Congress and signed into law by President Clinton.
- Complete analysis of the first term of the Clinton administration.
- A new and timely chapter on criminal justice that examines how the criminal justice system impacts American social welfare.

- An Internet Supplement. ***American Social Welfare Policy, 3/e,*** is the only social policy text on the market that features a user friendly guide to the basics of using the Internet for social policy research. This handy guide provides students with the basics of how to use the Internet and contains a comprehensive list of policy related web sites, listserv groups, and a glossary of Internet terms. From the "Internet-phobic" student to the more advanced Internet user, this guide has something for everyone.

The purpose of the supplement is not to dazzle students with computer technology, but to impress upon them the important contribution that the Internet can make to policy research. In fact, much of the information for this third edition was gleaned from a variety of Internet sources, including the vast array of federal documents now available on the Net. Among other things, the Internet can dramatically shorten the time between the release of information and the time it takes to access it. Although not the only source for policy information, the Internet remains an important vehicle for the policy student to master. The Internet supplement is free to students who purchase new copies of the text. Please visit our website at **http:\\longman.awl.com.** We have provided an index of on-line social policy resources for this text that is available through the Social Work area in the Academic Center.

A GOOD BALANCE

We have also tried to balance theory with program detail. However, we have omitted some of the details of program specifications that appear in other treatments of welfare policy. In doing so, we are less concerned with program detail—which practitioners become acquainted with during their first day on the job—than we are with defining the themes around which welfare policy is constructed. Given political developments since the mid–1970s, we believe that this corrects an error on the part of many liberal analysts. Specifically, while preoccupied with program intricacies, many welfare professionals have found, much to their chagrin, that ideologies of the political Right have in the past commanded public attention. Many Democrats and Republicans who have attained high public office have used these ideologies effectively to alter the rules of the game in the process executing punishing cuts in social programs. If welfare professionals are to redirect social welfare policy to liberal goals, they will have to abandon questions of program "puzzle solving" temporarily and return to defining the paradigm of social programs.[1] In other words, social workers need to play more than the notes—they also need to play the music.

Social work students often ask why they are required to study social policy. Many have entered social work to help people, and thus they believe their sole concern is with the provision of direct services. As experienced social workers, we recognize the distance between social welfare policy and direct practice, and we have come to appreciate the difficulties that clients and practitioners often encounter because of social welfare policy. Accordingly, we insist that direct service is inextricably linked to policy. Clients exist in a given society and are continually influenced by the larger social forces affecting that society. The more disenfranchised the clients, the more exposed they are to the maelstrom of social forces swirling about them. Social workers help clients not only by working with them individually but by protecting the collective interests of vulnerable populations—children, the aged, racial and ethnic minorities, the handicapped, and the poor, among others. There are many ways of helping; social workers must try to learn them all.

One of our major goals in writing this book was to encourage students to think critically about social policy. We hope that students and instructors will critique and even argue about the ideas they find here. For us, that is part of the joy of policy analysis. Unfortunately, the student who studies policy analysis will soon find that few things are carved in stone and that there are many gray areas. Although sometimes frustrating, these gray areas can provide an exciting challenge. Because social policy is not rigid in its methods, it demands creative ideas and solutions. The very openness of policy requires that each student come up with his or her own answers for the major social policy questions of our times.

American Social Welfare Policy is the product of two authors, both of the same mind. Over the years we have collaborated on so many projects that it is sometimes unclear who originated what. The interaction that has led us this far is what scholarship is all about, and we have found it immensely gratifying. There is a convention in publishing about junior and senior authors. In this regard, the listing of the authors on the title page and cover is alphabetical. Both authors contributed equally, and neither was more senior than the other in the preparation of this book.

ACKNOWLEDGMENTS FOR THE FIRST EDITION

We offer special thanks to Steve McMurty and Thomas Watts for their thorough and systematic critique of the original manuscript of the first edition. Thanks also to Larry Litterst, a good friend and a fine economist. His thorough critique of economic principles helped strengthen the book, especially in areas where his advice was heeded. Our deep appreciation goes to Stephen J. Boland, computer wizard; Paul Michaelewicz, data cruncher; Debbie Dycaico, "sleuth" reader; and Lucinda Roginske and Suzanne Cooper, table and glossary compilers, for their assistance in assembling technical materials. We also extend our appreciation to Michael Kelly for his generosity in sharing high tech equipment and to Karen Stout, Mary Ann Reitmeir, Joanne Mermelstein, Paul Sundet, and Roland Meinert, as well as other people too numerous to mention. To our associates at policyAmerica, a nonprofit research group established in 1985 to develop innovations in social welfare policy, we owe a special thanks. This band of intellectual guerrillas not only critiqued parts of the first edition but also convinced us that thinking about social welfare policy and dancing to zydeco music were not mutually exclusive.

We also extend our deep-felt appreciation to our colleagues at Longman. As former senior editor, David Estrin showed his confidence in us by accepting the idea for this book on principle and without formalities. The manner in which he directed this publication was a model for editorial coordination. Victoria Mifsud, former editorial assistant, helped keep the book on track by efficiently handling our requests and the details involved in the preparation of the manuscript.

ACKNOWLEDGMENTS FOR THE SECOND EDITION

For the second edition we owe special thanks to David Shapiro, senior editor; Susan Alkana, development editor; Owen Lancer, editorial assistant; and Linda Witzling, production editor, for putting this book on the fast track to and through production. Their shepherding of the second edition allowed us to be more contemporary and more relevant than is usually possible in a textbook. We also owe thanks to the reviewers who helped us to fashion a better book through their ideas and suggestions. These reviewers include: Patrick Leung, University of Houston; Thomas D. Watts, University of Texas at Arlington; Sally Alonzo Bell, Azusa Pacific University; Catherine Havens, University of Connecticut; Sharon M. Keigher, University of Wisconsin-Milwaukee; Nancy Gewirtz, Rhode Island College; Douglas K. Chung, Grand Valley State College; Jean Howard, Illinois State University; Doman Lum, California State University-Sacramento; and Barbara Kail, University of Texas at Arlington.

A warm thanks to Suzanne Tidwell for help in library research.

ACKNOWLEDGMENTS FOR THE THIRD EDITION

In the third edition, we would like to thank the people at Longman for not forgetting about our book despite the difficult corporate transitions that went on in the last four years. Thanks also to Janice E. Wiggins for keeping the book on track and for moving up the production schedule. Very special thanks to the reviewers for the third edition: Sally Alonzo Bell, Asuza Pacific University; Michel A. Coconis, University of Kentucky; Richard Hoefer, University of Texas, Arlington; Philip Jackson, University of Cincinnati; Deborah Jacobs, Shippensburg University; Esther Jones Langston, University of Nevada, Las Vegas; Kathleeen McInnis-Dittrich, Boston

College; and David F. Metzger, Indiana University. The students who sat through our policy classes also deserve special credit for their patience, insight, and ideas.

Thanks to Suzanne Boyd and William Beverly for their diligence in exploring the nonprofit and for-profit sectors, and Linda Naiditch for her assistance regarding the United Way.

D. S.
Richmond, VA
December 12, 1996

Thanks to Carolyn Brooks for baby-sitting the doctoral program while I was totally engrossed in writing this book. Also to Phil D'Amato for finding important materials that sped along the writing. A special thanks to Paul Raffoul who patiently listened to complaining and yet still had enough resilience left to carefully review the Internet supplement. His review was indispensable. Thanks to John Stroehlein for helping to keep me together during the difficult process of writing this third edition. A special thanks to Saul and Aaron for putting up with a very distracted father. Heartfelt thanks to Joanne Levine, my partner, colleague, friend, and the best critic I know. It is hard to imagine how I would have made it through this book without her support, patience, and critical insight.

H. J. K.
Houston, Texas
December 12, 1996

NOTE

1. See Thomas Kuhn, *The Structure of Scientific Revolutions* (Chicago: University of Chicago Press, 1956).

PART ONE

◆ ◆ ◆ ◆ ◆ ◆ ◆ ◆ ◆

American Social Welfare Policy

CHAPTER 1

Social Policy and the American Welfare State

This chapter provides an overview of the American welfare state. In particular, it examines various definitions of social welfare policy, the relationship between social policy and social problems, and the values and ideologies that drive American social welfare. In addition, the chapter examines the effects of ideology on the U.S. welfare state, including the important role played by conservatism and liberalism (and their variations) in shaping welfare policy. As part of examining the influence of ideology on social welfare, the chapter explores the political economy of American welfare, including the role played by the Keynesians, free market economics, socialism, and communitarianism, among others. Lastly, the chapter examines the place of pluralism in American social welfare policy, particularly the influence of established interests in shaping welfare policy.

American social welfare is in transition. Since the Social Security Act of 1935, advocates of the unfortunate have held that federal social programs were the best way to help the disadvantaged. Now, after a half-century of experimentation with the "welfare state," a discernible shift has occurred. The conservatism of American culture—so evident in the Reagan, the Bush, and even the Clinton presidencies—has left private institutions to shoulder more of the welfare burden. At the same time, many social programs were reduced or eliminated as federal and state governments struggled to prop up shaky budgets. For proponents of social justice, the suggestion that the private sector should assume more responsibility for welfare represents a retreat from hard-won governmental social legislation that for many years has provided essential benefits to millions of Americans. Justifiably, these groups fear the loss of basic goods and services during the transition in American social welfare.

A pluralistic mix of private and public services is an essential feature of American social welfare. Similar to other institutions, such as education, private institutions in social welfare coexist alongside those of the public sector. American social welfare has a noble tradition of voluntary groups of citizens taking the initiative to solve local problems. Today, private voluntary groups provide important services to patients with acquired immune deficiency syndrome (AIDS), the homeless, and refugees. Although voluntary activities represent the historical contribution by the private sector to American social welfare, a more recent development within the private sector raises fundamental questions for the future provision of social services.

Social welfare has become big business. During the last 25 years the number of human service corporations—for-profit firms providing social welfare through the marketplace—has increased dramatically. Human service corporations are prominent in long-term nursing care, health maintenance, child day care, psychiatric and substance abuse services, even corrections. For many welfare professionals, this proprietary provision of social services is troubling because it occurs at a time when government has reduced its commitment to social programs. Yet, human service corporations are likely to be prominent players in the shaping of the nation's social welfare policies. As long as American culture is open, democratic, and capitalistic, groups will be free to establish social welfare services in the private sector, both as nonprofit agencies and as for-profit corporations.

The pluralism of American social welfare, in which the voluntary, governmental, and corporate sectors coexist, poses important questions for social welfare policy. To what extent can voluntary groups assume responsibility for public welfare when their fiscal resources are limited? For which groups, if any, should government divest itself of responsibility? Can human service corporations be induced to care for poor and multiproblem clients while continuing to generate profits? Equally important, how can welfare professionals shape coherent social welfare policies given the inherent fragmentation in such pluralism? Clearly, the answers to these questions have much to say about how social welfare programs are perceived by human service professionals, their clients, and the taxpayers who continue to subsidize social programs.

The multitude of questions posed by the transition of American social welfare is in itself daunting. Indeed, the interaction of ideological, political, social, and economic factors has exacerbated the problem to the extent that the idea of "the welfare mess" has become a fixture in contemporary American folklore. Yet, past advocates of social justice such as Jane Addams, Whitney Young, Jr., and Wilbur Cohen, to name a few, interpreted the inadequacy of social provision and the confusion of their times as an opportunity to further social justice. It remains for another generation of welfare professionals to demonstrate the same imagination, perseverance, and courage to advance social welfare in the years ahead. Those accepting this challenge will need to be familiar with the various meanings of social welfare policy, differing political and economic explanations relating to social welfare, and the various interest groups that have emerged within the American social welfare system.

DEFINITIONS OF SOCIAL WELFARE POLICY

The English social scientist Richard Titmuss has defined *social services* as "a series of collective interventions that contribute to the general welfare by assigning claims from one set of people who are said to produce or earn the national income to another set of people who may merit compassion and charity."[1] Whether it is the product of governmental, voluntary, or corporate institutions, welfare policy is concerned with allocating goods, services, and opportunities in order to enhance social functioning.

Social welfare policy regulates the provision of benefits to people for the purpose of meeting basic life needs, such as employment, income, food, housing, health care, and relationships.[2] As such, it is a subset of social policy, which can be defined as the formal and consistent ordering of human affairs. Beyond this, social welfare policy is influenced to a large extent by the context in which benefits are provided. For example, social welfare policy is often associated with legislatively mandated governmental programs, such as the former Aid to Families with Dependent Children (AFDC). In the AFDC program, social welfare policy consisted of the rules by which the federal and state governments apportioned cash benefits to an economically disadvantaged population, poor families. AFDC benefits were derived from general revenues generated by government, often taxes on citizens who were better off. But this is a simplification of benefits provided to those deemed needy. Benefits provided through governmental social welfare policy include cash, but also noncash or in-kind benefits, including the personal social services.[3] Cash benefits can be further divided into social insurance and public assistance grants.

In-kind benefits (benefits provided as proxies for cash) include a variety of benefits such as food stamps, Medicaid, housing vouchers, Women, Infants, and Children (WIC) coupons, and low-income energy assistance. Personal social services are designed to enhance relationships among people as well as institutions, such as individual, family, and mental health treatment, child welfare services, rehabilitation counseling, and so forth. While complicated, this social welfare policy classification reflects a common theme, namely, the redistribution of resources from those who are better-off to those who are comparatively disadvantaged. This redistributional aspect of social welfare policy is generally accepted by those who view social welfare as a legitimate function of the State. Governmental social welfare policy is often referred to as "public" policy because it is the result of decisions reached through a process that involves a legislature that is representative of the entire population.

But social welfare is also provided by entities that are nongovernmental, in which case social welfare policy is not a manifestation of public policy but, rather, of "private" policy. For example, a nonprofit agency that has only limited resources but is inundated by a high demand for its services may establish a waiting list as agency policy. As other agencies in similar circumstances adopt the same strategy for rationing services, clients begin to pile up on waiting lists. Eventually, some clients are denied services because private agencies have established waiting lists. In this case, the policies of independent private agencies have a significant effect on the welfare of clients. Or consider the practice of "dumping," a policy of private health care providers by which uninsured patients are abruptly transferred to public hospitals even though they are suffering from traumatic injuries. In some instances, patients have died as a result of a policy that is essentially a private social welfare policy.

Because American social welfare has been shaped to a great extent by policies of the government and nonprofit agencies, a good deal of confusion has arisen about the role of for-profit firms that provide social services. Traditionally, the distinction between the public and private sectors was marked by the boundary between governmental and nonprofit agencies. However, for-profit firms are also private in that they are nongovernmental entities; but they differ from the traditional private voluntary agencies, which are run on a not-for-profit basis. Consequently, it is important to distinguish within private social welfare between policies of for-profit organizations and policies of nonprofit organizations. A logical way to redraw the social welfare map is to adopt the following usage: Governmental social welfare policy refers to decisions established by the State; voluntary social welfare policy refers to decisions reached by nonprofit agencies; and corporate social welfare policy refers to decisions made by for-profit firms.

SOCIAL PROBLEMS AND SOCIAL WELFARE POLICY

Social welfare policy is often developed as a response to social problems. The relationship between social problems and social welfare policy is, however, not simple, and not all social problems generate social welfare policies. In other instances, social welfare policies exist but are funded at such low levels that they are ineffectual. The Child Abuse Prevention and Treatment Act of 1974, for example, introduced standards that should have helped rectify the problem of child abuse, yet underbudgeting left Child Protective Service (CPS) workers in a Catch-22 situation. The act required CPS workers to investigate complaints of child abuse shortly after receiving them, yet agencies had inadequate staff resources to deal with the skyrocketing number of complaints. Caught in a resources crunch, CPS workers were unable to properly investigate allegations of abuse, and thus many children were seriously injured or died as a result.

In still other instances, social welfare policies aggravate social problems. For decades, states authorized mental hospitals to warehouse the mentally ill, a practice that further handicapped mental patients. To replace state mental hospitals, the federal Community Mental Health Centers (CMHC) Act of 1963 authorized the creation of community-based facilities. This reform proved short-lived and was subverted by a lack of support for CMHCs. Now, with a substantial number of the homeless having been hospitalized for past mental illness, the CMHC Act is associated with a worsening of care for the seriously mentally ill. Thus, what was once seen as mental health reform seems actually to have exacerbated a social problem.

As the relationship between social problems and social welfare policy suggests, social welfare is not merely an expression of social altruism; it contributes to the maintenance and survival of society. In this respect, social welfare policy can be instrumental in helping to hold together a society that tends to fracture along social, political, and economic stress lines. Social welfare policy can be useful in enforcing social control, especially as a proxy for other coercive forms of societal control, such as law enforcement and the courts.[4] In having their minimum basic needs provided, the disadvantaged are less inclined to revolt against the unequal distribution of resources. A population that has nothing to lose is highly volatile, as the 1992 Los Angeles riots demonstrated. Social welfare policies also subsidize the marketplace. Public social welfare benefits often supplement wages that are so low that people cannot survive on them alone. In this instance, social welfare policies supplement wages in effect subsidizing employers who would otherwise have to their raise wages. Social welfare also supports important industries, such as agriculture, housing, and health care. Indeed, if social welfare benefits were eliminated, a substantial segment of American business would collapse. In addition, social welfare redistributes income from one segment of the population to another, allowing the disadvantaged essential income and services. Without such social benefits, fundamental questions would arise about the moral, spiritual, and ethical quality of American society. Thus, social welfare policies relieve the social and economic dislocations caused by the uneven nature of economic development. Finally, social welfare policies are a means for rectifying past injustices. For example, affirmative action was intended to remedy historical racist and sexist practices that have denied African Americans and women access to economic opportunities and positions of power.

Social work practice is largely driven by social policies, which dictate how the work is done, with whom, for how much, and toward what ends. For example, a social worker employed in a public mental health center may have a caseload of well over 200 clients. Given that caseload, it is unlikely that this worker can engage in any kind of sustained psychotherapeutic intervention with clients, caseload constraints permitting little more than superficial case tracking. Or consider the JOBS (Jobs Opportunities and Basic Skills) worker required to find employment for mothers on public assistance who are about to lose benefits due to the imposition of time limits but who are unlikely to find adequate work because of high unemployment in the area. What are child welfare workers to do when demand for protective services exceeds funding for staff positions and workers begin to cut corners in order to respond to the most urgent cases, eventually leading to injuries or death of youngsters? In each of these instances, social, ideological, and economic factors contribute to policies that determine the ability of the social worker and the agency to accomplish their mission.

Since 1980, an ideological preference among policymakers that social service needs should be met in the private marketplace has resulted in less funding for public agencies. Thus, a conservative emphasis on cutting taxes has lead to reductions in public revenues, which in turn, has been translated into reductions for social programs. As a result of diminishing revenues, public agencies take predictable measures to adjust, including reductions in the number of qualified staff, administrators beseeching staff to do more with less, the introduction of short-term or group interventions designed to move more clients off the rolls (thereby allowing more new intakes and a shorter waiting list), reducing pay or benefits for professional staff—all of which conspire to shape an agency geared to managing clients and their demands rather than helping them in any real sense. Thus, what a trained social worker is able to accomplish depends, in part, on the available resources within the agency.

Although this may not be obvious at first glance, the same is true for many social workers in private practice who depend on managed care plans for reimbursement. Specifically, managed care plans can dictate how much a social worker is paid and how often the social worker will see a client and, as such, care management dictates the kinds of interventions that will be practical in the allotted time. The rationing of client services by managed care companies has become a volatile issue in the 1990s. Thus, social policy and its composites—economics, ideology, and values—are not abstract concepts that only marginally affect social work practice. Instead, they have as much impact upon clients and social workers as the microlevel theories that otherwise guide much of social work.

VALUES, IDEOLOGY, AND SOCIAL WELFARE POLICY

Social welfare policies are not created in a vacuum; they are shaped by a set of social and personal values that reflect the preferences of those in decision-making capacities. According to David Gil, "Choices in social welfare policy are heavily influenced by the dominant beliefs, values, ideologies, customs, and traditions of the cultural and political elites recruited mainly from among the more powerful and privileged strata."[5] Yet, even if social welfare policies were established through a more representative process, the odds are high that the result would not be straightforward. Charles Prigmore and Charles Atherton list no fewer than 15 values that influence social welfare policy: achievement and success, activity and work, public morality, humanitarian concerns, efficiency and practicality, material comfort, equality, freedom, external conformity, science and secular rationality, nationalism and patriotism, democracy and self-determination, individualism, racism and group superiority, and belief in progress.[6] How these values are played out in the world of social welfare is the domain of the policy analyst.

Despite the best of intentions, social welfare policy is not always based on a rational set of assumptions and reliable research. One view of a worthwhile social policy is that it should leave no one worse off and at least one person better off, at least as that person judges his or her wants. In the real world of policy that is rarely the case. More often, the policy game is played as a zero-sum game, where some people are advantaged at the expense of others. When value-laden stereotypes about welfare "cheats," insensitive bureaucrats, and "greedy" professionals are added to the script, social welfare policy begins to resemble a morality play. In fact, it can be argued that major social policies are made in relation to values, not the careful consideration of alternative policies.

Of course, there are serious consequences when social welfare policy is determined to a high degree by values. Since the late 1970s, social welfare policy has been largely shaped by values that emphasize individualism, self-sufficiency, work, and the omniscience of the marketplace. Because the disadvantaged were expected to be more independent, supports from government social programs were cut significantly. While these reductions saved money in the short run, most of the beneficiaries that fell to the budget ax were children. Eventually, these cuts in social programs are likely to lead to greater expenditures as the generation of children who went without essential services begins to require programs to remedy problems associated with poor maternal and infant health care, poverty, illiteracy, and family disorganization. As Silvia Ann Hewlett has poignantly observed, "Although the United States ranks No. 2 worldwide in per capita income, this country does not even make it into the top ten on any significant indicator of child welfare."[7]

Social values are organized through ideology. Simply put, *ideology* is the framework of commonly held beliefs through which we view the world. In other words, ideology is a set of assumptions about how the world works: what has value, what is worth living and dying for, what is good and true, and what is right. For the most part, these assumptions are rarely examined and are simply assumed to be true, a priori. Hence, the core of ideological tenets around which society is organized exists as a collective social consciousness that defines the world for its members. All societies reproduce themselves, in part, through reproducing ideology; in this way, each generation accepts the basic ideological suppositions of the preceding generation. When widely held ideological beliefs are questioned, society often reacts with strong sanctions. Lastly, ideological trends influence social welfare directly when adherents of one orientation hold a majority in decision-making bodies, such as the state or national legislature.

Ideology strongly influences social welfare during periods of social and economic instability. The continuity of American social history has been shattered intermittently when certain oppressed groups have asserted their rights in the face of mainstream norms. Too easily forgotten, perhaps, are the egregious conditions that provided justification for the militancy displayed by workers before the New Deal, by women during the struggle for suffrage, and by African Americans fighting for their basic civil rights. Periods of social unrest strain the capacity of conventional ideologies to explain social problems and offer solutions. Sometimes, social unrest is met with force, as during the period of the great labor strikes of 1877. In other instances, such as the Great Depression, social unrest is met with the expansion of social welfare programs. Frances Fox Piven and Richard Cloward have attributed the cyclical nature of social welfare programs to periods of social unrest.

> Relief arrangements are ancillary to economic arrangements. Their chief function is to regulate labor, and they do that in two general ways. First, when mass unemployment leads to outbreaks of turmoil, relief programs are ordinarily initiated or expanded to absorb or control enough of the unemployed to restore order; then, as turbulence subsides, the relief system contracts, expelling those who are needed to populate the labor markets.[8]

THE POLITICAL-ECONOMY OF AMERICAN SOCIAL WELFARE

The term *political-economy* refers to the interaction of political and economic institutions in a society. As such, the political-economy of the United States has been labeled "democratic-capitalist," reflecting an open, representative form of government coexisting with a market economy. The interaction of political and economic institutions is frequently irregular, and social welfare functions to make the society more stable. The main function of social welfare is to modify the play of market forces and to ameliorate the social and economic inequities that the market generates.[9] In order to accomplish that end, two sets of activities are necessary: State provision of social services (benefits of cash, in-kind, and personal social services) and State regulation of private activities to alter (but not necessarily improve) the lives of citizens. In short, social welfare bolsters ideology by helping to remedy the problems associated with economic dislocation, thereby allowing a society to remain in a state of more or less controlled balance.

While Americans are assured of their political rights through a Constitution that delineates a representative democracy, they have no corresponding document to guarantee their economic rights. Such a document would be undesirable for free market supporters because it would allow government to interfere in the operations of the marketplace. In the absence of any guaranteed economic rights, large numbers of Americans have found the economy unresponsive to their needs, with the political system being the only vehicle through which to seek redress. But because access to the political system often presupposes wealth and status, it is a less than optimal method for achieving social justice for many citizens. The political-economy of the United States thus increases the likelihood that disruptions in the political order will occur. Social welfare programs are one method of compensating for deficiencies in the American political-economy by appeasing dissident groups. This role of social welfare as a means for ensuring social stability was well established until recently, with both Democratic and Republican parties recognizing the importance of social programs in American culture. With the 1994 Congressional election triumph of conservative Republicans, many conservative leaders have called for a rollback, if not elimination, of the American welfare state.

An understanding of political-economy is important because of the breadth of social welfare and because of the intense disagreement as to the most desirable way to enhance the general welfare. For example, expenditures for health and welfare claim approximately 50 percent of the federal budget, more than any other category, including defense.[10] Despite such enormous expenditures, there is no common understanding of how the American political-economy *does* work or of how it *should* work. Instead, several competing schools of thought purport to explain not only how the political-economy functions but also the best way that it should be deployed to solve new problems. The stakes are high in that major institutions—government, corporations, organized labor, and the social welfare industry—stand to lose or gain once one school of thought has gained public confidence. Invariably, any given explanation of the political-economy will benefit some institutions more than others. Because social welfare is advantaged or disadvantaged depending upon which school of political-economy holds sway at any given moment, policy analysts pay close attention to important schools of thought.

THE AMERICAN POLITICAL CONTINUUM

Various understandings of the political-economy produce differing conceptions of what constitutes the best public good. As such, the uneasy relationship between competing notions of the best public good and the welfare state has long been a knotty issue in American political-economy. Because any shift in government policy is driven largely by an ideologically determined view of the public good, any analysis must be based on whose definition is being examined. In a pluralistic society, ideas about the public good often vary based on one's position in the social order.

The major American ideologies, (neo)liberalism and (neo)conservatism, hold vastly different views of social welfare and the public good. Conservatives believe that the public good is best served when individuals and families meet their welfare needs through marketplace participation. Accordingly, conservatives prefer private sector approaches over governmental welfare, while advocating for smaller government social welfare programs. Conservatives are not *anti*welfare per se; they simply believe that government should have a minimal role, as a "safety net," in ensuring the social welfare of citizens. Traditional liberals, on the other hand, view government as the only institution capable of bringing a measure of social justice to the millions of Americans who cannot participate in the American mainstream because of social obstacles such as racism, poverty, and sexism, among others. Traditional liberals therefore view governmental social welfare programs as a key factor in promoting the public good. Thus, one of the major differences between conservatives and liberals is their differing perceptions on how the public good is enhanced or hurt by the welfare state.

The definition of *the public good* is lodged in the political and ideological continuum that makes up American political-economy. An appreciation of this requires an understanding of how the interaction of schools of economic thought have evolved within the primary American ideologies, liberalism and conservatism. These, in turn, shape the major political parties, Democrats and Republicans.

Keynesian Economics

The engine that has driven liberalism is Keynesian economics. Albeit indirectly, John Maynard Keynes was the economic architect of the welfare state, and all welfare societies are built along principles of Keynesian economics. Sometimes called demand or consumer-side economics, Keynesian economics emerged from a model developed in 1936 by Keynes in *The General Theory of Employment, Interest and Money*.

An Englishman, Keynes took the classical model of economic analysis (self-regulating markets, perfect competition, the laws of supply and demand, etc.) and added the insight that macroeconomic stabilization by government is necessary to keep the economic clock ticking smoothly.[11] Keynes rejected the classical laissez-faire idea that because a perfectly competitive economy tended automatically toward a balance of full employment, the government should not interfere with the process. He observed that, instead of a self-correcting economy that pulled itself out of recessions easily, the modern economy was quite recession-prone and the attainment of full employment was problematic.

According to Keynes, periodic and volatile economic situations that brought new high unemployment were primarily caused by an instability in investment expenditures. The government could stabilize, that is, *correct*, recessionary or inflationary trends by increasing or decreasing total spending on output. This could be accomplished by the government increasing or decreasing taxes, thereby increasing or decreasing consumption, as well as by the transfer of public goods or services. For Keynes, the "good" government was an activist government in economic matters, especially when the economy got out of a full employment mode. Keynesians hypothesize that social welfare expenditures are investments in human capital that ultimately increase the national wealth and thereby boost everyone's net income.

Keynesianism emerged out of an attempt to understand the nature of recessions and depressions. Specifically, Keynes saw recessions and depressions as emerging from businesspeople losing confidence in investments (e.g., focusing on the risk rather than the gain), which, in turn, causes people to hoard cash. Eventually, this leads to a shortage of money as everyone tries to hoard cash simultaneously. Keynes's answer to this problem was for government to make it possible for people to satisfy their demand for more cash without cutting their spending, which would prevent the spiral of shrinking income and shrinking spending. According to Keynes, recessions can be cured by an expansionary money policy, thereby allowing companies and householders to continue to spend and produce. Simply put, the government should print more money and get it into circulation.[12]

Keynes also understood that this policy alone might not be enough if a recession was allowed to get out of hand (e.g., the Depression of the 1930s). In a depression, businesses and households may not increase spending regardless of how much cash they have. To exit this "liquidity trap," government must do what the private sector will not, namely, spend. This spending can take the form of public works projects (financed by borrowing programs) or by the direct governmental subsidization of demand (welfare entitlements). To be fair, Keynes saw public spending only as a last resort if monetary expansion failed. Moreover, Keynes sought an economic balance—specifically, print money in a recession, but stop spending once it's over, because more money in circulation (especially when production is active and there is full employment) leads to inflation. Although simple, Keynes's philosophy arguably represents one of the great insights of economic thought.[13] It also forms the economic basis for the modern welfare state.

Liberalism

Since Franklin Delano Roosevelt's New Deal, liberals have argued for advancing the public good by promoting an ever-expanding economy and the growth of universal, non-means-tested social welfare and health programs. As such, traditional liberals used Keynesian concepts as the economic justification for building the welfare state, and from the middle 1930s until the middle 1970s, the dominant domestic concept of the public good was liberal. As such, the general direction of policy from the 1930s to the middle 1970s was for the federal government to assume greater amounts of responsibility for the public good.

American liberalism established the welfare state with the passage of the Social Security Act of 1935. Motivated by a sense of the public good, the Social Security Act was also a political turning point for liberalism. Harry Hopkins—a social worker, the head of the Federal Emergency Relief Administration, a confidant of President Roosevelt, a coarchitect of the New Deal, and a consummate political operative—had developed a calculus for American liberalism: "tax, tax; spend, spend; elect, elect."[14] This liberal approach was elegant in its simplicity: The government would tax the wealthy, thereby securing the necessary revenues to fund social programs for workers and the poor. It was a calculus that would dominate social policy for close to fifty years. In fact, the momentum created by this approach was so strong that by 1980, social welfare programs accounted for 57 percent of all federal expenditures.[15]

By the late 1960s, the welfare state had become an important component of the American social landscape, and politicians sought to expand its benefits to more constituents. Focusing on the expansion of middle-class programs, such as FHA home mortgages, federally insured student loans, Medicare, and veterans' pensions, liberal policymakers could secure the political loyalty of a middle class that directly benefited from these programs. Even conservative politicians understood the support of voters for the middle-class welfare state. Not surprisingly the largest post–World War II expansion of social welfare spending occurred under Richard Nixon, a Republican president who understood that he could not gain reelection without the working- and middle-class vote.

Yet, the promise of the American welfare state's expansion to provide the social protection offered by the European model was compromised by the ambivalence of many Americans toward centralized government. "The emphasis consistently has been on the local, the pluralistic, the voluntary, and the business-like over the national, the universal, the legally entitled, and the governmental," observed policy analyst Marc Bendick.[16]

> Given such a consistent pattern of anti-government bias in the American response style, it is unfortunate that much of American social policy has looked to Europe for models of both specific programs and general approaches. Reflecting political, social, economic, and intellectual circumstances very different from those in the United States, most European nations have evolved an approach to social welfare services that is strongly state-centered. . . . When presented explicitly to the American public, the European welfare state approach has won few adherents outside of academic circles.[17]

This intrinsic problem of the American welfare state—distrust of centralized government—was exacerbated by the desertion of New Deal allies. Staunch defenders of social programs—Democratic politicians such as George McGovern, Hubert Humphrey, and Daniel Patrick Moynihan—have either retired, died, or modified their ideological stance. Even liberal holdouts have had second thoughts about the traditional goal of American social welfare. Speaking to the Women's National Democratic Club, Senator Edward Kennedy—"the last of the liberal lions"—questioned the basis of American social policy: "We now stand between two Americas, the one we have known and the one toward which we are heading. The New Deal will live in American history forever as a supreme example of government responsiveness to the times. But it is no answer to the problems of today."[18] All but confirming that the New Deal was dead, Harvard University's Michael Sandel stated that as early as the 1970s that "the New Deal agenda had become obsolete."[19]

During the 1980s, public ambivalence about social programs was exploited by the Reagan administration, placing liberals on the defensive. Having conceded the middle ground in the public policy debate, liberals were in a poor position to press for additional programs that would benefit vulnerable populations that remained unprotected by the "reluctant" American welfare state.[20] Cuts in social welfare programs executed by the Reagan administration were met with an ineffectual response, and the prospect of increasing welfare—even among leaders of the Democratic party, the traditional defenders of the welfare state—was jettisoned. Hence, by the middle 1970s, the goal of traditional liberals like Ted Kennedy, Tip O'Neill, George McGovern, and others to build a welfare state like those of Northern Europe was replaced by an incremental approach that narrowly focused on consolidating and fine-tuning the programs of the Social Security Act.

Liberalism also lost ground because of the way in which the American welfare state was structured. The hallmark of American liberalism—the Social Security Act of 1935—was essentially a self-financing social insurance program that rewarded working people. The public assistance programs—which contained less political capital and were therefore a better measure of public compassion—were rigorously means-tested, sparse in their benefits, and designed to be operated by the less than generous states. Thus, while Social Security benefits were indexed to the cost-of-living (COLA) in the mid–1970s, public assistance benefits deteriorated so badly that the former AFDC program lost about half of its value between 1975 to 1992. Although Social Security halved the poverty rate for the elderly, the plight of poor families worsened.

Liberal Welfare Philosophers

Many welfare professionals had built their careers around a vision of an American welfare state that was European in origin.[21] This vision was shared by virtually every social welfare scholar writing in the late 1960s and early 1970s.[22] Social workers in the United States have tended to adhere to a liberal philosophy toward welfare that assumed that a system of national programs would be deployed as a greater portion of the citizenry demanded a variety of services and benefits through governmental social programs. The implicit vision behind the expansion of the government-driven welfare state was the European model, especially the Scandinavian variant in which health care, housing, income benefits, and employment opportunities were available more equitably throughout the population than in any other region in the world.[23] It was this example that led Richard Titmuss to hope that the welfare state, as an instrument of government, would eventually lead to a "welfare world."[24] Ultimately, governmental programs, which were the basis of the welfare state, were treated by most welfare philosophers as synonymous with social welfare.

This convention was followed in the United States as well. For American welfare philosophers, government programs designed to ameliorate the caprices of capitalism were both desirable and inevitable. In their classic *Industrial Society and Social Welfare*, Harold Wilensky and Charles Lebeaux suggested that "under continuing industrialization all institutions will be oriented toward and evaluated in terms of social welfare aims. The 'welfare state' will become the 'welfare society,' and both will be more reality than epithet."[25] Accordingly, from the New Deal through the War on Poverty, the notion that government should be the primary institution for promoting social welfare was a persistent theme among American welfare philosophers.[26]

These explanations of the emergence of social welfare in American society were accepted by welfare professionals who took jobs with governmental agencies or with voluntary sector agencies that were heavily dependent on governmental contracts. In fact, the combination of a government bureaucracy and casework agency became so prevalent that Wilensky and Lebeaux concluded that "virtually all welfare service is dispensed through social agencies . . . and virtually all social workers operate through such agencies."[27] For most social welfare professionals, the welfare state was not a philosophical abstraction; it was the basis of livelihood.

Neoliberalism

By the late 1970s, the liberal view that the welfare state could advance the public good was in retreat. What remained of traditional liberalism was replaced by a *neo*liberalism that was more cautious of government, less antagonistic toward big business, and more skeptical of the value of universal entitlements.

While traditional liberals and most Democrats viewed government as the best institution for bringing social the justice to the millions of Americans who failed to participate in society, the defeat of Jimmy Carter and the election of a Republican Senate in 1980 forced many liberal Democrats to reevaluate their party's traditional position on domestic policy. This reexamination, christened "neoliberalism" by Charles Peters to differentiate the new ideology from both old-style liberalism and neoconservatism, attracted a small following in the early 1980s.[28] With the resounding defeat of Walter Mondale, a candidate who symbolized liberal social policy, neoliberalism moved to stage center of Democratic party politics. The defeat of presidential candidate Michael Dukakis in 1988 underlined the need for Democrats to reformulate their positions on domestic policy. By the late 1980s, several leading Democrats were identified as neoliberal. Moreover, the movement rapidly influenced social policy proposals advanced by the Democratic party. Randall Rothenberg charted the influence of neoliberalism on the Democratic domestic policy platform as early as 1982:

> The party's June 1982 midterm convention in Philadelphia did not endorse a large-scale federal jobs program, in spite of more than 9 million unemployed. It did not re-propose national health insurance, even though medical costs were still soaring. It did not submit yet again a plan for a guaranteed annual income, although the American welfare system was still not operating efficiently.[29]

In the late 1980s, a cadre of prominent mainstream Democrats, including Paul Tsongas, Richard Gephardt, Sam Nunn, and Bill Bradley, to name a few, established the Democratic Leadership Council (DLC). In part, their goal was to wrest control of the Democratic Party from traditional liberals, who were so easily exploited by the Republican Party, and thus create a new Democratic Party that was more attuned to the beliefs of the traditional core of voters and less antagonistic to corporate interests. In 1989, the DLC released *The New Orleans Declaration: A Democratic Agenda for the 1990s*. This agenda promised that Democratic Party politics would shift toward a middle ground that combined a corporatist economic analysis with a so-called Democratic compassion. Two of the founders of the DLC were Bill Clinton and Al Gore. In fact, Bill Clinton chaired the DLC just before announcing his candidacy for presidency.[30]

Neoliberals were also more forgiving than traditional liberals of the antisocial behavior of large corporations. Not coincidentally, they were opposed to economic protectionism. Adherents of *realpolitik*, neoliberals viewed New Deal philosophy (with the exception of Social Security) as too expensive and too antiquated to address the current mood of voters and the new global realities. To reestablish the credibility of the Democratic Party, neoliberals distanced themselves from the large-scale governmental welfare programs associated with Democrats since the New Deal. Like their neoconservative counterparts, they called for a reliance on personal responsibility, work, and thrift as an alternative to governmental programs. Accordingly, neoliberal welfare proposals emphasized labor market participation (workfare), personal responsibility (time-limited welfare benefits), meeting family obligations (child support enforcement), and frugality in governmental spending (reinventing government). In place of comprehensive welfare reform proposals, neoliberals argued for reducing governmental spending while encouraging businesses to assume more responsibility for the welfare of the population.

For Secretary of Labor Robert Reich, a former Harvard professor and advisor to the Democratic Leadership Conference, a postliberal formulation meant substituting social welfare entitlements with investments in human capital. Public spending was consequently divided into "good" and "bad" categories: "bad" being consumption, such as unproductive expenditures in welfare and price supports, and "good" being investments in human capital, such as expenditures in education, research, and job training.[31] Writing in 1983, Reich anticipated that a significant part of the present welfare system would be replaced by government grants to businesses that agreed to hire the chronically unemployed and made these further predictions:

> Other social services—health care, social security, day care, disability benefits, unemployment benefits, relocation assistance—will become part of the process of structural adjustment. Public funds now spent directly on these services will instead be made available to businesses, according to the number of people they agree to hire. Government bureaucracies that now administer these programs to individuals will be supplanted, to a large extent, by companies that administer them to their employees. Companies, rather than state and local governments, will be the agents and intermediaries through which such assistance is provided.[32]

Neoliberalism altered the traditional liberal concept of the public good. Instead of viewing the best interests of large corporations as antithetical to the best interests of society, neoliberals argued for free trade, less regulation of corporate activity, and a more laissez-faire approach to social problems. Moreover, longtime Democratic Party supporters such as labor unions were viewed with skepticism. For example, when labor unions fought to stop NAFTA (the North American Free Trade Agreement), Clinton continued to endorse it despite labor's threats to oppose his reelection in 1996. The same was true for the GATT (General Agreement on Tariffs and Trade) agreement. In both instances, Clinton was firmly aligned with conservative Democrats and Republicans. Traditional liberal Democrats therefore found themselves alone, bereft of support even from the first Democratic White House in 14 years. Long-standing Democratic allies such as the Rainbow Coalition and the minority caucuses were also treated with skepticism. Refusing to bow to the pressures of the minority caucus, Clinton continued to back the death penalty component of his 1994 crime bill. The new shapers of the public good had systematically excluded key actors of the old liberal coalition.

The neoliberal view of the public good reflects a kind of postmodern perspective. For neoliberals, the public good is elusive, and the form it takes is fluid and situational. Definitions of *the public good* change as the social order evolves and new power relationships emerge. As such, neoliberals do not define the public good as tethered to industrial era norms and allegiances but to a postindustrial society composed of new opportunities and new institutional shapes and forms. The State, then, is either good or bad depending upon the circumstances. Neoliberalism is therefore less of a political philosophy than a mode of pragmatic operation. In effect, neoliberalism can be characterized more as a political strategy and a technology (used in its broadest sense) than a well-defined ideology that holds a firm view on the public good. This feature is both its strength and its weakness. Specifically, the strength of neoliberalism lies in its ability to compromise and therefore accomplish things. Its weakness is that when faced with an ideological critique (such as the Republicans' Contract with America), neoliberals are incapable of formulating a cogent ideological response. When Reagan argued for staying the course in the early 1980s, voters knew exactly what he meant even if they disagreed with him. When Clinton argued for staying the course in 1994, the public was uncertain as to what the course was.

Accustomed to controlling the moral high ground in the debate over the public good since the 1930s, liberals were overwhelmed by aggressive neoconservative policymakers, planners, philosophers, and ideologues of a half-century later. By the 1980s, the social discourse on the public good came to be dominated by conservative perspectives.

Free Market Economics

If liberalism is guided by Keynesian economics, then the conservative view of social welfare is driven by free market economics. The ascendence of the conservative economic (and social) argument accelerated after 1973 when the rapid economic productivity and increased living standards began to slow to a crawl for most Americans. Conservatives blamed this economic downturn on governmental policies, specifically deficit spending, progressive taxes, excessive regulations, and monetary policies.[33]

Milton Friedman, sometimes considered the father of modern conservative economics, was one of Keynesianism's more ardent critics. In opposition to Keynes, Friedman argues that using fiscal and monetary policy to smooth out the business cycle is harmful to the economy and worsens economic instability.[34] Contradicting Keynes, Friedman contends that the Depression did not occur because people were hoarding money; rather, there was a fall in the quantity of money in circulation. He therefore argues that Keynesian economic policies should be replaced by simple monetary rules (hence the term *monetarism*). In effect, Friedman believes that the role of government should be to keep the money supply steady, growing slowly at a rate that is consistent with stable prices and long-term economic growth.[35]

Friedman's analysis undermines the case for active efforts to stabilize the economy, because instead of pumping money into the economy, government should simply make sure that enough cash is in circulation. He calls for a relatively inactive government in economic affairs, one that does not try to manage or intervene in the business cycle. In Friedman's framework, the logic of Keynesian demand-side economics is diminished, and welfare spending would exist for altruistic rather than economic reasons (a far less compelling argument for welfare expenditures).[36] To the right of Milton Friedman is Robert Lucas, 1994 Nobel Prize winner and developer of the Theory of Rational Expectations, who argues that Friedman's monetary policy is still too interventionist and will inevitably lead to more harm than good.[37]

Developing outside of conventional economics, supply-side theory enjoyed considerable popularity during the early 1980s. Led by Robert Barth, editorial page head of the *Wall Street Journal*, this group of journalists, policymakers, and maverick economists argued that demand- side policies and monetary policies are ineffective.[38] They maintained that the incentive effects of reduced taxation are so large that lowering taxes would dramatically increase economic activity to the point where tax revenues would rise not fall. (Bush referred to this as voodoo economics in 1980.[39]) Specifically, supply-siders argued that tax cuts would lead to a large increase in labor supply and investment and therefore to a large expansion in economic output. The budget deficit would not be problematic because taxes, increased savings, and higher economic output would offset the deficit. (Critics of supply-side economics complained that the only "trickle-down" would be in the form of massive debt.) In the early 1980s, supply-siders seized power not only from the Keynesians, but also from more mainstream conservative economists, many who believed in the same things but wanted to move more slowly.[40]

Supply-side economics stressed the concept of a self-regulating economy and posited an economic system based on "perfect competition." Transactions in the economy were likened to those that occur in simple marketplaces; the rationality of supply and demand served to provide the market with a "general equilibrium" that characterized the entire economy.[41] This model emphasized the efficiency of markets and focused on the supplier (hence the term *supply-side economics*) rather than the consumer.

Although some supply-siders preferred to think of it as pure economics, it contained enough political implications to qualify as a political as well as an economic theory. Popularized by ardent supporters such as Jack Kemp, Arthur Laffer, and, later, Ronald Reagan, supply-side economics provided the major rationale for the cuts in federal social programs executed during the Reagan administration.

Despite its popularity during the early years of the Reagan administration, supply-siders fell out of favor when it became evident that massive tax cuts for the wealthy and corporations did not result in increased capital formation and economic activity. Rather, the wealthy spent their tax savings on luxury items, and corporations used their tax savings to purchase other companies in a merger mania that took even Wall Street by surprise. Many corporations took advantage of temporary tax savings to transfer their operations abroad, further reducing the supply of higher-paying industrial jobs in the United States. For these and other reasons, the budget deficit during the Reagan administration grew at an unprecedented rate (from about $50 billion a year in the Carter term to $352 billion a year in 1992).[42]

In general, conservative economists maintain that large social welfare programs—including unemployment benefits and public service jobs—are detrimental to the society in two ways. First, government social programs erode the work ethic by supporting those who do not work. Second, public sector social welfare programs divert money that could otherwise be invested in capital formation from the private sector, because they are funded by taxes. Conservative economists also believe that only when government alters the patterns of rewards to favor work over leisure and investment over consumption, it does not foster the expansion of real economic demand. These economists believe that economic growth helps everyone, because overall prosperity creates more jobs, income, and goods, and these will eventually filter down to the poor. Investment is the key to prosperity for conservative economists; it is the raw material that fuels the economic machine, and without it the economy is frozen. Investment in capital creates the economic growth that results in more jobs, income, and goods. Accordingly, many conservative economists favor tax breaks for the wealthy. The more disposable after-tax income that is available, the greater the amount freed up for investment. High taxes are therefore an impediment to economic progress because they channel money into "public" investment and away from "private" investment.

Belief in the economic value of "insecurity" has also played a key role in developing the conservative agenda. Specifically, many conservative economists argue that economic insecurity is an important building block for entrepreneurial energy. Simply, unless people are *compelled* to work, they will choose leisure over work. Conversely, providing economic security for large numbers of people through welfare programs leads to diminished ambition and fosters an unhealthy dependence on the State, one that can become intergenerational. Conservatives further argue that self-realization can only occur through marketplace participation. Hence, social programs harm rather than help the most vulnerable members of society. Belief in the function of economic insecurity has formed the base for recent welfare reform initiatives calling for a maximum time-limit on welfare benefits. These and other economic ideas shaped the economic, political, and social agenda of the conservative movement in the 1980s and 1990s.

Classical Conservatives

On one level, American conservatives agree about important values relating to social policy. They are antiunion, opposed to aggressive governmental regulations and various forms of subsidies, demand lower taxes and less governmental spending, want local control of public education, oppose extending civil rights legislation, and are strong believers in states rights. Beneath this veneer, however, important differences are evident among various conservative groups.

Older, classical conservatives diverge with newer, cultural conservatives on a range of social issues. First, as strict constitutionalists, classical conservatives believe strongly in the separation of church and state. Matters such as prayer and religion are seen as personal choices for which government has no legitimate right to intervene. Second, while both classical conservatives and cultural conservatives advocate a less powerful federal government, at the same time cultural conservatives demand that the power of the federal government be used to implement their domestic agenda in areas they consider amoral, including abortion and homosexuality. Classical conservatives, to the contrary, are strongly pro-choice regarding reproductive freedom and are equally open toward the gay and lesbian communities.

Third, classical conservatives are more socially liberal than cultural conservatives. For example, Barry Goldwater, a quintessential conservative and former U.S. senator and 1964 presidential candidate, argues that "I have been, and am still, a traditional conservative, focusing on three general freedoms—economic, social, and political. . . . The conservative movement is founded on the simple tenet that people have the right to live life as they please, as long as they don't hurt anyone else in the process."[43] His outspoken support of homosexuals in the military is in direct opposition to the principles of cultural conservatives. Regarding reproductive freedom, classical conservatives challenge cultural conservatives on various measures to limit or ban abortions.

After the Reagan-Bush presidencies, factions within the conservative movement became more evident. Old-style conservatives such as Barry Goldwater, who were more concerned with foreign policy than with domestic issues, were replaced by a new breed of radical conservatives such as Dick Armey, Newt Gingrich, Phil Gramm, and others, who were adamant about reversing a half-century of liberal influence in social policy. Swept into power as a result of the 1994 congressional elections, these "young Turks" within the Republican Party brandished about their priorities in the Contract with America, a document that was intended to dismantle the welfare state. How the cultural conservatives have shaped social policy warrants elaboration.

Prior to the 1970s, conservative thought held that business activity and governmental programs were essentially independent of one another. Accordingly, conservatives seemed content merely to snipe at welfare programs, reserving their attention for areas more in line with traditional conservative concerns: the economy, defense, and foreign affairs. By the mid–1970s, however, younger conservative intellectuals recognized that this classically conservative stance vis-à-vis social welfare was no longer tenable: Welfare had become too important to be dismissed so lightly. Consequently, a *neo*conservative movement emerged that sought to contain the growth in governmental welfare programs while at the same time transferring as much welfare responsibility as possible from government to the private sector.[44] Many of the neoconservatives were former liberals who had become concerned about the consequences of the unchecked expansion of social programs. Government programs were faulted for a breakdown in the mutual obligation between groups, the lack of attention to efficiencies and incentives in the way programs were operated and benefits awarded, the induced dependency of beneficiaries on programs, and the growth of the welfare industry and its special interest groups, particularly professional associations.[45] Moreover, to counter the liberal goals of full employment, national health care, and a guaranteed annual income, neoconservatives argued that high unemployment was good for the economy, that health care should remain in the private marketplace, and that competitive income structures were critical to productivity. Neoconservative economists argued that income inequality was socially desirable because social policies that promote equality encourage coercion, limit individual freedom, and damage the economy.[46]

The neoconservative assault on liberal social policy was soon taken over by cultural conservatives, who raged against governmental intrusion in the marketplace while simultaneously attempting to use the authority of government to advance their social objectives in the areas of antiwelfare planks, sexual abstinence, school prayers, abortion, and anti–gay rights proposals. Cultural conservatives cleverly promoted a dual attitude toward the role of government. Mimicking their classical conservative predecessors in demanding a laissez-faire approach to economics, they steadfastly refused to translate that orientation to social affairs. Instead, cultural conservatives argued for social conformity and a level of governmental intrusion into private affairs that made most classical conservatives gag. In contrast to the classical conservative skepticism about blending religion and politics, cultural conservatives unashamedly and opportunistically embraced the rising tide of fundamentalist religion. In doing so, they attempted to rewrite the spirit, if not the letter, of the American Constitution. As a measure of their success, this cobbled-together coalition of economic conservatives, Right-wing Christian ideologues, and opportunistic politicians had by the early 1990s virtually decimated what remained of Republican liberalism (those Republicans who were conservative on economic and defense concerns but relatively liberal on domestic issues). In effect, liberal Republicans had gone the way of liberal Democrats—both had became an endangered species.

Neoconservatism

The neoconservative view of the public good differs dramatically from the liberal view. For liberals, the State represents either the best vehicle for achieving the public good or at least is an ally in promoting social change. In contrast, neoconservatives view the State (and, by implication, welfare state programs) as the cause rather than the solution to social problems. Neoconservatives argue that the very existence of the State is antithetical to the public good because it interferes with the maximization of individual self-interest. Hence, the neoconservative posture toward the State is predominantly adversarial, except when it uses the State to further its social agenda. In theory, neoconservatives see the primary role of government as protecting people, property, and those who own it (police and defense). On the surface, the best State for neoconservatives is a minimalist one that does not interfere with individual self-interest or the market economy. Beyond this, however, neoconservatives have been willing to compromise their libertarian tendencies by adopting the agenda of cultural conservatives in myriad social issues such as school prayer, abortion, sexual orientation, and drug testing.

Opportunity in the neoconservative paradigm is based on one's relationship to the marketplace. As such, legitimate rewards can only occur through marketplace participation. In contrast to the liberal emphasis on mutual self-interest, interdependence, and social equity, neoconservatives argue that the highest form of social good is realized through the maximization of self-interest. In the neoconservative view, the best society is one in which everyone actively pursues his or her own good. Through a leap of faith, the maximization of self-interest is to be transformed into a mutual good. In that sense, neoconservatives occupy the opposite end of the philosophical continuum from liberals.

The neoconservative critique of the welfare state gained plausibility, if only because it was repeated so frequently. Neoconservatives maintained that high taxation and government regulation of business served as disincentives to investment, while individual claims on social insurance and public welfare grants discouraged work. Together, critics of liberal social policies alleged, these factors led to a decline in economic growth and an increase in the expectations of beneficiaries of welfare programs. For neoconservatives, the only way to correct the irrationality of government social programs was to smash them completely. Charles Murray, in his much-celebrated *Losing Ground*, suggested that

> . . . The proposed program, our final and most ambitious thought experiment, consists of scrapping the entire federal welfare and income support structure for working-aged persons, including AFDC, Medicaid, Food Stamps, Unemployment Insurance, Worker's Compensation, subsidized housing, disability insurance, and the rest. It would leave the working-aged person with no recourse whatsoever except the job market, family members, friends, and public or private locally funded services. It is the Alexandrian solution: cut the knot, for there is no way to untie it.[47]

Neoconservative Think Tanks, Philosophers, and Social Policy

Neoconservatives relished making proposals to reform welfare; no policy institute from the right of the ideological spectrum could prove its mettle unless it could produce a plan to clean up "the welfare mess." Working with the neoconservative movement, the Hoover Institution of Stanford, California, helped shape the early neoconservative position on welfare. "There is no inherent reason that Americans should look to government for those goods and services that can be individually acquired," argued Hoover's Alvin Rabushka, who listed four strategies for reforming welfare: (1) letting users pay; (2) contracting for services; (3) funding mandated services through the states; and (4) emphasizing private substitution.[48] Martin Anderson, a Hoover senior fellow and subsequent domestic policy adviser to the Reagan administration, elaborated the neoconservative position on welfare in terms of the need to: (1) reaffirm the need-only philosophical approach to welfare and state it as explicit national policy; (2) increase efforts to eliminate fraud; (3) establish and enforce a fair, clear, work requirement; (4) remove inappropriate beneficiaries from the welfare rolls; (5) enforce support of dependents by those who have the responsibility and are shirking it; (6) improve the efficiency and effectiveness of welfare administration; (7) shift more responsibility from the federal government to state and local governments and private institutions.[49]

Complementing the work of the Hoover analysts, the American Enterprise Institute (AEI) commissioned Peter Berger, a sociologist, and Richard John Neuhaus, a theologian, to prepare a theoretical analysis of American society. Berger and Neuhaus's *To Empower People: The Role of Mediating Structures in Public Policy* identified the fundamental problem confronting American culture as the growth of megastructures (i.e., big government, big business, big labor, and professional bureaucracies) and the corresponding diminution in the value of the individual. The route to empowerment of people, then, was to revitalize "mediating structures," among them, the neighborhood, family, church, and voluntary associations.[50] In a subsequent analysis, an AEI scholar transferred the corporation from a megastructure to a mediating structure, thus leaving the basic institutions of liberal social reform—government, the professions, and labor—as the sources of mass alienation.[51] AEI also prepared *Meeting Human Needs*, an anthology detailing how the private sector could shoulder more of the public welfare burden;[52] and *The New Consensus on Family and Welfare*, the product of a distinguished panel of neoconservative scholars directed by Michael Novak.[53]

Not to be outdone by AEI, the Heritage Foundation featured *Out of the Poverty Trap: A Conservative Strategy for Welfare Reform* by Stuart Butler and Anna Kondratas.[54] Following along the same lines, the Free Congress Research and Education Foundation proposed reforming welfare through "cultural conservatism," that is, by reinforcing "traditional values: delayed gratification, work and saving, commitment to family and to the next generation, education and training, self-improvement, and rejection of crime, drugs, and casual sex."[55]

A handful of other works also served as beachheads for the neoconservative assault on the liberal welfare state. George Gilder's *Wealth and Poverty* argued that beneficent welfare programs represented a "moral hazard," insulating people against risks essential to capitalism and thus contributing to dependency. Instead of welfare, Gilder concluded, "In order to succeed, the poor need most of all the spur of their poverty."[56] Martin Anderson contended that the poverty-line figure should include the cash equivalent of in-kind benefits—food stamps, Medicaid, and housing vouchers—and that doing this would effectively lower the poverty rate by 40 percent. "The war on poverty has been won," Anderson proclaimed, "except for perhaps a few mopping-up operations."[57]

Apart from the above works, neoconservatives were also highly influenced by another important idea, that of "public choice" theory. The Public Choice school has become more prominent among neoconservative analysts, particularly as faith has ebbed in the supply-side school. Not widely known beyond academic circles until its major proponent, James Buchanan, was awarded the Nobel Prize for economics in 1986, the Public Choice school posits that a political economy with a large number of interest groups tends to generate budget deficits. As a result, government must be vigilant and very selective about making concessions to interest groups or their demands will eventually destabilize the economy. Briefly, the Public Choice model states that there are strong incentives for interest groups to make demands on government in that the concessions flow directly to the group while the costs of these concessions are spread among all taxpayers. Initial concessions lead to demands for further concessions, which are likely to be forthcoming so long as the interest group is vociferous in its demands. Under such an incentive system, different interests are also encouraged to band together to make demands because there is no reason for an interest group to oppose the demands of others. But while demands for goods and services increase, revenues tend to decrease. This is because interest groups resist paying taxes directed toward them specifically and because no interest group has much individual incentive to support general taxes. The result of such a scenario is predictable: Irresistible demands for government benefits accompanied by declining revenues lead to government borrowing to finance programs, which results in large budget deficits.[58] Critical of the demands posed by any interest group, the Public Choice school has been embraced by conservatives to explain the gradual expansion of government social programs. As a result, adherents of Public Choice theory view social welfare as a series of concessions to disadvantaged groups that could be endless, eventually bankrupting the government. On the other hand, it is just as logical to apply Public Choice analysis to interest groups related to the defense industry, which make similar demands on government while not paying corresponding taxes. Despite such contradictions in its analysis, the Public Choice school is likely to remain influential in shaping future social welfare policy by calling for further reductions in public expenditures for social programs.

As a collection, these works, ideas, and theories provided conservatives with a potent critique of liberal governmental welfare programs. Unlike classical conservatives of an earlier generation, who simply refused to deal with welfare policy questions, neoconservatives not only did their homework on social welfare policy, but had also prepared serious proposals for welfare reform.

The Neoconservative Impact on Social Welfare Policy

A half-century after the passage of the Social Security Act, the consensus on social policy became increasingly subject to redefinition. Even some traditional liberals became ambivalent about the ability of social programs to affect the public good. This reappraisal came about partly as a result of the chronic economic problems of the 1970s, including stagflation (the combination of recession and high inflation), high levels of unemployment, a mounting federal debt, and the failure of welfare advocates to demonstrate the effectiveness of social programs in combating social disorganization. Neoconservative griping about wasteful welfare programs—so easily dismissed only a decade earlier—had by the early 1980s turned into the dominant critique, replete with a policy agenda.

Ronald Reagan's election brought the nascent welfare crisis to a head. Appealing to the public in his crusade to cut welfare programs, Reagan argued that government was the cause rather than the solution to social and economic problems. As the neoconservative-inspired antiwelfare sentiment quickly spread, liberals were overwhelmed. Journalist Gregg Easterbrook wrote that "Neoconservative thinking has not only claimed the presidency; it has spread throughout our political and intellectual life and stands poised to become the dominant strain in American public policy"[59]

This agenda for social policy in the 1980s was fourfold: (1) end the liberal hegemony in social policy, (2) reroute public policy through the private sector, (3) preclude the possibility of a resurgence in social programs, and (4) stop costly social programs that allegedly lessen the profits and global competitiveness of corporations. In tandem with this agenda, the Reagan administration crippled social programs by using multiple strategies such as tax policy and federal budget deficits. These strategies had effectively prohibited the future growth of the welfare state by the mid–1980s.

Despite these victories, neoconservatives were unable to construct a programmatic alternative to the welfare state. This is even more surprising given the enormous power they enjoyed during the early part of the 1980s. It is also surprising given the number of voluntary agencies, independent practitioners, employee benefit programs, commercial human-services providers, and philosophers that the right employed to construct an alternative vision of welfare.

After a decade of hammering away at social programs, neoconservatives had accomplished relatively little in terms of replacing liberal social policies. By the late 1980s, the American welfare state remained intact, if a little battle-worn. Despite the neoconservative rhetoric, no major social programs were dismantled in either the Reagan or Bush terms. Moreover, costs for social insurance and entitlement programs such as Social Security, Medicare, and Medicaid continued to soar. In the end, neoconservatives had underestimated three important variables: (1) the resiliency of the American welfare state, (2) the continued support (however ambivalent) it enjoyed among the middle class, and (3) the difficulty of translating rhetoric into viable reform proposals. Overall, the most enduring joint legacy of the Reagan and Bush administrations was not their contribution to neoconservative social policy, but the $4.5 trillion federal debt left in the wake of fast and loose tax policies coupled with increased military spending. Had the neoconservatives of the 1980s not unwisely invested their political and economic capital in foreign adventures in Nicaragua and El Salvador, numerous scandals such as Irangate, and the deregulation of industries like the savings and loan associations, they might have reshaped the American welfare state in a manner consistent with their vision.

Despite the right's failure to reshape the welfare state in the 1980s, frustrated and fearful American voters seemed ready to give them a second chance in 1994. With control of both the Senate and the House, neconservatives had learned from their past mistakes. Instead of toying with incremental policies, they proposed bold new social initiatives. These reform measures emerged in their most sophisticated form in the Contract with America, a document signed by more than 300 House Republicans in 1994. The contract was designed to define the legislative debate and alter most of the safety net programs within a two-year period.[60]

Developed during a brainstorming weekend in Salisbury, Maryland, the group of House Republicans who developed the contract was headed by Newt Gingrich and consisted of Dick Armey and Tom DeLay of Texas, John Boehner and John Kasich of Ohio, Robert Walker of Pennsylvania, and Bill Paxon of New York. One of the most ambitious political agendas ever assembled by a mainstream political party, some of the main points of the contract included these:

> *The Fiscal Responsibility Act* was a balanced budget and tax limitation amendment that included a legislative line-item veto. The bill would have amended the Constitution to require that the total amount of money spent in any fiscal year does not exceed the total income for that year.[61]
>
> *The Taking Back Our Streets Act* included authorization of funds for states to prosecute capital cases, reform of death penalty procedures, mandatory minimum sentencing for drug crimes, mandatory victim restitution, and directed federal courts to dismiss any frivolous or malicious action brought by an incarcerated criminal. The bill also provided for the prompt deportation of an alien convicted of an aggravated felony.[62]
>
> *The Personal Responsibility Act* was generally thought of as welfare reform. This bill would have denied AFDC to minor mothers, denied increased benefits for additional children born while the mother is on AFDC, required mothers to establish paternity as a precondition for receiving AFDC, required states to move AFDC mothers into work programs if they have received AFDC for two years, dropped families from AFDC after they have received AFDC benefits for five years, allowed states to design their own welfare-to-work programs, capped the spending growth of major welfare programs, denied welfare benefits to noncitizens, and prohibited discrimination in adoption on the basis of race, color, or national origin.[63]
>
> *The Family Reinforcement Act* would have shielded parents from intrusive federally sponsored surveys, protected parental rights to supervise their child's participation in any federally funded program, required states to respect child support orders from other states, and strengthened child pornography penalties.[64]
>
> *The American Dream Restoration Act* would have provided an additional $500 tax credit per child for families with incomes up to $200,000, allowed up to $2,000 a year in tax deferred savings to be deposited into an American Dream Savings Account (i.e., money that could be used for retirement income, purchase of a first home, higher education, or medical costs), and would have provided $2 billion in tax relief to married couples who pay more than if they were filing as single.[65]
>
> *The Job Creation and Wage Enhancement Act* included a 50 percent capital gains tax cut, required federal agencies to assess the risk and cost of each imposed regulation, required federal agencies to publicly announce the cost of their policies, limited the government's ability to impose undue burdens

on private property owners, and lowered taxes on investments.[66]

Thus, the Contract with America represented the most direct challenge to the liberal social policies that formed the American welfare state.

While the liberal, neoliberal, conservative, and neoconservative schools represent the major current streams of political and economic thought in the United States, they do not reflect all of them. As the discussion of these major schools illustrate, ideas on the best way to address questions of the political-economy change over time. Some of the newer schools of thought deserve attention because they may become prominent in the future.

Other Schools of Thought

The Communitarians (sometimes known as civic republicans[67]) represent a loose-knit group of intellectuals that propose a "third way." In part, the communitarians arose as a response to the lacuna that emerged when the political center began to erode in the late 1970s and America moved markedly to the right. Groups that were once considered fringe—that is, the Christian fundamentalist Right—now found themselves in mainstream positions of power. At the same time, there was an uneasy sense among certain intellectuals and political leaders that the moral and social fabric of America was unwinding along with its political center.

According to Peter Steinfels, "Communitarians essentially staked out political territory somewhere between the liberal advocates of the welfare state and civil liberties entrenched in one corner, and conservative devotees of laissez-faire and traditional values on the other."[68] Communitarians generally agree with liberals on issues of individual rights, equality, and democratic change. They argue, however, that none of these values can be preserved unless America's basic communities and institutions (e.g., families, schools, neighborhoods, unions, local governments, religious institutions, and ethnic groups) succeed in rebuilding individual character and promoting the virtues of citizenship.[69]

Sociologist Amitai Etzioni maintains that communitarians are concerned with the social preconditions that enable individuals to maintain their psychological integrity, civility, and ability to reason. He argues that when community (social webs carrying moral values) deteriorates, the individual's psychological state is endangered. Communitarians also firmly believe in balancing rights with responsibilities.[70] For Etzioni, strong social rights entail strong social responsibilities.

Communitarians are concerned with rebuilding communities. For them, radical individualism is responsible for the breakdown of society. In addition, they also advocate for strong two-parent families (although they do acknowledge that some single parent families succeed), which is viewed as the main conduit for socialization and good citizenship. In communitarian philosophy, the family is where each new generation acquires its moral anchor.

Communitarians attempt to balance conservatism with liberalism. On the one hand, communitarians (like traditional conservatives) fault liberals for consistently citing economic and political forces as the causes of poverty, drug abuse, crime, and urban problems while neglecting the importance of personal responsibility and the forces that have historically nurtured it. On the other hand, they blame conservatives for overemphasizing the value of the free market and for promoting the pursuit of self-interest as the answer to social problems. As such, conservatives simply ignore the corrosive effects of the market and the subsequent economic pressure it places on family life and community spirit. Although priding themselves on being tough-minded, bold, and challenging, communitarians take no position on abortion or gay rights.[71]

On the surface, communitarians appear more conservative than traditional liberals. They argue for adolescent curfews, work requirements for welfare, family values, "drug free" zones, more emphasis on public safety, less access to legal redress for criminals, and the need for government to create more obstacles to divorce in terms of assuring child support. Communitarians also reject the view that America is so divided over basic values that teaching moral education is impossible. In effect, they argue that moral education and character building should be taught from kindergarten to college. While communitarians advocate the protection of basic rights, they also call for "sensible limits on freedom," which includes road sobriety checkpoints and mandatory drug testing for those in public jobs. Echoing anti–federal government sentiment, communitarians call for shifting power out of Washington and into the private sector and local government. Lest communitarians sound too conservative, they also advocate European-style child allowance benefits, extended paid and unpaid parental leaves, and flexible working hours. They also call for national service and an end to private gun ownership.

Communitarians maintain that such terms as *liberal* and *conservative* are antiquated. Etzioni argues that "When it comes to freedom of speech, enforcement of law, public safety, the family and schools, we find it better to talk about authoritarians who want to impose their moral solution on everybody, libertarians who oppose any voice other than that of the individual, and communitarians who want new moral standards reached through consensus."[72] Evidence of the possible bridging effects of communitarian thought was reflected in an agenda developed in the early 1990s that was endorsed by leaders across the political spectrum, including Democrats such as Daniel P. Moynihan and Al Gore, and Republicans such as David Durenberger and Jack Kemp.

Socialists differ significantly from both liberals and conservatives. In fact, liberalism and conservatism have more in common with each other than with a radical, leftist perspective. For example, socialists dislike Keynesianism because of its inherent belief that economic problems can be fixed by a simple technicality as opposed to a major institutional change. They dislike conservatism for more obvious reasons, such as the primary importance it places on markets, its belief in deferring individual interests to market relations, and its overall social conservatism.

According to Jeffry Galper, one of social work's most articulate proponents of a radical perspective, socialists see social problems as a logical consequence of an unjust society.[73] Galper and other Left-wing theorists maintain that it is the failure of capitalism that has led to political movements that have pressured institutions to respond with increased social welfare services. Socialists believe that real social welfare is structural and can only be accomplished through a redistribution of resources. In a just society—where all goods, resources, and opportunities were made available to everyone—all but the most specific forms of welfare (health care, rehabilitation, counseling, and so forth) would be unnecessary. In the context of a radical framework, poverty is inextricably linked to structural inequality. Therefore, people need welfare because they are exploited and denied access to resources. In an unjust society, welfare functions as a substitute, albeit a puny one, for social justice.

For socialists, social welfare is an ingenious arrangement on the part of business to get the public to assume the costs incurred by the social and economic dislocations attendant to capitalism. According to socialists, social welfare expenditures "socialize" the costs of capitalist production; in other words, they make public the costs of private enterprise. Social welfare, then, serves both the needs of people and the needs of capitalist expansion and production. In the final analysis, social welfare programs do respond to human needs, but they do so in a way that supports an unjust economic system which continues to generate problems requiring social programs.

Radicals maintain that social welfare programs function like junk food for the impoverished: They provide just enough subsistence to discourage revolution but not enough to make a real difference in the lives of the poor. Within the radical framework, social welfare is seen as a form of social control. In place of liberal social welfare reforms, the radical vision requires that the entire system—social, political, and, especially, economic—undergo a major overhaul. In short, the radical position is that real welfare reform—including a complete redistribution of goods, income, and services—can occur only in the context of a socialist system.

The inimical relationship between socialists and welfare state supporters began to shift dramatically with the changing political terrain of the 1980s and 1990s. Specifically, the Reagan presidency marked a turning point in the historically uneasy relationship between the Left and liberals. Traditional liberals who had vigorously promoted the public good through the expansion of the welfare state were forced to hunker down and cut their losses in the conservative onslaught of the 1980s. Despite their skepticism of welfare statism, many radicals in the United States and elsewhere were also unprepared for the conservative juggernaut. Put on the defensive by a international shift to the right, the American Left became a defender of the welfare state by the mid–1980s.[74] As such, the Left-wing opprobrium once reserved for liberals was now focused on neoconservatives.

As the public debate shifted rightward, and the most damaging political epithet to call an opponent became "liberal," liberals moved right and the Left was forced to defend social welfare policy as a critical basis for a progressive public good. However, in defending the welfare state, the Left had inadvertently forfeited the opportunity to develop innovative welfare proposals in the face of bold and aggressive conservative proposals. Aligning itself with the remnants of traditional Democratic liberals, the Left moderated its criticism of welfare state programs, viewing them as working class victories not simply mechanisms of social control.[75] This weakened the Left's ability to formulate salient proposals on issues such as the underclass, regressive tax policies, the failure of welfare programs to diminish poverty rates, and the creation of alternatives to centralized public programs and spending priorities. In short, the Left found its creativity hampered by its newly formed defense of the social welfare state.

The Left's reconceptualization of the welfare state contained the seeds of an important shift in strategy. In progressive periods, such as the middle 1930s and 1960s, it could be a gadfly of the welfare state, pushing society farther left. During these periods, the Left could push discussions on the public good and social policy toward increased inclusion and equality. In conservative periods, such as the 1980s and 1990s, the role of the Left takes on a more popular front strategy, which includes the creation of alliances with a wide range of progressive political forces. Despite its shortcomings, the Left has had a significant impact on shaping American social welfare policy, particularly during the New Deal of the 1930s and the Great Society of the 1960s.

The Traditionalists have a Christian religious orientation to social policy and emphasize the moral relationship between politics and religion. They are exemplified by evangelical groups such as the Moral Majority. According to Traditionalists, God's laws must be translated into politics, and "higher laws" must become the laws of the State. Because this group presumes the United States to be, for all practical purposes, a Christian nation, the separation of church and State is seen as unnatural. Apart from its belief in a strong military defense, this group emphasizes the Christian value of hard work and proposes little welfare, except for the most needy. Traditionalists have been highly critical of governmental social programs, which they associate with a liberal social philosophy (secular humanism), a philosophy which in their opinion has eroded traditional social institutions, particularly the family and the church. Lightning-rod issues for Traditionalists have been abortion, prohibition of prayer in school, affirmative action, and school integration—all of which are associated by them with the increasing liberalism of society. Traditionalists have been among the most severe critics of governmental social programs.

The Libertarians reflect another perspective. This relatively small but somewhat influential group believes in virtually no government regulation. According to the Libertarian plank:

> We, the members of the Libertarian Party, challenge the cult of the omnipotent state and defend the rights of the individual. We hold that all individuals . . . have the right to live in whatever manner they choose, so long as they do not forcibly interfere with the equal right of others to live in whatever manner they choose. We . . . hold that governments . . . must not violate the rights of any individual: namely, (1) the right to life—accordingly we support the prohibition of the initiation of physical force against others; (2) the right to liberty of speech and action—accordingly we oppose all attempts . . . [at] . . . government censorship in any form; and (3) . . . we oppose all government interference with private property. . . .[76]

Libertarians argue that the smaller the government the better because government invariably grows at the expense of individual freedom. They also believe that the only proper role for government is to provide a police force and a military. Moreover, the only weapons that the military should possess are defensive. Libertarians are highly critical of taxation, recognizing that government is dependent on tax revenues. Aside from advocating minimal taxation earmarked for military and police activities, Libertarians oppose the income tax. Because of their emphasis on individual freedom (and therefore individual responsibility), Libertarians advocate the decriminalization of narcotics. They also believe that government should only intercede in social affairs when the behavior of one individual threatens the safety of another. The Libertarian critique of social welfare is based on the belief that the State should not be involved in social and economic activities, save in very limited and extreme circumstances.

The Self-Reliance School offers a newly emerging perspective that is gaining adherents in economically distressed areas of the United States as well as in Third World countries.[77] This school maintains that industrial economic models are irrelevant to the economic needs of poor communities and are often damaging to the spiritual life of their peoples.[78] Adherents of self-reliance repudiate Western economic philosophies that stress economic growth and the idea that the quality of life can be measured by the material acquisitions of citizens. These economists stress a balanced economy based on the real needs of people, production designed for internal consumption rather than export, productive technologies that are congruent with the culture and background of the population, the use of appropriate and manageable technologies, and a small-scale and decentralized form of economic organization.[79] Simply put, proponents of self-reliance postulate that more is less and less is more. The objective of self-reliance is the creation of a no-poverty society in which economic life is organized around issues of subsistence rather than trade and economic expansion. Accepting a world of finite resources and inherent limitations to economic growth, proponents argue that the true question of social and economic development is not what people think they want or need but what people require for survival. The self-reliance school accepts the need for social welfare programs to ameliorate the social and economic dislocations caused by industrialization, but it prefers low-technology and local solutions to social problems. This contrasts with the conventional meaning of the welfare state, which describes a set of programs on a national scale, administered by large bureaucracies through sophisticated management systems.

The Greens/Green Party is a loosely knit national organization that is part of a worldwide movement that began in Germany. Greens promote ecological wisdom, social justice, grassroots democracy and nonviolence. In the United States, Greens are organized into state Green Parties and Green Locals. By 1996, the Green Party had run Senate candidates in Alaska, New Mexico, and Maine and candidates for the House in Alaska, California, New Mexico, Massachusetts, New York, and Rhode Island. Running as the Green Party's 1996 presidential candidate, Ralph Nader made it onto the ballot in 21 states, including Alaska, California, Washington, Oregon, Colorado, New Mexico, Louisiana, Wisconsin, Iowa, and Arkansas.[80] Despite the fact that Nader's campaign spent only $5,000, he received almost 550,000 votes, or 1 percent of the total popular vote. This was 150,000 votes more than the Libertarian party, which spent $1.1 million.[81]

As their fundamental orientation, U.S. Greens have adopted ten values, including: ecological wisdom, grassroots democracy, nonviolence, social justice, decentralization, community-based economics, feminism, respect for diversity, personal and global responsibility, and future focus. In addition, Greens argue for policies that promote economic and environmental sustainability. Greens encourage their members to live Green lifestyles, including organizing local Green groups in urban and rural areas; working on community issues like toxic dumping, homelessness, equal rights and recycling; fielding ballot initiatives and referendums, and challenging restrictive election laws; working for or against legislation; and taking nonviolent direct action.[82]

John Judis and Michael Lind argue that "Ultimately American economic policy must meet a single test: Does it, in the long run, tend to raise or depress the incomes of most Americans? A policy that tends to impoverish the ordinary American is a failure, no matter what its alleged benefits are for U.S. corporations or for humanity as a whole."[83] To this we would add: "What are the effects of an economic policy on the social health of the nation? Researchers at Fordham University's Institute for Innovation in Social Policy contend that the nations quality of life has become unhinged from its economic growth. "We really have to begin to reassess this notion that the gross domestic product—the overall growth of the society—necessarily is going to produce improvements in the quality of life."[84] Constructing an Index for Social Health that encompassed governmental data that went back to 1970, researchers found that in six categories—children in poverty, child abuse, health insurance coverage, average weekly earnings adjusted for inflation, out-of-pocket health costs for senior citizens, and the gap between the rich and the poor—the index had hit its lowest point ever in 1993 (the last year that data was recorded). While values, political and economic theories, and ideologies combine to help shape ideas about the public good and the American welfare state, social welfare policy is also defined by certain other realities. One of these is the omnipresent budget deficit.

The Federal Debt and the Budget Crisis

Skillfully brought to the foreground by Ross Perot's presidential bid in 1992, the federal debt is currently one of the most potent forces driving American social welfare policy. Arguably, this debt is almost as important a variable in shaping social welfare policy as conservative ideology or mainstream American values.

Before examining the debt, it is important to define budgetary terms. The budget problem can be understood as consisting of two parts: (1) the national debt, which is the federal government's *total* indebtedness at a given moment in time (i.e., the accumulation of previous deficits plus outstanding interest); and (2) the budget deficit (the *yearly* fiscal deficit accrued by the federal government).

At first glance, the budget deficit numbers are confusing. In 1996, for example, the total federal debt was more than $5 trillion, or 70 percent of the approximately $6.82 trillion gross domestic product (GDP) for that year. This is equivalent to someone having a debt totaling almost three-fourths of individual yearly income (a situation not unusual for homeowners with a high mortgage). On the other hand, it also translates into a debt of more than $18,500 for every American.[85]

The budget deficit can be better understood by placing it in historical perspective. For example, while the total current national debt totals a very high 70 percent of the GDP, the national debt was equal to 71.5 percent of the GDP in 1955, 65 percent in 1956, 62 percent in 1957, and 50 percent in 1964. The federal debt, however, has gone up and down. During the period of high social spending between 1965 and 1970, the national debt actually declined in relationship to the GDP. By 1981 the national debt was reduced to 33.5 percent of the GDP before it started its upward climb again in 1982. Moreover, federal outlays as a percentage of the GDP remained relatively constant between 1962 and 1991, hovering between 19 and 23.5 percent for those three decades.[86] Thus, contrary to conventional wisdom the national debt has been proportionately higher in previous years and, more important, it has also been reduced. Clearly, the national debt (at least as a percentage of the GDP) does not always spiral upward.

There is both good news and bad news about the federal debt. The good news is that the 1996 federal deficit of $144 billion was only 2.2 percent of GDP—the lowest since 1979.[87] This is on top of budget reductions that saw the federal deficit drop from $290 billion.[88] The bad news is that Congressional Budget Office (CBO) projections based on current policy show that it will rise to 4.0 percent of GDP by 2005. Without intervention, the annual deficits are projected to increase to $300 billion by 2000 and to continue upward to $472 billion by 2005.[89] Moreover, interest payments alone on the debt totaled well over $219 billion in 1996.[90] According to Gary Selnow, in

1993 the government could have purchased every single item listed below with the $213 billion in interest payments alone:

- Trained one million displaced workers
- Educated a half-million students for two semesters at public colleges
- Provided a year's salary for 50,000 workers to repair our worn national parks and forests
- Doubled federal contributions to victims of the Los Angeles earthquake and the Mississippi floods
- Built 150,000 quality homes for disaster victims and the homeless
- Funded all the highway construction, highway safety, mass transit and railroad projects for the year
- Picked up all the state spending for public libraries
- Bought 22 million hardback books (more than 7,000 for every county in the country)
- Given libraries from California to Maine 350 CD-ROM–equipped research computers
- Put a quarter-million police officers on the streets (575 for each congressional district)
- Paid the salaries of a quarter-million counselors and caseworkers to help troubled youth and to monitor released prisoners
- Paid the entire operating budgets of the legislature, the judiciary, and the executive office of the president
- Funded all the operations of the:
  FBI
  State Department
  U.S. Information Agency
  Small Business Administration
  Federal Trade Commission
  Interstate Commerce Commission
  Federal Aviation Administration
  Environmental Protection Agency
  National Endowment for the Humanities
- Paid half the annual salary of every man and woman in the armed forces
- Paid the full salary of all civilian workers in the Defense Department
- Paid for all space flight control and data communication activities
- Tripled the government's contribution to the Corporation for Public Broadcasting (and mercifully reduced the need for pledge drives)
- Paid for each household in the United States to have bought 435 postage stamps—one per thank-you note to every member of Congress for having done something real about the deficit.[91]

By the year 2000, interest payments are expected to reach $313 billion—a 52 percent increase. In that same year, interest payments are projected to surpass defense spending to become the second largest (the first being Social Security) federal expenditure.[92]

An increasing percentage of federal spending is on automatic pilot and therefore not subject to the congressional appropriations process. Such spending is mandatory and made up of interest payments on the federal debt and entitlement spending (e.g., Temporary Assistance to Needy Families, Social Security, food stamps, Medicaid, Medicare, etc.). Automatic pilot spending represents two-thirds of all federal outlays, double the percentage 25 years ago. By 2003, the CBO anticipates that such spending will exceed 70 percent of total federal outlay. In effect, more than 72 cents of each federal dollar spent will be on automatic pilot, which means that only 28 cents will be available for discretionary spending on education, research and development (R&D), crime prevention, public works, NASA, and the costs of operating the government.[93] Unless changes occur, projected spending for just four federal programs (Social Security, Medicare, Medicaid, and federal retirement programs) will consume all federal tax revenues by 2030.[94] As such, adults today would receive $14 trillion more in benefits than they paid in taxes. This translates into a $150,00 gap for every household.[95]

Other compelling arguments can be made for acknowledging the seriousness of the federal debt. First, the national debt (especially federal government borrowing) crowds out private investment. Specifically, the government competes in the funds market like any private citizen. When it needs to borrow large funds, it drives up interest rates, thereby crowding out, or lessening private investments. If the government uses the borrowed funds to pay for current expenses (e.g, welfare, Medicaid, the armed forces, etc.) rather than for investment purposes (e.g., highways, R&D, education, etc.), then the total investment as a nation is reduced. This lower rate of investment diminishes the rates of future economic growth, slowing the increase in living standards. For example, capital expenditures grew at a rate of 1.6 percent from 1969 to 1977; during the Reagan years they plummeted to 0.9 percent per year, or less than half the rate of overall growth.[96] The last figure, a social deficit, is reflected in the neglect of various domestic needs, which have contributed to high rates of poverty among children and others.[97] In short, those living two or three generations from now may have significantly lower standards of living than they might have had.

Contrary arguments can be made for a more sanguine approach to the budget problem. First, a point can be made that the importance of the debt is overstated. First, about 25 percent of the federal debt is owned by the U.S. government (with 15 percent of the debt owned by foreign investors). When one branch of the government runs a surplus and subsequently buys federal securities with the excess revenue, the total debt remains the same (except on the balance ledger). In effect, the federal government could have just as easily transferred the surplus revenue from one program (or budgetary category) to another. (This is the current situation with the surplus in the Social Security trust fund.) Second, the power of inflation makes the real interest payments of government smaller because the federal government pays back borrowed money at a later time. Third, the United States can carry much larger deficits than many countries because its economy is larger. Fourth, while the deficit imposes a fiscal burden on future generations, there is no reason why the next generation cannot pass on the debt. As long as the economy grows, future generations can continue to pass on ever-larger debts. Because payers and recipients of the debt are both Americans, income is simply redistributed from one group to another. Others, such as Nobel Prize–winning economist Robert McVickery, warn that balancing the budget could lead to a severe depression by reducing the demand for consumer items. McVickery argues that the nation can well sustain the federal debt, especially because the economy is in a growth mode.[98]

Despite such disclaimers, the national debt appears to warrant concern. When Richard Nixon took office in 1969, the federal government ran a $3 billion surplus. When Jimmy Carter took office in 1977, the deficit was $54 billion. By the time Ronald Reagan assumed the presidency, it had risen to $79 billion. During the eight years of the Reagan presidency, the yearly federal deficit nearly doubled to $152.5 billion. The Bush presidency saw the deficit nearly double again, this time to $300 billion. By the time Bill Clinton was elected to office in 1992, the budget deficit was more than $300 billion a year, with a combined national debt of much more than $4.3 trillion.[99]

Most budget deficit proposals presented in the 1980s and 1990s sought to reduce the budget deficit in ways that aggravated the social deficit. One such example is the balanced budget amendments that have repeatedly surfaced since the 1980s. These amendments would require a balanced budget by a given year, a goal necessitating deep budget cuts. Under a balanced budget act, governmental expenditures would have to match revenues. Where expenditures are greater than revenues, either more revenue must be raised or spending cuts must be enacted. In effect, the balanced budget amendments would deny the federal government the power to borrow money to finance its expenditures, including investments with long-term payoffs. Moreover, a balanced budget amendment would reverse the Keynesian strategy by requiring larger spending cuts or revenue increases in years of slow growth rather than in economically robust years.

The long-term effect of any governmental debt is based on how and where the deficit is spent. Specifically, if the bulk of the budget deficit is spent on physical and human capital improvements (e.g., roads, new schools, telecommunications, job training programs, etc.), then society can look forward to reaping long-term rewards in future economic growth. If the debt is spent entirely on entitlement programs and domestic consumption, then the long-term benefits of the debt become more spurious. Regardless of the political administration, the national debt will influence the funding of existing social programs and the creation of new ones well into the next century.

STRUCTURAL INTERESTS WITHIN SOCIAL WELFARE

Differences on how best to promote the general welfare also exist within the social welfare community. Considering the scope of social welfare in a postindustrial society, the divisive influences attributable to our national culture, and the ideologies that frequently guide social policy, it is not surprising that human-service professionals should have varying ideas about the best way to address human needs. A theory developed by David Stoesz posits that four such groups can be identified within American social welfare: traditional providers, welfare bureaucrats, clinical entrepreneurs, and human-service executives.[100] Because these groups have become integrated into the nation's political-economy, they are termed *structural interests*.

Traditional Providers

Traditional providers are both professionals and laypersons who seek to maintain and enhance traditional relations, values, and structures in their communities. Traditional providers hold an organismic conception of social welfare, seeing it tightly interwoven with other community institutions. According to traditional providers, voluntary nonprofit agencies offer the advantages of neighborliness, a reaffirmation of community values, a concern for community as opposed to personal gain, and freedom to alter programming so as to conform to changes in local priorities. Their base of influence consists of the private, nonprofit agencies, often referred to as the voluntary sector.

Much of the heritage of social welfare can be traced to this interest (e.g., Mary Richmond of the Charity Organization Society movement, and Jane Addams of the Settlement House movement). Charity Organization Societies and settlement houses were transformed by two influences: the need for scientifically based treatment techniques and the socialization of charity. Together, these factors functioned as an anchor for the social casework agencies in American industrial society. The agency provided the grist for scientific casework that was instrumental in the emergence of the social work profession. The new schools of social work, in turn, relied on casework agencies for internship training, a substantial portion of a professional's education. Once graduated, many professionals elected to work in the voluntary sector, ensuring agencies of a steady supply of personnel.

Voluntary agencies routinized philanthropic contributions by socializing charity. Beginning with Denver's Associated Charities in 1887, the concept of a community appeal spread so rapidly that by the 1920s more than 200 cities had community chests. The needs of workers for effective treatment techniques and the economic imperatives for organizational survival functioned together to standardize the social agency. Perhaps the best description of the casework agency is found in the Milford Conference Report of 1923, *Social Casework: Generic and Specific*, which comprehensively outlined the organization through which professional caseworkers delivered services.[101] By the 1940s, the social casework agency had become a predominant form of service delivery. Today, much social service provision exists in the form of United Way-subsidized sectarian and nonsectarian agencies, whose member groups collected $2.4 billion in 1986.[102]

Welfare Bureaucrats

Welfare bureaucrats are public functionaries who maintain the welfare state in much the same form in which it was conceived during the New Deal. "Their ideology," according to Robert Alford, "stresses a rational, efficient, cost-conscious, coordinated . . . delivery system."[103] They view government intervention vis-à-vis social problems as legitimate and necessary, considering the apparent lack of concern by the private sector and local government. Moreover, they contend that government intervention is more effective because authority is centralized, guidelines are standardized, and benefits are allocated according to principles of equity and equality.

The influence of welfare bureaucrats grew as a result of the Social Security Act of 1935. To a limited extent, the larger community chests "exerted a pressure toward rationalization of the professional welfare machinery,"[104] but this did not diminish the effect of the federal welfare bureaucracy, which soon eclipsed the authority of traditional providers. Actually, a unilinear evolution between these interests could have occurred had Harry Hopkins, head of the Federal Emergency Relief Administration, not prohibited states from turning federal welfare funds over to private agencies.[105] Denied the resources to address significantly the massive social problems caused by the Great Depression, private agencies lapsed into a secondary role while federal and state agencies ascended in importance. An array of welfare legislation followed the Social Security Act, including the Housing Act of 1937, the G.I. Bill of 1944, the Community Mental Health Centers Act of 1963, the Civil Rights Act of 1964, the Food Stamp Act of 1964, the Economic Opportunity Act of 1964, the Elementary and Secondary Education Act of 1965, the Medicare and Medicaid Acts of 1965, Supplemental Security Income in 1974, Title XX of the Social Security Act of 1975, and the Full Employment Act of 1978.

The flourishing of bureaucratic rationality concomitant with this legislative activity represented the institutionalization of liberal thought, which sought to control the caprice of the market, ensure a measure of equality among widely divergent economic classes, and establish the administrative apparatus that would ensure the continuity of these principles. Confronted with a rapidly industrializing society lacking basic programs for ameliorating social and economic catastrophes, progressives perceived the State as a vehicle for social reform. Their solutions focused on "coordinating fragmented services, instituting planning, and extending public funding."[106] Implicit in the methods advocated by welfare bureaucrats is an expectation, if not an assumption, that the social welfare administration should be centralized, that eligibility for benefits should be universalized, and that social welfare should be firmly anchored in the institutional fabric of society.

The influence of welfare bureaucrats had been curtailed by the mid–1980s. The Reagan administration all but capped the growth of social programs, expenditures of which as a percent of GDP fell from 12.4 in 1983 to 11.3 in 1991.[107] Even Democrats who had smarted from election losses in 1980, 1984, and 1988 began to voice a preference for private sector solutions to social problems. Still, the volume of resources and the number of people dependent on public welfare assure welfare bureaucrats of a dominant and continuing role in the near future.

Clinical Entrepreneurs

Clinical entrepreneurs are professional service providers, chiefly social workers, psychologists, and physicians, who work for themselves instead of being salaried employees. Important to clinical entrepreneurs is the establishment of a professional monopoly, the evolution of which represents a concern on the part of practitioners that their occupational activity not be subject to political interference from the State or the ignorance of the lay public. In the United States, the professions found that a market economy was conducive to occupational success. In the most fundamental sense, private practice reconciles the professionals' desire for autonomy with the imperatives of a market economy. The transition from entrepreneur to professional monopolist is a matter of obtaining legislation restricting practice to those duly licensed by the State. "Professionalism provides a way of preserving monopolistic control over services without the risks of competition."[108] As an extension of the entrepreneurial model of service delivery, professional monopoly offers privacy in practice, freedom to valuate one's worth through setting fees, and the security ensured by membership in the professional monopoly.

The social worker as clinical entrepreneur is a relatively recent phenomenon, and the National

Association of Social Workers (NASW) did not officially sanction this form of service delivery until 1964. Prior to that, privately practicing social workers identified themselves as psychotherapists and lay analysts. Typically, they relied on referrals from physicians and psychiatrists and, after World War II, they began to establish "flourishing and lucrative" practices.[109] By the 1970s, private practice in social work was developing as an important form of service delivery, although analysts disagreed about the number of social workers engaged in independent practice. In 1975, NASW estimated that from 10,000 to 20,000 social workers were engaged in private practice. By 1983, Dr. Robert Barker, author of *Social Work in Private Practice* and a column on private practice in *NASW News*, speculated that about 30,000 social workers, or 32 percent of all social workers, engaged in private practice on a full- or part-time basis.[110] By 1985, a large portion of psychotherapy was being done by social workers, and *The New York Times* noted that "growing numbers of social workers are treating more affluent, private clients, thus moving into the traditional preserve of the elite psychiatrists and clinical psychologists."[111] Yet, in the early 1990s, NASW reported that only about 15,000 of its members—11.1 percent—were in solo or partnership practice as private practitioners.[112]

Clinical entrepreneurs are an emerging interest in social welfare. Continued growth of this group is likely for several reasons. Through local and state chapters, NASW has been effective in expanding the scope of its professional monopoly. In 1983, 31 states had passed legislation regulating the practice of social work; by 1992, all 50 states regulated social work practice. At the same time, professional groups have lobbied for vendorship privileges that allow them more regular income through insurance held by clients. Finally, large numbers of students entering graduate schools of social work do so with the expressed intent of setting up a private practice.[113] Clinical entrepreneurs would be well positioned to become a more influential interest in American social welfare were it not for the incursion of managed care, the attempt of human-service corporations to diminish the influence of clinical entrepreneurs.

Human-Service Executives

Human-service executives share an important characteristic with clinical entrepreneurs: Both represent ways of organizing service delivery in the context of the market. However, in some important ways they differ. Unlike clinical entrepreneurs, human-service executives are salaried employees of proprietary firms and, as such, have less autonomy. As administrators or chief executive officers of large corporations, human-service executives advance market strategies for promoting social welfare. Welfare bureaucrats emphasize the planning and regulatory functions of the State, whereas human-service executives favor the rationality of the marketplace in allocating resources and evaluating programs. In the present circumstances, human-service executives advocate market reform of the welfare state—the domain of welfare bureaucrats—and thus are in a position to challenge this interest.

For-profit firms became prominent in American social welfare during the 1960s, when Medicaid and Medicare funds were paid to proprietary nursing homes and hospitals.[114] Since then, human-service executives have been rapidly creating independent, for-profit human-service corporations that provide an extensive range of nationwide services. Human-service corporations have established prominent, if not dominant, positions in several human-service markets, including nursing home care, hospital management, health maintenance, child care, home care, and corrections. Most recently, human-service corporations have aggressively exploited the managed care market. In 1981, 34 human service corporations reported annual revenues above $10 million; by 1985, the number of firms had increased to 66. Several corporations reported revenues higher than the total contributions to the United Way of America.[115]

As the proprietary sector expands to dominate different human-service markets, oligopolies emerge and a fundamental change occurs. No longer passively dependent on government appropriations, proprietary firms are in a strong position to shape the very markets they serve, influencing not only consumer demand but governmental policy as well. It is this capacity to determine or control a market that qualitatively distinguishes corporate welfare from the earlier form of business involvement in social welfare, that is, philanthropic contributions to nonprofit agencies of the voluntary sector. For these reasons, human-service executives are well positioned to influence welfare bureaucrats.

The structural interests just described can be located in relation to two variables: span of influence and type of economy. As Figure 1.1 indicates, power shifts as a result of significant social influences: privatization and bureaucratization. The consequences of these forces will be evident in subsequent chapters of this book.

Marginal Interests

Social welfare in America is populated by numerous groups that have *not* become as symbiotically attached to the social structure as have the structural interests described in the preceding section. These marginal interest groups usually represent special populations that have been ignored, excluded, or oppressed by mainstream society. The number of these groups reflects the capacity of American culture to maintain its equilibrium while excluding many groups from full social participation. A partial list of marginal interest groups includes African Americans, women, Native Americans, homosexuals, residents of isolated rural areas, and Hispanic Americans. These groups are of concern to welfare professionals because typically they have not had the same opportunities of mainstream populations; in other words, they have been denied social justice. Within the context of democratic capitalism, elevating marginal interests remains extraordinarily difficult.

The marginal status of many groups relates to the nature of the social welfare industry. In American culture, groups excluded from the mainstream are expected to gather their resources and identify leaders who will mount programs to serve their particular group. Although this expectation is congruent with traditional values, such as self-sufficiency and community solidarity, that approach does not necessarily ensure success. The voluntary sector may be able to accommodate only a limited number of marginal interests because of financial restraints, or it may be unresponsive to groups that violate traditional community norms. Programs to aid victims of domestic violence and the homeless, for example, have often struggled to mount and sustain minimal services because the United Way has funding priorities consonant with clientele more highly regarded in a community.

In a democratic polity, marginal groups can make claims on the social order by seeking benefits through governmental programs, but to do so presents other problems. Government programs are likely to be managed by welfare bureaucrats, who have their own understanding of what is best for the marginal interest. For a marginal group to get benefits through government programs, its claim must be interpreted, programmed, and monitored by agents of the welfare state, who have a welfare ideology that differs from that of oppressed groups. The result is likely to be a program that is more consonant with the ideology of the welfare bureaucrats than with that of the marginal group.

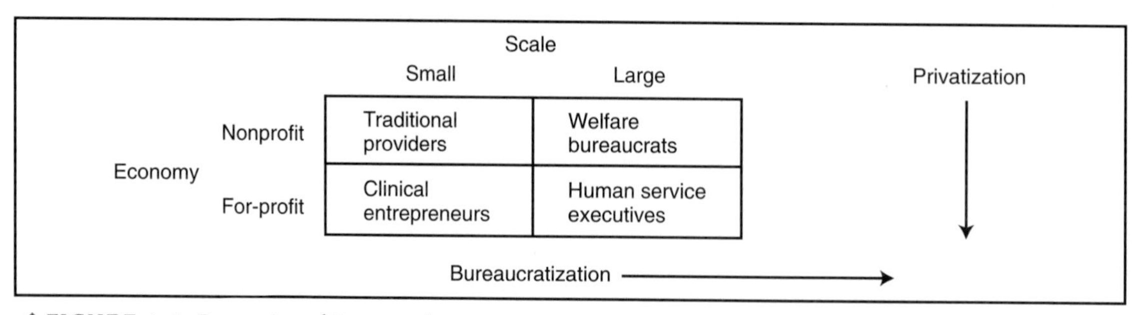

◆ **FIGURE 1.1 Dynamics of Structural Interests**

Source: David Stoesz, "A Theory of Social Welfare," *Social Work* (34) 2 (March 1989), p. 106.

The effort to combat AIDS has been plagued by volatile disagreements between gay advocacy organizations and the public health bureaucrats who run the Centers for Disease Control and Prevention.

Despite such obstacles, members of marginal groups have powerful incentives to work within existing structures if their needs are to be met at all. Usually, their success in this regard is mixed. As a result of affirmative action, African Americans have been able to secure positions within the welfare bureaucracy in relatively significant numbers and are now well established among welfare bureaucrats. White women have found independent practice a desirable auspice to provide services and are well represented among clinical entrepreneurs. On the other hand, many marginal groups continue to struggle against a welfare industry that is controlled by structural interests indifferent to minority concerns. The structural interest of human service executives, for example, remains a bastion of white patriarchy. Activists from the African American community struggle to contain gang violence, reduce the number of teen pregnancies, and halt the scourge of illegal drugs, often with inadequate resources. Indeed, one of the most glaring contradictions of American social welfare are state-of-the-art medical centers controlled by human-service executives located right next to inner city ghettoes inhabited by the poorest and most neglected Americans. How has the American welfare state come to assure wealth for health and human-service executives while generating, at the same time, an underclass?

CONCLUSION: PLURALISM AND RECENT SOCIAL WELFARE INITIATIVES

Consistent with the pluralism of thought evident in the various schools of political-economy, social welfare in the United States is characterized by a high degree of diversity. American social welfare is not a monolithic, highly centralized, and well-coordinated system of programs. Rather, a great variety of organizations provide a wide range of benefits and services to different client populations. The vast array of social welfare organizations contributes to what is commonly called the welfare mess. As the phrase suggests, different programs serving different groups through still different procedures have become part of an impenetrable tangle of institutional red tape that often functions poorly for administrators, human-service professionals, and their clients.

The complexity of social welfare can be attributed to several cultural influences, some of which are peculiar to the American experience. The U.S. Constitution outlines a federal system of government through which the states vest certain functions in the national government. Although the states have assumed primary responsibility for social welfare through much of the history of the United States, this changed with the New Deal of Franklin Delano Roosevelt, which ushered in a raft of federal programs. Over subsequent decades, federal social welfare initiatives took on a dominant role in the nation's social welfare effort. Still, states continued to manage important social welfare programs, such as mental health, corrections, and social services. Over time, then, the relationship between the federal government and the states has changed. From the New Deal of the 1930s through the Great Society of the 1960s, federal welfare programs expanded, forming the American version of the "welfare state." During the 1980s, however, the Reagan administration sought to return more of the responsibility for welfare to the states, a process called *devolution*.[116]

A second confounding element can be attributed to the relatively open character of American society. Often called the melting pot, the national culture is a protean brew of groups that have immigrated to the United States and then competed with each other to become an established part of national life.[117] An enormous influx of Europeans during the last century has given way to waves of Hispanics and Asians entering the United States a century later.[118] Historically, social welfare programs have played an important part in the acculturation of these groups. At the same time, many ethnic groups bring with them their own fraternal and community associations, which not only provide welfare benefits to members of the community but also serve to maintain its norms. Other groups that have exerted important influences on American social welfare are African Americans, the aged, women, and Native Americans. The very pluralism of American society—a diverse collection of peoples, each with somewhat different needs—contributes to the complexity in social welfare.

The American economic system is another reason why social welfare is complex. With some important exceptions, the economy of the United States is predominantly capitalist, with most goods and services being owned, produced, and distributed through the marketplace. In a capitalist economy, people are expected to meet their basic needs through the marketplace, and they ordinarily do this through participation in the labor market. When groups are unable to participate fully in the labor market because, like the aged or the handicapped, they are unable to work or because, like women and African Americans historically, they do not earn enough as a result of discrimination, "social" programs are deployed to support these groups. These programs take various forms. Many are governmental programs that are mandated by legislation. Private sector programs often complement those of the public sector. Within the private sector, two organizational forms are common—nonprofit organizations and for-profit corporations. Sometimes public and both forms of private sector organizations coexist, proximate to one another.[119] For instance, in many communities, family planning services are provided by the public health department, a governmental agency; by Planned Parenthood, a private, nonprofit agency; and by a private, for-profit health maintenance organization.

Finally, various religious organizations have influenced social welfare. This is most clearly seen in the range of sectarian agencies that appear in most American cities: Jewish Family Services, Lutheran Social Services, Catholic Charities, and the Salvation Army, among others. Because of the American tradition of the separation of church and State, these nongovernmental agencies are vehicles for providing services to groups that would not otherwise get them because government does not support religious activities or because corporations do not find them profitable. However, this is not to say that there is no relationship between the government and sectarian agencies. During the 1970s, the federal government experimented with contracting out some services to the private sector, and sectarian agencies frequently competed for these contracts. Today, many sectarian agencies receive federal funds for particular services they provide to the public. A more recent illustration of the influence of religion on social welfare has been the religious Right, which has sought to curtail the reproductive rights of adults through opposing federal funding of family planning programs and abortion services.

The pluralism of American culture is of increasing interest to social welfare policy analysts as the influence of the federal government in social policy diminishes. With reductions in many federal social programs and calls for the private sector to assume more responsibility for welfare, the prospect of molding the diverse entities involved in American social welfare into one unified whole under the auspices of a central authority—the federal government—seems remote. This vision is often implicit in the proposals of advocates for nationalized programs that ensure basic goods and services such as food, housing, education, health, and income to all as a right of citizenship. While programs of this nature have been integral to the welfare states of Northern Europe for decades, there is a serious question as to how plausible they are for the United States, which already has so much complexity built into its social welfare system.[120]

Questions about the correct role of the federal government in social welfare reached controversial proportions by the late 1980s. Proponents of a strong federal role conceded that the American welfare state was, by European standards, incomplete. For these analysts, the "reluctant welfare state"[121] or the "semi-welfare state"[122] required further elaboration through social programs in primary areas of need—income, health, and employment. The principle that social welfare should be a "national effort on behalf of those in need," noted Robert Reich, has been central to American social welfare for a half-century. According to Reich, "The theme permeated Roosevelt's New Deal, Truman's Fair Deal, Johnson's Great Society: America is a single, national community, bound by a common ideal of equal opportunity, and generosity toward the less fortunate. E Pluribus Unum."[123] To proponents of more State intervention in social welfare, the advocates of nongovernmental initiatives represented the abandonment of the most effective method for assuring protection of vulnerable populations. "Conservatives," some observed, "continually assert that many social services in the public sector can be transferred to the voluntary sector."[124]

Advocates of more nongovernmental activity in social welfare trace their argument to the Colonial era in America. Daniel Boorstin, former Librarian of Congress, has written passionately about the unique role played by voluntary organizations in the United States. Boorstin maintains that voluntary organizations "have many unique characteristics and a spirit all their own." Voluntary organizations are no less than "monuments to what in the Old World was familiar neither as private charity nor as governmental munificence. They are monuments to community. They originate in the community, depend on the community, are developed by the community, serve the community, and rise or fall with the community."[125]

But can the problems of postindustrial America be addressed adequately without massive federal social programs? Daniel Patrick Moynihan, an authority in Congress on welfare, claims that there is no choice but to begin to think about new ways to solve social problems. According to Moynihan, "The issues of social policy the United States faces today have no European counterpart nor any European model of a viable solution. They are American problems, and we Americans are going to have to think them through by ourselves."[126] To the extent that Moynihan is correct, future welfare initiatives are increasingly likely to reflect the diversity of American social welfare.

The complexity of American social welfare helps account for changes in welfare policies and programs. Since 1980, for example, a convergence of social, political, and economic forces has led to a reappraisal of welfare in the United States. Both liberal and conservative scholars have questioned the dominance of government programs in welfare provision. At the same time, a firestorm of fundamentalism swept across the nation, attracting the allegiance of groups associated with evangelicalism. The "traditionalist movement" flexed its muscles through the elections of Ronald Reagan and George Bush, the installation of a Republican Senate in the early 1980s, a conservative House of Representatives in 1994, and an effective grass-roots mobilization that challenged government policies on issues that ranged from the family to affirmative action. Current social policy initiatives that can be traced to conservative influences include:

- The designation of Enterprise Zones through which incentives would be offered to businesses in exchange for locating in distressed areas and employing poor workers.
- Supporting the expansion of the Earned Income Tax Credit, a negative income tax, through which the working poor are mailed payments by the Internal Revenue Service to make up for low income.[127]
- Incorporating "reciprocity" in public assistance programs, such as requiring mothers on AFDC to work, obtain immunizations for their children, and send them to school.

By the mid–1980s, social conservatism had begun to influence leaders of the Democratic Party, a traditional supporter of government welfare programs. In order to reestablish credibility in an increasingly conservative political climate, liberals distanced themselves from the large-scale government welfare programs with which Democrats had been associated since the New Deal. In their place, they called for a reliance on personal responsibility, work, and thrift. These values have partly realized in the Clinton presidency through emphasizing "civic liberalism" in social policy by engineering class-mixing situations, such as a National Service Corps, and extending the idea of child support enforcement to ensure a minimum benefit for all children from broken homes.

Conservative public sentiment toward social welfare serves as a backdrop for the debate on the future of welfare policy.[128] The conservative legacy for social welfare from the 1980s onward will continue to shape the welfare policy discussion. The classic trinity of liberal welfare reform—full employment, a guaranteed income, and a national health care system—is unlikely to be part of a near-future public debate.

The structural interests within social welfare have keenly felt the conservative shift. Having braced themselves against repeated blows to social programs during the 1980s, welfare bureaucrats are unlikely to feel any relief in the near future in view of the extraordinary fiscal problems troubling both federal and state government. As more of the responsibility for welfare is shifted to private institutions, the voluntary sector has been called upon to expand its programs. At the same time, the voluntary sector has struggled to maintain programming despite diminishing support from government, not to mention reductions in voluntary contributions associated with a nagging recession. Meanwhile, programs run by corporate human-service executives have prospered; at the same they are using managed care to muscle into the market that has been controlled by clinical entrepreneurs. The consequences of the conservative movement in social policy have been felt most acutely by marginal groups. Government programs that benefited African Americans, women, and the poor have been severely cut, leaving these groups more vulnerable. As the end of the century approaches, welfare professionals face a formidable challenge: How can basic goods and services be brought to vulnerable populations within a context of such complexity and uncertainty?

◆ ◆ ◆ *Discussion Questions* ◆ ◆ ◆

1. According to the authors, American social welfare is undergoing a transition. Which ideologies, schools of political economy, and interest groups within social welfare stand to gain most from this transition?

2. Ideology tends to parallel schools of political economy. From a sample of current social welfare issues—health care, long-term care of the aged, substance abuse, as examples—how would traditional conservatives and liberals address these problems? How would neoconservatives and neoliberals diverge from traditional conservatives and liberals in their proposals?

3. Welfare pluralism suggests that there are multiple definitions of welfare according to the different interest groups within social welfare. How would the various structural interests address current issues, such as abortion, the provision of adequate pay and benefits to poor workers, and ensuring that women have opportunities comparable to those of men?

4. If the structural interests in American social welfare tend to exclude marginal groups, how could social policy be changed to better include these groups? What would be the likely reaction of the different structural interests to proposals for wide-ranging reforms?

5. The concept of structural interests suggests that institutions tend to reinforce the status quo. How does the social work program at your school reinforce structural interests? Which ones? What could your social work program do to provide more opportunities to marginal interests?

6. What are the pros and cons of welfare pluralism? Does welfare pluralism enhance or detract from the chances of disenfranchised groups receiving high quality social services? Why?

7. Is the federal debt as serious a problem as some policymakers and legislators contend? Within the context of the budget deficit, which new programs, if any, are possible? How should they be funded?

8. Examining the schools of political, social, and economic thought discussed in this chapter, which one would come closest to being moderate? Why?

Notes

1. Richard Titmuss, *Essays on the Welfare State* (Boston: Beacon Press, 1963), p. 16.
2. Education would logically be included here, except that in the American experience it has been treated separately.
3. See Alfred Kahn, *Social Policy and Social Services* (New York: Random House, 1979).
4. Frances Fox Piven and Richard Cloward, *Regulating the Poor* (New York: Vintage, 1971).
5. David Gil, *Unraveling Social Policy* (Boston: Shenkman, 1981), p. 32.
6. Charles Prigmore and Charles Atherton, *Social Welfare Policy* (Lexington, MA: D.C. Heath, 1979), pp. 25–31.

7. Silvia Ann Hewlett, *When the Bough Breaks* (New York: Basic Books, 1991), p. 12.
8. Piven and Cloward, *Regulating the Poor,* pp. 3–4.
9. Claus Offe, *Contradictions of the Welfare State* (Cambridge, MA: MIT Press, 1984).
10. Diana DiNitto and Thomas Dye, *Social Welfare: Politics and Public Policy* (Englewood Cliffs, NJ: Prentice-Hall, 1987), p. 25.
11. John Maynard Keynes, *The General Theory of Employment, Interest and Money* (London: Macmillan, 1936).
12. Paul R. Krugman, *Peddling Prosperity: Economic Sense and Nonsense in the Age of Diminished Expectations* (New York: W.W. Norton, 1994).
13. Ibid.
14. Harry Hopkins, *Spending to Save: The Complete Story of Relief* (Seattle: University of Washington Press, 1936).
15. Neil Gilbert, Harry Specht, and Paul Terrell, *Dimensions of Social Welfare Policy* (Englewood Cliffs, NJ: Prentice-Hall, 1993).
16. Marc Bendick, *Privatizing the Delivery of Social Welfare Service* (Washington, DC: National Conference on Social Welfare, 1985), p. 1.
17. Ibid., p. 6.
18. Quoted in David Broder, "Reagan's Policies Are Standard for Would-Be Successors," *Omaha World-Herald* (January 24, 1988), p. A–25.
19. Michael Sandel, "Democrats and Community," *The New Republic* (January 22, 1988), p. 21.
20. Bruce Jansson, *The Reluctant Welfare State* (Belmont, CA: Wadsworth, 1988).
21. Daniel Patrick Moynihan, *Came the Revolution* (New York: Harcourt Brace Jovanovich, 1988), p. 291.
22. See Harold Wilensky and Charles Lebeaux, *Industrial Society and Social Welfare* (New York: Free Press, 1965); and Mimi Abramovitz, "The Privatization of the Welfare State," *Social Work,* 31 (July–August 1986), pp. 257–264.
23. R. Erikson, E. Hansen, S. Ringen, and H. Uusitalo, *The Scandinavian Model* (Armonk, NY: M. E. Sharpe, 1987).
24. Richard Titmuss, *Commitment to Welfare* (New York: Pantheon, 1968), p. 127.
25. Wilensky and Lebeaux, *Industrial Society and Social Welfare*, p. 147.
26. Mimi Abramovitz, "The Privatization of the Welfare State," *Social Work* 31 (July–August 1986), pp. 257–264.
27. Wilensky and Lebeaux, *Industrial Society and Social Welfare*, p. 231.
28. Charles Peters, "A New Politics," *Public Welfare* 41, no. 2 (Spring 1983): 34, 36.
29. Randall Rothenberg, *The Neoliberals* (New York: Simon and Schuster, 1984), pp. 244–245.
30. Stoesz, *Small Change*.
31. Robert Reich, *The Next American Frontier* (New York: Times Books, 1983).
32. Ibid., p. 248.
33. Krugman, *Peddling Prosperity*.
34. Milton Friedman, *Money Mischief: Episodes in Monetary History* (New York: Harcourt Brace, 1992).
35. Milton Friedman, *Capitalism and Freedom* (Chicago: University of Chicago Press, 1962).
36. Ibid.
37. Robert E. Lucas, *Studies in Business Cycle Theory* (Cambridge, MA: MIT Press, 1981).
38. Krugman, *Peddling Prosperity*.
39. Ibid.
40. Ibid.
41. Robert Kuttner, "The Poverty of Economics," *Atlantic Monthly*, February 1985, p. 74.
42. Congressional Budget Office, *The Economic and Budget Outlook: Fiscal Years 1993–1997* (Washington, DC: Congressional Budget Office, 1992), p. 28.
43. Barry M. Goldwater, *The Conscience of a Conservative* (New York: Putnam, 1960), pp. 109–110.
44. See Peter Steinfels, *The Neoconservatives* (New York: Simon and Schuster, 1979).
45. Interview with Stuart Butler, Director of Domestic Policy at the Heritage Foundation, October 4, 1984.
46. Alan Walker, "The Strategy of Inequality: Poverty and Income Distribution in Britain 1979–89. In I. Taylor (ed.), *The Social Effects of Free Market Policies* (Sussex, England: Harvester-Wheatsheaf, 1990), pp. 43–66.
47. Charles Murray, *Losing Ground* (New York: Basic Books, 1984), pp. 227–228.
48. Alvin Rabushka, "Tax and Spending Limits," in Peter Duignan and Alvin Rabushka (eds.), *The United States in the 1980s* (Stanford, CA: Hoover Institution, 1980), pp. 104–106.
49. Martin Anderson, "Welfare Reform," in Peter Duignan and Alvin Rabushka (eds.), *The United States in the 1980s*, pp. 171–176.

50. Peter Berger and John Neuhaus, *To Empower People: The Role of Mediating Structures in Public Policy* (Washington, DC: American Enterprise Institute, 1977).
51. Michael Novak, *Toward a Theology of the Corporation* (Washington, DC: American Enterprise Institute, 1981), p. 5.
52. Jack Meyer (ed.), *Meeting Human Needs* (Washington, DC: American Enterprise Institute, 1983).
53. Michael Novak, *The New Consensus on Family and Welfare* (Washington, DC: American Enterprise Institute, 1987).
54. Stuart Butler and Anna Kondratas, *Out of the Poverty Trap: A Conservative Strategy for Welfare Reform* (New York: Free Press, 1987).
55. William Lind and William Marshner, *Cultural Conservatism: Toward a New National Agenda* (Washington, DC: Free Congress Research and Education Foundation, 1987), p. 83.
56. George Gilder, *Wealth and Poverty* (New York: Basic Books, 1981), p. 118.
57. Anderson, "Welfare Reform," p. 145.
58. Privatization: Toward More Effective Government (Washington, DC: U.S. Government Printing Office, 1988), pp. 233–234.
59. Gregg Easterbrook, "Ideas Move Nations," *Atlantic Monthly* (January, 1986), p. 65.
60. Kristen Geiss-Curran, Sha'ari Garfinkle, Fred Knocke, Terri Lively, and Sue McCullough, "The Contract with America and the Budget Battle," unpublished manuscript, University of Houston, Spring 1996.
61. Fiscal Responsibility Act, *Contract with America*. On-line: http://www.house.gov.FISCREPSD.TXT, 1994.
62. Taking Back Our Streets Act, *Contract with America*. On-line: http://www.house.gov.SAFETYD.TXT, 1994.
63. Personal Responsibility Act, *Contract with America*. On-line: http://www.house.gov.PERSRESPD.TXT, 1994.
64. Family Reinforcement Act, *Contract with America*. On-line: http://www.house.gov.FAMILIESD.TXT, 1994.
65. American Dream Restoration Act, *Contract with America*. On-line: http://www.house.gov.AMDREAMD.TXT, 1994.
66. Job Creation and Enhancement Act, *Contract with America*. On-line: http://www.house.gov.CRE8JOBSDTXT, 1994.
67. Michael J. Sandel, *Democracy's Discontent* (Cambridge, MA: Belknap Press/Harvard University Press, 1996).
68. Peter Steinfels, "A Political Movement Blends it Ideas From Left and Right," *The New York Times* (May 24, 1992), p. B16.
69. Amitai Etzioni, *The Spirit of Community: Rights, Responsibilities, and the Communitarian Agenda* (New York: Crown Publishers, 1993).
70. Amitai Etzioni (ed.), *New Communitarian Thinking: Persons, Virtues, Institutions, Communities* (Charlottesville and London: University Press of Virginia, 1995).
71. Katha Pollitt, Subject to Debate. *The Nation*, (July 25/August 1, 1994), p. 118.
72. Richard Benedetto, "A New Approach to Nation's Problems. Interview with Amitai Etzioni," *USA Today* (April 23, 1992), p. 13A.
73. Jeffry Galper, "Introduction of Radical Theory and Practice in Social Work Education: Social Policy." Mimeographed paper, Michigan State University School of Social Work, ca. 1978.
74. See Michael Katz, *In the Shadow of the Poorhouse* (New York: Basic Books, 1986); Fred Block, Richard Cloward, Barbara Ehrenreich, and Frances Fox Piven (eds.), *The Mean Season: The Attack on the Welfare State* (New York: Pantheon, 1987); and Michael Harrington, *The New American Poverty* (New York: Basic Books, 1984).
75. See Frances Fox Piven and Richard Cloward, *The New Class War: Reagan's Attack on the Welfare State and its Consequences* (New York: Pantheon, 1982); and Ian Gough, *The Political Economy of the Welfare State* (London: Macmillan, 1979).
76. The Libertarian Party, "Statement of Principles," The Libertarian Party, 2600 Virginia Ave, NW, Washington, DC, 1996.
77. Bruce Stokes, *Helping Ourselves: Local Solutions to Global Problems* (New York: W. W. Norton, 1981).
78. Sugata Dasgupta, "Towards a No-Poverty Society," *Social Development Issues* 12 (Winter 1983), pp. 85–93.
79. Some of these economic principles were addressed by E. F. Schumacher, in *Small Is Beautiful* (New York: Harper and Row, 1973).
80. Politics Now. On-line: http://www.politicsnow.com/campaign/wh_house/green/index.htm

81. Politics Now. On-line: http://www.politicsnow.org
82. Nationwide Green Organizations in the USA. On-line: http://www.greens.org/usa/
83. John Judis and Michael Lind, "For a New Nationalism," *The New Republic* (March 27, 1995), p. 26.
84. Mitchell Landsberg, "Nation's Social Health Declined in '93," *Houston Chronicle* (October 16, 1995), p. 1C.
85. Representative Dick White, "Budget Deficit Facts." On-line: http://house.gov/white/budget/deficit.html
86. Ibid.
87. House Budget Committee Democratic Caucus, "Promises Kept: President Clinton Successfully Cuts Deficit in Half." On-line: http://www.house.gov/budget_democratic/06.htm, May 1996.
88. Ibid.
89. The Federal Reserve Bank, "The Federal Budget." On-line: http://clev.frb.org/research/jan96et/regcon1.htm1b
90. Representative Dick White, "Budget Deficit Facts."
91. Gary Selnow, Speech given on "Marketplace," American Public Radio, Washington, DC, April 16, 1994.
92. Representative Dick White, "Budget Facts."
93. Federal Reserve Bank, "The Federal Budget."
94. Bipartisan Commission on Entitlement and Tax Reform, "Interim Report," Bipartisan Commission on Entitlement and Tax Reform, 120 Constitution Ave, NE, Room SH-825, Washington, DC, August, 1994.
95. Ibid.
96. Robert Kuttner, *The End of Laissez-faire* (New York: Knopf, 1991), p. 275.
97. Robert Greenstein and Paul Leonard, *A New Direction: The Clinton Budget and Economic Plan* (Washington, DC: Center on Budget and Policy Priorities, March 1993), p. 1.
98. Interview with Robert McVickery, Marketplace, National Public Radio, October 7, 1996.
99. Ibid., p. 2.
100. David Stoesz, "A Structural Interest Theory of Social Welfare," *Social Development Issues* 10 (Winter 1985): 73–85.
101. National Association of Social Workers, *Social Casework: Generic and Specific* (Silver Spring, MD: NASW, 1974).
102. Conversation with United Way of America staff, Washington, DC, April 15, 1986.
103. Robert Alford, *Health Care Politics* (Chicago: University of Chicago Press, 1975), p. 204.
104. Roy Lubove, *The Professional Altruist* (New York: Atheneum, 1969), p. 197.
105. Walter Trattner, *From Poor Law to Welfare State* (New York: Macmillan, 1974), p. 237; and "The First Days of Social Security," *Public Welfare* 43 (Fall 1985), pp 112–119.
106. Alford, *Health Care Politics*, p. 2.
107. Congressional Budget Office, *The Economic and Budget Outlook*, p. 123.
108. Ibid., p. 199.
109. Trattner, *From Poor Law to Welfare State*, p. 250.
110. Robert Barker, "Private Practice Primer for Social Work," *NASW News* (October 1983), p. 13.
111. A. Goleman, "Social Workers Vault Into a Leading Role in Psychotherapy," *The New York Times*, (April 3, 1985), p. C–1.
112. Per conversation with NASW staff, November 16, 1992.
113. Maryann Mahaffey, "Fulfilling the Promise," *Proceedings*, Fifth Annual Association of Baccalaureate Program Directors Conference, Kansas City, 1987.
114. Donald Light, "Corporate Medicine for Profit," *Scientific American* 255 (December 1986), pp. 81–89.
115. David Stoesz, "Human Service Corporations and the Welfare State," *Society/Transaction* 26 (Fall 1989), pp. 321–332.
116. Domestic Policy Council, *Up from Dependency* (Washington, DC: White House Domestic Policy Council, December 1986).
117. For a classic description of the assimilation phenomenon, see Nathan Glazer and Daniel Patrick Moynihan, *Beyond the Melting Pot* (Cambridge, MA: MIT Press, 1970).
118. Thomas Muller et al., *The Fourth Wave* (Washington, DC: Urban Institute, 1985).
119. The three auspices of social welfare in the United States have been termed the *mixed economy of welfare*. See Sheila Kamerman, "The New Mixed Economy of Welfare," *Social Work* 28 (January–February 1983), pp. 43–50.
120. Marc Bendick, *Privatizing the Delivery of Social Welfare Service* (Washington, DC: National Conference on Social Welfare, 1985).
121. Bruce Jansson, *The Reluctant Welfare State* (Belmont, CA: Wadsworth, 1988).

122. Katz, *In the Shadow of the Poorhouse*.
123. Robert Reich, *Tales of a New America* (New York: Vintage, 1987), p. 11.
124. Robert Schilling, Steven Schinke, and Richard Weatherly, "Service Trends in a Conservative Era: Social Workers Rediscover the Past," *Social Work* 33 (January–February 1988), p. 7.
125. Daniel Boorstin, *Hidden History* (New York: Harper and Row, 1987), p. 194.
126. Original emphasis, Daniel Patrick Moynihan, *Came the Revolution* (New York: Harcourt Brace Jovanovich, 1988), p. 291.
127. The EITC can be considered a "conservative" policy because it is tied to labor force participation rather than being based solely on need.
128. For further details, see David Stoesz, "The Functional Conception of Social Welfare," *Social Work* 34 (March 1989), pp. 86–91.

CHAPTER 2

Social Welfare Policy Research: A Framework for Policy Analysis

This chapter examines one of the major tools used by the policy researcher—a structured framework for policy analysis—as well as the common components of such policy frameworks. We also propose our own model for policy analysis.

Policy analysis is concerned with the systematic investigation of a social policy or a set of policies. As such, policy analysts can be employed in a variety of settings, including federal, state, and local governments; think tanks (on both the Left and the Right); universities; social justice groups, public interest or community organizations; and in larger social agencies. The goals of policy analysis can range from pure research to information provided to legislators (congressional researchers) to advocacy research.

The previous chapter examined how ideology, economic theories, and interest groups influence the social welfare state and examined also the role that concepts such as social justice and equity play in the formation of social welfare policy. A policy framework—in other words, a systematic means for examining a specific social welfare policy or a series of policies—is one means for evaluating the congruence of a policy with the mission and goals of the social welfare state. Policy frameworks also assess whether key social welfare values (e.g., social justice, redistribution, equity) are incorporated within a given policy. Moreover, policy frameworks are useful in determining whether a policy fits within the theoretical guidelines of social welfare activities and whether a policy is consistent with established social welfare foundations, that is, with the historical precedents that guide social welfare initiatives. For example, let us consider the proposal that foster care should be abolished and that all children suspected of being abused or neglected should be placed in an orphanage. The use of a policy framework would show that this proposal represents a clear break with the general drift of late–twentieth-century social policy and, moreover, that it repudiates general social welfare values that stress self-determination, justice, equity, and compassion. In addition, a systematic analysis would show that this policy is not feasible—economically, politically, or socially.

Apart from examining a given policy, an analytic framework is also useful for comparing existing policies. For example, comparing the mental health policies of Missouri with those of Massachusetts and Minnesota would yield valuable information for all three states. A comparative analysis of the health systems of the United States, Canada, and Sweden would also provide useful information for decision makers. Lastly, analytic frameworks can be used to evaluate competing policies. Given alternative policies, the analytic framework could be used to help the analyst make a recommendation as to which policy would most effectively solve a problem or remedy a need.

Policy analysis frameworks can be useful for social work practitioners on several different levels. For one, policy analysis can be done on the agency level as well as on the national or state levels. Social work practitioners can look at agency policies around issues such as flextime, merit pay, agency-based day care services, job shifting, and so forth. Child welfare workers can use policy analysis to evaluate impending state or federal legislation and concomitant fiscal allocations. Social workers in health care can analyze managed care policies in terms of equity, effectiveness, and a whole range of other issues. Agency or other policies dictate what a social worker will do, with whom, and for how long. Policies define who a client is (or is not) and what services will be provided for them. Social work practice is clearly influenced—if not driven—by social policy.

Social welfare policies and programs are complex phenomena. For example, it is easy to propose a social policy such as mandatory drug testing for all governmental employees. On the surface, the policy may appear simple: Drug users are discovered by the tests and are then forced to seek treatment. On closer scrutiny, however, the hidden issues appear more problematic. Is it constitutional to require drug treatment if a positive result is found? Is occasional use of marijuana sufficient grounds for mandatory drug treatment? Because it is a legal substance, tests do not measure the appearance of alcohol. Is alcohol therefore less debilitating than marijuana? Can the policy of mandatory drug testing be misused by supervisors to harass employees? Will the policy produce the intended results? Although these questions must be addressed, without a way to analyze the effects of an intended policy systematically, decisions become arbitrary and may produce side effects worse than the original problem.

All well-designed policy frameworks are characterized by eight key elements:

1. Policy frameworks attempt to analyze a social policy or program *systematically*.
2. Policy frameworks reflect an understanding that social policy is not created in a vacuum but is, rather, context-sensitive and that policy options usually contain a set of competing priorities.
3. Policy frameworks employ rational methods of inquiry and analysis. The evidence used for the analysis of a policy is derived from scientific inquiry, and all data must be collected from reliable and legitimate sources. Furthermore, the data should be interpreted and analyzed as objectively as possible.
4. Although open to interpretation, the analytic method is explicit, and all succeeding analysts should be able to approximate the same conclusion.
5. The objectives of policy analysis reflect a commitment to deriving the largest possible social benefit at the least possible social cost. Thus, a good social policy is one that benefits at least one person (as that person perceives his or her own best self-interest) while at the same time hurting no one. In the real world of finite resources—and of proliferating claims upon them—that goal is rarely achieved. Nevertheless, analysts should strive to realize that aim.
6. Policy frameworks should take into account the unintended consequences of a particular policy or program.
7. Policy frameworks examine a particular policy in the context of alternatives, that is, alternative social policies or alternative uses of the resources allocated to a given policy.
8. Policy frameworks examine the potential impact of a policy (or series of policies) on other social policies, social problems, and the public.

In the end, the analysis of social policy—often through utilizing a policy framework—provides decision makers and the general public with information, an understanding of the possible ramifications of the policy on the target problem as well as on other problems and policies, and a series of alternative policies that could be more effective in dealing with the problem. Untoward costs and injuries are more likely to result when a systematic framework for policy analysis is not used.

History is replete with examples of well-intentioned policies that proved to be catastrophic. For example, the prohibition to manufacture, sell, or transport alcohol was enacted by the U.S. Congress in 1919 in order to cut down on crime, familial instability, unemployment, and many other social problems. Proponents of Prohibition, including many social workers, touted the end of alcohol as a major step forward in the social evolution of the United States. However, when Prohibition was repealed 13 years later in 1932, most of the original supporters did not vigorously argue for its continuance. Despite the hopes of its backers, Prohibition did not decrease crime and familial instability or encourage social order; instead, Prohibition encouraged the growth of an organized crime industry that fed the ongoing taste of Americans for alcohol. Instead of eliminating an alcohol-related nightlife, Prohibition fostered the growth of illegal but well-attended speakeasies. Even many supporters conceded that alcohol was almost as abundant as before Prohibition. Had a systematic policy analysis of Prohibition been undertaken, good policy analysts might have demonstrated the futility of the measure.

A similar argument can be made for the current policy of drug interdiction and enforcement. After almost a century of vigorous drug enforcement, heroin, cocaine and other drugs continue to be readily available. The latest round of drug enforcement (which began in the 1980s) did not result in less drug use, but in a doubling of the prison population from 1980 to 1996 (more than one million people are now incarcerated). It also resulted in the added public expense of new prison construction (as opposed to new school construction), the creation of drug cartels whose wealth and power rival that of many national governments and multinational corporations, a dramatic increase in the homicide rate associated with drugs, and the deterioration of inner city neighborhoods wracked by a gang warfare rooted in the lucrative drug culture. Moreover, while drug enforcement polices have not led to the diminished use of drugs, they have resulted in the creation of a "drug industry" that includes governmental officials, contractors, private correctional corporations, police departments, and large parts of the legal and judicial system. Instead of curbing drugs, these groups have a vested interest in maintaining a status quo drug policy, regardless of its efficacy. In short, a social problem has led to a social policy, which in turn, has led to a powerful industry that depends for its very existence on the continuation of an ineffective policy.

In that sense, social policy is often driven by politics and is rarely, if ever, systematically analyzed. Policy analysis often occurs only after a bill or policy is enacted, and analysts are occasionally asked to perform an autopsy to determine why a specific bill or policy failed.

The purpose of a policy framework is to provide the analyst with a model—a set of questions—for systematically analyzing a policy.[1] As such, the choice of a framework must fit the requirements of the project as well as those of the analyst. Every existing policy framework can either be fine-tuned or substantially modified. In fact, the best policy framework may result from a synthesis of existing models. In short, a policy framework is simply a set of questions that is systematically asked of a past, present, or future policy to determine its desirability.

A PROPOSED MODEL FOR POLICY ANALYSIS

The policy analyst is expected to evaluate a policy and make recommendations. In order to succeed in this charge, the analyst must accept his or her own values while, at the same time, basing the analysis on objective criteria. The policy framework that we propose here is divided into four sections: (1) the historical background of the policy, (2) the description of the problem that necessitated the policy, (3) the description of the policy, and (4) the policy analysis.

Policy Framework

The Historical Background of the Policy. Understanding the historical antecedents of a particular policy is important to the policy analyst for two reasons: The analyst needs to know the historic problems that led to the creation of the policy, and he or she needs to know the historical background of the policy under consideration. Questions that are addressed should include: What historical problems led to the creation of the policy? How important have these problems been historically? How was the problem previously handled? What is the historical background of the policy? When did the policy originate?

How has the original policy changed over time? What is the legislative history of the policy (e.g., what similar issues have been discussed and debated in the House and the Senate)? In addition, the policy analyst must examine similar policies that were adopted in the past and how they fared.

Apart from providing continuity, a historical analysis helps to curb the tendency of decision makers to reinvent the wheel. Policies that were previously unsuccessful may continue to be so, or the analyst may come to realize that historical circumstances have changed, thus creating a climate in which a previously failed policy might now be viable. In addition, a historical analysis helps the analyst to understand the forces that were previously mobilized to support or oppose a given policy. In short, a historical analysis locates a particular policy within a historical fabric, thus helping to explicate the often evolutionary nature of a specific social policy or series of policies.

Description of the Problem That Necessitated the Policy. The second major step in analyzing a policy addresses the problem(s) that led to the creation of the policy. In order to assess the ability of a policy to remedy successfully a social problem, the analyst must understand the parameters of the problem. Furthermore, the analyst must be familiar with the nature, scope, and magnitude of the problem and with the populations affected by the problem. In this way, the policy analyst is able to discern early the appropriateness of the policy for tackling the problem it is expected to remedy. Specific questions that the policy analyst might ask include: What is the nature of the problem? How widespread is the problem? How many people are affected by the problem? Who is affected and how? What are the causes of the problem? How will the policy help to address the problem?

Description of the Policy. The next step in this policy framework is the description of the policy. This section requires a detailed explanation of the policy, including a description of: (1) the way the policy is intended to work; (2) the resources or opportunities the policy is expected to provide (i.e., power, cash, economic opportunity, in-kind services, status redistribution, goods and services, and so forth); (3) who will be covered by the policy and how (e.g., universal versus selective entitlement, means testing, and so forth); (4) how the policy will be implemented, including means for coordination; (5) the intended short- and long-term goals and outcomes of the policy; (6) the administrative auspices under which the policy will be lodged, including the roles of the private sector and of local, state, and federal governments in the development and implementation of the policy; (7) the funding mechanism for the policy, including long- and short-term funding commitments; (8) the agencies or organizations that have overall responsibility for overseeing, evaluating, and coordinating the policy; (9) the criteria, formal or informal, that will be used, to determine the effectiveness of the policy and its appropriateness; (10) the length of time the policy is expected to be in existence—for example, is it a "Sunset Law" (a law designed to end at a certain date)? (11) the knowledge base or scientific grounding on which the policy rests.

Policy Analysis. In this section, the policy analyst goes beyond a simple description of the policy and engages in a *systematic* analysis of the policy (the heart of any good policy analysis).

Policy Goals. The goals of the policy are the criteria by which all else is measured. Oftentimes the goals of a policy are not overtly stated, and the analyst must tease out or conjecture as to what the overall goals of the policy are. The following questions may help to explicate the goals of a particular policy.

- Are the goals of the policy legal?
- Are the goals of the policy just and democratic?
- Do the goals of the policy contribute to greater social equality?
- Do the goals of the policy positively affect the redistribution of income, resources, rights, entitlements, rewards, opportunities, and status?
- Do the goals of the policy contribute to a better quality of life for the target population? Will the goals adversely affect the quality of life of the target group?
- Does the policy contribute to positive social relations between the target population and the overall society?

- Are the goals of the policy consistent with the values of professional social work (i.e., self-determination, client rights, self-realization, and so forth)?

Other, perhaps more difficult questions should also be asked. Analysts must understand the value premises of the policy as well as the ideological assumptions underlying it. To this end, several questions should be asked: What are the hidden ideological suppositions contained within the policy? How is the target population viewed in the context of the policy? What social vision, if any, does the policy contain? Does the policy encourage the continuation of the status quo or does it represent a radical departure? Who are the major beneficiaries of the policy—the target population or some other group? In whose best interest is the policy? Is the policy designed to foster real social change or merely to placate a potentially insurgent group? Uncovering the hidden ideological dimensions of a policy is often the most difficult task for the policy analyst.

Feasibility. Despite the good intentions of a prospective policy, its goals must be achievable for it to be successfully implemented. American history is littered with good policies that were simply not viable at the time they were proposed. For example, during the middle 1930s (at the height of the Great Depression), a California physician named Francis Townsend proposed that all citizens over the age of 65 be given a flat governmental pension of $200 per month. Although in more prosperous times this proposal might have been given at least a cursory hearing, in the midst of one of the greatest depressions in American history, policymakers summarily dismissed the proposal as not viable. The overall feasibility of a policy is based on three factors: political feasibility, economic feasibility, and administrative feasibility.

Political Feasibility of a Policy

The political feasibility of a particular policy is always a judgment call. In order to evaluate a policy, the analyst must assess which groups will oppose and which groups will support a particular policy, as well as estimate the constituency and power base of each group. In American politics, however, the size of the constituency base and its relative power are sometimes unrelated. For example, despite its relatively small numbers, the American Medical Association (AMA) is a powerful lobby in American politics. Conversely, although more than 30 million people in the United States are poor, their political clout at this point is negligible. Thus, the analyst must carefully weigh the political salience of each side in the policy struggle.

The political viability of a policy is always subject to the public's perception of its feasibility. In other words, for a policy to be feasible, it must be *perceived* as being feasible by the public. For example, although some observers maintain that a sizable portion, if not the majority, of the public would like to see some form of guaranteed full employment, none exists. In part, a viable full employment program has not been enacted because the public believes that it cannot happen and, in part, because of the power of the business lobby. Therefore, the United States lacks a full employment program not because the public rejects it, but because it believes that it cannot occur. Thus is born a public myth around what is possible and impossible. Many good policy options are not enacted because of the public mythology surrounding what is feasible.

To assess the political feasibility of a policy, the analyst must also examine the public sentiment toward it. Is a large segment of the public concerned about the policy? Do people feel that they will be directly affected by the policy? Does the policy address a problem that is considered to be a major political issue? Does the policy threaten fundamental social values? Is the policy compatible with the present social and political climate? What is the general public sentiment toward the policy? What is the possibility that either side will be able to marshal public sentiment for or against the policy? The answers to these questions help the policy analyst determine the political feasibility of the policy.

The politics of political feasibility also encompass a smaller, but no less important, dimension. In order to do a thorough assessment, the analyst must understand the relationship between the policy and external factors in agencies and institutions. For example, which social welfare agencies, institutions, or organizations support or oppose the policy? What is the relative strength of each group? How strong is their support or opposition to the policy? What are the major federal, state, or local agencies affected by this policy? How are they affected? The world of social policy is heavily political, with some governmental and private social welfare agencies having political power that is on a par with that of elected decision makers. These groups often coalesce around issues, problems, or policies that directly affect them, and through their lobbying strength they have the ability to defeat legislation. In cases where they cannot defeat a policy outright, these administrative institutions can choose to implement a policy in such a way as to ensure its failure. The analyst must therefore take into account whether these administrative organs support or oppose a proposed or existing social policy.

Economic Feasibility of a Policy

Many, if not most, social policies require some form of direct or indirect funding. In assessing the economic feasibility of a policy, the analyst must ask several hard questions: What is the minimum level of funding required for the successful implementation of the policy? Does adequate funding for the policy currently exist? If not, what is the public sentiment toward reallocating resources for the policy? Is the funding called for by the policy adequate? What are the future funding needs of the policy likely to be?

Given the magnitude of the current federal debt (around $5.1 trillion in 1996), it appears unlikely that new social policy initiatives requiring large revenues will be successful. Perhaps new policy legislation necessitating additional revenues will be based on the reallocation of existing resources (budget-neutral policies) rather than on new revenue sources, a situation that may result in taking money away from one program to fund another. (This is referred to in Congress as "paygo" funding.) The inherent danger in this approach is that by thinning out fiscal resources among many programs none will be adequately funded. The analyst must therefore decide whether a new policy initiative should be recommended regardless of the funding prospects. The positive and negative aspects of this decision are complex. If a new policy is recommended, despite insufficient resources, the chances of its failure are greater. However, if a policy is not recommended, the possibility exists that adequate fiscal resources might be allocated in the future. Many policy analysts lean toward incremental approaches, thus tending to recommend policies in the hope that suitable funding will become available in the future.

Administrative Feasibility of a Policy

The analyst must also be concerned with the administrative viability of the policy. Whatever the potential value of the policy, responsible administrative agencies must be capable of effectively implementing it. In other words, administrative and supervisory agencies must possess the personnel, resources, skills, and expertise needed to implement the policy effectively. If the requisite personnel are lacking, agencies must have the fiscal resources to hire qualified employees. In addition, directors and supervisors must be sympathetic to the goals of the policy, have the expertise and skill necessary to implement or oversee the policy, and possess an understanding of the fundamental objectives of the policy initiative.

Effectiveness. Effectiveness refers to the likelihood that the policy can meet its stated objectives. In short, is the policy likely to accomplish what its creators intended? The answer to this question encompasses several further questions: Is the policy broad enough to accomplish its stated goals? Will the benefits of the policy reach the target group? Are the side effects of the policy likely to cause other social problems? What ramifications does the policy have for the nontarget sector (e.g., higher taxes, reduced opportunity, diminished freedom, fewer resources, and so forth)?

An important question facing policy analysts involves the nature and extent of the unintended consequences of a policy. Virtually all policies have certain consequences that are unforeseen. An example of the unforeseeable consequences of a social policy can be seen in the case of methadone, a drug legally administered to addicts as a substitute for heroin. When introduced in the 1960s, methadone was thought to be a safe way to wean addicts away from heroin. By the mid–1970s, however, health experts realized that methadone was almost as addictive as heroin and that some addicts were selling their methadone as a street drug. Despite this outcome, some addicts were able to withdraw from heroin and, in hindsight, the methadone program was probably a positive development. Because policy analysts cannot see into the future, they make their recommendations on the basis of available data. Nevertheless, an attempt must be made to predict possible adverse future consequences.

Efficiency and Alternative Policies. These refer to the cost-effectiveness of the proposed policy compared to that of alternative policies, no policy, or the present policy. Social policy always involves a trade-off. Even in the best of economic times, societal resources are always inadequate compared to the breadth of human need. For example, virtually everyone could benefit from some form of social welfare allocation, whether it be counseling services, food stamps, or free health care. But because resources are finite, society must choose the primary beneficiaries of its social allocations. Publicly financed services are often awarded on the basis of two criteria: (1) the severity of the problem, with services going to those who most require the allocation; and (2) means, with services provided to those who can least afford them. As a result of finite resources, the adequate funding of one policy often means denying or curbing allocations to another. This is the essential trade-off in social welfare policy. When analysts evaluate a policy, they must be cognizant that promoting one policy means that needs in other areas may go unmet. Thus, a primary question remains: Is this policy important enough to justify the expenditure of scarce resources? Also, are there other areas where resources could be better used?

The policy analyst is also concerned with the cost-effectiveness of a given policy compared to the cost-effectiveness of alternative policies. Given the additional expenditure of money, will the new policy provide results that are better than either the present policy or no policy at all? Is it advantageous to enlarge or modify the present policy as opposed to creating a new one? Can an alternative policy provide better results at lower cost? What alternative policies could be created that would achieve the same results? How do these alternative policies compare with each other and with the proposed policy? These questions must be answered in any thorough policy analysis.

In conclusion, the policy analyst must address several key questions: Is the proposed policy workable and desirable? What, if any, modifications should be made in the policy? Does the policy represent a wise use of resources? Are there alternative policies that would be preferable? How feasible is the implementation of the policy? What barriers, if any, are there to the full implementation of the policy? These questions represent the core of policy analysis.

RESEARCHING AND ANALYZING SOCIAL POLICIES

There are two major hurdles in policy analysis. The first is focusing on a manageable social policy, and the second is finding or generating information relevant to it.

One of the most difficult tasks in analyzing a social policy is the choice of the actual policy. In order to do a careful policy analysis, the analyst must choose a policy that is both discrete and specific. For example, it would be difficult, if not impossible, to do an exhaustive analysis of child welfare policy in the United States. For one thing, the United States does not have *one* specific child welfare policy. The American policy on child welfare is composed of myriad programs that constitute a patchwork quilt of social policies. Given the limitations of time and resources, the question then becomes *which* policy will be analyzed. Second, the differences in child welfare policies on the national versus the state or community levels make such a policy analysis even more daunting. Thus, defining and narrowing down a specific and manageable social policy constitutes one of the most formidable tasks in policy analysis. A second task involves locating relevant information on a specific social policy.

Technology and Social Policy

One of the most dramatic changes since the late 1980s has been the widespread use of communications technology. The use of E-mail, listervs, the Internet, the World Wide Web (WWW), Gopher, and

FTP (File Transfer Protocol) sites has made the job of the policy analyst immeasurably easier, more efficient, and more fun. More important, by narrowing the distance between policy analysis and policy research (through shortening the period between the acquisition of data and the publication of a policy), technology has created a minirevolution in policy analysis. No longer does the policy analyst (or the student doing policy research) have to wait months before their library receives the report or data they are seeking; no longer does the analyst have to contend with lost, misplaced, or checked-out documents, or wade through large stacks filled with dozens of feet of government reports. Instead, with the touch of a finger the policy analyst can download reams of the newest government data, legislative reports, and governmental bills. The Internet has created a virtual library of millions of sources for the policy analyst, one that can be accessed even from the comfort of home.

Some of the most important communications changes have occurred under the Clinton administration. While a modest amount of on-line policy-relevant government data was available during the latter part of the Bush administration, the software available to view and download the data required arcane typing commands like "push," "dir," "get," etc. Finding and downloading this data was a daunting task for all but the most computer-literate. However, with the introduction of new software using graphical interfaces (user-friendly software designed to provide an intuitive visual environment for the user) and the widespread use of graphical WWW pages, the chore has been made considerably easier. As a result of the Clinton administration's emphasis on quickly moving the federal government onto the information superhighway, mounds of federal documents on the WWW can now be read or downloaded. This includes volumes of material from the departments of Health and Human Services, Transportation, Commerce, and Housing and Urban Development and Centers for Disease Control, among others. Many of the documents of the Government Printing Office are on-line as are reports from a growing number of policy institutes. For the policy analyst this represents a savings of untold hours of library research and frustration. Apart from documents, magazines such as *Time* and *Newsweek* can also be accessed on-line, as can parts of such major newspapers as *The New York Times*, the *Washington Post*, and the *Wall Street Journal*.

A clear challenge exists for social policy analysts to both view and post information on the Internet. For example, it was recently estimated that by the end of the decade there will be 300 million Internet users.[2] One observer noted that traffic on the Internet increased 1,713 percent in 1994 alone.[3] Even if these figures are exaggerated, the advances in communication technology remains an important cultural phenomenon. Internet opportunities that are the most useful for social workers can be broken down into the following areas:[4]

- E-mail is becoming a growing substitute for telephone and postal communications. Letters are written on the computer and sent over telephone lines via the Internet. Recipients usually receive the letter within hours (sometimes minutes) after it is sent.
- Listservs function like bulletin boards for people with similar interests. Subscribers to a specific listserv can post a message that will be received as E-mail by all other subscribers on that listserv. Replies to messages are also received by all subscribers to that specific listserv. Conversely, subscribers to listservs can simply be spectators that read (but don't reply to) posted messages. There is one main listserv for social work, along with several different ones, each specializing in a subarea.
- The WWW is like a network of sources of information scattered around the world. Using a web browser such as Netscape or Microsoft Explorer, one can visit various pages (which can be sources of information or entertainment), download data, copy the page, or, in some cases, reply to the person(s) who have set up the WWW page. WWW pages are often interconnected (through "hot links") to similar pages either locally or across the globe. Because WWW pages are set up as graphical interfaces, they can be attractive, or even in some cases artistic.
- Newsgroups are like listservs, except that they are more public and can be accessed by anyone on the Internet. One simply drops in on a newsgroup.

Those accessing a newsgroup can either read or respond to messages. Web browsers such as Netscape allow users to access the more than 30,000 newsgroups currently on-line.

Policy Research

Apart from the Internet, there are seven major avenues for finding information on a specific policy. First, policy analysts may choose to generate their own data through conducting primary research, including surveys, opinion polls, experimental research, longitudinal studies, and so forth. Although this method can yield a rich body of information, the time and cost constraints may prove an impossible obstacle. Moreover, the same research may already exist in other places, in which case the replication of the effort would be unwarranted.

Second, governmental or agency records are often an important source of relevant data on a specific policy. These records can include archives, memos, and the minutes of the meetings of boards of directors, governmental officials, and staff. This research method can also include an examination of policy manuals, departmental records, and minutes of public meetings. A surprising amount of this information can be found on-line in government or agency WWW sites.

A third avenue for policy research involves use of the records and published minutes of legislative bodies and committees. On the federal level, this includes the *Congressional Record* and the minutes of the various House and Senate committees and subcommittees (much of which can be accessed online). All state legislatures have similar record-keeping procedures, and most of these legislative records can be found in regional or university libraries or on-line through the Internet.

A fourth source of information is found in governmental publications. For example, the U.S. Government Printing Office maintains catalogues of all government documents published. Other documents include the Census Bureau's population studies (many of which are updated annually), publications of the Departments of Labor, Commerce, Housing, and Health and Human Services, and the House Committee on Ways and Means' *Green Book* (a yearly publication containing the most comprehensive information available on social programs and participants). Many of these publications can be found in regional and university libraries and on-line.

A fifth source of policy-relevant information is provided by think tanks, advocacy organizations, and professional associations. All think tanks (many of which also function as advocacy organizations) employ research staff who evaluate and analyze social policies. Examples of these think tanks include the Brookings Institute, the American Enterprise Institute, the Heritage Foundation, the Hoover Institute, the Urban Institute, the Center for Budget and Policy Priorities, the Reason Foundation, the Hudson Foundation, the Progressive Policy Institute, the Economic Policy Institute, and the Independent Sector. Again, at least some of the information can be accessed through the Internet. Because most, if not all, of these think tanks are affiliated with a particular political ideology, their evaluation of data and their policy recommendations should be viewed critically.

Many national advocacy organizations retain research staff and publish reports that may be helpful to the policy analyst. Some of these organizations are the Urban League, the NAACP, the Children's Defense Fund, the National Farm Organization, and the National Organization for Women. Many professional associations, such as the American Medical Association, the American Public Welfare Association, and the American Psychological Association, also publish policy-relevant information. A listing of these organizations can be found in any major library. Updated lists can also be found by using one of several search engines found on the Internet.

A sixth procedure used by policy analysts is to consult professional journals, books, and monographs. Articles or books on specific policy areas can be found in various places, including the *Social Science Index*, the subject headings in card catalogues, in on-line library systems, and in electronic databases, which are becoming increasingly common in the larger professional associations. Electronic databases are also becoming common commercial ventures.

Seventh and last, policy-relevant information may be gathered from interviews with principals in the policy process, advocates, recipients of services, and government officials. Personal interviews may be useful in determining the background of the issue, in assessing the opposition to a particular policy, or in gauging the public reaction to a policy. Taken together, these sources can be a gold mine for the policy analyst.

THE INCOMPLETENESS OF POLICY ANALYSIS

The choice of a framework for policy analysis is dependent upon a number of considerations, including: (1) the kind of problem or policy that must be analyzed; (2) the available resources of the policy analyst, including time, money, staff, facilities, and the availability of data; (3) the requirements of the decision maker requesting the analysis; and (4) the time frame in which the analysis must be completed.

No policy analysis is ever complete. Because it is impossible to discover *all* of the data (data are essentially infinite) and to ask *all* of the possible questions, policy analysis is never either complete or perfect. Policy analysis is always an approximation of the ideal and, as such, decisions are always made on the basis of incomplete data. How incomplete the data are and how close an approximation of a rational decision is provided to decision makers will depend on the skills of the analyst, the available resources, and the time allotted for the project.

Despite its reliance on an analytic framework, social policy analysis in the real world is to some degree always subjective. Because policy is analyzed by human beings who are only human, it is always done through the lens of the analyst's value system, ideological beliefs, and particular understanding of the goals and purposes of social welfare. Subjectivity may be seen in the omission (conscious or otherwise) of facts or questions or in the relative weight given to one variable at the expense of others. Subjectivity may also be expressed by asking the wrong questions of the policy, evaluating it on the basis of expectations that it cannot meet, and by expecting it to tackle a problem that it was not designed to address. Finally, political pressure may be put on the policy analyst to come up with recommendations that are acceptable to a certain interest group. Regardless of the causes of subjectivity, policy analysis is always an approximation of the ideal, in effect an informed hunch as to the effects of a policy or a set of policies.

◆ ◆ ◆ *Discussion Questions* ◆ ◆ ◆

1. What are the main advantages of using a systematic framework for social policy analysis? Describe the benefits of using such a framework. What, if any, are the potential drawbacks?

2. Although by definition the *unintended* consequences of a social policy are unpredictable, what specifically can a policy analyst do to minimize the risks of a policy producing harmful and unintended consequences? Describe a recent social policy that has produced unintended consequences that were either positive or harmful.

3. Is it possible to neutralize a policy researcher's personal values when conducting a policy analysis? If so, describe ways in which this can be done.

4. What specific components could be added to the proposed policy framework presented in this chapter? Which of the components provided in this framework are the most important and why?

5. Are most social policies analyzed thoroughly and rationally? If not, why not? Describe the factors that stand in the way of a systematic and rational analysis of social policy in American society. How much value do decision makers place on social policy research before reaching a decision?

6. Because any analysis of social policy is by nature incomplete, should decision makers therefore not rely heavily on policy studies? What alternatives, if any, can be used in lieu of a thorough and systematic policy analysis?

7. Describe the value of the Internet in policy research. What are some of its strengths and possible pitfalls?

Notes

1. Many social policy writers, including Elizabeth Huttman, *Introduction to Social Policy* (New York: McGraw-Hill, 1981); Neil Gilbert and Harry Specht, *Dimensions of Social Welfare Policy*, 2nd ed. (Englewood Cliffs, NJ: Prentice-Hall, 1986); Gail Marker, "Guidelines for Analysis of a Social Welfare Program," in John E. Tropman et al. (eds.), *Strategic Perspectives on Social Policy* (New York: Pergamon Press, 1976); David Gil, *Unraveling Social Policy* (Boston: Shenkman, 1981); and Charles Prigmore and Charles Atherton, *Social Welfare Policy* (New York: D. C. Heath, 1979), have developed excellent policy frameworks.
2. Gary Holden, Gary Rosenberg, and Andrew Weissman, "World Wide Web Accessible Resources Related to Research on Social Work Practice," *Research on Social Work Practice* 6, no. 2 (April 1996), pp. 236–262.
3. Ibid.
4. All of these technological avenues require a modem or a hardwired network connection, and an Internet provider. Internet service providers can be a university (sometimes free to students and faculty) or a private provider like CompuServe America OnLine or MCI Mail. Other options are finding a local Internet provider that can be located in magazines, telephone books, and newspaper advertisements. More specific information on the available technologies, including a sampling of policy sites, is contained in the supplement to this book.

CHAPTER 3

The Origins and Future of American Social Welfare

The American social welfare state did not emerge from a vacuum. To grasp its complexity, the student of social welfare policy must understand the historical foundations on which it has been built. This chapter examines the historical antecedents of the American social welfare state, taking the reader from its distant roots before the English Poor Laws to the more recent developments that mark the emergence of the modern social welfare state.

EARLY ANTECEDENTS OF WELFARE STATISM

Virtually all societies—including tribal, agricultural, and technologically based ones—have developed some form of welfare-related activities. In general, these structures—whether they be governmental, societal, familial, or cultural—often involve several goals: (1) to help ameliorate the individual suffering of those judged worthy of help, (2) to enhance the common good by helping to better distribute economic and social resources from one social group to another, (3) to extend the rights of citizenship to groups generally considered outside of the societal mainstream, and (4) to promote social stability (and thereby social control) by helping to remedy and manage individual and group suffering. Different societies often highlight different parts of these welfare functions.

In ancient Judaism, for example, it was expected that a brother marry the widow of his deceased brother. The custom of mandatory interfamilial marriage was more often found in traditional societies where polygamy was widely practiced. In effect, a widow and her children were protected from the harsh vicissitudes of daily life by entering the home (and thereby the physical and economic protection) of an immediate family member. While sexist by contemporary standards, these cultural systems served a purpose in maintaining at least a modicum of economic security for women and children.

Walter Trattner notes that Hammurabi, the Babylonian ruler who lived 2,000 years before Christ, made the protection of women and children part of his famous code. The Greeks and Romans also instituted welfare functions which included daily allowances for the handicapped, public distribution of grain for the needy, and institutions for the custodial care of various unfortunates.[1] Notwithstanding these important ancient precedents, the more immediate roots of the modern welfare state is found in Judeo-Christianity.

Judeo-Christian Doctrine and Social Welfare

From its early beginnings, Judaism contained strict laws for dealing with the poor and for giving *tzedakah* (Hebrew for "charity"). In many ways it also contained the seeds of the modern welfare state. For one, Jewish law required farmers to leave a minimum of one-sixtieth of their field crops unharvested, which was to be left for the poor. In order to deter dependence and promote ability and aggressiveness, this remaining crop was to be left standing for the poor to gather. Hence, the poor were encouraged to be competitive in gathering the *peah* (the standing allotment), and each was allowed to take as much as could be gathered.

Jewish Rabbinic law also established one of the earliest-known means tests. A person who had 200 *zuz* or above (which was established by the Rabbis as constituting enough to purchase one year's supply of food) was considered to be above the poverty line and therefore ineligible for assistance. Like modern means tests, exemptions in calculating the 200-*zuz* poverty level were complex. For example, the primary residence, household utensils, religious articles, and certain of the wife's property were exempt. As such, the poor were not forced to give up essential elements of their lifestyle in order to be entitled to assistance.

The process of Jewish charity itself was highly organized. In biblical times, it was common for each community to have two types of charity organizations—one for poor travelers and the other for the resident poor. The organization of the charity was administered by a tax committee and each family was assessed a fixed tax which was distributed to the resident poor every Friday. In addition, plates of prepared food were to be collected for the traveling poor. The law also prescribes what is to be given. If a person is hungry, that person must be given food; if people are without sufficient clothing, they must be given dress. In short, each person should be supplied with what is needed.

Jewish law is somewhat complicated in terms of taking charity, reflecting the ambiguity contained in the modern welfare state. On the one hand, poor people who are entitled to alms but who, instead of burdening the public, work exceptionally hard, thereby raising their standard of living and managing to support themselves, are worthy of high praise and long life. Instead of living a life where they need others for help, people will come to them for assistance. On the other hand, people who are so old, sick, or incapable of eking out the barest of existence and yet refuse help and therefore deprive themselves of essentials, thus endangering their lives, are condemned as ruthless and unworthy of pity. False pride is clearly scorned upon in the scriptures.

It is forbidden in Jewish law to turn away a poor person empty-handed. However, of the degrees of Jewish charity, the highest form is assisting the poor with a gift or a loan or by accepting them into a business partnership or by helping them find employment. In other words, the highest form of giving is easing the poor into situations where they can be self-sufficient. Conversely, the lowest level of charity is giving it morosely. Charity is expected to be given with an open heart: "Whoever gives charity to a poor man ill-mannerdly and with downcast looks has lost all the merit of his action even though he should give him a thousand gold pieces."[2] The next level of Jewish charity is when the giver knows not to whom s/he gives and the recipient is unaware of the source of the gift. The idea of providing anonymous charity to strangers also forms the backbone of the modern welfare state; namely, the modern welfare state is predicated on the payment of taxes to help strangers who will neither reciprocate nor recognize the charity provided by an individual.

Because most of the early Christians including Jesus, Paul, Peter, and the other early founders of the Christian church were Jews, it is not surprising that Jewish customs were adopted into Christian doctrine. Beginning in the sixth century, monasteries became important sources of relief for the poor, and some monastic orders were specifically designed to help the needy. The money to run charitable endeavors came from rents received on church lands, donations, endowments, collections, and the formal tithing of 10 percent or more of a person's income. Some of these monies were used to tend to the needy by providing food, provisions, and medical services.

THE ENGLISH POOR LAWS

The feudalistic system that dominated Europe throughout the Middle Ages helped protect (at least in theory) the poor from untoward hardship and distress. Specifically, most people were serfs living on large estates whose basic needs for employment, food, clothing, and aid in sickness were met by the lords of the manor. In return, most serfs functioned as quasi slaves and were forbidden to leave the estates without permission.

In turn, many of those living in medieval towns and cities were helped by service, craft or merchant guilds. While the first responsibility of guilds was to protect and meet the social and economic needs of their members, they sometimes helped others. This might include feeding the needy by distributing crops and by providing free lodging to itinerant travelers. In addition to the guilds, medieval hospitals (usually connected to monasteries) also provided an important service by offering free medical services and care for weary travelers, the old, orphans, and the destitute. Many of those hospitals, especially those in the burgeoning cities, were later taken over by municipal authorities. The growth of cities combined with the increased power of the state and the collapse of feudalism eventually led to the creation of the English Poor Laws, the first modern codification of laws and responsibilities relating to the poor.

The English Poor Laws in many ways functioned as an early model for American social welfare. Early social welfare relief in England was considered a private and church matter. For example, individual benefactors took responsibility for building almshouses, hospitals, and even bridges and roads. Despite private philanthropy, the main burden for the poor rested on the shoulders of the church. Most European governments, including that of England, assumed little responsibility for the care of the poor. This situation would change, however, with the emergence of industrialization and its stark realities.

As a result of rapid industrialization and the transformation of farmland into more profitable pasture areas for sheep—a transformation that was necessary to feed the hungry wool mills of England—the ensuing urban migration of displaced and impoverished peasants produced untoward social consequences, including begging and vagrancy. In 1349, after the Black Death had drastically reduced the population of England, King Edward III created the Statute of Labourers, which fixed maximum wages, placed travel restrictions on unemployed persons, forced the jobless to work for any employer willing to hire them, and outlawed giving alms to the able-bodied.[3] In 1531, the English Parliament outlawed begging for the able-bodied. Although repressive, the act also instructed local officials to seek out the worthy poor and to assign them areas where they could beg.[4]

The passage of the Act for the Punishment of Sturdy Vagabonds and Beggars in 1536—the Poor Law—further mandated the English government to take limited responsibility for the poor. Although this act increased the punishment for begging, it also ordered officials to obtain resources—through voluntary church donations—to care for the poor, the sick, the lame, and the aged. In addition, the statute required local officials to find work for the able-bodied and to arrange for the apprenticeship of poor children aged 5 to 14. In 1572, the English Parliament enacted yet another poor law, this time requiring local officials to implement a mandatory tax for the provision of economic relief to the poor.[5]

In 1601, the English government established the Elizabethan Poor Laws. These laws were developed primarily to control those poor who were unable to obtain employment in the new industrial sector and who, because of that, might become disruptive. Taxes were levied to finance the law, but the rules were, by our standards, harsh. Again a primary theme of the law was to distinguish the "deserving" from the "undeserving" poor. The worthy poor were the lame, the blind, orphaned children, and those who were unemployed through no fault of their own. The unworthy poor were vagrants, drunkards, and those considered slothful. The Elizabethan Poor Laws, which with minor modifications were to stand for 250 years, contained positive and repressive features. For example, parents with means were legally responsible for supporting their children and grandchildren. Children were responsible for supporting their parents and grandparents. On the repressive side, the unworthy poor were sent to workhouses and forced to do menial work for the minimum necessities of life. Poor people who refused to work could be sent to jail or, in some cases, executed. In addition, the English Poor Laws established the principle of "less eligibility," the idea that welfare will be less than the lowest prevailing wage.

In essence, these laws established the responsibility of the English government to provide relief to the needy. Furthermore, the laws decreed that the needy had a legal right to receive governmental assistance. In order to define the boundaries of government help, the law distinguished among three classes of dependents and proposed remediative measures: Needy children were given apprenticeships, the able-bodied were given work, and the worthy poor were provided either indoor (institutional) or outdoor (home) relief. Finally, the law ordered local governments to assume responsibility for the needy.[6] The English Poor Laws formed the basis for statutes that were enacted in both colonial and postcolonial America.[7]

THE POOR IN COLONIAL AMERICA

Many aspects of the Elizabethan welfare system were adopted by the American colonists. Like its English corollary, the parish, the colonial town was responsible for its residents. Up to about 1700, when almshouses began to appear, cases of pauperism were handled on an individual basis in town meetings. When the number of poverty cases increased as a result of indentured servants and abandoned children, the English system of overseers was introduced.

Most settlers in colonial America were poor.[8] However, unlike their European ancestors, they were not destitute. Therefore, despite the poverty in Colonial America, pauperism was not widespread. According to Robert Morris, fewer than 1 percent of American colonists received help from outside sources.[9]

In smaller towns unable to support an almshouse, it was not uncommon for the town council to auction off the poor to neighboring farmers, apprentice out children, place the poor in private homes at public expense, or send them to privately operated almshouses. Settlers believed that children should be part of a family unit, and thus the practice of indenture became widespread. However, by the end of the colonial period, the locus of responsibility for the poor began to shift from the town to the province.[10]

While the settlers had compassion for indigent townspeople, they showed considerably less compassion for destitute strangers. As the numbers of poor increased, some communities enacted laws of settlement. Residency requirements were strictly enforced through the policies of "warning out" or "passing on." The former term meant that newcomers were urged to move on if they appeared to be indigent. *Passing on* meant returning the transient poor to their former counties of residence. In addition to these warning-out practices, some colonies established residency requirements to determine eligibility for public assistance. The "fit" poor in colonial America were treated harshly. Idleness was regarded as a vice and the able-bodied loafer was either indentured, expelled from town, whipped, or jailed. By the eighteenth century the able-bodied unemployed were placed in workhouses or almshouses.[11]

By the early 1800s, the process for helping the poor had changed radically. The quasi benevolence of the town council was replaced by a reliance on workhouses. In some areas, the use of outdoor relief was all but abandoned in favor of institutional care. Moreover, it was not until the mid–1800s that the national government conceded even limited responsibility for the poor. Local government activities were based on a belief that poverty was a consequence of moral weakness, a theory that was linked to Puritan values and hence more prevalent in the New England than in the Middle Atlantic states and that thus demanded reeducation and an economical system of relief.[12]

SOCIAL WELFARE IN THE CIVIL WAR ERA

Historically, the federal government's role in providing relief has been a contentious issue. This question was to be advanced by the reform activities of Dorothea Dix, a name that has become synonymous with the movement for the humane care of the mentally ill. As a result of volunteering as a Sunday school teacher for an insane asylum in 1841, Dix went through a form of emotional conversion. Appalled by the conditions she saw at the asylum, Dix committed herself to fighting for reform in the care of the mentally ill.

The majority of mentally ill people in the 1840s were placed in public mental institutions, jails, or almshouses. Their treatment was often brutal and consisted of beatings, being chained, or being sequestered in cages or pens. Dix decided that neither private philanthropy nor local action could remedy the problem. For Dix, the solution to caring for the insane lay in state and federal intervention.

After having successfully lobbied for state action, Dix decided that, because of the large expenditures required, federal intervention was necessary. With the support of well-known members of the clergy, prominent citizens, newspaper staff members, and public and private organizations, a bill was passed in 1854 by both houses of Congress that provided federal support for the mentally ill. Unfortunately, President Franklin Pierce vetoed the bill, claiming that, "If Congress has the power to make provisions for the indigent insane . . . it has the same power for the indigent who are not insane. . . . I cannot find any authority in the Constitution for making the Federal Government the great almoner of public charity throughout the United States."[13] Pierce's veto was in large part based on his belief in states' rights, but, more important, for the next 75 years his veto provided the rationale for the federal government's refusal to provide social welfare services.[14]

The Civil War ushered in a new period for relief activities. Families who had lost a breadwinner or who had a breadwinner return from the war permanently disabled could not be blamed for their misfortunes. As a response to the hardship created by the Civil War, localities passed laws that raised funds for the sick and needy and, in some instances, for the founding of homes for disabled soldiers.

Other welfare issues during the Civil War included the disease and filth rampant in army camps and hospitals and the shortage of trained medical personnel. In an effort to remedy this situation, a group of citizens (composed mainly of women) in 1861 organized the U.S. Sanitary Commission, the first important national public health group. Functioning as a quasi-governmental body, the commission was financed and directed by the private voluntary sector. Working initially in the area of preventive health education, the commission eventually became involved in a variety of direct and indirect ways of serving the needs of soldiers.[15]

Another social welfare institution that emerged from the Civil War was the Freedmen's Bureau. By the close of the war, political leaders realized that the emancipation of millions of slaves would create serious social problems. Former slaves having no occupational training, land, or jobs would require assistance. In 1865, therefore, Congress established the Bureau of Refugees, Freedmen, and Abandoned Lands. The Freedmen's Bureau, as it was commonly called, was responsible for directing a program of temporary relief for the duration of the war and one year afterward. After a bitter struggle, Congress extended the Freedmen's Bureau for an additional six years.

The bureau, under General Oliver Howard, performed a variety of services designed to help African Americans make the transition from slavery to freedom. For example, the bureau served as an emergency relief center that distributed 22 million rations to needy Southerners. The bureau also functioned as an African American employment agency, a settlement agency, a health center that employed doctors and operated hospitals, an educational agency that encouraged the funding of African American colleges and provided financial aid, and, finally, as a legal agency that maintained courts in which civil and criminal cases involving African Americans were heard. The Freedmen's Bureau set a crucial precedent for federal involvement in a variety of human services. In 1872 the bureau was dissolved by Congress.[16]

INDUSTRIALIZATION AND THE VOLUNTARY SECTOR

Private efforts to enhance the welfare of the community have been a prominent part of social welfare throughout the history of the United States. During his travels through the young nation early in the nineteenth century, Alexis de Tocqueville commented on the proclivity of Americans to band together voluntarily to solve the problems besetting their communities:

> Americans of all ages, all conditions, and all dispositions, constantly form associations. They have not only commercial and manufacturing companies, in which all take part, but associations of a thousand other kinds—religious, moral, serious, futile, extensive or restrictive, enormous and diminutive. The Americans make associations to give entertainments, to found establishments for education, to build inns, to construct churches, to diffuse books, to send missionaries to the antipodes; and in this manner they found hospitals, prisons, and schools. If it be proposed to advance some truth, or to foster some feeling of encouragement of a great example, they form a society. Wherever, at the head of some new undertaking, you see the Government of France, or a man of rank in England, in the United States you will be sure to find an association.[17]

Reliance on voluntary associations to solve problems corresponded with the nature of the community in that era. Prior to industrialization, most people lived in communities with an array of institutions that afforded a high degree of self-sufficiency. Survival necessitated a degree of solidarity, or interdependence, that was taken as a law of nature. Cohesiveness of this kind can still be found among certain religious sects, such as the Amish, which manage human needs through the voluntary impulses of members, who see good deeds as a normal extension of their daily activities.

With industrialization, however, this method of managing welfare proved inadequate for most groups, and special entities were designated to provide for social welfare.[18] The fact that institutions specializing in welfare would emerge at this time is related to the spreading industrialization of America and to the subsequent social dislocation that resulted in the relocation of millions of families. From 1890 to 1920, 22 million immigrants came to the United States. At the same time, the American people became more urban. Seventy-five percent of foreign immigrants lived in the cities, and during the decade following 1920, 6 million people moved from farms to cities.[19]

Life in late–nineteenth-century America was hard. The dream of milk and honey that motivated many immigrants to leave their homelands became, for many, a nightmare. The streets of American cities were not paved with gold; instead, they were overcrowded, rampant with disease and crime, and economically destitute. Many tenement houses in the larger cities contained neither windows nor indoor plumbing. Tuberculosis was widespread, and among some groups, infant mortality ran as high as 50 percent. Scant medical care existed for the poor; there was no public education, and insanity and prostitution rates among immigrants were high.[20] The industrial and economic prospects were equally bleak. Factory conditions were abominable: Workers were expected to labor six or seven days a week (often on Sunday), and 18-hour days were not unusual, especially in summer.[21] Factories were poorly lit and unsanitary, easily turned into fire traps, and offered almost no job security. Moreover, homework (taking piecework home, usually for assembly by whole families in one- or two-room tenements) was common. Women were forced to work night shifts and then take care of their homes and children by day.[22] No special protective legislation for women existed until the early 1900s, and child labor was legal. According to Richard Hofstadter, industrial accidents affected one out of every 10 to 12 workers, and employees had neither worker's compensation nor disability insurance.[23] When these conditions are added to the fact that every 15 or 20 years there was another depression, it is obvious that the lot of the immigrant and of most working-class Americans was very hard. The extent of their suffering is evident in a modern scholar's description of New York City during the period:

> With the shift of population from the grange to the tenement house came a degree of over expansion and under management that brought large cities to the crisis point: sanitation and health were plainly inadequate; there was a constant fear of rioting and crime; the police used their night sticks against the people they were sworn to protect. Fed by immigrants streaming through Castle Garden and, after 1891, Ellis Island, New York's East Side was the end point of all cities. With over 500 people for

> each acre, nearly five times the average for the rest of Manhattan, the Tenth Ward was the most densely settled area in the world, and its ghetto was larger than Warsaw's. It was "the suicide ward" and "the typhus ward," and the breeding place of the "white plague" of tuberculosis, epidemics of all kinds, crime, pauperism, alcoholism, sweated labor, hopelessness, and a frightful mortality rate.[24]

Faced with this dilemma, a growing middle class struggled to explain and cope with the mounting social debris in American cities. There was an urgency to this task. Through the germ theory, medical science had identified the cause of many contagious diseases but had yet to develop preventive vaccines or cures. Thus, it was no accident that Charles Loring Brace, a pioneer of child welfare, entitled his book *The Dangerous Classes of New York*. Moreover, graft and corruption became rife as urban immigrants competed for scarce food, housing, and jobs, eking out a marginal existence in squalid city tenements. Eventually, political machines emerged that converted city governments into fiefdoms of patronage. In an exposé of graft in New York City, Jacob Riis, a muckraking journalist, alleged that the political machine of Boss Tweed's Tammany Hall was nothing more than "a band of political cutthroats." Not particularly surprising, Riis noted that Tweed was the product of a Fourth Ward tenement.[25] Yet, even when muckrakers uncovered abuses and railed against them in banner headlines, political bosses were so confident of the indispensability of "the machine" that they responded to accusations with defiance. For example, upon hearing of an exposé by Lincoln Steffens, George Washington Plunkett, a Tammany Hall crony, quipped: "Steffens means well but, like all reformers, he don't know how to make distinctions. He can't see no difference between honest graft and dishonest graft and, consequently, he gets things all mixed up."[26]

Social Darwinism

Many people looked to the developing social sciences for guidance in redefining social policy. There, prominent scholars drew lessons from the natural sciences that could be used for purposes of social engineering. Borrowing from biology, some American proponents of the new science of sociology applied the idea of natural selection to social affairs.

Social Darwinism was a bastard outgrowth of Charles Darwin's theory of evolution as described in his 1859 classic, *The Origin of Species*.[27] Social theorists such as Herbert Spencer and America's William Graham Sumner reasoned that if Darwin's laws of evolution determined the origin and development of species, then they might also be applied to understanding the laws of society.[28]

Applying Darwin's rules to society and then adapting laissez-faire principles of economics to sociology led to a problematic set of assumptions. First, if the "survival of the fittest" (a term coined by Spencer) was a law governing the lower species, then it must also govern the higher species. Because subsidizing the poor allowed them to survive, this circumvented the law of nature, and because the poor reproduced more rapidly than the middle classes, society was thus subsidizing its own demise. Social Darwinists believed essentially that the poor would eventually overrun society and bring down the general level of civilization.

Second, if as Darwin maintained, competition for resources was the law of life, then the poor are impoverished because they cannot compete. Conversely, the economic elite are entitled to their spoils because of their "fitness" and competitive abilities. In any case, by subsidizing the poor, thus allowing them to reproduce, society artificially alters the laws of nature and, in doing so, weakens the human gene pool.

Finally, Social Darwinists believed that, although unfortunate, the poor must pay the price demanded by nature and be allowed to die out. According to the Social Darwinists, social welfare thwarts nature's plan of evolutionary progress toward higher forms of social life. Speaking for many intellectuals, the British theorist Herbert Spencer drew this conclusion:

> It seems hard that widows and orphans should be left to struggle for life or death. Nevertheless, when regarded not separately but in connexion with the interests of universal humanity, these harsh fatalities are seen to be full of beneficence—the same beneficence which brings to early graves the children of diseased parents, and singles out

> the intemperate and the debilitated as the victims of an epidemic.[29]

While some thinkers promoted the harsh strictures of Social Darwinism, and socialists saw poverty as a manifestation of an unjust class society, Christianity provided yet another answer.

Religion and Social Welfare

Religion and social welfare in nineteenth-century America were inextricably linked. Almost all forms of relief emanated from church groups, and all major denominations had some mechanism for providing social welfare.[30] For example, as early as 1880 there were 500 private, church-related social welfare organizations in New York City alone, with the largest network for social services provided by Protestant churches.

Poverty was seen as a moral failing in the context of orthodox Protestant theology. Martin Luther viewed work as a responsibility to God. Furthermore, work conferred dignity and was a "calling" by God. In Luther's view, a person served God by doing the work of his vocation. Therefore, those who are able-bodied and yet unemployed are sinners. John Calvin took Luther's argument one step further by claiming that work carried out the will of God and, as such, would ultimately help to create God's kingdom on earth. According to both Luther and Calvin, God-fearing people must work regardless of their wage or type of employment.[31]

Because the command to work came from God, economic success was seen as a sign of favor. Poverty, therefore, was also a sign of God's will. This Protestant ethic fueled the creation of a work-oriented society and provided a religious foundation for the indifference of the elite classes toward the poor. In addition, by adding a religious dimension to poverty, conservative Protestantism more sharply focused the distinction between the worthy and the unworthy poor.[32]

Conservative theologians used a religious framework to connect poverty and improvidence: People were poor because they engaged in drinking, slothfulness, licentious behavior, and gambling. Some critics have argued that despite the social welfare services provided by the churches, in the final analysis Protestant theology was basically opposed to social welfare.[33]

It was thought that in order to reclaim providence the poor must be taught to live a moral and self-disciplined life. While early religious social workers clung tenaciously to their desire to teach the moral life, they also understood the need to provide material assistance.[34] The major emphasis of the early social worker, however, was more often on spiritual guidance than on material aid.

The relief assistance provided by these evangelical social workers was often linked to harsh criteria. For example, it was not uncommon for social workers to appraise the worth of the family's possessions and then instruct them to sell off everything in order to qualify for relief. Nor was it uncommon for social workers to deny relief because they felt that the poor family was intemperate and not sufficiently contrite. If the family refused to accept moral guidance, it could be deemed ineligible for relief. Despite the fact that these social workers dispensed relief, they were basically opposed to the concept of it. They believed that distributing relief was imprudent because a reliance on charity would weaken the moral fabric of the poor and provide a disincentive for work.

The reign of conservative Protestant theology was not without opposition. In the late nineteenth and early twentieth century, a movement known as the Social Gospel emerged. Composed of theologians concerned with the abuses created by industrialization and the excesses of capitalism, Social Gospelists such as Josiah Strong, Graham Taylor, and others believed that the church should recapture the militant spirit of Christ by taking on the issues of social justice and poverty. The critique posed by the Social Gospelists called for fair play and simple justice for the worker.[35]

Proponents of the Social Gospel movement maintained that churches wrongfully stressed spirituality rather than morality.[36] The condemnation of classical economics, business ethics, and the lawlessness of the plutocracy was centered on a moral rather than a spiritual plane. For the Social Gospelists, social reformation could not occur without a regeneration of character.[37] Although the movement contained degrees of radicalism, all Social Gospelists were moved by a sense of social crisis, and all believed in the necessity of a Christian solution.[38] The legacy of the Social Gospel movement is evident in the current rise of Liberation Theology, a grass-roots movement of progressive theologians that is gaining strength in many Latin American and African nations. In any case, the combination of Social Darwinism and Christian charity suffused the organizations that assumed a major share of the responsibility for social welfare during the industrial era—Charity Organization Societies and Settlement Houses.

Charity Organization Societies

First evident in the 1870s, Charity Organization Societies (COSs) had offices in most American cities by 1900.[39] With the exception of meager state-sponsored indoor and outdoor relief, the COS movement was a major provider of care to the destitute. COSs varied in their structures and methods. In general, they coordinated relief giving by operating community-wide registration bureaus, providing direct relief, and "educating" both the upper and lower classes as to their mutual obligations.

The work of the COS was carried out by a committee of volunteers and agency representatives who examined "cases" of needy applicants and decided on a course of action. The agent of the COS was the "friendly visitor," whose task was to conduct an investigation of the circumstances surrounding the cases and to instruct the poor in ways of better managing their lives. Friendly visitors, drawn from the upper classes, often held a morally superior attitude toward their clientele, and their intervention in the lives of the poor was interpreted by some observers as a form of social control[40] as well as a means of providing assistance. In any case, the charity provided by these organizations was often less than generous. Leaders of the movement drew an important lesson from Social Darwinism in believing that beneficent charity was counterproductive because it contributed to sloth and dependency. Josephine Shaw Lowell, president of the New York Charity Organization Society, believed that charity should be dispensed "only when starvation was imminent."[41]

To be sure, it was difficult for friendly visitors to maintain a sense of Christian duty in the midst of immoral behavior. In such instances, when some wretched soul seemed beyond instruction and charity, more radical measures were in order. Charles Loring Brace, head of the New York Children's Aid Society, described his approach to dealing with a German mother who worked as a "swill-gatherer" in "Dutch Hill":

> On the eastern side of the city, in the neighborhood of Fortieth Street, is a village of squatters, which enjoys the title of "Dutch Hill." The inhabitants are not, however, "Dutch," but mainly poor Irish, who have taken temporary possession of unused sites on a hill, and have erected shanties which serve at once for pig-pens, hen-coops, bed-rooms, and living-rooms. They enjoy the privilege of squatters in having no rent to pay; but they are exposed to the penalty of being at any moment turned out from their dens, and losing land and house at once. . . . The village is filled with snarling dogs, which aid in drawing the swill or coal carts, for the children are mainly employed in collecting swill and picking coals through the streets.
>
> [An] old rag-picker I remember whose shanty was a sight to behold; all the odds and ends of a great city seemed piled up in it—bones, broken dishes, rags, bits of furniture, cinders, old tin, useless lamps, decaying vegetables, ribbons, cloths, legless chairs, and carrion, all mixed together, and heaped up nearly to the ceiling, leaving hardly room for a bed on the floor where the woman and her two children slept. Yet all these [children] were marvels of health and vigor, far surpassing most children I know in the comfortable classes. The woman was German, and after years of effort could never be induced to do anything for the education of her children, until finally I put the police on their track as vagrants, and they were safely housed in the "Juvenile Asylum."[42]

What happened to the children who had been placed in the "Juvenile Asylum"? Brace's solution was as ingenious as it was compatible with the tenets of Social Darwinism and Christian charity. The Children's Aid Society transported between 50,000 and 100,000 "orphans" westward by train, where they were placed with farm families.[43] The advertisement in Figure 3.1, posted in McPherson, Kansas, provides some detail on the procedures devised by Brace and his associates.

Settlement Houses

The settlement house movement, which began in the 1880s and emerged in most of the big cities over the next two decades, was also a response to the urban conditions of the times. Settlement houses were primarily set up in immigrant neighborhoods by wealthy people, college students, unattached women, teachers, doctors, and lawyers, who themselves moved into the slums as residents. Rather than simply engaging in friendly visiting, the upper- and middle-class settlement leaders tried to bridge class differences and to develop a less patronizing form of charity. Rather than coordinate existing charities as had the COSs, they sought to help the people in the neighborhoods to organize themselves. Because they actually lived in the same neighborhoods as the impoverished immigrants, settlement workers could provide fresh and reliable knowledge about the social and economic conditions of American cities.

Jane Addams established Hull House in 1889. She approached the project—and the Chicago ethnic community in which it was based—with a sense of Christian Socialism that was derived from a "rather strenuous moral purgation"[44] rather than a sense of noblesse oblige. The cofounder of Hull House, Ellen Gates Starr, described the values of the settlement house worker.

> After we had been here long enough and people see that we don't catch diseases and that vicious people do not destroy us or our property . . . we have well founded reason to believe that there are at least half a dozen girls in the city who will be glad to come and stay a while and learn to know the people and understand them and their ways of life; to give out of their culture and leisure and overindulgence and to receive the culture that comes from self-denial and poverty and failure which these people have always known.[45]

By 1915, this altruism was shared by enough settlement workers so that more than 300 settlements had been established, and most of the larger American cities could boast at least one or more settlement houses.[46]

While providing individual services to the poor, the larger settlements were essentially reform-oriented. These reforms were achieved not only by organizing the poor to press for change but also by using interest groups formed by elite citizens, as well as by the formation of national alliances. Settlement-pioneered reforms included tuberculosis prevention, the establishment of well-baby clinics, the implementation of housing codes, the construction of outdoor playgrounds, the enactment of child labor and industrial safety legislation, and the promotion of some of the first studies of the urban black in America, such as W. E. B. Du Bois's *The Philadelphia Negro*.

Homes For Children

WANTED

A Company of Homeless Children from the East Will Arrive at

McPherson, Friday, September 15.

These children are of various ages and of both sexes, having been thrown friendless upon the world. They come under the auspices of the Children's Aid Society, of New York. They are well disciplined, having come from various orphanages. The citizens of this community are asked to assist the agent in finding good homes for them. Persons taking these children must be recommended by the local committee. They must treat the children in every way as members of the family, sending them to school, church. Sabbath school and properly clothe them until they are 18 years old. Protestant children placed in Protestant homes and Catholic children in Catholic homes. The following well known citizens have agreed to act as a local committee to aid the agents in securing homes:

Dr. Heaston H. A. Rowland C. W. Bachelor
F. A. Vaniman W. J. Krehbiel K. Sorensen

Applications must be made to and endorsed by the local committee.

An address will be given by the agents. Come and see the children and hear the address. Distribution will take place at

Opera House, Friday, September 15

at 10:00 a. m. and 2:00 p. m.

Miss A. I. HILL and MISS C. B. COMSTOCK, Agents, 105 East 22nd Street, New York City. W. W. BUGBEE, Eldorado, Kansas, State Agent.

◆ **FIGURE 3.1 Handbill Promoting Orphan Train, McPherson, KS, 1911**

Source: Reprinted from Martha Nelson Vogt, *Searching for Home* (Martha Nelson Vogt and Christina Vogt, 1062 Edison NW, Grand Rapids, MI, 1979).

Many of the leaders of the New Deal had worked in settlements. For example, alumnae of Hull House included Edith Abbott, drafter of the Social Security Act; her sister, Grace Abbott, and Julia Lathrop, who became directors of the U.S. Children's Bureau; and Frances Perkins, Secretary of Labor and the first woman to be appointed to a cabinet post.[47]

African American Associations

If the conditions of immigrants were difficult, those of African Americans were even more trying. In the absence of government programs, African Americans had to rely on private sources of welfare, even though many of these voluntary agencies frequently discriminated against them. Consequently, a number of fraternal and benefit associations emerged within the African American community, such as the Knights of Tabor, the Knights of Pythias, the Ancient Sons of Israel, and the Grand United Order of True Reformers.[48] These organizations, many of them indigenous to the African American community, were instrumental in binding the fabric of a community that suffered from continual distress compounded by limited resources. As an example, consider some of the constitutional provisions of one health and burial society:

Sec. 1. This society shall be known as the Sons and Daughters of Zion.

Sec. 2. The object of this society shall be to care for its sick and bury its dead members and all moneys paid therein shall be expended for same. By a two-thirds vote, however, of all the active members, money may be expended for other purposes.

Sec. 5. The monthly fee of all members in Sons and Daughters of Zion shall be 25 cents.

Sec. 17. The Society shall not employ more than three doctors, who shall be elected annually, and shall purchase all medicine from one drug store.

Sec. 18. The burial expenses shall in no case exceed $25.00, and in all cases the hearse shall be used in conveying the body to the cemetery.

Rule 19. The chairman of the sick and burial committee shall summon as many male members as are necessary to dig a grave. In his absence the male messenger shall discharge this duty. Members who fail to assist in digging a grave after having been appointed, and who don't get anyone in their place, shall pay a fine of 75 cents or be suspended for six months.

Rule 26. The society shall not be responsible for the following bills: Bills caused from accident or death in disreputable places, self-abuse among men as diseases brought on by lewd habits, women confined, accident or death from stealing or anything dishonorable.[49]

Before government played a prominent role in guaranteeing the basic rights of citizens, important events in the history of African Americans were often connected with voluntary associations that arose within the African American community. Talladega College, the first distinguished liberal arts college serving rural African Americans, had its origin in a carpenter shop where David White, Sr., a freedman, and Leonard Johnson, "a black man who had in some way acquired the rudiments of learning," began a school.[50] Morehouse College, the alma mater of Martin Luther King, Jr., began in 1867 as a night school in the Springfield Baptist Church of Augusta, Georgia.[51] When it appeared that the industrial education approach of Booker T. Washington would not guarantee African Americans full citizenship, W. E. B. Du Bois galvanized a group of reformers, among them social workers such as Ida B. Wells, Mary White Covington, and Jane Addams, into the Niagara Movement. Marshaling support through meetings at centers of abolitionist sentiment, the Niagara Movement became the National Association for the Advancement of Colored People. Meanwhile, a concern for economic justice led George Edmund Haynes, a Columbia University graduate student, to write *The Negro at Work in New York City*. The attention attracted by this study contributed to the formation in 1911 of the National Urban League on Urban Conditions. Using philanthropic assistance from foundations, the League established a program for social work training that "made possible the education of many of America's most distinguished social work leaders in the next generation."[52]

Prior to World War I, social welfare in the United States consisted almost exclusively of private agencies voluntarily established by groups for the purpose of enhancing the public welfare. Indeed, many of the community agencies with which most Americans are familiar were established at this time, as shown in the following list of the founding dates of selected organizations:

1851—Young Men's Christian Association
1858—Young Women's Christian Association
1880—Salvation Army
1881—American Red Cross
1896—Volunteers of America
1902—Goodwill Industries
1907—Boys' Clubs of America
1910—Boy Scouts of America
1910—Catholic Charities
1911—Family Service Association of America
1912—Girl Scouts of America

The Social Casework Agency

Charity Organization Societies and settlement houses served as models for the delivery of social welfare services in the voluntary sector organizations that emerged during the Progressive Era. Similar in many respects, these organizations evolved to form the social casework agency. Both were of modest size in terms of staff, both were located in the communities of the clientele they served, both served a predominantly poor population, and both relied on contributions from a variety of sources—private donations, the Community Chest, and foundations.[53] Typically, workers in these agencies were female volunteers. COS techniques for investigation were refined, their aim being the identification of a "social diagnosis" as the basis for case intervention.[54] Subsequently, these activities, along with the community-oriented work of the settlement reformers, gave birth to the profession of social work.

Despite the efforts of these early women social workers, their professional status was not highly esteemed or even recognized. At the time, the caricature of the journalist H. L. Mencken was perhaps typical of public sentiment:

> The social worker, judging by her own pretensions, helps to preserve multitudes of persons who would perish if left to themselves. Thus her work is clearly dysgenic and anti-social. For every victim of sheer misfortune that she restores to self-sustaining and social usefulness, she must keep alive scores of misfits and incompetents who can never, for all her help, pull their weight in the boat. Such persons can do nothing more valuable than dying.[55]

As predominant service delivery forms, COSs and settlement houses were transformed by two influences: the need for scientifically based treatment techniques, and the socialization of charity. Together, these factors contributed to the emergence of the social casework agency. COSs and settlement houses had provided meaningful activity for upper- and middle-class women who found it necessary to ground their work in treatment techniques that were derived from science. This necessity had been driven home in 1915 during the National Conference of Charities and Correction, when Abraham Flexner, a renowned authority on professional graduate education, was asked to address the question of whether social work was a profession. Much to the disappointment of the audience, Flexner judged that social work lacked all the requirements of a profession, particularly a scientifically derived knowledge base that was transmittable.[56] Subsequently, the Milford Conference Report of 1923 underscored the importance of a scientific base for social work knowledge.

> The future growth of social casework is in large measure dependent upon its developing a scientific character. Its scientific character will be the result of a scientific attitude in social caseworkers towards their own problems, and as part of increasingly scientific adaptations from the subject matter of other sciences.[57]

Scientific social work served the manifest function of improving the effectiveness of social work practice and thereby increased the status of the new profession. At the same time, it served a latent function. Describing the social worker's client in scientific terms functioned to elevate the image of the client from one of an inept wretch to one characterized by specific afflictions that were mutable.

At the same time, the funding of COSs, settlement houses, and other service organizations had proven undependable because of the competition among agencies for donors' funds and the fact that these gifts were dependent on a largesse that fluctuated with an unstable economy. The solution to this problem emerged in the form of a collective approach to philanthropic giving. As early as 1887, Denver's Associated Charities had pioneered the concept whereby a group of agencies appealed to the conscience of the community for operating funds. By the 1920s, more than 200 cities had adopted community chests, thus reducing the need for the independent agency to curry favors on its own.[58] The socialization of charity provided agencies with a relatively steady income while demanding uniformity in operations. Uniformity was allied with efficiency, a guiding principle of the Progressive Era,[59] and this resulted in an organizational form that served to rationalize a previously haphazard array of social services.[60] Together, the needs of workers for effective treatment techniques and the economic imperatives for organizational survival functioned to standardize the social casework agency.

Perhaps the best description of the casework agency evolved from the Milford Conference of 1923, when 16 executives and board members from six national organizations drafted a document endorsing agency-based service delivery. The Milford Conference Report provided a comprehensive outline of the organization through which professional caseworkers delivered services. The social casework agency was located in a community and derived its objectives and purposes from it. The agency was governed by a board of directors that hired the agency director and met monthly to monitor agency affairs. Caseworkers functioned under supervision, thus combining the need for administrative and professional accountability. Most important, workers had a repertoire of more than 25 methods—among them diagnosis, interviewing, prognosis, planning, treatment, and reeducation. Moreover, some or all of these methods were useful for countering a host of "deviations" from "normal social life," such as alcoholism, delinquency, family antagonisms, mental ill health, pauperism, and vagrancy. The social casework agency concept encompassed the fields of child welfare, family welfare, visitor teaching, medical social work, psychiatric social work, and probation work. They accomplished this charge within administrative procedures that were "in accordance with accepted business standards and practice, including audits of accounts at least annually by an accredited public accountant."[61]

This characterization of the social agency was prophetic and served as a model for human service delivery over the following decades. Child guidance clinics, probation departments, mental health clinics, family planning clinics, and public welfare offices resembled the casework agency envisaged by the Milford Conference Report. Despite differences in auspices and service mandate, the fundamental elements remained intact. The social casework agency provided a service delivery model through which the emerging profession of social work could apply its skills.

Economically, the social casework agency met the accountability requirements of different funding sources. In the case of private donations—corporate, individual, and foundation—the casework agency was managed by an executive officer and operated in accordance with established business practices. In the case of other charities—the Community Chest and United Way—the casework agency was under the guidance of a board of directors that upheld the best interests of the community. In the case of public (governmental) funding, the casework agency was administered on the basis of governmental regulations by the executive director who was part of the government bureaucracy. According to the needs of the professional social work community and the fiscal requirements of philanthropic and governmental funding sources, the casework agency was perceived to be professionally managed and economically efficient. Through much of the twentieth century, the social casework agency was a common setting for the provision of human services, reflecting the basic principles outlined in the Milford Conference of 1923.

The Progressive Movement

A reaction to the heartlessness that characterized a large segment of American society came in the form of the Progressive movement, a social movement that was popular from the early 1900s to World War I.

Progressive Era philosophy, intended to inject a measure of public credibility and Christian morality into social, political, and economic affairs, was a unique blend of social reform encompassing anti–big business attitudes, a belief that government should regulate the public good, a strong emphasis on ethics in business and personal life, a commitment to social justice, a concern for the "common man," a strong sense of paternalism, and, not surprisingly, a tendency toward jingoism. Progressives believed that the state had a responsibility for protecting the interests of the public, especially people who were vulnerable. The Progressive Party, supported by the nation's most respected social workers, including Jane Addams, Lillian Wald, and Paul U. Kellogg, presented a presidential ticket in 1912.

Impressive governmental reforms were enacted during the Progressive period. For example, President Theodore Roosevelt made great strides in the areas of natural resource conservation and civil service reform, and also strengthened the power of the Interstate Commerce Commission. President Woodrow Wilson's administration enacted major reforms in the areas of tariffs and banking, and curbed monopolistic practices through the Clayton Antitrust Act of 1914. Other reforms enacted during Wilson's administration included better credit facilities and agricultural education for farmers, better working conditions in the Merchant Marine, a worker's compensation law for all federal civil service employees, the establishment of the eight-hour day for all workers on interstate railroads, a law excluding the products of child labor from interstate commerce, and federal aid to states for highway construction.[62]

Progressive reformers also experienced limited successes in protecting the rights of working women. By 1912, a total of 11 states had legislated a floor under which women's wages could not fall. In 1919, Massachusetts passed a bill that limited the maximum number of hours (for most classes of working women) to 44 per week. New York followed suit in 1919 with a 54-hour week for a limited number of women workers.[63] In addition to minimum wage and maximum hour legislation, many states enacted laws prohibiting night work for women in certain industries, as well as lifting restrictions regulating the maximum weight a woman could be required to handle.[64]

The advent of World War I helped diminish the liberal fervor that had characterized the Progressive Era of the late 1800s and early 1900s. In the wake of the disillusionment that followed the war, the mood of the country became conservative. Progressive ideas were treated skeptically in the 1920s; frequently the proponents of those ideas were accused of being Bolsheviks. By 1924, the situation was even worse: Congress had curtailed immigration, the child labor amendment was all but defeated, political repression became common, many foreign radicals were deported as a result of the raids conducted by Attorney General A. Mitchell Palmer, the Ku Klux Klan was gaining strength, labor unrest exploded everywhere, and corruption in high places was rampant.[65] Americanization and intolerance became operational concepts, and even the settlement houses lost much of their sway during the conservative post–World War I era. Despite the suffrage movement, which gave women the right to vote, the 1920s represented an extremely conservative period in American history.

Although we think of the 1920s as a period of prosperity, more than one-third of the American population at this time lived in poverty.[66] Many of the reforms enacted during the Progressive Era of the early 1900s were rescinded in the Roaring Twenties. By the late 1920s, some states had enacted widows' pensions and workers' compensation laws, but most charity still occurred by way of private social service organizations.

THE GREAT DEPRESSION AND THE MODERN WELFARE STATE

In the election of 1928, Herbert Hoover ran for President against the Catholic and Democratic governor of New York State, Alfred E. Smith. Known as a militant prohibitionist and a strong humanitarian (because of his relief activities at the end of World War I), Hoover handily beat Smith, in the process winning the support of many social workers, including Jane Addams.[67]

In October 1929 the stock market crashed. A year later, 6 million men and women were walking the streets looking for work. By 1932, more than 600,000 were jobless in Chicago, and 1 million in New York City. In Cleveland, 50 percent of workers were unemployed, in Akron 60 percent, and in Toledo 80 percent of the population was looking for work. Only three years after the crash, more than 100,000 workers were being fired in an average week.[68] By the early 1930s, the gross national product (GNP)—the sum total of all the goods and services produced in the country—had dropped to a half of what it had been prior to the Depression. The national income dropped from $81 billion in 1929 to $40 billion in 1932.[69] By 1932, manufacturing output had fallen to 54 percent of what it had been in 1929, a little less than the total production in 1913. In that same year the automobile industry was operating at only one-fifth of its 1929 capacity. Steel plants operated at only 12 percent of their potential, and the output of pig iron was the lowest since 1896. In addition, factory wages shrank from $12 billion in 1929 to $7 billion in 1932. Unemployment reached a high of 24 percent, and for the first time, more people emigrated from America than migrated to it (in 1932, 35,329 people emigrated to America and 103,295 left). Even the birthrate was cut almost in half—from 30 births per thousand in 1929 to 18 births per thousand in 1940. By 1932, 20 million people were on the relief rolls.[70]

In search of work, or perhaps just motion, thousands of Americans aimlessly wandered the country. In 1929, the Missouri Pacific Railroad reported 13,745 migrants; in 1931, 186,028; and by 1932, between 1 and 2 million people were roaming the country.[71] The unemployed who chose to stay close to home often frequented the thousands of soup lines that sprang up across the country.

Relief under the Hoover administration proved wholly inadequate. Private charities and local governments soon exhausted their coffers. Relief payments, which in 1929 totaled $5 per week for an entire family, were cut to $2.39 in New York and still less elsewhere. Dallas and Houston refused relief to all Hispanic American and African American families. Detroit slashed its relief rolls by one-third. New Orleans refused all new relief applicants, and St. Louis cut its relief rolls in half. Except for New York, Illinois, Pennsylvania, New Jersey, and Wisconsin, state governments did almost nothing to aid the victims of the Great Depression. More than 100 cities had no relief appropriations in 1932.[72]

Having seen little of the acclaimed prosperity of the 1920s, most farmers were devastated by the Depression. American foreign trade declined from $10 billion in 1929 to $3 billion in 1932. Crop prices registered new lows: Wheat fell from $1.05 a bushel in 1929 to 39 cents in 1932, corn from 81 cents to 33 cents a bushel, cotton from 17 to 6 cents a pound, and tobacco from 19 to 10 cents a pound. As a result, gross farm income fell from nearly $12 billion in 1929 to only $5 billion in 1932.[73] Farmers responded to these economic conditions with angry protests. From Pennsylvania to Nebraska, farmers banded together to prevent banks and insurance companies from foreclosing on mortgages. When sheriffs attempted to break up these actions, some farmers brandished pitchforks and hangman's nooses to make their point.

Herbert Hoover's response to the Depression was, for the most part, inaction. Hoover opted to rely on the voluntary social welfare sector, justifying his position by the belief that federal relief would weaken the social and moral fiber of the society, impair the credit and solvency of the government, and delay the ability of the natural forces at work to restore the economy. Moreover, according to Hoover, federal relief was illegal and a violation of states' rights.[74]

The voluntary social welfare sector responded to the Depression by organizing massive fund drives, but, because of the sheer scope of the problem, these proved ineffective. Although a large segment of the social work community and most voluntary social welfare agencies agreed with Hoover in his opposition to federal aid, by 1932 he was forced to propose an unemployment assistance program in which the federal government paid 80 percent of the costs. By the time Hoover was defeated by Franklin Delano Roosevelt (FDR) in the election of 1932, Hoovervilles (shantytowns sarcastically named in Hoover's honor) had sprung up in most large cities. Soup lines became a part of the urban landscape, economically motivated suicides were commonplace, and such legendary robbers as Dillinger, Baby Face Nelson, and Bonnie Parker and Clyde Barrow were the rage.

When FDR assumed the presidency in 1933 he faced a country increasingly divided between Right- and Left-wing political factions, an industrial system experiencing convulsions in the form of violent labor strikes, a class society at the breaking point, and a banking system on the verge of collapse. As one of his first acts, FDR declared a "bank holiday." While the banks were closed, FDR put in place the Federal Deposit Insurance Corporation (FDIC) program (later called FSLIC to include *savings and loan* as distinct), which guaranteed depositors that the federal government would insure their deposits (up to a certain dollar amount) if a member bank became insolvent. FDR's response to the Depression involved a massive social experiment whose objectives were relief, recovery, and reform.[75] Despite the accusations made by his critics, FDR was not a socialist. The philosophy of the New Deal was neither socialistic nor Marxian. In the final analysis, FDR was not a proponent of radicalism, and his New Deal programs served to salvage capitalism. Faced with an economic system at the breaking point, Roosevelt plunged into relief activities to save capitalism. In that sense, FDR was the quintessential liberal capitalist.

Roosevelt's first task was to alleviate suffering and provide food, shelter, and clothing for the millions of unemployed workers. In 1933, Congress established the Federal Emergency Relief Administration (FERA), which distributed over $5.2 billion of emergency relief to states and local communities. In 1933, FDR initiated the National Recovery Act (NRA), which provided a comprehensive series of public works projects. Under the umbrella of the NRA, Congress instituted the Public Works Administration (later changed to the Works Progress Administration—WPA) to coordinate the system of public works. Workers employed by this make-work program built dams, bridges, and other important public structures. In 1935 the WPA was expanded to provide more employment through an emphasis on long-range projects that had a positive value for the country. WPA projects employed white- and blue-collar workers as well as unskilled laborers. The WPA ultimately cost about $11.3 billion, employed 3.2 million workers a month by 1938, and produced roads, public parks, airports, schools, post offices, and various other public buildings. In addition, the white-collar division of the WPA provided work opportunities through the Federal Writers' Project, the Federal Arts Project, and the Federal Theater Project.[76]

FDR created the Civilian Conservation Corps (CCC) and the National Youth Administration (NYA) to address the problem of unemployed youth. The purpose of the CCC was to employ poor youths (ages 17 to 23) to replant forests and to help conserve the soil. Apart from obtaining employment, the 2.5 million young men served by the CCC received a leisure-time educational program as well as vocational and academic training. The NYA, on the other hand, was designed for young adults who wanted to stay at home and for needy high school and college students. Begun in 1935, the NYA eventually provided part-time employment for more than 1.7 million young people and assisted more than 1.8 million high school and college students.

Other experiments followed suit: In 1933, Congress established the Tennessee Valley Authority (TVA), a radical technological and social experiment that brought electricity to the South, helped control flooding, reclaimed land, improved river navigation, and produced nitrates; the Farm Security Administration (FSA) aided farmers and migratory workers by attempting to raise prices of farm goods; and in 1934, Congress established the Federal Housing Administration (FHA), an agency designed to provide insurance to lenders against losses on secured and unsecured loans for repairs and improvements, and on first mortgages for residential property. In addition, in 1937, Congress began a slum clearance and low-income housing program under the auspices of the WPA.[77]

In 1937, Congress passed the Fair Labor Standards Act (FLSA), which established a minimum wage (25 cents an hour) and a maximum work week (44 hours, and then time and a half for additional hours). The FLSA also abolished child labor for those under 16. In addition, the passage of the National Labor Relations Act (NLRA) gave private-sector workers the right to collectively bargain, organize, and strike.

The apogee of FDR's New Deal was the Social Security Act of 1935. This legislation included: (1) a national old-age insurance system; (2) federal grants to states for maternal and child welfare services, relief to dependent children (ADC), vocational rehabilitation for the handicapped, medical care for crippled children, aid to the blind, and a plan to strengthen public health services; and (3) a federal-state unemployment system. Conspicuously omitted was a national health insurance plan, a policy that was included in virtually every other social security plan adopted by nations in the industrialized world. The Social Security Act of 1935 was clearly the most enduring of all FDR's programs.

Although the New Deal programs were important, some argue that they did not represent a real change of direction. Most of FDR's policies were based on past employment and thus did not help the hard-core poor, who had a meager work record, if any. FDR's policies had several long-range effects. Federal policy was used to make income more equal (through minimum wage laws, and establishment of the right of workers to strike and collectively bargain); and the New Deal programs, especially the Social Security Act, established the framework for the modern social welfare state.

THE POST–WORLD WAR II WELFARE STATE

The end of World War II brought with it a repression similar to what had occurred after World War I. Progressive ideas were labeled as Communist-inspired, and the House Un-American Activities Committee hearings, chaired by Martin Dies, frightened away all but the most intrepid social reformers. Welfare programs also suffered. The antiwelfare reaction was so strong that some major newspapers published lists of welfare recipients in an attempt to shame them off the rolls. Virtually no new welfare programs were proposed, and the existing ones were in constant jeopardy. Many political leaders balked at the need for welfare programs, given the relatively healthy economy of the period.

The 1950s were marked by a kind of smugness. Americans believed that for the most part poverty had been eradicated, and even though small pockets of poverty remained, the age of affluence had arrived. The concept of a poverty-free America was ruptured by several social reformers, including Michael Harrington, whose book *The Other America: Poverty in the United States* became a classic. Harrington and others maintained that American society encompassed a subculture of poverty. These poor were hidden from the middle classes but, like specters, haunted the cities, towns, and villages. This poor subculture was composed of African Americans, Native Americans, Mexican Americans, and whites.[78] Harrington and others were correct, because in 1959, about 22 percent of the nation lived below the poverty level.[79]

The relative quiet of the 1950s gave way to the quasi-revolutionary spirit of the 1960s. After John F. Kennedy was assassinated in 1963, President Lyndon Johnson exploited the sentiments of the nation and declared a "War on Poverty." This War on Poverty—whose name was later changed to the Great Society—comprised many social programs designed to cure poverty in America. Driven by massive urban riots in African American communities during the middle and late 1960s, Johnson's programs were aimed at empowering poor communities to arrest poverty and increase economic opportunity within their own neighborhoods. Operating under the umbrella of the Office of Economic Opportunity (OEO), various programs were tried, including Volunteers in Service to America (VISTA), a domestic peace corps; Upward Bound, a program that encouraged poor and ghetto children to attend college; a Neighborhood Youth Corps for unemployed teenagers; Operation Head Start, a program that provided preschool training for lower-income children; special grants and loans to rural families and migrant workers; a comprehensive Community Action Program (CAP) designed to mobilize community resources; the Legal Services Corporation; the Model Cities Program; the Job Corps, a manpower program providing job training for disadvantaged youths from 16 to 21; and the Economic Development Act of 1965, which provided states with grants and loans for public works and technical assistance. The Economic Opportunity Act of 1964 (incorporated in 1973 under the Comprehensive Employment and Training Act, CETA) emphasized education and job training.

A key phrase in Johnson's Great Society program was "the maximum feasible participation of the poor," a concept that informed poor communities that they should invoke self-determination in their attempt to politically and economically empower themselves. The major thrust of Johnson's War on Poverty was fueled by the belief that job creation, education, and other incentives can alleviate poverty.

By 1968, the Great Society programs had become unpopular with the American public. Despite the huge amounts of money the Johnson administration spent on the poverty problem, critics claimed that the programs were ineffective. Several causes emerge as plausible explanations for this phenomenon. For one, Johnson was faced with a costly war in Vietnam at the same time that he was constructing his war on poverty. Although America was wealthy, it became increasingly clear that it could not afford to conduct two wars simultaneously. In addition, confusion in Washington, inexperienced personnel, delays in funding, corrupt local politicians, intransigent bureaucrats, and ineffective community leaders all contributed to massive problems in the programs. Despite the grim postmortem offered by subsequent scholars, however, during the Great Society period the number of people living below the poverty line was cut almost in half, from about 25 percent in the early 1960s to around 12 percent by 1969.

Richard Nixon assumed the presidency in 1969 and promptly began to dismantle the Great Society. As one of his first moves, he curbed the power of the then-influential OEO. Determined to clean up the welfare mess, Nixon in 1969 proposed another type of welfare reform—a guaranteed annual income for all poor persons. Under Nixon's Family Assistance Plan (FAP), every unemployed family of four would receive $2,400 a year from the federal government. The working poor would be allowed a minimum of $1,600 per year until their earned income reached $4,000, after which the payments would be discontinued. In order to be eligible for assistance, the able-bodied—including women with children over three years of age—would be required to work or to be enrolled in a job-training program. The program was eventually to be turned over to the states.[80] Although parts of this plan were adopted, notably the Supplemental Security Income (SSI) program in 1972, for the most part the concept of a guaranteed income was rejected by Congress. The biggest problems with this plan involved what the minimum income should be and the forced work approach.

Between 1965 and 1975, America's national priorities, in terms of the money spent on them, were reversed: In 1965 defense expenditures accounted for 42 percent of the federal budget while social welfare expenditures accounted for only 25 percent, but by 1975 defense expenditures accounted for only 25 percent of the federal budget while social welfare outlays accounted for 43 percent. Social welfare is currently the major expenditure in the federal budget. Even in Ronald Reagan's conservative budget of 1986, characterized by large increases in defense spending, only 29 percent was so earmarked, while 41 percent was allocated to social welfare.[81]

Beginning with Reagan's election in 1980, the years of his presidency saw a reappraisal of the welfare state. Reagan's ideological stance assumed that (1) federal government expenditures for social welfare should be minimal, (2) only those who were "truly needy" should receive welfare, and (3) welfare should be provided only on a short-term basis. As a result of Reagan's position, the American social welfare state was marked, at best, by inattention. In terms of real dollars, benefits for those on public assistance fell precipitously. Uneven economic development accelerated during this same period: While some people found themselves better off, larger segments of American society experienced greater economic hardship. Homelessness grew at unprecedented rates for a nondepression period. Real income continued to fall as higher-paying industrial jobs were lost and replaced by jobs in a burgeoning but relatively low-paid service sector. At the same time, most redistributive mechanisms, including social welfare allocations, experienced cuts or freezes. This situation was complicated by enormous budget and trade deficits that further justified curtailing the welfare functions of the federal government.

The parsimonious policies of the Reagan years continued throughout the administration of President George Bush. Despite his call for "a thousand points of light," Bush's policies fostered a rise in the number of those in poverty and a buildup of extreme racial, economic, and social pressures. Moreover, these policies resulted in the dramatic growth of hungry Americans and in increased unemployment, homelessness, racially based incidents, and a 5 percent increase in the AFDC rolls from 1989 to 1991. Some argue that the lack of a coherent domestic policy climaxed in the bloody Los Angeles riots of spring 1992. Based on a platform of change, Bill Clinton was elected President of the United States on November 3, 1992.

Progressives initially rejoiced at Clinton's election—the first time in 14 years that a Democrat had captured the presidency. By the end of Clinton's first term, many of those same liberals were left more cautious or, in some cases, despondent because even the important policy successes of the Clinton administration were tinged with conservatism. Moreover, the pace of legislation under Clinton's first term is best described as dizzying. An overall assessment (at least domestically) of Clinton's first term reveals important policy accomplishments and failures. Of those, perhaps the most important defeat was the administration's failure to pass its comprehensive health care reform bill (discussed in greater depth in Chapter 12). This failure is especially disappointing given the enthusiasm that health care reform enjoyed in the early 1990s.

On the other hand, Clinton was successful in passing a large urban stimulus package; AmeriCorps, a national service corps initiative; and a crime bill that added 100,000 police officers to the streets, locked up third-time felons for life, allocated $10.5 billion for new prisons, and created 50 new death penalty crimes.[82]

Clinton also made Social Security a separate cabinet department, fully funded the Ryan White Care Act, strengthened the Office of AIDS research at the National Institute of Health, and placed HIV/AIDS victims under the Americans with Disabilities Act.[83] Overall, the Clinton administration failed in expanding job training and placement, education, and child care programs. The most dramatic move, however, was signing into law the Personal Responsibility and Work Opportunity Act of 1996, a bill then capped public assistance benefits (see Chapter 11), ended AFDC, and eliminated recipients' entitlement to public assistance.

The end of the Clinton administration's first term left liberals baffled and dispirited. To be fair, Clinton entered the White House in a difficult period. Cold War policy was made obsolete by the dismantling of the Soviet Union, the economy was lethargic, and a huge $4 trillion-plus federal debt precluded the possibility of any new large social expenditures. By the end of Clinton's first two years in office, his reelection to a second term seemed all but doomed. However, in a remarkable comeback, Clinton became the first Democratic president to be elected to a second term since FDR. Clinton's coattails were not long enough to bring with it a change in Congress, and Republicans maintained control of both houses, making it difficult for the Clinton administration to implement any far-reaching social welfare initiatives.

SOCIAL WORK'S LEADERSHIP IN SOCIAL WELFARE

Although the history of the welfare state is clearly linked to the social and economic history of the United States, there are nevertheless important actors, many of them social workers, who also helped shaped the direction of social welfare.

Throughout the history of American social welfare, advocates of care for vulnerable populations have been instrumental in shaping social policies. If one looks beneath the surface of policy statements, one finds a rich and often exciting account of the skirmishes fought by advocates for social justice. In some respects, social policy innovations can be looked upon as individual and collective biography written in official language. In an age of mass populations, often manipulated by private and public megastructures, it is easy to forget how powerful some individuals have been in shaping American social welfare policy. Many of these leaders are known because they achieved national prominence; yet some of the more heroic acts to advance social justice were performed by individuals whose names are not widely recognized. Not to be forgotten in this regard is Michael Schwerner, a social worker who was murdered while working in a voter registration drive in the South during the Civil Rights movement.[84]

Early social welfare leaders emerged during the Progressive Era, a period when educated and socially conscious men and women sought to create structures that would advance social justice in America. The settlement house gained a reputation as the locus for reform activity, leading one historian to conclude that "settlement workers during the Progressive Era were probably more committed to political action than any other group of welfare workers before or since."[85] From this group, Jane Addams quickly surfaced as a leader of national prominence. Through her settlement home, Hull House, she not only fought for improvements in care for slum dwellers in inner-city Chicago but also for international peace. Social work for Jane Addams *was* social reform. Instead of focusing solely on restoration and rehabilitation, Addams claimed that there was a superior role for the profession: "It must decide whether it is to remain behind in the area of caring for the victimized," she argued, "or whether to press ahead into the dangerous area of conflict where the struggle must be pressed to bring to pass an order of society with few victims."[86] In that struggle, Addams served nobly, receiving an honorary degree from Yale University and serving as president of the Women's International League for Peace and Freedom. In 1931, Jane Addams was awarded the Nobel Peace Prize, a suitable distinction for a social worker who once had herself appointed a garbage collector in order to improve sanitation in the slums around Hull House.

Hull House proved a remarkable institution, and some of its tenants made lasting and important contributions to the New Deal:

Edith Abbott, president of the National Conference of Social Welfare, Dean of the University of Chicago School of Social Service Administration, and participant in the drafting of the Social Security Act of 1935

Grace Abbott, organizer of the first White House Conference on Children, director of the U.S. Children's Bureau, and participant in the construction of the Social Security Act

Julia Lathrop, developer of the first juvenile court and of the first child mental health clinic in the United States, and the first director of the U.S. Children's Bureau

Florence Kelley, director of the National Consumer League, cofounder of the U.S. Children's Bureau, and a member of the National Child Labor Committee

Frances Perkins, director of the New York Council of Organizations for War Services, director of the Council on Immigrant Education, and the first Secretary of Labor.[87]

The activity around Hull House was never limited to those with a narrow view of reform. A regular participant in the settlement was John Dewey, in his time "America's most influential philosopher, educator, as well as one of the most outspoken champions of social reform."[88]

Settlement experiences crystallized the motivations of other reformers as well. Harry Hopkins, primary architect of the New Deal and of the social programs that comprised the Social Security Act, had resided in New York's Christadora House Settlement. Ida Bell Wells-Barnett led the Negro Fellowship League to establish a settlement house for African Americans in Chicago; Lillian Wald, with Florence Kelley, a cofounder of the U.S. Children's Bureau, had earlier established New York's Henry Street Settlement, an institution that was to achieve distinction within the African American community. Under the guidance of Mary White Ovington, a social worker, the first meetings of the National Association for the Advancement of Colored People were held at the Henry Street Settlement.[89]

Early social welfare leaders championed causes that improved the conditions of children and immigrants, but they did not always forsake African Americans. When it became apparent that Booker T. Washington's program of "industrial education" was unable to contend effectively with ubiquitous racial discrimination, social reformers—Jane Addams, Ida Bell Wells-Barnett, and John Dewey—joined W. E. B. Du Bois in the Niagara Movement. The early organizations spawned by the Niagara Movement were later consolidated into the National Urban League, with George Edmund Haynes, a social worker, as one of its codirectors. In 1910, Haynes had been the first African American to graduate from the New York School of Philanthropy, so it is not surprising that an important Urban League program was the provision of fellowships for African Americans to the school.[90] Later, during the height of the Civil Rights movement, the National Urban League, under the direction of social worker Whitney Young, Jr., collaborated in organizing the August 28, 1963, march on Washington, memorialized by Martin Luther King, Jr.'s ringing words, "I have a dream!"[91]

If the New Deal bore the imprint of social workers, the Great Society was similarly marked some 30 years later. Significantly, one leader of the War on Poverty was Wilbur Cohen, a social worker who had been the first employee of the Social Security Board created in 1935. Eventually, Cohen was to be credited with some 65 innovations in social welfare policy, but his crowning achievement was the passage of the Medicare and Medicaid Acts in 1965. The Secretary of Health, Education and Welfare during the Johnson administration, Cohen was arguably the nation's most decorated social worker, receiving 18 honorary degrees from American universities.[92] In the end, the history of social work has always been inextricably bound up with the history of the American welfare state, a condition that may not prevail well into the future.

SOCIAL WORK, POLITICS, AND ADVOCACY ORGANIZATIONS

The formulation of social welfare policy in the United States is a complicated and often arduous process. Much of this can be attributed to the nature of American culture—to the competing interests that contribute to a pluralistic society, to the federal system of government that authorizes decision making on several levels at once, to the public and private bureaucracies that serve large numbers of consumers, to economic and technological developments that lead to specialization. Under these circumstances, the prospect of changing social welfare policy toward preconceived ends that improve the circumstances of disadvantaged groups can be a daunting task. Regrettably, few welfare professionals consider social policy an enterprise worthy of undertaking. Most social workers prefer direct service activity, where they have little opportunity for direct involvement in social welfare policy. Some social workers have attained important positions in federal and state human service bureaucracies and are much closer to the policy process. Unfortunately, these managers are often administering welfare policies that have been made by legislatures and that do not necessarily represent either clients or human-service professionals. Perhaps most troubling, the involvement of social workers in the formulation of social policy has been diminishing in recent years. In a provocative statement, June Hopps, dean of the Boston College School of Social Work and former editor-in-chief of *Social Work*, acknowledged that "Since the late 1960s and early 1970s, the [social work] profession has experienced a dramatic loss of influence in the arenas where policy is shaped and administered."[93]

If one indicator of good social policy is the correspondence between the policy and the social reality of its intended beneficiaries, then social welfare policy should be enhanced by the input of social workers. However, social workers have left much of the decision making about social welfare to professionals from other disciplines. "There are increasing numbers of non-social workers, including psychologists and urban planners," observed Eleanor Brilliant, "taking what might have been social work jobs in service delivery and policy analysis."[94] The consequences of welfare professionals opting to leave social policy in the hands of others are important. For direct service workers, it can mean having to apply eligibility standards or procedures that, while logical in some respects, make little sense in the social context of many clients. For the public, it may mean a gradual disenchantment with social programs that do not seem to work. While the causes of the retrenchment affecting social programs since the late 1970s are complex, it is worth noting that public dissatisfaction with social programs has escalated as welfare professionals have retreated from active involvement in social welfare policy.

For welfare professionals to reassert their voice in the formulation and execution of social policy will take concerted effort. Individual leadership is a necessary, but no longer sufficient, precondition for achieving this objective. Essential to the undertaking is the ability to understand and manipulate complex organizations and programs. In fact, this skill may be the most critical for welfare professionals to acquire if they are to advance social justice, for it addresses a question central to the postindustrial era. During the Industrial Revolution, Karl Marx suggested that the central question was "Who controls the means of production?" A mature industrial order and the expansion of civil bureaucracy led Max Weber to ask, "Who controls the means of administration?" The evolution of a postindustrial order where primary economic activity occurs in a service sector dependent on processed information raises another question: "Who controls the means of analysis?" If social workers are to shape social policy as effectively as they have in the past, they will have to learn to control the means of analysis. This means conducting research on social problems, surveying public opinion about welfare programs, analyzing existing social policy for opportunities to enhance welfare provision, and winning elected office in order to make decisions about proposed social welfare policies.

Advocacy Organizations and the New Welfare Institutes

In order to be successful in an increasingly complex political climate, social reformers must be able to take advantage of sophisticated advocacy methods. In social work, the organization that provides assistance to candidates is PACE, "the political arm of the National Association of Social Workers." PACE uses a variety of tactics to "expand social workers' activity in politics," including voter registration, support in political campaigns, and analysis of incumbents' voting records.[95] In 1986, PACE donated $110,000 to candidates running for national office; and 39 NASW chapters supported candidates for state and local office.[96] According to Toby Weismiller, NASW staff director for political affairs, PACE encourages social workers to view holding public office as a practice option. In her summary of the 1986 election, Weismiller noted that social workers who have "learned how to solve problems by working within the community" can use this to great political advantage,[97] as did Barbara Mikulski.

While PACE attempts to influence social welfare policy by sponsoring candidates for public office, other organizations focus on the policy process itself. Policy analysis organizations have been instrumental in shaping social policy from as early as the New Deal period. Subsequently, policy institutes have had liberal or conservative labels ascribed to them, with the liberal organizations achieving dominance up until the late 1970s, when conservative institutes began gaining popularity. The failure of government social programs to expand during the Carter presidency, followed by the profoundly negative impact of the Reagan and Bush administrations, led social reformers to look to the traditional policy institutes—the Brookings Institution and the Urban Institute—for leadership. But the inability of these organizations to shape the debate on American social welfare policy compelled increasingly impatient reformers to establish a new group of policy analysis organizations.

Children's Defense Fund. Begun by Marian Wright Edelman in 1974, the Children's Defense Fund (CDF) sought to address the health, educational, and income needs of the nation's children.[98] By the mid-1980s, CDF had become a major voice in children's policy and had successfully advocated programs at the federal and state levels. CDF helped pass the Child Health Assurance Program in 1984, which expanded Medicaid eligibility to poor pregnant women and to children. Following the federal devolution of social programs to the states, CDF deployed field offices in five states and provided services to groups in many more. Notably, CDF has not winced at championing groups that have benefited least by welfare programs. Recently, CDF established the Adolescent Pregnancy Prevention project, an imaginative initiative relying on local groups to identify resources for teens.

In less than a decade, the CDF budget had grown to more than $4 million and its staff to more than 70. Contributions have been received from important foundations, and support has been secured from influential persons, including Hillary Rodham Clinton. In addition to distributing educational packets to poor mothers, CDF regularly sends editorial packets to 200 newspapers across the nation. CDF also prints eye-catching posters and a number of publications for public education purposes. Its annual *The State of America's Children* is an authoritative compendium of issues and programs concerning children.

Independent Sector. In 1978, former Secretary of Health, Education, and Welfare John Gardner and philanthropic executive Brian O'Connell merged the Coalition of National Voluntary Organizations and the National Council on Philanthropy to enhance the capacity of the nonprofit sector to deal with social problems. An organizing committee comprised of

Gardner, O'Connell, John Filer (CEO of Aetna Insurance Company and chairperson of the Commission on Private Philanthropy and Public Needs), and Richard Lyman (president of the Rockefeller Foundation) chartered Independent Sector (IS) in 1980 to further voluntary sector activities. By 1986, IS had cultivated a board of directors numbering 40, which represented influential corporations and nonprofit organizations. From the dues of its 650 institutional members and from contributions, IS boasted a budget exceeding $4.5 million in 1986.[99]

IS quickly became an influential voice for the nonprofit sector, occupying a suite of executive offices in Washington, D.C. In addition to annual seminars on policies affecting nonprofit organizations, IS has sponsored seminal studies of the contributions of nonprofit organizations to the national culture. In an effort to extend the scope of its activities, IS has helped establish research centers in major universities, such as the Mandel Center for Nonprofit Management at Case Western Reserve University.[100]

The Center on Budget and Policy Priorities. Established in 1981 by Robert Greenstein, former administrator of the Food and Nutrition Service in the Agriculture Department, the Center on Budget and Policy Priorities (CBPP) has fought to defend social programs for low-income people against budget cuts. With a modest staff, CBPP distributes its analyses to congressional staffs, the media, and grass-roots organizations. Despite its small size, CBPP provided much of the program analysis to refute arguments presented by officials of the Reagan administration to cut means-tested social programs. Significantly, CBPP and CDF have developed a close working relationship. CBPP regularly provides data to CDF on the health and income status of children, and Greenstein is a regular contributor to CDF reports.[101]

The National Center for Social Policy and Practice. Still in the early stages of its development, the National Center for Social Policy and Practice (NCSPP) originated with the National Association of Social Workers (NASW). In launching NCSPP, NASW sought an institute that would serve as an advocate for a more just and equitable society through analyses of social problems, policy, and social work practice. Toward that end, NASW commenced a capital campaign to raise $10 million and began a series of symposia designed to inform human-service professionals about NCSPP and solicit their financial support. In the fall of 1986, Karen Orloff Kaplan, a clinical social worker with expertise in health policy and extensive legislative experience, was named director of NCSPP. Among the projects begun by NCSPP are a survey of benefits for employees of corporations that cover catastrophic illness and long-term care, an AIDS ethics forum, and a policy statement on welfare reform. Located near Washington, D.C., NCSPP is potentially well positioned to influence social welfare policy.[102]

Social Work's Impact on Social Welfare Policy

The capacity of social workers to reassert their role in social welfare policy depends on the willingness of individuals to consider public office as a setting for social work practice and the ability of the new policy institutes to prepare sophisticated policy analyses. Despite the openness of the American political system, only the naive would ignore the very real obstacles to progressive social reform. Corporate contributions to candidates for federal office, $38.9 million in 1983 and 1984,[103] far exceeded the NASW-PACE effort. Without a strong economic base, new candidates for national office are unlikely to be successful in elections where massive campaign war chests are a prerequisite for office. The development of the new policy institutes is an encouraging sign, but even the more prominent of these—CDF and IS—are operating on budgets half the size of the more established policy organizations.

Political Practice. Although many welfare professionals began their careers advocating for social welfare policy and then assumed administrative positions managing social programs, others used elected office to advance social reform. The first woman elected to the House of Representatives was Jeannette Rankin, who won a seat in 1916 running as a Republican in Montana. As a social worker who had studied under Frances Perkins, Rankin voted for early social welfare legislation and against military expansion. More recently, social workers in political practice have included Maryann Mahaffey, a member of the Detroit City Council, and Ruth Messinger, a member of the New York City Council. Other social workers became mayors of major American cities. Sidney Barthelemy earned his Master of Social Work degree and directed the New Orleans City Welfare Department. In 1974, Barthelemy became the first African American elected to the Louisiana State Senate since Reconstruction. After serving on the New Orleans City Council, he was elected mayor in 1986.[104]

By the late 1980s, four social workers had attained national office. Ronald Dellums, a Marine Corps veteran, earned his Master of Social Work degree and then served on the Berkeley (California) City Council from 1967 to 1971, when he was elected to Congress. Since then he has proposed an alternative military budget based on arms reduction, fought for greater employment opportunities for minorities, and sought services for the homeless. Dellums is perhaps best known for his proposed National Health Service Act, "the most comprehensive health care legislation ever introduced in Congress."[105]

Barbara Mikulski received her Master of Social Work degree in 1965 and then served on the Baltimore City Council and in the United States House of Representatives. In 1986, Mikulski became the first Democratic woman to be elected to the United States Senate in her own right. Through appointments to the powerful Appropriations Committee and the Labor and Human Resources Committee, Mikulski is well positioned to advocate programs in health and social services.[106]

Edolphus "Ed" Towns received his Master of Social Work degree in 1973. Elected as the Democratic state committeeman and then the first African American deputy borough president in Brooklyn's history, Towns was elected to serve as the representative of the eleventh Congressional District of New York in 1982, with 90 percent of the vote. Towns's appointments to committees overseeing government operations, public works, and narcotics directly address the primary concerns of his inner-city constituents.[107]

Perhaps the best indicator of social work's future influence on social policy appears at the local level. Social workers have lobbied successfully on behalf of nonprofit agencies facing threats to their tax-exempt status,[108] encouraged students to engage in election campaigns and to become more knowledgeable about politics,[109] and managed a campaign for the election of a state senator.[110] In each of these instances, social workers were gaining experience that is essential to political involvement at higher levels.

A good example of what social workers can accomplish at the local level can be found in Tim Dee, the alderman from St. Louis's Seventeenth Ward from 1977 to 1987. Early in his tenure as alderman, Dee documented that the Seventeenth Ward had lost about one-third of its population during the 1970s, a demographic hemorrhage he attributed to the absence of employment opportunities in this inner-city political district. Using a little-known state law that provided for the creation of enterprise zones, Dee created legislation establishing the Seventeenth Ward as an enterprise zone that allowed businesses tax abatement and other advantages if they located in Dee's ward. The strategy paid off. In a few years following the creation of the enterprise zone in September 1983, the Seventeenth Ward boasted some 15 new businesses and 1,200 new jobs, and Dee's enterprise zone was noted as one of the 10 best nationally. But Dee was not content to allow his district to be manipulated by businesses seeking concessions from local government as a justification for their relocation. In order to make the enterprise zone responsive to the needs of local residents, Dee built into the enabling legislation an intriguing provision that established an enterprise zone commission, representing business and residents, to oversee the economic development of the area. It is difficult to imagine a better example of a social worker using the local political process to improve the conditions of so many disadvantaged people than Tim Dee's innovative work as an alderman in St. Louis.[111]

Social workers disinclined to engage in high-visibility activities such as campaigning for public office could make their imprint on politics through "constituent services." Writing of new developments in Congress, Pulitzer Prize–winning journalist Hedrick Smith observed that members of Congress are increasingly relying on constituent services in place of pork barrel projects as domestic expenditures dry up.

Using a term familiar to most social workers, politicians call constituent services "casework—which includes having your staff track down missing Social Security checks, inquire about sons and husbands in the armed services, help veterans get medical care, pursue applications for small-business loans."[112] The importance of political casework has been noted by political scientists who attribute up to 5 percent of the vote to such activities, a significant amount in close elections. David Himes of the National Republican Congressional Committee claimed that "our surveys have shown that constituency service—especially in the House—is more important than issues."[113]

The cultivation of practice skills in the political arena at the local level offers perhaps the most promise for social workers to regain influence in social welfare policy. Such activity can be undertaken by virtually any professional interested in the opportunity. On a volunteer basis, social workers would find few politicians willing to turn down their professional assistance in the provision of constituent services. With experience, enterprising social workers might find that political practice can be remunerative, providing that they possess the skills—such as conducting surveys, maintaining data banks of contributors, organizing public meetings, and keeping current on legislation important to constituents—needed by elected officials. From another perspective, however, the prospect of political practice should be taken seriously indeed. If social workers are sincere about making essential resources available to their clients—a responsibility stated in the *NASW Code of Ethics*—then some form of political practice is a professional obligation. "To do less," noted Maryann Mahaffey, "to avoid the political action necessary to provide these resources, is to fail to live up to the profession's code of ethical practice."[114]

◆ ◆ ◆ Discussion Questions ◆ ◆ ◆

1. Many commentators argue that the English Poor Laws continue to form the basis of current social welfare policy in America. How are the English Poor Laws reflected in modern social welfare policy? Specifically, which current values or social welfare policies can be traced to the influence of the English Poor laws?

2. Are there any residual social welfare policy values that have persisted from colonial times to the present? Describe specific social welfare policies or values that have their origin in colonial times.

3. What lasting legacy, if any, did the Freedmen's Bureau have for contemporary U.S. policy toward African Americans? Describe any influence that the Freedmen's Bureau had on the U.S. welfare state in terms of specific policies and programs.

4. The concept of Social Darwinism clearly had a big following in the late 1800s. Is this concept dead today or does a modified form of it continue to exercise influence? If you answer yes, describe how this idea is expressed in terms of values or specific social welfare policies or programs.

5. Religion clearly played an important role in the development of professional social work, especially in the late 1800s and early 1900s. What role, if any, does religion currently play in the creation of social welfare policy? Specifically, are religious impulses an important factor in decisions relating to social programs and policies? If you agree, describe specific policies and programs that reflect religious influences.

6. Although the Charity Organization Societies and the Settlement Houses seemed to be at opposite poles, some commentators argue that there were strong similarities between the two. Describe the similarities, in terms of both values and approaches, between the two organizations.

7. The Progressive Era was an important period in American history. Describe the major contributions of the Progressive Era, in terms of its programs and policies, for the later American welfare state.

8. FDR is often thought of as the father of the American welfare state, and most policy analysts agree that his New Deal policies formed the basis for the current welfare system. What is the most enduring legacy of the New Deal and why?

9. Most pundits across the political spectrum agree that Ronald Reagan had a major impact on the American welfare state. His impact included both concrete fiscal cuts and new ideas about welfare. What, if any, permanent legacy was left by this president? Specifically, in what ways did Reagan help shape current values and attitudes toward social programs?

10. Evaluate Bill Clinton's contribution to the American welfare state? What are the successes and the failures of the first Clinton term?

11. The history of American social welfare is marked by the formidable accomplishments of key leaders in social work. These include Jane Addams, Lillian Wald, the Abbott sisters, and Wilbur Cohen, among many others. In effect, these leaders dominated the field of social welfare for more than a half-century. Some critics point out that there are no leaders on the social work scene today who have the stature of those mentioned. What do you believe are the reasons for this predicament?

Notes

1. Walter Trattner, *From Poor Law to Welfare State* (New York: Free Press, 1974), p. 2.
2. Anatoly Twersky, *A Maimonides Reader* (New York: Ketev Press, 1972), p. 136.
3. Robert Morris, *Rethinking Social Welfare* (New York: Longman, 1986), pp. 7–8.
4. Karl de Schweinitz, *England's Road to Social Security* (Philadelphia: University of Pennsylvania Press, 1943).
5. Ibid.
6. Ibid.
7. Ibid., p. 12.
8. David Rothman and Sheila Rothman (eds.), *On Their Own: The Poor in Modern America* (Reading, MA: Addison-Wesley, 1972).
9. Morris, *Rethinking Social Welfare*, p. 143.
10. Nathan Edward Cohen, *Social Work in the American Tradition* (New York: Holt, Rinehart and Winston, 1958), pp. 23–24.
11. Trattner, *From Poor Law to Welfare State*, p. 17
12. Morris, *Rethinking Social Welfare*, p. 153
13. Quoted in Trattner, *From Poor Law to Welfare State*, p. 62.
14. Cohen, *Social Work in the American Tradition*, p. 36.
15. Trattner, *From Poor Law to Welfare State*, p. 63.
16. Ibid., p. 87.
17. Alexis De Tocqueville, *Democracy in America*, vol. 2, (New Rochelle, NY: Arlington House, 1966), p. 114.
18. Ibid.
19. June Axinn and Herman Levin, *Social Welfare* (New York: Dodd, Mead, 1975), p. 129.
20. Robert Bremner, *From the Depths: The Discovery of Poverty in the United States* (New York: New York University Press, 1956).
21. David Montgomery, *Workers' Control in America* (Cambridge, England: Cambridge University Press, 1979).
22. Ibid.
23. Richard Hofstadter, *The Age of Reform* (New York: Vintage Books, 1955), p. 242.
24. Justin Kaplan, *Lincoln Steffens* (New York: Simon and Schuster, 1974), pp. 50–51.
25. Jacob Riis, *How the Other Half Lives* (New York: Charles Scribner and Sons, 1890), p. 15.
26. Kaplan, *Lincoln Steffens*, p. 51.
27. Charles Darwin, *On the Origin of Species by Means of Natural Selection* (London: John Murray, 1859).
28. See Herbert Spencer, *An Autobiography*, 2 vols. (New York: D. Appleton, 1904); William Graham Sumner, *Social Darwinism* (Englewood Cliffs, NJ: Prentice-Hall, 1963); and Richard Hofstadter, *Social Darwinism in American Thought* (Boston: Beacon Press, 1959).
29. Spencer, *An Autobiography*, p. 186.
30. David Macarov, *The Design of Social Welfare* (New York: Holt, Rinehart and Winston, 1978).
31. Ibid.
32. Ibid.
33. Herbert G. Guttman, *Work, Culture and Society* (New York: Vintage Books, 1977).
34. Roy Lubove, *The Professional Altruist: The Emergence of Social Work as a Career, 1880–1930* (New York: Atheneum Books, 1975).

35. Charles Howard Hopkins, *The Rise of the Social Gospel in American Protestantism, 1865–1915* (New Haven, CT: Yale University Press, 1940).
36. Ibid.
37. Henry F. May, *Protestant Churches in Industrial America* (New York: Octagon Books, 1963).
38. Howard Jacob Karger, *The Sentinels of Order: A Study of Social Control and the Minneapolis Settlement House Movement, 1915–1950* (Lanham, MD: University Press of America, 1987).
39. Lubove, *The Professional Altruist*, pp. 1–21.
40. Ibid., p. 14.
41. Axinn and Levin, *Social Welfare*, p. 100.
42. Charles Loring Brace, *The Dangerous Classes of New York* (New York: Wynkoop and Hallenbeck, 1872), pp. 151–152.
43. Jean Quam, "Charles Loring Brace," *Encyclopedia of Social Work*, 18th ed. (Silver Spring, MD: NASW, 1987), p. 916.
44. Hofstadter, *The Age of Reform*, p. 211.
45. Allen F. Davis, *American Heroine: The Life and Legend of Jane Addams* (New York: Oxford University Press, 1973), p. 57.
46. Ibid., p. 92.
47. *Encyclopedia of Social Work*, 18th ed., pp. 913–936.
48. John Hope Franklin, *From Slavery to Freedom* (New York: Knopf, 1979), p. 288.
49. *Constitution of the Sons and Daughters of Zion*, author's collection.
50. Addie Louise Joyner Butler, *The Distinctive Black College: Talladega, Tuskegee, and Morehouse* (Metuchen, NJ: Scarecrow Press, 1977), pp. 17–18.
51. Ibid., p. 102.
52. Franklin, *From Slavery to Freedom*, pp. 318–321.
53. H. L. Weissman, "Settlements and Community Centers," *Encyclopedia of Social Work*, 18th ed., p. 21.
54. Mary Richmond, *Social Diagnosis* (New York: Russell Sage Foundation, 1917).
55. H. L. Mencken, *Minority Report* (New York: Knopf, 1956), p. 153.
56. Maryann Syers, "Abraham Flexner," *Encyclopedia of Social Work*, 18th ed., p. 923.
57. National Association of Social Workers, *Social Casework: Generic and Specific* (Washington, DC: NASW, 1974), p. 27.
58. Trattner, *From Poor Law to Welfare State*, pp. 221–222.
59. Larry Hirschhorn, "The Social Service Crisis and the New Subjectivity," (Berkeley, CA: University of California, Berkeley, Institute of Urban and Regional Development, December 1974).
60. Lubove, *The Professional Altruist*, pp. 172, 185.
61. National Association of Social Workers, *Social Casework*, pp. 16–50.
62. See Cohen, *Social Work in the American Tradition*; and William E. Leuchtenburg, *The Perils of Prosperity, 1914–32* (Chicago: University of Chicago Press, 1958).
63. Clarke A. Chambers, *Seedtime of Reform: American Social Service and Social Action, 1918–1933* (Ann Arbor, MI: University of Michigan Press, 1967), p. 118.
64. Hofstadter, *Age of Reform*.
65. See Karger, *The Sentinels of Order*; and Chambers, *Seedtime of Reform*.
66. Chambers, *Seedtime of Reform*, p. 211.
67. Ibid., p. 219.
68. Leuchtenburg, *Perils of Prosperity*, p. 247.
69. Cohen, *Social Work in the American Tradition*, p. 161.
70. Ibid., p. 162.
71. Leuchtenburg, *Perils of Prosperity*, p. 254.
72. Ibid., pp. 252–253.
73. Ibid., p. 248.
74. Trattner, *From Poor Law to Welfare State*, p. 230.
75. Cohen, *Social Work in the American Tradition*, p. 169.
76. Ibid.
77. Ibid.
78. Michael Harrington, *The Other America: Poverty in the United States* (New York: Penguin, 1962).
79. Robert Morris, *Social Policy of the American Welfare State* (New York: Longman, 1985), p. 63.
80. Trattner, *From Poor Law to Welfare State*.
81. Diane M. DiNitto and Thomas R. Dye, *Social Welfare: Politics and Public Policy* (Englewood Cliffs, NJ: Prentice-Hall, 1987), p. 56.
82. David Stoesz, *Small Change* (New York: Longman, 1995).
83. Joanne Szabo, Phyllis Tonkin, Veronique Vailancourt, Philip Winston, and Deidre Wright, "The Clinton Scorecard." Unpublished manuscript, Graduate School of Social Work, University of Houston, Houston, Texas, April 25, 1996.
84. Maryann Mahaffey, "Political Action in Social Work," *Encyclopedia of Social Work*, 18th ed., p. 290.
85. Allen Davis, "Settlement Workers in Politics, 1890–1914," in Maryann Mahaffey and John

Hanks, (eds.), *Practical Politics: Social Work and Political Responsibility* (Silver Spring, MD: National Association of Social Workers, 1982), p. 32.

86. Davis, *American Heroine*, p. 292.
87. Biographical information from *Encyclopedia of Social Work*, 18th ed.
88. Richard Bernstein, "John Dewey," *Encyclopedia of Philosophy*, vol. II, Paul Edwards, Ed. (New York: Macmillan and The Free Press, 1967), p. 380.
89. Mahaffey, "Political Action in Social Work," p. 286.
90. Franklin, *From Slavery to Freedom*, pp. 319–321.
91. Ibid., pp. 471–472.
92. Charles Schottland, "Wilbur Joseph Cohen: Some Recollections," *Social Work* (32)5 (September–October 1987), pp. 371–372.
93. June Hopps, "Reclaiming Leadership," *Social Work* 31 (September–October 1986), p. 323.
94. Eleanor Brilliant, "Social Work Leadership: A Missing Ingredient?" *Social Work* 31 (September–October 1986), pp. 328.
95. Interview with Toby Weismiller, NASW, Washington, DC, January 11, 1988.
96. National Association of Social Workers, *Annual Report 1987* (Washington, DC: NASW, 1987), p. 23.
97. Interview, Weissmiller, January 11, 1988.
98. For details on CDF, see Joanna Biggar, "The Protector," *Washington Post Magazine* (May 18, 1986), p. C–4; and *The Children's Defense Fund Annual Report 1984–85* (Washington, DC: Children's Defense Fund, 1985).
99. "CONVO: Background Information and Initial Statements by John Gardner and Brian O'Connell" (Washington, DC: Independent Sector, n.d.); Annual Report 1986 (Washington, DC: Independent Sector, 1986).
100. Brian O'Connell, *Philanthropy in Action* (New York: Foundation Center, 1987), pp. 103–104.
101. Information on CBPP was obtained from an interview with David Kahan at CBPP on March 12, 1984.
102. Interview with Karen Orloff Kaplan on January 11, 1988, at NCSPP; *National Association of Social Workers, Annual Report 1987* (Silver Spring, MD: NASW, 1987), p. 18.
103. Steven Lydenberg, *Rating America's Corporate Conscience* (Reading, MA: Addison-Wesley, 1986), p. 39.
104. Biographical profile, courtesy of the Office of the Mayor, New Orleans, n.d.
105. Biographical sketch, courtesy of Congressman Dellums' Office, n.d.
106. Biographical sketch, courtesy of Senator Mikulski's Office, n.d.
107. Congressman Ed Towns, courtesy of the Congressman Towns' office, n.d.
108. Elliot Pagliaccio and Burton Gummer, "Casework and Congress: A Lobbying Strategy," *Social Casework* 69 (March 1988), pp. 321–330.
109. Grafton Hull, "Joining Together: A Faculty-Student Experience in Political Campaigning," *Journal of Social Work Education* 23 (Fall 1987), pp. 116–123.
110. William Whittaker and Jan Flory-Baker, "Ragtag Social Workers Take on the Good Old Boys and Elect a State Senator," in Maryann Mahaffey and John Hanks (eds.), *Practical Politics: Social Work and Political Responsibility* (Silver Spring, MD: National Association of Social Workers, 1982).
111. Telephone interview with Tim Dee, March 20, 1988.
112. Hedrick Smith, *The Power Game* (New York: Random House, 1988), p. 124.
113. Ibid., p. 152.
114. Mahaffey and Hanks, *Practical Politics* (see Chapter 10, "Political Action in Social Work"), p. 284.

CHAPTER 4

Discrimination and Social Stigma in American Society

Discrimination and poverty are inextricably linked in the fabric of American social welfare. Economic, social, and political discrimination often leads to poverty for most of its vulnerable victims and, in turn, results in income maintenance and poverty programs designed to address the effects of poverty. Realizing that discrimination encourages poverty, some policymakers have attempted to address this cycle of misery by attacking discrimination and social stigma, one of its core components. In the end, these policymakers hope that by curtailing discriminatory practices and attitudes, vulnerable populations will be given equal opportunities for achievement and success, thereby reducing the need for expensive and often inadequate social welfare programs. This chapter probes discrimination based on race, gender, sexual orientation, disability, and age.

DISCRIMINATION AND OPPRESSION

The causes of discrimination in American society are complex and elusive. A range of literature attempts to explicate the motives for discrimination. Broken down, these theories fit into three broad categories: psychological, normative-cultural, and economic.

Psychological interpretations attempt to explain discrimination in terms of intrapsychic variables.[1] A theory called the frustration-aggression hypothesis, formulated by J. Dollard, maintains that discrimination is a form of aggression that is activated when individual needs become frustrated.[2] According to Dollard, when people cannot direct their aggression at the real sources of their rage, they seek a substitute target. Thus, relatively weak minority groups become an easy and safe target for the aggression and frustration of stronger discontented groups. For example, poor whites have often been thought of one of the more outwardly racist groups in Southern society. Exploited by the rigid economic and social class system of the old South, poor whites often focused their rage on African Americans, a group even weaker than themselves. African Americans thus served a twin function for poor whites: On the one hand, they formed a lower socioeconomic group making poor whites feel better about their own standing; on the other, they functioned as a scapegoat for the frustrations of poor whites. Women, racial minorities, homosexuals, and other disenfranchised groups can serve the same function for those on a slightly higher social rung.

The "authoritarian personality" theory, developed by Theodore Adorno and other psychoanalytic authors, posited that discriminatory behavior is determined by personality traits that involve a reaction to authority.[3] Persons who exhibit the traits of irrationality, rigidity, conformity, xenophobia, and so forth, are more likely to discriminate against minorities than are people lacking those traits. Other authors, such as Wilhelm Reich, argued that discriminatory attitudes arise from a sense of insecurity, self-hatred, deep-seated fears, and unresolved childhood needs and frustrations.[4]

The normative-cultural explanation suggests that individuals hold prejudicial attitudes because of their socialization. Through both overt and covert messages, a society teaches discrimination and rewards those who conform to prevailing attitudes and behaviors. Because societal pressures to conform to established norms are great, resistance to discriminatory practices becomes difficult.[5] For example, particular wrath in the old South was reserved for liberal whites who broke the norms regarding interactions with African Americans. Often, societies are more tolerant of "outsiders" who break the norms than they are of "insiders" who "betray" them. This theory suggests that as the social and institutional norms supporting discriminatory practices change, individual attitudes follow suit.

One variation of the economic argument contends that dominant groups discriminate in order to maintain their economic and political advantages. This theory is grounded in the belief that relative group advantages are gained from discrimination. For example, male workers may discriminate against women because they perceive them as encroaching on their employment prospects. These male workers may fear that they will replaced by a female who is satisfied with lower wages. On the other hand, employers may uphold discriminatory attitudes because, as long as women workers are stigmatized, they will command a lower salary and thereby serve as a cheap pool of labor. In that sense, the increasing racial tensions in American society can be partly understood as a reaction to the job advancements made by minority groups, and the fears of whites that this may affect their job opportunities and/or upward mobility or even result in the loss of their jobs.

A more Marxian economic analysis sees sexism, racism, homophobia, and other forms of discrimination as economically useful to the capitalist class. Specifically, industrialization requires a mobile labor force willing to relocate to available employment. Discrimination has thus helped force disenfranchised groups to relocate (usually westward) in order to flee persecution based on ethnic, religious, or racial differences. According to Marxists, capitalism requires a marginal and unskilled labor pool willing to take jobs refused by economically enfranchised groups. The use of stigma reduces the economic currency of whole populations and thus creates an underclass forced to take whatever jobs are available at whatever wages are offered. Furthermore, by threatening relatively well-paid workers with replacement by a stigmatized group, employers are able to force wage concessions. By manipulating stigmatized groups against each other, employers can keep wage demands in these groups relatively low. Moreover, because stigmatized groups are often employed in unstable jobs, they can be moved around as the economy requires. Paradoxically, the reduction in the economic currency of disenfranchised groups increases their value to the economic order.

To maintain an air of legitimacy, discrimination must have a moral, social, and theological underpinning. To that end, some have used the Bible to explain the inferiority of women, the "sin" of homosexuality, and the necessity of separating the races. To augment or replace biblical interpretations, spurious scientific explanations have been developed that are rooted in quasi-psychoanalytic theory, Social Darwinism, and pseudomedical "insights" concerning the attributes of stigmatized groups. For example, some people maintain that menstrual cycles cause severe mood swings that make women incapable of being in positions of power. Others believe that African Americans are descended from Ham and have therefore committed biblical sins that justify discrimination. Some members of the Ku Klux Klan argue that African Americans are racially inferior on the basis of theories grounded in shaky anthropological research confirmed by even more dubious intelligence testing. Without the legitimation offered by moral, religious, social, and "scientific" sources, discrimination is devoid of social validity and becomes mere exploitation.

Social stigma and discrimination can lead to the transformation of disenfranchised groups into a lower economic class. Alternatively, discrimination and social stigma can result in social marginalization, as in the case of gays, lesbians, and the aged, without triggering statistically observable economic discrimination. For example, while the individual incomes of gays and lesbians (and the assets of the elderly) are higher than the national average, they often experience economic discrimination in the form of constricted career choices, including forced occupational clustering, limited access to upper managerial positions, discrimination in hiring practices, forced retirement, and so forth. In addition, discrimination can also turn violent. For example, according to federal officials, there were more than 243 attacks against religious institutions—black churches and white churches, synagogues and mosques—since May 1990. More than half of those attacks occurred from January 1995 to May 1996. Most disturbing, 78 percent of all suspicious church fires in the Southeast occurred at black churches. In response, Congress passed the Church Arson Prevention Act of 1996, which broadened the ability of the federal government to seek criminal penalties in cases involving vandalism or destruction of religious institutions. The following sections will examine some core components of discrimination and social stigma, including racism, sexism, homophobia, agism, and the discrimination against people with disabilities.

RACISM

American society is typically divided along the lines of whites and people of color. However, clumping white American society into a single category is almost as misleading as not understanding the important cultural differences between people of color. For example, in 1850, it was relatively easy to describe a white American. In all probability, they were of Anglo-Saxon background and Protestant. However, after the Civil War, immigrants began to immigrate from Southern and Central Europe. They were not Protestant, not Anglo-Saxon, and had different languages and cultures from those who preceded them. Therefore, it is difficult in the 1990s to describe an American exactly because about 200 million white Americans can trace some of their ancestry back to the following groups (in descending size order): English, German, Irish, French, Italian, Scottish, Polish, Dutch, Swedish, Norwegian, Russian, Czech, Slovakian, Hungarian, Welsh, Danish, and Portuguese.[6] In addition, there are many white Americans of Hispanic background. Although each of these groups has generally assimilated into American life, many still maintain some of the characteristics that have contributed to the uniqueness of white American society.

Racism refers to the discrimination and prejudicial treatment of a racially different minority group. This prejudicial treatment may take the form of differential hiring and firing practices, promotions, differential resource allocations in health care and education, a two-tier structure in transportation systems, segregation in housing policies, discriminatory behavior of judicial and law enforcement agencies, and stereotypical and prejudicial media images. A pattern of racial discrimination that is strongly entrenched in a society is called institutional racism.

Discrimination Against African Americans

Between 1970 and 1989, the black population of the United States increased by 35.3 percent, from 22.6 to 30.6 million. Between 1985 and 1989, the African American population grew at double the rate of the white population, increasing by 6.2 versus 3.1 percent for whites. By 1995, African Americans composed almost 13 percent of the U.S. population (33.5 out of 265 million). The African American population is primarily urban, with more than 86 percent living in metropolitan areas. About 58 percent of African Americans live in the South; the remainder live in the Midwest (19 percent), the Northeast (17 percent), and the West (8 percent).[7] In 1980, approximately 60 percent of the black population lived in central cities (e.g., New York, Los Angeles, Washington, D.C.,) with black populations greater than 100,000. This number rose to 69 percent in the 1990 census figures, indicating an increasing Black migration towards the inner cities.[8]

Many African Americans have not only improved their socioeconomic position in recent years, but have done so at a relatively faster rate than whites. The most noticeable gains have occurred in the areas of professional employment, incomes, including two-earner family incomes, higher education, and home ownership. Examples include:

- The typical black family income in 1995 was $3,000 higher than in 1992.[9] In fact, African Americans are the only group whose inflation-adjusted median income exceeds what it was in 1989, the year before the last recession. In 1995, African American married couples earned 87 percent as much as white married couples. In 1989, they only earned 79 percent as much as white married couples.[10] In African American households where couples were between the ages of 24 and 35, and where both the husband and wife were employed, the difference in annual income between African Americans and whites was less than $3,000, a significant improvement over earlier decades. The fraction of African American families earning $25,000 a year or more (calculated in 1982 dollars) increased from 10.4 percent in 1960 to 24.5 percent in 1982.
- The number of African American businesses in the United States increased 46 percent (from 424,165 to 620,912 businesses) between 1987 and 1992. (The total number of the nation's firms increased only 26 percent in that same period.) Receipts for black firms increased by 63 percent, from $20 to $32 billion.[11]
- The percentage of African Americans in poverty fell in 1995 to 29.3 percent, the lowest level since poverty statistics were first collected in 1959.[12]
- The number of African Americans in technical, professional, and managerial positions increased by 57 percent (from just under 1 million to over 1.5 million) from 1973 to 1982 By comparison, the number of whites in such positions increased by only 36 percent.
- African Americans recorded a 47 percent increase in home ownership during the 1970s compared to a 30 percent for whites.[13]
- African American youngsters recorded a substantial gain in SAT scores from 1976 to 1989, earning 19 percent higher in verbal and 32 percent higher in math scores. By comparison, white students SAT scores dropped by 5 percent and 2 percent, respectively.[14] The above gain may have contributed in part to the halving of the African American dropout rate from 11 percent in 1968 to 5 percent in 1993, a dropout rate almost identical to that of whites.[15] By 1994, 73 percent of African Americans were high school graduates and 13 percent had graduated college.[16]
- The rate at which African Americans people were murdered in 1995 dropped 17 percent.[17] Despite this relative improvement, millions of African Americans did not experience progress during the last decade; instead, they experienced a significant erosion in living standards.

Evidence of Racism

Discrimination against African Americans is evident in all sectors of social, political, and economic life. The effects of discrimination are illustrated when examining key socioeconomic indicators in the areas of poverty, housing, employment, family composition, health, education, crime, and welfare dependency.

The results of individual and institutional racism manifest themselves most clearly in impoverishment.

- By 1995 the poverty rate for all Americans was 13.8 percent; for African Americans it was 29.3 percent.[18]
- In 1994, 44 percent of African American children were poor, up from 40 percent in 1974. This figure compares unfavorably with the 1994 poverty rate of 12.5 percent for white children.[19]

The higher African American poverty rate is also evident when disaggregating the data.

- The poverty rate in 1994 for *all* families was 12 percent compared to 27 percent for all black families.
- For female-headed black families, the poverty rate was 50 percent, compared with 29 percent for female-headed white families.
- In that same year, the poverty rate for male-present African American families was 8.7 percent compared with 4.3 percent for similar white families.[20]
- In general, the poverty rate for African Americans is almost two times higher than for comparable whites, even when controlling for family composition and geographic differences.[21]

Housing patterns reflect the economic differential between African Americans and whites. Minority (African American, Hispanic, and Native American) households are both poorer and more likely to be renters than white households. In addition:

- Minority households make up 41 percent of households with yearly incomes below $5,000, but only 13 percent of those with incomes above $50,000.[22] This encourages a home ownership rate of 43 percent for African Americans compared with 69 percent for whites.[23]
- About 29 percent of African American households lived in severely or moderately deficient housing in 1989; by comparison, about 13 percent of poor white households lived in these conditions.[24]
- In 1989, 39 percent of African American households spent at least 30 percent of their income for housing compared with 25 percent of white households. Among poor African American households, almost 54 percent paid 50 percent or more of their monthly income for housing.[25]

Employment and wages are other areas where discrimination is evident. While laws and regulations that fight racial discrimination in employment have had some success, they have not adequately prevented widespread discrimination against young African American men. The Urban Institute recently compared the experiences of comparable African American and white male job seekers. Using hiring audits, the study found that black applicants were subject to unfavorable treatment during the application process 20 percent of the time, compared with 7 percent for the white applicants. Unfavorable treatment went on to include: (1) not advancing to the next level of the hiring process; (2) encountering more questions or resistance before receiving an application form; (3) being steered toward less desirable positions than white counterparts; (4) being forced to wait longer for interviews; (5) receiving only cursory interviews; (6) hearing discouraging or derogatory remarks; and (7) being turned down for a position when it was offered to a white applicant.[26]

In part, discrimination also carries into incomes. Not surprisingly, the lowest income gap is found among blacks and whites without a high school diploma. The two highest gaps are found among the two highest education levels. Hence the more education a minority member receives, the less s/he can expect to make in proportion to a white counterpart. For example, in 1994 the mean earnings for a White college graduate was $45,387; for the equivalent African American male it was $32,360[27] (see Table 4.1). While the mean earnings of white college graduates increased by 10.5 percent from 1979 to 1989, it *decreased* for African Americans by 2.8 percent.[28]

In 1994, black male executives had an average income of $41,385 compared with $56,310 for white executives. African American families with children in 1994 had a median family income of $36,670; for whites the median income was $48,630 (33 percent higher). (Single female-headed black families had a median income of only $10,380—28 percent that of black married couples). In 1994, African Americans working full-time, year-round, had a median income

◆ TABLE 4.1
1989 Yearly Mean Income of African American, Hispanic American, and White Families by Educational Level

Years of Education	*White*	*Black*	*Hispanic*
0–8 years	$19,164	$13,800	$14,255
9–11 years	19,780	15,180	15,413
12 years	26,509	19,020	19,942
13–15 years	31,116	23,119	24,811
16 years	39,331	28,287	31,297
17 years plus	44,396	34,344	36,863

Source: Adapted from U.S. House of Representatives, *Overview of Entitlement Programs, 1992 Green Book* (Washington, DC: U.S. Government Printing Office, 1992), p. 598.

of $21,132 ($22,405 for males and $20,628 for females). For whites, the median income was $29,916 ($34,387 for males and $24,487 for females).[29]

This wage differential is even more marked when the percentage of employed men with low earnings is examined on the basis of educational level. In 1989, slightly more than 12 percent of white males with 12 years of schooling were considered to have low earnings. For African American males that figure was 25.5 percent.[30] Moreover, 34 percent of African American males earned poverty-level wages in 1987 (up from 18.4 percent in 1979), compared with 16.3 percent of white men.[31] Perhaps the group hardest hit is the young black worker. While the average young worker aged 25 to 34 earned 7.2 percent less in 1987 than in 1979, the average black worker earned 21.6 percent less.[32] African Americans earned less than whites irrespective of household composition, education, region, or religion.

Another indicator of economic discrimination is unemployment. Since the middle 1950s, the black unemployment rate has been twice the white rate. Despite narrowing differences between the two groups in the areas of education, occupational mobility, and earnings during the 1970s, the unemployment rate for blacks was still more than twice that of whites in 1994 (11 percent compared to 5 percent).

Questions remain as to why this employment/income phenomenon is occurring. Jared Bernstein proposes several explanations for why wage gaps grew faster for African Americans with more education (wages of black college graduates fell in the 1980s relative to their white counterpart). These explanations include: discrimination in employment (helped partly by the lax enforcement of antidiscrimination laws); more frequent employment in vulnerable sectors of the labor economy; a combination of regional, industrial, and occupational choices; lower rates of unionization in the labor market; and the general erosion of worker rights.[33] Another explanation suggests that as middle-class African Americans advanced, greater unemployment occurred among those with less education and skills. This explanation, however, does not address the large African American/white unemployment differential among college-educated men, a disparity that is greater in central cities of the East and North. According to Franklin Wilson, the cause of this discrepancy can be found in two factors: (1) the decline during the 1980s in the number of jobs traditionally filled by college-educated African American men (e.g., public sector jobs dealing with affirmative action, social welfare, and criminal justice); and (2) the inability of educated African Americans to penetrate the professional/technical occupations that involve managerial or supervisory responsibilities, positions that usually have more security.[34] The recent personnel cutbacks in federal and state governments is likely to exacerbate the income differential of African Americans. This is especially true because one of the major opportunities for the employment of African Americans has been in the governmental sector.

Health is another important indicator of discrimination. Compared to white women, African American women:

- have a 68 percent higher death rate from heart disease;
- are 86 percent more likely to die from strokes;
- have roughly twice the rate of cervical cancer; and
- have a higher death rate from breast cancer than white women who were diagnosed at the same time.[35]

Also

- African American women are 15 times more likely to have AIDS than white women.[36] (AIDS is the second leading cause of death among African American women aged 25 to 44.[37])
- African American women have one of the highest rates of infant mortality of any group in the United States, a rate that equaled 16.5 deaths per 1,000 in 1993 compared with 6.8 deaths per thousand for white women.[38] If the black infant mortality rate had been the same as the white rate over the past 50 years, more than 400,000 babies would have survived.
- A major factor affecting infant mortality is low birth weight. Although the definitive cause is unknown, what is clear is that low birth weight

(defined as less than 5.5 pounds) increases the chances of infant death during the first month by 40 times.[39] Also known is that low birth weight is often correlated with inadequate nutrition in mothers during pregnancy. Of the roughly 40,000 infant deaths each year, about 23,000 are estimated to result from low birth weight. In 1993, 7.2 percent (288,482 thousand) of babies were born at low birth weight; for African American babies it was 13.3 percent.[40] Moreover, less than half of all African American children in 1985 had been fully immunized against measles, rubella, diphtheria, polio, and mumps.[41]

- African American mothers are also four times more likely to die in childbirth than are white mothers.[42] Higher infant mortality and higher deaths in childbirth are often correlated with poor early prenatal care. In 1993, only 66 percent of African American births were to women who had received early prenatal care. By comparison, almost 82 percent of white births were to women who had such care.[43]
- These variations are even sharper when the amount and frequency of care is considered. In 1988, 73 percent of babies were born to white mothers who had received care that began before the seventh month of pregnancy and included more than four visits; for African Americans the figure was only 51 percent.[44] The combination of these factors caused the African American infant mortality rate to rank twenty-seventh internationally in 1989, behind such countries such as Hungary, Poland, and Cuba. Table 4.2[45] ranks countries according to their infant mortality rates.

◆ TABLE 4.2.
Infant Mortality Rates and Ranks: Selected Countries, 1991 *

Rank	*Country*	*Rate*
1	Japan	4.4
2	Singapore	5.4
3	Finland	5.9
4	Sweden	6.1
5	Switzerland	6.2
6	Norway	6.4
7	Canada	6.4
8	Netherlands	6.5
9	Hong Kong	6.6
*	U.S. (White Rate)	6.8
10	German F.R.	7.0
11	Australia	7.0
12	Scotland	7.1
13	Denmark	7.2
14	France	7.3
15	England & Wales	7.4
16	Northern Ireland	7.4
17	Austria	7.6
18	Ireland	7.6
19	Spain	7.7
20	Belgium	7.9
21	Italy	8.2
22	New Zealand	8.4
23	U.S. (total)	8.9
24	Greece	9.0
25	Israel	9.8
26	Cuba	10.7
27	Portugal	10.8
28	Czechoslovakia	11.5
29	Puerto Rico	13.8
30	Costa Rica	13.8
31	Poland	15.0
32	Chile	15.4
33	Hunary	15.6
*	U.S. (Black Rate)	16.5
34	Bulgaria	16.9
35	Russian Federation	18.1
36	Romania	22.7

*Infant deaths per 1,000 births
Source: Adapted from March of Dimes, "Infant Mortality Rates and Ranks: Selected Countries, 1991." On-line: http://www.modimes.org/stats/mortal.htm

The variation in health indicators between African Americans and whites goes beyond infant mortality. From age 1 until age 24, the African American mortality rate is close to double that of whites, except in the area of suicide, where the African American rate is almost half the white rate. This higher mortality follows African Americans throughout their lives, and the life expectancy of African Americans is 6.4 years less than it is for whites.[46] However, when environmental and economic variables are controlled, the effect of race on the African American mortality rate is reduced by 75 percent.[47] In other words, the lessened longevity of African Americans is based on poverty, not race.

Education is another indicator that illustrates the "diswelfare" of African Americans. Education is thought to be one of the most important variables in determining economic security. Despite the relatively high unemployment rate of college-educated African American men, discussed earlier, those with college degrees were much less likely to have low earnings than those with only a high school education. In short, as a high school education alone becomes less valuable in the marketplace, only educational upgrading can protect men from large income losses. In fact, the incomes of college graduates rose from 20 percent above the earnings of high school graduates in the 1950s to about 40 to 50 percent higher than high school graduates' incomes by the mid–1970s. Also, while the annual wage of a high school graduate fell 8.6 percent from 1979 to 1987, the income of a college graduate rose by 9.2 percent.[48] Partly as a result of market conditions, African American men have increased their schooling more than whites since the mid–1970s.[49]

From 1968 to 1990, the white high school dropout rate remained relatively flat, falling from 14.7 to 12.0 percent. By contrast, the African American dropout rate fell dramatically from 27.4 to 13.2 percent.[50] According to Lawrence Mishel and David Frankel, more than 73 percent of African Americans completed high school in the 1980–1988 period, compared to 61 percent in the 1967–1973 period.[51] Although these figures may seem comforting, they also contain inconsistencies. For example, in 1988 only 58.4 percent of African Americans completed high school between ages 18 and 19, a figure that increased to 81.5 percent for the 20- to 21-year-old age group. Moreover, almost 29 percent of African American students who entered ninth grade in 1984 failed to graduate from high school by 1988. These figures are exacerbated by a stagnant high school completion rate for African Americans, which rose only three percentage points in the past 20 years.[52]

The failure to complete high school is clearly correlated with poverty. According to the American Public Welfare Association, in 1989 nearly half of all female heads of families and 60 percent of parents receiving welfare in 36 of the previous 60 months did not finish high school.[53] Furthermore, an estimated 85 percent of juveniles appearing in court are functionally illiterate.[54]

While high school graduation rates have steadily, if slowly, improved among African Americans, college enrollment stagnated during the 1980s. Among 1989 high school graduates, about 60 percent of whites and 53 percent of African Americans entered college the following fall. Among 1980 high school graduates, however, only 10 percent of African Americans had completed their degree by 1986, compared with 20 percent of similar white college enrollees.[55] Moreover, while white college enrollment rates improved slightly from 1974 to 1988 (from 26 to 28 percent), African American college enrollment was stuck between 20.4 and 20.5 percent. Also, fewer minority college graduates have gone on to obtain advanced degrees. For example, in 1986–1987, whites made up 81 percent of all undergraduates: They received 88 percent of the bachelor's degrees, 88 percent of the master's degrees, and 89 percent of all doctorates. By contrast, African Americans accounted for 9 percent of all undergraduates but received only 6 percent of the bachelor's degrees, 5 percent of the master's degrees, and 4 percent of the doctorates.[56]

African American college enrollment rates peaked in 1976. Much of that bubble was attributable to civil rights legislation and variables like increased student aid. However, while overall financial aid decreased slightly between 1980 and 1989, public college costs for tuition and room and board (adjusted for inflation) rose from $3,838 in 1978–1979 to $4,899 in 1987–1988. Private college costs soared from $9,060 to $13,840 in the same period. The average financial aid award had so eroded by 1989 that it paid for less than 21 percent of the yearly costs of a private college and for only 61 percent of the costs of a public university.

Crime is another indicator of economic and social distress. Although African Americans constitute slightly more than 12 percent of the population, they account for 30 percent of all arrests and for 51 percent of all violent crime arrests. Moreover, they are 8.5 times more likely than whites to go to prison.[57] Harvard economist Richard Freeman calculated that 35 percent of all African Americans aged 16 to 35 were arrested in 1989.[58] In 1986, almost 47 percent of the inmates in state prisons were African American, four times their numerical representation in the population. According to the U.S. House Committee on Ways and Means, "Juveniles in public facilities are predominantly male, and disproportionately Black, and four-fifths were 14 to 17 years old."[59] In fact, of the 56,000 juveniles held in public juvenile facilities, almost 34,000 were from minority groups, and of the 144 felons executed from 1977 to 1990, 40 percent were African American and another 5 percent Hispanic American.[60]

Perhaps one of the most startling statistics is the death rate for African Americans through homicide and legal intervention. In 1989, 102 African American men in every 100,000 were killed through homicide or legal intervention. This compares with 11.5 per 100,000 white men. In effect, African American men are almost 10 times more likely to die in this manner than white males. For African American females the rate is 17.5 per 100,000, higher than the 11.5 death rate for white males and over four times higher than the death rate for white females.[61]

Welfare dependency is still another indicator of racism. Although African Americans comprise only 12 percent of the U.S. population, they make up roughly 41 percent of all public assistance recipients, 35 percent of all food stamp recipients, 31 percent of Medicaid recipients, and 25 percent of SSI beneficiaries.[62]

Hispanic Americans and Poverty

Because of the large number of undocumented aliens coming from Central America and Mexico, the Hispanic population of the United States is difficult to accurately measure. Although some estimates of the number of undocumented workers in the United States (most of them from Spanish-speaking countries) are in the 12 million range, other researchers have estimated this population to be from 3 to 6 million.[63] Still other estimates are that by 1988, approximately 1.8 million illegal immigrants from Mexico and Central and South America were in the United States.[64] The total Hispanic population grew by 96 percent from 1987 to 1994, reaching about 25 million, or close to 9 percent of the U.S. population.[65] The Hispanic population is also geographically concentrated, with 65 percent of Hispanics living in just three states: California, Texas, and New York. Eighty-eight percent of all Latinos live in nine states, and 88 percent live in urban areas (a figure 13 percent higher than the national average).[66]

The poverty status of Hispanics has worsened in the last two decades in relation to other groups, including African Americans. For example, while the overall poverty rate for African Americans decreased slightly from 1992 (33 percent) to 1995 (29.3 percent), the poverty rate for Hispanics rose to 30.3 percent, surpassing the black poverty rate for the first time.[67] In 1979, 28 percent of Hispanic children were below the poverty line; by 1990 that number had risen to 38 percent (well over twice the poverty rate of 16 percent for white children). By 1990, some 2.8 million Hispanic children were living in poverty, the highest level ever recorded since the Census Bureau began to keep data on Latinos in 1973.[68] The high poverty rate for children is clearly correlated with the 48 percent of Hispanic female-headed families that fell below the poverty line in 1990, a number significantly higher than the 25 percent of white female-headed families in this category, and slightly above the 47 percent of African American female-headed families in poverty.[69]

The median earnings of Hispanic males ($21,697) were also low, and in 1988 they were lower than those of African Americans ($23,374). (Almost the same wage differential existed between Hispanic American and African American women—$16,860 versus $17,811.) The loss of income for both Hispanic men and women represents a change from 1978, when they earned slightly more than African Americans.[70] More importantly, this translates into a loss of one-tenth of a percent in family income (adjusting for inflation in 1989 dollars) from 1973 to 1989, thus making Hispanic families the only minority group in the United States to have experienced a net loss of income in that period.[71] By 1995, Hispanics replaced African Americans as the most impoverished group in America. Scott Barancik sums up the economic position of Hispanics:

> Hispanics account for a disproportionately large share of the American households with low incomes and a disproportionately small share of those with high incomes. Census Bureau data show that of all the households in the top income fifth in

1987, just over three percent were Hispanic. By contrast, nine percent of those in the bottom fifth were Hispanic, meaning that Hispanics were about three times as likely to be among the poorest fifth of U.S. households as among the wealthiest fifth.[72]

Traditionally, Hispanic women have had higher fertility rates than non-Latinas. In 1992, the total fertility rate was 3.04 births per woman, compared with 1.94 for white women. Since 1980, Hispanic fertility has risen by about 20 percent, while white fertility has risen by less than 7 percent. The increase in teenage fertility is even more dramatic. Hispanic teen birthrates increased by 30 percent between 1980 and 1992 while white rates increased by only 6 percent.[73]

Although for statistical purposes the Hispanic population is often considered as a single group, the various Latino subgroups have distinct social and historical backgrounds. For example, Cubans living in Florida may have little in common historically and politically with Mexican Americans living in California, and Puerto Ricans living in New York may have little understanding of the culture of either Cuban Americans or Mexican Americans. These sociocultural differences are also reflected in the significant differences in incomes and family patterns among these groups. One study noted that:

> . . . Latina mothers displayed patterns that fell intermediate to the patterns of Anglo and Black mothers, though there was no single pattern that characterized all Latino subgroups. Puerto Rican mothers stand out as being considerably worse off than other groups: they are less likely to be married, less likely to be living with parents or other adults, more likely to be living in poverty and more likely to be receiving welfare. Cuban mothers stand out in the opposite way, with the highest household incomes of any group and the lowest rates of receiving welfare. Mexican and Central and South American mothers look more like Anglos than any other group in terms of their marriage patterns and living arrangements, although their poverty rates are much higher.[74]

These differences are also reflected in incomes. Two in three U.S. Hispanics, or 17.1 million, are of Mexican origin. The average earnings of Mexican men was $17,700 in 1994, down 8 percent from 1987 (in constant 1994 dollars). The average earnings of all Hispanic men also dropped 8 percent over the period, to $19,100. Cuban American men, however (4 percent of the Hispanic population), saw their income increase 12 percent, to $31,400 in constant 1994 dollars.[75]

According to the Bureau of the Census, there were about 13 million Mexican Americans in the United States in 1989, a 100 percent increase over the 1970 census. Mexican Americans constitute about 63 percent of all Hispanic Americans in the United States and are the fastest growing of the Spanish-speaking subgroups. Moreover, the continuation of this growth rate will result in Mexican Americans being the largest minority group in the United States by the year 2010.[76]

In part, the poverty of Mexican Americans is correlated to deficits in educational attainment. Although Mexican Americans have made educational gains, in 1980 their median attendance in school was 9.8 years, the lowest of any Hispanic subgroup.[77] Moreover, they have the highest dropout rate in the United States. In 1980, over 62 percent of those between the ages of 25 and 64 had less than a high school education, and only 4.4 percent had some college.[78]

Puerto Ricans constitute 12 percent of all Hispanics in the United States and less than 1 percent of the total U.S. population. In the past 25 years, Puerto Ricans have steadily lost ground in labor force participation, earnings of family heads, and poverty status. In 1988, Puerto Ricans had one of the lowest family incomes of any minority group in the United States—$18,932.[79] From 1960 to 1984, Puerto Rican family income dropped relative to other minority groups, and over 43 percent of all Puerto Rican families lived below the poverty line in 1984.[80]

While Hispanic incomes have dropped relative to other minority groups, Hispanic businesses increased 76 percent (from 490,00 to 862,600) between 1987 and 1992. Receipts for Hispanic businesses increased by 134 percent during this period.[81] Regardless, the overall statistics clearly suggest a worsening economic picture for America's Hispanic communities.

Native Americans and Poverty

Oppression and exploitation are by no means limited to African Americans and Hispanics. Native Americans, in some ways the most destitute group in the

United States, experience the same intensity of oppression as other disenfranchised populations.

Although there are 504 federally recognized tribes (including 197 Alaskan Native groups) and 304 Indian Reservations, there is no single definition of a Native American. The Bureau of Indian Affairs (BIA) considers someone Indian if the person is a member of a recognized Indian tribe and has one-fourth or more Indian blood. The Bureau of the Census uses self-identification.

The history of Native Americans is marked by hardship, deprivation, and gross injustice. Before the arrival of Christopher Columbus, the Indian population in the territorial United States was somewhere between 900,000 and 12 million.[82] As a result of the westward expansion of whites—and the wars and genocidal policies that ensued—the indigenous Indian population was dramatically reduced. By 1880, the census reported the existence of only 250,000 Indians.[83] Moreover, Native Americans were not granted citizenship until 1924, and New Mexico did not allow them to vote until 1940. Some Native Americans remained virtual slaves until 1935.[84]

From 1970 to 1989, the Native American population grew from 574,000 to almost 2 million.[85] According to BIA estimates, about 864,500 Indians live on or near Indian reservations. This population rise was due to a lower infant mortality rate, a high birthrate, and the fact that more individuals of mixed Indian descent were reporting their race as Indian. This last factor may be partly correlated with the resurgence of Native American pride that began in the 1970s.

In 1980, about 25 percent of Native Americans (400,000) lived on 278 federal and state reservations. However, because of the federal policy of selling or leasing reservation land, only 49 percent of the inhabitants of reservations are Native Americans, the rest being non-Indian spouses, ranchers, merchants, teachers, doctors, and government employees. With the exception of the Navajo nation (containing more than 100,000 Indians and 16 million acres), most reservations are small, having less than 1,000 residents.[86] Because 63 percent of Native Americans live away from reservations, more than half the Native American population is now urban.

As a group, Native Americans experience severe social and economic problems. For example, 30 percent of Native Americans live below the poverty line compared to slightly more than 13 percent of the general population. In 1989, Native Americans had the lowest per capita income of any ethnic group in the United States ($13,678).[87] In 1985, their median Indian income was about 48 percent of the national median. While unemployment in the United States is about 5 percent, 41 percent of American Indians are unemployed. Unemployment on reservations range from 45 to 90 percent on the more isolated reservations. Housing is a major problem. Sixteen percent of Native American homes are without electricity, while the U.S. average is only 0.1 percent.[88] It is estimated that about 38,000 Native American homes lack safe water and adequate sanitation. Only 56 percent of Native American children graduate from high school.

Most health indicators for Native Americans are dismal. Roughly 43 percent of Native Americans who live beyond infancy die before age 55 (this compares to slightly more than 16 percent for the general population). Many of these deaths are attributable to accidents. For example, in 1984 the Native American death rate from accidents was 81 per 100,000, 42 of which were related to motor vehicles (frequently alcohol related and three times the national average). These figures are much higher than the 1984 age-adjusted death rate for all races—35 per 100,000.[89]

Native Americans also have a maternal death rate 20 percent higher than the national average; the death rate for tuberculosis is six times higher than that for the population as a whole; for chronic liver disease it is four times the norm; for diabetes, influenza, and pneumonia, two times; and suicide rates are twice the national average, with rates tending to be highest among young people. Moreover, Native Americans have the highest rate of alcoholism of any ethnic group in the United States.[90] Poor education, alcoholism, gambling, and high suicide rates plague many Native American urban and reservation communities.

Caught in the paternalistic and authoritarian web of the Bureau of Indian Affairs, Native Americans struggle for their identity. Having been robbed of their land, murdered indiscriminately by encroaching white settlers (as well as the U.S. Cavalry), and treated alternately as children and pests by the federal government, Native Americans were further oppressed by having their children taken away by welfare officials. This widespread abuse by welfare workers, who evaluated Native American childrearing practices as neglectful in the context of white middle-class family values, was partially remedied by the Indian Child Welfare Act of 1978, which restored child-placement decisions to the individual tribes. As a result of this act, priority for the placement of Native American children was given to tribal members rather than white families. In an attempt to remedy historical injustices, the Indian Self-Determination Act of 1975 emphasized tribal self-government, self-sufficiency, and the establishment of independent health, education, and welfare services. Despite these limited gains, the plight of Native Americans serves as a reminder of the mistakes made by the United States both in its past and present policies toward disenfranchised minority groups.

Asian Americans

The 1990 census reported more than 20 Asian-Pacific subgroups in the United States, including Chinese, Filipino, Japanese, Asian-Indian, Korean, Vietnamese, Laotian, Thai, Cambodian, Polynesian (Hawaiian, Samoan, and Tongan), Micronesian (Guamanian), and Melanesian (Fijan). The five largest Asian population groups in the United States are: Chinese (1.6 million), Filipino (1.4 million), Japanese (850,000), Asian-Indian (815,000), and Korean (800,000).[91] In 1970, there were 1.5 million Asians living in the United States. By 1980, that rose to 3.7 million; by 1990, 7.3 million, representing almost a 100 percent increase in the last decade and an astounding 475 percent increase in the last 20 years. This rapid increase has made Asians the fastest growing segment of the U.S. population. Demographers predict that this growth will continue at a greater rate throughout the 1990s and into the twenty-first century because of above average birthrates and accelerating legal and illegal immigration. If these predictions are correct, by 2080 Asians will constitute 12 percent of the U.S. population, compared to 3 percent in 1990.[92]

While the social and economic data is mixed, perhaps the most striking feature is that Asian Americans had the highest median family income in 1995 (see Figure 4.1). Economic and social data also point to a population that has made great strides, especially in the educational area. For example, In 1990, 82 percent of Asians were high school graduates, compared with 78 percent of whites, 65 percent of blacks, and 51 percent of Hispanics.[93] In 1989, college-bound Asian seniors had a high school grade point average of 3.25/4.0 versus 3.08/4.0 for all other students.[94] In 1992, the nation's most elite universities reported 14 percent Asian American enrollment, almost five times the percentage in the total population.[95] While Asians made up only 3 percent of the population in 1990, they represented 12 percent of the students at Harvard University, 20 percent at Stanford, and 30 percent at the University of California, Berkeley campus.[96] In 1986, all five top scholarships of the Westinghouse Science Talent Search scholarships went to Asians.[97] In 1990, 39 percent of Asian Americans 25 years or older had graduated from college, as opposed to 22 percent for whites and 12 percent for blacks.[98]

In 1990, Asian Americans had approximately the same unemployment rate (4.6 percent) as whites (4.5 percent),[99] and median earnings for Asians with four years of college was $34,469 compared to $36,134 for whites. Japanese Americans earned 37 percent more than the median family income for all Americans.[100] In 1987, Asian-Pacific Americans owned 355,000 businesses, a 328 percent increase in just 10 years. From 1987 to 1992 the number of Asian businesses grew 61 percent (from 439,271 to 705,672). Receipts from Asian businesses increased 163 percent in that same period, from $36.5 to $96 billion.[101] Census data indicate that Asian poverty levels range from less than 5 percent for Japanese Americans to 35 percent for newly arrived Southeast Asian immigrants.[102]

While the above economic statistics are impressive, they conceal several things. First, most

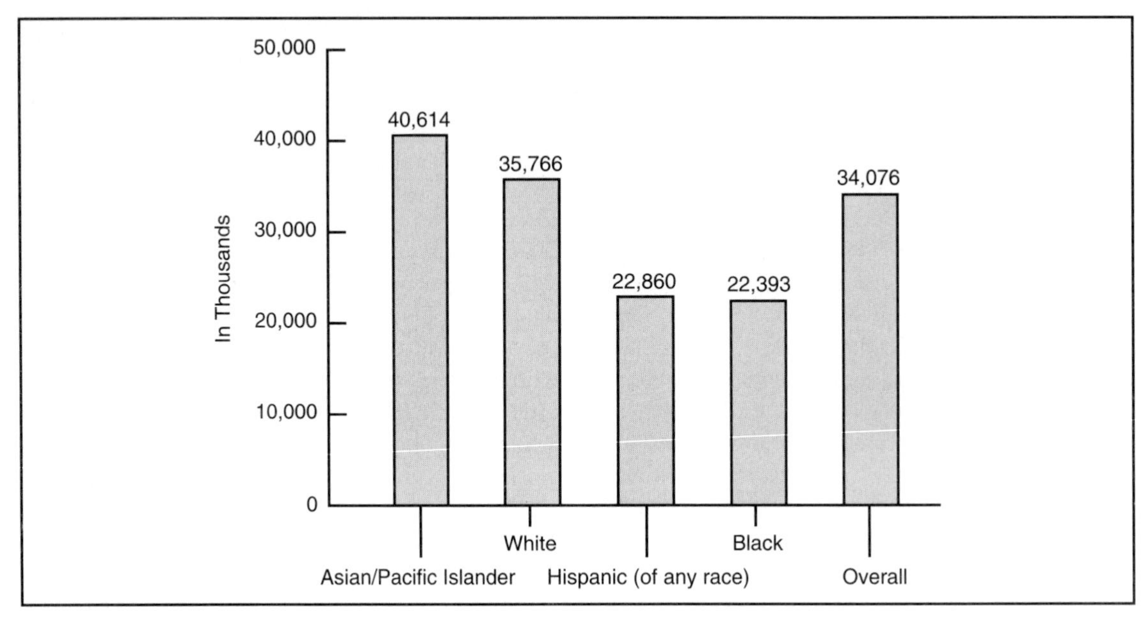

◆ **FIGURE 4.1 Median Family Income, 1995**
Source: U.S. Census Bureau, "The Income Outlook, 1995" (Washington, DC: US Census Bureau, 1996).

Asians live in expensive urban areas where salaries are higher than the U.S. average. Second, statistics indicating economic success for Asian Americans conceal the problems of many recent low-wage immigrants who work in sweatshops in "Chinatowns." For example, the average suburban Chinese household earned $16,790 in 1980 compared to $9,059 for the average Chinatown household.[103] Third, while Chinese and Japanese Americans do reasonably well economically, Southeast Asians are at higher risk of poverty than whites. Fourth, Asians are underrepresented in the higher-salaried public and private positions. Fifth, while a large number of Asian immigrants have become successful entrepreneurs and own and operate their own small retail businesses, for some it was forced on them as a result of discrimination.

Asian Americans have been stigmatized in American society in a number of ways. Most dramatic was the internment of Japanese Americans in detention camps during World War II. However, they have also experienced more subtle forms of discrimination. For example, Asians are often thought of as a model minority. Because of this status, many experience pressure from the white majority as well as from other minority groups. An example of this tension is evident in the hostility between Korean shopkeepers and inner-city African American residents. Asians have also been the victims of hate crimes, some motivated by the mudslinging that has been going on between Japan and the United States over recurrent trade problems. Specifically, the U.S. trade deficit with Japan and the resulting displacement of American blue-collar workers have often been blamed on Asians. In addition, some Asian Americans complain that they are discriminated against in colleges and universities because of their superior academic performance.[104] Facing this backlash, some Asians are redoubling their efforts to become mainstream players in American society. As such, they want to be in the center of American society rather than on the margins as "hyphenated-Americans." They also want to bolster their clout in the political arena by helping to shape American public policy.

Many Asians point to contributions to American society that can result from the input of Oriental cultural values. For example, Asian culture often includes a sense of frugality that leads to environmental conservation, greater consideration for the feelings of others, and a sense of balance between group and individual welfare. According to sociologist Tu Weiming, the less individualistic nature of Asians, their lower sense of self-interest, their less adversarial nature, and their less legalistic approach to society may have important applications for the United States.[105] In the end, the cross-fertilization of cultures is an important factor that has made America a strong and resilient society.

Immigrants and Immigration

Immigration, one of the knottiest social and legal issues to reemerge in the past decade, has long had a major economic and social impact on American society. A 1992 Urban Institute study estimated that 3.4 million illegal immigrants lived in the United States, with 86 percent settling in 7 states. Critics point out that these seven states paid $4 billion in benefits and incarceration for illegals, while illegals paid only $1.9 billion in taxes.[106] Moreover, a significant portion of Hispanic poverty is attributable to the large numbers of illegal immigrants entering the United States and to the low-paying, menial jobs they occupy. Asian Americans have also felt the backlash from mainstream Americans who are worried about the consequences of admitting non-Europeans into the American economy.

As a reaction to immigration, groups such as the Federation for American Immigration Reform (FAIR) have promoted exclusionary messages in both national and international forums. For these groups, immigration is a time bomb in terms of its negative impact on the U.S. economy and its effects on the interests of American workers. Moreover, this hostility is also rooted in the fear of losing an already vaguely defined American identity. In 1992, Republican presidential candidate Pat Buchanan made immigration policy a major plank in his bid for the presidency. According to Buchanan, "[One] reason that we are beset with conflict is that since 1965 a flood tide of immigration has rolled in from the Third World, legal and illegal, as our institutions of assimilation—public schools, popular culture, churches—disintegrated."[107] For their part, Asian and Hispanics argue that immigrants are a productive sector of American society, one that puts in more than it takes out. In fact, while poverty rates are higher for immigrants, naturalized citizens have lower poverty rates—10.5 percent than—native-born Americans.

In response to political pressures, Congress passed the Immigration Reform and Control Act (IRCA) (PL 99–603) in 1986, which was partly an attempt to "legalize" immigrants already in the United States. According to Fariyal Ross-Sheriff, the three main objectives of IRCA were: (1) to decrease the number of illegal aliens currently living in the United States; (2) to regain control of U.S. national boundaries; and (3) to increase the number of legal or migrant farm and agricultural workers.[108]

IRCA was a mixed blessing for undocumented workers, most of whom were Hispanic. For one thing, it included an employer sanction provision that specified imprisonment and fines of up to $10,000 a worker for employers who knowingly hired undocumented workers. In a controversial approach, the Immigration and Naturalization Service (INS) relied on employers to determine the legitimacy of each worker, thereby making it more risky to hire alien workers. Under the amnesty provision of the act, undocumented persons who could prove they entered the United States before 1982 were eligible to apply for temporary resident status. After 18 months, they were permitted to apply for permanent resident status. Provided they had no criminal record and did not apply for benefits from a federally subsidized welfare program for a period of five years, they were allowed to stay in the United States. After that, they were permitted to apply for citizenship. Therein lies the hitch. Forced to accept low-paying jobs because of language and educational deficits, these workers became banished to the netherworld of minimum-wage employment. These immigrants were thus forced to rely on family or nongovernmental aid, deprived of the welfare safety net guaranteed to most Americans.[109] By October 1988, 2 million people had applied for citizenship, including the one million who had entered the country illegally before January 1, 1992, and the 510,000 agricultural workers who were in the country before 1986.[110]

In 1996, Congress passed the Personal Responsibility and Work Opportunity Act (PRWOA). The most comprehensive welfare reform legislation passed since the New Deal of 1935, the 900-page bill contained profound implications for both legal and illegal immigrants (PRWOA will be discussed more fully in Chapter 11).[111] Specifically, the PRWOA disentitles most legal immigrants (including many who have been living in the United States for years but elected not to become citizens) from food stamps, Aid to Families with Dependent Children (AFDC), and Supplemental Security Income (SSI). (Illegal immigrants were never entitled to these benefits.) The only immigrants still entitled to benefits are: (1) those who have become citizens or who have worked in the United States and paid Social Security taxes for at least 10 years; and (2) veterans of the U.S. Army who are noncitizens. In addition, the bill gives states the option to deny Medicaid benefits to immigrants. In Texas alone, the PRWOA is expected to disqualify 187,000 legal immigrants from food stamps, 22,000 from AFDC benefits, and 53,000 from SSI.[112]

In September 1996, Congress revisited immigration, this time voting to double the size of the Border Patrol, stiffen penalties for document fraud and immigrant smuggling, bar illegal immigrants from qualifying for Social Security benefits or public housing, give states the right to deny illegal immigrants drivers' licenses, and slightly increase the earnings requirements for U.S. residents wanting to sponsor foreign family members.[113]

Immigration policies have been questioned on several other fronts. For one, the current focus on Latino immigration distorts the diversity of illegal immigrants. As such, these policies have failed to address the largest source of immigration—those who overstay their visas. For example, 107,000 Poles, 106,000 Filipinos, 79,000 Italians, and 78,000 Canadians overstayed their visas. Nevertheless, as a result of these and other U.S. immigration policies, the steepest sustained drop in immigration since WWII occurred in 1995. Current legal immigration is 700,000 a year in a U.S. population of more than 260 million.

LEGAL ATTEMPTS TO REMEDY RACISM

Concerted attempts to eliminate racism are a relatively recent phenomenon. Although the Fourteenth Amendment of the Constitution guaranteed all citizens equal protection under the law, it was also used to perpetuate discrimination by forming the grounds for separate but equal treatment. In fact, segregation existed in the South until the middle of the twentieth century, and separate but (supposedly) equal public facilities characterized much of the social and economic activity of America. The extensive system of Southern segregation included public transportation, schools, private economic activities, and even public drinking fountains. It was only in the middle-1950s that the U.S. Supreme Court overturned the *Plessy v. Ferguson* (1896) decision that had formed the basis for the separate but equal doctrine.

In 1954 the Supreme Court, in its landmark decision on *Brown v. Board of Education of Topeka, Kansas*, ruled that separate but equal facilities in education were inherently unequal. The Court ruled that separating the races was a way of denoting the inferiority of African Americans. In addition, the court stated that segregation retarded the educational and mental development of black children. Although the Supreme Court ruled against officially sanctioned segregation in public schools, de facto segregation was not addressed until the *Swann v. Charlotte-Mecklenburg Board of Education* ruling of 1971. This ruling approved court-ordered busing to achieve racial integration of school districts that had a history of discrimination.

The legal gains made by African Americans were won only through considerable, often bitter struggle. Up to the middle-1960s, Southern blacks enjoyed few rights, with total segregation enforced in almost all spheres of social, economic, political, and public activity. (Segregation in the North occurred through de facto or unofficial, rather than de jure, or legal, means, although the net effect was in many ways the same.) In 1955, Rosa Parks, too tired to stand in the "colored" section in the back of a bus in Montgomery, Alabama, sparked a nonviolent bus boycott led by Martin Luther King, Jr. Still another protest was begun when African American students in North Carolina were refused service at an all-white lunch counter. The Civil Rights movement grew and resulted in widespread demonstrations (in Selma, Alabama, one march drew more than 100,000 people), picket lines, sit-ins, and other forms of political protest. Gaining international publicity, the protests attracted Northern religious leaders, students, and white liberals—some of whom would lose their lives. By the time Reverend Martin Luther King, Jr., was assassinated in 1968, many demands of the Civil Rights movement had been incorporated in the Civil Rights Act of 1964. Paradoxically, Congress exempted itself from complying with the act until 1988. The 1964 Civil Rights Act did not live up to its implicit promise. The balance of racial power did not shift, and, for the most part, African Americans and other minority groups continued to be disenfranchised economically and politically. It soon became apparent that other remedial methods were required, one of which was affirmative action, a set of policies designed to achieve equality in admissions and employment opportunities for minorities and women.

Affirmative Action

Two basic strategies have been employed to address racial, economic, and other injustices. The first is nondiscrimination, which means that no preferential treatment is given to selected groups. The second is affirmative action, whose overall goal is to admit, hire, and promote women and minorities in direct proportion to their representation in the population. Affirmative action policies and legislation represent an aggressive step beyond the largely reactive stance taken by simple nondiscrimination policies. As such, rigorous affirmative action policies give preferential treatment to minority and female applicants. The ostensible purpose of affirmative action policies are to right past wrongs done to groups of people throughout the country's history of slavery, Jim Crow laws, and institutionalized racism and sexism.

Federal affirmative action began in 1941 when President Franklin Roosevelt issued an executive order barring discrimination against black contractors in the federal government and the war industry. Without staff or enforcement authority, the policy was rendered useless. As a response to the Civil Rights movement, Presidents Kennedy, Johnson, and Nixon initiated affirmative plans to move the country toward nondiscrimination. Targeted initially to address discrimination against African Americans, affirmative action policies were expanded to address discrimination based on gender, age and disability.

There are three types of affirmative action and admissions action programs: (1) Employers and schools can adopt voluntary programs to increase the hiring of minorities and women; (2) the courts can order an employer or school to create an affirmative action plan; and (3) federal, state, and local governments may require contractors to adopt affirmative action plans to remain eligible for government contracts.[114]

As Table 4.3 illustrates, affirmative action and civil rights legislation affect a much wider group of Americans than minorities. Moreover, as the following table demonstrates, rulings on affirmative action and civil rights cases have been inconsistent, characterized by two steps forward and one or two steps backward. In the final analysis, modern civil rights and affirmative policies have been forged from an often conflicting blend of legislation and court decisions.

Affirmative action became a hotly contested issue in the middle 1990s. While the Republican Contract with America did not specifically target affirmative action programs, some conservatives, including a presidential candidate, former Senator Bob Dole, supported legislation that would prohibit the federal government from granting preferences based on race, gender, or national origin in employment, contracting, or any other federal program. In 1995, California Governor Pete Wilson issued an executive order dismantling affirmative action programs under his authority. In 1996 California voters approved Proposition 209 (the California Civil Rights Initiative), that would prohibit racial or gender preferences in public education, employment, and state contracting.

◆ TABLE 4.3
Milestones in Civil Rights and Affirmative Action Rulings

Legislation or Court Ruling	*Summary*
Plessy v. Ferguson (1896)	The U.S. Supreme Court established the "separate but equal" doctrine.
Fair Employment Practices Committee (1935)	Asked employers not to discriminate in hiring based on race.
Brown v. Board of Education of Topeka, Kansas (1954)	The Supreme Court ruled that "separate but equal" facilities in education were inherently unequal.
Equal Pay Act of 1963	Men and women have a right to equal pay for doing the same work
Civil Rights Act of 1964, including amendments added in 1972, 1978, and 1991	1. Voter registration is a legal right that cannot be tampered with. 2. It is unlawful to discriminate or segregate based on race, color, religion, or national origin in any public accommodation, including hotels, motels, theaters, and other public places. 3. The attorney general will undertake civil action on the part of any person who is denied access to a public accommodation. If the owner continues to discriminate, a court fine and imprisonment will result. 4. The attorney general must represent anyone who undertakes the desegregation of a public school. 5. Each federal department must take action to end discrimination in all programs or activities receiving federal assistance. 6. Public or private employers, employment agencies, or labor unions with more than 15 employees cannot discriminate against an individual because of their race, color, religion, national origin, or sex. An Equal Opportunity Commission will be established to enforce this provision. A 1968 amendment to this act prohibited discrimination in housing.
Age Discrimination Act of 1967	Protects persons over 40 in any terms or conditions of their employment.
Griggs v. Duke Power Co. (1971)	The Supreme Court prohibited discriminatory employment practices. It put the burden of proof on the employer to show that hiring criteria have a direct relationship to the job. Griggs was overturned by Wards Cove Packing Co., Inc. v. Atonio (1989), where the Supreme Court imposed tougher standards for proving discrimination and shifted the burden of proof onto the employee.
Swann v. Charlotte-Mecklenburg Board of Education (1971)	The Supreme Court ruled in favor of court-ordered busing to achieve racial integration of school districts that had a history of discrimination.
Title IX of Education Amendments of 1972	Institutions receiving federal financial assistance cannot discriminate based on sex.
Rehabilitation Act of 1973	Prohibited discrimination on the basis of mental or physical disability.
Vietnam Era Veterans Readjustment Act of 1974	Required employers with federal contracts to take steps to employ and advance qualified disabled veterans.
Milliken v. Brady (1974)	The Supreme Court ruled that mandatory school busing across city-suburban boundaries to achieve racial integration was not required unless the segregation had resulted from an official action.
Marco DeFunis v. University of Washington Law School (1974)	DeFunis claimed that he was denied admission to law school even though his grades and test scores were higher than those of minorities who were accepted. The Supreme Court ruled in his favor.
Age Discrimination Act of 1975	Employers who receive federal financial assistance cannot discriminate based on age.

(continued)

◆ **TABLE 4.3** ***(continued)***

Legislation or Court Ruling	*Summary*
Regents of the University of California v. Bakke (1978)	The Supreme Court ruled that Alan Bakke was unfairly denied admission to the University of California-Davis Medical School. Like DeFunis, Bakke argued that his qualifications were stronger than those of many of the minority candidates who were admitted.
United Steelworkers v. Weber (1979)	The Supreme Court upheld an affirmative action plan to erase entrenched racial biases in employment.
Fullilove v. Klutznick (1980)	Federal public works contracts may require 10% of the work to go to minority firms.
Firefighters Local Union No. 1784 v. Stotts (1984)	The Court ruled that an employer may use seniority rules in laying off employees, even when those rules adversely affect minority employees. This ruling was a blow to affirmative action because it perpetuated the dilemma that minorities are the last to be hired and the first to be fired. The Department of Justice used this decision to force Indianapolis and 49 other jurisdictions to abandon their use of quotas.
Wyatt v. Jackson Board of Education (1986)	An affirmative action plan must have a strong basis in evidence for remedial action.
United States v. Paradise (1987)	A judge may order racial quotas in promoting and hiring to address "egregious" past discrimination.
Johnson v. Transportation Agency (1987)	The Supreme Court permitted the use of gender as a factor in hiring and promotion.
City of Richmond v. J.A. Croson (1989)	Imposed standards of "strict scrutiny." Racial or ethnic classifications must serve a compelling interest and be narrowly tailored.
Martin v. Wilks (1989)	Imposed tougher standards for Asian Americans to be included in affirmative action plans and made it easier to challenge settlements of those plans.
Metro Broadcasting Inc., v. FCC (1990)	Allowed minority preferences to promote diverse viewpoints across the airwaves.
Adarand Constructors, Inc. v. Pena (1995)	The Supreme Court ruled that federal affirmative measures using racial and ethnic criteria in decisionmaking must meet the same standards of strict scrutiny imposed in Croson.
Hopwood v. State of Texas (1996 5th Cir.)	The appeals court ruled that achieving a diverse student body at the University of Texas did not justify its affirmative action program, suggesting that achieving diversity does not represent a compelling state interest.

Sources: Adopted from ACLU, "Affirmative Action," ACLU Briefing Paper No. 17 (New York: ACLU, n.d.); American Council on Education, "Major Civil Rights and Equal Opportunity Legislation Since 1963" (On-line: http://www.berkshire-aap.com/ace) n.d.,; American Council on Education, "The Major Affirmative Action Cases: A Digest of the Record," (On-line: http://www.berkshire-aap.com/ace), n.d.; and Winnie Chen, Vilma Hernandez, Erin Townsend, and Carol Wyatt, "Affirmative Action," unpublished class paper, Graduate School of Social Work, University of Houston, Houston, TX, 1996.

Conservative opponents of affirmative action argue that it leads to racial quota systems (employers can use quotas to avoid lawsuits), preferential treatment, and reverse discrimination. They argue that it violates equal protection under the laws guaranteed in the Fourteenth Amendment. Still others argue that affirmative action policies benefit minorities who were not victims of discrimination and that they place whites who are innocent of any wrongdoing at a disadvantage. These critics maintain that rights inhere in individuals, not in groups. Other conservatives, such as Supreme Court Justice Antony Scalia, argue that there was never a justification for affirmative action because the Constitution is "colorblind."[115] Moderates such as President Bill Clinton note that: "Affirmative action has been good for America. Affirmative action has not always been perfect, and affirmative action should not go on forever. . . . We should reaffirm the principle of affirmative action and fix the practices. We should have a simple slogan: Mend it, but don't end it."[116]

Attacks on affirmative action have also come from liberal quarters. Columnist Roger Hernández argues that:

> Admittedly, affirmative action offers protection from discrimination. But the price it exacts is too high. Affirmative action reinforces the degrading notion that certain cultures are so inferior they render all individuals brought up in it—regardless of their socioeconomic status—into incompetent fools who cannot get along without special attention.
>
> . . . The sense of ethnic inferiority such a philosophy encourages does more harm than the outright discrimination affirmative action is supposed to prevent.
>
> . . . Ending affirmative attacks the idea that every member of certain ethnic groups is a muddle of social pathologies.[117]

William Julius Wilson, a progressive African American sociologist, criticizes the ability of affirmative action strategies to help the most disadvantaged members of society:

> Programs based solely on . . . [race-specific solutions] . . . are inadequate . . . to deal with the complex problems of race in America. . . . This is because the most disadvantaged members of racial minority groups, who suffer the cumulative effects of both race and class subjugation . . . are disproportionately represented amongst the segment of the general population that has been denied the resources to compete effectively in a free and open market. . . .
>
> On the other hand, the competitive resources developed by the *advantaged minority* [original emphasis] *members* [original emphasis] . . . result in their benefitting disproportionately from policies that promote the rights of minority individuals by removing artificial barriers to valued positions. . . . [If] policies of preferential treatment . . . are developed in terms of racial group membership rather than real disadvantages suffered by individuals, then these policies will further improve the opportunities of the advantaged without necessarily addressing the problems of the truly disadvantaged such as the ghetto underclass.[118]

Affirmative action is one of the most controversial issues in American social policy. Apart from the above critique, affirmative action is open to other problems. For example, how much discrimination does a group have to encounter in order to justify preferential treatment? While Asian Americans as a group have certainly encountered (and are continuing to encounter) significant discrimination, their income levels and educational attainment may mitigate against the need for preferential treatment. Moreover, if social discrimination were a basis for affirmative action, then Jews, Catholics, Irish, Eastern Europeans, and other groups who have been historically squeezed out of the American social mainstream should also be eligible. For example, it is unlikely that an American Jew will be elected president in the next decade. The conventional wisdom is that the country is not yet ready for a Jewish president. Given this, should Jews claim affirmative action status? Moreover, poor whites are discriminated against in U.S. society because of their class background. Should they, too, be covered under affirmative action? Women who grow up in upper-class backgrounds and are educated at top-rated universities are covered under affirmative action by virtue of their gender. Do they experience more discrimination than a poor white male who is marked by language, culture, and class background? These are some issues that plague the enforcement of clear and fair affirmative action guidelines. While racial prejudice is one form of discrimination found in America, gender discrimination also represents a major obstacle to the social, political, and economic well-being of at least half of society.

SEXISM: HOW DO WE KNOW THAT IT EXISTS?

Sexism is a term that denotes the discriminatory and prejudicial treatment of women based solely on their gender. It is a problem that American society has wrestled with since the beginning of the republic. Moreover, sexism is widespread and permeates every aspect of social and political life in America.

Sexism can manifest itself in a variety of ways. For one, it can be social, such as keeping women out of military academies, private clubs, and certain sports. It can take the form of erecting occupational boundaries that keep women from operating heavy construction machinery, being involved in such skilled trades as bricklaying, or flying commercial and military jets. Sexism can take political forms, for example, appointing or electing token women to key offices or cabinet positions or creating offices or cabinet positions solely to placate feminist groups. In addition, sexism can also manifest itself in crime and family life.

According to the Department of Justice, almost 5 million American women ages 12 years and older were raped, robbed, assaulted, or were the victim of a threatened or attempted violent crime in 1992 and 1993. Almost three-quarters of these attacks were committed by someone the victim knew.[119] In response to this violence, Congress passed the Violence Against Women Act (VAWA), which was signed into law by President Bill Clinton in 1994. VAWA attempts a comprehensive approach to domestic violence and sexual assault, combining a broad array of legal and other reforms. Specifically, it was designed to improve the response of police, prosecutors and judges to these crimes, force sex offenders to pay restitution to their victims, and increase funding for battered women's shelters. As such, VAWA establishes the nationwide enforcement of protection of abuse orders entered in any court and provides penalties for crossing state lines to abuse a spouse or violate a protection order. VAWA also prohibits anyone facing a restraining order for domestic abuse from possessing a firearm.[120] The act provides grants for training police, prosecutors and judges in domestic abuse; provides grants for battered women's shelters; assists victims of sexual assault, including providing educational seminars, hotlines, and more programs to increase awareness (as well as targeted efforts to underserved racial and ethnic minority communities); provides grants for safety-related improvements to public transportation, national park systems and public parks; funds efforts to prevent youth violence; assists funding for rape crisis centers; and allocates funds for the treatment and counseling of youth subjected to or at risk of sexual abuse (e.g., runaways, homeless, street people).[121]

Sexism also has a distinct economic face. The fact that women's wages are lower than those of men and that they more often have to resort to public welfare programs has led some scholars to coin the term the "feminization of poverty." Advocates of this idea maintain that the feminization of poverty is illustrated by the demographics of poverty. For example, there were 12 million families maintained by women in the United States in 1992—a figure that has more than doubled since 1970 when there were only 5.6 million such families.[122] Not coincidentally, the poverty rate for female-headed households was 32 percent in 1995.[123] Moreover, the number of poor families headed by women increased 54 percent by 1981, while at the same time the number of poor families headed by men dropped nearly 50 percent. Two out of three poor adults are women.[124] Not surprisingly, this has led to a high dependence of women on the welfare system. This pattern of dependency is illustrated by the huge increase in the welfare rolls from 1960 (3 million) to 1992 (13.5 million).[125]

The causes of this feminization of poverty are complex. When women are deserted or divorced, many have to find jobs immediately or go on welfare. Those who choose welfare are held in poverty by the low benefits; those who opt to work are kept in poverty by the low wages that characterize service jobs, the most rapidly expanding sector in the American labor market. Low-paying service jobs, such as servers in fast-food restaurants and salesclerks, make welfare benefits seem attractive because at least there are no child-care costs if a mother stays at home.

The entrance of women into the workforce is often through the service and retail trades—for example, clerical work, cleaning, food preparation or service, personal service work, and auxiliary health service work. These occupations are characterized by low pay, a low level of union organization, little status, meager work benefits, and limited prospects for job advancement. Thus, much of the increase of women in the workforce was in the secondary labor market, a marginal area of employment that provides few work benefits and little hope for economic betterment. When economists cite the millions of jobs that were created in the 1980s, much of what they refer to has been in this secondary labor market, the underbelly of the work world. For example, of the 18.8 million jobs created between 1979 and 1989, 14.4 million were in retail trade and services (i.e., business, personal, and health services), the two lowest-paid economic sectors.[126]

The economics of low-wage service work are gloomy. For example, if a single mother[127] with two children chooses to avoid the stigma of welfare and finds work at near the minimum wage, her prospects for economic survival are dismal. The mock budget in Table 4.4 illustrates the dilemma of a single mother who finds full-time employment at $6.00 an hour (95 cents an hour above the minimum wage).

◆ TABLE 4.4
Monthly Budget for a Working Mother with One Child in School and One Infant in Day Care Gross Monthly Income for Full-Time Work
@ $6.00 per hour: $960.00

Expenses	
Day Care for 1 child	$ 250.00[1]
Rent	$ 450.00[2]
Health Care	$ 93.75[3]
Utilities	$ 60.00[3]
Food	$ 235.00[4]
Clothing	$ 62.00[1]
Transportation	$ 200.00[3]
Entertainment	$ 50.00[3]
Sundry Items (e.g.,soap, cleaners, repairs, sheets, blankets, etc.)	$ 100.00[3]
Total Approximate Cost	$1,500.75[3]
Monthly Deficit between Income and Budget	– $ 540.75[3]

1 Child care costs are calculated based on the Urban Institute's 1995 national estimate of $3,000 a year for child care.

2 Rent was calculated on the basis of the average of HUD-determined fair market rents in the lowest-cost metropolitan areas in a state. The average rent of all these states totaled $450.00 for 1989. See U.S. House of Representatives, Committee on Ways and Means, *Overview of Entitlement Programs, 1992 Green Book* (Washington, DC: U.S. Government Printing Office, 1992).

3 This amount was based on figures provided in John E. Schwartz and Thomas J. Volgy, "A Cruel Hoax Upon the Poor," *The San Diego Union Tribune*, November 9, 1992, p. 5.

4 The amount for food is based on the maximum Food Stamp allocation that this mother would receive in 1991 if she had no countable income.

Work at close to the minimum wage is impractical, limiting the economic choices for the unskilled female head of a household. Moreover, the National Commission on Children estimates that the typical family spends about $6,000 annually on expenses associated with raising a child.[128] This would mean that, excluding a mother's personal expenses, having two children requires a minimum income of $12,000 per year. According to the National Commission on Children, "If a single mother with two children moved from welfare to a full-time, minimum wage job in 1991, her net income would have increased by only about $50 per week."[129] Neither welfare nor low-income work provides single female-headed households with viable economic choices.

Single-mother families in the United States fare worse than their counterparts in many European industrial nations. In a study of the relative economic well-being of single-mother families in eight nations, Yin-Ling Wong, Irwin Garfinkel, and Sara McLanahan found that compared with two-parent families, single mothers in the United States are in considerably worse financial shape. Of the eight countries surveyed, the United States ranked last on the list, surpassed by Canada, Australia, France, Germany, Norway, Sweden, and the United Kingdom.[130]

Inequities in public transfer programs also exacerbate the economic problems of low-income women. For example, Social Security and public assistance are often the only viable options for women, and about eight out of ten poor female-headed families rely on public cash transfers through public welfare programs.[131] Although median transfers to women are lower, they constitute a higher share of their total income, about one-third for female-headed households as compared with one-tenth for male-headed households. Moreover, Social Security is the only source of income for 60 percent of elderly women, and, in 1990, some 15 percent of these women were in poverty compared with 8 percent of elderly men. Like other public transfer programs, Social Security is riddled with pitfalls. In large part, many problems with Social Security are based on the assumptions that all families are nuclear and that families with young children need more per capita income than aged couples or single individuals.

Some women have cited the mistreatment by Social Security:

1. Because women's wages are lower than men's, their retirement benefits are also lower.
2. Married female workers fare better on Social Security than those who are single.
   Individuals who never worked can benefit from Social Security payments made by a spouse.
3. Couples in which one worker earned most of the wages may fare better than couples in which the husband and wife earned equal wages.
4. Homemakers are not covered on their own unless they held a job in the past. Widows do not qualify for benefits unless they are 60 years old or have a minor in the house.
5. Regardless of how long they were married, divorced women are entitled to only one-half of their ex-husband's benefits. If this partial payment is the only income of a divorced woman, it is usually inadequate. Furthermore, divorced women must have been married to the beneficiary of Social Security for at least 10 years to qualify for his benefits.
6. Because women are less likely to spend as much time in the workforce as men—owing to child care responsibilities—their benefits are usually lower.[132]

As result of the Social Security Amendments of 1983, several sex-based qualifications were eliminated: Divorced persons were able to qualify for benefits at age 62 (even if the ex-spouse has not yet claimed benefits), and divorced husbands could claim benefits based on the earnings records of their ex-wives.[133] While these changes are important, they have led to only minor improvements in the system. Other reforms under discussion include an earnings-sharing option that would equally divide a couple's income between husband and wife (thereby eliminating the category of a primary wage earner and a dependent spouse) and a double-decker option in which everyone would be eligible for basic benefits regardless of whether they contributed to the system (individuals who contributed to the paid labor force would receive a higher benefit). These options are in the discussion phase, but with a $5 trillion plus federal debt in 1996, their adoption seems unlikely in the near future.

Women and Work

Myths abound in attempts to explain why women consistently earn less than men. These myths include:[134]

Myth 1. A working mother's wages are not necessary to her family's survival, and her job is a secondary activity that usually ceases with marriage or childbirth.

Fact. Most families require two paychecks to maintain the same standard of living as their parents. Twenty percent of working mothers are heads of households; two out of three working mothers report that they cannot decrease their working hours because of economic need. In 1984, one-third of women who worked had a spouse who earned less than $15,000 per year.[135] Moreover, 18 percent of all working women bring home larger paychecks than their husbands. Sixty-six percent of working African American women provide more than half of the median family income.

Myth 2. A working mother is unreliable because her family is her basic concern.

Fact. Although some working mothers choose the "mommy track," others are forced into it by a lack of quality and affordable day care. (Parenthetically, many men would choose the family as their first priority if they were forced to make the decision. However, they are usually not asked to make this choice.) Seventy-five percent of mothers return to work within a year after childbirth. Even without family assistance programs, most working mothers continue to maintain employment.

Myth 3. Large numbers of working women leave the workforce to return home to raise their children.

Fact. Statistics show that an opposite trend is occurring. In 1978, mothers of infants had a labor force participation rate of 35.7 percent; by 1988 it had risen to 50.8 percent. The choice of mothers to become full-time homemakers is the exception, not the rule.

Myth 4. The cost of providing benefits to assist working mothers with families is prohibitive. Small businesses cannot afford to provide benefits and services such as child care, maternity leave, and flextime. Even large businesses complain that such costs decrease their international competitiveness.

Fact. Family assistance programs raise productivity, increase worker loyalty, lower turnover, and curb absenteeism costs. The majority of employers report no change in costs owing to family leave legislation.[136]

Myth 5. Women are doing better economically. In fact, they are rapidly closing the wage gap and are shooting ahead of men.

Fact. The wage gap between men and women is shrinking, although very slowly. In 1979, women made 64 percent of a male wage; by 1993 the gap was reduced to 71 percent. A study by the Economic Policy Institute covering the years from 1973 to 1993, showed that the typical worker's wages fell 7.5 percent, after adjusting for inflation. Wages for males dropped by 12 percent, while female worker's pay rose by 6 percent in general, and by 16 percent for women in upper-level jobs.[137] While this may seem like a step forward for women, the increase in female wages may be more a result of declining male wages than of increasing female wages. Although household wages rose 2.7 percent from 1994 to 1995, womens' wages fell by $255.[138]

To further dispel myths about working women, it is important to examine the characteristics of the female labor force. In 1995, there were 103 million women age 16 and over in the United States. Of that total, a record 61 million were in the civilian labor force (persons working or looking for work). Nearly six out of every ten women—58.9 percent—age 16 and over were labor force participants. Women between the ages of 20 and 54 had labor force participation rates of at least 70 percent. Even half of U.S. teenage women ages 16–19 were labor force participants—52 percent. In 1990, nearly 40 percent of the 56.6 million workers in the United States were mothers, an increase of 4.4 million since 1980.[139] Women's labor force participation grew from 37.7 percent in 1960 to 48 percent in 1995, a rise that accounted for 60 percent of the total growth in the workforce.[140] Almost 67 percent of mothers with children under 18 worked for pay in 1990, compared with 56.6 percent in 1980. When the figures are broken down, almost 50 percent of women with children under age one were in the labor force in 1990 (about 9.4 million working mothers of preschool children). Of the total female labor force, nearly 75 percent are married, and 81 percent of divorced women with children (2.6 million) under age 18 currently work.[141] The high labor force participation rates of women also extend to African Americans. Although African American women are more than three times as likely to be single heads of families than white women, those with children under 18 have the same labor force participation as their white counterparts.[142]

There is a strong relationship between poverty and working mothers, especially single working mothers. For example, 44 percent of mothers living in poverty are in the workforce. In 1995, the median income of a married couple with children ($50,052) was roughly triple that of a single female-headed household with children ($17,936).[143] Working women are almost twice as likely to earn the minimum wage than men. Sixty-three percent of all workers earning the minimum wage or less are women.[144]

Income Disparities Between Men and Women

Some of the income disparity between men and women can be traced to female occupational clusterings. Roughly half of all working women are employed in occupations where 80 percent of the other workers are women.[145] In fact, 97 percent of secretaries are women, as are 93 percent of bookkeepers, 93 percent of nurses, and 82 percent of administrative/clerical staff. In 1988 only 9 percent of women worked in occupations classified as nontraditional (i.e., where 75 percent of the employees are men). Women still comprise only 3 percent of firefighters; 8 percent of state and local police officers; 1.9 percent of construction workers; 11.8 percent of college presidents; and 3–5 percent of senior level management positions in corporations.[146] (See Table 4.5.) From 1983 to 1988 the greatest increase in women entering nontraditional jobs took place in the professional sphere. From 1983 to 1995, the number of female attorneys increased from 15 to 20 percent; female physicians rose from 16 to 20 percent; and marketing and advertising managers from 22 to 32 percent.[147]

Women consistently earn less than men, both within and outside these clusterings (See Table 4.6.) As Table 4.7 illustrates, women earn less than men even in traditionally female occupational clusterings. For example, female attorneys earn only 63 percent of their male counterparts; female sales representatives earn between 62 and 72 cents of every dollar earned by a male in the same position; and female social workers earn only 73 cents for each dollar earned by a male social worker.[148] When women work in the same occupations as men, they usually earn less pay.

Upward mobility is a key factor in male/female wage discrepancies. Surveys of the top Fortune 1,000 industrial and 500 service companies show that 95 percent of the senior level managers are men, and of that 95 percent, 97 percent are white. That translates into slightly more than 2,100 senior women executives (out of a workforce of 58.4 million women) in these companies. Only 5 percent of senior women executives are minorities.[149] Parenthetically, a survey of male CEOs and female vice presidents on the existence of a glass ceiling revealed that 73 percent of male CEOs didn't think there was a ceiling; 71 percent of the women did.[150]

Despite these numbers, women are slowly moving up the corporate ladder. Surveys show that between 1982 and 1992, the proportion of women holding the title of executive vice president rose from 4 to 9 percent. Those at the senior vice president level rose from 13 to 23 percent, and a recent study shows a growth in the number of women on the boards of directors of the Fortune 500. Eighty-one percent (404 companies) now have one or more female directors, up from 376 companies in 1995. Yet despite the steady increases, women still hold only 1 in 10 board seats.[151] At the current level of advancement, it will take women 475 years to reach equality with men in upper management positions.[152]

Employment and earnings rates rise with educational attainment for both females and males. Of all labor force participants age 25 years and over in 1995, women were more likely than men to have completed high school. Ninety-one percent of female labor force participants held the minimum of a high school diploma, compared with 88 percent for men. A slightly lower percentage of female labor force participants than men were college graduates—27 percent compared with 29 percent. Despite this, as Table 4.6 illustrates, earnings are considerably less for females with the same education as males.[153]

Many women face extraordinary challenges in finding and securing adequate employment for fair wages. Some of the obstacles faced by working women include the difficulty of finding good and affordable day care, the existence of limited family leave policies, inflexible working conditions, inadequate health insurance coverage, and problems of sexual harassment.

◆ TABLE 4.5
Employed Women by Occupational Group *(in millions)*

Occupation	*No. Employed*
Total	57.5
Management and profession specialty	16.9
Technical, sales and administrative support	24.1
Service occupations	10.2
Precision production, craft, and repair	1.2
Operators, fabricators, and laborers	4.4
Farming, forestry, and fishing	0.7

Source: U.S. Department of Labor, Bureau of Labor Statistics, *Employment and Earnings* (Washington, DC: U.S. DOL, January 1996).

◆ **TABLE 4.6**
1996 Salary Survey

	Women	*Men*	*Average*
Accounting Auditor	$ 28,340	$ 37,648	$ 32,032
Advertising CEO	100,800	126,800	123,160
Art Director	45,600	50,700	48,609
Computer Systems Analyst	39,572	45,760	43,992
Computer Operator	19,084	26,000	21,268
College Dean of Arts & Sci.	106,428	104,030	106,088
College Prof., Pub. Inst.	56,050	63,000	62,000
Teacher, Secondary School	34,528	37,856	35,880
Engineering, 10–14 yrs exp.	64,108	63,520	64,000
Engineering, 3–4 yrs exp	44,000	45,577	45,000
Financial Serv. Salesperson	26,936	48,932	37,366
Food Serv. Supervisor	15,288	19,344	16,848
Medicine Health Manager	30,212	44,200	32,396
Insurance Sales Person	30,160	36,660	31,772
General Counsel	291,096	304,658	297,877
Attorney	84,200	89,500	88,862
Lawyer (overall)	47,684	64,324	58,032
Orthopedic Surgeon	222,478	298,444	292,000
Internist	119,258	138,240	133,581
Psychiatrist	115,297	143,739	132,929
Family Practitioner	109,000	125,333	122,000
Registered Nurse	35,360	36,868	35,464
Pharmacist, Chain	56,577	56,844	59,176
Real Estate Salesperson	24,908	37,960	30,836
Retail/Personal Sales	12,584	19,032	14,712
Executive Travel Services	30,800	38,600	32,500
Front-line Travel Agent	22,000	27,200	22,700
Mixed Animal Vet	35,500	40,900	39,700

Source: *Working Woman*, "Working Woman's 1996 Salary Survey." Cited in DeWayne Peebles, Susan Robinson, Dorothy Rogers, and Fiona Stephenson, "Scorecard of Women's Issues in 1996." Unpublished paper, Graduate School of Social Work, University of Houston, Houston, TX.

Day Care: A Barrier to Female Employment

A major barrier to female employment involves the problem of day care and of subsidized child-care leaves. For many working families child care has become a necessity. A 1982 Census Bureau survey found that 45 percent of single mothers would seek employment if affordable, quality child care were available. But infant and toddler care costs more than care for preschoolers, and care provided in a center is more expensive than family day care. There are serious shortages of quality child care, and rates vary widely around the country. According to the Urban Institute, the average yearly cost of child care is $3,000.[154] However,

◆ **TABLE 4.7**
Median Weekly Earnings, Selected Traditionally Female Occupations, 1995

	Earnings	
Occupation	*Women*	*Men*
Registered nurses	$693	$715
Elementary school teachers	627	713
Cashiers	233	256
General office clerks	360	389
Health aides, except nursing	285	345

Source: U.S. Department of Labor, Bureau of Labor Statistics, *Employment and Earnings* (Washington, DC US DOL, January 1996).

◆ **TABLE 4.8**
Median Income of Persons, by Educational Attainment and Sex, Year-Round, Full-Time Workers, 1994

Level of Education	*Women*	*Men*
9th to 12th grade (no diploma)	$15,133	$22,048
High school graduate	20,373	28,037
Some college, no degree	23,514	32,279
Associate degree	25,940	35,794
Bachelor's degree or more	35,378	49,228

Source: U.S. Department of Commerce, Bureau of the Census, *Income, Poverty, and Valuation of Noncash Benefits: 1994* (Washington, DC, U.S. Department of Commerce, 1995).

costs can vary widely. For example, the annual costs of an infant in day care can range from around $4,000 a year in Dallas, Texas, to $11,000 a year in Boston, Massachusetts.[155] A single mother in Boston earning a minimum wage would have to spend almost 150 percent of her salary just to afford day care for one child! Low-income mothers seeking publicly funded day care may have to experience long waits. For example, Texas has a waiting list of 40,000 children needing day care; California's list is 225,000. Mothers in these states have expected waits of two years for children aged 2 to 5 and one year for infants.[156]

Title XX is the largest federal program for child-care services. In 1990 the U.S. Congress passed legislation that was an important step in increasing the supply of child care and in expanding early childhood education. Through the Child Care and Development Block Grant and amendments to Title IV-A of the Social Security Act, Congress provided new funds to help families with child-care costs and to help states improve the quality and supply of child-care services.[157]

The lack of subsidized child-care leaves poses a major problem for American working women. Sheila Kammerman reported on a study of working mothers in five industrialized countries—Sweden, East and West Germany, Hungary, and France.[158] In all these countries, except for West Germany, a higher proportion of women were employed than in the United States. All nations, except the United States, provided a tax-free family allowance that ranged from $300 to $600 yearly. Guaranteed maternity leave (in Sweden the leave also pertained to fathers) ranged from 14 weeks in West Germany to 8 months in Sweden. Guaranteed maternity leave also included full pay in most places. No national guaranteed maternity leave exists at present in the United States.

The child-care system in the United States is two-tiered: Those with adequate incomes can afford to purchase first-rate child care or, if they desire, they can stay at home; those with low wages are at the mercy of the ebb and flow of political support for publicly supported day care.[159]

Other Obstacles to Women and Work

Apart from problems involving low wages and difficulties in securing child care, many working mothers also require a flexible family leave program. Although 30 states had some form of parental or medical leave law in the past, no such national statute existed until 1993. In 1992, President George Bush vetoed the Family and Medical Leave Act (FMLA) after it had passed the House and Senate for a second time. With the election of President Bill Clinton, the FMLA was rushed through Congress and was signed into law on February 5, 1993. The FMLA is designed to allow workers to receive unpaid leave for up to 12 weeks in the event of childbirth, adoption, or the serious illness of an immediate family member. Should a worker use the leave, he or she is guaranteed the same or a comparable job upon returning to work and continued health benefits. The FMLA applies to all firms with 50 or more employees. However, those who work in firms with less than 50 employees are not protected by federal family leave legislation.

Another issue affecting working women is that of health insurance. Women working in traditionally female occupations (the largest share of working women) have the highest uninsured rate. More than 15 million women of childbearing age in the United States have no public or private medical coverage for maternity care, even though the average cost of having a baby is over $4,300. Half of all women earning $5.00 per hour or less are without health care, and divorced and separated women are twice as likely to be uninsured as married women. Of the 4 million births each year in the United States, 500,000 are not covered by any health care plan.

About 5 million American women of reproductive age have private insurance policies that don't cover maternity care. Moreover, health insurance often does not cover important services for women's health, including family planning services, long-term care, reproductive care and elective abortions, and maternity care and childbirth.[160] If women are to participate more fully in the labor force, health care insurance obstacles must be overcome.

Another issue affecting women in the workplace is sexual harassment, an issue brought to the fore by Anita Hill in the 1990 Senate confirmation hearings of Supreme Court Justice Clarence Thomas. Sexual harassment is defined as unwelcome behaviors including jokes, teasing, remarks, questions, and deliberate touching; letters, telephone calls, or materials of a sexual nature; pressure for sexual favors; and sexual assault. Although sexual harassment is against the law (Title VII of the 1964 Civil Rights Act has been interpreted as prohibiting sexual harassment), it remains all too common in the workplace. Moreover, women in nontraditional jobs are at greater risk of sexual harassment.[161]

Finally, a major obstacle for many working women is the inflexibility of work. Because women often take on the major responsibility for child care, elder care, and home management, they often forgo educational or training opportunities. In order for women workers to better balance family and work responsibilities, options such as flexible hours, job sharing, and part-time work with benefits need to be expanded.

Fighting Back: The Equal Rights Amendment and Comparable Worth

In 1920 the Nineteenth Amendment to the Constitution gave women the right to vote. That, however, did not seem to lessen their economic and social plight, and shortly after winning the vote the Women's Party proposed the first Equal Rights Amendment (ERA). Although at first glance it seemed a good idea, progressive social workers such as Jane Addams, Florence Kelley, and Julia Lathrop, among others, saw the ERA as endangering the hard-fought protection won for women workers. For example, reformers had successfully fought for a maximum weight limit on lifting for women workers, the establishment of maximum workday laws in many states, and mandatory work breaks. These social workers saw the ERA as having the potential to eradicate protective legislation for women workers. Moreover, these reformers saw the ERA as mainly benefiting middle-class professional women at the expense of poor, working-class women. Many female trade unionists continued to oppose the ERA well into the 1970s.

In 1972, Congress passed the ERA and set a 1979 date for state ratification. When the ERA had not been ratified by 1978, Congress extended the deadline to June 30, 1982. Despite the endorsement of 450 organizations representing 50 million members, opponents of the ERA were able to defeat the amendment in 1982, just 3 states short of the 38 required for ratification.

Cutting through the controversy surrounding the ERA, the act reads as follows: "Equality of rights under the law shall not be denied or abridged by the United States or any other State on account of sex. . . . The Congress shall have the power to enforce, by appropriate legislation, the provisions of this article. . . . This amendment shall take effect two years after the date of ratification."[162]

Contrary to the myths surrounding it, the ERA would not have nullified all laws on the basis of sex; instead, it would have required that men and women be treated equally. Most alimony, child support, and custody laws would not have been invalidated, although laws giving preference to one sex would have been struck down. On the other hand, special restrictions on the property rights of married women would have been invalidated; married women would have been free to manage their own separate finances and property. Again, contrary to popular myth, the ERA would have affected only public employment; private employment practices would not have been changed. In the areas of military service and jury duty, women would have been subject to participation under the same conditions as men. Like men, women would have been eligible for the draft.[163]

Surrounded by fear and misinformation—much of it purposeful—the ERA became a symbolic struggle. Opponents feared what *might* happen if the ERA were passed. Often couched in hyperbolic language, these fears suggested that the passage of the ERA would result in men and women being forced to share the same bathrooms, in the drafting of women to serve on the front line, and in granting women the legal right to refuse to cook for their husbands. In essence, the struggle around the ERA was a conflict about the future of gender relations in America.

Another front on which sexism has been fought is the issue of comparable worth—the idea that workers should be paid equally when they do *different* types of work requiring the same level of skill, education, knowledge, training, responsibility, and effort. The desire to rectify incomes through comparable worth is based on the belief that the dual labor market has created a situation in which "women's work" (i.e, secretarial, teaching, social work, nursing, child care) is automatically less highly valued than traditionally male occupations.

An illustration of the debate around comparable worth is provided in Table 4.9, which compares the pay for jobs typically occupied by women with the pay for those usually held by men. Although a controversial notion, 20 states passed laws making comparable worth a requirement or goal of state employment. While a good idea in theory, comparable worth brings up a difficult question: What criteria should be used to determine that different jobs are comparable? Moreover, comparable worth has been rejected by some people on the grounds that the inherent economic cost is infeasible.

Legal protection for women workers is not a recent phenomenon. As early as the turn of the century, protective legislation restricted the amount of weight a woman was required to lift, mandated rest and lunch periods, prohibited hours of work beyond a specified number, regulated night work, and prohibited employment in particular occupations. In 1963, Congress passed the Equal Pay Act, which required employers to compensate male and female workers equally for performing the same job under the same conditions (not all jobs were covered by the bill). Another protective measure was Title VII of the Civil Rights Act of 1964, which prohibited sex discrimination in employment practices and provided the right of redress in the courts. In 1972, Presidential Executive Order 11375 mandated that employers practicing sexual discrimination be prohibited from receiving federal contracts. Title IX of the Educational Amendments of 1972 prohibited discrimination in educational institutions receiving federal funds. Finally, the Equal Credit Act of 1975 prohibited discrimination by lending institutions on the basis of sex or marital status.

◆ TABLE 4.9
Comparable Worth and Average Annual Income, 1988

1988 Average Annual Income	
Secretary	$14,976
Mechanic/Repairer	$18,816
Child Care Worker	$ 8,592
Motor Vehicle Operator	$13,488
Textile Sewing Machine Operator	$ 9,168
Mail Carrier	$21,120
Data Entry Keyer	$14,304
Construction Worker	$16,080

Source: This data is drawn from the National Commission on Working Women of Wider Opportunities for Women, "Women and Nontraditional Work," Washington, DC: Wider Opportunities for Women, n.d., n.p.

Abortion and Women's Rights

Feminists often point to the abortion debate as another arena in which women's rights are threatened. Specifically, pro-choice advocates argue that where abortion is concerned, some male legislators and judges (with the exception of the nine male judges who decided on *Roe v. Wade*) have promulgated laws and regulations to control the behavior of women, in this case by denying them their reproductive freedom. They argue that the choice of an abortion is a personal matter involving only a woman and her conscience. Antiabortion forces claim that life begins at conception and therefore abortion is murder. Moreover, they point to the 28 million legal abortions performed in the United States from 1973 to 1992 (there are 1.5 million abortions performed each year, half of which are done on women age 15 to 19),[164] while at the same time the search for adoptable infants has become an almost insurmountable task. This argument becomes even more focused when abortion statistics are examined: in 1987, 59 percent of those having abortions were younger than 25; 65 percent of them were white; 58 percent had experienced no previous abortion; and 82 percent were unmarried.[165]

In 1973, Sarah Weddington, a young attorney from Austin, Texas, argued *Roe v. Wade* before the Supreme Court. Though her client had long since relinquished her child for adoption, Weddington argued that a state could not unduly burden a woman's right to choose an abortion by making regulations that prohibited her from carrying out that decision. The Court ruled in favor of Weddington, and abortion was legalized in the United States, thereby nullifying all state laws that made abortion illegal during the first trimester of pregnancy. (Before 1970, four states—New York, Alaska, Hawaii, and Washington—had already made abortion legal contingent upon the agreement of a physician.) Within a decade after *Roe v. Wade* was successfully argued, almost 500 bills were introduced in Congress, most of which sought to restrict abortions by promoting a constitutional amendment outlawing abortion, by transferring the power to regulate abortion decisions to the states, or by limiting federal funding of abortions.[166]

The abortion issue has been marked by Byzantine maneuvers and complex twists and turns. In 1977 the Hyde Amendment prohibited the federal government from paying for abortions except to preserve the mother's life. The 1980 Supreme Court decision in *Harris v. McRae* upheld the constitutionality of the Hyde Amendment. In 1977, the federal government lifted its ban on providing abortions for promptly reported cases of rape and incest and in cases where severe and long-lasting harm would be caused to a woman by childbirth. In 1981, the government again reversed its position, this time curbing federal funding of abortions except to save the life of the mother.[167] By 1990, federal funds paid for only 165 abortions, a dramatic drop from the almost 300,000 federally funded abortions in 1977.[168]

The major strategy of the antiabortion movement has been to whittle away at *Roe v. Wade* by attempting to restrict abortions on the state level. For example, in Akron, Ohio, rules were promulgated that required a minor to receive parental consent for an abortion and that imposed a one-day moratorium on the time between a woman's signing the consent form and the actual performance of the abortion. In 1986, the Supreme Court struck down a Pennsylvania law designed to discourage women from obtaining abortions. Yet in a 1989 landmark decision, the Supreme Court upheld a Missouri law that prohibited public hospitals and public employees from performing an abortion (except to save the life of the mother), required physicians to determine whether a woman who is at least 20 weeks pregnant is carrying a fetus able to survive outside the womb, and declared that life starts at conception.[169] During the 1990–1991 term, the Court in *Rust v. Sullivan* ruled that the United States can prohibit federally financed family planning programs from giving out abortion information. On January 22, 1993, President Bill Clinton's second day in office, he signed a bill overturning this "gag rule," and in another blow to antiabortion advocates, on the same day overturned the federal ban on using fetal tissue matter gained from abortions in scientific experiments.

The abortion debate again picked up steam in 1994–1995. During those years the number of antichoice legislation increased by 260 percent and the number of states enacting these laws rose by 225 percent.[170] In 1996, the Congress passed a law that would have outlawed late-term abortions and the D&C Procedure. Abortion advocates feared that this bill would have applied to all abortions performed in the second or third trimester of pregnancy.[171] In April 1996, Clinton vetoed the bill, claiming that it would not allow an exception to protect the mother's health.[172] In August 1996, the Congressional attempt to overturn the Clinton veto failed by a margin of only nine votes.

Since 1973, the question of abortion has proved to be one of the most divisive issues in public life. Although nearly three out of four voters polled in national surveys believe that abortion should be legal, 56 percent oppose the use of federal money to fund abortions for women who cannot afford them.[173] Nevertheless, this highly charged issue has led to murder, firebombings of abortion clinics, large demonstrations on both sides of the issue, and widespread civil protest.

Sexual discrimination operates in all areas of social, political, and economic life. Like racism and other forms of discrimination, it is usually present, although occasionally hidden from view. Arguably, the intense competition for a dwindling economic pie is bringing these and other forms of discrimination into clearer focus. Another form of discrimination that has occupied the public consciousness for the past two decades revolves around the stigma associated with gays and lesbians.

GAYS AND LESBIANS: TWO POPULATIONS AT RISK

In America's "culture wars," one of today's most intense controversies rages around the issue of whether homosexuality is an acceptable lifestyle, and if so, whether those who are openly gay and lesbian should enjoy protected "minority" status under civil rights laws. Only 40 years ago, few in public or religious sectors even dared to raise the possibility that it might be acceptable to be openly gay in America. For example, in 1960, all 50 states maintained laws criminalizing sodomy by consenting adults. In 1970, 84 percent of respondents to a national Gallup poll agreed that homosexuality was "social corruption that can cause the downfall of a civilization." Two-thirds of those polled thought homosexuals should not be allowed to work as schoolteachers, church pastors, or even government employees. Yet, recent decades have seen slow but dramatic shifts in public attitudes toward homosexuality.

After several years of concerted pressure by gay activists, the American Psychiatric Association decided in 1993 to remove homosexuality from its DSM III list of "objective disorders" and declare it "a normal, if divergent lifestyle." Throughout the 1970s and 1980s, laws forbidding sodomy were repealed in state after state. By 1995, 29 states had rescinded laws criminalizing consensual sodomy, 9 states had statewide gay rights laws in force, and more than 100 local communities had placed gay rights ordinances (recognizing sexual orientation as a protected minority class distinction) on the books. In a landmark vote in 1992, Oregonians rejected Ballot Measure Nine by 55 percent to 45 percent. This referendum would have branded gays and lesbians as "abnormal and perverse" and would have required schools to teach that homosexuality is wrong. The referendum would also have barred antidiscrimination protection for gays and lesbians.[174] Some 75 percent of Americans polled nationwide in the early 1990s felt that homosexuals should not be discriminated against in employment, housing and public accommodations.[175] These policies and polls reflect a significant shift in American public opinion about homosexuality.

Despite these limited successes, many homosexuals continue to be forced to live in the "closet," thereby concealing their sexual orientation in order to survive in a hostile world. Often the objects of ridicule, homosexuals have been denied housing and employment, harassed on the job, and beaten, assaulted, and even killed because of their sexual orientation. In many states homosexuality is still considered a criminal or felony offense, and in some of these the police systematically raid homosexual bars and randomly arrest the patrons. In 24 states, women are at risk of prosecution for being in a lesbian relationship.[176] Twenty-five states have no legislation or ordinances protecting gays and lesbians from discrimination based on sexual orientation.[177]

Represented in all occupations and socioeconomic strata, gays and lesbians make up anywhere between 1 and 10 percent of the general population.[178] (Later research suggests that the 10 percent figure cited in the early Kinsey studies was exaggerated, and that the real percentage of gays and lesbians in the population is between 1 and 2 percent.[179]) Like Asian Americans, discrimination against gays and lesbians is not always reflected in income. For example, male homosexuals have per capita incomes ranging from $37,800 to $42,100 versus about $12,300 for heterosexuals.[180] More than three times as many homosexuals as heterosexuals are college graduates (59.6 percent versus 18 percent). According to one market analyst, "America's gay and lesbian community is emerging as one of the nation's most educated and affluent, and Madison Avenue is beginning to explore the potential for a market that may be worth hundreds of billions of dollars. . . . It's a market that screams opportunity."[181]

Regardless of the their numbers or relative affluence, when gays and lesbians have decided to "come out of the closet" and demand equal rights under the law, the result has been mixed, although generally negative. During the 1970s, Miami gays tried to pass a civil rights amendment that would have prevented discrimination based on sexual orientation. The referendum failed in Miami, and similar ones were defeated in St. Paul and other cities. In 1986, Houston voters defeated two gay rights proposals, one calling for an end to discrimination based on sexual orientation in city employment practices, the other calling for an end to the maintenance of sexual orientation data in city employment records.[182] In 1992, Colorado voters unexpectedly banned laws protecting gays and lesbians from discrimination (later struck down by the U.S. Supreme Court in 1996); in Tampa, Florida, and in Portland, Maine, voters overturned city ordinances protecting gays and lesbians.[183]

For almost 20 years the Supreme Court refused to hear cases concerning gay rights, but in 1985 it heard the case of *Oklahoma City Board of Education v. the National Gay Task Force*. In this case the Supreme Court ruled that public schoolteachers cannot be forbidden to advocate homosexuality (e.g., by way of public demonstrations), but they can be prohibited from engaging in homosexual acts in public. In a major setback for gay rights, the Supreme Court in 1986 refused to strike down laws in Georgia and Texas that forbid homosexuals from engaging in similar types of activity. In 1988 the Supreme Court ruled that the Central Intelligence Agency could not dismiss a homosexual without a reason for justifying the dismissal. On the other hand, the Supreme Court has refused to rule on whether homosexuals have equal protection under the Fourteenth Amendment of the U.S. Constitution, including the right to serve in the military.

The United States armed forces have generally not tolerated homosexuality in their ranks. In 1940, draft board physicians were ordered to screen out homosexuals on the basis of such characteristics as a man's lisp or a woman's deep voice. However, these instructions were often overlooked when World War II created a desperate need for soldiers. After the war, however, gay and lesbian military personnel were discharged, and exclusionary policies were again enforced. A similar situation occurred during the Vietnam War; once the conflict ended, gays and lesbians were again persecuted and their careers terminated.[184] The policy of the U.S. armed forces that excludes gays and lesbians from military service reads as follows: "Homosexuality is incompatible with military service. The presence in the military environment of persons who engage in homosexual conduct or who, by their statements, demonstrate a propensity to engage in homosexual conduct, seriously impairs the accomplishment of the military mission."[185] Individuals who admit to homosexuality at the time of enlistment are rejected; if homosexuality comes to light later on, the individual is separated. Although more liberal policies were put into effect during the 1970s and 1980s, they were directed at the type of separation, not at the morality of the separation itself.[186]

One of the principal justifications for excluding gays and lesbians from military service has been their supposed vulnerability to blackmail by enemy agents threatening to expose their sexuality. The Defense Department has conducted at least three separate studies to justify this belief. None of these studies supported the exclusionary policy.[187] In fact, the Personnel Security Research and Education Center of the Defense Department conducted an examination of the homosexual exclusion policy and found no evidence that gays and lesbians disrupt any branch of the military; instead, it praised their dedication and superior performance.[188] Support for homosexuals in the military came from other sources, including former conservative Senator Barry Goldwater who argued that "you don't need to be straight' to fight and die for your country, you just need to shoot straight."[189]

The policy of excluding homosexuals from the military has far-reaching consequences. First, it adversely affects the career prospects of multitudes of gays and lesbians. Second, people discharged from military service without an honorable discharge may find it difficult to secure employment and may not be eligible to obtain many benefits associated with military service. Even an honorable discharge given on the grounds of homosexual conduct will carry with it grave and important consequences for the future of ex-servicepeople.

One campaign promise of Bill Clinton was to end discrimination against homosexuals in the military. As one of his first official acts, President Clinton signed an order that prohibited military recruiters from inquiring about the sexual orientation of potential recruits. Shortly afterward, Clinton proposed wide-ranging reforms that would ensure equal rights for gays and lesbians serving in the military. Proponents of such plans argued that discrimination against homosexuals in the military was no different than the discrimination practiced against African American soldiers in World Wars I and II. For these activists, discrimination against homosexuals in the military was a civil rights issue. On the other side, critics argued that homosexuality was a lifestyle choice rather than a factor of birth, such as skin color. Facing criticism from the Joint Chiefs of Staff and many influential members of Congress, Clinton retreated from his earlier position and instead supported a "don't ask, don't tell" policy that prohibited the military from asking questions as long as a homosexual behaved discreetly. In 1996, Congress gave the Pentagon the right to discharge all service members who tested HIV positive, even if they were healthy and showed no signs of illness.

A long-standing issue for gays and lesbians has been the recognition of gay unions. Jeffrey Levi, former executive director of the National Gay and Lesbian Task Force, stated that:

> [We] are no longer seeking just a right to privacy and a right to protection from wrong.
>
> We also have a right—as heterosexual Americans have already—to see government and society affirm our lives.
>
> Now that is a statement that may make our liberal friends queasy. But the truth is, until our relationships are recognized in the law—through domestic partnership legislation or the definition of beneficiary, for example—until we are provided with the same financial incentives in tax law and government programs to affirm our family relationships, then we will not have achieved equality in American society.[190]

By 1996, the recognition of gay marriages became more feasible, given the likelihood that Hawaii would recognize such marriages. Other states were quick to react, and by late 1996, one-third of all states had already passed legislation prohibiting the recognition of same-sex marriages from another state. Congress entered the fray by passing the Defense of Marriage Act (DOMA), which effectively established that the only legitimate marriage could be with members of the opposite sex. In the same session, Congress defeated the Employment Non-Discrimination Bill, which, among other things, would guarantee homosexuals protection from job-based discrimination. Ironically, in the same month that Congress passed DOMA, both IBM and the city of Denver, Colorado, extended domestic partnership benefits (e.g., health insurance) to their gay and lesbian employees.

The AIDS crisis gave voice to omnipresent homophobic attitudes. The early days of the epidemic saw suggestions for quarantining AIDS victims, renewed attempts at punishing homosexual behavior, increased job discrimination, and a generally hostile climate for both gays and lesbians. At the federal level, Right-wing Senator Jesse Helms (R–NC) successfully introduced a bill that prevented the Centers for Disease Control from using AIDS education funds in ways that could foster homosexuality. Although AIDS is still predominantly a disease affecting selected population groups—gay and bisexual men (58 percent) and intravenous drug users (25 percent)—the movement of AIDS into the heterosexual community (now about 8 percent of victims) has fueled, among some people, a certain sympathy toward the gay population. But positive change has come only after the documentation of more than 513,000 AIDS cases in the United States, resulting in more than 320,000 deaths through mid–1996.[191] Robert Walker describes the early days of the AIDS epidemic:

> This was the time, the early 1980s, when the AIDS epidemic and its costs might have been contained, but effectively raising the alarm entailed serious political risks in all the affected communities—the political, the religious, and the homosexual. Political leaders took their cue from President Reagan's deafening silence, and most national, state, and local public and private institutions dithered through the critical years.[192]

The AIDS crisis has had a devastating effect on the lives of gay men. There are few gays in larger cities who have not lost either a lover or many close friends to the disease. This suffering, combined with AIDS education, has led to the galvanizing of the gay community. Comprehensive medical and support services have been developed in several of the larger cities, and many members of the gay community are exercising increased caution in the choice of sexual partners and in the sexual act itself. As a result of these measures, there has been a perceptible decrease in the numbers of AIDS cases in some cities. Despite these advances, AIDS remains one of the most significant health problems facing both gay and heterosexual communities.

Homophobia—the irrational fear of homosexuality—is a social phenomenon that has led to attempts to limit the civil rights and legal protections of gays and lesbians. Justifications for this attitude have been found in traditional religious dogma that treats homosexuality as a sin against God, and in psychological explanations that view homosexuality as a disease, as a symptom of an arrested developmental process or a fear of intimacy.

Nevertheless, the self-perception of gays and lesbians has undergone a dramatic change in the past 20 years. Gays and lesbians have begun to identify themselves as members of an oppressed minority, similar in many ways to other oppressed minority groups. As gays and lesbians have become more visible, they have organized support groups, religious groups (Dignity [Roman Catholics], Integrity [Episcopalians], Mishpachat Am [Jews], and Lutherans Concerned [Lutherans]), social service organizations, subchapters of professional associations, and political action groups. The political power of gays and lesbians has grown to the point that in 1984 they succeeded in inserting a gay civil rights plank in the platform of the Democratic Party. These changing attitudes have encouraged some political leaders to court the gay vote openly by supporting gay issues. Moreover, this change is seen most clearly in the Clinton presidency, which was the first administration to endorse gay rights openly (albeit erratically). For example, although Clinton signed the DOMA bill, his administration also backed the Employment Non-Discrimination Act (a gay civil rights bill); appointed more than 100 openly gay and lesbian persons to administrative jobs; nominated the first-ever open lesbian to the United States District Court; helped defeat anti-gay initiatives in Oregon, Maine, and Idaho; mandated that all federal agencies add sexual orientation to their affirmative action policies; outlawed the practice of denying security clearance based on sexual orientation; granted political asylum to people who fear persecution in their home countries based on their sexual orientation; and increased public health spending on AIDS.[193]

Gays and lesbians continue to face discrimination in social and economic areas. This discrimination is often manifested in the absence of gay and lesbian rights in employment and employment benefits, housing, immigration and naturalization, insurance, custody and adoption, and neighborhood covenants that bar home sales to nonrelated couples.[194] Moreover, social service agencies routinely refuse to allow foster care in gay or lesbian homes; insurance companies deny workers the right to cover same-sex spouses or lovers under health insurance; and gays and lesbians are often refused the right to name a lover as next of kin in medical emergencies. Discrimination can also manifest itself in the aged population.

AGEISM

The increase in the number of elderly pose one of the greatest challenges to social policy in the coming decades. During the twentieth century, the number of persons in the United States under age 65 has tripled. At the same time, the number age 65 or over has jumped by a factor of 11. Consequently, the elderly, who comprised only 1 in every 25 Americans (3.1 million) in 1900, made up 1 in 8 (33.2 million) in 1994. According to Census Bureau projections, the elderly population will more than double between 1996 and the year 2050, to 80 million. By 2050, as many as 1 in 5 Americans could be elderly, and there will be more persons who are elderly (65 or over) than young (14 or younger). Most of this growth should occur between 2010 and 2030, when the "baby boom" generation enters elderly years.[195]

The "oldest old"—those age 85 and over—are the most rapidly growing elderly age group. Between

1960 and 1994, their numbers rose 274 percent. The over-85 age group numbered 3 million in 1994, making them 10 percent of the elderly and slightly more than 1 percent of the total population. It is expected the 85+ group will number 19 million in 2050, making them 24 percent of the elderly and 5 percent of all Americans. In addition, elderly women outnumbered elderly men in 1994 by a ratio of 3 to 2 (20 million to 14 million). At ages 65 to 69, it was only 6 to 5; at age 85 and over, it reached 5 to 2.[196]

As more people live long enough to experience multiple chronic illnesses, disability, and dependency, there will be more relatives in their fifties and sixties faced with the responsibility and expense of caring for them. The parent-support ratio equals the number of persons age 85 and over per 100 persons age 50 to 64. Between 1950 and 1993, the ratio tripled from 3 to 10. Over the next six decades, it will triple again, to 29. The elderly are also becoming more ethnically and racially diverse. In 1994, 1 in 10 elderly were other than white. In 2050, this proportion will rise to 2 in 10. Similarly, the proportion of elderly who are Hispanic is expected to climb from 4 percent to 16 percent over the same period.[197]

The implications of these current and future trends for social welfare policy are profound. For one, as the numbers of elderly increase, their demands on society for housing, health, and recreational services also become more pronounced. The stresses put on the health care system by an increasingly aging population are already significant. For example, in 1989 the elderly accounted for 33 percent of all hospital stays and 45 percent of all days of hospital care. The average stay for older people was 8.9 days compared with 5.3 days for persons under 65. The average length of stay for older people has increased 5.3 days since 1968 and 1.8 days since 1980. Moreover, while the elderly account for about 12 percent of the population, they account for 36 percent of personal health care expenditures. These expenditures totaled $162 billion in 1991 and averaged more than $5,300 a year for each older person. Benefits from Medicare ($72 billion) and Medicaid ($20 billion) covered about 63 percent of those costs in 1987, compared with only 26 percent for persons under age 65.[198] As more of the population ages in the coming decades, and as the number in the 85+ group rapidly increase, the burden of paying for health care costs will likely become even more problematic.

How the costs of caring for the elderly will be resolved is an important policy question. For one, elderly women live longer than men. In 1992, the median income for men was $14,548 compared to $8,189 for women. Moreover, income drops and poverty rates increase with old age (partly because the COLA adjustments in Social Security do not keep up with real inflation). Because elderly women live longer than men and yet have only 56 percent of their income, it is expected that more of their health care costs will either have to be picked up by the state or by their families, putting increasing burdens on both. In addition, as people live longer and require more care—especially in-home care—more pressure will be put on family members to provide or pay for that care. Already stressed by increasing workloads, family pressures, and the often large geographic distances between children and parents, the state may ultimately have to provide even more intensive care for greater numbers of elderly.

The perception of the elderly as being poor has changed in recent years to a view that the noninstitutionalized elderly are better off than other Americans. Both views are simplistic because there is great variation among elderly subgroups. On the one hand, the elderly—those over 65—recorded (as they have for a number of years) some of the largest gains in median income in 1995, about 4.3 percent. This compares to the more modest 1.3 percent income gain made by traditional working age households.[199] On the other hand, income stagnated for many of the elderly after 1991 when interest rates paid on certificates of deposit and savings accounts dropped to less than 4 percent per annum. This cut into the investment income that many elderly had relied on in the early and mid–1980s.[200]

In 1992, the poverty rate—15 percent for those under age 65—rose with age among the elderly from 11 percent for 65- to 74-year-olds to 16 percent for those age 75 or older. Elderly women had a higher poverty rate (16 percent) than elderly men (9 percent). The rate was higher for elderly blacks (33 percent) and Hispanics (22 percent) than for whites

(11 percent). Elderly white men, on the other hand, had much higher median incomes than other groups. In 1992, their income was more than double that of elderly black and Hispanic women ($15,276 versus $6,220 and $5,968, respectively). Moreover, 71 percent of elderly African American women who lived alone in 1990 were poor.

Ageism, or discrimination against older persons, is an important problem in a consumer-oriented society that idolizes youth. Like other minority groups, the aged have significant social and economic obstacles to overcome. Workers over 50, for example, often find it difficult to find new or equivalent employment if they lose their jobs. The aged in America are seldom revered or respected for their wisdom and experience, nor do they occupy elevated social positions protected by tradition. Instead, once they have lost their earning potential, the aged are often perceived as a financial albatross around the neck of an economically productive society. This intergenerational animosity is fueled by the looming crisis in the Social Security system. Socially isolated in retirement communities, low-income housing, or other old-age ghettos, the aged often become invisible.

Because the elderly vote in large numbers, their voices have been heard more clearly by politicians than those of African Americans and other minorities. In the 1960s, policymakers responded to the needs of the elderly by passing the Older Americans Act (OAA) of 1965. The objectives of the OAA included: (1) an adequate retirement income that corresponds to the general standard of living; (2) the achievement of good physical and mental health, regardless of economic status; (3) the provision of centrally located, adequate, and affordable housing; (4) the necessity of meaningful employment, with the elimination of age-specific and discriminatory employment practices; (5) the pursuit of meaningful activities in the area of civic, cultural, and recreational opportunities; and (6) adequate community services, including low-cost transportation and supported living arrangements.[201]

Perhaps the clearest expression of ageism is seen in employment policies. The Age Discrimination in Employment Act (ADEA) of 1967 protects most workers from ages 40 to 69 from discrimination in hiring, job retention, and promotion. However, for most workers the protection of the ADEA stops when they reach age 70. Legislation to remove the "70" cap has consistently failed in Congress, as employer lobbies have persuasively argued that they require a free hand in personnel policies.

Despite the attempts made by the American Association of Retired Persons (AARP) and other advocacy groups, such as the Gray Panthers, discrimination still persists. Negative stereotypes of elderly persons continue to be perpetuated by the media and the film industry. These stereotypes also exist in the public consciousness. Moreover, the elderly continue to the victimized by crime, elderly abuse by family members, and job discrimination. For many of the elderly, especially minorities and women, their economic well-being is precarious. Like race, gender, and sexual orientation, age is a liability that makes older populations vulnerable to oppression and injustice.

PEOPLE WITH DISABILITIES

People with disabilities represent yet another group that experiences the effects of discrimination. About 8 to 17 percent of the population between the ages of 20 and 64 have disabilities that limit their ability to work, and about half that number are disabled to the point that either they cannot work or can work only irregularly.[202]

Disability is a difficult concept to define. The medical definition is based on the assumption that it is a chronic disease requiring various forms of treatment. Another definition derived from the medical model—also used as a basis for determining eligibility in the Social Security Disability Insurance program—sees people with disabilities as unable to work (or unable to work as frequently) in the same range of jobs as nondisabled people.[203] People with disabilities are thus viewed as inherently less productive than the able-bodied. A third model defines disability in terms of what people with disabilities cannot do, seeing the disabled in terms of their inability to perform certain functions expected of the able-bodied population. As William Roth maintains: "The functional limitation, economic, and medical models all define disability by what a person is not—the medical model as not healthy, the economic model as not productive, the functional limitation model as not capable."[204]

A newer definition—the psychosocial model—views disability as a socially defined category. In other words, people with disabilities constitute a minority group, and if the person with disabilities is poor, it is less a result of personal inadequacy than of a discriminatory society. This definition situates the problem of disability in the interaction between the disabled person and the social environment. Therefore, the adjustment to disability is not merely a personal problem but one requiring the adjustment of society to people with disabilities. This definition requires that society adjust its attitudes and remove the barriers it has placed in the way of self-fulfillment for people with disabilities—through, architecture and transportation systems designed for the able-bodied and subtle stereotypes that impugn the competence of people with disabilities. In part, this newer definition of disability was expressed in Section 504 of the Rehabilitation Act of 1973 (PL 93–112).

Although the range of disabilities is great, people with disabilities share a central experience rooted in stigmatization, discrimination, and oppression. Like other stigmatized groups, people with disabilities experience poverty and destitution in numbers proportionately larger than the general population. Perhaps not surprisingly, rates of disability are greatest among the aged, African Americans, the poor, and blue-collar workers.[205] Compared to the able-bodied, people with disabilities tend to be more frequently unemployed and underemployed and, as a consequence, often fall below the poverty line. Moreover, because disability is often correlated with poor education, age, and poverty, it is not surprising that African Americans are twice as likely to be disabled as whites (their representation is even greater in the fully disabled population), and that more women are disabled than men. The problems of low wages and unemployment are exacerbated because people with disabilities often need more medical and hospital care than others, are less likely to have health insurance, and spend three times more of their own money on medical care than do the able-bodied.[206]

Although discrimination continues to exist, major strides have been made in the integration of people with disabilities into the social mainstream. These advances have often resulted from organized political activity on the part of people with disabilities and their families. For example, an outgrowth of this political activity is Title V of the Rehabilitation Act of 1973, which mandates the following rules for all programs and facilities that receive federal funds:

1. Federal agencies must have affirmative action programs designed to hire and promote people with disabilities.
2. The Architectural and Transportation Barriers Compliance Board must enforce a 1968 rule mandating that all buildings constructed with federal funds—including buildings owned or leased by federal agencies—be accessible to people with disabilities.
3. All businesses, universities, and other institutions having contracts with the federal government must implement affirmative action programs targeted for people with disabilities.
4. Discrimination against people with disabilities is prohibited in all public and private institutions receiving federal assistance.[207]

Perhaps the greatest stride was made on July 26, 1990, when former President George Bush signed the Americans with Disabilities Act (ADA) (PL 101–336) into law. This act is the most comprehensive piece of legislation for people with disabilities ever passed in the United States. The ADA lays a foundation of equality for people with disabilities, and it extends to the disabled civil rights similar to those now available on the basis of race, sex, color, national origin, and religion through the Civil Rights Act of 1964. For example, the ADA prohibits discrimination on the basis of disability in private sector employment, in state and local government activities, and in public accommodations and services, including transportation that is provided by both public and private entities. While some policies of the

ADA went into effect immediately, others were to be phased in over several years.[208]

In particular, the ADA is divided into five titles and covers the following areas:

I. Employment
   A. Employers may not discriminate against an individual with a disability in hiring or promotion if the person is otherwise qualified for the job.
   B. Employers can ask about one's ability to perform a job but cannot inquire if someone has a disability; nor can employers subject a person to tests that tend to screen out people with disabilities.
   C. Employers will need to provide "reasonable accommodation" to employees with disabilities. This includes job restructuring and modification of equipment. Employers do not need to provide accommodations that impose an "undue hardship" on business operations.
   D. All employers with 15 or more employees must comply with the act.

II. Transportation
   A. New public transit buses and rail cars must be accessible to individuals with disabilities.
   B. Transit authorities must provide comparable paratransit or other special transportation services to individuals with disabilities who cannot use fixed bus services, unless an undue burden would result.
   C. Existing rail systems must have one accessible car per train.
   D. New bus and train stations must be accessible. Key stations in rapid, light, and commuter rail systems must be made accessible, with extensions up to 20 years for commuter rail (30 years for rapid and light rail). All existing Amtrak stations must be accessible by July 26, 2010.

III. Public Accommodations
   A. Private entities such as restaurants, hotels, and retail stores may not discriminate against individuals with disabilities.
   B. Auxiliary aids and services must be provided to individuals with vision or hearing impairments, unless an undue burden would result.
   C. If removal is readily achievable, physical barriers in existing facilities must be removed. If readily achievable, alternative methods of providing services must be offered. All new construction and alterations of facilities must be accessible.

IV. State and Local Government
   A. State and local governments may not discriminate against individuals with disabilities.
   B. All government facilities, services, and communications must be accessible, consistent with the requirements of Section 504 of the Rehabilitation Act of 1973.

V. Telecommunications
   A. Companies offering telephone service to the general public must offer telephone relay services to individuals who use telecommunications services for the deaf (TDD's) or similar devices.[209]

In spite of large loopholes, the ADA represents an important step forward for people with disabilities.

Federal laws discouraging discrimination notwithstanding, discrimination against people with disabilities is still widespread. For instance, most buildings still do not meet the needs of the physically challenged in terms of access, exits, rest rooms, parking lots, warning systems, and so forth. Many apartment complexes and stores continue to be built without recognizing the needs of people with disabilities. The struggle for full integration remains an ongoing battle.

CONCLUSION

Taking many forms, discrimination is an omnipresent part of the American social landscape. It can be targeted against many groups, including African Americans, Hispanic Americans, Native Americans, Asian Americans, women, gays and lesbians, the physically challenged, and poor whites. Because discrimination often results in poverty, it can lead to the creation of income maintenance and poverty programs designed to meliorate its effects. Those who are forced into income programs because of discrimination, soon find themselves with a second handicap. Namely, the stigma of being on public assistance.

Some policymakers have tried to reduce the need for long-term and expensive social welfare programs by attempting to arrest the cycle of discrimination, poverty, welfare receipt, and stigma. This is often done by advocating for policies and legislation designed to attack discrimination at its roots. Antidiscrimination programs, policies, and legislation include affirmative action programs, women's rights legislation, gay and lesbian city and state ordinances, and legislation for the physically and mentally challenged. To this end, policymakers hope that by curtailing overt discrimination, vulnerable populations will be given equal opportunities for achievement and success. At best, the scorecard on programs and policies designed to end discrimination has been mixed. Despite a strong start, affirmative action programs have not led to widespread economic success for women and minorities. Gays and lesbians continue to be discriminated against, even in places which have passed civil rights legislation. Although women have made significant gains over the last few decades, they continue to earn less than males in similar jobs.

Out of the insidious brew of discrimination and social stigma comes oppression—the enforcement of discrimination and unequal power relationships. It is perhaps a truism that oppression flows from prejudice in the same way that opportunity flows from tolerance. Discrimination is a likely manifestation in a society that breeds an individualistic and competitive ethos, status fears among marginal groups, and the need for visible scapegoats upon which to blame the alienating quality of life. In the final analysis, discrimination and social stigma help promote poverty, destitution, and social isolation.

◆ ◆ ◆ *Discussion Questions* ◆ ◆ ◆

1. The results of racism are manifested in a variety of ways, including outright discrimination, poverty, housing problems, high rates of under- and unemployment, wage differentials, family composition, inferior educational opportunities, crime statistics, and welfare dependency. Moreover, the relationship between racism and poverty is clear. What is less clear, however, are the causes of racism. Describe what you believe to be the primary causes of both individual and institutional racism. How are these causal factors nourished or condemned by society?

2. Over the past decade there has been a marked increase in the number of racially based incidents, especially against African Americans and Asian Americans. What are some of the reasons for the rise in such incidents?

3. Over the past three decades many legal attempts have been made to eradicate the effects of racism, including the 1964 Civil Rights Act and a number of Supreme Court rulings. Were these legal attempts successful? If not, why? Could anything have been done legally to eliminate the impact of racism? If yes, what?

4. It is generally acknowledged that sexism is a powerful and pervasive force that permeates much of society. Describe some of the most important ways that sexism is expressed in American society. What strategies, if any, should be adopted to lessen the impact of sexism in society?

5. Most women in American society are forced to work either to provide a second household income or as the family's primary wage earner. What are the major obstacles faced by working women?

6. Gays and lesbians face severe economic and social problems, even apart from the AIDS epidemic. What are some of the most important social, political, and economic hurdles faced by gays and lesbians in achieving full equality?

7. Being elderly in our society is in many ways a social handicap. Describe some key social, economic, and political indicators that illustrate this idea.

8. It is generally agreed that people with disabilities face a difficult kind of discrimination. What is the evidence, if any, to support this idea?

9. The Americans with Disabilities Act (ADA) is often considered the most important piece of legislation affecting people with disabilities. Why do policy analysts consider the ADA such an important act? What are its loopholes, if any?

10. Reviewing the various causes of discrimination discussed in this chapter, describe what you believe to be the major cause of discrimination today. Why is this cause more important than others? Using this cause as a framework for understanding discrimination, state what can be done to counteract the effects of discrimination.

Notes

1. Billy J. Tidwell, "Racial Discrimination and Inequality," *Encyclopedia of Social Work*, 18th ed. (Silver Spring, MD: NASW, 1987), p. 450.
2. J. Dollard et al., *Frustration and Aggression* (New Haven, CT: Yale University Press, 1939).
3. Theodore W. Adorno et al., *The Authoritarian Personality* (New York: Harper and Row, 1950).
4. Wilhelm Reich, *Listen Little Man* (Boston: Beacon Books, 1971).
5. Tidwell, "Racial Discrimination and Inequality," p. 450
6. Stephanie Bernardo, *The Ethnic Almanac* (Garden City, NY: Doubleday, 1981).
7. U.S. Census Bureau. On-line: http://www.census.gov/population/socdemo/race/black/black.html
8. U.S. Bureau of the Census. *Statistical Abstract of the United States, 1991*, 111th ed. (Washington, DC: U.S. Government Printing Office, 1991), p. 32.
9. "Family Income Finally Rises," *The New York Times* (September 27, 1996), p. 18.
10. Steven A. Holmes, "Quality of Life is Up for Many Blacks, Data Say," *The New York Times* (November 18, 1996), pp. A1, A13.
11. U.S. Census Bureau, "Black-Owned Business Firms Up 46 Percent over Five Years, Census Bureau Survey Shows," December 12, 1995. On-line: http://www.census.gov/ftp/pub/agfs/smobe/view/b_press.txt
12. "Family Income Finally Rises," *The New York Times*, p. 18.
13. William Julius Wilson, *The Truly Disadvantaged: The Inner City, the Underclass, and Public Policy* (Chicago: University of Chicago Press, 1987), p. 109.
14. Lawrence Mishel and David M. Frankel, *The State of Working America* (Armonk, NY: M. E. Sharpe, Inc., 1991), p. 251.
15. U.S. House of Representatives, Committee on Ways and Means, *Overview of Entitlement Programs: 1992 Green Book* (Washington, DC: U.S. Government Printing Office, 1992), p. 1073.
16. U.S. Census Bureau. On-line: http://www.census.gov/population/pop-profile/blackpop.html
17. Holmes, "Quality of Life is Up for Many Blacks, Data Says."
18. Barbara Vobjeda and Steven Pearlstein, "Household Income Climbs," *Washington Post* (September 27, 1996), p. A1.
19. Jon D. Haverman, Sheldon Danziger, and Robert D. Plotnick, "State Poverty Rates for Whites, Blacks, and Hispanics in the late 1980s," *Focus* (13)1 (Spring 1991), p. 3.; U.S. Census Bureau. On-line: http://www.census.gov/population/socdemo/race/black/black.html
20. U.S. Census Bureau, "Selected Characteristics of the Population Below the Poverty Level in 1994, by Region and Race." On-line: http://www.census.gov/population/socdemo/race/black/black.html
21. Claudette E. Bennett and Kymberly A. DeBarros, "The Black Population," U.S. Census Bureau, August 16, 1996. On-line: http://www.census.gov/population/pop-profile/blackpop.html
22. Joint Center for Housing Studies, *The State of the Nation's Housing, 1992* (Boston: Joint Center for Housing Studies, Harvard University, 1992), p. 33.
23. Cushing N. Dolbeare, *The Widening Gap* (Washington, DC: Low Income Housing Information Service, 1992), p. 11.

24. Center on Budget and Policy Priorities, *A Place to Call Home* (Washington, DC: Center on Budget and Policy Priorities, December 1991), p. xx.
25. Edward B. Lazere and Paul A. Leonard, *The Crisis in Housing for the Poor: A Special Report on Hispanics and Blacks* (Washington, DC: Center on Budget and Policy Priorities, 1989), p. 3.
26. Jared Bernstein, *Where's the Payoff?* (Washington, DC: Economic Policy Institute, 1995).
27. Bennett and DeBarros, "The Black Population."
28. Mishel and Frankel, *The State of Working America*, p. 201.
29. U.S. House of Representatives, *1992 Green Book*, p. 590.
30. Ibid., p. 598.
31. Mishel and Frankel, *The State of Working America*, p. 218.
32. Ibid., p. 213.
33. Bernstein, *Where's the Payoff?*.
34. Franklin D. Wilson, Marta Tienda, and Lawrence Wu, "Racial Equality in the Labor Market: Still an Elusive Goal?" Institute for Research on Poverty, Madison, WI., 1992, Discussion Paper no. 968–992.
35. "Detroit Study Looks for Clues to Breast Cancer Development," *Michigan Citizen* (October 2, 1994), p. 5.
36. Larry Lucas, "Health Care Reform: Let Get It Right." *Oakland Post* (July 17, 1994), p. 2.
37. M.J. McCollum, "Study: Number of HIV-infected Black Women up Dramatically," *Philadelphia Tribune* (September 13, 1994), p.1.
38. March of Dimes, "Leading Infant Health Indicators United States, 1993: By Race of Mother." On-line: http://www.modimes.org/stats/datatab.htm
39. Children's Defense Fund, *The State of America's Children*, p. 61.
40. March of Dimes, "Leading Infant Health Indicators, 1993."
41. Ibid.
42. Council on Interracial Books for Children, Inc., "Fact Sheets on Institutional Racism" (New York: Council on Interracial Books, November 1984).
43. March of Dimes, "Leading Infant Health Indicators, 1993."
44. Ibid., p. 63.
45. Ibid., p. 60.
46. U.S. House of Representatives, *1992 Green Book*, p. 247.
47. "Poverty and Mortality Rates," *Insights* 3 (January 1991), p. 1.
48. Mishel and Frankel, *The State of Working America*, p. 219.
49. Gregory Acs and Sheldon Danziger, "Educational Attainment, Industrial Structure, and Male Earnings, 1973–1987," Institute for Research on Poverty, 1991, Discussion Paper no. 945–991.
50. The figures on high school dropout rates are highly variable, with ranges of several percentage points between low and high figures. For a discussion of these measurement problems, see Robert M. Hauser, "What Happens to Youth After High School?" *Focus* (13)3 (Fall & Winter 1991), pp. 1–13. See also U.S. House of Representatives, *1992 Green Book*, p. 1073.
51. Mishel and Frankel, *The State of Working America*, p. 253.
52. Children's Defense Fund, *The State of America's Children*, p. 76.
53. Ibid., p. 25.
54. Ibid., p. 92.
55. Ibid.
56. Mishel and Frankel, *The State of Working America*, p. 253.
57. Robert Elias, *The Politics of Victimization* (New York: Oxford University Press, 1986), p. 56.
58. Quoted in Jonathan Marshall, "Targeting the Drugs, Wounding the Cities," *Washington Post Weekly*, (May 25–31, 1992), p. 23.
59. U.S. House of Representatives, *1992 Green Book*, p. 1136.
60. Leon Ginsberg, *Social Work Almanac* (Silver Spring, MD: National Association of Social Workers Press, 1992), pp. 54–55.
61. U.S. House of Representatives, *1992 Green Book*, p. 1135.
62. Diana M. DiNitto, *Social Welfare: Politics and Public Policy* (Englewood Cliffs, NJ: Prentice-Hall, 1991), p. 247.
63. L. Lowell, F. Bean, and R. De La Garza, "The Dilemmas of Undocumented Immigration: An Analysis of the 1984 Simpson–Mazzoli Vote," *Social Service Quarterly* 67 (1986), pp. 118–126.
64. Fariyal Ross-Sheriff, "Displaced Populations," *Encyclopedia of Social Work, 1990 Supplement*, 18th ed. (Silver Spring, MD: National Association of Social Workers, 1990), p. 85.
65. Hispanic News Link, "Hispanics Who Defy Averages," *The Numbers News* (September 1995), p. 1.

66. U.S. Bureau of the Census, *The Hispanic Population in the United States* (Washington, DC: U.S. Government Printing Office, March 1989).
67. See U.S. House of Representatives, *1992 Green Book*, p. 1275; and Vobjeda and Pearlstein, "Household Income Climbs."
68. Ibid., p. 1072.
69. Ibid.
70. Ibid., pp. 590–591.
71. Mishel and Frankel, *The State of Working America*, p. 16. It should be noted that although Hispanic American family income dropped in that period, it was still over $3,000 more yearly than African American family income.
72. Scott Barancik, *Falling Through the Gap: Hispanics and the Growing Income Disparity Between Rich and Poor* (Washington, DC: Center on Budget and Policy Priorities, 1990), p. 3.
73. Joan R. Kahn and Rosalind E. Berkowitz, "Sources of Support for Young Latina Mothers." (Washington, DC: The Urban Institute, August 16, 1995.)
74. Ibid., p. 6.
75. "Hispanics Who Defy Averages," Hispanic News Link, p. 2.
76. Guadalupe Gibson, "Mexican Americans," *Encyclopedia of Social Work*, 18th ed. (Silver Spring, MD: NASW, 1987), p. 139.
77. Ibid., p. 140.
78. Marta Tienda, "Puerto Ricans and the Underclass Debate," *The Annals of the American Academy* 501 (January 1989), p. 115.
79. Barancik, *Falling Through the Gap*, p. 25.
80. Marta Tienda, "Race, Ethnicity and the Portrait of Inequality: Approaching the 1990s," *Sociological Spectrum* 9 (1989), p. 32.
81. U.S. Census Bureau, "Number of Hispanic Businesses Up 76 Percent in Five Years, Census Bureau Reports," July 10, 1996. On-line: http://www.census.gov/Press-Release/cb96-110.html
82. H. F. Dobyns, *Native American Historical Demography: A Critical Bibliography* (Bloomington, IN: Indiana University Press, 1976), p. 32.
83. H. E. Fey and D. McNickle, *Indians and Other Americans: Two Ways of Life Meet* (New York: Harper and Row, 1970), pp. 9–12.
84. DiNitto, *Social Welfare*, p. 257.
85. Evelyn Lance Blanchard, "American Indians and Alaska Natives," *Encyclopedia of Social Work*, 18th ed. (Silver Spring, MD: NASW, 1987), p. 61; Bureau of the Census, 1990 *Census of Population and Housing Summary* (Washington, DC: U.S. Government Printing Office, 1990), p. 93.
86. Blanchard, p. 142.
87. Leon Ginsberg, "Selected Statistical Review," *Encyclopedia of Social Work, 1990 Supplement*, 18th ed. (Silver Spring, MD: National Association of Social Workers, 1990), p. 280.
88. University of Arizona Library, "Contemporary Indian Affairs: A Bibliography of U.S. Government Documents." On-line: http://www.lib.ua.edu/indians.htm
89. Ibid.
90. Ibid., pp. 143–144.
91. Margaret L. Usdansky, "Asian Immigrants Changing Face of Rural USA," *USA Today* (September 10, 1992), p. 9A.
92. Felicity Barringer, "U.S. Asian Population Up 70% in 80's," 18th ed. *The New York Times National* (March 2, 1990), p. 1.
93. U.S. Bureau of the Census. *Statistical Abstract of the United States: 1992*, 111th ed. (Washington, DC: Government Printing Office, 1984), p. 139.
94. Daniel Goleman, "Probing School Success of Asian-Americans," *The New York Times* (September 11, 1990), p. B5.
95. Arthur Hu, "Hu's on First: Asian Males Lose Again," *Asian Week* (February 12, 1993), p. 15.
96. Goleman, "Probing School Success of Asian-Americans."
97. Goleman, "Probing School Success of Asian-Americans."
98. U.S. Bureau of the Census. *Statistical Abstract of the United States: 1992*.
99. See Rich Connell and Sonia Nazario, "Affirmative Action: Fairness or Favoritism?" *Los Angeles Times* (September 10, 1995), pp. A1, A26–A28; and U.S. Commission on Civil Rights, "Civil Rights Issues Facing Asian-Americans in the 1990s" (Washington, DC: U.S. Commission on Civil Rights, February 1992), p. 17.
100. Ibid., pp. 16–17.
101. U.S. Census Bureau, "Large Increases in Number of Asian, Pacific Islander, American Indian, and Alaska Native Businesses Between 1987 and 1992, Census Bureau Reports," August 1, 1996. On-line: http://www.census.gov/Press-Release/cb96-127.html
102. S. B. Gall and T. L. Gall, *Statistical Record of Asian-Americans*. (Cleveland, OH: Eastwood Publications Development, Inc., 1993), p. 44.

103. Rockefeller Foundation, Research Briefs on Poverty, "Poverty and Asian Americans," n.d. On-line: http://www.cdinet.com/Rockefeller/Briefs/brief27.html
104. Susumu Awanchara, "Hit by a Backlash," *Far Eastern Economic Review* (155)2 (March 26, 1992), p. 30.
105. Ibid.
106. Jeffrey Rosen, "The War on Immigrants," *The New Republic* (January 7, 1996), pp. 8–12.
107. Quoted in Ibid., p. 32.
108. Ross-Sheriff, "Displaced Populations," p. 84.
109. David Stoesz, "What Amnesty Means to All of Us," *Newsday* (May 18, 1987), p. 77.
110. Immigration and Naturalization Service, *Report* (Washington, DC: U.S. Government Printing office, 1988).
111. HR 3734: Personal Responsibility and Work Opportunity Act (Immigration Provisions)—Conference Committee Version. Title IV-Restricting Welfare and Public Benefits for Aliens. (Washington, DC: U.S. House of Representatives, Conference Committee, August 5, 1996), p. 16.
112. Patty Reinert, "Federal Welfare Plan Hits Legal Immigrants," *Houston Chronicle* (August 2, 1996), pp. 1A and 16A.
113. Greg McDonald, "House Passes $600 Billion Spending Bill," *Houston Chronicle* (September 29, 1996), pp. 1A and 32A.
114. Kathy Brown, "Mend It, Don't End It," *Outlook* (90)3 (Fall 1996), p. 9.
115. Bryan, "Mend It, Don't End It," p. 11.
116. Bill Clinton, Mend, Don't End, Affirmative Action," *Congressional Quarterly Weekly Report* 53 (July 22, 1995), pp. 2208–2209.
117. Roger Hernández, "End Affirmative Action, But For the Right Reason," Syndicated Column, King Features, 1995.
118. Wilson, *The Truly Disadvantaged*, pp. 146–147.
119. U.S. Department of Justice, "National Crime Victimization Survey," August 1995. Quoted in U.S. Department of Justice, "The Violence Against Women Act," September 23, 1996. On-line: http://www.usdoj.gov/vawo/vawafct.htm
120. U.S Ibid.
121. Update on VAWA, *National NOW Times* (January 1995). On-line: http://www.now.org
122. Women's Bureau, "Women Who Maintain Families, U.S. Department of Labor, June, 1993. On-line: http://bubba.dol.gov/dol/wb/public/wb_pubs/wwmf1.htm
123. U.S. House of Representatives, *1992 Green Book*, pp. 591–596.
124. Ruth Sidel, *Women and Children Last* (New York: Harper, 1984).
125. National Commission on Children, *Poverty, Welfare and America's Families: A Hard Look* (Washington, DC: National Commission on Children, 1992), p. 3.
126. Mishel and Frankel, *The State of Working America*, p. 105.
127. While we have stressed single female-headed families here, it is important to acknowledge that single male-headed families are growing even more rapidly. From 1959 to 1989, single male-headed families grew from 350,000 to 1.4 million, compared with 7.4 million mother-only and 25.5 million two-parent households. From 1960 to 1990, the percentage of father-only households increased 300 percent. See Daniel R. Mayer and Steven Garasky, "Custodial Fathers: Myths, Realities, and Child Support Policy," Institute for Research on Poverty, Madison, WI, August 1992, Discussion Paper no. 982–992, pp. 8–9.
128. National Commission on Children, "Poverty, Welfare and America's Families," p. 3.
129. National Commission on Children, *Beyond Rhetoric: A New Economic Agenda for Children and Families* (Washington, D.C.: National Commission on Children, 1991), p. 90.
130. Yin-Ling Irene Wong, Irwin Garfinkel, and Sara McLanahan, "Single-Mother Families in Eight Countries: Economic Status and Social Policy," Institute for Research on Social Policy, Madison, WI, 1992, Discussion paper no. 970–992.
131. Winifred Bell, *Contemporary Social Welfare* (New York: Macmillan, 1983), p. 129.
132. Martha N. Ozawa, "Gender and Ethnicity in Social Security," *Conference Proceedings*, Nelson A. Rockefeller Institute of Government, State University of New York at Albany, November 1985, pp. 2–6.
133. Ibid.
134. Most of the following section, unless otherwise noted, is based on information found in Wider Opportunities for Women, *Making Both Ends Meet* (Washington, DC: Wider Opportunities for Women, Inc., 1991), pp. 4–9.

135. Nina Totenberg, "Why Women Earn Less," *Parade* (June 10, 1984), p. 5.
136. Family assistance was one of the major thrusts of the Clinton campaign. It is also an issue that seems to cross racial and social class lines.
137. Quoted in D. Harris, "How Does Your Pay Stack Up? *Working Women* (February 1996), pp. 27–28.
138. U.S. Census Bureau, "Income and Poverty 1995," September 26, 1996. On-line: http://www.census.gov/hhes/income/income95/prs96asc.html
139. National Commission on Working Women of Wider Opportunities for Women, "Women, Work and Family: Working Mothers—Overview" (Washington, DC: Wider Opportunities for Women, n.d.), n.p.
140. Harrington, *Who Are the Poor?* p. 7; see also Women's Bureau, "20 Facts About Women Workers."
141. National Commission on Working Women of Wider Opportunities for Women, "Women, Work and Family: Working Mothers—Overview."
142. Ibid.
143. U.S. Census Bureau, "Income 1995," September 26, 1995. On-line: http://www.census.gov/hhes/income/income95/in95med2.html
144. National Commission on Working Women of Wider Opportunities for Women, "Women, Work and Family."
145. Bell, *Contemporary Social Welfare*, p. 126.
146. Feminist Majority Foundation, "Women in Business," 1995. On-line: http://www.feminist.org/research/ewb_myths.html
147. National Commission on Working Women of Wider Opportunities for Women, "Women and Nontraditional Work," (Washington, DC: Wider Opportunities for Women, n.d.), n.p.
148. DiNitto, *Social Welfare*, p. 237.
149. Rene Redwood, "Breaking the Glass Ceiling"—A Summary of Reports," adapted by Dawn Hyde. On-line: http://www.berkshire-aap.com
150. Ibid.
151. Ibid.
152. Feminist Majority Foundation, "Women in Business."
153. See Nijole V. Benokraitis and Joe R. Feagin, *Modern Sexism: Blatant, Subtle, and Covert Discrimination* (Englewood Cliffs, NJ: Prentice-Hall, 1986); and Women's Bureau, "20 Facts About Women Workers."
154. The Urban Institute, "Services for Low-Income Children." On-line: http://www.urban.org
155. Children's Defense Fund, *The State of America's Children*, p. 42.
156. Ibid., p. 8.
157. Children's Defense Fund, *The State of America's Children*, p. 37.
158. Sheila B. Kammerman, "Child Care and Family Benefits: Policies of Six Industrialized Countries," *Monthly Labor Review* 103 (November 1980), p. 23–28.
159. Sidel, *Women and Children Last*, p. 123.
160. National Commission on Working Women of Wider Opportunities for Women, "Women, Work and Health Insurance" (Washington, DC: Wider Opportunities for Women, n.d.), n.p.
161. National Commission on Working Women, "Women and Nontraditional Work."
162. Jim Harris, *The Complete Text of the Equal Rights Amendment* (New York: Ganis and Harris, 1980), p. 7.
163. "Fighting Discrimination," *The Legal Advisor* (Spring 1982), pp. 457–458.
164. Alan Gutmacher Institute, *Facts of Abortion* (Washington, DC: Alan Gutmacher Institute, September 1995).
165. S. K. Henshaw, L. M. Koonin, and J. C. Smith, "Characteristics of U.S. Women Having Abortions, 1987," *Family Planning Perspectives* 23 (March/April, 1991), pp. 75–81.
166. Nanneska Magee, "Should the Federal Government Fund Abortions?: No." In Howard Jacob Karger and James Midgley (eds.), *Controversial Issues in Social Policy* (New York: Allyn and Bacon, 1993).
167. DiNitto, *Social Welfare*, p. 241.
168. R. B. Gold and D. Daley, "Public Funding of Contraceptive, Sterilization and Abortion Services, Fiscal Year 1990," *Family Planning Perspectives* 23 (September/October 1991), pp. 204–211.
169. DiNitto, *Social Welfare*, p. 241.
170. National Abortion and Reproduction Rights Action League Foundation, *The Road to the Back Alley* (Washington, DC: NARAL, April 1996).
171. Ibid.
172. "Abortion Bill Vetoed," *Houston Chronicle* (April 11, 1996), pp. 1 and 6.
173. M. Clements, "Should Abortion Remain Legal?" *Parade* (May 17, 1992), pp. 4–5.
174. Ibid.; see also *Lesbian and Gay Civil Rights in the U.S.* (New York: National Gay and Lesbian Task Force, 1992).

175. Robert Williams, *Just As I Am* (New York: Crown, 1992).
176. Natalie Jane Woodman, "Homosexuality: Lesbian Women," *Encyclopedia of Social Work*, 18th ed. (Silver Spring, MD: NASW, 1987), p. 809.
177. Lambda Legal Defense and Education Fund, Inc., "Information Sheet" (New York: Lambda, 1991).
178. A. P. Bell and M. S. Weinberg, *Homosexualities: A Study of Diversity Among Men and Women* (New York: Simon and Schuster, 1978), p. 101.
179. See *Newsweek*, "The Homosexual Numbers" (March 22, 1993), p 9.; *Springs Gazette Telegraph*, "Homosexual Activity Lower Than Believed, Study Shows" (April 15, 1993), p. A18.
180. See the *Wall Street Journal*, "Overcoming a Deep Rooted Reluctance, More Firms Advertise to Gay Community" (July 18, 1991), p. 48; and The *San Francisco Chronicle*, "Gay Market a Potential Gold Mine" (August 27, 1991), C30.
181. Ibid.; *Travel Weekly*, "For Gays, Ship Charters Are a Boon, Say Two Travel Companies" (August 5, 1991), p. 2; and the *Bay Areas Reporter*, "Where the Money Is: Travel Industry Eyeing Gay/Lesbian Tourism" (September 19, 1991), p. 53.
182. DiNitto, *Social Welfare*, p. 109.
183. Kent Kilpatrick, "Oregon Voters Reject Stigmatizing Homosexuals," *The Advocate*, (November 5, 1992), p. 2C.
184. Much of this section on the military and gays and lesbians was derived from Rivette Vullo, "Homosexuals in the Military," unpublished paper, School of Social Work, Louisiana State University, Baton Rouge, LA, December 4, 1991. See also K. Dyer, ed., *Gays in Uniform: The Pentagon's Secret Reports* (Boston, Alyson Publications, 1990).
185. Ibid., p. xiv.
186. Joseph Harry, "Homosexual Men and Women Who Served Their Country," *Journal of Homosexuality* 10 (1984): 117–125.
187. Dyer, *Gays in Uniform*, p. xv.
188. Conrad K. Harper and Jane E. Booth, "End Military Intolerance," *National Law Journal* 13 (1991), pp. 17–18.
189. Barry M. Goldwater, "Ban on Gays is Senseless Attempt to Stall the Inevitable" *Los Angeles Times* (September 23, 1993), C7.
190. Tony Marco, "What Does the Bible REALLY Say About Homosexual Issues?" On-line: http://www.qrd.tcp.com/qrd/religion/anti/CFV/christian.american
191. Centers for Disease Control, "DHAP Basic Statistics,"June 13, 1996. On-line: http://www.cdc.gov/nchstp/hiv_aids/statisti/exposure.htm
192. Robert Searles Walker, *AIDS: Today, Tomorrow* (New Jersey: Humanities Press, 1992), p. 119.
193. Joann Szabo, Phyllis Tonkin, Veronique Vaillancourt, Philip Winston, and Deidre Wright, "The Clinton Scorecard." Unpublished paper, Graduate School of Social Work, University of Houston, Houston, TX, April 25, 1996.
194. Norman Wyers, "Is Gay Rights Necessary for the Well-Being of Gays and Lesbians?" In Howard Jacob Karger and James Midgley (eds.), *Controversial Issues in Social Welfare Policy* (Boston: Allyn and Bacon, 1994).
195. U.S. Census Bureau, "Sixty-Five Plus in the United States," May 1995. On-line: http://www.census.gov/socdemo/agebrief.html
196. Ibid.
197. Ibid.
198. Ibid.
199. John Anderson, "Poverty Rates for Elderly, Blacks are Lowest on Record," *Washington Post* (September 27, 1996), p. A1.
200. American Association of Retired Persons, *A Profile of Older Americans, 1991* (Washington, DC: AARP, 1991).
201. L. D. Haber, "Trends and Demographic Studies on Programs for Disabled Persons," in L. G. Perlman and G. Austin (eds.), *A Report of the Ninth Annual Mary E. Switzer Memorial Seminar* (Alexandria, VA: 1985), pp. 27–29.
202. Ibid., pp. 35–37. See also Bell, *Contemporary Social Welfare*, p. 174.
203. William Roth, "Disabilities: Physical," *Encyclopedia of Social Work*, 18th ed. (Silver Spring, MD: NASW, 1987), p. 86.
204. Ibid.
205. Haber, "Trends and Demographic Studies on Programs for the Disabled," p. 32.
206. Bell, *Contemporary Social Welfare*, p. 174.
207. DiNitto, *Social Welfare*, p. 104.
208. Administration on Developmental Disabilities, *Fact Sheet* (Washington, DC: Administration on Developmental Disabilities, n.d.).
209. Ibid.

CHAPTER 5

Poverty in America

This chapter examines the characteristics of poverty in America. Particular attention is focused on the definition of terms and concepts used in the study of poverty, the examination of its demographic aspects, the relationship between poverty and income distribution, and the connection between poverty and work-related issues such as the minimum wage, structural unemployment, dual labor markets, and job training programs. In addition, the authors look at a wide range of theories used to explain why some people become poor and why many stay there. Lastly, this chapter provides an overview of key strategies developed to combat poverty.

Poverty is at once a complex and a simple phenomenon. Nevertheless, there are three general categories of poverty: (1) those making only minimum wage (the working poor); (2) the unemployed; and (3) those who have an occupational disability or poor health (i.e., a deficit in human capital such as poor education or a low quality and quantity of training and skills).

Poverty can be defined as deprivation and, in particular, as absolute and relative deprivation. *Absolute poverty* refers to an unequivocal standard necessary for survival (e.g., the calories necessary for physical survival, adequate shelter for protection against the elements, and proper clothing). Those who fall below that absolute standard of poverty are considered poor. Relative poverty refers to deprivation that is relative to the standard of living enjoyed by other members of society. Although basic needs are met, a segment of the population may be considered poor if they possess fewer resources, opportunities, or goods than other citizens. For example, if most families in a society have two cars and a family can afford only one, they are relatively poor. Relative poverty (or deprivation) can be understood as inequality in the distribution of income, goods, or opportunities. Little attention is currently being focused on relative deprivation.

The University of Michigan's Panel Study of Income Dynamics (PSID) followed 5,000 American families for almost ten years (1969–1978). Researchers found that only 2 percent of families were persistently poor (i.e., poor throughout the entire period),[1] suggesting that poverty is a fluid rather than a static condition. The data showed that as people gained (or lost) jobs, as marriages were created (or dissolved), or as offspring were born (or left home), people were either pushed into poverty or escaped from it. Moreover, the data showed that most people who were poor in a given year had not been poor for an extended period of time.[2] In fact, about one-third of the individuals who were poor in any given year escaped from poverty the following year, and only about one-third of the poor families in any given year had been poor for at least eight of the preceding years. Family composition, and especially divorce or separation, were the leading causes of poverty. Conversely, spells of poverty were most often ended by family reconstitution (e.g., remarriage).

MEASURING POVERTY

Set by the Social Security Administration (SSA), *absolute deprivation* in the United States is defined by a poverty line drawn at a given income. The poverty line used by the federal government was developed in the mid–1960s and was created by taking the cost of the least expensive food plan (the Thrifty Food Plan) developed by the Department of Agriculture and multiplying that number by 3. The rationale was based on 1955 survey data showing that the average family spent about one-third of its budget on food.[3] Formally adopted by the SSA in 1969, the official measure provides a set of income cutoffs adjusted for the size of the household, the number of children under age 18, and the age of the household head. To ensure the same purchasing power, the SSA adjusts the poverty line yearly using the Consumer Price Index (CPI). This absolute figure is known as the poverty index or poverty line.

In 1995 the federal poverty index for a family of four was $15,569,[4] up from $8,414 in 1980.[5] (See Table 5.1 for a long-term view of the poverty index). These increases in the poverty index do not represent more liberal standards but are due almost solely to the effects of inflation. Poverty is assumed to be eliminated when the income of a family exceeds the poverty line.

The poverty index is plagued with structural problems. For example, in recent years there has been a heated debate over the poverty count. Households falling below the poverty line because of in adequate income from private market sources are called the pretransfer poor. But, after receiving food stamps, housing assistance, and Medicaid, many of these families are raised above the poverty line. Some conservatives argue that if the value of noncash benefits (e.g., Medicaid and Medicare) were counted as income, fewer people would be classified as poor. According to the Census Bureau, valuing benefits and subtracting taxes would have reduced the 1995 poverty rate from 13.8 to 10.3 percent, resulting in about 9 million fewer people being counted as poor. While these criticisms have some validity, placing a dollar value on noncash benefits produces a new set of problems. For instance, how should these benefits be valued? Some critics who favor placing a dollar value on noncash benefits (the "market value" approach), believe that these benefits should be highly valued. Under this approach, elderly persons with no cash income would be considered as living above the poverty line simply because they possess a Medicare card (assumed to have greater monetary value than the poverty line figure).

Another problem with the poverty index relates to the dollar threshold. Some policy analysts argue

◆ TABLE 5.1
Changes in Poverty Levels Based on Income and Family Size, 1970–1995

	Income, Selected Years					
Family Size	*1970*	*1975*	*1980*	*1985*	*1990*	*1995*
1	$1,954	$2,724	$ 4,190	$ 5,250	$ 6,652	$ 7,763
2	2,525	3,506	5,363	7,050	8,509	9,933
3	3,099	4,293	6,565	8,850	10,419	12,158
4	3,968	5,500	8,414	10,650	13,359	15,569
5	4,680	6,499	9,966	12,450	15,572	18,408
6	5,260	7,316	11,269	14,250	17,839	20,804
7	6,468	9,022	13,955	16,050	20,241	23,552

Source: Compiled from U.S. Bureau of the Census, *Technical Paper 56*, series P–60, Nos. 134 and 149 (Washington, DC: U.S. Government Printing Office, 1992); and U.S. Census Bureau, "Poverty 1995," September 26, 1996. On-line: http://www.census.gov/hhes/poverty/pov95/thresh95.html

that the federal poverty line is out of date. For example, the proportion of the U.S. household budget spent on food has declined since the 1950s, whereas the proportion of the family budget spent on health care, housing, and child care has increased. The American family currently spends less than one-fifth of its income on food. If the poverty line were revised using the Thrifty Food Plan, but this time multiplying it by a factor of five rather than three, the poverty line would be significantly higher.[6] Moreover, the Thrifty Food Plan is based on an emergency diet that assumes the existence of an educated consumer able to identify nutritious and inexpensive foods. The Nationwide Food Consumption Survey in 1977–1978 indicated that fewer than one-tenth of the families spending an amount equivalent to the cost of the Thrifty Food Plan were able to purchase a diet that met the recommended dietary allowance for all major nutrients. Food cost data from 1981 indicated that the diets of low-income families cost 24 percent more than the amount allotted in the Thrifty Food Plan.[7] Some critics argue that the federal poverty line, established almost 30 years ago, does not reflect current employment realities. For instance, 30 years ago relatively few mothers of young children worked outside the home; today, child care costs consume a substantial share of the budgets of most young families.

The poverty line is also not adjusted for differences in the regional cost-of-living. In 1981 the Bureau of Labor Statistics (BLS) calculated the cost of three family budgets in 24 metropolitan and 4 nonmetropolitan areas. The lower family budget was 19 percent higher in the highest-cost metropolitan area (Seattle-Everett, Washington) than in the lowest-cost metropolitan area (Dallas). The BLS also found that the cost of living in metropolitan areas was 6 percent higher than in nonmetropolitan areas.[8] It is difficult to believe that the costs of food and housing are similar in New York City and Houma, Louisiana.

In 1989, the Gallup Organization polled a sample of Americans on what they thought would be a fair poverty line for a family of four in their communities. The poll showed that Americans believed the poverty line should be higher than what it was: The average figure reported by respondents was $15,017 yearly, which was nearly $3,000, or 25 percent, higher than the federal poverty line for that year. If this poverty line had been adopted, the number of poor people would have increased from 32 to 45 million. Moreover, the poverty rate would have been 18 percent rather than 13.5 percent. The percentage of children in poverty would have gone from 19 percent to 26 percent; for the elderly it would have risen from 12 percent to 23 percent.[9]

Poverty analysts have recently begun to explore other ways of defining the poverty line. One alternative is to base the poverty line on an inflation-sensitive "market basket," which includes food, housing, clothing, medical care, child care, transportation, and other necessities. The contents of this market basket would be updated periodically, and items would be added (or deleted) as they became necessities instead of luxuries. Despite the SSA's calculations, it is clear that $15,559 is insufficient for the survival of an urban or a rural family of four, particularly if they are renters.

WHO MAKE UP THE POOR?

"Who are the poor in America?" (Table 5.2 describes the characteristics and numbers of poor over a 30-year period.) In 1995, about 36.4 million Americans were poor, or about 13.8 percent of the population. This was down from 38 million (14.5 percent of the population) in 1994. However, this was an increase of almost 12 million above the 1978 figure of 24.5 million. Moreover, the 1995 poverty rate was higher than in any year of the 1970s, including the recession years of 1974 and 1975.[10] In short, almost one out of every seven Americans was poor in 1995.

One of the most striking features of poverty in America involves hunger. The Harvard School of Public Health estimated that in 1985 some 20 million Americans were hungry. In 1992, Dr. Vincent Breglio, a national survey researcher, estimated that 30 million Americans now experience hunger. Estimates of hunger in America range from a low of 22.1 million to a high of 41.2 million.[11] A 1991 study of 28 major cities by the U.S. Conference of Mayors found that requests for emergency food assistance increased by about 26 percent in the cities surveyed; 17 percent of these requests went unmet.[12] An Urban Institute study found that between 8 percent and 16

◆ **TABLE 5.2**
Persons Below the Poverty Line, Selected Years and Characteristics, 1959-1995
(Number and percentage below poverty, in thousands)

Year	Overall	Aged	Children[1]	Individuals in Female-Headed Families[2]	Blacks	Hispanic Origin[3]	White
1995	36,425	3,318	13,999	12,315	9,872	8,574	24,423
Rate	13.8%	10.5	20.2	32.4	29.3	30.3	11.2
1990	33,585	3,658	14,431	12,578	9,837	6,006	22,326
Rate	13.5%	12.2	20.6	37.2	31.9	28.1	10.7
1986	32,370	3,477	12,876	11,944	8,983	5,117	22,183
Rate	13.6%	12.4	20.5	38.3	31.3	27.3	11.0
1980	29,272	3,871	11,543	10,120	8,579	3,491	19,699
Rate	13.0%	15.7	18.3	36.7	32.5	25.7	10.2
1978	24,497	3,233	9,931	9,269	7,626	2,607	16,259
Rate	11.4%	14.0	15.9	35.6	30.6	21.6	8.7
1969	21,147	4,787	9,961	6,879	7,095	NA	16,659
Rate	12.1%	25.3	14.0	38.2	32.2	NA	9.5
1959	39,490	5,481	17,552	7,014	9,927	NA	28,484
Rate	22.4%	35.2	27.3	49.4	55.1	NA	18.1

1 All children, including unrelated children.
2 Does not include females living alone.
3 People of Hispanic origin may be of any race; it is an overlapping category.
Sources: Compiled from Committee on Ways and Means, U.S. House of Representatives, *Overview of Entitlement Programs: 1992 Green Book* [Washington, DC: U.S. Government Printing Office, 1992], Tables 2 and 3, pp. 1274–1275.); and U.S. Census Bureau, "Poverty 1995," September 26, 1996. Online: http://www.census.gov/hhes/poverty/pov95/thresh95.html

percent of elderly Americans experience food insecurity in a six month period.[13]

In absolute numbers, half of the nation's poor population are white. In 1995, they accounted for 24.4 out of the 36.4 million poor people in the United States. As such, more whites were poor in 1995 than African Americans (9.8 million), Asians (1.4 million), and Hispanics (8.6 million) combined. In contrast to popular stereotypes:

- Whites constitute the single largest group of poor people in every region of the country and in the vast majority of states. In rural areas, about 70 percent of the poor population is white.
- From 1989 to 1991, the poverty rates for whites rose by 14 percent—more than the 10 percent increase for blacks.
- From 1989 to 1991, the population of poor white children grew from 11.5 percent to 13 percent.
- The proportion of white workers earning wages too low to lift a family out of poverty grew from 20 percent in 1973 to 28 percent in 1991.
- Even in America's metropolitan areas, there are four poor whites for every three poor African Americans.[14]

On a proportional basis, however, whites make up only 11.2 percent of those in poverty compared to 29 percent for blacks, 30.3 percent for Hispanics, and 14.6 percent for Asians. African Americans and Hispanics are almost three times as likely to experience poverty as whites.[15]

Family Composition and Poverty

Family composition is an important indicator of poverty, and the group at greatest risk of poverty in the United States are single female-headed families.

In 1995 the poverty rate for male-present families was 5.6 percent; for female-headed households it was 32.4 percent. When disaggregated, the figures become even starker: families headed by white women had a poverty rate of 36.6 percent; families headed by African American and Hispanic women had poverty rates of 45.1 percent and 49.4 percent, respectively.[16]

More than one million children see their parents divorce or separate each year, and more than half of all children will spend some time in a single-parent family. Using six nationally representative data sets containing more than 25,000 children, Sara McLanahan and Gary Sandefur found that children raised with only one biological parent are disadvantaged in a multitude of ways. Compared to children who grow up in two-parent families: (1) they are twice as likely to drop out of school, (2) 2.5 times more likely to become teen mothers, and (3) 1.4 times more likely to be idle—out of work and out of school; (4) they also have lower grade point averages, lower college aspirations, and poorer attendance records, and they have higher rates of divorce in adulthood. These patterns persist even after adjusting for differences in race, the education of parents, the number of siblings, and the child's geographic and residential location.[17]

"Deadbeat Dads"

The feminization of poverty is in some measure influenced by the refusal of fathers to pay child support. A recent Census Bureau study reported that slightly more than half of families with an absent parent have child support orders in place. Of those with orders, half received full payment and half received partial or no payment.[18] Federal authorities allege that only $14 billion is collected in child support payments out of a potential $48 billion. Thus, the supposed gap between what fathers could and actually do pay is $34 billion. Moreover, federal officials claim that if all the money due custodial parents were collected, approximately 800,000 children could be moved off welfare.[19]

The recent attention focused on "deadbeat dads" risks oversimplifying a complex problem. Specifically, the problem of deadbeat dads has taken on distinct political overtones. Some argue that focusing on deadbeat dads has allowed policymakers to blame a variety of social ills, from poverty to high welfare costs to social pathology, squarely on the shoulders of fathers.[20] Given this, it is important to separate the hype from the fact. According to the Census Bureau, 64 percent (6.2 million out of 11.5 million) of custodial parents, including single fathers, do not receive child support. Of the 4.9 million payments, 76 percent received at least a portion of the amount owed. While more than 5 million custodial parents went without financial support from their child(ren)'s other parent, about one-third of those chose not to pursue them. Two common reasons were: (1) they did not want an award or (2) the noncustodial parent was unable to pay.[21] According to Stuart Miller, of the 30 percent of child support payments not collected, a significant number are owed by imprisoned fathers. A high percentage of prisoners have child support obligations, and as many as one-third of the inmates in many county jails are incarcerated because of child support noncompliance. Many of the other delinquent fathers are addicts, alcoholics, disabled, mentally ill, unemployed, or otherwise unable to pay pre-set child support amounts.[22] In 1992, the General Accounting Office found out that 14 percent of fathers who owed child support were dead. The report further stated that 56 percent of fathers who owed child support "cannot afford to pay the amount ordered."[23]

Recent bipartisan governmental initiatives have characterized deadbeat dads as a virtual goldmine of untapped revenue and a way out of paying for expensive welfare benefits. Health and Human Services Secretary Donna Shalala testified that if all of the child support owed by Americans were collected, the $200 billion in welfare costs would be reduced by 25 percent or $50 billion. While both Republicans and Democrats have used increased child support collections as a cornerstone of welfare reform, the Census Bureau's own projections show that "A total of $11.9 billion was paid in child support in 1991, $5.8 billion less than the amount due."[24] This $5.8 billion figure is a far cry from federal estimates of close to $50 billion in unpaid child support collections. Clearly, public policy around child support and reduced welfare expenditures is predicated on the existence of a goldmine of resources, one that apparently does not exist.

Policy analysts Irwin Garfinkel and David Ellwood have suggested the creation of a Child Support

Assurance program, consisting of three components: (1) setting child support as a percentage of an absent parent's income; (2) automatically deducting child support payments from income, as is done with Social Security taxes; and (3) ensuring a minimum benefit to children if the absent parent defaults on payments.[25] Some policy analysts argue that if these or similar policies were enacted, the poverty rate could be reduced by 8 to 10 percent, with a corresponding 12 to 20 percent reduction in welfare dependency.[26] As many as 16 million children living in single-parent families could benefit from this system.[27] As a result of these and other findings, child support enforcement guidelines have been considerably strengthened in recent years. First, new laws in the Family Support Act of 1988 contained major provisions for establishing paternity. This was important because paternity is currently established for fewer than half of children born to never-married parents in child support cases.[28] Second, the laws require states to set uniform guidelines for child support awards and withhold the wages of an absent parent for payment of child support on behalf of AFDC families who seek assistance from a state enforcement agency. Moreover, many states require immediate wage withholding of child support payments from all noncustodial parents.

Despite vigorous implementation, Child Support Enforcement (CSE) has yielded diminishing dividends on investment. For 1993, $9 billion was collected through CSE, but this cost the government $2.2 billion. Having obtained collections from 2.8 million families removed 241,880 families, or about 10 percent, from AFDC. For that year, 12 percent of AFDC payments were retrieved through CSE. As a welfare prevention strategy, CSE is available to the nonpoor as well as those on welfare, a feature that obscures the limited effectiveness of the program as a welfare reform measure. Thus, of the $9 billion in CSE collections, most—$6.5 billion—came for families not on AFDC; only $2.4 billion was collected for AFDC families. While CSE is a strong performer in overall collections, it barely breaks even with the welfare population, obtaining only $1.08 in collections for every dollar in program costs. In terms of its total impact on public revenues, CSE is actually a loser, in 1993 reporting a $278 million *loss*, so much of which was borne by the federal government that the states received a benefit of $462 million.

During the two decades since its inception, several changes have been introduced to CSE in order to make it more effective, such as requiring establishment of paternity in order to receive AFDC and garnishing wages for absent parents whose payments are in arrears. These have improved CSE, but modestly. For example, from 1978 to 1989, the percent of families with a child support order increased 45 percent; yet this increased the income for poor families only 23 percent. During this period, the percent of families receiving full child support payments increased only 4 percent, while those receiving partial payment increased only 6 percent.

Much of the variation in child support payments can be attributed to social class: wealthier absent parents pay more than poorer parents. Researchers from the Urban Institute found that in 1990, "60 percent of noncustodial fathers in the highest income quartile paid child support for that year" while "only 27 percent of noncustodial fathers in the lowest income quartile paid."[29] Absent fathers who are dropouts who fathered children out of wedlock and who have a new family with children are less likely to pay child support. On the other hand, the formality of family life is an indicator of paying child support. Noncustodial fathers who were married longer, who recently left a family, and who have a child support court order are more likely to pay support. Absent fathers who move out of state are *more* likely to pay support, presumably because they relocate in pursuit of job opportunities.

The most ambitious initiative to enhance child support payments to poor families is Parents' Fair Share (PFS), a pilot project operated from 1992 through 1993. PFS attempted to increase the child support payments of some 4,000 noncustodial parents (97 percent of whom were male) who had support orders for families on AFDC. Attributes of the noncustodial parents recruited for PFS suggested poor candidacy for full and regular payment of child support: nearly two-thirds reported working three months or less during the previous year; almost three-fourths stated their most recent wage was less than $7 per hour; almost 40 percent stated they had gone hungry during the previous three months; nearly one-third had trouble paying rent during the past quarter;

and three-fourths reported having been arrested at least once since their sixteenth birthday. Typically, the noncustodial parent was $4,252 in arrears for child support.[30] PFS was a comprehensive program including employment and training services, peer support groups, enhanced support payment activities, and conflict mediation. Preliminary analysis indicated that the average monthly child support payment for noncustodial parents decreased from $22.95 for those four months before referral to PFS to $22.62 four months afterwards. When those PFS participants who had made no previous support payments were excluded, the amount decreased from $63.80 to $62.89.[31] PFS not only failed to increase child support payments among participants, but has yet to incorporate the costs of mounting the program into outcomes. The PFS experiment illustrates how difficult it is to alter behaviors relating to child support.

Teenage Pregnancy

Out-of-wedlock pregnancies have been on the rise for several years. By 1994, 20 percent of never-married U.S. women had at least one child. Contrary to popular stereotypes, this surge is being led by white women whose out-of-wedlock birth rate rose from 18 to 20 percent between 1992 and 1994. The percentage of African American women having children outside of marriage declined during that period. By 1994, 46.2 percent of never-married black women, 27.1 percent of Hispanic women, and 12.9 percent of white women had given birth.[32] Much of the rise in out-of-wedlock births has been fueled by teenage mothers.

Teenage pregnancy is a powerful indicator of current and future poverty. Approximately one million U.S. teenagers—6.5 percent of all 15- to 19-year-olds—become pregnant in 1994. This translates into the highest teen pregnancy rate in the industrialized world. Eighty percent of teens who gave birth lived in poor or low-income households before they became pregnant. While the rate of teens becoming mothers for the first time has apparently stabilized in recent years (after increasing by 24 percent from 1986 to 1991),[33] teen pregnancy rates remain alarmingly high.

About 85 percent of teen pregnancies are unplanned. Half end in births, about one-third are terminated by abortions, and the rest end in miscarriages. Only about one-third of teen births involve teen fathers; adults father about two-thirds of children born to teenage mothers. According to the Alan Gutmacher Institute, 39 percent of 15-year-old mothers report that the father is 20-years-old or older; for 17-year-olds that number rises to 55 percent.[34]

Overall, a high percentage of births to *all* teenagers are to unmarried women:

- In 1989 out-of-wedlock births accounted for 93 percent of all births to females under age 15 and for 77 percent of all births to teenagers 15 to 17.
- Of teenagers aged 15 to 19, 57 percent of all white births and 92 percent of all African American births were to unmarried teens.[35] In the 20- to 24-year-old age group, as many as 35 percent of all births are to unmarried women, with 25 percent of all white births and 70 percent of all African American births occurring among unmarried mothers. This number represents a significant increase in the out-of-wedlock birth rate for African American women, which soared from about 22 percent of all births in 1960 to almost 68 percent by 1995. The white rate also increased during the same period, going from 2 percent in 1960 to about 19 percent of all births in 1995.
- In 1993, these numbers translated into 450,000 out-of-wedlock births to African American women and 598,000 out-of-wedlock births to white women. As a result, over 56 percent of all African American families in 1990 were headed by single females as compared with 18.8 percent of white households.[36]

Out-of-wedlock births have grave economic consequences. This is especially true because teenage mothers are now more likely to keep their children regardless of their income.[37] The out-of-wedlock birth rate translates into important economic realities. For one, teenage mothers are twice as likely to be poor as nonteen mothers, and a teenage mother earns only half the lifetime wage of a woman who waits until she is 20 to have her first child.[38] Secondly, a strong correlation exists between single, young mothers and high welfare dependency. In 1993, 77 percent of unmarried adolescent mothers became welfare recipients within five years of the birth of their first child.[39] Mothers with children age three and under are at the greatest risk of long-term welfare receipt. In 1989, teenage childbearing cost taxpayers almost $40 billion in AFDC, food stamps, and Medicaid costs.[40] Moreover, teenagers who had been on AFDC were more than twice as likely to be welfare reliant themselves.[41] Thus, high rates of teenage pregnancy increase the likelihood of future welfare dependency.

Policymakers and analysts have long struggled with ways to curb teenage pregnancy. Although many programs have been developed to reduce teenage pregnancy, evaluations of these attempts have yielded mixed results. One early evaluation of a teen pregnancy prevention program was Project Redirection. From 1980 to 1982, 805 AFDC-eligible mothers aged 17 or younger received intensive services to optimize educational, employment, and life-management skills. Evaluation of Project Redirection mothers one, two, and five years after participation in the program was mixed. Of the five outcomes—education, employment, welfare dependence, childbearing, and parenting/child development—the only significant improvement of Project Redirection participants over the control group was the last. Regarding education, Project Redirection teens fared no better than the control group in obtaining a high school diploma or GED certificate. Project Redirection participants were more likely to be employed one year after exiting the program; however, their weekly earnings five years later were only $23 more than those in the control group. Five years later, the household income of the control group exceeded the Project Redirection group by $19. The affect of Project Redirection on welfare dependence was also ambiguous. Two years after participation, 7 percent of Project Redirection teens were on welfare; however, five years later, 10 percent fewer of the control group were on welfare contrasted to the Project Redirection teens. Regarding childbearing, Project Redirection teens reported fewer pregnancies in the first and second years after the program, yet they exceeded the control group in the number of pregnancies, as well as the number of live births five years after the program. Researchers noted that many of the improvements of Project Redirection teens had disappeared after two years, leading "the evaluators to conclude that the program impacts were largely transitory."[42]

Transitory benefits through Project Redirection were to prove superior to those generated by a larger initiative mounted a few years later. From 1989 to 1992 researchers randomly assigned 2,322 poor young mothers, age 16 to 22, to New Chance, a program through which they received health, education, and welfare assistance coordinated by a case manager, or to a control group which received no special services. At the 18-month followup, the experimental group fared worse than the control group in two important respects. First, New Chance participants were more likely to get pregnant again. New Chance mothers were less likely to be using contraception, were more likely to become pregnant, and were more likely to abort their pregnancies than the control group. Second, New Chance mothers were participating less in the labor market. New Chance participants were less likely to be working after entering the program, were earning less, and during the fourth to the sixth months more likely to be on AFDC.[43] To compound matters, New Chance cost $5,073 per participant, excluding child care (if child care were included, $7,646 was spent on each New Chance mother).[44] The apparent failure of these prevention programs illustrates how little policymakers understand both the motivation and the behaviors associated with teenage pregnancy. It also illustrates how little is known about the interpersonal, social and cultural components that support and encourage teenage pregnancy.

Children in Poverty

In 1995, there were 14.7 million poor children in America. Although children under 18 make up 27 percent of the total population, they make up 40 percent of those in poverty. In fact, the poverty rate for children is higher than for any other age group, 20.2 percent in 1995. For children under age 6, the poverty rate was even higher, at 23.7 percent. While high, this rate is eclipsed by the 62 percent poverty rate for children under 6 who are living in a female-headed household with no spouse present. (By comparison, children living in two-parent households have a poverty rate of 11 percent.)[45]

In 1990, 44.8 percent of African American children were poor, or almost one out of every two black children. For Hispanic children the poverty rate was 38.4 percent, up sharply from 28 percent just 11 years earlier.[46] More children fell deeper into poverty during the 1980s. In 1978, 34 percent of all poor families lived below 50 percent of the poverty line; by 1989, that number had risen to 41 percent.[47] The probability of children growing up poor is strongly correlated with family circumstances. The Census Bureau estimated that 61 percent of the children born in 1987 will spend some part of their childhood in single-parent families, which are five times more likely to be poor than a two-parent family.[48]

Although the rate of child poverty is increasing in every racial and ethnic group, white children account for the highest number of children added to the poverty rolls: Poverty rates for white children rose more than 25 percent in the past decade, putting about 1.4 million more children into poverty.[49] In 1991, some 41.2 percent of the children living in poverty were white, and in 1991 more than half (55.4 percent) of poor married couples with children were white.[50]

One major cause of child poverty is the high cost of raising a child. According to the National Commission on Children, the typical family spends about $6,000 a year to raise a child. To reduce child poverty the commission recommended a flat $1,000 refundable tax credit for each child. This proposal would function like the child allowances provided by most Western European nations, and for middle-class families it would be worth three times the current exemption. Because it would function like a negative income tax, poor families would receive the tax credit regardless of whether they filed tax returns.[51]

Elaine Kamarck and William Galston propose the restoration of the child exemption allowance on federal taxes that has eroded since 1948. Kamarck and Galston call for raising the personal exemption to between $6,000 and $7,500 per young dependent, much closer to the actual cost of raising a child. Because this would entail huge costs—about $43 billion in 1990—the increase would have to be targeted in two ways. First, the increased exemption would be targeted at families with young preschool-age children, where the costs of day care substantially reduce a low-income parent's income. Secondly, the exemption would be reduced as family income increases. For families earning $64,000 a year or more (double the median income) only the present exemption would apply.[52]

Poverty and the Elderly

On the surface, the poverty picture for the elderly (once the poorest group in America) seems less bleak. (See Figure 5.2.) In 1959 the poverty rate for those over 65 was 35.2 percent; by 1995 it was reduced to 10.3 percent. Elderly poverty has followed a downward trajectory since 1959, the opposite of the trajectory followed by child poverty. Despite economic gains, almost 3.7 million elderly citizens still live in poverty, with another 2.1 million (about 7 percent of the elderly population) classified as "near poor." Elderly women experience a disproportionate share of poverty: In 1990, elderly women had a higher poverty rate (15 percent) than elderly men (8 percent). Poverty data reveals that the elderly of color experience a greater share of poverty. In 1990 the poverty rate for elderly African Americans was 34 percent; for Hispanics it was 22 percent.[53]

The federal government's estimate of the number of the elderly poor is spurious. Presently, the poverty line is divided into two classifications: families headed by persons under age 65, and families headed by persons 65 or older, the latter group having a lower poverty line. In 1995, the poverty line for a two-person family headed by someone 65 or older was $9,219, exactly $714 lower than the poverty line for younger two-person families. This lower poverty line is based on the belief that the elderly spend less on food and other expenses. Had the poverty line for the elderly been the same as for the rest of the population in 1990, their poverty rate would have *exceeded* the rate for the population as a whole, raising the number of elderly poor by 25 percent.[54]

The Rural Poor

People living in rural areas were more likely to be poor than those living in America's metropolitan areas. In 1995, about 16 percent of rural residents had income levels below the poverty line, a rate only 4.6 percentage points higher than the 20.6 percent poverty rate in central cities. Rural African

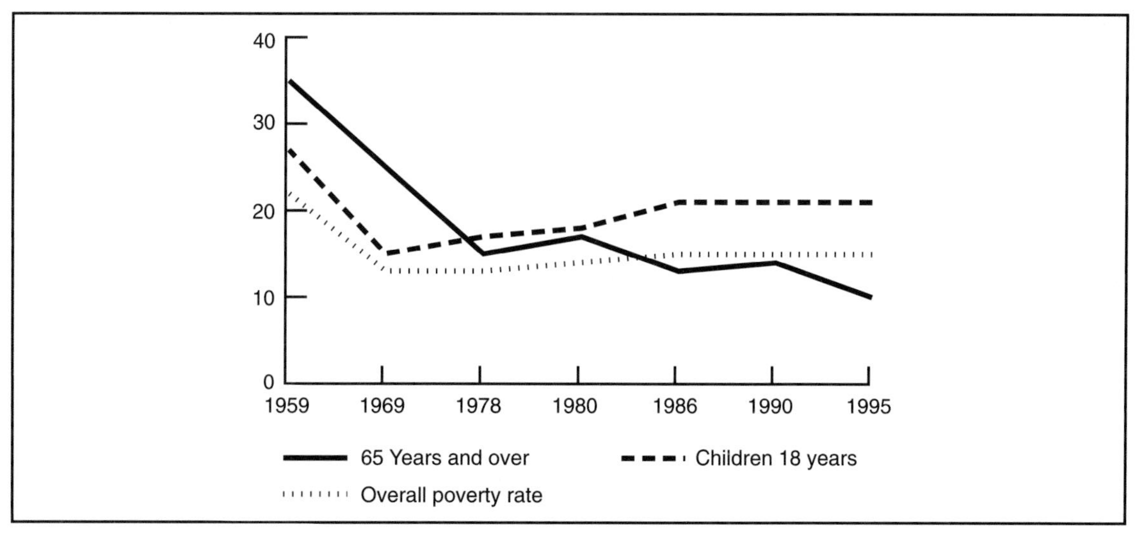

◆ **FIGURE 5.1 Poverty Rates by Age: Selected Years, 1959–1995**

Source: Compiled from U.S. House of Representatives, *Overview of Entitlement Programs: 1992 Green Book* (Washington, DC: US GPO, 1992); and U.S. Census Bureau, "Poverty 1995: Graphs," September 26, 1996. On-line: http://www.census.gov/hhes/poverty/pov95/povage/95.html

Americans did worse in 1987 than those living in central cities: 44 percent of rural African Americans were poor compared with 33 percent of African Americans who lived in central cities. For Hispanics, the elderly, and single female-headed families, the poverty rates in rural areas were as high as they were in central cities.[55]

The composition of the rural poor is different from the poor who live in central cities. For one thing, the proportion of the poor living in two-parent families (61 percent) is much greater than in central cities (42 percent). The rural poor are also more likely than the urban poor to have at least one working family member. In addition, more family heads among the rural poor work full-time, year-round than do central city family heads. The rural poor are also more likely to be elderly than their urban counterparts.[56]

International Comparisons

While it is difficult to compare U.S. poverty rates to those of other countries, an attempt has been made by an international team of researchers known as the Luxembourg Income Study (LIS). The LIS has undertaken an extensive study comparing poverty rates and income levels in several Western nations, including the United States. The LIS study defines poor households as those with incomes below 40 percent of their country's median income (adjusted for family size), which produces a poverty line for the United States that is close to the official poverty threshold used by the Census Bureau.[57]

The results of the LIS study show that poverty rates in the United States are much higher than in other industrialized economies. Comparing poverty rates for whites only[58] (the lowest percentage of those in poverty) reveals interesting results. Specifically, the data shows that for every age group in the United States the poverty rate is significantly higher than it is for the other nations studied, with the gap being greatest for children and the elderly. For example, in 1986 the poverty rate for whites was 9 percent, nearly twice the poverty rate (5 percent) of the other countries.

In 1991, the U.S. poverty rate for children of the pretransfer poor (those people who have not yet received any government income) was 25.9 percent; the postransfer rate was 21.5 percent. In comparison, the pretransfer poverty rate for children in Canada was 22.5 percent; the posttransfer rate was 13.5 percent. The poverty rate for U.S. children ranks highest among the industrialized countries in the LIS study.[59] Table 5.3 lists the pre- and posttransfer rates of children in the 17-nation LIS study.

The United States also scored badly on other social indicators. In infant mortality and mortality for children under age five, the United States ranked nineteenth worldwide; in the percentage of low-birth-weight babies, twenty-eighth; in the percentage of one-year-old children fully immunized against polio, it ranked seventeenth (for nonwhite babies, the United States ranked fifty-sixth). Among industrial nations, the United States ranked fourteenth in spending on elementary and secondary education as a percentage of the gross domestic product; it ranked nineteenth in the number of school-age children per teacher.[60]

INCOME DISTRIBUTION AND INEQUALITY

Today, the net worth of the world's richest 358 people is equal to the combined income of the poorest 45 percent of the world's population—2.3 billion people.[61] In large part, poverty can be understood as inequality in the distribution of income. (Table 5.4 illustrates this unequal distribution and how it has grown in recent years.) According to the Census Bureau, the long-term trend in the United States has been toward increasing income inequality. Census data illustrate that the highest income quintile received 43.8 percent of household income in 1967, rising to 48.7 percent in 1995. Conversely, the bottom quintile saw their share of household income decline from 5.7 percent in 1977 to 3.7 percent in 1995. The middle 60 percent of the income distribution (households with incomes from $14,401 to $65,124 in 1995) saw their share decline from 52.3 percent of household income in 1967 to 47.6 percent in 1995.[62] By examining the distribution of wealth in society, it becomes clearer why poverty rates have not declined and why social welfare programs have only managed to keep poverty relatively constant rather than alleviate it.

One of the prime causes of income disparity has been the low wage and salary structure characteristic of much of the U.S. economy. For example, while household income grew by 2.7 percent from 1994 to 1995, this was the first time it had done so in six years. In effect, tax and investment policies have pushed the nation toward a two-tiered society in which the top 20 percent of wealth holders received 99 percent of the total gain in marketable worth from 1983 to 1989. The bottom 80 percent of the population received only 1 percent. Moreover, between 1983 and 1989 the top 1 percent of income recipients received about one-third of the total increase in real income. The richest 1 percent received 62 percent of the new wealth that was created during that period. As a result, the concentration of wealth reached a new postwar high by 1992.[63] The economic gap between upper- and lower-income American families is now wider than at any time since the Census Bureau began to collect this data in 1947.

According to Edward Wolff, the super-rich (the richest 1 percent of Americans) generally held about one-third of the nation's wealth from 1945 until 1965. However, by 1979 their share of the national wealth had dropped to 22 percent. Since 1979 the share of wealth owned by the super-rich has doubled to 42 percent of the nation's wealth. Viewed another way, the super-rich own 46 percent of all outstanding stock, 54 percent of bonds, 56 percent of business

◆ TABLE 5.3
Children Under Age 6 at Poverty Level and Effect of Government Programs

Country	*Before %*	*After %*
United States (1991)	25.9	21.5
Australia (1989)	19.6	14.0
Canada (1991)	22.5	13.5
Ireland (1997)	30.2	12.0
Israel (1986)	23.9	11.1
U.K. (1986)	29.6	9.9
Italy (1991)	11.5	9.6
Germany (1989)	9.0	6.8
France (1984)	25.4	6.5
Netherlands (1991)	13.7	6.2
Norway (1991)	12.9	4.6
Luxembourg (1985)	11.7	4.1
Belgium (1992)	16.2	3.8
Denmark (1992)	16.0	3.3
Switzerland (1982)	5.1	3.3
Sweden (1992)	19.1	2.7
Finland (1991)	11.5	2.5

NOTE: Dates of latest data used in parentheses; government programs include: child tax credits, day care credits, health care and child support when father's won't pay.
Source: Luxembourg Income Study, 1995 (Luxembourg: LIS, 1995).

◆ TABLE 5.4
Percentage Share of Aggregate Pre-Tax Family Income Received by Each Fifth of Families, and Family Income at Selected Levels, 1950–1995

	Percentage of Aggregate Income Received by					
	Lowest 5th	*Second 5th*	*Middle 5th*	*Fourth 5th*	*Highest 5th*	*Top 5%*
1995	3.7	9.1	15.2	23.4	50.2	26.4
1988	4.3	9.8	15.1	21.4	49.8	25.2
1985	4.4	10.1	15.3	22.0	49.0	23.4
1980	5.4	11.4	16.2	22.6	44.9	19.7
1977	5.7	11.6	16.3	22.7	44.0	18.5
1970	5.4	12.2	17.6	23.8	40.9	15.6
1965	5.2	12.2	17.8	23.9	40.9	15.6
1960	4.8	12.2	17.8	24.0	41.3	15.9
1955	4.8	12.3	17.8	23.7	41.3	16.4
1950	4.5	12.0	17.4	23.4	42.7	17.3

Sources: Compiled from U.S. Bureau of the Census, "Consumer Income 1984," *Current Population Reports*, Series P–60, No. 151, Table 12 (Washington, DC: U.S. Government Printing Office, 1985); and Isaac Shapiro and Robert Greenstein, *Selective Prosperity: Increasing Income Disparities Since 1977* (Washington, DC: Center on Budget and Policy Priorities, July 1991), p. 4; U.S. Census Bureau, "Income 1995," September 26, 1995. On-line: http://www.census.gov/hhes/income/income95/in95agg1.html

equity, 40 percent of non–home real estate, and 53 percent of trusts. The top 10 percent of families as a group account for about 90 percent of stock shares, bonds, trusts, and business equity, and 80 percent of non–home real estate. The bottom 90 percent are responsible for 70 percent of the indebtedness of American households. By the 1980s, America had become the most unequal industrialized country in terms of wealth.[64]

More conservative estimates contend that in 1983 the richest 1 percent of the population held 20 percent of all household wealth. However, more than 75 percent of the wealth of the top 1 percent was held by the top one-half percent, a group whose net worth in 1983 was $2.5 trillion and whose net income was almost $131 billion. In other words, the net worth of the top one-half percent in 1983 was 75 percent of the total net worth of 90 percent of the American population.[65]

Income data also suggest that the center of the middle class is eroding. While the rich are getting richer, real earnings for most Americans have either stagnated or fallen during the past decade. From 1977 to 1990 the median income for the wealthiest 5 percent of the population grew by $12,819 (in 1990 dollars); for the wealthiest 10 percent it grew by $9,256. By contrast, median income for the poorest 40 percent of the population was actually $1,088 *lower* (in 1990 dollars) in 1990 than it was in 1977.[66]

In 1988, the income of the typical poor family fell further below the poverty line than at any time since the Census Bureau began to collect income data in 1959. In particular, 38 percent of poor persons were below 50 percent of the poverty line in 1988; another 28 percent were between half and three-quarters of the poverty line. This compares with 32.9 percent of the poor who were under 50 percent of the poverty line in 1979.[67] In effect, this means that a three-person family that fell below 50 percent of the poverty line in 1988 had a combined yearly income of less than $4,528.

An issue closely related to the skewed distribution of incomes is the skewed distribution of assets. In 1993 the average net worth of all households was $37,587. For African American and Hispanic American households, it was $4,418 and $4,656, respectively. Moreover, while the median net worth for white female householders was $22,099 in 1988, it was $757 and $736, respectively, for African American and Hispanic American female householders. This asset inequity led Washington University's Michael Sherraden to pioneer the concept of "stakeholding," the substitution of assets for income transfers through social policy. Accordingly, Sherraden has proposed the creation of Individual Development Accounts (IDAs) to bolster the assets of the working poor. IDAs would be designated for specific purposes: housing (home equity remains the largest share of a household's networth—44 percent[68]), postsecondary education, self-employment, and retirement. The heart of the IDA concept is that the federal or state government would match the IDA deposits made by people in qualifying low-income families. The amount of the governmental supplement would vary with the activity—say $5 a in governmental match for $1 saved for housing, or $2 in governmental match for $1 saved for retirement.[69] The IDA concept was incorporated in the 1996 welfare reform act.

Tax Policy and Incomes

Federal and state tax policies have played a major role in promoting income inequality. One form of tax inequality is illustrated by a simple case. For example, a family living on $6,000 a year pays roughly 6.4 percent of those resources in federal taxes. As its income increases to $25,000, the share it pays in taxes nearly triples to 16.8 percent. If the same family increased its income twenty-fold to reach $500,000, its tax burden would only double to 32.7 percent. Tax inequality contains other features. For instance, families in the middle fifth of all wage earners pay roughly as much in federal taxes as they did in 1977, but families in the top fifth (and especially in the top 1 percent) pay significantly less. Congressional Budget Office data indicated that in 1993 the richest 1 percent of households would have owed an additional $43 billion in federal taxes if they had paid the same percentage of taxes as in 1977.[70] Finally, the tax burden for at least 90 percent of American families was higher in 1995 than it was in 1977. The combination of federal, state, local, and Social Security taxes equaled about 14 percent of the average family's income in 1960; by 1995 they accounted for more than 25 percent.[71]

The poor often experience the unequal burden of taxation through regressive state and local taxation policies. A 1991 study by Citizens for Tax Justice found that in all but six states, the middle fifth of families pay a larger proportion in state income taxes than do the richest fifth. Similarly, in all but seven states the poorest fifth pays a larger share of its income in state and local taxes than the richest fifth.[72] In 1989, only 19 percent of all state tax revenues were collected through individual and corporate income taxes; 37 percent of state revenues were collected through general and selective sales taxes.[73]

Corporate taxes are generally thought to be progressive because the tax received from the corporation is based on the extent of profit. However, the corporate tax is no longer an important source of federal revenues. In the 1950s and 1960s, corporate taxes provided 25 percent of all federal government revenues. By 1991, that figure was only 7 percent. Because of special exclusions, the corporate tax base has shrunk by more than $175 million a year, reducing 1994 corporate tax revenues by more than $60 billion—enough to fully fund AFDC and food stamps. When Citizens for Tax Justice surveyed 44 major American companies in 1989, all had paid no federal taxes despite a collective total profit of $53.6 billion. In addition, all had reduced their capital spending and reduced their work forces. The money saved went for higher stock dividends, higher pay for CEOs (an average pay hike of 54 percent), and to pay for corporate mergers and acquisitions.[74]

Income taxes are also thought to be progressive. At least theoretically, the rich pay more and the poor less. By contrast, general and selective sales taxes are regressive, being based not on the ability of people to pay but solely on purchases. Therefore, an affluent family that purchases $75 worth of clothing will pay the same amount of sales tax as a poor family, even though that purchase represents a greater share of the poor family's income. As a general rule, the poor—when compared with the wealthy—spend a larger proportion of their income on items subject to sales taxes. Although the tax burden on the poor can be partially relieved by exempting certain necessary items from a sales tax, of the 46 states that had a general sales tax in 1987, only 29 exempted most grocery purchases, while 32 states exempted utilities.[75] Despite attempts by more progressive states to equalize the tax burden, inequities continue. For example, the average poor family in Alabama spent $363 on sales taxes in 1989 compared with $280 in 1980; in Florida, the poor family's sales tax went up from $183 to $442; in Idaho, from $192 to $452; in Kansas, from $192 to $358; in South Carolina, from $276 to $452; and in Texas, from $183 to $390.[76]

Although Americans complain about the burden of taxes, U.S. taxation is relatively light when compared with other industrialized nations. In 1970, governments in all of the major industrial countries claimed roughly 30 percent of their national incomes in taxes. Today, American government at all levels still takes about 30 percent of the Gross Domestic Product (GDP) in taxes, while the average for other industrialized countries has reached nearly 38 percent. America is the lowest taxing country in the G-7 (i.e., United States, Great Britain, Italy, Germany, Canada, France, and Japan). The three levels of government in the United States claim about 34 percent of GDP for public purposes, as compared to an average of about 46 percent for the other G-7 countries.[77]

Income distribution is an important indicator of social equity. In the United States, it reveals a highly stratified economic system in which the rich are getting richer while the poor get poorer. Given this income disparity, it is not surprising that welfare programs are losing the battle to eradicate poverty. Despite the limitations of these programs, without the redistributive function of welfare the economic stratification in American society would worsen. Yet, in the American context, welfare programs have not shown themselves capable of raising significant numbers of people out of poverty. Consequently, conservatives and many liberals argue that the best welfare program is a job.

WORK AND POVERTY

Labor force participation is a key variable in determining poverty. More than two-thirds of the poor in the United States are children, the aged, or the disabled. Apart from these groups—who for the most part are unable to work—poverty is also widespread within the workforce. The number of working individuals (ages 22 to 64) who are poor has escalated sharply, increasing more than 50 percent between 1979 and 1991.[78] Forty-one percent of all poor people now work some time during the year. Moreover, the number of poor people who are employed full-time on a year-round basis stands at 2 million, an increase of more than two-thirds since 1978.[79]

The rise in the number of the working poor is attributable to several factors, chief among them being the replacement of high-paying industrial jobs with low-paying service jobs. Currently, about 20 percent of jobs will not support a worker and two dependents. In 1986, 35 percent of all people who worked part- or full-time earned less than $8,500 a year. Moreover, according to the Joint Economic Committee, about 44 percent of the new jobs created between 1979 and 1985 paid less than $7,400 a year.[80]

This employment trend reflects a clear movement away from higher-paying manufacturing jobs to low-wage service employment. For example, from the 1950s to the 1970s, businesses added about 1.5 million new manufacturing jobs a decade. By the 1980s, corporations had eliminated 300,000 manufacturing jobs. If this trend continues, a million more manufacturing jobs will be eliminated during the 1990s. These statistics, however, grossly underestimate the problem. For example, 33 percent of all workers in the 1950s were employed in primary manufacturing jobs (cars, radios, refrigerators, clothing). Only 17 percent were employed in those industries by 1992, a number that is falling. While manufacturing jobs have declined, retail service jobs have increased by 32.5 percent. By the late 1980s, retail-trade workers, whose ranks are growing, earned $204 per week; manufacturing workers, whose ranks are declining, earned $458 per week.[81]

The absence of adequate employment opportunities contributes to a variety of psychological and physiological problems; therefore, a range of social programs have been deployed to aid Americans who are unemployed or underemployed. The history of employment policy in the United States shows a gradual expansion of programs until the policies of the Reagan administration reduced them sharply. Employment policy has become increasingly important for social welfare, as the popularity of AFDC workfare programs demonstrates. At the same time, the lack of employment opportunity contributes to a growing American underclass.

In a market economy, most people are expected to meet their needs by participating in the labor market. Work provides them income with which to purchase goods and services as well as benefits that provide some security against the costs of health care, sickness, and old age. The labor market in capitalist economies, however, is not well synchronized, thus resulting in the failure of employment to provide the basic needs of all people. As a consequence, many people who could work must depend on social welfare programs for economic support. A little more than half—56 percent—of the poor people in the United States are adults of working age.[82]

The failure of the labor market to meet the economic needs of the population has been the source of important distinctions in employment policy. One set of distinctions focuses on the experiences of workers. People over 16 looking for work are counted by the Department of Labor as unemployed. But the unemployment rate does not assess the adequacy of employment. For example, part-time workers who wish to work full-time are counted as employed, and workers holding jobs below their skill levels are not identified, even though such workers are underemployed. Finally, discouraged workers who simply give up and stop looking for work, relying on other methods to support themselves, do not appear in the unemployment statistics because they are not actively looking for work.

A second set of distinctions relates to economic performance. In a robust economy, businesses start up and close down in significant numbers, leaving workers temporarily out of work until they find other jobs. Such frictional unemployment is considered unavoidable and the cost of a constantly changing economy. Structural unemployment "refers to deeper and longer-lasting maladjustments in the labor market," such as changes in the technical skills required for new forms of production.[83] Because of swings in economic performance, unemployment may be cyclical, as when recessions pitch the rate upward, and because certain groups of workers in certain regions have persistent difficulty finding work owing to an absence of jobs, unemployment is sometimes chronic. Michael Sherraden has examined how these components vary in the composition of the unemployment rate and concludes that structural and frictional factors account for about one-third, the cyclical factor for about one-fourth, and chronic unemployment for about one-half.[84]

These distinctions are important because social welfare is connected directly to the employment experience of Americans. When people are out of work, they frequently rely on welfare benefits to tide them over. Thus, welfare programs are often designed to complement the labor market. This has led some observers to refer to welfare as a "social wage" or, in other words, the amount paid workers by the government through welfare programs when they are not able to participate in the labor market. Logically, much of welfare could be eliminated if well-paying jobs were plentiful, but such has not been the case in the United States. Policymakers have tacitly accepted an unemployment rate of 5–7 percent, which means that at any given time between 5 million and 8 million workers are not employed.[85] Yet in 1978, Congress enacted the Humphrey-Hawkins Full Employment Act, which set an unemployment rate of 3 percent—equivalent to frictional unemployment—as a national goal. Since then, many government programs to aid the unemployed, underemployed, and discouraged workers have been reduced or eliminated, leaving many Americans dependent on welfare programs for support.

Moreover, absence of employment opportunity contributes to other social dysfunctions. Research by Dr. M. Harvey Brenner shows that a seemingly small increase in the unemployment rate is associated with an increase in several social problems. For example, during the 1973–1974 recession, the unemployment rate increased by 14.3 percent and was associated with the pathologies shown in Table 5.5. Brenner calculated that the combination of the 1973–1974 increase in the unemployment rate, the decrease in real per capita income, and an increase in the business failure rate was related to "an overall increase of more than 165,000 deaths [from cardiovascular disease] over a ten-year period (the greatest proportion of which occurs within three years)." Overall, the total economic, social, and health care costs of this seemingly slight increase in unemployment came to $24 billion.[86]

The Minimum Wage

The low minimum wage is yet another factor that has increased the ranks of the working poor. Currently, an estimated 3.7 million hourly workers make the minimum wage; another 7.7 million hourly workers earned less than the $5.15 minimum wage before it was raised in 1997.[87]

The minimum wage covers about 90 percent of all nonsupervisory workers. In 1950 the minimum wage brought a worker to 56 percent of the average

◆ **TABLE 5.5**
Consequences of Increases in Unemployment

Pathological Indicator	*Percentage Increase Due to Rise in Unemployment Increase*	*Rise in Incidence of Pathology*
Total mortality	2.3	45,936
Cardiovascular mortality	2.8	28,510
Cirrhosis mortality	1.4	430
Suicide	1.0	270
Population in mental hospitals	6.0	8,416
Total arrests	6.0	577,477
Arrests for fraud and embezzlement	4.0	11,552
Assaults reported to police	1.1	7,035
Homicide	1.7	403

Source: Reprinted from M. Harvey Brenner, *Estimating the Effects of Economic Change on National Health and Social Well-Being* (Washington, DC: U.S. Government Printing Office, 1984), p. 2.

wage. Throughout the 1950s and 1960s (as can be seen from Table 5.6), the minimum wage hovered between 44 and 56 percent of the average wage. However, by 1980 the minimum wage had fallen to 46.5 percent of the average wage, and in 1988 it dropped even further to 35.7 percent. Overall, the minimum wage dropped 29 percent from 1979 to 1996. Even with the increase in the minimum wage to $5.15 an hour in 1997, it equaled only 42 percent of the average wage, bringing a family of three to 83 percent of the poverty line[88] (considerably lower than the 120 percent of the poverty level reached by the minimum wage in 1968).[89] Moreover, the minimum wage would have to be $6.07 (almost $1.00 higher than its current level) to have the purchasing power as it did in the 1970s.[90]

For workers stuck with a $3.35 an hour minimum wage that was frozen from 1981 to 1990, the drop in earnings relative to the median income was significant, especially in light of the 48 percent jump

◆ **TABLE 5.6**
Value of the Minimum Wage, Selected Years

Year	*Percent of Poverty Line For a Family Of Three*	*Percent of Average Wage*	*Value of the Minimum Wage, 1995 Dollars*	*Minimum Wage Nominal Dollars*
1955	73	44	$3.94	$0.75
1960	88	48	4.75	1.00
1965	103	51	5.59	1.25
1968	120	56	6.49	1.60
1970	107	50	5.92	1.60
1975	101	46	5.71	2.10
1980	98	47	5.76	3.10
1985	81	39	4.76	3.35
1988	73	36	4.33	3.35
1989	71	35	4.13	3.35
1990	79	38	4.44	3.80
1993	75	39	4.50	4.25
1995	72	37	4.25	4.25
1997	83	42	NA	5.15

Source: Adapted from Isaac Shapiro, *The Minimum Wage and Job Loss* (Washington, DC: Center on Budget and Policy Priorities, 1988), p. 3; U.S. Census Bureau, "Income 1995," September 26, 1996; and Center on Budget and Policy Priorities, "Assessing the $5.15 an Hour Minimum Wage," March 1996. On-line: http://epn.org/cpbb/cbwage.html.

in the cost of living during that period. This low minimum wage is especially troubling because some 18 million Americans—including 8 million children—live in a household with a working family member whose income remains below the poverty line.[91] The average share of household income earned by a minimum wage worker is 50 percent; 36 percent of minimum wage workers are sole breadwinners for their households.[92]

Despite its meager benefits, the minimum wage has been criticized by both conservatives and liberals. Looking at the persistently high unemployment rate among younger workers—about 35 percent of African American teenagers[93]—some conservatives have argued that the minimum wage deters employers from hiring unproven workers. Lowering (or eliminating) the minimum wage would encourage employers to make more jobs available to the disadvantaged. On the other hand, liberals have contended that the minimum wage is far from adequate. At its present level, a worker employed 40 hours per week would earn approximately $9,888 per year, $2,270 below the 1995 poverty line of $12,158 for a family of three. The controversy surrounding the minimum wage is compounded by the fact that a portion of the service industry—notably convenience stores and fast food franchises—have taken advantage of the large number of younger workers available to hire them on a part-time basis for limited periods of time in order to avoid the expenses of paying benefits associated with full-time employment. In this instance, an industry has clearly profited from the use—or abuse—of young workers who rely on the minimum wage.[94]

Underemployment and Unemployment

Another major factor determining poverty is under- and unemployment. Between 1981 and 1986, 10.8 million workers lost their jobs because of plant shutdowns, layoffs, or other forms of job termination. Five million of these workers had been at their jobs for at least three years.[95] From 1979 to 1984 the Department of Labor conducted a special study of 5.1 million workers whose jobs were abolished between January 1979 and January 1984. This study reported that in 1984, 40 percent of these workers were still unemployed or out of the workforce. Of the remainder, close to half were employed at either part-time jobs or jobs with lower weekly earnings than they had previously received, and the majority experienced significant economic losses for a lengthy time after their jobs were terminated.[96]

Unemployment benefits reflect the nature of a selective recession that is disproportionately felt by the poor and lower-middle classes. Throughout most of the 1970s, the majority of unemployed workers received unemployment benefits each month. For example, 75 percent of the jobless received benefits in 1975. By 1986, the percentage of unemployed workers receiving benefits had dropped to the lowest levels in the history of the program, with only 32.9 percent of jobless workers receiving benefits in a given month. Although the number of those covered under unemployment insurance rose slightly to 36.8 percent by 1990, 4.3 million of the 6.9 million unemployed workers were not receiving benefits.[97]

As unemployment coverage has declined, so too have the benefits. In 1986, the total insurance benefits were 59 percent lower than they were in 1976 (after adjusting for inflation). These figures are complicated by the fact that from 1980 to 1986, the number of long-term unemployed (those looking for work for more than a year) rose from 820,000 to 1.2 million. These factors, coupled with federal budget cuts in 1981 that largely eliminated unemployment benefits for those unemployed for more than six months, contributed to the falling rates of unemployment coverage and the subsequent increase in poverty rates for the unemployed.

The economic data suggest that the private sector is not presently creating the kinds of jobs necessary to raise large numbers of low-income workers above the poverty line. In order to remedy this situation, the Progressive Policy Institute (PPI) has called for a nonpoverty working wage that would be sufficient to enable any full-time, year-round worker to support a family above the poverty line. This proposal calls for restructuring the Earned Income Tax Credit (EITC) so that, in combination with food stamps, the poor working family would be lifted out of poverty. According to the PPI, this proposal would cost $7.8 billion ($3.8 billion for increased EITC benefits and an additional $4 billion to accommodate more food stamp beneficiaries), or less than one-half percent of the 1996 federal debt.[98]

Job Training Programs

The failure of the labor market to provide adequate employment opportunities to large numbers of workers led to a series of governmental efforts to better prepare the unemployed and underemployed. The first of these was the Manpower Development and Training Act (MDTA) of 1962. Intended as a program to assist workers displaced by technological and economic change, MDTA was also expected to serve the disadvantaged when the Office of Economic Opportunity was established in 1964. As one of the primary weapons in the newly declared War on Poverty, the MDTA grew rapidly, from $93 million in 1964 to $358 million in 1973. In 1973, 119,600 people were enrolled in MDTA. Still, the program was only one of several War on Poverty job programs to aid the disadvantaged, including the Neighborhood Youth Corps (for high school students), the Job Corps (for young adults), and the Work Incentive Program (for AFDC recipients).[99]

By the mid–1970s the proliferation and cost of job training programs prompted the Nixon administration and Congress to consolidate MDTA and other job training programs under the Comprehensive Employment and Training Act (CETA) of 1973. In addition to consolidating federal job training programs, CETA also decentralized program responsibilities for local governments. By 1978, CETA was budgeted at $11.2 billion and enrolled 3.9 million persons[100] (by comparison, the unemployed numbered 6.2 million in 1978).[101] Yet the nation's most ambitious program for contending with joblessness soon became the center of controversy. The recession of the 1970s placed financial burdens on local government, and budget-limiting acts, such as California's Proposition 13 (1978), capped the fiscal capacity of local government. Consequently, strong incentives were created for local governments to use the CETA program to fill civil service positions left vacant because of the retrenchment by local government. Because many of these jobs required work experience, CETA became a means by which a local government could subsidize its personnel budget—often by hiring relatively skilled persons and neglecting the chronically unemployed. This inflamed white-collar labor organizations, which saw civil service rosters being decimated while state and municipal employees were replaced by CETA workers. Moreover, Ronald Reagan, governor of California during the Proposition 13 revolt, was angry that the federal government would subsidize local government activities that the taxpayers had determined to be excessive. As president, Reagan would move quickly to clip the CETA program. Finally, many critics—both conservatives and liberals—charged that the chronically unemployed were often given dead-end, make-work jobs that failed to integrate them fully into the private sector.

Superseding CETA, the Job Training and Partnership Act (JTPA) of 1982 attempted to focus training on the hard-core unemployed in order to make them economically self-sufficient through private sector employment. Approximately 600 Private Industry Councils were created locally to synchronize training and job opportunities. Initially, the Reagan administration allocated $2.8 billion for the first year of JTPA, approximately three-quarters of what had been spent on CETA in 1980.[102] But appropriations were reduced in later years even though the unemployment rate rose above 7 percent. In 1992, appropriations for JTPA were approximately $1.7 billion. During 1990, 565,200 enrollees were terminated from JTPA; of these, 55 percent found private employment at an average hourly wage of $5.54,[103] on an annual basis considerably below the poverty level for a family of four.

Dual Labor Markets

Despite the large enrollments in government employment programs and the substantial expenditures of public funds, the difficulty of elevating people out of poverty through job training programs led several scholars to examine the nature of the work that participants are expected to find. Labor market analysts such as Peter Doeringer, Michael Piore, and David Gordon found that "a group of low-wage, and often marginal, enterprises and a set of casual, unstructured job opportunities where workers with employment disadvantages tend to find work" characterized job seekers and employers participating in job training programs.[104] These researchers reasoned that the segmentation of the labor market—into better jobs versus disadvantaged jobs—explained much of the problem at the root of government employment programs.

According to Piore, the labor market can be divided into two segments, or "dual labor markets"—a primary labor market and a secondary labor market:

> The primary market offers jobs which possess several of the following traits: high wages, good working conditions, employment stability and job security, equity and due process in the administration of work rules, and chances for advancement. The other, secondary sector, has jobs which, relative to those in the primary sector, are decidedly less attractive. They tend to involve low wages, poor working conditions, considerable variability in employment, harsh and often arbitrary discipline, and little opportunity to advance. The poor are confined to the secondary labor market.[105]

Piore noted that to the extent that employment is expected to solve the poverty problem, the trick is to see that the poor "gain access to primary employment."[106]

The magnitude of the secondary labor market has been explored by researchers who calculated that 36.2 percent of workers in 1970 fell into the secondary labor market, a modest increase over the number in 1950, 35 percent.[107] By the 1980s, however, two factors increased the proportion of workers in the secondary labor market. First, membership in labor unions—the best security for nonprofessional workers—fell from 30.8 percent of nonagricultural workers in 1970 to about 17 percent in 1996, leaving millions of workers vulnerable to the employment insecurity typical of the secondary labor market.[108] Second, a higher proportion of the new jobs created were in the service sector of the economy, which consists largely of secondary labor market jobs. Between 1979 and 1985, 44 percent of new jobs paid less than $7,400 per year.[109]

For workers in the secondary labor market, social welfare is an important source of support, whether this is in the form of income payments, such as AFDC, or in-kind benefits, such as Medicaid and food stamps. Yet, the relationship between public assistance and the secondary labor market is a poor fit. Generally, no state provides benefits above the poverty level, even when the cash equivalent of food stamps is added to welfare benefits.[110] Consequently, most families have strong incentives to work in order to supplement their meager welfare benefits. The relatively punitive treatment of earnings under welfare programs encourages families to under report their income from work. The circularity of the dilemma is as frustrating for administrators of public assistance programs as it is for public assistance beneficiaries, especially those with children, who often resort to deception for purposes of survival. In an investigation of income sources of AFDC recipients, Kathryn Edin and Christopher Jencks found that low AFDC benefits produced a perverse consequence: Virtually every recipient supplemented AFDC with other income sources, but only one in four reported any portion of this to welfare authorities.[111]

The Underclass

The current discussion of the underclass was started in the 1980s by journalist Ken Auletta, who descriptively identified four groups that comprise the underclass: (1) the "passive poor," usually those dependent on welfare; (2) hostile "street predators," often dropouts and addicts; (3) "hustlers," or opportunists, who do not commit violent crimes; and (4) "traumatized" alcoholics, shopping bag ladies, and casualties of deinstitutionalization.[112] In the late 1980s, William Julius Wilson revived the term and defined the underclass as:

> [a] heterogeneous grouping of families and individuals who are outside of the mainstream of the American occupational system. Included . . . are individuals who lack training and skills and either experience long-term unemployment or are not members of the labor force, individuals who are engaged in street crime and other forms of aberrant behavior, and families that experience long-term spells of poverty and/or welfare dependency.[113]

Another definition of the *underclass* is offered by Erol Ricketts and Isabel Sawhill, who define it as a subpopulation characterized by a cluster of behaviors and attitudes that are considered outside of current middle-class social norms.[114] In *The Black Underclass*,

Douglas Glasgow attributed the existence of an underclass to "structural factors found in market dynamics and institutional practices, as well as the legacy of racism, [that] produce and then reinforce the cycle of poverty and, in turn, work as a downward pull toward underclass status."[115] These groups share characteristics that, according to Robert Reischauer of the Brookings Institution, differentiate them from "lower-class" status, with its connotation of merely being further down on the socioeconomic ladder.[116]

The definitions of the *underclass* fall into two broad categories: those used by the structuralists (e.g., Wilson) and those used by the behavioralists (e.g., Sawhill, Ricketts). The structuralists view the underclass as emerging from broad societal forces that cause neighborhoods to deteriorate and economic opportunities to evaporate. For example, according to Wilson, the emergence of an underclass is related to changing employment opportunities (reduced demand for low-skilled labor), declines in African American marriage rates, and selective outmigration (the movement of the African American middle class away from the urban ghettoes). This sociological concept is used as a referent for disadvantaged persons living in census tracks with abnormally high rates of dysfunctional family and employment conditions. The structuralists argue that those left behind in the ghetto are outside the economic opportunity structure, and as such, structural poverty generates cultural poverty. The behavioralists, on the other hand, focus on individuals and categorize them on the basis of their behaviors.[117]

A more precise definition of the term *underclass* is hard to come by, and this leads to a set of difficult conceptual problems. Specifically, the absence of a clear operational definition for the *underclass* results in its taking on an air of subjectivity. In other words, although people may not be able to define the *underclass*, they believe that they know it when they see it. For example, proponents of the underclass concept point to the "wilding" of New York teenagers who savagely beat and raped a female jogger in Central Park, an event replicated when a gang of Boston youths raped and murdered a young mother.[118] Moreover, they point to gang killings in Los Angeles, which soared 69 percent during the first eight months of 1990.[119] They also point to gang-related murders in the nation's capital, which reached a three-year high and prompted the police department's spokesperson to quip, "at the rate we're going the next generation is going to be extinct."[120] But while these events make for interesting journalism, the ambiguity of what is meant by the term *underclass* produces problems for policymakers trying to operationalize the term in order to develop social programs for this group.

Despite problems in defining the underclass, relevant social science research has shown that this group increased from 1970 to 1980. Moreover, some researchers have estimated that in 1980 between 1 and 2 million people could be characterized as members of the underclass. According to Ricketts and Sawhill, who are considered to have done some of the best empirical research on the subject, the definition of underclass applies to 1 percent of the American population, roughly one-thirteenth of all people living under the poverty line. Using Ricketts and Sawhill's guidelines, more than 2.4 million people would be classified as an underclass in 1992.[121]

The seriousness of the underclass phenomenon was underscored in research conducted by David Ellwood and Mary Jo Bane. In an examination of the Michigan Panel Study of Income Dynamics, Bane and Ellwood discovered that, although most people are in poverty for short periods of time, a significant number have protracted spells in poverty. Significantly, 18 percent of poverty is long-term, and almost 60 percent of the people who are poor at any given time are experiencing a long-term spell of poverty. When the costs of this poverty are borne by minority families who are disproportionately poor, the consequences are disastrous. Since 1970, poor urban families have been more likely to have poor neighbors, evidence of a continuing deterioration in the socioeconomic condition of poor communities that makes it increasingly difficult to alleviate the pathology of "ghetto culture."[122]

SOME THEORETICAL FORMULATIONS ABOUT POVERTY

A question that has plagued contemporary social scientists is, "Why have African Americans remained consistently poor when other groups, such as the

Irish, Jews, and Poles, have been able to climb out of poverty?" The attempts made to answer this question have run the gamut from the alleged genetic deficiency of African Americans to the difficulty of African Americans in assimilating because of their color. Cultural, racial, and family explanations have all been touted as the correct answer at some point over the past 30 years.

One of the most controversial theories offered to explain black poverty was offered by Daniel Patrick Moynihan, now a U.S. senator from New York. In his 1969 book, *Maximum Feasible Misunderstanding*, Moynihan stated his argument:

> At the heart of the deterioration of the fabric of Negro society is the deterioration of the Negro family. It is the fundamental source of weakness for the Negro community at the present time. . . . The white family has achieved a high degree of stability. By contrast, the family structure of lower class Negroes is highly unstable, and in many centers is approaching a complete breakdown! . . . the circumstances of the Negro community in recent years have been probably getting worse, not better . . . the fundamental problem, in which this is most clearly the case, is that of family structure . . . so long as this structure persists, the cycle of poverty and disadvantage will continue to repeat itself. . . . A national effort is required that will give a unity of purpose to the many activities of the federal government in this area, directed to a new kind of goal: the establishment of a stable Negro family structure.[123]

Moynihan argued that the bonds holding the black family together had been ruptured both during slavery and at the beginning of the twentieth century, when the large migration of African Americans to the urban areas of the North occurred.[124] Prompted by the intense debate over the Moynihan report, Herbert Guttman demonstrated that the black family was not profoundly disrupted either during slavery or urban migration; instead, the problems of the contemporary African American family were associated with modern forces.[125] In any case, Moynihan's perspective situated the problem of black poverty within the fabric of African American family life. For Moynihan, the problem of poverty lay in the matriarchal African American family: The supposed emasculation of the black male by a strong matriarch coupled with the absence of powerful black men as role models for youngsters contributed to an identity crisis for male teenagers, a problem that would play itself out in terms of crime and violence. Outraged by Moynihan's analysis, African American leaders launched an attack on his pseudopsychoanalytic explanation of black family life. What emerges from the speculation about the causes of black poverty is an understanding that its causes are complex and rooted in the social, political, and economic realities of contemporary America. In some measure, Moynihan's theories grew out of an earlier belief that America's urban landscape was dominated by a culture of poverty.

The Culture of Poverty

Another group, the culture of poverty (COP) theorists, maintain that poverty and, more specifically, poverty traits are transmitted intergenerationally. These theorists, led by Edward Banfield and Oscar Lewis, argued that poverty is a way of life passed on from one generation to the next in a self-perpetuating cycle. According to this theory, the COP transcends regional, rural/urban, and national differences, and everywhere shows striking similarities in family structure, interpersonal relations, time orientation, value systems, and patterns of spending.[126]

Oscar Lewis maintains that the COP flourishes in societies where: there is a cash economy, wage labor, and production for profit; there is a high rate of under- and unemployment for unskilled workers; low wages are common; there is a failure to provide low-income groups with social, political, and economic organization, either on a voluntary basis or by governmental imposition; a bilateral kinship system rather than a unilateral one exists; and a set of values held by the dominant class stresses the accumulation of wealth and property, the possibility of upward mobility, thrift, and the idea that low economic status results from personal inadequacy.

According to Lewis, the COP is characterized by hopelessness, indifference, alienation, apathy, and a lack of effective participation in or integration into the social and economic fabric of society; a present-tense time orientation; cynicism toward and mistrust of those in authority; strong feelings of marginality, helplessness, dependence, and inferiority; a high incidence of maternal deprivation, orality, and a weak ego structure; confusion of sexual identification; lack of impulse control and the inability to defer gratification; a sense of resignation and fatalism; a widespread belief in male superiority; a high tolerance for psychological pathology of all kinds; a provincialism coupled with little sense of history; the absence of childhood as a specially protected and prolonged state, and thus early initiation into free sexual unions or consensual marriages; a high incidence in the abandonment of wives and children; a matriarchal family structure containing an emphasis on family solidarity that is never achieved because of sibling rivalry and competition for maternal affection; a proclivity toward authoritarianism; and a minimum level of organization beyond the nuclear or extended family, a low level of community organization, and a strong sense of territoriality.

Adherents believe that simply being poor does not initiate one into the culture of poverty. Banfield and Lewis both argue that most people who experience poverty through the loss of a breadwinner, involuntary unemployment, or illness are able to overcome their impoverishment. The poverty that these people endure is not the squalid, degrading, and self-perpetuating kind found among COP victims. Lewis suggests that only 20 percent of those living under the poverty line are actually ensconced in the culture of poverty. Nevertheless, according to Banfield, those who are in the culture of poverty will be poor regardless of their external circumstances, and improvements in their environment will only superficially affect their poverty.

Some opponents of the COP argue that this theoretical orientation diverts attention from the real factors that cause poverty. These critics maintain that an unjust society encourages the attitudes that Lewis and Banfield have observed. Other critics argue that many of Lewis's observations about the COP are also true of the middle and upper classes. For example, the inability to defer gratification underlies many credit card purchases. Free sexual unions and consensual (nonlegal) marriages are a common occurrence among the middle classes; they are also well publicized in Hollywood. A lack of community and provincialism are earmarks of the modern suburb as well as of the slum. The inability to achieve family solidarity, and feelings of indifference, helplessness, alienation, and dependence probably afflict middle-class people as often as they do the slum dweller. Consequently, either a culture of poverty does not exist or it has been usurped by the middle classes in the same way that marijuana and jazz have been.

Eugenics and Poverty

Eugenic theories, based on a belief that poverty is grounded in genetic inferiority, have surfaced periodically as plausible explanations for poverty, crime, and disease. In 1877 Richard Dugdale wrote *The Jukes*, a study of the New York penal system that found that crime, pauperism, and disease were transmitted intergenerationally and were closely related to prurient behavior, feeblemindedness, intemperance, and mental disorder.[127] A second major book of the Eugenics Movement was Henry Goddard's *The Kallikak Family*, an account of a Revolutionary War soldier who had an affair with a feebleminded servant girl before his marriage to a "respectable woman."[128] As part of his analysis, Goddard meticulously listed the disreputable descendants of the servant girl and compared them with the respectable achievers who emerged from the wife's descendants. Dugdale's and Goddard's findings were reaffirmed by similar pseudoscientific research that further established poverty as an inherited characteristic. Generations of students were taught the dogma of eugenics.

The Eugenics Movement went into remission when it became obvious to what extent racial and genetic theories had formed the groundwork for Hitler's genocidal policies. However, the movement reemerged after close to 40 years—albeit in a modified form—with the publication in 1969 of Arthur Jensen's article "How Much Can We Boost IQ and Scholastic Achievement."[129] Jensen concluded that compensatory education was doomed to failure because 80 percent of intelligence (as measured by intelligence tests) was inherited. He pointed to the fact that the average IQ scores of African Americans were 15 points lower than the scores of their white counterparts, and concluded therefore that money spent on compensatory education was wasted.[130]

Jensen's theories were taken one step further by William Shockley, a Nobel laureate in physics who became interested in genetics in 1974. Shockley advocated paying the "unfit poor" (those who paid no income taxes) $1,000 for each point they fell below an IQ of 100, if they agreed to be sterilized. The money they received would be placed in a trust fund and dispensed to them throughout their lives.[131] To encourage the propagation of brilliant people like himself, Shockley invited other Nobel Laureates to follow his lead and contribute to a sperm bank.[132]

Richard Herrnstein, a Harvard psychologist and a colleague of Shockley and Jensen, claimed that income and wealth are distributed among Americans on the basis of their abilities, which, in the final analysis, are related to their IQ. Herrnstein maintained that America was becoming a "hereditary meritocracy," and thought that the most capable citizens should receive the greatest rewards, which would serve as incentives to them to take the responsibility of leadership.[133]

A recent book rekindling the eugenics movement was Richard Herrnstein and Charles Murray's *The Bell Curve*.[134] In it, they argue that socioeconomic inequality in the United States is due not to the effects of capitalism or institutionalized racism but to lack of genetic intelligence. Armed with statistics, tables and charts, Herrnstein and Murray try to demonstrate that those in the lower socioeconomic strata have lower intelligence, which is reflected in lower IQ scores. Intelligence, they argue, determines success. Much of their discussion focuses on stereotyped groups such as unwed teenage mothers and chronically unemployed males. Herrnstein and Murray claim that whites, and in particular, white males, score higher on intelligence tests,[135] which explains why they control so much of society's institutions. Conversely, the poor have been bypassed by economic opportunity because of lower intelligence. Hence, affirmative action programs run counter to intellectual meritocracy, and expending large sums of money to educate and improve the lot of the poor is wasted given their innate cognitive deficiencies.

Herrnstein and Murray's solution lies in creating policies that better the lives of the poor by removing governmental interference, thus restoring social control to neighborhoods and municipalities. This includes eliminating bureaucratic mechanisms that complicate the lives of the poor. They argue that the best way for society to raise the mean IQ is for smarter, not duller, women to have children. They also argue against what they see as a governmental policy that encourages "the wrong women" to have children.

The scholarship in the *The Bell Curve* and the bias of its authors have been subject to attacks from a wide range of the scientific and educational community. Herrnstein and Murray's arguments have been compared to those of Nazi eugenicists.[136] Critics also note that they exaggerate IQ as a predictor of job performance by attributing inaccurate validities to IQ test scores and by substituting hypotheticals for reality. Stephen Jay Gould compares the arguments of Herrnstein and Murray to those of Joseph-Arthur, comte de Gobineau, the "father of all modem racist science."[137]

The theories of Shockley, Jensen, Herrnstein, and Murray have been repudiated by scores of educators, psychologists, sociologists, and anthropologists. Critics claim that IQ scores do not guarantee success in life, and in fact, many incarcerated criminals have high IQ scores. Moreover, several studies have shown that compensatory education does significantly raise IQ scores.[138] Finally, a variety of studies have found that IQ tests are biased in favor of middle-class and upper-socioeconomic-level students. In short, assertions about genetic inferiority fail to hold up under scrutiny.

The Radical School and Poverty

Radicals define *poverty* as the result of exploitation by the ruling or dominant class. According to Marxians, one function of poverty is to provide capitalists with an army of surplus laborers who can be used to depress the wage structure of society. For example, applying the law of supply and demand to the wage marketplace means that employers can use an oversupply of workers to pay low wages in the knowledge that there will always be an abundance of takers. Moreover, when there is an oversupply of labor, employers can more easily threaten recalcitrant workers with dismissal because each worker is aware of the competition for his or her job. The oversupply of workers is inextricably linked to the fabric of poverty and, as such, the threat of poverty becomes a way to discipline the labor force and thereby force concessions from it.

A second function of poverty is to increase the prestige of the middle class by providing a class directly below it. As long as an underclass exists, the middle class has a group it can feel superior to. The superiority felt by the middle class encourages a bond with the upper class around the issue of social stability because both classes fear the loss of their social position. The existence of the poor thus obscures the class tensions between the upper and the middle class over the issue of resource distribution. In that sense, an efficient way to defuse a conflict between two potential enemies is to create a third enemy (the poor), one that appears to threaten both parties.

According to David Gil, poverty can also be understood in view of status and resource allocations and the division of labor.[139] Most developed societies must perform several universal processes. For instance, they must develop resources—symbolic, material, life-sustaining, and life-enhancing goods and services. They must also develop a division of labor, which is usually related to the allocation of statuses, as well as assign individuals or groups to specific tasks related to developing, producing, or distributing the resources of a society. The division of labor is used as the basis for assigning statuses to individuals and groups; that is, the more highly a society prizes the function the individual or group is expected to perform, the higher the status and the reward that group or individual will accrue. By manipulating the division of labor, a society is able to assign individuals to specific statuses within the total array of statuses and functions available. These status allocations involve corresponding roles and prerogatives.

Complementing the assignment of status roles is the issue of rights distribution. Higher-status roles implicitly demand greater compensation than lower-status roles, and such rewards come by way of the distribution of rights. Higher-status groups are rewarded by a substantial and liberal distribution of specific rights to material and symbolic resources, goods, and services through general entitlements. Conversely, lower-status groups are denied these resources by formal and informal constraints. The entire process is couched in the language of the marketplace. This form of status and goods allocation is rationalized by a belief in the omniscient quality of the marketplace, and so as to make it appear rational, the market is mystically endowed with an internal sense of logic. The implicit ideology is so well masked that it often appears fail-safe, and its rationality is rarely questioned.

Although it often appears to do so inequitably, society must allocate goods and statuses because all valuable resources are finite, with their worth judged by the available quantity. For example, gold is a valuable commodity because its quantity is limited. In that sense, opportunity is a valuable commodity because it, too, is limited. Harvard University is prestigious in part because it accepts only a limited number of students yearly, and its policy of admissions is thought to be stringent. If Harvard University adopted an open-door admissions policy, one might expect its prestige to plummet. High-status occupations or social positions are also a scarce commodity and are thus socially distributed.

Nevertheless, the question remains as to how statuses are distributed and how the division of labor is determined. In American society, both the division of labor and status allocation—and their by-product, the distribution of rights—are differentially determined by sex, race, and social class. In large part, those occupying high-status positions determine their successors and, more often than not, the heirs apparent belong to the same social class.

Radicals argue that poverty is a logical outgrowth of an inequitable system of resource, status, and rights distribution. Those who live in poverty have been assigned specific social tasks and roles, and the status of the group often corresponds to the nature of the task. Through the assignment of status, role, and rights distribution, societies attempt to reproduce themselves and the ideologies that justify their existence. In the end, the main job of any society is to reproduce itself and, in doing so, it reproduces the relations of production and power.

Although on the surface this argument appears to explain social inequity, it does not necessarily explain poverty. For instance, is it possible for status allocation to be based on the need of a society to reproduce itself, and yet for that society to obviate poverty? Adherents of the radical approach argue that so long as society reproduces itself on the basis of the private ownership of the means of production, poverty will be omnipresent. On the other hand, many radical theorists argue that even though status must be allocated, poverty can still be eliminated through the equitable distribution of goods and resources. But although it may be possible to eradicate poverty and, at the same time, allocate status, most radicals believe that it cannot be done under the aegis of capitalism. According to radical critics, the social function of the poor cannot be altered without fundamentally rearranging the social fabric of American society. In short, poverty is an immutable reality in a society marked by discrimination and the inequitable distribution of resources.

A NOTE ON STRATEGIES DEVELOPED TO COMBAT POVERTY

Social scientists and policy analysts have identified three basic strategies for combating poverty. The first strategy, used by Lyndon Johnson in the War on Poverty and Great Society programs, was an attempt to apply a curative approach to the problems of the poor. The curative strategy aims to end chronic and persistent poverty by allowing the poor to become self-supporting through bringing about changes in their personal lives as well as in their environment. By breaking the self-perpetuating cycle of poverty, the poor are initiated into the employment marketplace, and, later, the middle class. The goal of the curative approach is rehabilitation rather than relief, and its target is the causes of poverty, not the consequences.

The second antipoverty strategy is the alleviative approach. This perspective is best exemplified by public assistance programs that attempt to ease the suffering of the poor rather than ameliorate the causes of poverty.

The third approach is the preventive strategy, best exemplified by the nation's social insurance programs such as Social Security. In this approach, people are required to save money to insure their future against accidents, sickness, death, old age, unemployment, and disability. The preventive strategy sees the State as a large insurance company whose umbrella shelters its productive members against the vicissitudes of life.

In 1958, John Kenneth Galbraith, later to become one of John F. Kennedy's principal economic advisers, wrote *The Affluent Society*. In this landmark book, Galbraith identified two kinds of poverty: case poverty and area poverty. According to Galbraith, case poverty was a product of personal deficiency, or deficit in human capital. Area poverty was related to economic problems endemic to a region. "Pockets of poverty" or "depressed areas" resulted from a lack of industrialization in a region or the inability of an area to adjust to technological change. This kind of poverty was a function of the changing nature of the marketplace.[140]

One example of a case poverty approach is the federal government's attempt to promote education as a means to increase human capital. Poverty is highly correlated with educational deficits, and adolescent parenthood is strongly associated with low levels of basic skills and high dropout rates. For example, youths with the weakest reading and math skills are eight times as likely to have out-of-wedlock children and seven times as likely to drop out of high school as students with above-average skills.[141] To help address these educational deficits, the federal government instituted the Head Start program which was targeted at poor children aged three to five and their families. The High/Scope Educational Research Foundation's 20-year follow-up study of Head Start (and similar preschools) found that compared to nonparticipants, graduates were more likely to complete high school, receive additional vocational or academic training, be employed, be self-supporting, have fewer problems with the law, have lower instances of teenage pregnancy, and not become public assistance recipients.[142]

Area poverty is illustrated by examining poverty rates on a state-by-state basis. (See Table 5.7.) In 1995 the poverty rate for all persons in the United States was 13.8 percent. Some states that were poverty pockets had much higher poverty rates, including New Mexico (25.3 percent), Mississippi (23.5 percent), the District of Columbia (22.2 percent), Alabama (20.1 percent), and South Carolina (19.9 percent). In addition, almost 1 in 5 (18.6 percent) people in the city of Los Angeles was below the poverty line. By contrast, states like New Hampshire (5.3 percent), Alaska (7.1 percent), New Jersey (7.8

percent), and Utah (8.4 percent) had poverty rates below the national average.[143] Depressed states such as Mississippi, Alabama, Louisiana, New Mexico, South Carolina and West Virginia, among others, typically experience a recession regardless of the economic prosperity enjoyed by the rest of the nation.

These approaches to poverty are not merely hypothetical formulations; they formed the basis for social welfare policy throughout much of the 1960s and beyond. Between 1965 and 1980, social welfare policies were grounded in the view that public expenditures should be used to stimulate opportunities for the poor. As a result, major social welfare legislation was enacted and billions of dollars earmarked for the remediation of poverty. Beginning with the Reagan administration in 1980 (and later with the Bush presidency), there was a move away from reliance on social welfare expenditures to an emphasis on ending poverty through economic growth. Consequently, public expenditures for poverty programs decreased as tax cuts to provide incentives to work and save money increased. The Reagan approach assumed that it would be more in the interests of the poor to wait for gains realized through increased economic activity rather than to rely on welfare programs. This perspective assumed that the trickle-down effect of economic growth would benefit the poor more than direct economic subsidies. However, according to analyst Kevin Phillips, "Low-income families, especially the working poor, lost appreciably more by cuts in government services than they gained in tax reductions."[144] Despite the

◆ TABLE 5.7
Percent of Persons in Poverty by State, 1993–1995

State	*1995*	*1994*	*1993*
Alabama	20.1	16.4	17.4
Alaska	7.1	10.2	9.1
Arizona	16.1	15.9	15.4
Arkansas	14.9	15.3	20.4
California	16.7	17.9	18.2
Colorado	8.8	9.0	9.9
Connecticut	9.7	10.8	8.5
Delaware	10.3	8.3	10.2
Dist. of Columbia	22.2	21.2	26.4
Florida	16.2	14.9	17.8
Georgia	12.1	14.0	13.5
Hawaii	10.3	8.7	8.0
Idaho	14.5	12.0	13.1
Illinois	12.4	12.4	13.6
Indiana	9.6	13.7	12.2
Iowa	12.2	10.7	10.3
Kansas	10.8	14.9	13.1
Kentucky	14.7	18.5	20.4
Louisiana	19.7	25.7	26.4
Maine	11.2	9.4	15.4
Maryland	10.1	10.7	9.7
Massachusetts	11.0	9.7	10.7
Michigan	12.2	14.1	15.4
Minnesota	9.2	11.7	11.6
Mississippi	23.5	19.9	24.7
Missouri	9.4	15.6	16.1
Montana	15.3	11.5	14.9
Nebraska	9.6	8.8	10.3
Nevada	11.1	11.1	9.8
New Hampshire	5.3	7.7	9.9
New Jersey	7.8	9.2	10.9
New Mexico	25.3	21.1	17.4
New York	16.5	17.0	16.4
North Carolina	12.6	14.2	14.4
North Dakota	12.0	10.4	11.2
Ohio	11.5	14.1	13.0
Oklahoma	17.1	16.7	19.9
Oregon	11.2	11.8	11.8
Pennsylvania	12.2	12.5	13.2
Rhode Island	10.6	10.3	11.2
South Carolina	19.9	13.8	18.7
South Dakota	14.5	14.5	14.2
Tennessee	15.5	14.6	19.6
Texas	17.4	19.1	17.4
Utah	8.4	8.0	10.7
Vermont	10.3	7.6	10.0
Virginia	10.2	10.7	9.7
Washington	12.5	11.7	12.1
West Virginia	16.7	18.6	22.2
Wisconsin	8.5	9.0	12.6
Wyoming	12.2	9.3	13.3
Los Angeles CMSA	18.6	19.8	20.0
New York CMSA	15.0	14.9	15.5

Source: Adapted from U.S. Census Bureau, "Poverty 1995," September 1996. On-line: http://www.census.gov/hhes/poverty/pov95/statepov.html

emphasis on eradicating poverty through market incomes, the major factors influencing the general decrease in poverty from the 1960s to the late 1970s were governmental cash and in-kind transfers.[145]

A decade of Manpower Research Development Corporation (MDRC)-sponsored work experiments served to reinforce a suspicion among social policy analysts that, associated with the deterioration of employment opportunities, a growing number of poor were emerging in the United States. That the life circumstances of the minority poor were being severely attenuated was evident as early as the 1970s. Census tract data indicated that ghettoization was increasing significantly, further isolating poor urban minorities from the American mainstream (see Table 5.8). Moreover, while poverty continued to affect poor neighborhoods (census tracts with 20 percent poor), it considerably worsened the conditions of still poorer neighborhoods (census tracts with 40 percent poor).

Compounding the erosion of income and assets, urban minority communities were further disadvantaged by the exodus of middle-income African Americans to the suburbs and by the replacement of better-paying, manufacturing jobs with low-wage service jobs. The interaction of middle-class flight and technological transformation proved devastating for the minorities residing in older industrial cities. During the 1980s, to be young, African American, and out of school was bad enough; the prospects were even worse for those who lived in the Northeast, particularly as compared with those living in the West. In 1985, 68 percent of young blacks living in the Northeast were unemployed, not in school, or not working, compared with 39 percent of those who lived in the West.

Under these circumstances, it is not surprising that the social and economic status of the minority poor plummeted. In 1983 the median worth of nonwhite and Hispanic families was only $6,900, 12.7 percent of that of white families; but by 1989 that had fallen to $4,000, 6.8 percent of white families.[146] By the middle 1990s, the poverty rate of African Americans was three times that of whites.[147] But financial data provided only a statistical portrait of a social tragedy that was evolving. In 1990, a criminal justice reform organization, the Sentencing Project, reported that one-fourth of all African Americans between the ages of 20 and 29 were incarcerated, on parole, or on probation. Incredibly, Harvard economist Richard Freeman calculated that 35 percent of all African Americans aged 16 to 35 had been arrested in 1989.[148] Predictably, all this reached the flash point with the 1992 Los Angeles riot.

Of the few proposals advanced to reduce poverty, most emphasize employment. New Deal-type job programs were proposed in works that received wide circulation, such as Nicholas Lemann's article "The Origins of the Underclass" in the *Atlantic Monthly*[149] (later expanded in *The Promised Land*)[150] and Mickey Kaus's article "The Work-Ethic State" in *The New Republic*[151] (later rewritten as *The End of Equality*).[152] According to William Julius Wilson, increasing job opportunities for the employable poor would have

◆ TABLE 5.8
Trends in Social Conditions in Large Central Cities, 1970-1980
(In percentages)

	Census Tracts with 20% Poor			*Census Tracts with 40% Poor*		
Indicator	*1970*	*1980*	*Change*	*1970*	*1980*	*Change*
Employment rate						
Males, age 16+	63.3	56.0	–13	56.5	46.0	–22
AFDC families	19.8	28.0	+40	30.2	42.0	+40
Black persons	27.2	26.5	– 3	6.3	8.3	+32
Poor blacks	28.3	30.5	+ 8	9.4	13.1	+40

Source: Adapted from Sara McLanahan, Irwin Garfinkel, and Dorothy Watson, "Family Structure, Poverty, and the Underclass," in M. McGeary and L. Lynn (Eds.), *Urban Change and Poverty* (Washington, DC: National Academy Press, 1988), p. 130.

several related payoffs. For example, much welfare dependency among female heads of households can be attributed to the fact that large numbers of young men in poor neighborhoods are not good candidates for marriage because of their poor education, engagement in illicit activities, and unemployment. According to Wilson, employment programs that would make young men more marriageable would not only reduce the social costs of their current status but also those of the women with children who are dependent on welfare.[153]

Experience with employment training programs over the past two decades suggests that the earlier proposition advanced—that a substantial portion of the welfare problem could be solved if people on welfare found adequate employment—is not likely to be achieved solely through workfare. Although workfare programs may enhance the sense of self-worth of welfare beneficiaries, make for good public relations, and assuage irate taxpayers, these programs—whether coercive or voluntary—have achieved only marginal success in terms of their ability to get welfare beneficiaries into jobs that can make them economically self-sufficient. Given the experience of the MDRC demonstrations, to say nothing of the growing underclass, a more effective strategy would be a national labor policy directed at the secondary labor market. Such a policy would include further raising or supplementing the minimum wage or developing a benefit package to complement the minimum wage. In addition, tight labor market policies or the certification of completion of tough government training programs would make the disadvantaged more desirable workers to employers. Without a national labor market strategy that addresses the secondary labor market—and therefore the plight of the unemployed, underemployed, and discouraged workers—workfare programs is likely to be punitive and the number of poor is likely to grow.

CONCLUSION

Poverty is one of the most intractable problems facing American society. Because poverty is both a political and social issue, the policies surrounding it are often less than objective. For example, one can halve the poverty rate simply by redefining the poverty index. Conversely, one can swell the ranks of the poor by moving the poverty line downward, that is, by increasing the income level at which people are defined as poor. Poverty rates can also be cut by placing a high dollar value on in-kind benefits such as food stamps and Medicaid. Like all social policies, poverty-related policies exist in a context marked by political exigencies, public opinion, the economic health of a society, and the complex mask of ideology.

Although various kinds of poverty-related data are available, policymakers remain uncertain as to the precise causes of poverty. What is known is that its causes are complex and involve, among other things, the effects of discrimination; the composition of family life, including the rise in single female-headed families and teenage pregnancies; geographical location; and age. In large measure, the determination of whether a child is poor depends on chance, that is, which family the child is born into. Policymakers also know that the skewed distribution of income in society and governmental tax and investment policies also has a major impact on the numbers of those in poverty and the extent of their poverty.

Most policymakers agree that employment is the best antipoverty program. As such, work-related policies such as the value of the minimum wage (especially its relationship to mean incomes), the level of under- and unemployment, the rise or decrease in family incomes, and the general state of the economy all have a major impact in determining the level and extent of poverty. The availability of job training programs and the regulation of the dual labor market help determine which workers will make which salaries. Taken together, these factors have caused poverty rates to remain higher in the United States than in many other industrialized nations. It has also helped make poverty seem like an intractable problem with few viable solutions.

Questions of poverty have long plagued social scientists. Specifically, these questions revolve around why some groups are able to rise out of poverty while others appear only to fall deeper into the poverty trap. Although theorists such as Daniel Patrick Moynihan, Oscar Lewis, and others have offered explanations for poverty, none apparently hold up to empirical testing. This is because there is no simple or single answer to poverty. The causes of poverty are complex and involve a wide range of social, economic, political, and cultural factors. Poverty is one of the most elusive—if not the most elusive—problems facing American social policy. Theories and strategies that address single explanations or single causes of poverty are doomed to failure, only aggravating an American public that is already suspect of most antipoverty measures.

◆ ◆ ◆ *Discussion Questions* ◆ ◆ ◆

1. The measurement of poverty is at once both complex and controversial. Nevertheless, the way in which poverty is measured has important implications for the development of social policy in America. Describe some of the potential pitfalls in measuring poverty rates and discuss how the calculation of poverty rates affects the creation of social policy.

2. Economic and social indicators suggest that when compared to similar countries, the United States ranks poorly in terms of overall poverty rates, health indicators, and child welfare. What are the main causes of this low ranking? Can and should the United States concentrate on improving its ranking?

3. Income inequality is often seen as an important causal factor in determining poverty. Is income inequality a cause or a symptom of poverty? What specific policy initiatives can be undertaken to narrow income inequality or lessen its effects?

4. Working families comprise a growing and important segment of the poor. What are some of the causes of the increase in the numbers of working poor as a percentage of the total population in poverty? What specific policies could be implemented to reduce the number of working poor families?

5. A number of theories have been advanced to explain why some individuals and groups of people are poor while others are not. Theorists who have tried to tackle this problem include Daniel Patrick Moynihan, Oscar Lewis, and Edward Banfield, among others. Although all these theories of poverty have intrinsic flaws, which theory (or combination of theories) described in this book or elsewhere do you think best explains the dynamics of poverty?

6. Over the past several years an intense debate has arisen over the existence of an underclass in American society. Some critics claim that there is little real evidence to prove the existence of an underclass as a *distinct* subgroup of people in poverty. These critics argue that what is referred to as the underclass is simply a normal group of very poor people. Others argue that the evidence points to the existence of a distinct subgroup of poor people who indeed qualify as an underclass. According to these critics, these people have values and behaviors that are so at odds with those of the mainstream that they qualify as a distinct subgroup of the poor. Is there an underclass in America? If so, what kinds of values and behaviors do they exhibit that qualify them as a special subgroup of the poor?

7. Many strategies have been developed to fight poverty, including the curative approach, the alleviative approach, and the preventive approach. Of these strategies, which is the most effective in fighting poverty and why? What alternative strategies, if any, could be developed that would be more effective in combating poverty?

8. Policy analysts have traditionally argued that jobs are preferable to welfare and that the lack of employment opportunities results in increasing needs for social welfare. Is this relationship evident in your community? What is your evidence?

9. A commonly held belief is that government make-work jobs are inferior to private sector employment. Yet, many New Deal jobs programs have made important contributions to the infrastructure of the nation's cities. What New Deal projects are evident in your community? What were the resources used for these projects? If a new governmental jobs program were initiated, what community needs might it address?

10. The Job Training and Partnership Act has attempted to enhance opportunities for workers in the secondary labor market. What has been the track record of this and other programs in your community? Has one been more successful than the other? How would you change these programs to more adequately address the needs of the poor in your community?

11. The idea of an American "underclass" has been debated by scholars for more than a decade. To what extent can an underclass be said to exist in your community? What are its demographic characteristics? How might employment policy be changed to better integrate the long-term poor into the labor market?

Notes

1. Blanche Bernstein, "Welfare Dependency," in Lee D. Bawden, Ed., *The Social Contract Revisited* (Washington, DC: Urban Institute Press, 1984), p. 129.
2. Greg J. Duncan et al., *Years of Poverty, Years of Plenty* (Ann Arbor, MI: Institute for Social Research, 1984).
3. William O'Hare, Taynia Mann, Kathryn Porter, and Robert Greenstein, *Real Life Poverty in America: Where the Public Would Set the Poverty Line* (Washington, DC: Center on Budget and Policy Priorities, and Families USA Foundation Report, July 1990), p. viii.
4. U.S. Census Bureau, "Poverty 1995," September 26, 1996. On-line: http://www.census.gov/hhes/poverty/pov95/thresh95.html
5. Committee on Ways and Means, U.S. House of Representatives, *Overview of Entitlement Programs: 1992 Green Book* (Washington, DC: U.S. Government Printing Office, 1992), p. 1272.
6. O'Hare et al., *Real Life Poverty in America*, p. vii.
7. Ibid., p. 6.
8. Ibid., p. 8.
9. Ibid., p. vi.
10. Center on Budget and Policy Priorities, "Number in Poverty Hits 20-Year High as Recession Adds 2 Million More Poor, Analysis Finds" (Washington, DC: Center on Budget and Policy Priorities, September 3, 1992), n.p.
11. Letter, September 8, 1992, from J. Larry Brown, director of the Tufts University School of Nutrition, to the Hon. Tony Hall, chairman of the House Select Committee on Hunger, Washington, DC.
12. U.S. Conference of Mayors, "Status Report on Hunger and Homelessness in America's Cities: 1991" (Washington, DC: U.S. Conference of Mayors, 1991).
13. Urban Institute, "Hunger Among the Elderly: Local and National Comparisons" (Washington, DC: Urban Institute, 1992).
14. Isaac Shapiro, *White Poverty in America* (Washington, DC: Center on Budget and Policy Priorities, 1992), pp. 8–9.
15. U.S. Census Bureau, "Poverty 1995."
16. U.S. Census Bureau, "Poverty 1995."
17. Sara McLanahan and Gary Sandefur, *Growing Up with a Single Parent* (Cambridge, MA: Harvard University Press, 1997).
18. ACF Press Release, Department of Health and Human Services, Washington, DC, December, 1995. On-line: http://www.acf.dhhs.gov/ACFNews
19. Philip D'Amato, Joseph Ekwere, and Gina Vitale, "American Child Support Enforcement: Now and in the Future." Unpublished paper, Graduate School of Social Work, University of Houston, Houston, TX, spring 1996.
20. Ron Dean, "Myths, Legends and the American Way: Deadbeat Dads," August 15, 1995. On-line: Newsgroups: soc.men
21. U.S. Census Bureau, U.S. Department of Commerce, Economics and Statistics Administration, "Who Receives Child Support?" (Washington, DC: U.S. Department of Commerce, May 1995).
22. Stuart A. Miller, "The Myth of Deadbeat Dads" (Washington, DC: American Fathers Coalition, 1996).
23. Quoted in ibid.
24. U.S. Census Bureau, "Who Receives Child Support?" May 1995, p. 5.

25. Irwin Garfinkel, "Bringing Fathers Back In: The Child Support Assurance Strategy," *The American Prospect* (Spring 1992); David Ellwood, "Child Support Enforcement and Insurance," Harvard University, Kennedy School of Government, March 1992.
26. Daniel Meyer, Irwin Garfinkel, Philip Robins, and Donald Oellerich, "The Costs and Effects of a National Child Support Assurance System," Institute for Research on Poverty, March 1991, Discussion Paper 940–991, p. 28.
27. Bureau of the Census, *Child Support and Alimony*, 1989, p. 1.
28. U.S. Department of Health and Human Services, Administration for Children and Families, Office of Child Support Enforcement, *Child Support Enforcement: Fifteenth Annual Report to Congress, For the Period Ending September 30, 1990* (Washington, DC: National Child Support Enforcement Center, n.d.), pp. 15–16.
29. Mark Turner and Elaine Sorensen, "Noncustodial Fathers and Their Child Support Payments," (Washington, DC: Urban Institute, 1995), p. 9.
30. Dan Bloom and Kay Sherwood, *Matching Opportunities to Obligations* (New York: MDRC, 1994), pp. xxx–xxxi.
31. Bloom, *Matching Opportunities to Obligations*, p. 131.
32. Mark Potok, "Out-of-Wedlock Childbirth Rising," *USA Today* (November 8, 1995), p. 2A.
33. Carol Claverie, Lilly Cuff, Robin Ferris, Kristina Friman, and Alyssa Sanders, "Teenage Pregnancy." Unpublished paper, Graduate School of Social Work, University of Houston, Houston, TX.
34. Ibid.
35. Children's Defense Fund, *The State of America's Children 1991* (Washington, DC: The Children's Defense Fund, 1991), p. 94.
36. U.S. House of Representatives, *1992 Green Book*, p. 1078.
37. "Teenaged Childbearing and Welfare Policy," *Focus* (10)1 (Spring 1987), p. 16.
38. Michael Harrington, with the assistance of Robert Greenstein and Eleanor Holmes Norton, *Who Are the Poor?* (Washington, DC: Justice for All, 1987), p. 12.
39. The Urban Institute, "Welfare Reform: Issues Before the Nation" (Washington, DC: The Urban Institute, 1995).
40. Ibid., p. 1100.
41. U.S. House of Representatives, *Overview of Entitlement Programs* (Washington, DC: U.S. GPO, 1994), p. 448.
42. Denise Polit, Janet Quint, and James Riccio, *The Challenge of Serving Teenage Mothers* (New York: MDRC, 1988), Tables 2 and 3, p. 17.
43. Janet Quint, Denise Polit, Hans Bos, and George Cave, *New Chance* (New York: MDRC, 1994), Tables 5 and 6.
44. Quint, *New Chance*, p. xxxi.
45. U.S. Census Bureau, "Poverty 1995."
46. U.S. House of Representatives, *1992 Green Book*, p. 1072.
47. Children's Defense Fund, *The State of America's Children* (Washington, DC: Children's Defense Fund, 1991), pp. 23–24.
48. *Congressional Record*, Senate, vol. 133, no. 120 (Washington, DC: U.S. Government Printing Office, July 21, 1987), pp. S10400–S10404.
49. Children's Defense Fund, *The State of America's Children*, pp. 23–24.
50. Shapiro, *White Poverty*, pp. 8–9.
51. National Commission on Children, "Poverty, Welfare and America's Families: A Hard Look" (Washington, DC, National Commission on Children, n.d.), p. 5.
52. Elaine Kamarck and William A. Galston, *Putting Children First: A Progressive Family Policy for the 1990s* (Washington, DC: The Progressive Policy Institute, September 27, 1990), pp. 22–25.
53. American Association of Retired Persons, "A Profile of Older Americans" (Washington, DC: AARP, 1991), n.p.
54. O'Hare et al., *Real Life Poverty in America*, p. 9.
55. Kathryn Porter, *Poverty in Rural America* (Washington, DC: Center on Budget and Policy Priorities, 1989), pp. 3–11.
56. Ibid.
57. Shapiro, *White Poverty*, pp. 10–11.
58. This poverty rate is based on the threshold set by the Luxembourg Income Study. Thus, it does not always *exactly* mirror the official poverty rate used by the Census Bureau.
59. Luxembourg Income Study, 1995. (Luxembourg).
60. Ibid., pp. 137–142.
61. James Gustave Speth, "World's 358 Richest Have Some Sharing to Do?" *Houston Chronicle* (September 3, 1996), p. 19A.
62. Daniel H. Weinberg, "Press Briefing on 1995 Income, Poverty, and Health Insurance Estimates"

(Washington, DC: U.S. Census Bureau, September 26, 1996).
63. Edward N. Wolff, "How the Pie is Sliced," *The American Prospect* 22 (Summer 1995), pp. 58–64.
64. Ibid.
65. U.S. House of Representatives, *1992 Green Book*, p. 1568.
66. Lawrence Mishel and David M. Frankel, *The State of Working America* (Armonk, NY: M. E. Sharpe, Inc., 1991), p. 24.
67. Mishel and Frankel, *The State of Working America*, p. 169.
68. U.S. Census bureau, "Median Value of Interest-Earning Assets Down and Home Equity Up in 1993 Compared With 1991," September 25, 1995. On-line: http://www.census.gov:70/Is/Bureau/Pr/Subject/Income/cb95-167.txt
69. See Michael Sherraden, *Stakeholding: A New Direction in Social Policy* (Washington, DC: Progressive Policy Institute, 1990); and Michael Sherraden, *Assets and the Poor* (Armonk, NY: M. E. Sharpe, Inc., 1991).
70. Quoted in Scott Barancik and Isaac Shapiro, *Where Have All the Dollars Gone?* (Washington, DC: Center on Budget and Policy Priorities, August 1992), p. xvi.
71. National Commission on Children, "Poverty, Welfare and America's Families," p. 3.
72. Robert S. McIntyre, Michael Ettlinger, Douglas P. Kelly, and Elizabeth A. Fray, *A Cry from Afar* (Washington, DC: Citizens for Tax Justice, 1991), p. 18.
73. Ibid.
74. Robert Shapiro, "Tax Fairness" (Washington, DC: Progressive Foundation, 1995).
75. Isaac Shapiro and Robert Greenstein, *Holes in the Safety Nets* (Washington, DC: Center on Budget and Policy Priorities, 1988), pp. 27–28.
76. U.S. House of Representatives, *1992 Green Book*, pp. 1488–1490.
77. Mishel and Frankel, *The State of Working America*, p. 48.
78. Center on Budget and Policy Priorities, "Number in Poverty Hits 20-Year High," p. 4.
79. Mishel and Frankel, *The State of Working America*, p. 183.
80. Michael Harrington, with the assistance of Robert Greenstein and Eleanor Holmes Norton, *Who Are the Poor?* (Washington, DC: Justice for All, National Office, 1987), p. 10.
81. Donald L. Bartlett and James B. Steele, *America: What Went Wrong* (Kansas City, MO: Andrews and McMeel, 1992), p. 18.
82. Michael Novak (ed.), *The New Consensus on Family and Welfare* (Washington, DC: American Enterprise Institute, 1987), p. 58.
83. Michael Sherraden. "Chronic Unemployment: A Social Work Perspective," *Social Work* (September–October 1985), p. 403.
84. Ibid., pp. 404–406.
85. As Sherraden notes, the common understanding that an unemployment rate of 7 percent is "normal" is not supported by economists who calculate that structural and frictional unemployment can be reduced to 3 percent through propitious social policies.
86. M. Harvey Brenner, *Estimating the Effects of Economic Change on National Health and Social Well-Being* (Washington, DC: U.S. Government Printing Office, 1984), pp. 2–4.
87. "House Passes Minimum Wage Increase of 90 Cents," *Houston Chronicle* (March 30, 1996), p. A1.
88. Center on Budget and Policy Priorities, "Assessing the $5.15 an Hour Minimum Wage," March 1996. On-line: http://epn.org/cpbb/cbwage.html
89. Isaac Shapiro, *The Minimum Wage and Job Loss* (Washington, DC: Center on Budget and Policy Priorities, 1988).
90. Center on Budget and Policy Priorities, "Assessing the $5.15 an Hour Minimum Wage."
91. Center on Budget and Policy Priorities, "Many Black and Hispanic Workers Harmed by Minimum Wage Bill Veto, Analysis Finds" (Washington, DC: Center on Budget and Policy Priorities, June 15, 1989).
92. Democratic National Committee, "America Needs a Raise" (Washington, DC: Democratic National Committee, March 25, 1996).
93. Michael Novak, *The New Consensus on Family and Welfare*, p. 32.
94. Amitai Etzioni, "The Fast-Food Factories: McJobs Are Bad for Kids," *Washington Post* (August 24, 1986), p. 6.
95. Harrington, *Who Are the Poor?* p. 10.
96. Center on Budget and Policy Priorities, *Smaller Pieces of the Pie* (Washington, DC: Center on Budget and Policy Priorities, 1987).
97. Center on Budget and Policy Priorities, *Unemployed and Uninsured* (Washington, DC: Center on Budget and Policy Priorities, March 1991), p. 4.

98. Robert J. Shapiro, "An American Working Wage: Ending Poverty in Working Families," *Policy Report*, No. 3. (Washington, DC: Progressive Policy Institute, February 1990), p. 1.
99. Sar A. Levitan and Joyce Zickler, *The Quest for a Federal Manpower Partnership* (Cambridge, MA: Harvard University Press, 1974), pp. 1–6.
100. Lawrence Mead, *Beyond Entitlement* (New York: Free Press, 1986), p. 27.
101. U.S. Bureau of the Census, *Statistical Abstract of the United States 1982–83* (Washington, DC: U.S. Government Printing Office, 1983), p. 391.
102. David Rosenbaum, "Federal Job Program Aids the More Able, According to Critics," *The New York Times* (July 22, 1984), p. 9.
103. U.S. House of Representatives, *1992 Green Book*, pp. 1690–1692.
104. Peter B. Doeringer and Michael Piore, *Internal Labor Markets and Manpower* Analysis (Armonk, NY: M. E. Sharpe, 1985), p. 163.
105. Michael Piore, "The Dual Labor Market," in David Gordon, Ed., *Problems in Political Economy* (Lexington, MA: D. C. Heath, 1977), p. 94.
106. Ibid.
107. David Gordon, Richard Edwards, and Michael Reich, *Segmented Work, Divided Workers* (New York: Cambridge University Press, 1982), p. 211.
108. U.S. Bureau of the Census, *Statistical Abstract of the United States 1982–83*, p. 409.
109. Michael Harrington, et.al., *Who Are the Poor?* (Washington, DC: Justice for All, 1987), p. 10.
110. National Conference on Social Welfare, *To Form a More Perfect Union* (Washington, DC: National Conference on Social Welfare, 1985).
111. Kathryn Edin and Christopher Jencks, "Reforming Welfare," in Christopher Jencks, *Rethinking Social Policy* (Cambridge, MA: Harvard University Press, 1992), Chap. 6.
112. Ken Auletta, *The Underclass*, (New York: Vintage, 1982), p. xvi.
113. William Julius Wilson, *The Truly Disadvantaged* (Chicago: University of Chicago Press, 1987), p. 8.
114. Erol Ricketts and Isabel Sawhill, "Defining and Measuring the Underclass," *Journal of Policy Analysis and Management* 7, no. 2 (Winter 1988): 316–325.
115. Douglas Glasgow, *The Black Underclass* (New York: Vintage, 1981), p. 4.
116. Robert Reischauer, "America's Underclass," *Public Welfare* 45, no. 4, (Fall 1987): 28.
117. See Prosser, "The Underclass," p. 3.
118. "Eight Boston Teenagers Charged in Savage Slaying of Young Mother," *Los Angeles Times* (November 21, 1990), p. A–4.
119. Louis Sahagun, "Gang Killings Increase 69%, Violent Crime Up 20% in L.A. County Areas," *Los Angeles Times* (August 21, 1990), p. B–8.
120. Gabriel Escobar, "Slayings in Washington Hit New High, 436, for 3rd Year," *Los Angeles Times* (November 24, 1990), p. A–26.
121. Kathleen Heffernan Vickland, "Is There an Underclass: No," in Howard Jacob Karger and James Midgley (eds.), *Controversial Issues in Social Policy* (New York: Allyn and Bacon, forthcoming 1993).
122. Christopher Jencks, "Deadly Neighborhoods," *The New Republic* (June 13, 1988), p. 30.
123. Daniel Patrick Moynihan, *Maximum Feasible Misunderstanding* (New York: Free Press, 1969), p. 61.
124. Daniel Patrick Moynihan, *The Negro Family: The Case for National Action* (Washington, DC: Office of Policy Planning and Research, U.S. Department of Labor, 1965).
125. Herbert G. Guttman, *The Black Family in Slavery and Freedom, 1750–1925* (New York: Pantheon, 1976).
126. See Edward C. Banfield, *The Unheavenly City* (Boston: Little, Brown, 1966); and Oscar Lewis, *La Vida* (New York: Harper and Row, 1965).
127. Richard Dugdale, *The Jukes* (New York: G. P. Putnam's Sons, 1910).
128. Henry Goddard, *The Kallikak Family* (New York: Arno Publishers, 1911).
129. Arthur R. Jensen, "How Much Can We Boost IQ and Scholastic Achievement," *Harvard Educational Review* 39 (Winter 1969): 1–23.
130. Winifred Bell, *Contemporary Social Welfare* (New York: Macmillan, 1983), p. 261.
131. William Shockley, "Sterilization: A Thinking Exercise," in Carl Bahema (ed.), *Eugenics: Then and Now* (Stroudsburg, PA: Doidon, Hutchinson and Ross, 1976).
132. Bell, *Contemporary Social Welfare*, p. 263.
133. Richard Herrnstein, *IQ and the Meritocracy* (Boston: Little, Brown, 1973).
134. Richard Herrnstein and Charles Murray, *The Bell Curve* (New York: Free Press, 1994).
135. Winnie Chen, Vilma Hernandez, Erin Townsend, and Carol Wyatt, "Affirmative Action."

Unpublished paper, Graduate School of Social Work, University of Houston, Houston, TX, May 1, 1996.

136. T. Beardsley, "For Whom the Bell Curve Really Tolls," *Scientific American* (272)1 (1995), pp. 14–17; Stephen Gould, "Ghosts of Bell Curves Past," *Natural History* (104)2 (1995), pp. 12–19; and C. Lane, "The Tainted Sources of the Bell Curve," *The New York Review of Books* (41)20 (1994), pp. 14–19.
137. Gould, "Ghosts of Bell Curves Past," p. 14.
138. Bell, *Contemporary Social Welfare*, p. 264.
139. David Gil, *Unraveling Social Policy* (Boston: Schenkman, 1981).
140. John Kenneth Galbraith, *The Affluent Society* (Boston: Houghton Mifflin, 1958).
141. Harrington, *Who Are the Poor?* p. 17.
142. Ibid., p. 22.
143. Christine M. Ross, "Poverty Rates by State, 1979 and 1985: A Research Note," *Focus 10*, no. 3 (Fall 1987): p. 1–5.
144. Kevin Phillips, *The Politics of Rich and Poor* (New York: Random House, 1990), p. 87.
145. Danziger, "Poverty," pp. 301–302.
146. Ibid., p. 1449.
147. Lawrence Mishel and David Frankel, *The State of Working America* (Armonk, NY: M. E. Sharpe, 1991), p. 171.
148. Jonathan Marshall, "Targeting the Drugs, Wounding the Cities," *Washington Post Weekly* (May 25–31, 1992), p. 23.
149. Nicholas Lemann, "The Origins of the Underclass," *Atlantic Monthly* (June/July 1986), pp. 8–18.
150. Nicholas Lemann, *The Promised Land* (New York: Knopf, 1991).
151. Mickey Kaus, "The Work-Ethic State," *The New Republic* (July 7, 1986), p. 8.
152. Mickey Kaus, *The End of Equality* (New York: Basic Books, 1992).
153. William Julius Wilson, "American Social Policy and the Ghetto Underclass," *Dissent* (Winter 1988), pp. 84–91.

PART TWO

◆ ◆ ◆ ◆ ◆ ◆ ◆ ◆ ◆

The Voluntary and For-Profit Social Welfare Sector

CHAPTER 6

The Voluntary Sector Today

This chapter describes the voluntary sector, made up of those private, nonprofit organizations that are important on the American social welfare scene. Philanthropic contributions have been an important source of revenues for social service initiatives. Prominent human service agencies, such as the Red Cross, the Family Service Association of America, and the Salvation Army, are identified. In addition, the role of voluntary agencies in advocating social justice is described. Finally, the fiscal crisis of the voluntary sector is discussed, as are the recession and the scandal that shook the United Way during the early 1990s, thus further compounding the funding problems of nonprofit service agencies.

Approaching the twenty-first century, welfare professionals are reassessing the capacity of the voluntary sector to meet the nation's social welfare needs. The primary reason for renewed interest in the voluntary sector is the reluctance of taxpayers and politicians to authorize major new governmental welfare initiatives. As governmental expenditures for social welfare fail to increase in the face of rising demand for human services, the voluntary sector has been called upon to shoulder more of the welfare burden. This was stated explicitly by President Reagan, who appealed to the charitable impulses of Americans as a way of addressing human needs while reducing federal appropriations to social programs, and was restated by George Bush in his reference to "a thousand points of light" during his 1988 presidential campaign. Although President Clinton has made no comparable gesture to the nonprofit sector, his statement that "the era of big government is over" has enormous implications for nonprofit agencies. If government is no longer expected to shoulder those responsibilities, what is to fill the void? The obvious, though unstated, answer is the voluntary sector.

While many liberals were skeptical about the sincerity of the Reagan and Bush administrations in championing the virtues of the nonprofit sector—suspecting that it was a ruse to gut governmental social programs—other events conspired to focus attention on the voluntary sector. A wave of conservatism stalled the introduction of liberally inspired social legislation, most recently the Clinton administration's proposal for health reform. But the conservative imprint on social welfare is not new; early influences can be traced to the late 1970s. During the Carter presidency, conservatives began to challenge welfare programs on the grounds that they divided the family, eroded the work ethic, and subverted communal norms. A widely distributed monograph by analysts from the American Enterprise Institute criticized social "megastructures," which contributed to alienation among Americans, and called for stronger "mediating structures"—voluntary entities—to empower people.[1] Reacting to these conservative trends, Democrats jettisoned from their party platform traditional welfare planks that called for new federal social programs in favor of more pluralist strategies that included the private sector. Responding to the new emphasis on the voluntary sector, welfare advocates established a new organization, Independent Sector, to promote the interests of nonprofit organizations. By 1986, six years after its inception, Independent Sector was able to boast more than 650 corporate, foundation, and voluntary organization members.

THE "FORGOTTEN SECTOR"

Despite this flurry of activity, the role of the voluntary sector in American social welfare has not been either fully appreciated nor well understood.[2] Following the triumph of the New Deal, leading welfare theoreticians expected government to dominate in the creation and administration of the welfare state. In fact, so complete was the expectation that the government-driven welfare state would dominate social welfare in the United States that references to private voluntary agencies became scant in the professional literature. There was little room within welfare state ideology for a dynamic voluntary sector, and references to private, nonprofit agencies virtually disappeared from discussions of American social welfare. When discussed at all, voluntary agencies were viewed as quaint holdovers from an earlier time. Rediscovered during the 1980s, the voluntary sector quickly attracted converts. Perhaps the most notable of the new adherents to the promise of nonprofits was business guru Peter Drucker. Citing the capacity of the "social sector" to address local problems, Drucker not only recited the virtues of the nonprofit sector in books, such as *The New Realities*,[3] but went so far as to establish the Peter F. Drucker Foundation for Nonprofit Management in 1990.[4]

To the extent that the voluntary sector has been included as a part of the governmental welfare state, it has been considered a subcontractor of social service. This role was made possible through an amendment to the Social Security Act, Title XX, which allowed for the "purchase of service" from private providers. Under purchase-of-service contracts, government could avoid the costs and responsibilities of administering programs directly. Because of an open-ended funding formula, however, federal costs for Title XX services escalated sharply. Congress later capped Title XX expenditures, initially at $2.5 billion, in order to contain program costs, and later the Reagan administration was successful in having the program placed under a Social Services Block Grant, with further funding restrictions.[5] Consequently, in response to Title XX, many voluntary social service agencies secured purchase-of-service contracts, the funding for which allowed nonprofit agencies to expand programs in the late 1960s and early 1970s. However, when funding was reduced, voluntary sector agencies were heavily penalized. Federal expenditures for Title XX fell from $2.8 billion in 1980 to $2.7 billion in 1992, a significant reduction in that it occurred at a time when demand for service was rising sharply.[6] As a result, voluntary social welfare agencies were hard-pressed to maintain such services as home-based care, child day care and protective services, self-support education, and adoption and family counseling services, among others. Although federal assistance to voluntary sector social service agencies became critically important to them, accounting for up to half of agency funding, purchase of service continued to be a relatively minor portion of governmental welfare expenditures. In 1986, for example, Title XX accounted for only about 2 percent of all federal expenditures for welfare programs benefiting low-income people.[7]

Consequently, when policymakers turned to the voluntary sector in the 1980s to compensate for reductions in the governmental welfare effort, little was known about nonprofit social service agencies. Lester Salamon and Alan Abramson, authorities on the voluntary sector, observed that "despite their importance, these organizations have tended to be ignored in both public policy debates and scholarly research."[8] As government assumed a dominant role in American social welfare, the voluntary sector receded in importance. If the Reagan and Bush presidencies rekindled interest in the voluntary sector, the Republican takeover of the One-hundred-fourth Congress to create a small firestorm. As part of their Contract with America, congressional Republicans promised to reform welfare as part of an extensive overhaul of the American welfare state. Government, they argued, had induced dependency of millions of families on public assistance, welfare programs largely benefited the health and human service professionals who worked in them, and all of this diluted the influence of community institutions. Congressional conservatives had a strategy in mind when they critiqued federal social programs: replace governmental welfare programs with private, voluntary sector initiatives. "The crisis of the modern welfare state is not just a crisis of government," contended conservative scholar Marvin Olasky. "The more effective provision of social services will ultimately depend on their return to private and especially religious institutions."[9] Suddenly, after half a century of neglect, the "forgotten sector" was being called upon to assume unprecedented responsibilities in caring for the needy.

Only in recent times have researchers begun to investigate the scope of the voluntary sector. Their task has not been an easy one. The voluntary sector is composed of tens of thousands of organizations, many of which are not associated with a national umbrella association. The picture that is emerging from these preliminary investigations reveals a sector that, if small by economic standards, is extraordinarily rich socially. Perhaps the most convenient measure of the scale of the voluntary sector is to count those voluntary and philanthropic associations that have received tax-exempt status as social service agencies from the Internal Revenue–Service 689,000 in 1992.[10] Despite the large number of voluntary sector organizations, they account for only 6.9 percent of the national income, compared with 78.0 percent attributed to commerce and 15.1 percent to government.[11] Indeed, the strength of the voluntary sector lies in its incorporation into the social fabric of American life. Some 89 million Americans 18 years or older volunteered an average 4.2 hours per week in 1993.[12] A substantial majority of Americans (73.4 percent in 1993) made charitable contributions to voluntary sector agencies, averaging $880.[13] Contrary to popular assumption, the voluntary sector is not bankrolled by wealthy philanthropists and their foundations. Foundations and corporations account for only 13 percent of voluntary sector contributions; "about half of all charitable dollars comes from families with incomes under $25,000."[14] Table 6.1 breaks down the sources of funds for the independent sector in four intervals.

In 1992, nonprofit social and legal service agencies accounted for $55.9 billion in revenues, a significant increase from the $32.2 billion budgeted in 1987.[15] Voluntary social service agencies vary considerably in their dependence on various sources of revenue, as can be seen in Table 6.2. These data reveal an important attribute of voluntary social service agencies: governmental and private giving account for about 80 percent of revenues. Fees charged to clients of voluntary social service agencies account for about 12 percent of revenues, which

TABLE 6.1
Independent Sector: Sources of Funds

	(Billions of dollars)							
Sources	*1977 amount*	*%*	*1982 amount*	*%*	*1987 amount*	*%*	*1992* amount*	*%*
Private contributions	$29.2	26.3	$46.2	21.8	$72.6	22.9	$93.7	18.4
Private payments	41.7	37.5	82.1	38.7	129.2	40.8	198.7	39.1
Government sector	29.5	26.6	59.5	28.1	88.5	27.9	159.4	31.3
Other	10.7	9.6	24.1	11.4	26.4	8.4	56.7	11.2
Total	111.1	100	211.9	100	316.7	100	508.5	100

*preliminary
Source: Virginia Hodgkinson and Murray Weitzman, *Nonprofit Almanac* (Washington, DC: Independent Sector, 1996), Table 4.2.

dispels any thought that these organizations as a group could become self-sufficient through the collection of client fees. Although some organizations are able to derive more of their revenues from fees, most social service agencies depend on other revenue sources, as Tables 6.1 and 6.2 illustrate.[16]

Proponents of private, nonprofit organizations contend that economic indicators alone do not adequately represent the significance of the voluntary sector in the national culture. Consistent with the label *voluntary*, nonprofit social service agencies attract the commitment of millions of volunteers who see human service organizations as a vehicle for improving the quality of life in their communities. During 1993, Americans volunteered 15 billion hours, representing 8.8 million full-time employees. In 1993, about 20 percent of volunteers were involved in human service and youth development activities, a significant reduction from the 30 percent so volunteering in 1989.[17]

As measured by revenues and volunteers, the voluntary sector of American social welfare is robust, indeed. Nonprofit human service organizations have their share of organizational difficulties, of course—reductions in government assistance and detrimental changes in tax law during the Reagan presidency, as examples—but it seems remarkably resilient. As the service sector of the postindustrial economy continues to expand, the voluntary sector will grow accordingly.

ADVANCING SOCIAL JUSTICE

In addition to providing social services, the voluntary sector has been important in American social welfare because it has been the source of events that have advanced the rights of disenfranchised populations. In this respect, the voluntary sector is essential to American culture in that it is a correcting influence to the indifference often shown to minority populations by governmental and corporate bureaucracies. This case has been argued vigorously by John W. Gardner, former secretary of Health, Education, and former chairperson of the Board of Independent Sector. According to Gardner, the voluntary sector fosters much of the pluralism in American life, taking on those concerns that do not attract the broad spectrum of public support necessary for the legislation that mandates governmental programs or concerns that do not represent the commercial prospects necessary to attract the interests of the business community. In other words, the voluntary sector serves as the best—and, in some cases, the only—vehicle for addressing certain social

◆ **TABLE 6.2**
Agency Funding Sources, 1986
(In percent of contributions)

	Private Support	*Government Support*	*Fees and Dues*	*Other**
Boys Clubs	66	7	8	19
Catholic Charities	21	47	12	19
Child Welfare Agency	15	65	6	14
Family Service Agency	28	46	17	9
Goodwill Industries	29	19	19	33
Jewish Community Centers	16	7	54	23
Salvation Army	57	14	10	20
Volunteers of America	13	45	8	34
YMCA, YMCA–YWCA	17	4	67	12
YWCA	29	21	36	14

* Other includes such sources of income as bequests, investment income, sale of capital goods, and sale of merchandise. The relatively high percentage of support in the "other" category for Goodwill Industries, the Salvation Army, and Volunteers of America comes from sales of donated merchandise.
Source: Virginia Hodgkinson and Murray Weitzman, *Dimensions of the Independent Sector* (Washington, DC: Independent Sector, 1986), p. 21. Reprinted with permission.

needs. Indeed, much of what Americans would identify as central to their culture can be attributed to organizations of the voluntary sector: hospitals, schools, religious institutions, welfare agencies, fraternal associations, symphonies, and museums, as a partial list. According to Gardner,

> Institutions of the nonprofit sector are in a position to serve as the guardians of intellectual and artistic freedom. Both the commercial and political marketplaces are subject to leveling forces that may threaten standards of excellence. In the nonprofit sector, the fiercest champions of excellence may have their say. So may the champions of liberty and justice.[18]

Gardner's last reference here is not merely rhetorical, but has its basis in history. As Alexis de Tocqueville observed more than a century ago, Americans have depended on voluntary organizations to solve communal problems. In doing so, the voluntary sector has claimed an impressive list of positive additions to American life. Those seeking solutions to current problems often find inspiration in voluntary sector initiatives of the past. Gardner noted that, "At a time in our history when we are ever in need of new solutions to new problems, the private sector is remarkably free to innovate, create, and engage in controversial experiments." He went on to observe that, "In fact, virtually every far-reaching social change in our history has come up in the private sector: the abolition of slavery, the reforms of populism, child labor laws, the vote for women, civil rights, and so on."[19]

Important social welfare initiatives have also originated in the voluntary sector. The War on Poverty—during which new social programs such as Medicaid, food stamps, and the Job Corps were launched—can be traced to the Mobilization for Youth, a voluntary sector poverty program in New York City funded by the Ford Foundation. Two champions of community organization, the late Saul Alinsky and the late César Chávez of the United Farm Workers Union, were also influenced by the privately run Industrial Areas Foundation in Chicago. More recently, services to battered women, patients with AIDS, and the homeless have been pioneered by voluntary sector organizations. Given public apathy toward these groups for so many years, the voluntary sector was the only source of service for these groups.

That social change begins in the voluntary sector has a particular lesson for human service professionals: The openness of democratic American culture means that anyone is free to organize for purposes of rectifying past injustices. The building blocks of a voluntary sector initiative are well within the reach of social welfare professionals—recruiting participants, forming a board of directors, filing for tax-exempt status under Internal Revenue Service Code 501(c)(3) or (4), soliciting contributions, and applying for grants and contracts. Wendy Kopp's Teach For America (TFA) is a good illustration. Having a vision of a Peace Corps–like program for inner cities and rural areas, 23-year-old Kopp began to hustle corporate contributions in 1988 to match idealist professionals to disadvantaged communities. By 1996, TFA boasted a $5.5 million budget and was graduating 500 volunteers annually.[20] What Wendy Kopp has accomplished in New York City illustrates the promise of the voluntary sector in every American community.

CONTEMPORARY NONPROFIT HUMAN SERVICE ORGANIZATIONS

The voluntary human service sector consists of a large constellation of organizations. The more than 81,700 nonprofit social agencies in 1992, accounting for $56 billion in revenues, employed 1.4 million staff to provide a range of services, including individual and family services, job training, child care, residential care, and social services.[21] The best depiction of the voluntary sector is not provided by statistics, however, but by a description of the organizations that are instantly recognizable by most Americans (see Table 6.3).

The United Way

Perhaps the best-recognized of voluntary sector organizations is the United Way. Local United Ways, as well as the United Way of America, are nonprofit organizations themselves. The purpose of local United Ways is to raise funds that are then disbursed to nonprofit agencies in the community, most of which are United Way members. Local United Ways also contribute a small percentage of funds to the national headquarters, the United Way of America, which is located in suburban Washington, D.C. Because the United Way is a confederation of organizations, power resides within the local United Ways. The United Way of America provides support services nationwide but has no direct authority over local United Ways. The influence of local United Ways over the United Way of America will be highlighted momentarily.

In 1995 the United Ways in the United States raised $3.15 billion, an amount that, once adjusted for inflation, was comparable to contributions in 1984.[22] Revenues of the United Way are derived from multiple sources, as shown in Figure 6.1. As is generally true of charitable contributions, most of the funds contributed to the United Way are from employees and small businesses. Corporations account for somewhat less than a fourth of United Way revenues. Financial support that the United Way provides to local agencies is also varied, as indicated in Figure 6.2. Health, family services, and youth services account for the largest categories of expenditures. Of course, the amounts actually allocated in communities vary considerably according to the different priorities of each local United Way.

In order to focus local responses on increasing national problems, the United Way of America has established priorities for the nation. Inaugurating its second century in American social welfare, the United Way identified significant social problems as foci for its affiliates: *illiteracy* (programs to help the 23 million people who are functionally illiterate in the United States); *housing and community development* (an initiative to compensate for the fourfold decrease in federal housing assistance between 1980 and 1990); *AIDS* (initiatives to prevent and combat increases in HIV infection); *Mobilization for America's Children* (efforts to improve the health of all American children); *alcoholism and drug abuse* (programs to counter the epidemic of substance abuse among teenagers and minorities); *The Diversity Initiative* (seeks to increase the volunteer activities of minorities of color); and *The Youth Service Initiative* (efforts to encourage volunteering on the part of the nation's youth).[23] Certainly, the extent to which the voluntary sector is able to respond to these and other worthwhile objectives depends on its ability to deploy new programs to address significant social changes.

The Aramony Scandal and Elite Philanthropy

In 1992 the capacity of the nonprofit sector to address mounting social problems was rocked by newspaper reports of financial improprieties by William Aramony, president of the United Way of America. In more than two decades of leadership, Aramony had effectively promoted the United Way of America as the equivalent of a major corporation with hundreds of local franchises. A corporate mentality, evident in modern, spacious offices, was spread throughout local United Ways by the National Academy of Volunteerism, which trained local officials. Opulence of corporate proportions was evident during the centennial celebration of the United Way when President Reagan spoke before 3,000 guests who had been invited to attend the event at the National Gallery of Art. Mimicking the behavior of corporate executives who contributed increasing amounts to the United Way of America, Aramony appeared to have vaulted the United Way out of the public relations doldrums associated with social welfare and into a new, dynamic era of human services. To many United Way professionals, William Aramony "walked on water."[24]

The transition was not without its price, however. Muckraking journalists reported that Aramony had supplemented his $390,000 annual salary by authorizing excessive "perks," including a New York penthouse, limousine service, and European trips on the Concorde. Using United Way funds for seed money, Aramony had also authorized the creation of three independent corporations, which later employed his son.[25] Local United Way chiefs recognized that a decadent lifestyle was utterly inconsistent with their attempt to raise contributions, made more difficult by a nagging recession,

◆ TABLE 6.3
Nonprofit Human Service Organizations, 1996

Name	*Budget ($ Millions)*	*Affiliates*	*Services*	*Current Issues/Goals*
American Foundation for the Blind	11.969*	New York City Headquarters and 6 field offices+	Policy research; professional publishing house; information referral and public education; and advocacy on special education, vocational rehabilitation, independent living services, accessible jobs and communities for people who are blind or severely visually impaired; Talking Book Program+	Maintain specialized blindness/low vision services appropriate for each age group, infants to elderly; promote descriptive video and access to electronic information; improve collection and use of demographic statistics; expand braille literacy+
American Red Cross	1.8 billion†	1,672 chapters; 43 blood service regions†	Disaster services; armed forces emergency services; biomedical services (blood services); transplantation services; health and safety services; HIV/AIDS education; international services.†	Improving the quality of human life; enhancing self-reliance and concern for others; helping people avoid, prepare for, and cope with emergencies.†
Arthritis Foundation	84+	64 chapters and more than 150 service points+	Health and exercise programs for those with arthritis; research on the causes and relief of arthritis+	To support research to find the cure for and prevention of arthritis and to improve the quality of life for those affected by arthritis+
Association for Retarded Citizens of the United States	4.4 (Nat'l Office)*	1,200 local groups; 46 state groups	Research, education, and prevention of mental retardation; provide resources to local chapters*	Participate in global Human Genome Project to map human genetic structure; ARC's role is to explore ethical issues of project*
Big Brothers and Big Sisters of America	3.8+	512 agencies+; 11 regional groups; 4 district groups	Provide adult guidance for children from single-parent households+	Increase minority recruitment+
Boys and Girls Clubs of America	13 (Nat'l)+	1,875 local groups serving 2.4 million youth+	Programs in six core-program areas: citizenship and Leadership Development; personal Development; Social Recreation; Health and physical Education; Cultural Enrichment; Health and physical Education and Outdoor Environmental Education; primary focus on disadvantaged youth+	Gang prevention/intervention; support to families; substance abuse and pregnancy prevention; and outreach/growth to unserved communities

Boy Scouts of America	62.5+	314 local councils+	Leadership and citizen training; drug and child abuse awareness+	Increase number of youth and leaders+
Camp Fire Boys and Girls	3.5 (Nat'l)+	130 local councils	Serves 700,000 youth through clubs, camping, self-reliance programs, child care and leadership services+	Enhance revenue volunteer assistance and membership in order to continue to provide opportunities for youth to realize their potential and to function effectively as caring, self-directed individuals, responsive to themselves and others.+
Catholic Charities USA	1.8 billion+	1,400 affiliates+	Full range of social services including counseling, adoption, emergency support, housing+	Reducing poverty, supporting families, building communities+
Child Welfare League of America	8.3	5 regional groups; 900 member agencies*	Variety of services to children and families including child protective services, foster care, adoption, residential services, services to children with HIV, etc.*	To improve the service delivery system children and families, especially foster care and adoption services; to use managed care model for the delivery of child welfare services*
Council of Jewish Federations	8.1*	200+ in North America*	Services to families and the aged; community organization and planning; Jewish cultural development*	Make up for decreased United Way funding; develop worldwide satellite transmissions; strengthen relationship with Israeli and North American Jewry and a sense of Jewish identity*
Family Service America	3.3	260+ in North America	Services vary but include: parent-child tensions; marital difficulties; drug and alcohol problems; teenage pregnancy; elder care; child abuse and neglect; family violence; work-related problems; consumer counseling; resettlement to immigrants*	Education issues, specifically the FAST Program (Families and Schools Together) which promotes the relationship between family and school for at-risk kids*
Girl Scouts of the U.S.A.	36+	323 local councils+	Providing a values-based, informal education program to help girls develop their full potential+	Promote pluralism; understand and address the needs of girls; prepare girls for leadership roles+

(continued)

◆ **TABLE 6.3** ***(continued)***

Name	*Budget ($ Millions)*	*Affiliates*	*Services*	*Current Issues/Goals*
Goodwill Industries International	1.04 billion+	186 member organizations in North America; 53 associate member organizations in 37 countries worldwide+	Education, employment and job-training programs for people with disabilities and other barriers to employment+	Welfare reform issue in putting people with barriers to employment, including dependency public assistance, to work; expansion of programs and services to people with disabilities and other barriers to employment in light of cuts in government funding; focus on high-tech industry for necessary training for job placement of people with disabilities and other barriers to employment+
National Council on Alcoholism and Drug Dependence Inc	1.5+	125 local groups+	Provide information and referrals to appropriate services for individuals and families seeking treatment for alcoholism and dependence or other drugs; offer community-based and education programs and local media advocacy campaigns; raise local awareness through presentations at schools, senior citizen centers, civic organizations and other groups; advocate for alcoholic and other drug dependent persons and their families at the city and state levels of government; serve as resource centers for literature and audiovisual materials+	Advocates prevention, intervention, research and treatment on alcoholism and other drug addictions, and is dedicated to ridding these diseases of its stigma and its sufferers from their denial and shame+
National Easter Seal Society	382.8	135 affiliates in the U.S. operating nearly 500 service sites+	Speech and language therapies; audiology services; medical treatment, physical therapy and prosthetic care; vocational evaluation, occupational therapy, training, and placement; psychosocial evaluation and counseling; educational evaluation and services; early intervention; camping, recreation, and social services; technological assistance; prevention and screening or potentially disabling conditions; and advocating on behalf of people with disabilities+	To help people with disabilities achieve independence through providing quality rehabilitative services; technological assistance; and disability prevention, advocacy, and public education programs+

(continued)

National Mental Health Association	2.4*	325 state and local affiliates*	Advocacy for adults and children with biological-based and emotional and behavior problems; prevention of mental illness; public education on depression; child mental health program; mental health information center*	Advocacy, specifically inclusion of mental health parity in the Mental Health Reform Act; public and community educational campaign on depression and children's campaign; prevention program to build coalitions based in school called Voices vs. Violence*
National Urban League	18.9+	115 affiliates+	Advocating equality for minorities; public education; policy monitoring+	Improve behavior of adolescent males; mobilize communities to fight crime+
Planned Parenthood Federation of America	405	169 affiliates in more than 900 locations worldwide†	Reproductive health services; sexual, reproductive and patient education; school and community education; professional training of other service providers; advocacy; counseling and referrals†	To provide comprehensive reproductive and complementary health care services in settings that preserve and protect the essential privacy and rights of individuals; to advocate for public policies that guarantee these rights and ensure access to such services; to provide educational programs that enhance understanding of individual and societal implications of human sexuality; to promote research and the advancement of technology in reproductive health care and encourage understanding of their inherent bioethical, behavioral, and social implications†
The Salvation Army	1.4 billion+	9505 units of operation+	Food; shelter; professional services; training; education; child and elderly day care; senior housing and congregate meals; advocacy; support groups; individual and family counseling; addiction treatment; character building; recreational and skill development for all ages; missing persons; camps; disaster relief; full range of Christian denominational programming+	Assistance for the poor commensurate to their needs; restoration of moral standard; family and youth character-building; comprehensive Christian witness+

(continued)

◆ TABLE 6.3 *(continued)*

Name	*Budget ($ Millions)*	*Affiliates*	*Services*	*Current Issues/Goals*
USO (United Service Organizations)	29+	3 regional groups; 70 state groups+	Airport, fleet and family support centers; cultural and recreational programs for U.S. military families+	Provide programs and services to low-income military families+
Visiting Nurses Association of America	2*	More than 200 members*	Home health and community health services regardless of ability to pay*	To provide home health and community health to all*
Young Men's Christian Association	2.1 billion†	961 members YMCA's operated 1,207 branches, units, and camps†	Community-based health and fitness; child care; camping; aquatics; sports; community development; international work†	Character development; programs in low-income communities; collaboration as a dominant way of work within the YMCA and with those outside the organization; develop nationally integrated information system; self esteem; values; family; health; cultural diversity; world; leadership; environment†
Young Women's Christian Association	42†	363 member associations; 4,000 locations nationwide†	Safety, shelter, child care; physical fitness programs; counseling and social, health, and educational and job-related services to women and girls and their communities annually†	National public education campaign on violence specifically sexual assault; child care campaign; campaign for Affirmative Action; advocating for increased funds for breast and cervical cancer; Women's Vote Project; opposing Proposition 187†

* denotes information obtained via telephone contact with public relations or communications department
† denotes information obtained from written documents on the organization
\+ denotes information obtained from organization via fax

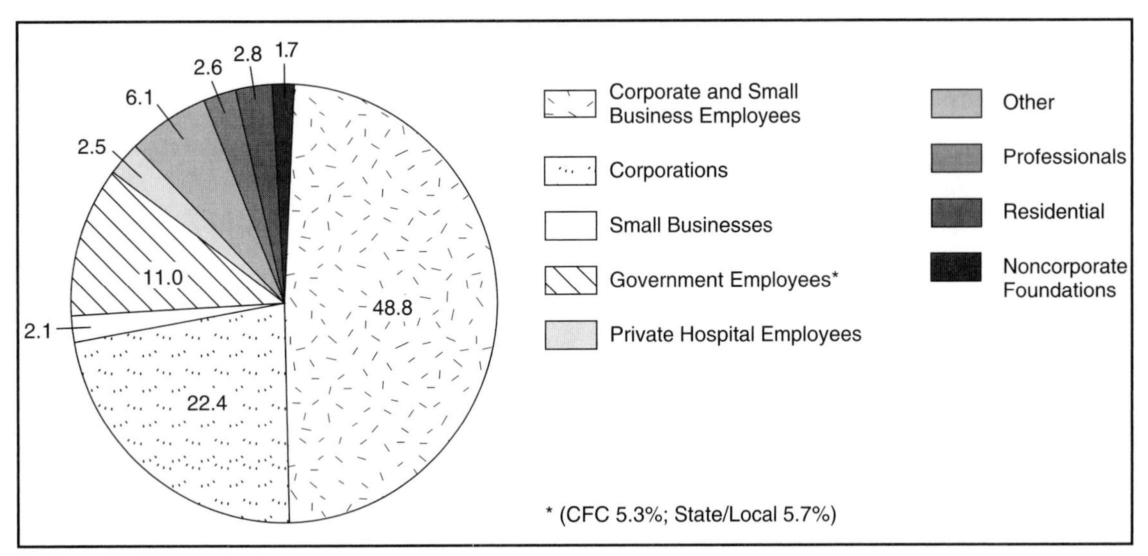

◆ FIGURE 6.1 Where the Money Comes From, 1992–93: Sources of United Way Capaigns (In percent of contributions).

(Source: United Way of America Research Services.)

and in protest withheld their membership dues to the United Way. Prominent philanthropists called for Aramony's resignation, forcing the issue. To the relief of local United Way officials, Aramony soon resigned from the United Way after 22 years as its head,[26] temporarily replaced by IBM vice president Kenneth Dam.[27] Eventually, Elaine Chao, former director of the Peace Corps, was appointed United Way director at a salary of $195,000, less than half what her predecessor had commanded.[28]

Quickly, the United Way of America moved to ascertain the amount of damage caused by the Aramony scandal. A poll conducted in April 1992 indicated that the number of people who had negative views about the United Way had increased from 14 percent in 1990 to 26 percent in 1992.[29] By July 1992 the Aramony story was more widely known, leaving 49 percent of poll respondents with a more negative view toward the United Way. But the damage seemed to be abating. Although 32 percent of respondents in April 1992 stated that they would give less to the United Way, only 23 percent stated this intention three months later.[30] By the end of 1992 the situation appeared to have subsided. A December 1992 poll indicated that 49 percent of respondents had given the same as usual to the United Way; only 7 percent had reduced their contributions.[31] Yet this could hardly be interpreted as good news. With social needs escalating but the fiscal capacity of voluntary agencies limited by the recession, nonprofit agencies needed a substantial boost in revenues from the United Way. Negative perceptions of the United Way of America undoubtedly diminished how altruistic many Americans were willing to be with their checkbooks. Thus, a final accounting of the Aramony scandal would be translated into the millions of dollars that nonprofit agencies failed to receive in 1992 because of public doubt about the management of the United Way of America.

The final chapter in the Aramony scandal was not written until 1995. In April, a jury found Aramony and two associates guilty of multiple counts of conspiracy, fraud, and filing false tax returns. Aramony was found to have misappropriated $1.2 million in United Way funds, was sentenced to seven years in federal prison, and was fined $522,000. During the following spring, Aramony's new attorney,

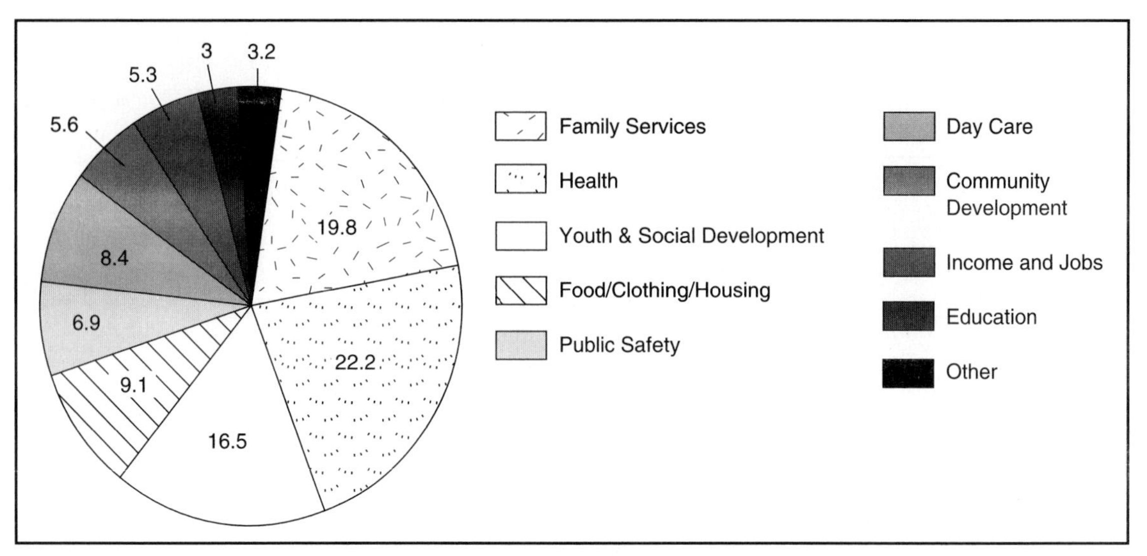

◆ **FIGURE 6.2 Where the Money Goes—1992: United Way Funding to Service Areas (In percent of expenditures).**
(Source: United Way of America Research Services.)

Harvard Professor Alan Dershowitz, appealed the sentence on the basis of Aramony's age—68—and a brain disorder that impaired his impulse control; however, the U.S. Court of Appeals for the Fourth Circuit upheld the majority of the counts.[32]

The Aramony flap refocused attention on the norms of propriety informally generated within the philanthropic community. In the aftermath of the scandal, *The Chronicle of Philanthropy* surveyed 117 of the nation's largest nonprofits and determined that one-fourth reported paying chief executives annual salaries of more than $200,000. As examples, Ben Love, chief executive of the Boy Scouts, is paid $223,375; Robert Ross, who heads the Muscular Dystrophy Association, claims $284,808; and Dudley Hafner, executive vice president of the American Heart Association, earns $246,000.[33] Why are nonprofit executives paid so well? Presumably because, in order to secure charitable contributions, they are expected to associate with the cultural elites who populate American corporations and foundations. To do so requires a substantial enough salary to cover the entertainment, club memberships, and other incidental costs associated with such socialization. Considering the upscale lifestyle of executives of prominent nonprofits, it is easy to understand how this could occur.

Unfortunately, the Aramony scandal was not an isolated event. Not long after Aramony reported to prison, federal attorneys returned an 82-count indictment against John G. Bennett, Jr., the founder of the Foundation for New Era Philanthropy, for cheating nonprofit organizations and philanthropists out of $115 million. Bennett was alleged to have promised future participants in New Era a doubling of their money through contributions by anonymous donors. By the time the indictments were handed down, New Era had recruited universities, museums, the Philadelphia Orchestra, the United Way of Southeast Pennsylvania, and several Christian social agencies into its program. Unknown to these institutions, Bennett's "anonymous donors" were fictional; the doubling of contributions was to come out of future donations, according to Justice Department allegations. Before dissolving New Era in light of questionable management, Bennett is alleged to have used $4.2 million for his own use.[34]

The Aramony and Bennett scandals have another lesson, and that is the distinction between "elite" and "bourgeois" philanthropy. For purposes of simplification, bourgeois philanthropy supports the relatively modest pursuits of the United Ways that dot the American landscape. Elite philanthropy, on the other hand, has much grander expectations. "Elite American philanthropy serves the interests of the rich to a greater extent than it does the interests of the poor, disadvantaged, or disabled," argues Teresa Odendahl; it "is a system of 'generosity' by which the wealthy exercise social control and help themselves more than they do others."[35] In 1987, for example, Odendahl calculates that $47 billion, about one-half of all gifts itemized on income tax returns, were made by the wealthy.[36] For what purposes do the rich demonstrate such beneficence? They give to institutions that "sustain their culture, their education, their policy formulation, their status—in short, their interests."[37] In other words, wealthy Americans usually use the tax code to maintain institutions of elite culture, such as private schools, museums, the symphony, and the opera. Generosity of sufficient magnitude is often announced to the public by naming an important institution after the benefactor, a tradition that is maintained by cultural elites in major American cities. Using funds that have been withdrawn from public use by the tax code in order to reproduce the social institutions of the rich is unacceptable to Odendahl, who proposes reforms so that philanthropy will be more truly put to public benefit.

Because elite philanthropy functions through the same tax code as its more modest cousin, bourgeois philanthropy, insults by the likes of Aramony and Bennett are acutely discomforting to the more affluent philanthropies. By late 1995, leaders of major American foundations met in New York to survey the damage. Noting that the philanthropic community "seems to have lost a large part of its claim on the sympathies of the American public," Lester Salamon, Director of the Johns Hopkins Institute for Policy Studies, suggested the establishment of a special commission that would "rethink the role, function and operation of the nonprofit sector for the next century." Citing "a growing mismatch between the actual operation of the voluntary sector and popular conceptions of what this sector is supposed to be like," Salamon argued that the major philanthropies were vulnerable to "cheap shots and exposés" when management scams gain the headlines.[38]

CONCLUSION: THE FUTURE OF THE VOLUNTARY SECTOR

During the early 1980s, the organizations comprising the voluntary sector made substantial headway in responding to increases in the demand for their services. Funding for nonprofit legal and social services increased steadily, representing 9.3 percent of voluntary sector revenues in 1977, increasing to 9.6 percent in 1982, to 10.2 percent in 1987, to 10.9 percent in 1992. Annually, the social and legal services sector increased 6.3 percent between 1977 and 1992.[39] Gradual expansion notwithstanding, the nonprofit human service sector must contend with important issues.

The most significant issue facing the social and legal subsector is the loss of services to for-profit competitors. Thus, while this nonprofit subsector continued to expand during the 1980s, that expansion lagged behind the more robust growth of other subsectors of the voluntary sector. Had for-profit providers not entered the new human services market, the social and legal subsector would have grown more, commensurate with evolution of the service economy. For example, relative to the general growth of the voluntary sector, the number of social service agencies lagged by 11 percent, the number of individual and family services fell behind by 9.9 percent, the number of employment-related services slowed by 16.2 percent, the number of child day care providers fell by 24.5 percent, and the number of residential care services lagged by 6.2 percent.[40] The dynamics of the for-profit health and human sector are described in greater detail in Chapter 7.

Within the nonprofit subsector competition has increased for charitable revenues. For example, traditional United Way agencies are faced with diminishing revenues as a result of nontraditional organizations seeking charitable contributions. An example of this can be found in the united giving campaign directed at federal employees, the Combined Federal Campaign, the largest of such fund-raising drives in the United States. Until recently, the United Way claimed about 90 percent of all campaign contributions not specifically designated for other purposes. As a result of challenges brought by agencies as diverse as environmental groups and the National Rifle Association, nondesignated contributions are now apportioned among a larger number of organizations. Consequently, the United Way has received less than it had in the past from the Combined Federal Campaign.[41]

In response to increased competition for charitable dollars, many United Ways have evolved donor-friendly policies. For example, 76.9 percent of United Ways offer individuals the option of designating the recipient agency, and 37.7 of United Ways will even allow the designation of recipient agency even if it is not a United Way member.[42] An unintended consequence of "donor choice" has been the diversion of United Way contributions from urban agencies serving the chronically ill to suburban agencies providing service to a less disadvantaged clientele. In Washington, D.C., for example, more than 70 percent of United Way contributions are designated to suburban agencies. This coupled with diminishing revenues as a result of the Aramony scandal left urban United Way member agencies with fewer resources. Subsequently the Salvation Army withdrew from the United Way on the basis that its services were not adequately valued by contributors.[43]

Tax law has a significant influence on revenues contributed to nonprofit activities. In 1986 legislation removed the deduction for charitable contributions on the part of taxpayers who did not itemize their tax returns. Because itemizers are more affluent, this change in tax law affected primarily blue-collar and middle-income families, the families that account for most of the revenues to nonprofit agencies. As a result, charitable contributions by this group of households has declined continuously since 1989. Since 1990, tax policy changed the amount of charitable contributions on the part of wealthier families, limiting the amount that could be deducted to no more than 3 percent of income for those earning more than $100,000 annually. Thus, incentives for charitable contributions for more affluent families were also diminished. As a result, charitable contributions by itemizers has also flatlined since the early 1990s.[44]

Charitable contributions by corporations have also stagnated since the mid–1980s. Corporations gave $5.2 billion to nonprofit ventures in 1993, or 1.14 of their pretax income. Controlling for inflation, however, corporate contributions are unchanged since 1987. Approximately 27 percent of corporate grants are dedicated to health and human services.[45] If individual and corporate donations to the voluntary sector have remained static, gifts from private foundations have increased substantially. A significant amount of the "new wealth" generated from financial deregulation during the 1980s has resulted in increased charity. From 1980 to 1993, the number of charitable foundations increased from 22,088 to 37,571, an increase of 71 percent. For 1993, foundation grants totaled $11.1 billion, a fivefold increase since 1975.[46] The inflation-adjusted lag in contributions by individuals and corporations, as well as the increase in revenues from foundations highlight the importance of tax law for the fiscal viability of the voluntary sector.

As a result of increased competition for funding from traditional sources, voluntary sector organizations have been forced to consider the entrepreneurial option, that is, engaging in commercial activities to raise needed revenues. It is already standard practice for nonprofit service providers to charge fees for service and to bill public and private insurance programs to recoup expenses. Thus, "vendorism" is a common practice of nonprofit social service agencies. But, "entrepeneurialism" is a newer and more significant development. Although it may seem innocuous for financially hard-pressed nonprofit agencies to engage in commercial ventures, some small business operators have complained about the unfair competitive advantage enjoyed by these nonprofits because of their tax-exempt status. The issues related to entrepreneurial ventures on the part of nonprofit organizations and the extent these represent "unfair competition" for commercial firms is considered in more detail in Chapter 8. Needless to say, many welfare professionals are uncomfortable about commercial behavior by nonprofit organizations. Ralph Kramer, an authority on nonprofit social services, has well stated this concern: "In competing with for-profit and other nonprofit organizations for governmental service contracts and for customers for their income producing subsidiaries, it is feared that voluntary agencies can lose their distinctive identity and become more like a commercial organization." Thus, the negative response of the business community and the ambivalence felt by many welfare professionals themselves impose limits on the use of commercial methods to enhance the fiscal capacity of the voluntary sector.

As the question of commercial activities by nonprofit agencies suggests, the voluntary sector is dynamic to an extent that is unprecedented. Overall, this portends well for American social welfare. To the extent congressional Republicans are able to contain the growth of government social programs, and insofar as President Clinton follows through on his conviction that "the era of big government is over," the voluntary sector becomes an essential vehicle for addressing social problems. Yet, nonprofit interventions are not a panacea for social provision. It is unlikely, for example, that Tuesday night bingo for the elderly will supplant Social Security or that YMCA-sponsored sports leagues will replace Child Protective Services. A fundamental problem of the voluntary sector is the unequal distribution of wealth from which the very resources of nonprofit agencies are derived. Economically disadvantaged states, such as West Virginia; regions, such as Indian reservations; and cities, such as Detroit, have significantly less capacity to generate the resources necessary for health and human service programming. For this reason alone, public benefits and services are necessary.

The dominant influence of public programs notwithstanding, the voluntary sector possesses a social significance that is greater symbolically if for no other reason than it strikes to the heart of the American experience. Nonprofit agencies are the source of important services that community residents define as important for themselves; the independent sector is an essential avenue for social change; and the voluntary sector makes extensive use of citizens who donate their time, a first lesson in civic citizenship for many. Because of these inherent virtues, nonprofit activities are able to hold their own when boundaries between commerce and government are crossed. When the Girl Scouts' cookie drive in Fort Collins, Colorado—intended to fund a summer camp—ran into trouble after city officials instituted a sales tax on every box of cookies sold, citizens objected.[47] When the Marriott Corporation challenged a student bake sale to fund a high school foreign exchange program because it competed with the company's food service contract, students pointed out that Marriott was a $5-billion company and then boycotted the food service until the company dropped its objection to the bake sale.[48] As these instances suggest, advocates of the voluntary sector may claim as their ultimate resource the allegiance of their neighbors.

◆ ◆ ◆ *Discussion Questions* ◆ ◆ ◆

1. What are the most prominent nonprofit human service agencies in your community? Are they members of the United Way? What do agencies perceive to be the advantages of United Way membership? Do they perceive disadvantages to United Way membership?

2. Has the United Way in your community failed to achieve its goals in contributions in recent years? If so, what are the causes—the recession, the Aramony scandal? Is your local United Way doing anything special to maintain a positive public image?

3. What are the newer nonprofit agencies in your community? What populations do they serve? Are these agencies members of the United Way? If not, how do they attract the necessary resources? What is their perception of the United Way?

4. If there are unmet needs in your community, how would you create a nonprofit agency to meet them? Whom would you recruit for your board of directors? Where would you solicit resources, both cash and in-kind? Whom would you recruit for staff? What would you name your agency? Would your agency focus on providing services or advancing social change?

5. In response to diminishing resources, many nonprofit social agencies have resorted to entrepreneurial strategies to raise money. What innovative projects have agencies deployed in your community? What entrepreneurial strategies can you think of that might be successful for nonprofit agencies in your community?

Notes

1. Peter Berger and Richard Neuhaus, *To Empower People: The Role of Mediating Structures in Public Policy* (Washington, DC: American Enterprise Institute, 1977).
2. Ralph Kramer, "The Future of Voluntary Organizations in Social Welfare," in *Philanthropy, Voluntary Action, and the Public Good* (Washington, DC: Independent Sector/United Way, 1986).
3. Peter Drucker, *The New Realities* (New York: HarperCollins, 1989).
4. Peter Drucker, "It Profits Us to Strengthen Nonprofits," *Wall Street Journal* (December 19, 1991), p. 18.
5. Neil Gilbert, *Capitalism and the Welfare State* (New Haven: Yale University Press, 1983), pp. 6–7; Neil Gilbert and Harry Specht, *Dimensions of Social Welfare Policy*, 2nd ed. (Englewood Cliffs, NJ: Prentice-Hall, 1989), pp. 46–47.
6. Committee on Ways and Means, U.S. House of Representatives, *Overview of Entitlement Programs, 1992 Green Book* (Washington, DC: U.S. Government Printing Office, 1992), p. 830.
7. Ibid.
8. Alan Abramson and Lester Salamon, *The Nonprofit Sector and the New Federal Budget* (Washington, DC: Urban Institute, 1986), p. xi. See also Waldemar Nielsen, *The Third Sector: Keystone of a Caring Society* (Washington, DC: Independent Sector, 1980).
9. Marvin Olasky, "Beyond the Stingy Welfare State," *Policy Review* (Fall 1990), p. 14.
10. Virginia Hodgkinson and Murray Weitzman, *Nonprofit Almanac* (Washington, DC: Independent Sector, 1996), p. 37.
11. Ibid., p. 40.
12. Ibid., p. 69.
13. Ibid., p. 92.
14. Brian O'Connell, *Origins, Dimensions and Impact of America's Voluntary Spirit* (Washington, DC: Independent Sector, 1984), p. 2.
15. Hodgkinson and Weitzman, *Nonprofit Almanac*, p. 190.
16. W. Harrison Wellford and Janne Gallagher, *The Role of Nonprofit Human Service Organizations* (Washington, DC: National Assembly of Voluntary Health and Social Welfare Organizations, 1987), Chapter III, p. 15.
17. Hodgkinson and Weitzman, *Nonprofit Almanac*, pp. 69, 71.
18. Gardner quoted in O'Connell, *Origins, Dimensions and Impact of America's Voluntary Spirit*, p. 6.
19. John W. Gardner, *Keynote Address* (Washington, DC: Independent Sector, 1978), p. 13.
20. Irene Lacher, "Teaching America a Lesson," *Los Angeles Times* (November 11, 1990), p. E1; personal communication, Teach for America, October 7, 1996.
21. Hodgkinson and Weitzman, *Nonprofit Almanac*, p. 200.
22. "National Amounts Raised 30-year History," (Alexandria, VA: United Way of America, n.d.).
23. "1996 United Way Fact Sheets," (Alexandria, VA: United Way of America, 1996).
24. Eleanor Brilliant, *The United Way: Dilemmas of Organized Charity* (New York: Columbia University Press, 1990), pp. 278–291.
25. David Lauter, "United Way's Chief Quits in Funds Dispute," *Los Angeles Times*, (February 28, 1992), p. A1.
26. Sara Fritz, "United Way Dues Withheld Over President's Lifestyle," *Los Angeles Times* (February 27, 1992), p. A1.

27. "Former United Way Chief Still Drawing $390,000 Pay," *Los Angeles Times* (March 7, 1992), p. A2.
28. Michael Ross, "Peace Corps Director to Head United Way," *Los Angeles Times* (August 27, 1992), p. A18.
29. United Way of America Research Services, "April 1992 Public Opinion Poll" (Fairfax, VA: United Way of America, 1992).
30. Ibid.
31. Ibid.
32. "Key Dates in the Adjudication of Former Management," (Fairfax, VA: United Way of America, 1996).
33. Lynn Simross, "When Sharing the Wealth, Let the Donor Beware," *Los Angeles Times* (April 5, 1992), p. A6.
34. "Man Accused in Charity Scheme Faces 82 Charges," *The New York Times* (September 28, 1996), p. 8.
35. Teresa Odendahl, *Charity Begins at Home* (New York: Basic Books, 1990), pp. 3, 245.
36. Ibid., p. 49.
37. Ibid., p. 232.
38. Karen Arenson, "Woeful '95 Leads U.S. Charities to Introspection, *The New York Times* (December 10, 1995), p. 38.
39. Hodgkinson and Weitzman, *Nonprofit Almanac*, pp. 158–159.
40. Ibid., p. 182.
41. Judith Havemann, "Federal Charity Drive Opened to More Groups," *Washington Post*, (January 2, 1988), p. A1.
42. *Designations and Donor Choice in United Way Campaigns* (Fairfax, VA: United Way of America, 1996), Table 1.
43. Tracy Thompson, "United Way Contributors Exercise Their Options," *Washington Post* (September 21, 1996), p. A–1.
44. Hodgkinson and Weitzman, *Nonprofit Almanac*, pp. 59–63.
45. Ibid., pp. 81–84.
46. Ibid., pp. 76–79.
47. "Girl Scouts View Sales Tax on Cookies as Crummy," *San Diego Tribune* (December 17, 1987), p. C–6.
48. National Public Radio, November 20, 1987.

CHAPTER 7

Human-Service Corporations

This chapter considers the role of the business community in American social welfare. Historically, business leaders have made important contributions to the health and welfare of their employees by envisaging utopian work environments and pioneering the provision of benefits to employees. Business leaders were also instrumental in fashioning early governmental welfare policies. More recently, emphasis on the "social responsibility" of corporations has encouraged business leaders to assess the broader implications of corporate activities. Corporations also shape social welfare policy through influencing the political process and subsidizing policy institutes. Finally, proprietary human-service firms have become well established in several markets: nursing care, hospital management, managed care, child care, life/continuing care, and corrections.

The business community in the United States influences social welfare in several important ways. Benefit packages for employees, which are usually available to dependents, provide important health and welfare benefits to a large segment of the working population. Corporate philanthropy has sponsored important—and, in some cases, controversial—social welfare initiatives. And policy institutes reflecting the priorities of the business community have made substantial changes in American "public philosophy." More recently, the corporate sector has begun to exploit the growing human-service markets in long-term care, health maintenance, and corrections. These instances reflect the significant role that the corporate sector has played in American social welfare.

Among welfare theorists, corporate activities have tended to be underappreciated. Many progressive scholars attributed the cause of much social and economic dislocation to industrial capitalism, and therewith implicated its institutional representative, the corporation. Thus, the corporation was not a source of relief, but rather the perpetrator of social and economic hardship. As a result, liberal theorists concluded that the government was the only institution capable of regulating capitalism and compensating the victims of its caprices. Welfare state ideology, as it evolved, left little room for the corporation, viewing it as the source of much suffering and as generally unwilling to pay its share of the tax burden to remediate the problems it had spawned. For example, advocacy groups such as the Public Interest Groups associated with Ralph Nader and Citizens for Tax Justice regularly criticize the corporate sector for pursuing economic and political self-interest, sacrificing the general welfare in the process. A frequent target of criticism is "corporate welfare," the direct subsidies and tax expenditures granted American businesses, which total at least $75 billion annually.[1] In his 1996 campaign for the presidency, Ralph Nader contended that corporate influence was unprecedented in public affairs: "Indeed the corporate government's takeover of our political government, so pronounced since 1980, has reached levels of pervasiveness without precedent in modern American history."[2] The sacrifice of civic values in pursuit of profits have been well chronicled by liberal advocacy groups. These include the disruption, then abandonment, of Love Canal because of improper disposal of toxic waste; the exploitation of Mexican agricultural workers in the Southwest; the extortion of huge sums from New York City housing officials by landlords who provide single-room occupancy for the homeless; and the deceit of tobacco companies about the harmful effects of smoking. To corporate critics, chief executive officers (CEOs) flaunt their positions by commanding salaries way out of proportion to their productivity. When opulent CEOs downsize production, lay off thousands of workers, and thereby decimate a local economy,[3] they become cultural pariahs. At the same time, few would doubt that such wealth and status are enormously influential when wealthy executives leave private life and run for public office. "It's no accident that the [U.S.] Senate is a citadel of multi-millionaires," observed one long-time Washington journalist.[4]

Their privileges, power, and wealth notwithstanding, the corporate sector has made contributions to the commonweal, and these are less often recognized. Consider that in 1993 corporate contributions to nonprofit activities totaled $5.2 billion, substantially more than the $3.0 billion contributed to the nation's United Ways. Certainly most Americans would be able to identify the largest corporate philanthropies shown in Table 7.1.

Through a variety of activities, from corporate philanthropy to workers's benefits, corporate executives have made significant improvements in American social welfare. Ironically, many welfare advocates who had leveled blanket indictments of the corporate sector during the 1960s found themselves furtively seeking grants from corporate

TABLE 7.1
20 Largest Company Sponsored Foundations by Total Grants

	Circa 1994	
Foundation	*Grants*	*Assets*
General Motors Foundation	$34,918,915	$113,458,520
AT&T Foundation	32,201,548	128,925,271
US WEST Foundation	23,673,008	24,801,558
General Electric Foundation	23,321,240	11,492,941
UPS Foundation	22,095,097	62,267,425
Shell Oil Company Foundation	20,511,367	48,317,126
Amoco Foundation	20,354,359	73,886,279
Exxon Education Foundation	19,846,586	3,998,013
GTE Foundation	19,496,822	28,551,298
Procter and Gamble Fund	19,146,977	19,561,836
Southwestern Bell Foundation	17,674,280	45,462,974
General Mills Foundation	17,456,689	46,584,182
Ford Motor Company Fund	16,804,535	8,954,670
Prudential Foundation	16,599,151	131,705,000
BankAmerica Foundation	14,854,325	97,564
RJR Nabisco Foundation	14,024,533	59,855,310
Wal-Mart Foundation	13,492,280	22,538,595
Merck Company Foundation	12,747,290	7,691,983
Bristol-Myers Squibb Foundation	12,617,655	2,320,620
American Express Foundation	12,436,900	14,019,227

Source: Virginia Hodgkinson and Murray Weitzman, *Nonprofit Almanac* (Washington, DC: Independent Sector, 1996), p. 125.

foundations when government funds for new social programs dried up in the 1980s.

At this point, many welfare theorists are beginning to reexamine the role of the corporate sector in American social welfare. The concept of "the mixed welfare economy" combines the corporate proprietary sector with the governmental and voluntary sectors as primary actors in social welfare.[5] And the issue of privatization has provoked a vigorous argument about the proper balance between the public and private (including corporate) welfare sectors.[6] Although Neil Gilbert's *Capitalism and the Welfare State* provides a timely review of the issues posed by "welfare capitalism,"[7] empirical investigations of for-profit human-service corporations have only begun.[8] Thus, the role of the corporate sector in American social welfare, while expanding, is not well documented.

HISTORY OF THE CORPORATE SECTOR

For most of the history of the United States, private institutions have been the basis of welfare provision. During the colonial era, the town overseer contracted out the poor to the resident who was willing to provide food and shelter at the lowest bid. Similarly, medical care for the poor was subsidized through purchase of physicians' services. Through the eighteenth and nineteenth centuries, this practice contributed to the emergence of private institutions—hospitals and orphanages, among others—that served the needy.[9] Although many of these early welfare institutions were communal efforts and not developed as private businesses, others were precisely that. Thus, many early hospitals in the United States were owned and operated by physicians who became wealthy by providing health care to the community. By 1900, approximately 60 percent of hospitals were privately owned by physicians.[10]

With industrialization, however, the business community took a new interest in the health and welfare of employees. To be sure, certain captains of industry saw employee welfare as a concession to be made as a last resort, sometimes only after violent confrontation with organized workers. Such was not always the case, however. Early in the Industrial Revolution, before government assumed a prominent role in societal affairs, altruistically minded businessmen saw little recourse but to use their business firms as an instrument for their social designs. In some cases, their experiments in worker welfare were nothing less than revolutionary. During the early 1820s, the utopian businessman Robert Owen transformed a bankrupt Scotch mill town, New Lanark, from a wretched backwater populated by paupers into a "marvelously profitable" experiment in social engineering. Owen abolished child labor, provided habitable housing for his workers, and implemented a system to recognize the efforts of individual employees. Soon New Lanark attracted thousands of visitors, who were as awed by the contrast between the squalor of other mill towns and the brilliance of New Lanark as they were by the substantial profits—eventually BP60,000—Owen realized from the venture. A humanist, Owen believed that the solution to the problem of poverty lay not in the stringent and punitive English Poor Laws but in "making the poor productive." An irrepressible idealist, Owen later transported his utopian vision to the United States, where he attempted to establish a rural, planned community in New Harmony, Indiana. Ultimately, this American experiment in local socialism failed.[11]

Business leaders in the United States began to acknowledge that industrial production on a grand scale required a healthy and educated work force. Locating such workers was not easy amid the poverty and ignorance that characterized much of the population of the period. To improve the dependability of labor, several large corporations built planned communities for workers. During the early 1880s, the Pullman Company, manufacturer of railroad sleeping cars, "constructed one of the most ambitiously planned communities in the United States—a company town complete with a hotel, markets, landscaped parks, factories, and residences for over 8,000 people."[12] Although some industries later built communities and facilities as a means of controlling and, in some cases, oppressing workers—for example, "the company store" operated by mining companies to keep miners forever in debt—many expressions of corporate interest in employee well-being clearly enhanced the welfare of the community.

In other instances, businesspeople experimented with alternative forms of business ownership. Current "workplace democracy" and "employee ownership" programs can be traced to the Association for the Promotion of Profit Sharing, established in 1892. In 1890, Nelson Olsen Nelson, a founder of this association, set aside a 250-acre tract in Illinois for workers in his company. Naming the village Leclair after a French pioneer of profit sharing, Nelson included in the town plan gardens, walkways, and a school and encouraged employees to build residences in the community. Consistent with his philosophy, Nelson offered employees cash dividends as well as stock in the company; and by 1893, 400 of the 500 employees held stock, thus earning 8 to 10 percent in addition to their wages. Not content with an isolated experiment in industrial socialism, Nelson advanced his ideas in a quarterly journal that promoted profit sharing. Eventually, Nelson went so far as to convert his company into a wholly employee-owned cooperative, but overexpansion and irregular earnings led to his ouster in 1918.[13]

It is important to recognize that such experiments in the social function of the business firm were not solely the work of utopian crackpots, nor were they always the product of peculiar circumstances. Welfare capitalism, "industry's attending to the social needs of workers through an assortment of medical and funeral benefits, as well as provisions for recreational, educational, housing, and social services," was a popular idea among some business leaders prior to World War I.[14] Indeed, concern about the optimal purpose and value of business in the national culture was a frequent subject of discussion among the elite of American commerce. Even a staunch capitalist such as John D. Rockefeller took a relatively progressive stance on the corporate role when, in 1918, he asked on behalf of the Chamber of Commerce of the United States:

> Shall we cling to the conception of industry as an institution, primarily of private interest, which enables certain individuals to accumulate wealth, too often irrespective of the well-being, the health and happiness of those engaged in its production? Or shall we adopt the modern viewpoint and *regard industry as being a form of social service*, [authors' emphasis] quite as much as a revenue-producing process? . . . The soundest industrial policy is that which has constantly in mind the welfare of employees as well as the making of profits, and which, when human considerations demand it, *subordinates profits to welfare*. [authors' emphasis][15]

As often ill-begotten fortunes accumulated in the hands of the few, some wealthy individuals felt compelled to return a portion of their wealth to the commonweal. "In the latter part of the nineteenth century, men who had great fortunes from the massive industrial growth of the post–Civil War period developed a humanistic concern which was manifested in lavish contributions toward social betterment."[16] Andrew Carnegie, who in 1886 had hired "an army of 300 Pinkerton detectives" to put an end to the violent Haymarket strike,[17] wrote seven years later that massive wealth was a public trust to be put toward the public interest. Eventually, Carnegie donated some $350 million through foundations for this purpose, most visibly for community libraries (often bearing his name) that began to dot towns across the country. For his part, John D. Rockefeller contributed about $530 million.[18]

Although largely based on the guilt associated with the great fortunes won by a handful of individuals in the midst of cruel circumstances for many, philanthropic foundations also fostered enduring contributions to social welfare. The Commonwealth Fund proved instrumental in the execution of a series of child guidance experiments during the 1920s, and these served as prototypes for today's juvenile-service departments.[19] The Russell Sage Foundation funded the publication of important works on the development of social welfare, including the classic *Industrial Society and Social Welfare* as well as a series of volumes that were precursors of the *Encyclopedia of Social Work*.[20]

The Rockefeller Foundation took a leading role in providing health care to a Southern African American population that was neglected by state officials.[21] The active role of the Rockefeller Foundation in the eradication of hookworm warrants particular mention. Shortly after the turn of the century, Charles Wardell Stiles was appointed zoologist of the U.S. Department of Agriculture. Hypothesizing that hookworm was caused by a parasite, Stiles convinced his superiors to fund his trip to the South for the purpose of confirming his theory. Yet, the confirmation of his theory notwithstanding, Congress refused to finance an eradication program. So Stiles turned to the Rockefeller Foundation. In 1909 it established the Rockefeller Sanitary Commission for the Eradication of Hookworm Disease, naming Stiles as an officer. Having diagnosed and treated millions of the rural poor—mostly African Americans—shortly before World War I, the commission was well on its way to eradicating the disease that had caused such extensive malaise and listlessness among the poor, in the process contributing to one of the most vicious characterizations of blacks in American culture.[22]

The American business community was also involved in early insurance programs designed to assist injured workers. Although court decisions initially absolved employers of liability for injuries incurred by employees, a swell in jury-awarded settlements to disabled workers convinced corporations of the utility of establishing insurance funds to pool their risk against employee suits. Eventually, companies realized that they would pay lower premiums through state-operated workers' compensation programs than they had been paying through commercial insurance. Consequently, between 1911 and 1920, all 45 states enacted workers' compensation laws.[23] Later, when the Great Depression overtaxed voluntary social welfare agencies, and when labor volatility resulting from high unemployment threatened political stability, it is not surprising that politicians, businessmen, and labor leaders drew on their workers' compensation experience in designing the New Deal. Instrumental in creating federal social programs in the Roosevelt era was Gerald Swope, an executive with the General Electric Company. Having envisaged a "corporate welfare state," including "a national system of unemployment, retirement, life insurance, and disability programs and standards," Swope helped fashion the Social Security program from his position as chairman of Roosevelt's Business Advisory Council.[24] The Social Security program clearly bore the imprint of the business community. As conceived, only workers who had contributed to a trust fund would be able to draw benefits, thus ensuring that no public funds would be required to operate the program.[25] What became known as the "social security concept" illustrated a public pension program that was in fact modeled on programs of the private sector. As such, it "represented the acceptance of approaches to social welfare that private businessmen, not government bureaucrats had created."[26]

The Social Security Act, the crown jewel of the New Deal, meant that the social and economic security of millions of Americans would be underwritten by the state. Although benefits from programs mandated by the Social Security Act became a staple of the American welfare state, the business community continued to make independent decisions regarding the welfare of workers. Major corporations, such as General Electric, General Motors, and IBM, began to offer "fringe" benefits as supplements to salaries, and these became important incentives in attracting desirable employees. By the standards of the time, the benefits offered by large corporations were quite generous, including annual vacations, health care, recreation, life insurance, and housing. Business historians Edward Berkowitz and Kim McQuaid have suggested that the conscientiousness with which some corporations cared for their employees was "almost as if these firms were consciously demonstrating that the true American welfare state lay within the large and progressive American corporation."[27] Private sector activity in health, income maintenance, and education are detailed in Table 7.2. Although private expenditures lagged behind public expenditures, its share of the welfare market increased between 1980 and 1992. During this period, public social welfare declined from 68.9 percent of all social welfare expenditures to 63.6 percent, while the private sector increased from 34.8 percent to 40.9 percent.

◆ **TABLE 7.2**
Private Social Welfare Expenditures, by Category and as a Percent of GDP
(In millions)

Category	1980	1985	1990	1992
Private social welfare expenditures	$255,320	471,223	727,523	824,871
Health	145,000	259,400	410,000	462,900
Personal health care	133,000	232,500	368,900	420,700
Income maintenance	53,564	118,871	164,772	185,724
Private pensions	37,605	98,570	138,114	157,258
Life insurance	5,075	7,489	9,278	10,184
Short-term disability	8,630	10,570	13,680	14,566
Long-term disability	1,282	1,937	2,926	3,143
Supplemental unemployment	972	305	774	573
Education	33,180	54,038	87,864	100,491
Elementary & secondary	11,302	16,782	25,235	27,814
Commercial & vocational	4,661	7,520	15,218	16,832
Higher education	16,042	28,036	43,311	51,245
Welfare & other services	22,776	38,914	64,887	75,756
As a percent of GDP				
Total	27.0	28.8	30.0	33.5
Public	18.6	18.4	19.2	21.3
Private	9.4	11.7	13.1	13.7

Source: *Social Security Bulletin, Annual Statistical Supplement* (Washington, DC: U.S. GPO, 1995), p. 151.

CORPORATE SOCIAL RESPONSIBILITY

The corporation has also influenced American social welfare as a result of accusations that it has been insensitive to the needs of minorities, the poor, women, and consumers. During the 1960s, criticism of the corporation focused on American business's neglect of minorities and of urban blight. A decade later, issues relating to affirmative action, environmental pollution, and consumer rip-offs were added to the list. These problems contributed to a public relations crisis, as a leading business administration text noted.

> The corporation is being attacked and criticized on various fronts by a great number of political and citizens' organizations. Many young people accuse the corporation of failing to seek solutions to our varied social problems. Minority groups, and women, contend that many corporations have been guilty of discrimination in hiring and in pay scales.[28]

Melvin Anshen, Paul Garret Professor of Public Policy and Business Responsibility at Columbia University's Graduate School of Business, bemoaned the fact that "profit-oriented private decisions are now often seen as antisocial."[29]

In order to improve their public image, many corporations established policies on social responsibility. Corporations that were reluctant to take the social implications of their operations seriously ran the risk of inviting the surveillance of public interest groups. As an example, the Council on Economic Priorities (CEP), founded in 1969, developed a reputation for investigating the social responsibility of American corporations. In 1986, CEP released *Rating America's Corporate Conscience*, a rating of 125 large corporations based on their standing with respect to seven issues: charitable contributions; representation of women on boards of directors and among top corporate officers; representation of minorities on boards of directors and among top corporate officers; disclosure of social information; involvement in South Africa; conventional weapons-related contracting; and nuclear weapons-related contracting.[30] Social responsibility audits such as this one provide a guide for consumers to select companies according to their own social consciences and thereby create an incentive for companies to follow socially responsible practices.

Although the facade of public relations frequently glosses over the substantive abuses of business interests, specific corporate social responsibility policies have advanced social welfare. General Electric and IBM instituted strong policies on equal opportunity for and affirmative action toward minorities and women during the late 1960s. Under the title Public Interest Director, Leon Sullivan assumed a position on the General Motors board of directors, from which he presented principles governing ethical practices for American corporations doing business in South Africa.[31] The "Sullivan principles" that dissuaded American firms from investing in South Africa contributed to the fall of apartheid.

More recently, financial consultants have pioneered the concept of socially responsible investments. The practice of excluding from investment funds certain industries because their activities are contrary to those of investors gained considerable ground during the 1980s. An illustration of socially responsible investing is the Domini Social Index (DSI), an investment strategy that screens-out businesses in five areas: military contracting, alcohol and tobacco, gambling, nuclear power, and South Africa. Initially after its inception in 1988, the DSI performed comparably to the Standard & Poors 500 Index, but by the early 1990s was generating a return on investment superior to Standard & Poors.[32]

In another instance, Control Data Corporation has actually sought out "major unmet social needs, designed means for serving them within the framework of a profit-oriented business enterprise, and brought the needs and the means for serving them together to create markets where none had existed before."[33] These and other initiatives demonstrate that the corporate sector has been willing to undertake significant programs to support troubled communities.[34]

Corporate practices have also been applied directly to social problems. In a venture reminiscent of Robert Owen, developer James Rouse established the Enterprise Foundation in 1981. While technically a foundation that supports charitable projects, what makes it different is that within the foundation is the Enterprise Development Company, a wholly owned taxpaying subsidiary. Profits from the Development Company, projected at $10–$20 million by 1990, are transferred to the foundation to fund projects. By the late 1980s, this fiscally self-sufficient "charity corporation" had developed innovative projects for low-income housing in dozens of cities.[35] In 1995, the Enterprise Foundation reported that, since its inception, $1.7 billion had been committed for loans, grants, and equity investments in order to develop 61,000 new and renovated homes. Since the establishment of neighborhood-based employment centers in 11 cities, the Enterprise Jobs Network aided in employing 26,000 people.[36]

Recognizing the tendency of community institutions in poor areas to become dependent on government or philanthropy for continuing operations, the Ford Foundation sought contributions from corporations for a program to apply business principles to social problems. By 1983, the Local Initiatives Support Corporation (LISC) had developed investment funds in 24 regions supporting 197 community-development projects.[37] LISC projects provided jobs and commodities needed in disadvantaged communities, including a fish processing and freezing plant in Maine, a for-profit construction company in Chicago, and a revolving loan fund to construct low- and moderate-income housing in Philadelphia.[38] Fifteen years after its inception, LISC had helped 1,400 community-based organizations leverage $2.9 billion. LISC contributions were credited with the construction of more than 64,000 homes. During the later 1990s, LISC plans to invest $302 million in rural communities to combat poverty.[39]

The success of initiatives, such as the Enterprise Foundation and LISC, have lead imaginative social activists to use market strategies to accelerate the upward mobility of the poor. Chicago's South Shore Bank, for example, has brought $270 million in new investments to deteriorating neighborhoods and rehabilitated 350 large apartment buildings. By the end of 1990, the bank had increased its assets fivefold, and was the exemplar for the community development bank component of the Clinton administration's Empowerment Zone initiative.[40]

By the early 1990s, South Shore Bank was consulting with community development activists in Poland, through collaborating in the Polish-American

Enterprise Fund, and Bangladesh, with the Grameen Bank, which has pioneered peer lending among poor women and in the process become one of the largest development banks in the world. The concept of providing loans to low-income women in order to encourage self-employment has been operationalized in the San Francisco metropolitan area through WISE, the Women's Initiative for Self-Employment. Since its inception in 1988, WISE has trained 3,500 poor women about running a business, in the process helping start or expand more than 500 businesses.[41] As South Shore Bank, the Polish-American Enterprise Fund, the Grameen Bank, and WISE indicate, the application of capital to promote social development has spawned a nascent network of international organizations.

In the light of such ventures, some business leaders have become enthusiastic about the activist response on the part of the corporation toward social problems. David Linowes, a corporate leader, foresaw a new role for business in public affairs.

> Mounting evidence proves that the private sector is uniquely well qualified to fulfill many of the social goals facing us more economically and expeditiously than government working alone. . . . I can visualize a wholesale expansion of existing incentives along with a spate of new reward strategies introduced to America's socio-economic system. Increasingly, I believe, this will help to change the attitude of businessmen regarding social involvement. I look forward to the day, in fact, when competition to engage in government-business programs will be every bit as spirited as competition for the consumer dollar is today.[42]

As chairman of the President's Commission on Privatization, Linowes worked to define ways in which the private sector could complement the responsibilities of government.[43]

CORPORATE INFLUENCE ON SOCIAL WELFARE POLICY

Corporate social responsibility notwithstanding, it would be naive to think that the corporate sector is above self-interest in its orientation toward social welfare. The conservative political economist Irving Kristol stated as much when he wrote that "corporate philanthropy is not obligatory. It is desirable if and only if it serves a corporate purpose. It is expressly and candidly a self-serving activity, and is only legitimate to the degree that it is ancillary to a larger corporate purpose. To put it bluntly: There is nothing noble or even moral about corporate philanthropy."[44] Corporate influence in social welfare is not exerted simply through myriad corporations acting independently. Special interest organizations, such as the National Association of Manufacturers and the United States Chamber of Commerce, have routinely pressed for public policies that clearly reflected the priorities of the business community. The influence that the business community brings to public policy is discussed in greater detail in Chapter 9.

Less well known has been the way in which corporations have funded policy institutes, or "think tanks," for purposes of shaping public policy. Prominent policy institutes favored by the business community have been the American Enterprise Institute for Public Policy Research (AEI) and the Heritage Foundation. Established as nonpartisan institutions for the purpose of enhancing the public's understanding of social policy, these policy institutes distanced themselves from the special interest connotations of earlier business advocacy groups. At the same time, conservative think tanks served as vehicles for the business community to take a less reactive stance regarding social policy. Conservative policy institutes, then, addressed the complaint voiced by Lawrence Fouraker and Graham Allison of Harvard's Graduate School of Business Administration: "Public policy suffers not simply from a lack of business confidence on issues of major national import, but from a lack of sophisticated and balanced contribution by *both* business and government in the process of policy development."[45]

The American Enterprise Institute (AEI)

Once noted for its slavish adherence to probusiness positions on social issues, AEI, by the early 1980s, had developed an appreciation for American "intellectual politics."[46] With a budget and staff comparable to that of a prestigious college, AEI was able to recruit an impressive number of notable scholars and individuals, and to maintain projects in several domestic policy areas: economics, education, energy, government regulation, finance, taxation, health, jurisprudence, and public opinion. The significance of these activities for social welfare was stated by AEI's then-president, William J. Baroody, Jr.

> The public philosophy that has guided American policy for decades is undergoing change. For more than four decades, the philosophy of Franklin Delano Roosevelt's New Deal prevailed, in essence calling upon government to do whatever individual men and women could not do for themselves.
>
> Today we see growing signs of a new public philosophy, one that still seeks to meet fundamental human needs, but to meet them through a better balance between the public and private sectors of society.
>
> The American Enterprise Institute has been at the forefront of this change. Many of today's policy initiatives are building on intellectual foundations partly laid down by the Institute.[47]

For such an ambitious mission, AEI empaneled a staff of influential and talented personnel. At the height of its influence, from the late 1970s through the mid–1980s, AEI maintained a stable of more than 30 scholars and fellows *in residence*, who prepared analyses on the various policy areas.[48] The institute's senior fellows included the previously mentioned Irving Kristol; Herbert Stein, an economist and chairman of the President's Council of Economic Advisors in the Nixon administration; and Ben Wattenberg, a veteran public opinion analyst. The AEI "distinguished fellow" was Gerald R. Ford, who had served as thirty-eighth president of the United States.

Michael Novak, director of AEI's project on democratic capitalism, prepared analyses that focused on social welfare policy. Under the direction of Novak, the project on democratic capitalism intended to reform public philosophy by depicting the corporation as a promoter of cultural enlightenment rather than as a perpetrator of inequality. "The social instrument invented by democratic capitalism to achieve social goals is the private corporation," he proselytized. "The corporation . . . is not merely an economic institution. It is also a moral and a political institution. It depends on and generates new political forms. . . . Beyond its economic effects, the corporation changes the ethos and the cultural forms of society."[49] At the same time, Novak took careful aim at the public sector, explaining, "I advise intelligent, ambitious, and morally serious young Christians and Jews to awaken to the growing danger of statism. They will better serve their souls and serve the Kingdom of God all around by restoring the liberty and power of the private sector than by working for the state."[50]

Through the late 1970s and early 1980s, AEI lay the groundwork for the conservative revolution in American domestic policy. Much of the conceptual work was done by conservative scholars, but the execution depended on building a network between the business community and government. By the election of Ronald Reagan in 1980, that network was in place. This ensured that no social policy proposal would receive serious consideration without first passing the review and comment of AEI.

The Heritage Foundation

In 1986, AEI faltered, and organizational problems led to the resignation of Baroody. With the weakening of AEI, the Heritage Foundation assumed leadership in defining a probusiness and antigovernmental outlook on social policy. Established in 1973 by a $250,000 grant from the Coors family,[51] the Heritage Foundation's 1983 budget of $10.6 million already approximated those of the liberal Brookings Institution and the conservative American Enterprise Institute.[52] Espousing a militantly conservative ideology, Heritage influenced social policy by proposing private alternatives to establishing governmental programs and by slanting its work to the religious Right. By breaking new ground while building mass support for policy initiatives, Heritage complemented the less partisan analyses of AEI.

Heritage social policy initiatives emphasize privatization, which, in this case, means transferring activities from government to business. Implicit in this is an unqualified antagonism toward government intrusion in social affairs. Government programs are faulted for breaking down the mutual obligations between groups, for their lack of attention to efficiencies and incentives in the way programs are operated and benefits awarded, for inducing dependency in the beneficiaries of programs, and for the growth of the welfare industry and its special interest groups, particularly professional associations.[53]

This critique served as a basis for the aggressive stance taken by the Heritage Foundation in urban development, income security, and social welfare policies. With regard to urban development, Heritage proposed the Urban Enterprise Zone (UEZ) concept, which would enable economically disadvantaged communities to attract industry by reducing taxes, employee costs, and health and safety regulations.[54] The UEZ concept came to the attention of then-Congressman Jack Kemp, who convinced the Reagan administration to make it the centerpiece of its urban policy, thus replacing the Economic Development Administration and Urban Development Action Grant programs in which government had provided technical assistance and funds for urban development.[55] When UEZ legislation stalled in Congress, Heritage changed tactics and targeted states and localities directly. By late 1984, 30 states and cities had created more than 300 UEZs.[56] As secretary of Housing and Urban Development in the Bush administration, Kemp was well placed to reintroduce the enterprise zone concept as a way of aiding troubled communities; yet this initiative failed to materialize at the federal level.

In the area of income security, the Heritage Foundation—in conjunction with the conservative CATO Institute—prepared an oblique assault on the Social Security program, promoting a parallel system of Individual Retirement Accounts (IRAs). Under "The Family Security Plan," proposed by Peter Ferrara, former senior staff member of the White House Office of Policy Development, the initial IRA provisions of the 1981 Economic Recovery and Tax Act would be expanded to allow individuals "to deduct their annual contributions to . . . IRAs from their Social Security payroll taxes."[57] Although the idea of substituting IRA investments for Social Security contributions was blocked by liberal politicians, Heritage was clearly banking on future support from workers of the baby boom generation. "If today's young workers could use their Social Security taxes to make . . . investments through an IRA," hypothesized Ferrara, "then, assuming a 6 percent real return, most would receive three to six times the retirement benefits promised them under Social Security."[58] According to this calculus, the interaction of demographic and economic variables would lead to increasing numbers of young workers salting away funds for themselves because of high investment returns as well as the fear that Social Security would provide only minimal benefits on retirement. If correct, the result would be a surefire formula for eroding the popular and financial support for Social Security.

Regarding welfare policy, Heritage was instrumental in scouting Charles Murray, whose *Losing Ground* provided much of the rationale for the conservative assault on federal welfare programs. In 1982, a pamphlet Murray had written for Heritage, entitled "Safety Nets and the Truly Needy," came to the attention of the Manhattan Institute, a conservative New York think tank.[59] Traded by Heritage to Manhattan, Murray elaborated his allegation that government social programs during the War on Poverty had actually worsened the conditions of the poor. Murray's wrecking-ball thesis advocated no less than a "zero-transfer system," which consisted of "scrapping the entire federal welfare and income support structure for working-aged persons."[60] Remembering his earlier sponsor, Murray returned to Heritage on December 12, 1984, to promote his book to a standing-room-only audience at a symposium entitled "What's Wrong with Welfare?"

By the mid–1990s, the Heritage domestic policy strategy was coming to fruition. UEZs had become modified and incorporated into the Clinton administration's Empowerment Zone program. The prospect of substituting private pension contributions for Social Security withholding had become a serious policy option for the restructuring of that program. Most notably, the Personal Responsibility and Work Opportunity Act of 1996 included a five-year lifetime limit on receipt of public assistance, with states having the option of limiting benefits for less than two years.

The conservative triumph in domestic policy was not coincidental. Not long after the Reagan inauguration, Heritage Vice-President Burton Pines had likened the conservative cause to a crusade. Pines noted the pivotal role of think tanks in the effort to transform public philosophy, acknowledge a debt to AEI, an organization he described as focusing "primarily on long (sometimes very long) range and fundamental transformation of the climate of opinion." Bringing the conservative Hoover Institution of Stanford into the fold, Pines characterized their work in military terms. "Together," he concluded, "Hoover, AEI and Heritage can today deploy formidable armies on the battlefield of ideas"[61]—forces that were to prove enormously influential in shifting domestic policy to the Right.

THE FUTURE OF CORPORATE INVOLVEMENT IN SOCIAL WELFARE

Corporations will continue to influence social welfare policy reflecting the preference of business leaders that the corporate sector assume a primary role in activities of both the voluntary and governmental sectors. Rather than assume a reactive role in corporate involvement in social policy and programming, human-service advocates should engage the business community proactively. A creative illustration of this appears in the "Decency Principles" proposed by Nancy Amidei, a social worker and syndicated columnist. Noting that the Sullivan principles addressed the responsibilities of firms doing business in South Africa, Amidei wondered about the responsibilities of firms doing business in the United States. Her standards for responsible business practices include:

1. *Equitable wages* (high enough to escape poverty, comparability across lines of race, age, sex, and handicapping conditions);
2. *Employee rights* (to equal opportunity, to organize for collective bargaining, to affordable child care, to safe working conditions, and to health coverage);
3. *Housing* (working for more affordable housing, helping relocated or migrant workers obtain affordable housing);
4. *Environmental* (responsible use of resources, sound handling of dangerous substances, conformance with environmental protection laws).

Amidei suggested that a corporation's adherence to the "Decency Principles" be a basis for government decisions on such matters as providing tax abatements to corporations to attract new industry or awarding government contracts.[62]

At the macroeconomic level, government and industry can collaborate through "industrial policy." The idea that government should intervene to aid the business community was reinforced by an increasingly rapid loss of economic advantage to the economies of Japan and Germany, both of which received substantial assistance from their governments. Industrial policy was endorsed by liberal economists, such as Lester Thurow, who proposed "the national equivalent of a corporate investment committee" to coordinate economic policy.[63] He argued that subsequent industrialization would provide increased revenues for welfare programs but, more important, create jobs for the unemployed. In the final analysis, further improvement in the economic circumstances of the poor and the unemployed was politically feasible only under conditions of an expanding economy.

Another advocate of fusing social needs and economic requirements is Secretary of Labor Robert Reich. According to Reich, much of the American industrial malaise was attributable to under investment in human capital. However, human capital investments can be wasteful, leading to nonproductive dependency, when not coupled with the needs of industry. "Underlying many of the inadequacies of American social programs, in short, is the fact that they have not been directed in any explicit or coherent way toward the large task of adapting America's labor force."[64] The attachment of social needs to industrial productivity would fundamentally alter social welfare. "Government bureaucracies that now administer these programs to individuals will be supplanted, to a large extent, by companies that administer them to their employees," suggested Reich. "Companies, rather than state and local governments, will be the agents through which such assistance is provided."[65]

Significantly, industrial policy has attracted conservative adherents as well. Influential analyst Kevin Phillips has proposed a more business-directed version of industrial policy. In Phillips's "business-government partnership," labor and business would agree to work cooperatively with government so that the United States could regain its dominant role in the international economy. For Phillips, however, industrial policy offers less for social welfare:

> Political liberals must accept that there is little support for bringing back federal agencies based on New Deal models to run the U.S. economy, and that much of the new business-government cooperation will back economic development and nationalist (export, trade competition) agendas rather than abstractions like social justice or social welfare.[66]

The primacy of business interests in public policy is not accepted by many social welfare advocates. While "corporatism" may seem plausible to corporate executives, government officials, and labor unions, it offers little to the unemployed and welfare or working poor.[67] In fact, some critics of industrial policy suggest that its very emergence signifies the inability of advanced capitalism to ensure the provision of basic goods and services to the economically disadvantaged through the welfare state.[68] If these critics are correct, industrial policy is an indication of the demise of welfare capitalism rather than a blueprint for enhancing social welfare. Exactly how the relationship among business, labor, and government will be articulated in the future has much to do with the development of public policy. Although the precise nature of such policy must be left to conjecture, the increasing sophistication of the corporate sector in shaping social policy suggests that social welfare policy of the future will show greater congruence with the priorities of American business.

HUMAN-SERVICE CORPORATIONS

As the postindustrial service sector expands, continued demand for human-services has drawn the corporate sector directly into social welfare in the United States. Corporate exploration of the growing human-services market has proceeded rapidly while government welfare programs have failed to keep pace. Heavily dependent on government support and the contributions of middle-income Americans who have experienced a continual erosion of their economic position, the voluntary sector is unlikely to meet all of future service demands. By contrast, relatively unfettered by government regulation and with easy access to capital from commercial sources, the corporate sector has made dramatic inroads into service areas previously reserved for governmental and voluntary sector organizations.

Significantly, the incentives for corporate entry into human-services were initially provided through government social programs. Between 1950 and 1991, government expenditures for social welfare increased from $23.5 billion to $1.16 *trillion*, a factor of 50. As a percent of Gross Domestic Product, public welfare expenditures more than doubled, from 8.8 percent in 1970 to 20.5 percent in 1991. Health care allocations figured prominently in the expansion of public welfare expenditures. In 1970, government spent $24.9 billion on health care; by 1991 that figure had grown to $317.0 billion.[69] The potential profits for corporations entering the rapidly expanding health and human-services market were unmistakable.

Concomitantly, public policy decisions have encouraged proprietary firms to provide health and human-services. This was the case when Medicaid and Medicare were enacted in 1965. By using a market approach to ensure the availability of health care for the medically indigent and the elderly, Medicaid and Medicare avoided the costs of constructing a system of public sector facilities and, in so doing, contributed to the restructuring of American health care. What had been essentially a haphazard collection of mom-and-pop nursing homes and small private hospitals was transformed, in a short period, into a system of corporate franchises, complete with stocks traded on Wall Street. Incentives offered through Medicaid and Medicare to encourage the corporate sector to become involved in hospital care were replicated in the health maintenance industry almost a decade later. The Health Maintenance Organization Act of 1973 stimulated a sluggish health maintenance industry that has since grown at an explosive rate.

Initially dependent on government welfare programs, the corporate sector has developed a life of its own. Exploitation of the nursing home, hospital management, and health maintenance markets has led to corporate interest in other markets. By the 1980s, human-service corporations had established prominence in child care, ambulatory health care, substance abuse and psychiatric care, home health care, as well as life- and continuing-care.[70] By the 1990s, managed care firms were restructuring health and mental health services and fattening corporate profits. Increasingly, proprietary firms were able to obtain funds for facilities through commercial loans or sales of stock, and to meet ongoing costs by charging fees to individuals, companies, and nongovernmental third parties. Insofar as resources for human-service corporations are not financed by the state, firms are free to function relatively independent of government intervention.

The Scope of Human-Service Corporations

How big is the corporate sector in American social welfare? By the mid–1990s, several of the largest firms—Columbia HCA, CIGNA, and United HealthCare Corp.—reported annual revenues that were far greater than all contributions to the United Way of America.[71] Each of these corporations employed thousands of workers, some more than the number of state and local workers for public welfare programs in any state in the union.[72] Some of the more salient features of the larger human-service corporations are depicted in Table 7.3.

Human-service corporations in the United States share several striking features. First, virtually all were incorporated after World War II, the benchmark of the postindustrial era, and the great majority of these were incorporated after 1960. All told, the overwhelming majority of these large firms have been in business for less than 25 years. Second, health and human-service corporations have experienced rapid growth. As Figure 7.1 shows, in the early 1980s, 34 firms reported annual revenues exceeding $10 million; by the mid–1990s, the number had ballooned to 186. Human-service corporations seemed immune from the recession of the early 1980s and continued to thrive despite attempts by the Carter and Reagan administrations to contain costs for health and human-service programs. Although most of the companies focus on health-related services, many diversify into other service areas and, in some instances, other types of corporations acquire human-service firms in order to balance their operations.

NEW HUMAN-SERVICE MARKETS

Within social welfare, human-service corporations have become prominent, if not dominant, in several areas: nursing homes, hospital management, health maintenance organizations (HMOs), child care, and

◆ TABLE 7.3
Prominent Health and Human-Service Firms, 1995

Firm	*Revenues*	*Markets*	*Employees*
Columbia/HCA	$20.1 billion	health care	131,600
CIGNA Corp.	19.0 billion	health care	44,700
United Health Care	5.5 billion	health care	28,500
FHP International	3.9 billion	health care	13,000
PacifiCare Health	3.7 billion	health care	4,400
Humana*	3.7 billion	health care	12,000
U.S. Healthcare	3.6 billion	health care	5,000
Tenet Healthcare	3.3 billion	health care	69,000
Wellpoint Health	3.1 billion	health care	3,800
Beverly Enterprises*	3.0 billion	health care	82,000
Wackenhut	748 million	corrections	46,000
Comm. Psych Ctrs.	507million	mental health	9,400
Kinder Care	507 million	child care	22,000

*Earnings for 1994, others for 1995.
Source: Standard & Poors, New York, 1996.

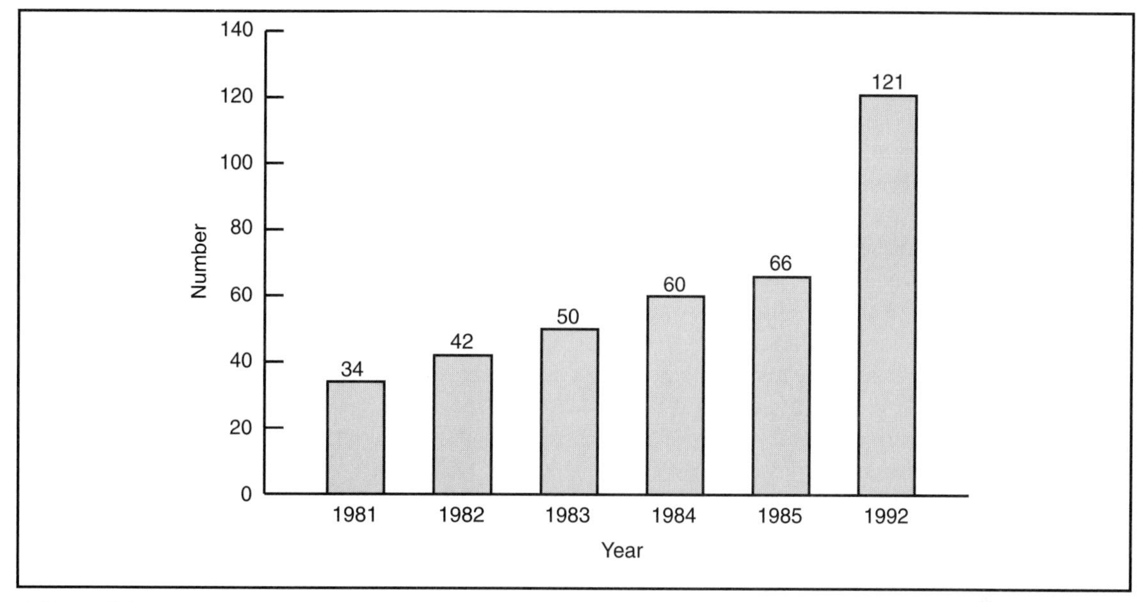

◆ Figure 7.1 **Human-Service Corporations Reporting Annual Revenues above $10 Million. (Source: *Standard and Poor's,* 1993.)**

home care. More recently, proprietary firms have established beachheads in other markets, notably life and continuing care and corrections.

Nursing Homes

Among corporate initiatives in social welfare, expansion into the nursing home industry is unparalleled. Between 1965 and 1978, expenditures for nursing home care increased 16.9 percent *annually*.[73] By the early 1980s, nursing homes had become a $25-billion-a-year industry, and the number of nursing home beds exceeded those in acute care facilities for the first time.[74] At that time, 70 percent of nursing homes were under proprietary management. Market conditions such as these led to the following observation in *Forbes* magazine: "This is a guaranteed opportunity for someone. How the nursing home industry can exploit it is the real question."[75] Under favorable market conditions, nursing home corporations proliferated. David Vaughan, president of a real estate firm specializing in facilities for the elderly, noted:

> The overall affluence of the over fifty-five population makes investments in special care facilities an extremely attractive venture. The need of capital in meeting the housing needs of this segment of the U.S. population has been so great that we have been able to invest in these facilities with only limited competition.[76]

Guaranteed growth of the nursing home market led to the consolidation of proprietary firms and the emergence of an oligopoly. As early as 1981, the following three corporations held more than 10,000 nursing home beds: Beverly Enterprises held 38,488; ARA Services held 31,325; and National Medical Enterprises (NME) held 14,534.[77] Beverly Enterprises attained first ranking by its purchase, in 1979, of Progressive Medical Group, which was the eleventh largest chain of nursing homes. NME attained third ranking in 1979 by purchasing Hillhaven, then the third-largest operation. ARA Services grew 26 percent in 1979, thereby attaining second ranking, by consolidating smaller operations in Indiana, Colorado, and California.[78] Undeterred by the filing of the first antitrust action in the nursing home industry, nursing home firms continued such acquisitions and mergers.[79] In 1984, using its Hillhaven subsidiary, NME acquired Flagg Industries, which held 12 facilities in Idaho, bringing its total holdings to 339 health care facilities with 42,000 beds. Not to be outdone, Beverly Enterprises acquired Beacon Hill

America for $60 million, thereby retaining its top ranking. By the mid–1980s, Beverly Enterprises controlled 781 nursing homes with a total of 88,198 beds in 44 states and the District of Columbia.[80] Given this trend, one industry analyst believed that the industry would eventually fall into the hands of "five or six corporations."[81]

A decade later, Beverly continued as the largest corporation focusing on long-term care, managing 703 nursing homes, 30 assisted living centers, 6 hospices, 11 transitional hospitals, and 4 home health centers. Yet, Beverly's share of the nursing home market did not go unchallenged. On March 1, 1995, Beverly's primary competitor, NME, merged with American Medical International to form Tenet Healthcare Corporation, a $5.5 billion company.[82]

Hospital Management

The growth of the nursing home industry is matched by corporate involvement in hospital management. Between 1976 and 1982, the number of investor-owned or investor-managed hospitals increased from 533 to 1,040, accruing gross revenues of approximately $40 billion.[83] Richard Siegrist, Jr., a Wall Street analyst, concluded that the future for the industry looked bright, noting that revenues and bed ownership for the five largest companies had roughly tripled between 1976 and 1981. According to this analyst, in 1978 Humana doubled its size through an unfriendly takeover of American Medicorp (worth $450 million), gaining 39 hospitals and 7,838 beds. Meanwhile, Hospital Corporation of America (HCA) purchased Hospital Affiliates (worth $650 million), gaining 55 hospitals, 8,207 beds, and 102 hospital management contracts; General Care Corporation (worth $78 million) gained eight hospitals with 1,294 beds; and General Health Services (worth $96 million) gained six hospitals with 1,115 beds. At the same time, American Medical International (AMI) acquired Hyatt Medical Enterprises (worth $69 million), with eight hospitals, 907 beds, and 26 hospital management contracts, as well as Brookwood Health Services (worth $156 million), with nine hospitals, 1,271 beds, and five hospital contracts.[84]

AMI's strategy of purchasing financially troubled community hospitals proved so successful that the company reported a 29 percent increase in net income for 1983 as compared with 1982, accomplished a four-for-three stock split in February 1983, and declared a 21 percent dividend per share. Moreover, in 1984, AMI acquired Lifemark's 25 hospitals and three alcoholism treatment centers through a $1 billion stock transfer.[85] Despite such large-scale growth, AMI continued to rank second behind HCA, which owned 393 hospitals having 56,000 beds.[86] But Humana was to hold the trump card in hospital management. Boldly gambling on its offer to implant artificial hearts in 100 heart patients at no cost, Humana captured the public's attention in 1984. Even though the artificial hearts failed to perform as planned, the project reflected a management strategy that pushed Humana to the head of the pack. By 1993, Humana had forged ahead of its competitors to become the largest health and human-service corporation in the world.

The mid–1990s witnessed the largest mergers among health care corporations that had occurred up to that point. As noted above, NME and AMI merged to form Tenet Healthcare Corp., effectively approximating the market share controlled by Humana. This paled, however, in comparison to the acquisition of HCA by Columbia. The Columbia/HCA merger created a $20 billion behemoth that dwarfed Tenet and Humana. By the mid–1990s the holdings of Columbia/HCA included 292 general hospitals, 28 psychiatric hospitals, and 125 outpatient and auxilliary facilities.[87]

Health Maintenance Organizations

Pioneered by the nonprofit Kaiser-Permanente in California, the concept of health maintenance organizations (HMOs) was slow to attract the interest of the corporate sector. However, from 1973 to 1981, the Health Maintenance Organization Act of 1973 authorized funds for the establishment of facilities in a large number of favorable marketing areas. This funding, coupled with the growth in the nursing home and hospital management industries, reversed investor apathy. By 1983, 60 HMOs were operating on a proprietary basis.[88]

An early leader in the HMO industry was HealthAmerica, a for-profit HMO begun in 1980.

Within a few years HealthAmerica enrolled almost 400,000 members in 17 locations across the nation, becoming the largest proprietary HMO (second in size only to nonprofit Kaiser-Permanente). Seeking capital for further expansion, HealthAmerica offered stock publicly in July 1983 and raised $20 million for 1.5 million shares. One month later, Phillip Bredesen, chairman and president of HealthAmerica, reported that he anticipated "dramatic growth in the HMO segment of the health care business," and that "HealthAmerica [was] well-positioned with the people and systems that this growth [would] represent."[89]

HealthAmerica's growth did not go unnoticed by Fred Wasserman, founder of Maxicare, a proprietary HMO. Wasserman suspected that Bredesen had stretched his company too thin in an ambitious expansion into new market areas. In November 1986, HealthAmerica was purchased by Maxicare for $372 million. Coupled with its earlier acquisition of HealthCare USA for $66 million, the purchase of HealthAmerica enabled Maxicare to claim more than 2 million members nationwide and annual revenues approaching $2 billion. After the HealthAmerica takeover, Wasserman spoke optimistically about overtaking Kaiser-Permanente in pursuit of a health maintenance market[90] expected to consist of 30 million members and $25 billion in revenues by 1990.[91] Wasserman's optimism was misplaced, however. The firm proved unable to manage the debt incurred by its appetite for mergers in the mid–1980s. Maxicare sought protection against creditors, filing for bankruptcy under Chapter 11 in the late 1980s. The collapse of Wasserman's HMO empire was evident in his firm's revenues. Peaking in 1987, Maxicare reported earnings of $1.8 billion; three years later, the firm earned $387 million, less than a fourth of its earlier value.

The HMO market surged in the late 1980s as managed care became the method of choice for containing health care costs. As business and labor groups attempted to limit the fiscal drain caused by escalating costs of health care, proprietary firms stepped forward to manage care more efficiently. By the early 1990s, more than a dozen managed care companies were reporting hefty revenues. Humana, for example, controlled 17 HMOs as well as the health care provided by some 40,800 physicians, in addition to its 630 hospitals. A rapidly growing competitor, PacifiCare, had established HMOs in six states and enrolled 1.2 million members. The largest firm focusing on health management was United HealthCare Corporation, with facilities in 24 states and Puerto Rico, and enrolling 13.5 million members. FHP International was in second place, reporting annual revenues of $3.9 billion. Yet the insurance giant CIGNA dominated the industry, controlling 46 HMOs in which 3 million people were subscribers.[92]

Child Care

As a human-services market, child care is exploited effectively by proprietary firms. In an important study of child welfare services delivery, Catherine Born showed the influence of for-profit providers relative to that of providers in the voluntary and public sectors. She noted that:

> . . . In the case of residential treatment, among all services purchased, 51 percent was obtained from for-profit firms, 26 percent from voluntary organizations, and 22 percent from other public agencies having contractual agreements with the welfare department. For contracted institutional services, 48 percent was provided by proprietary concerns, 14 percent by voluntary vendors, and 38 percent by other public agencies. The pattern was similar in the case of group home services where 58 percent was proprietarily contracted, 17 percent was obtained from the private, nonprofit sector, and 25 percent was purchased from other public agencies.[93]

The day care market—along with its largest provider, Kinder-Care—has expanded rapidly. Begun in 1969, Kinder-Care has demonstrated prodigious growth, claiming approximately 825 "learning centers" in 1983, representing $128 million in revenue. The net earnings for Kinder-Care in fiscal year 1983 represented a 68 percent increase over fiscal year 1982. The company executed a five-for-four stock split in November 1982 and a four-for-three stock split in May 1983. Also, during fiscal year 1983, the company entered the market of freestanding immediate medical care by purchasing First Medical Corporation and its 10 facilities for an undisclosed sum.[94] By the second quarter of 1984, Kinder-Care reported that more than 100 new learning centers and 20 new clinics were under construction.[95]

By the early 1990s, Kinder-Care's 1,236 centers and annual revenues of $411 million dominated the market, but new competitors emerged to serve a seemingly infinite need for organized child care. Children's Discovery Centers of America claimed 93 centers and $57.2 million in revenues in 1991; Rocking Horse Child Care Center of America owned 87 preschool and elementary learning centers in 1991 and reported earnings of $34.7 million; Sunrise Preschools—the new kid on the block—earned $10.4 million in 1991 through its 15 preschool programs.

By the mid–1990s, Kinder Care had consolidated to 1,133 child care centers serving 116,000 children. Yet, the smaller Discovery Centers more than doubled the number of its facilities, claiming 193 centers serving 17,500 children. Newcomer, Sunrise Preschools actually lost market share, reporting 1995 revenues of $9.7 million for its 29 facilities that cared for 2,700 children.[96]

Home Care

Several companies in the home care market have replicated the success of corporations in the nursing home industry. Home Health Care of America, renamed Caremark, began in 1979. A leader in the field, the company has grown particularly quickly. Caremark generated net revenues of $1 million in 1980, $35.8 million in 1983, and $133.2 million in 1986. In 1983, Caremark increased the number of its regional service centers from 10 to 31 and, despite the costs incurred by this expansion, net income for the year increased 129 percent. By the mid–1990s, Caremark was reporting annual revenues of $2.4 billion and claimed health care facilities in Canada, France, Germany, the United Kingdom, the Netherlands, and Japan.[97]

Growth of this magnitude led Elsie Griffith, chief executive officer of the Visiting Nurse Service of New York and chair of the board of the National Association for Home Care, to observe that home health care "is expanding at a phenomenal rate."[98]

Accordingly, during the early 1990s home health companies adjusted their services to meet earlier hospital discharges resulting from implementation of Medicare's prospective payment system. As patients went home sooner, the need for a range of specialized in-home health services grew. Quickly, home health companies began to offer a variety of services to patients. In markets where conventional home health companies failed to offer such specialized care, new firms entered the market and expanded rapidly.

Corrections

Among the more ambitious of human-service corporations is the Correction Corporation of America (CCA), founded in 1983 by Tom Beasely with the financial backing of Jack Massey, founder of the Hospital Corporation of America. CCA officials noted that many states were unable to contend with overcrowding of facilities and proposed contracting with state and local jurisdictions for the provision of correctional services. As CCA acknowledged in its 1986 annual report, court orders to upgrade facilities, coupled with governmental reluctance to finance improvements, provided strong incentives for jurisdictions to consider contracting out correctional services.

> Government response to . . . [overcrowding] . . . has been hampered by the administrative and budgetary problems traditionally plaguing public sector facilities. Most systems have suffered a lack of long-term leadership due to their ties to the political process, and many jurisdictions have placed a low priority on corrections funding. The outcome has been a proliferation of out-dated facilities with a lack of sufficient capacity to meet constitutional standards.[99]

By 1986, CCA operated nine correctional facilities, totaling 1,646 beds, and was negotiating with the Texas Department of Corrections "to build and manage two minimum security prisons which will provide an additional 1,000 beds."[100]

Most analysts expect that proprietary correctional facilities will grow in popularity as governmental agencies recognize the cost savings of contracting out correctional services. CCA's per diem charge in 1986 was $29.77, about 25 percent less than the cost in public facilities.[101] In the near future, Texas, Oklahoma, and Arkansas are to put 3,000 correctional "beds" out to bid, perhaps signifying the willingness of states to use proprietary firms on a large scale.[102] The most dramatic example of the prospective growth of for-profit corrections almost occurred in 1985, when CCA startled Tennessee state officials by offering to take over the state's entire prison system. Like 30 other states and the District of Columbia, Tennessee's system was characterized by too many prisoners in archaic facilities and was operating under court supervision. When CCA offered the state $250 million for a 99-year contract, state officials were hard-pressed not to give it careful consideration. Ultimately, state officials balked at the idea, primarily because of a conflict of interest between CCA and leaders of state government.[103]

Undaunted, CCA moved steadily ahead, capitalizing on the dire need of local and state governments for greater prison capacity. By 1991, CCA managed 17 facilities and reported annual revenues of $67.9 million. Although these earnings were small when compared with other human-service firms, they were astonishing in light of the $7.6 million CCA had earned just six years earlier.

By the mid–1990s CCA's reported revenues of $207 million from holdings that had expanded to 49 correctional facilities totaling 33,153 beds, with plans to develop or expand 16 more. Despite CCA's expansion, the largest for-profit provider of correctional services was Wackenhut, a firm with prisons and detention facilities in the United States, Great Britain, and Australia. For 1995, Wackenhut reported income of $796 million from 24 owned or managed facilities, representing 16,000 beds.[104]

Life and Continuing Care

The graying of the American population has led some corporations to construct special residential communities that include health care as a service. Life care, or continuing care, provides more affluent elders an opportunity to purchase a higher level of long-term care than is ordinarily found in nursing homes. Life care communities usually feature recreational, cultural, and other services in addition to health care. By the mid–1980s, 275 life care communities housed 100,000 elders.[105] Robert Ball, former commissioner of Social Security, estimated that perhaps 15 million elders could afford this type of care.[106]

Despite well-publicized bankruptcies of several life care communities, the prospect of a market of this magnitude has attracted the interest of several corporations. Beverly Enterprises, the largest nursing home operation, declared its intent to build or acquire several such communities.[107] Subsequently, the Marriott Corporation announced plans to have 200 Lifecare Retirement Communities in operation by the year 2000.[108] Despite the recession of the early 1980s, the interest of brokerage houses in life care remained high. Harold Margolin, a vice president of Merrill Lynch, stated that "the financial climate could impact on the growth of the continuing care segment of the health care industry, but only on the timing. It's going to be a very large industry."[109]

Electronic Benefit Transfer

If it is surprising that corporations have discovered a market in corrections, an emerging market in income maintenance is even more so. Since the late 1980s, states have explored the dispersion of public assistance benefits through Electronic Benefit Transfer (EBT). In EBT, government deposits benefits for the eligible population in a jurisdiction with a financial institution and beneficiaries access these through Automatic Teller Machines (ATMs). A variation of the same technology is Point of Service deductions through which the EBT card can be encoded to deduct food commodities from the user's Food Stamp or WIC account. EBT offers several advantages. States can achieve significant efficiencies because an EBT transaction costs 2 cents compared to the 43 cents for cutting a check.[110] Beneficiaries find that EBT is less stigmatizing because they use mainstream financial institutions and avoid onerous vouchers, such as food stamps. For both, security is enhanced because having to recover misplaced or stolen checks is avoided. By mid–1996, 11 states had deployed EBT for food stamps, and 23 states and the District of Columbia had begun conversion to EBT.[111]

New Mexico illustrates how EBT has become a market in dispersion of public assistance benefits. Since 1989, First Security Bank of Utah has subcontracted with the New Mexico State Department of Social Services to convert public assistance checks to EBT. By 1995, EBT was used statewide for AFDC and food stamps, and plans were to include SSI and WIC in EBT also. First Security Bank's interest in EBT was twofold. Having ATM technology already in place for its regular customers, little additional cost was incurred by folding in AFDC and food stamp recipients. Moreover, the bank had use of funds between the time they were deposited by government and withdrawn by beneficiaries. For example, by the spring of 1996, federal and state government deposited $29.7 million monthly in AFDC and food stamp funds. State officials reported that public assistance recipients adapted readily to EBT. The primary problem in EBT was accessing benefits in rural areas without commercial ATMs, but this was solved by installing an ATM in a county government building.[112]

As additional states convert to EBT, commercial banks will compete for contracts to disperse income maintenance benefits. Citibank, the largest EBT provider with contracts from 11 states, estimated that by late 1995, $111 billion was being dispersed through EBT.[113] Expanding EBT beyond public assistance to include social insurance benefits raises the specter of an enormous market, indeed. Unfortunately, proponents of welfare liberalism have been so capital adverse that community-oriented financial institutions that could serve as repositories for such accounts, using them to leverage community development projects in poor neighborhoods, are a rarity even in the largest American metropolitan areas. Institutions such as Chicago's South Shore Bank and the Central Brooklyn Federal Credit Union in New York City illustrate how such capital can be trapped in poor communities and used to leverage community development ventures.

CONCLUSION: IMPLICATIONS FOR HEALTH AND HUMAN-SERVICE PROFESSIONALS

Despite the proliferation of human-service corporations, health and human-service professionals have been slow to adopt the corporate sector as a setting for practice. Considering that organizations under traditional auspices—the voluntary and governmental sectors—are limited in their capacity to provide services, it is probable that health and human-service professionals will discover that corporations are a suitable location for practice.

Actually, for-profit firms can be advantageous for several reasons. Proprietary firms may provide access to the capital needed for expanding social services. A primary explanation for the rapid growth of human-service corporations is their ability to tap commercial sources of capital. Through loans and the sale of stock, they can quickly obtain the funds necessary for expansion. This has given them an enormous advantage over their competitors in the voluntary sector, which often resort to arduous and painstaking fund-raising campaigns, and competitors in the governmental sector, which must rely on the even more protracted methods of bond sales or tax increases to raise funds. For human-service corporations, the cost of commercially derived capital can be reduced by depreciating assets and writing off the interest against income during the first years of operation. This presents obvious advantages for human-service administrators who are faced with diminishing revenues derived from charitable or governmental sources. Perhaps the best example of this advantage is the meteoric rise of long-term care corporations, which were almost nonexistent 20 years ago. By convincing commercial lenders and investors that long-term care was viable, for-profit firms eventually gained control over the industry.[114]

In some instances, the corporate sector more readily offers opportunities for program innovation than what is possible under other auspices. Governmental programs must be mandated by a public authority, and this requires a consensus on how to deal with particular concerns. Voluntary sector agencies are ultimately managed by a board of directors that reflects the interests of the community in organizational policy. When human-service issues are controversial, welfare professionals can encounter stiff opposition to needed programs. Some of this can be obviated by a corporate organizational form that is not so directly wedded to the status quo. An example of how a human-service corporation offers opportunities not possible through traditional human-service organizations is the ability of for-profit correctional companies to expand the scope of correctional facilities when government is reluctant to finance new construction and the voluntary sector is unable to raise the necessary capital.

A compelling illustration of the advantages afforded by the for-profit sector is United American Healthcare Corporation, an HMO with 212,000 members. Started in the early 1980s by three physicians, including an African American gynecologist, Julius Combs, United American focused on the health care needs of the minority poor, many of whom were on Medicaid. In targeting the urban poor, United American offered primary care as well as preventive health care services, such as childhood vaccinations and prenatal care not readily available to Medicaid recipients. For 1994, United American reported revenues of $40 million, $6.5 million above expenses;[115] the next year revenues had jumped to $67 million.[116] Thus, in the span of a decade, minority health professionals had enhanced access and quality of health care to a substantial urban population that had been underserved, by incorporating a health care firm.

As the example of United American Healthcare suggests, the corporate sector offers greater organizational flexibility than that usually found in governmental agencies and a level of sophistication in managerial innovation not often found in the voluntary sector. To be sure, economic advantages enjoyed by the corporate sector make this possible, but the track record in organizational experimentation by the corporate sector is undeniable. In fact, examples of alternatives that could be of value to traditional welfare organizations are frequently derived from the corporate sector, as such popular books as *In Search of Excellence* and *The ChangeMasters Attest*.[117]

Of course, some human-service professionals are skeptical about the assurance of social welfare through human-service corporations. According to the critics of proprietary human-service delivery, the corporate sector is the organizational manifestation of a capitalist economy that is at the root of much social injustice and human need. For these welfare advocates, professional practice within a corporate context is antithetical to the very idea of "social" welfare. In fact, studies of the organizational practices of human-service corporations raise important questions about their suitability for promoting the commonweal. Human-service corporations have been found to be less cost-effective than nonprofit and governmental agencies, engage in a discriminatory selection of clients that penalizes the poor, and attract clients away from voluntary social service agencies. Despite the undesirable attributes of proprietary human-service providers, they are likely to continue to play an active role in defining social welfare. The economy of the United States, after all, is capitalistic, and entrepreneurs are free to establish businesses in whatever markets they consider profitable. Unless government strictly regulates—or prohibits—the for-profit provision of human-services, human-service corporations will influence American social welfare to an even greater extent in the future.

◆ ◆ ◆ Discussion Questions ◆ ◆ ◆

1. What are the major corporate philanthropic organizations in your community? What activities have they funded traditionally? To what extent do they incorporate social welfare projects in their funding priorities? Can you determine how priorities and funding decisions are made within these organizations?

2. If you were the director of a nonprofit welfare agency, which sources of philanthropy would you approach in your community to obtain contributions? How would you know which person or persons to approach in the organization? How would you approach them? If a major contribution were secured, how would you recognize the donor?

3. If you were inclined to establish a business providing a human-service, what population would you focus on? How would you get capital to start the business? Would you own the business or would you share ownership with stockholders? How would you market your service? What would you do with the profits—provide stockholders with dividends, enlarge the business, or make contributions to nonprofit agencies? What would be the name of your business?

4. Think tanks exist in Washington, D.C., and most state capitals. Obtain a copy of the annual report of a think tank. Who funds the think tank? Is there a relationship between the funding source and the ideological character of reports that the think tank publishes? What is the think tank's track record in social welfare issues?

Notes

1. Stephen Chapman, "Politicians Protect Corporate Welfare," *Richmond Times-Dispatch* (October 23, 1996), p. A13.
2. Ralph Nader, ". . . And What about Corporate Welfare Reform?" *Washington Post Weekly* (October 14–20, 1996), p. 22.
3. Jinlay Lewis, "CEOs' Presence in Bush Party Draws Attention to their Pay," *San Diego Union* (January 13, 1992), p. E3.
4. Fred Barnes, "The Zillionaires Club," *The New Republic* (January 29, 1990), p. 23.
5. Sheila Kamerman, "The New Mixed Economy of Welfare," *Social Work* 28 (January–February 1983), p. 76.
6. Paul Starr, "The Meaning of Privatization," and MDRC Bendick, "Privatizing the Delivery of Social Welfare Service" in *Working Paper* 6 (Washington, DC: National Conference on Social Welfare, 1985); David Stoesz, "Privatization: Reforming the Welfare State," *Journal of Sociology and Social Welfare* 16 (Summer 1987), p. 139; Mimi Abramovitz, "The Privatization of the Welfare State," *Social Work* (31)4 (July–August 1986), pp. 257–264.
7. Neil Gilbert, *Capitalism and the Welfare State* (New Haven: Yale University Press, 1983).
8. David Stoesz, "Corporate Welfare," *Social Work* (31)4 (July–August 1986), p. 86; "Corporate Health Care and Social Welfare," *Health and Social Work* (Summer 1986), p. 158; and "The Gray Market," *Journal of Gerontological Social Work* 16 (1989), p. 31.
9. Abramovitz, "The Privatization of the Welfare State," p. 257.
10. Theodore Marmor, Mark Schlesinger, and Richard Smithey, "A New Look at Nonprofits: Health Care Policy in a Competitive Age," *Yale Journal of Regulation* (3)2 (Spring 1986), p. 322.
11. Robert Heilbroner, *The Worldly Philosophers* (New York: Simon and Schuster, 1967), pp. 98–106.
12. Edward Berkowitz and Kim McQuaid, *Creating the Welfare State* (New York: Praeger, 1980), p. 4.
13. Ibid., pp. 5–10.
14. Gilbert, *Capitalism and the Welfare State*, p. 3.
15. Original emphasis, quoted in Norman Furniss and Timothy Tilton, *The Case for the Welfare State* (Bloomington: Indiana University Press, 1977), p. 156.
16. Murray Levine and Adeline Levine, *A Social History of Helping Services* (New York: Appleton-Century-Crofts, 1970), p. 237.
17. Harold Wilensky and Charles Lebeaux, *Industrial Society and Social Welfare* (New York: Free Press, 1965), p. 88.
18. James Leiby, *A History of Social Welfare and Social Work in the United States* (New York: Columbia University Press, 1978), p. 170.
19. Levine and Levine, *A Social History of Helping Services*, pp. 236–243.
20. Wilensky and Lebeaux, *Industrial Society and Social Welfare*, p. 9; National Association of Social Workers, *Encyclopedia of Social Work*, 18th Ed. (Silver Spring, MD: NASW, 1987), p. 781.
21. James Jones, *Bad Blood* (New York: Free Press, 1981), p. 34.
22. Thomas DiBacco, "Hookworm's Strange History," *Washington Post* (June 30, 1992), p. 14 (health section).
23. Berkowitz and McQuaid, *Creating the Welfare State*, pp. 33–36.
24. Ibid., p. 83.
25. Michael Boskin, "Social Security and the Economy." In Peter Duignan and Alvin Rabushka (Eds.), *The United States in the 1980s* (Stanford, CA: Hoover Institution, 1980), p. 182.
26. Berkowitz and McQuaid, *Creating the Welfare State*, p. 103.
27. Ibid., p. 136.
28. Michael Misshauk, *Management: Theory and Practice* (Boston: Little, Brown, 1979), p. 6.

29. Melvin Anshen, *Managing the Socially Responsible Corporation* (New York: Macmillan, 1974), p. 5.
30. Steven Lydenberg, *Rating America's Corporate Conscience* (Reading, MA: Addison-Wesley, 1986).
31. Theodore Purcell, "Management and the 'Ethical' Investors." In S. Prakash Sethi and Carl Swanson (Eds.), *Private Enterprise and Public Purpose* (New York: John Wiley, 1981), pp. 296–297.
32. Lloyd Kurtz, Steven Lydenberg, and Peter Kinder, "The Domini Social Index." In Peter Kinder, Steven Lydenberg, and Amy Domini (Eds.), *The Social Investment Almanac* (New York: Henry Holt, 1992), Chap. 25.
33. James Worthy, "Managing the 'Social Markets' Business." In Lance Liebner and Corrine Schelling (Eds.), *Public-Private Partnership: New Opportunities for Meeting Social Needs* (Cambridge, MA: Ballinger, 1978), p. 226.
34. Melanie Lawrence, "Social Responsibility: How Companies Become Involved in Their Communities," *Personnel Journal* (61)7 (July 1982), p. 381; James Chrisman and Archie Carroll, "SMR Forum: Corporate Responsibility—Reconciling Economic and Social Goals," *Sloan Management Review* (25)2 (Winter 1984), p. 173.
35. Enterprise Foundation, *Annual Report 1983* (Columbia, MD: Enterprise Foundation, 1983), p. 1.
36. Enterprise Foundation, *Annual Report* (Columbia, MD: author, 1995).
37. Brian O'Connell, *Philanthropy in Action* (New York: The Foundation Center, 1987), p. 218.
38. Local Initiatives Support Corporation, *The Local Initiatives Support Corporation* (New York: LISC, 1980); "A Statement of Policy for Programs of the Local Initiatives Support Corporation" (New York: LISC, 1981).
39. Local Initiatives Support Corporation, *Making Change Happen: Annual Report* (New York: author, 1995).
40. Joan Shapiro, "Community Development Banks." In Peter Kinder, Steven Lydenberg, and Amy Domini (Eds.), *The Social Investment Almanac* (New York: Henry Holt, 1992), Chap. 42.
41. "Would You Like to Be Your Own Boss?" (San Francisco: Women's Initiative for Self Employment, n.d.).
42. David Linowes, *The Corporate Conscience* (New York: Hawthorn Books, 1974), p. 209.
43. *Privatization: Toward More Effective Government* (Washington, DC: U.S. Government Printing Office, 1988), pp. 2–3.
44. Irving Kristol, "Charity and Business Shouldn't Mix," *The New York Times* (October 17, 1982), p. 18.
45. Lawrence Fouraker and Graham Allison, "Foreword." In John Dunlop (Ed.), *Business and Public Policy* (Cambridge, MA: Harvard University Press, 1980), p. ix.
46. Peter Steinfels, "Michael Novak and His Ultrasuper Democraticapitalism," *Commonweal* (February 15, 1983), p. 11.
47. William J. Baroody, Jr., "The President's Review," *AEI Annual Report 1981–82* (Washington, DC: American Enterprise Institute, 1982), p. 2.
48. Peter Stone, "Businesses Widen Role in Conservatives' 'War on Ideas,'" *Washington Post* (May 12, 1985), p. C5.
49. Ibid., p. 50.
50. Ibid., p. 28.
51. Richard Reeves, "How New Ideas Shape Presidential Politics," *The New York Times Magazine* (July 15, 1984), p. 18.
52. Heritage Foundation, *The Heritage Foundation Annual Report* (Washington, DC: Heritage Foundation, 1983).
53. Interview with Stuart Butler, at the Heritage Foundation, Washington, DC, October 4, 1984.
54. George Sternlieb, "Kemp-Garcia Act." In George Sternlieb and David Listokin (Eds.), *New Tools for Economic Development* (Piscataway, NJ: Rutgers University Press, 1981), p. 42.
55. Stuart Butler, "Enterprise Zones," in Sternlieb and Listokin, *New Tools for Economic Development*, pp. 73–94.
56. Gilbert Lewthwaite, "Heritage Foundation Delivers Right Message," *Baltimore Sun*, (December 9, 1984), p. 2.
57. Peter Ferrara, *Social Security Reform* (Washington, DC: Heritage Foundation, 1982), p. 51.
58. Peter Ferrara, *Rebuilding Social Security* (Washington, DC: Heritage Foundation, 1984), p. 7.
59. Chuck Lane, "The Manhattan Project," *The New Republic* (March 25, 1985), p. 34.
60. Charles Murray, *Losing Ground* (New York: Basic Books, 1984), pp. 226, 227.

61. Burton Pines, *Back to Basics* (New York: William Morrow, 1982), p. 254.
62. Nancy Amidei, "How to End Poverty: Next Steps," *Food Monitor* (Winter 1988), p. 52.
63. Lester Thurow, *The Zero-Sum Society* (New York: Basic Books, 1980), p. 95.
64. Robert Reich, *The Next American Frontier* (New York: Times Books, 1983), p. 223.
65. Ibid., pp. 247–248.
66. Kevin Phillips, *Staying on Top: The Business Case for a National Industrial Policy* (New York: Random House, 1984), pp. 5–6.
67. Yeheskel Hasenfeld, "The Changing Context of Human-Services Administration," *Social Work* (29)4 (November–December 1984), p. 524.
68. James O'Connor, *The Fiscal Crisis of the State* (New York: St. Martin's Press, 1973); Ian Gough, *The Political Economy of the Welfare State* (London: Macmillan, 1979).
69. Social Security Administration, *Social Security Bulletin, Annual Statistical Supplement* (Washington, DC: U.S. GPO, 1994), p. 140.
70. Life/continuing care refers to residential communities for the elderly that have a complete range of health services available to residents. Such communities usually require residents to purchase their homes and to pay a monthly fee for a comprehensive range of services, including health care.
71. David Stoesz, "Human-Service Corporations and the Welfare State," *Transaction/Society* 16 (1989), pp. 80–91.
72. Bureau of the Census, *Statistical Abstract of the United States, 1986* (Washington, DC: U.S. Government Printing Office, 1986).
73. U.S. Department of Commerce, *1982 U.S. Industrial Outlook for 200 Industries with Projections for 1986* (Washington, DC: U.S. Government Printing Office, 1982), p. 406.
74. J. Avorn, "Nursing Home Infections—The Context," *New England Journal of Medicine* 305 (September 24, 1981), p. 759.
75. J. Blyskal, "Gray Gold," *Forbes* (November 23, 1981), p. 84.
76. D. Vaughan, "Health Care Syndications: Investment Tools of the '80s," *Financial Planner* (December 1981), p. 49.
77. Blyskal, "Gray Gold," p. 80.
78. V. DiPaolo, "Tight Money, Higher Interest Rates Slow Nursing Home Systems Growth," *Modern Health Care* (June 1980), p. 84.
79. National Senior Citizens' Law Center, "Federal Antitrust Activity" (Los Angeles: National Senior Citizens' Law Center, 1982), p. 2.
80. "NME Makes More Health Care Acquisitions," *Homecare News* (February 17, 1984), p. 4.
81. Quoted in W. Spicer, "The Boom in Building," *Contemporary Administrator* (February 1982), pp. 13–14.
82. "Beverly Enterprises" and "Tenet Healthcare Corp," *Standard and Poor's Stock Report* (October 1995), p. 89.
83. B. Gray, "An Introduction to the New Health Care for Profit," in B. Gray (Ed.), *The New Health Care for Profit* (Washington, DC: National Academy Press, 1983), p. 2.
84. R. Siegrist, Jr., "Wall Street and the For-Profit Hospital Management Companies."In B. Gray (Ed.), *The New Health Care for Profit*, p. 36.
85. American Medical International, *1983 Annual Report* (Beverly Hills, CA: AMI, 1983).
86. "GAO Says Proprietary Hospital Chain Mergers Raise Medicare/Medicaid Costs," *Homecare News* (February 17, 1984), p. 6.
87. "Columbia/HCA" *Standard and Poor's Stock Reports* (October 1996), p. 80.
88. National Industry Council for HMO Development, *Ten Year Report 1971–1983* (Washington, DC, 1983).
89. HealthAmerica, *Company Profile* (Nashville, TN: HealthAmerica, 1983).
90. M. Abramowitz, "Maxicare HMO Soars with Farsighted Founder," *Washington Post*, (November 30, 1986), p. 12.
91. National Industry Council, *Ten Year Report*, p. 22.
92. "PacifiCare," "United HealthCare Corp.," and "CIGNA," *Standard and Poor's Stock Reports* (October 1996), 102.
93. Catherine Born, "Proprietary Firms and Child Welfare Services: Patterns and Implications," *Child Welfare* 62 (March–April 1983), p. 112.
94. Kinder-Care, *Annual Report 1983* (Montgomery, AL: Kinder-Care, 1983).
95. Kinder-Care, *Second Quarter Report* (Montgomery, AL: Kinder-Care, March 16, 1984).
96. "Kinder Care," "Children's Discovery Centers," and "Sunrise Preschools," *Standard and Poor's Stock Reports* (October 1996).

97. "Home Health Care of America," *Standard and Poor's Stock Reports* (March 1984; October 1995).
98. "Interview with Elsie Griffith," *American Journal of Nursing* 18 (March 1984), p. 341.
99. "Digest of Earnings Reports," *Wall Street Journal* (August 13, 1987), p. 41.
100. Stephen Boland, "Prisons for Profit." Unpublished manuscript, School of Social Work, San Diego State University, 1987, pp. 5–6.
101. Ibid., p. 8.
102. Eric Press, "A Person, Not a Number," *Newsweek* (June 29, 1987), p. 63.
103. D. Vise, "Private Company Asks for Control of Tennessee Prisons," *Washington Post* (September 22, 1985), p. D2.
104. "Correction Corporation of America" and "Wackenhut," *Standard and Poor's Stock Reports* (October 1996).
105. U.S. Senate Special Committee on Aging, *Discrimination Against the Poor and Disabled in Nursing Homes* (Washington, DC, U.S. Government Printing Office, 1984), p. 8.
106. Ibid.
107. "Sun City—With an Add-On," *Forbes* (November 23, 1981), p. 84.1.
108. Paul Farhi, "Marriott Corp. Caters to America's Rapidly Aging Population," *Washington Post* (January 2, 1989), p. 5.
109. "Merrill Lynch: Bullish on Health Care," *Contemporary Administrator* (February 1982), p. 16.
110. "Direct Federal Electronic Benefit Transfer Fact Sheet," (Washington, DC: U.S. Department of Treasury, n.d.).
111. Ibid.
112. Conversation with Marlee Torres, EBT Coordinator, New Mexico State Department of Social Services, Albuquerque, July 2, 1996.
113. "Treasury Names Citibank for Major EBT Project in 8 Southern States," (press release) (New York: Citibank, October 18, 1995).
114. D. Stoesz, "The Gray Market," p. 45.
115. Udayan Gupta, "United American Healthcare Proves Naysayers Wrong," *Wall Street Journal* (August 22, 1994), p. B2.
116. "United American Healthcare Corporation," *Standard and Poor's Stock Reports* (October 1996).
117. Thomas J. Peters and Robert W. Waterman, Jr., *In Search of Excellence* (New York: Harper and Row, 1982); and Rosabeth M. Kanter, *The Changemasters* (New York, Simon and Schuster, 1983).

CHAPTER 8

Privatization and Private Practice

This chapter reviews privatization of social welfare. Historically, much social welfare has been provided by the private not-for-profit sector. Since the 1980s, however, conservatives have called for down-sizing government, in the process shifting service responsibility to the private sector. "Governments in the United States spend roughly half a trillion dollars per year paying public workers to deliver goods and services directly," observed John Donahue. "If only one-quarter of this total turned out to be suitable for privatization, at an average savings of, say, 25 percent—and neither figure is recklessly optimistic—the public would save over $30 billion."[1] Such savings could be used to lower taxes or to extend existing programs.

Yet, many health and human-service professionals have trepidations about privatization. Significant downsizing of government coupled with the astronomical growth of for-profit health and human-service firms, presents a significant challenge to the American welfare state. As a result, many liberal, social activists object to privatization often citing research that identifies weaknesses in relying on the private sector for certain activities. Research on for-profit firms generally confirms liberal doubts about privatizing welfare.

The irony in the critical stance toward privatization assumed by many health and human-service professionals is that many of them prefer private practice as a method of service delivery. Thus, private practice on a small scale is condoned, but corporate exploitation of the new health and human-service markets is met with considerable skepticism. This issue has become volatile as corporate managed care firms have penetrated markets once controlled by private practitioners. It also raises a profound question for the social work profession: to the extent that social workers engage in private practice there are fewer human-service professionals in the public sector to work with people presenting more serious disorders. As a result, what limited influence social work has is invested in promoting its self-interest at the expense of the poor, a point underscored by the late Harry Specht and Mark Courtney in *Unfaithful Angels*:

> there has been an increasing tendency of the [social work] profession to use its political power to support licensing of clinical social workers and third-party payments for social workers who are so licensed, to the relative neglect of efforts to improve the lot of social workers employed in the public social services and their clients.[2]

For many human-service professionals, private practice represents a retreat from a service ethic that transcends self-interest: the public welfare.

Finally, the chapter considers collective bargaining as a response to privatization. Health and human-service professionals have been reluctant to join unions, primarily because they fear doing so would taint their professional status. Yet, continuing privatization means that unions may be the only aggregate defense for professionals who have become employees of health and human-service corporations.

THE PRIVATIZATION OF HEALTH AND HUMAN-SERVICES

As a function of public dissatisfaction with governmental social programs, increasing reliance on the private sector to finance and deliver social services has emerged as an important theme in American social welfare. *Privatization*, as this idea has been termed, addresses the problem of the proper relationship between the public and private spheres of the national culture. In this case, *privatization* has come to refer to "the idea that private is invariably more efficient than public, that government ought to stay out of as many realms as possible, and that government should contract out tasks to private firms or give people vouchers rather than provide them services directly."[3] That government should not hold a monopoly on social welfare is not a novel idea. Even liberal policy analysts have entertained ways in which the private sector could complement governmental welfare initiatives.[4] Liberal proponents of welfare programs are often willing to concede a viable role to the private sector—even an innovative role—but insist that government must be the primary instrument to advance social welfare. Conservatives, of course, see the proper balance as one in which the private sector is the primary source of protection against social and economic calamity, and believe that government activity should be held in reserve. According to conservative doctrine, government can deploy the "safety net" of social programs, but these should provide benefits only as a last resort.

A clear articulation of the conservative vision of reinforcing the role of the private sector in social affairs appeared in the 1988 Report of the President's Commission on Privatization. "In the United States . . . the growth of government has been based on the political and economic design that emerged from the Progressive movement around the turn of this century," noted the report. "The American privatization movement has represented in significant part a reaction against the themes and results of Progressive thought."[5] Specifically, the report targeted government social programs and the professional administrators who manage them as the undesirable consequences of the progressive state of mind, which can be corrected by privatization. The implications of this analysis are broad: Not only should benefits be removed from government and provided by the private sector, but the administration of social programs should also be removed from the public sector and placed under private auspices. Accordingly, the President's Commission on Privatization identified three "techniques for the privatization of service delivery": (1) the selling of government assets; (2) contracting with private firms to provide goods and services previously offered by government; and (3) the use of vouchers, whereby the government would distribute coupons authorizing private providers to receive reimbursement from the government for the goods and services they had provided.[6] While all these methods have been used to restructure welfare programs at one time or another, the report introduces an unprecedented idea into the debate by characterizing the issue as a "zero-sum game," one in which the advantage to one party is at the expense of the other. In this case, proponents of privatization suggest that the private sector should assume more responsibility for welfare, but with government social programs reduced. It is this sacrifice of the government's obligation to ensure the general welfare that makes the current debate on privatization so important.

A new question in the debate on the balance between private and public responsibility for welfare was introduced with the recent emergence of health and human-service corporations. This is: If government is to divest itself of its welfare obligation, can the business community pick up the slack? If the answer is yes, proponents of privatization have two options for the private provision of social welfare: the nonprofit, voluntary sector, and the for-profit, corporate sector. In the years following President Lyndon Johnson's Great Society programs, government began to experiment with contracting out services through both nonprofit and for-profit providers. The for-profit, corporate sector capitalized on the contracting-out provisions of the Medicare and Medicaid programs. Through the purchase-of-service concept introduced in Title XX, nonprofit agencies became contractors providing a range of social services on behalf of public welfare departments. Unfortunately, studies comparing the performance of these sectors have been few and their findings debatable.[7]

In the absence of definitive studies showing the advantages of one sector over another, the privatization debate has become heated. Advocates of *voluntarization*, or reliance on the voluntary sector to assume more of the responsibility for welfare, point to its historical contribution to the national culture, the rootedness of its agencies in the community, and the altruistic motive behind its programs. Proponents of *corporatization*, or dependence on the corporate sector to provide welfare, argue that it offers more cost-effective administration, is more responsive to consumer demand, and pays taxes. Whether voluntarists or corporatists prevail in the privatization debate will rest largely on the ability of each party to manipulate the social policy process in its favor. Whatever the outcome, this process is certain to be lengthy and complex, as one might expect with the remaking of an institutional structure that has become as essential as social welfare is in the United States. Whether voluntarization or corporatization defines the future of American social welfare, privatization has already highlighted several important issues.

Commercialization

For welfare professionals the idea of subjecting human need to the economic marketplace is often problematic. It is hard to condone health care advertising, when opponents, notably the Health Insurance Association of America, spent $100 million to defeat the Clinton Health Security Act even though the United States is still without a universal program for expectant mothers and infants, to say nothing of the 40 million Americans without health insurance.[8] When research on the AIDS virus led to a diagnostic test, some private physicians exploited the AIDS panic and charged as much as $300 for each test, whereas the U.S. Army negotiated a test price of 82 cents.[9] As objectionable as these market-induced practices may be, the commercialization of health and human-services is a reality that welfare professionals cannot simply dismiss out of a sense of moral indignation.

In one of the earliest treatments of the matter, Richard Titmuss's *The Gift Relationship* explored the differences in the way nations manage their blood banks. Unlike the practice in the United Kingdom, blood in the United States is "treated in laws as an article of commerce;" as such, rules of the market affect the supply and quality of blood. Titmuss observed the growth of blood and plasma businesses with alarm because they bought blood from a population that was often characterized by poverty and poor health. Quite apart from the health hazard posed by a blood supply derived from such a population—a hazard highlighted by the AIDS pandemic—Titmuss was concerned that the profit motive would disrupt the voluntary impulses of community life. "There is growing disquiet in the United States," he observed, "with expanding blood programs that such programs are driving out the voluntary system."[10] Indeed, by 1976, 63.3 percent of blood banks in the United States were commercial.[11]

The commercialization issue is particularly important for financially strapped nonprofit agencies. Faced with static, if not declining revenues, some voluntary sector agencies have experimented with commercial activities in order to supplement income derived from traditional sources: contributions, grants, and fees. That nonprofit organizations should be allowed to engage in commercial endeavors without restriction is "unfair competition," according to business operators, who note that nonprofits do not ordinarily pay taxes on their income.

Limits on the freedom of nonprofit organizations to engage in commercial activities were highlighted in a celebrated case involving New York University Law School and the Mueller Macaroni Company. Seeking a way to enhance revenues to the law school, thereby avoiding the burden of contributing to their alma mater, enterprising alumni acquired the Mueller Company and reorganized it as a nonprofit organization registered in Delaware.

Income from the macaroni company was thus redefined as nontaxable income and diverted to the law school as a charitable contribution. This clever arrangement, however, did not go unnoticed by Mueller's competitors, who recognized the possibility of Mueller being able to use its newly acquired tax-exempt status to cut prices and drive other macaroni companies from the market. Further, they argued, what was to prevent any well-endowed nonprofit institution from acquiring profitable businesses as a way of supplementing its income while dodging its tax obligation? The situation soon proved so embarrassing to the law school that it sent no representatives to the congressional hearings that deliberated on the ethics of the arrangement. Eventually, the tax code was altered, thereafter making income from commercial activities that are not related to the service function of the agency taxable.[12]

Since 1950, revenue obtained by nonprofit organizations from commercial activity has been taxable under the unrelated business income tax (UBIT). While the Mueller case served as an adequate measure against gross breaches of business propriety, subsequent developments raised further questions around the commerce issue. For example, a nonprofit hospital association in Virginia attempted to maintain its competitive edge by acquiring several commercial ventures, including an advertising agency, two health clubs, an interior decorating firm, a pharmacy, and a helicopter ambulance service. These acquisitions were criticized by nearby businesses.[13] Even the YMCA has come under fire. In this case, the 1,100-member International Racquet Sports Association complained that "Ys" held an unfair competitive advantage over for-profit racquet clubs.[14] These and other conflicts between nonprofit and for-profit organizations were aired during hearings held by the House Ways and Means Committee in 1987.[15]

During the hearings, representatives of the business community complained that nonprofits were engaged in "unfair competition" with for-profit businesses. According to business representatives, this unfair competition occurred in two ways. First, the UBIT failed to distinguish between related and unrelated business activities. For example, a nonprofit hospital's pharmacy is considered related to the hospital's mission and is therefore exempt from paying taxes on profit, but a for-profit hospital's pharmacy is part of the business and its profit is therefore taxable. Second, nonprofit organizations benefit from the "halo effect"—that is, the public's perception that their services are superior because they do not operate from the profit motive. Thus, health spas complain that the philanthropic image of Ys is inaccurate because Ys use many commercial business practices—such as marketing and advertising—to promote their services. Yet the revenues of the Ys are tax-exempt.

Although complaints of unfair competition on the part of nonprofit organizations appear to be academic, the accusations open the possibility of further restricting the revenue base of voluntary sector agencies. For example, some Ys have stopped advertising their programs for fear that local authorities may interpret that activity as commercial and thereby attempt to tax income derived from them. Thus, the unfair competition issue presents some very disturbing questions for administrators of nonprofit organizations. If a nonprofit family service agency bills a client's insurance company for a "usual, customary, and reasonable" fee comparable to what is charged by a private practice group that must pay taxes on such income, should this income remain tax-exempt? Should tax-exempt income be limited to charitable contributions only? Do program outreach and public education activities constitute marketing and advertising and, if so, should they be limited if a nonprofit organization is to retain its tax exemption? Questions like these strike at the heart of the function of the voluntary sector. How these questions are resolved will be of great concern to proponents of nonprofit community service agencies, particularly those organizations faced with dwindling revenues.

Preferential Selection

If privatization has implications for program administrators, as evident in the commercialization of human-services, it also has significant implications for clients. The application of market principles to client service introduces strong incentives for providers to differentiate clients according to their effect on organizational performance. Such selection can be at variance with professional standards, which emphasize the client's need for service over organizational considerations. But the marketplace tends to penalize providers who are imprudent about client selection, at the same time rewarding providers who are more discriminating. The subtle or blatant practice of choosing clients according to criteria of organizational performance—as opposed to client need—is defined as *preferential selection*. Under marketplace conditions, providers who do not practice preferential selection are bound to serve a disproportionate number of clients with serious problems and with less ability to pay the cost of care, thereby running deficits. By contrast, providers who select clients with less serious problems and who can cover the cost of care often claim surpluses. For example, an analysis of psychiatric patients admitted to a public and a private hospital found that the latter selected patients of higher social status. The researchers concluded that "patients in the marginal/uncredentialed social class were comparatively more likely to be admitted to state mental hospitals than to private hospitals."[16]

Preferential selection could be excused, perhaps, as a benign method through which organizations determine those clients who are likely to be best served—if it were not for the odious practice of client "dumping." Dumping occurs when clients, already being served by an organization (usually a for-profit firm), are abruptly transferred to another organization (ordinarily a nonprofit or governmental agency) because they represent a drain on the institutional resources of the former.

Critics of privatization complain that creaming the client population through preferential selection is unethical and should be prohibited. Simply ruling out the practice is, however, easier said than done. Accusations of preferential selection are not new; private, nonprofit agencies were accused of denying services to welfare recipients well before proprietary firms became established.[17] Yet recent reports of dumping when life-threatening injuries are evident have drawn the ire of many human-service professionals. In some instances, private hospitals have transferred indigent patients with traumatic injuries to public facilities without providing proper medical care, thus contributing to the deaths of several patients.

Incidents of dumping are directly related to the patient's ability to pay for service, and transfers of poor patients have increased as Medicaid is cut. For example, the transfer of poor patients to the publicly owned Cook County General Hospital in Chicago increased from between 90 and 125 per month to 560 patients in August 1981, one month after Illinois instituted cuts in its Medicaid program.[18] In another instance, researchers at Highland General Hospital, the public health care facility in Alameda County, California, examined the transfer disposition of 458 patients over a six-month period. The researchers concluded that "the transfer of patients from private to public hospital emergency rooms is common, involves primarily uninsured or government-insured patients, disproportionately affects minority group members, and sometimes places patients in jeopardy."[19] In Denver, where public hospitals have borne heavy deficits for carrying a disproportionate burden of the medically indigent, the problem has become critical. Jane Collins, director of clinical social work for the Denver Department of Health and Hospitals, described public hospitals in the city as having become "social dumps."[20]

Given the market, preferential selection on the part of a large number of providers is likely to be adopted by others who wish to remain in a competitive position. In analyzing the practice in health care, a team of researchers from Harvard University and the American Medical Association noted that, "in the same way that competition from for-profit providers leads to reduction in access, the more competitive the market for hospital services generally, the more likely are all hospitals in that market to discourage admissions of Medicaid and uninsured patients."[21] In other words, nonprofit providers—who are exempt from taxes because they contribute to the community's welfare—are compelled to adopt the discriminatory practices of for-profit providers in a competitive market, unless the nonprofits are willing to underwrite the losses that more costly clients represent to for-profit providers. "When competitive pressures are great," researchers from Yale and Harvard universities, have noted, "the behavior of for-profit and nonprofit institutions often converge."[22]

Cost-Effectiveness

Proponents of privatization frequently cite the discipline imposed by a competitive environment on organizational performance as a rationale for market reforms in social welfare. A competitive environment provides strong incentives for firms to adopt cost-effective practices that reduce waste. This claim has led to a handful of studies of for-profit versus nonprofit service providers. In 1981, Lewin and Associates compared 53 nonprofit hospitals with a matched set of for-profit hospitals in the South and Southwest. They concluded that investor-owned hospitals were more expensive than nonprofit hospitals, largely due to higher ancillary (laboratory, radiology services) and administrative service costs. Also, investor-owned hospitals used fewer full-time equivalent staff to provide care than did nonprofit hospitals.[23] This last finding is unsettling because lower staff-to-patient ratios have been associated with higher rates of contagious disease in nursing homes.[24] The Florida Hospital Cost Containment Board released a 1980 analysis comparing 72 proprietary and 82 nonprofit hospitals in that state. With results similar to the Lewin study, the Board reported a 15 percent higher charge for patient care and an 11 percent higher collection rate by investor-owned hospitals more than their nonprofit counterparts.[25]

In an ambitious study, researchers from the Western Consortium for the Health Professions compared 280 private voluntary, public, and investor-owned hospitals. The Western Consortium investigators reached conclusions that were even less supportive of subjecting health care to the marketplace. For example, they suggested that investor-owned hospitals used emergency services and room and board as loss-leaders, funneling patients into pricing situations where higher-cost ancillary services would be used. Investor-owned hospitals cared for the smallest proportion of patients dependent on Medicaid. The researchers concluded that "the data do not support the claim that investor-owned chains enjoy overall operating efficiencies or economics of scale in administrative or fiscal services."[26]

Significantly, the higher cost of proprietary hospitals cannot be attributed to longer periods of hospitalization, because the average stay at for-profit hospitals, 7.8 days, was (along with government institutions) less than that of sectarian and other nonprofit institutions.[27] In a comprehensive review of the issue, the Institute of Medicine of the National Academy of Sciences concluded that there is "no evidence to support the common belief that investor-owned organizations are less costly or more efficient than are not-for-profit organizations."[28]

More recently, Robert Kuttner summarized analyses conducted by an association of nonprofit hospitals and found that "investor-owned hospitals in 1994 were 13.7 percent more expensive on a charge basis than nonprofit and public hospitals." Not only were for-profit hospitals more expensive, but they also provided less care to the poor, admitting only half as many Medicaid patients as nonprofit hospitals. Another analysis of proprietary hospitals by the nonprofit hospital association found that investor-owned hospitals were 30 percent more expensive than not-for-profit hospitals.[29]

Although skeptics of market strategies in welfare use such studies to criticize the false economies of the human-services market, it appears that the practices of for-profit firms are nevertheless influencing nonprofit human-service organizations. Many nonprofits have adopted features of for-profit firms—bulk buying, sophisticated information systems, staff reductions—to enhance organizational efficiency. As noted, when nonprofits compete with for-profit firms in the same market, the adoption of competitive practices is inevitable in order to ensure organizational survival. As a result, competitive practices characteristic of human-service corporations may become standard organizational procedure, not because they serve the public interest better but because the rules of the marketplace require their adoption.

The promise of cost containment through privatization has not been borne out, and this presents an enormous problem for the governmental sector. Under a privatized system, government is in a weak position to control the prices charged by contracting agencies unless it is prepared to deploy its own set of public institutions, thereby avoiding the private sector altogether. A good example is provided by the Medicare program through which the government subsidizes health care, most of which is provided by the private sector. In response to runaway Medicare costs, Congress enacted the Diagnosis Related Group (DRG) prospective payment plan in 1983, whereby hospitals are reimbursed fixed amounts for medical procedures. Three years after the DRG system was in place, the Congressional Budget Office reported that hospitals had increased their surplus attributed to Medicare by 15.7 percent during 1985. This surplus occurred despite a reduction in the number of Medicare patients admitted to hospitals.[30]

Proponents of privatization often claim that noncompetitive markets and governmental regulation, as in the case of the DRG prospective payment system, impose additional costs that must be passed on to consumers. Research, however, does not bear this out. In a study of 6,000 hospitals sponsored by the National Center for Health Services Research and Health Care Technology Assessment, a research team found that "hospitals located in areas with 11 or more neighboring facilities within a 15 mile radius—the most competitive type of hospital market—have admission costs and patient day costs that are 26 percent and 15 percent higher, respectively, than corresponding figures for hospitals with no competitors." Significantly, the hospitals were surveyed before 1983, so governmental regulation through the DRG system could not have contributed to increased costs.[31]

Standardization

Privatization induces human-service organizations to accept an industrial mode of production in which the accepted measure of success is not necessarily the quality of service rendered but the number of people processed. Organizational surplus, essential for investor-owned facilities, tends to be derived from increasing the intensity of production and lowering labor costs. Because the logic of the market dictates that the goal of production is to process the largest number of people at the lowest possible cost, the standardization of services is an important method for lowering organizational costs.

Such uniformity of care has become an issue in the nursing home industry. Because Medicaid regulations stipulate standards of care, providers deriving a large portion of their revenues from Medicaid are induced to standardize care for all patients. Paradoxically, well-to-do patients are unable to purchase better care from a nursing home even though they have the resources to do so. The standardization of care has became a cause for serious concern among nursing home corporations. Richard Buchanan, professor of business administration at Bowling Green State University, noted the social consequences of standardized care:

> The nursing home industry's identical treatment of everyone creates a one-class social system for all patients. This constitutes a denial of the affluent person's rights to purchase the quality of life that had been his or hers until stricken with illness or infirmity. This phenomenon represents creeping socialism of a major order, and creates an atmosphere ripe for either legal or market reprisal.[32]

That standardization of care within an industry dominated by for-profit firms would be equated with socialism is perhaps the best measure of the acuity of the problem.

Under these circumstances, life care—or the continuing-care retirement community—has emerged as an attractive alternative to the nursing home for the provision of long-term care. Under life care, residents can purchase cottages or apartments in self-contained communities that include a range of human-services. In many respects, the life care community provides more affluent residents an opportunity to purchase a higher level of long-term care. One continuing-care facility boasted wall-to-wall carpeting, maid service, and a designer courtyard. "Already, the facility has shown its first in-house movie . . . and soon residents will be soaking up steam in the saunas, relaxing in the Jacuzzi, exercising on the mechanical bicycles, or browsing in the library," noted a visitor.[33] Among the amenities found in the more posh life-care communities are cocktail lounge, billiards room, sports facilities, and elegantly furnished restaurants serving continental cuisine. Amenities such as these "provide a lifestyle of grace and activity for seniors with the ability to pay for it," observed an industry reporter.[34] "We sell a style of life," explained David Steel, vice president of Retirement Centers of America Inc., a subsidiary of Avon.[35]

Entry into life-care communities can be equivalent to purchasing a home. Nationwide, in the early 1980s the average entrance fees were $35,000 for a single person and $39,000 for a couple. Monthly fees for medical care, dining and laundry, recreation, and transportation averaged $600 for a single person and $850 for a couple.[36] In more exclusive communities, one- and two-bedroom units sell for from $100,000 to $170,000.[37] By the mid–1980s, 275 life-care communities were housing 100,000 elders.[38] But this was only the tip of a very large iceberg. Robert Ball, former commissioner of Social Security, estimated that perhaps 15 million elders could afford this type of care.[39] Despite the well-publicized bankruptcies of several life-care communities, the prospect of a market of this scale has attracted the interest of several corporations.[40] Beverly Enterprises, the largest nursing home corporation, announced plans to build or acquire several life care communities.[41] Subsequently, Marriott Corporation stated its intention to build a number of life-care communities serving between 300 and 400 residents each.[42] Despite the recession of the early 1980s, the interest of brokerage houses in continuing care remained high.[43] By the year 2000, as many as 15 million Americans will need some form of long-term care.[44]

The prospect of extensive proprietary involvement in life care troubles some analysts. Lloyd Lewis, director of a nonprofit life care community, fears that "well-funded proprietary interests" will "drain off the more financially able segment of our older population, widening the gap between the 'haves' and the 'have nots.'"[45] To a significant extent this is already occurring. Robert Ball noted that life-care communities operating under even not-for-profit auspices are beyond the means of "the poor, the near poor, or even the low-income elderly."[46]

The accommodation of long-term care facilities to the desire for amenities on the part of affluent residents is likely to produce significant change in how the nation cares for its elderly. In 1982, for example, *The New York Times* reported a nationwide shortage of nursing home beds for those "whose nursing care is financed by the government through Medicaid."[47] As human-service corporations divert capital to care for those who represent profit margins, economic and political support diminishes for the care of those less fortunate. "Those who cannot gain admission to [a private] institution will be forced into boarding homes . . . or bootleg boarding homes," commented Milton Jacobs, vice president of American Medical Affiliates. "These boarding homes will be filled with what are literally social rejects. We're reverting back to the way the industry was in the fifties and sixties."[48] Left unchecked, long-term care is likely to divide into two clearly demarcated systems: the affluent enjoying the generous care of completely—some would say excessively—provisioned life-care communities and the elderly poor dependent on the squalid institutions willing to accept government payment for their care. To a great extent, dual systems of long-term care will be attributed to the desire of the affluent to escape the standardization of care associated with the economies of privatization.

Oligopolization

The privatization of human-services invites the development of oligopolies, or the control of a market by few providers, as organizations seek to reduce competition by acquiring competitors. Within the corporate sector, three waves of acquisition can be identified: acquisitions affecting long-term care, acquisitions affecting hospital management, and acquisitions affecting health maintenance organizations. As firms control major shares of markets, they are in a strong position to leverage influence through trade associations to shape social policy.

Driven by the same competitive pressures, the consolidation of proprietary health providers has encouraged nonprofit providers to form franchises. In terms of number of beds, five of the ten largest hospital systems are nonprofit. Of these, three are operated by religious organizations; one—the New York City Health and Hospital Corporation—is a public conglomerate, while another—Kaiser Foundation Hospital—is a private nonprofit entity. Increasingly, nonprofit health providers are having to join together in order to compete with the aggressive proprietary providers, which has led to oligopolies within the voluntary sector.[49]

Oligopolization of human-services presents a daunting specter in that a small number of wealthy and powerful organizations are in a strong position to shape social policy to conform with their interests. Within health care, this development has led Arnold Relman, editor of the *New England Journal of Medicine*, to voice alarm at the growing influence of the "new medical-industrial complex" in defining health policy in the United States.[50] A good illustration of the influence of health providers on public policy was the Clinton administration's ill-fated Health Security Act (HSA).

The HSA was designed to incorporate for-profit health care providers through regional health alliances, which would compete for members. Even though this incorporated the interests of the larger health care firms, it threatened to wipe out many smaller firms. Soon after HSA was rolled-out, the Health Insurance Association of America (HIAA) broadcast $2 million worth of ads, alleging that the HSA would ration health care under socialized medicine.[51] Michael Bromberg, director of the Federation of American Health Systems (FAHS) representing 1,400 for-profit hospitals, announced preference for a less restrictive proposal than the HSA. Bromberg threatened Hillary Rodham Clinton with an adversarial campaign if the administration did not adjust its plan to accommodate FAHS. The threat was not hollow; FAHS routinely contributed $250,000 to the campaigns of strategically placed Senate and House candidates.[52] Within weeks lobbyists besieged Capitol Hill. Anticipating the 1994 election, health industry interest groups contributed $26 million to Congressional campaigns.[53] Eventually, observers would put the price tag on influence peddling around failed health care reform at $100 million.[54]

The primary question relating to oligopolization of social markets is the emergence of a "welfare-industrial complex"—a network of CEOs and governmental appointees who represent an "interlocking directorate" that defines health and human-service policy. An illustration of such networking is evident in plans by Texas to privatize its public welfare department. One of the bidders for the contract was Lockheed Martin, a defense firm that was diversifying into human-services. Because of the magnitude of the Texas contract, $500 million, Lockheed deftly maneuvered to the inside track by offering Gerald Miller, Michigan's director of welfare reform as well as president of the American Public Welfare Association, a senior vice-presidency.[55] Undoubtedly, Lockheed's acquisition of Miller would prove a significant advantage given the firm's lack of experience in welfare programming.

THE CHALLENGE OF PRIVATIZATION

Privatization is a disquieting prospect for health and human-service professionals. For those committed to increasing government's responsibility for ensuring social and economic equality, privatization is simply a retreat from a century of hard-won gains in social programs. Their case is argued cogently by Pulitzer Prize–winning sociologist Paul Starr:

> A large-scale shift of public services to private providers would contribute to further isolating the least advantaged, since private firms have strong incentives to skim off the best clients and most profitable services. The result would often be a residual, poorer public sector providing services of last resort. Such institutions would be even less attractive as places to work than they are today. And their worsening difficulties would no doubt be cited as confirmation of the irremediable incompetence of public managers and inferiority of public services. Public institutions already suffer from this vicious circle; most forms of privatization would intensify it.[56]

For defenders of government social programs, the problems attributed to privatization—commercialization, client creaming, inflated costs, standardization, and oligopolization—make it a poor vehicle for advancing social welfare.

Most profoundly, privatization reinforces a tendency in market economies to evolve dual structures of benefits, services, and opportunities: adequate and varied services for the affluent, substandard and uniform services for the poor. As Robert Kuttner has pointed out: "in a purely for-profit enterprise or system, there is no place for uncompensated care, unprofitable admissions, research, education, or public health activities—all chronic money losers from a strictly business viewpoint."[57]

For many human-service advocates, the purpose of social welfare is to correct for the inherent tendency of markets to direct resources toward the affluent and away from the poor. From this perspective, the idea of privatization of social welfare is apostasy. Thus, when Texas proposes to put public welfare out to bid, or when New Jersey plans to privatize child welfare, or when the partial privatization of Social Security is proposed, the Left objects.[58]

Yet reliance on the private sector at a time when public social programs are under assault is a reality that must be faced by those concerned about social welfare. In the absence of an effective Left and the diminishing influence of a progressive labor movement, there appears little chance of launching new government social programs, as the demise of health reform during the first Clinton term demonstrated. If the public is unwilling to authorize and pay for new governmental social programs, welfare professionals have little choice but to reconsider privatization as a basis for welfare provision. In seeking to understand the conditions under which privatization is an appropriate policy response, for example, William Gormley has suggested that privatization is indicated less for "regulation than for distribution of goods, less for social services than for physical services, and less for less for core services than for auxiliary services."[59]

In some instances, private sector analogues to public services have demonstrated surprising success. Take, for example, job placement of the hard-core unemployed. Traditional public sector approaches to this population include policies realized in the Job Training and Partnership Act and the Family Support Act. Yet in New York and Connecticut an innovative program called America Works has evolved from the private sector:

> Each year the company finds jobs for more than 700 of the state's hard-core unemployed, 68 percent of whom are (as a result) permanently weaned from the welfare rolls. The company gets paid only after the former welfare recipient has been working for four months and its $5,000 fee is less than half of what it costs New York State to support an average welfare family of three. All told, America Works is saving taxpayers approximately $4.5 million annually and providing many of the state's hard-core unemployed with meaningful work.[60]

Upon inspection, it could be argued that there are compelling reasons to believe that privatization could be a strategy for promoting social welfare. Through commercial loans and issuance of stock, for-profit organizations have faster access to capital than does the governmental sector (which requires a lengthy public expenditure authorization process) or the voluntary sector (which relies on arduous fund-raising campaigns) for purposes of program expansion. The example of United American Healthcare providing prenatal and primary health care for Medicaid recipients, described in Chapter 7, illustrates how the for-profit sector can be a vehicle for advancing the public good. The private sector has also been the source of important innovations in programs and organizational administration, which have often become the exemplars for effective administration.[61] It could be argued further that welfare-conscious administrators have missed opportunities for promoting social welfare by ignoring opportunities for professional practice associated with privatization. In this regard, welfare professionals might wonder if patient abuses in the nursing home industry, chronicled in *Tender Loving Greed,* would have been lessened had socially conscious administrators managed long-term care facilities.[62] After years of lobbying, human-service advocates have finally secured a regulation "requiring nursing homes with more than 120 beds to employ full-time at least one [undergraduate] social worker," which is hardly enough to ensure compliance considering past abuses.[63]

Privatization will continue to challenge the moral and rational impulses of human-service professionals. The President's Commission on Privatization notes that "the impact of the privatization movement, broadly understood, is only beginning to be felt. Privatization in this broad sense may well be seen by future historians as one of the most important developments in the American political and economic life of the late 20th century."[64] How health and human-service professionals choose to respond to the challenge of privatization—whether by reaction or innovation—will be critical for the future of American social welfare. Privatization may come to be a rallying cry for defenders of established programs that have been discredited as being wasteful, inflexible, and currying the favors of special interests, or privatization may ultimately mean discovering new ways to exploit the social carrying capacity of the private sector. As David Donnison has suggested, welfare professionals would be wiser to reconsider their aversion to the private sector and to try to find the "progressive potential in privatization."[65]

UNIONS AND THE PRIVATE SECTOR

Unions of health and welfare professionals are one response to privatization. Since the Depression, social welfare professionals have organized collectively in order to obtain better wages and benefits, to enhance working conditions, and improve services to clients. Two pioneers of American social welfare, Bertha Capen Reynolds and Mary van Kleek vigorously urged social welfare workers to view unions as a vehicle for social justice. Today, members of the Bertha Capen Reynolds Society advocate collective bargaining in order to empower human-service professionals.

Social workers in the public sector often hold memberships in unions, most often the American Federation of State, County and Municipal Employees (AFSCME) with 55,000 social work members in 1993, or the Service Employees International Union (SEIU) with 26,000 social work members. Altogether about one in four social workers belongs to a collective bargaining unit.[66] Because of the dispersion of social work activities, however, social workers have been less successful in using unions to achieve their ends compared to nurses and teachers.

Collective bargaining is the foundation of the union process. Collective bargaining refers to the face-to-face interaction between unionized employees and management for the purpose of negotiating a union contract. Such bargaining is done in good faith with the legal rights of workers protected by the National Labor Relations Act. If these rights are attenuated, workers can petition the National Labor Relations Board to address grievances. The ultimate power of unions is to exercise the right to strike when the bargaining process breaks down. Theoretically, both parties have an interest in a successful collective bargaining process because strikes hurt both union members and their employers.

Collective bargaining can also address professional issues, such as caseload size, benefits relating to educational benefits like tuition reimbursement, conference release time and reimbursements, payment for professional dues and subscriptions, and flexible work hours. One union leader noted that, "To the professional—the teacher or caseworker—things like class size and caseload size become as important as the number of hours in a shift is to the blue collar worker."[67] In one organizing campaign, for example, caseload size, career ladders and training, pay equity, and classification downgrading were the primary issues. In a nonprofit mental health clinic, safe working conditions, benefits for part-time workers, workloads, and participation in agency decision making were the focus of organizing efforts.[68]

A significant question before human-service professionals has been the extent to which union objectives are consistent with professional values. Despite the constructive influence that unions could serve in response to cuts in public welfare during the Reagan presidency or wholesale privatization of state and local governmental programs, social workers have approached unions with great apprehension. Opponents to collective bargaining contend that (1) unions cost employees money; (2) strike losses are never retrieved; (3) members have little voice in union affairs when they are not purposely kept uninformed by union leadership; (4) bureaucratic union hierarchies control the economic destiny of members; (5) union corruption is rampant; (6) union opposition to attempts by management to increase productivity arrests organizational growth; (7) union "featherbedding" results in unneeded employees and unnecessary payroll expenses; (8) union activities foster conflict rather than collaboration; and (9) unions fail to extrapolate the effects of wage increases on future employment, inflation, and taxes.

A fundamental concern among social welfare professionals revolves around the ultimate strategy that unions can bring to employer-employee relations: job actions, particularly strikes. For social workers who have pledged to place client welfare as a priority, the prospect of denying services as a result of job actions makes union and professional collaboration contradictory. In covering a 1984 strike by Local 1199 of the Retail Drug Employees Union that included the social work staffs of more than 50 hospitals and nursing homes, Dena Fisher observed that

> Standards for professional practice conflict with the [NASW] Code of Ethics with regard to behavior during a labor strike when the prescribed behavior includes withholding service, failing to terminate clients properly, and picketing activity directed toward consumers. . . . The problem is that participation in a strike is a nonprofessional activity. . . . Standards of professional behavior conflict with union membership requirements.[69]

Yet, proponents of union membership cite ways in which collective bargaining complements professional objectives. In an attempt to encourage a better relationship with professional social workers, Jerry Wurf, former AFSCME president, stated that

> AFSCME's involvement . . . [with social issues] . . . is part of a larger commitment to improving public services and programs. But more importantly, these vital efforts prove the true mission of a labor organization to be closely linked to that of social work. AFSCME's growth in the last decade was due in large part to its role as a social missionary. This precious pursuit has undoubtedly been enhanced by the growing number of social workers in our ranks.[70]

The few studies that have examined the issue have found little incongruity between the loyalties of social workers who belong to unions. Leslie Alexander and his colleagues studied 84 union members with M.S.W degrees and found that "they view their work as solidly professional and, for the most part, do not see unionism and professionalism as incompatible."[71] Ernie Lightman reported similar findings when studying 121 randomly chosen professional social workers in Toronto. According to Lightman, "the vast majority saw no incompatibility; indeed, many felt unionization may facilitate service goals, offsetting workplace bureaucracy."[72] Reporting on child welfare agencies in Pennsylvania and Illinois, Gary Shaffer found that "workers did not find unionism incompatible with their educational or professional goals."[73]

Such complementarity notwithstanding, social work "exceptionalism" pervades the debate about professionalism and unions. This exceptionalism implies that tasks performed by social workers are more important than those performed by many other workers, especially nonprofessionals, and that normal labor relations principles are therefore not applicable. Proponents of social work exceptionalism must address two matters: First, how is it that other semiprofessions—teachers and nurses—have reconciled their professional priorities with union activities and become more powerful in the contexts of their work as a result? Are social service activities to be considered more essential than education or health care? Second, does social work exceptionalism contribute to the powerlessness of social workers? If social work places such value on the empowerment on of clients, why should social workers themselves not also be so empowered? The idea of American social work's exceptionalism was put in bold relief in 1991 when members of Canada's Public Service Alliance—many of whom are social workers—participated in one of the largest strikes in the nation's history, inspired by the government's plan to reduce wage increases.[74] If Canadian human-service professionals can reconcile professional and union differences, why is this beyond American social workers?

While social workers in the United States procrastinate about an alliance with unions, events such as privatization and government cuts in funding, make the issue ever more urgent. Social workers and unions can collaborate in problem solving, fostering a public debate on social issues and promoting class-aware groupings in an adverse social climate. Facilitating social change is the goals of several organizations, including Jobs with Justice. As Heckscher points out, while new approaches to unionization "are still in their infancy . . . the rich variety of innovations being tried today has the potential to restore an essential pillar of labor's strength: the sense among the wider public that employee organization contributes to the general good."[75]

PRIVATE PRACTICE

Rather than confront for-profit providers of human-services, many professionals have pursued a more accommodating strategy: establishing private practices. As a form of independent practice, private practice is influenced by the policies of the states regulating it, by professional associations, and by the insurance companies that pay clinicians for their services. Private social work practice has been controversial within the social work profession, as reflected in this depiction.

> In increasing numbers, social workers are flocking to psychotherapeutic pastures, hanging out their shingles to advertise themselves as psychotherapists just as quickly as licensing laws will permit. For the most part, professional associations of social workers and schools of social work are active participants in the great transformation of social work from a professional corps concerned with helping people deal with their social problems to a major platoon in the psychotherapeutic armies.[76]

Despite this, private practice continues to be a popular form of practice.

Private practice has become an attractive vehicle for delivering clinical social services. As Table 8.1 shows, social workers in for-profit settings are increasing in numbers beyond those in more traditional settings. Of all NASW members the number in private solo practice increased from 10.4 percent in 1988 to 12.2 percent in 1991.[77]

For some time, many of the health and mental health services have been delivered by physicians and psychologists who work predominantly out of private offices. The upsurge of social workers' interest in private practice is such that today a large portion of students entering graduate programs in social work—as

◆ TABLE 8.1
Primary Auspice of Working NASW* Members

	1988		1991	
Primary Auspice	n	%	n	%
Public local	12,309	18.4	15,368	18.5
Public state	11,937	17.9	12,461	15.0
Public federal	2,185	3.3	2,399	2.9
Public military	513	0.8	653	0.8
Private nonprofit	7,697	11.5	10,078	12.2
Private nonprofit sectarian	18,926	28.3	22,168	26.7
Private for profit	13,223	19.8	19,753	23.8
Total respondents	66,970		82,880	

*National Association of Social Workers
Percentages do not total 100 because of rounding.
Source: Margaret Gibelman and Philip Schervish, *The Social Work Labor Force as Reflected in the NASW Membership* (Washington, DC: NASW, 1993), p. 56.

high as 80 percent[78]—do so with the expressed intent of establishing a private practice. Professional schools of social work are specifically equipped to prepare graduate students for private practice. "M.S.W. programs appear to offer more to the practitioner bound for private practice than to the social worker who would prefer to work in an agency setting," concluded researchers in a study of private and agency-based social workers.[79]

The current enthusiasm for private practice can be attributed to several factors. Private practitioners often enjoy a prestige and income that set them apart from salaried professionals. A 1993 survey of salaries of members of the National Association of Social Workers (NASW) revealed that the mean salary of private practitioners was $50,008, well above that of any other practice setting,[80] while they worked significantly fewer hours per week compared to colleagues in public and nonprofit settings.[81] It is not surprising that social workers, who are usually female and underpaid—social work salaries are significantly less than those of nurses or teachers[82]—would see private practice as a way to increase their earnings and status. In fact, women are more likely to engage in private practice than to work in traditional social service agencies; two-thirds of private practitioners are women.[83]

Private practitioners also have a degree of autonomy that is not available to professionals who are bound by the personnel policies of traditional agencies. Srinika Jayaratne and his associates found that "whereas 55 percent of the private practitioners report a high level of congruence between their expectations and their activities, only 18.3 percent of the agency practitioners do so."[84] This is important for experienced professionals who find continued supervision unnecessary or intrusive and who require some flexibility in their work schedules to make room for other priorities. Finally, private practice allows professionals to specialize in activities at which they are best instead of having to conform to organizational requirements of the private agency or governmental bureaucracy. Again, 66.5 percent of private practitioners reported that they were able to do those things at which they excelled, while only 22.9 percent of agency practitioners said they could do so.[85]

The image of private practice that has emerged is one of freedom and opportunity, sans rules and regulations. This is somewhat misleading. Although private practice may involve comparatively fewer compliance requirements than does salaried employment, it is anything but unfettered practice. In actuality, private practice involves a number of policies with which practitioners must be familiar if they are to be successful. The policies that affect private practice originate primarily from two sources: the professional community (a private entity), a government regulatory authority (a public entity), and as recent influences of managed care demonstrate, corporate firms. This situation is complicated by the provision of service through the marketplace of a capitalist economy that traditionally discriminates against groups—minorities, women, the aged, the handicapped—that do not participate fully in the labor market. These groups frequently lack the resources to purchase the goods and services provided by private practitioners. For this reason, private practice is not easily reconciled with the traditional values of the human-service professions, which emphasize service to the community and to the disadvantaged. Paradoxically, private practice has become a popular, yet controversial, method of social work practice.

Private Practice in Social Work

The private practice of social work is a relatively recent phenomenon and the National Association of Social Workers (NASW) did not officially sanction this form of service delivery for its members until 1964.[86] Prior to that, privately practicing social workers identified themselves as psychotherapists and lay analysts. Typically, they relied on referrals from physicians and psychiatrists,[87] and, after World War II, they began to establish "flourishing and lucrative" practices.[88] By 1991, 10,458 NASW members were primarily involved in private practice, another 9,325 indicated private practice as secondary employment.[89]

By 1987, all 50 states regulated social workers, with the majority of these requiring a master's degree in social work (M.S.W.). However, a social work license is not automatically awarded to those holding the M.S.W. degree. Many states require candidates for licensure to have two years of post–M.S.W. experience under the supervision of a Licensed Certified Social Worker (LCSW) and to have passed an examination. Beyond these common requirements, states vary greatly in their regulatory practices. Maryland, for example, has a three-tier system: the LCSW for M.S.Ws who have two years of post–M.S.W. experience and who have passed an examination; the Licensed Graduate Social Worker (LGSW) for newly graduated M.S.Ws; and the Social Work Associate (SWA) for those with baccalaureate degrees in social work. To further complicate matters, new licensing legislation often allows candidates who have practiced professionally to become licensed without first meeting the requirements of the licensing legislation. This practice, called "grandfathering," is characteristic of new licensing legislation and, in that social work licensing is a relatively recent development in many states, there are many LCSWs who would not otherwise meet the technical requirements for a license. Moreover, because some states exempt state employees from licensing requirements, many "social workers" in public welfare do not meet the licensing requirements necessary for the title of social worker. As a result, many social workers are licensed but have not met the requirements with which their colleagues must comply. Consequently, states often establish additional requirements for professionals to be eligible for vendorship. Special registries for clinical social workers may be used to identify LCSWs who are eligible for third-party payments.

Professional associations also designate practitioners who have expertise in particular areas. In social work, the most common distinction is membership in the Academy of Certified Social Workers (ACSW). Requirements for the ACSW are two years of post–M.S.W. experience under the supervision of an ACSW and passage of an examination. These are similar to those for the LCSW, but the two designations should not be confused. Because states have the legal authority to license professions, special distinctions established by professional associations are neither equivalent to nor a substitute for state licensure. Thus, it is common for experienced clinicians to list both LCSW and ACSW after their names as indications of professional competence. Recently, the NASW (which administers the ACSW) developed a "diplomate," which identifies those practitioners with skills above those required for the ACSW. Credentials such as the ACSW serve the function of distinguishing expertise among members of the professional community. Such credentials are determined by policies of the professional community and not by a public authority, as in the case of state licensure.[90]

Clinicians who successfully cultivate private practices stand to do quite well economically. Financial gain does not appear to be the sole motivation for social workers to enter private practice, however. In research on the motives of private social work practitioners versus social workers employed in agencies, Jayaratne and his associates concluded that stress reduction played an important part in the decision to go private. "Those in private practice reported fewer psychological and health strains, reported higher levels of performance, and, in general, felt better about their life circumstances," concluded the researchers. "On every measure, those in private practice scored significantly better than those in agency practice."[91]

Despite the popularity of private practice, it has provoked a great deal of controversy within the professional community. There are several aspects to this controversy, not the least of which is that many practitioners who have committed themselves to helping the disadvantaged through working with the voluntary and governmental sectors view the instant popularity of private practice as antithetical to everything that is "social" about social work. The extent to which private practice has grown at the expense of traditional auspices of employment is evident in data from California. A 1990 survey of California members of NASW found that 29.5 percent were employed in private, for-profit settings, compared with 34.5 percent in public social services and 36 percent in private, nonprofit agencies.[92] Given trends evident during the 1980s, social work in private, for-profit agencies will eclipse other auspices of practice at some time during the 1990s.

For professionals who have committed themselves to furthering social justice through careers in the voluntary and governmental sectors, private practice is often viewed with disdain. Donald Feldstein, head of the Federation of Jewish Philanthropies of New York, suggested that private social work practice is similar to private medical practice in that it presents "new opportunities for rip-offs by the privileged." Private practice, he maintained, replaced social decision making with market decision making. According to Feldstein, "Social decision making is preferable to marketing human-services like soap. . . . The private practice of social work is still against everything that is social about the term social work."[93] Another critic impugned the motives of social workers in private practice:

> Over 15 years ago, when I first had exposure to private practitioners, they were objects of envy, never of nonacceptance. Obviously this envy has continued. For we see more social workers developing private practices. But why all the sham? Let's be honest enough to say it's usually done for the money.[94]

Defenders of private practice emphasize the benefits of the method for practitioners and clients. Why should social workers not enjoy the same professional freedom and responsibility as other professions that use private practice extensively, for instance, law, medicine, and psychiatry? Moreover, "some clients prefer the opportunity to choose their own practitioner and a service they consider more personal and confidential."[95] Concern for the client's perceptions means that practitioners must be concerned about their image. This is evident in one privately practicing social worker's description of her office:

> It is decorated with comfortable chairs, built-in book cases, soft lighting, etc., and is arranged in such a way as to offer several different possibilities for seating. It is commensurate with most of the socio-cultural levels of my client group and provides him or her the opportunity for free expression without being overheard. . . . Dealing with only one socio-cultural client group allows me to provide physical surroundings which facilitate the client's identification with the worker.[96]

On the surface, then, private practice often provokes strong responses from welfare professionals who perceive private practitioners as avoiding efforts by the voluntary and governmental sectors to advance social equity. On the other hand, some believe that private practice offers an opportunity to enhance their status and to provide services to a middle class that the profession has neglected.

Beneath this surface issue, there are more substantial problems raised by private practice. Perhaps the most important of these is "preferential selection," the practice of selecting certain clients for service while rejecting others. In an era of specialization, professionals will refer clients with problems that are inappropriate for their practice to other providers. An important finding of Jayaratne's research was that private practitioners do not perceive their clients in the same way that agency-based social workers do. The latter "were significantly more likely to agree with the statement that 'my personal values and those of my clients differ greatly' than those in private practice."[97] Preferential selection becomes an issue when private practitioners elect to serve less troubled clients (who are able to pay the full cost of care) while referring multiproblem clients (who are unable to pay the practitioner's fee for service directly or indirectly through insurance) to agencies of the voluntary sector. Such "creaming" of the client population places an enormous burden on public agencies, which are left to carry a disproportionate share of the chronically disturbed and indigent clients. In effect, then, the public sector absorbs the losses that would be suffered by private practitioners if they served this population. Preferential selection has become so pronounced that researchers have facetiously identified it as a syndrome. According to Franklin Chu and Sharland Trotter, the commercialization of private practice contributes to the "YAVIS syndrome"—the tendency of clients of private practitioners to be *young*, *attractive*, *verbal*, *intelligent*, and *successful*. One might add *W* to the syndrome because the clients also tend to be disproportionately white.[98] Consequently, clients of private practitioners are less likely to be poor, unemployed, old, and uneducated.

The Business of Private Practice

Aside from preferential selection, another set of issues relates directly to the business nature of private practice. Because private practice is a business, economic considerations figure prominently in a professional's activities. Robert Barker, an authority on private social work practice, explains how economic factors shaped a new practice he established with a colleague: "We hired a good secretary, employed interior decorators to redo our offices and waiting room. We hired an investment counselor and established retirement accounts and insurance programs. Most of all we became more serious about getting our clients to meet their financial obligations."[99]

The market nature of private practice, coupled with economic entrepreneurship, presents the possibility of questionable accounting practices, such as the creation of "uncollectible accounts," the use of "deliberate misdiagnosis," and the practice of "signing off." These practices involve income derived from third-party sources, usually health insurance. As private practitioners become more dependent on insurance reimbursement, these questionable accounting practices become important for the professional community at large.

Health insurance frequently covers outpatient psychiatric care at a "usual, customary and reasonable" (UCR) rate that is determined by the insurance companies. The UCR is what the therapist charges, not necessarily what he or she expects to collect from cash-paying clients. The practice of charging a fee higher than what is expected to be collected is termed holding an "uncollectible account," and is frequently used with third-party fee payment arrangements. This practice is encouraged because insurance coverage rarely covers all of the practitioner's fee but leaves a certain percent to be paid by the client. For example, a social worker may have a UCR of $50 per session while the client may have insurance paying only 50 percent of the UCR, which leaves the client responsible for the remaining $25. If the client is unable to pay $25 per session, but can afford $10, a clinician will bill the insurance company directly, using an assignment of benefits procedure, for $50. Meanwhile, the client pays $10 per session, as opposed to the implied obligatory contractual amount of $25. Although the therapist may collect a total of $35 per session and not the UCR of $50, it may be economical to prefer that amount over an extended period of treatment or possibly until the client can afford the full amount of the copayment. At question here is a professional practice that is contrary to the implied contractual relationship among the client, the clinician, and the third-party payer. Yet, it is in the interest of the clinician to establish this as a regular accounting procedure owing to the dependence on income through fees and the fear that the insurance company may lower the practitioner's UCR if a significant number of billings are below the customary rate, usually 50 percent.

A second example is "deliberate misdiagnosis," an intentional error in client assessment on the part of clinicians. In a survey of clinical social workers, 70 percent of whom had engaged in private practice, Stuart Kirk and Herb Kutchins found that 87 percent of practitioners frequently or occasionally used a less stigmatizing, or "mercy," diagnosis to avoid labeling their patients. On the other hand, clinicians frequently misdiagnose in order to collect insurance payments.

> Seventy-two percent of the respondents are aware of cases where more serious diagnoses are used to qualify for reimbursement. At least 25 percent of the respondents . . . indicated that the practices occurred frequently. Since reimbursement is rarely available for family problems, it is not surprising that 86 percent are aware of instances when diagnoses for individuals are used even though the primary problem is in the family. The majority of respondents said that this occurred frequently.[100]

Of course, such "overdiagnosis" is unethical because it places the economic benefit of the clinician before the service needs of the client. Still, overdiagnosis continues to be a prevalent practice. Kirk and Kutchins suggest that "reimbursement systems, which have become increasingly important for psychiatric treatment for the last decade, are undoubtedly a major factor in encouraging over-diagnosis."[101] The undesirable consequences of a reimbursement-driven diagnosis system are multiple. First, of course, is the possibility that clients will be done harm, particularly if confidentiality is breached and the diagnosis becomes known to others outside the therapeutic relationship. Second, if the prevalence of severe mental disorders is over reported to public officials, they may make errors in program planning as a result. Third, and perhaps most important, overdiagnosis violates the "professional's obligation to their profession to use their knowledge and skill in an ethical manner."[102] While individual digressions can be reported to professional and governmental bodies for investigation, a greater problem exists for practitioners as a whole. Widespread misdiagnosis violates the social contract between the professional community and the state, and thus threatens to "corrupt the helping professions."[103] For these reasons, ethical problems associated with the relationship between diagnosis and reimbursement are of greater concern to the professional community.[104]

Finally, there is the practice of signing off. Signing off has become important because some insurance covers services provided only by psychiatrists or psychologists. In other instances, insurance will reimburse at a higher rate when the services are provided by a psychiatrist or psychologist than when they are rendered by a social worker. The sign-off practice is one in which the psychiatrist or psychologist signs the insurance claim, even though the services were provided by a social worker, in order to maximize reimbursement. In some instances, psychiatrists and psychologists may recruit social workers, paying them half the fees charged to insurance companies and pocketing the difference. Signing off is a type of fee splitting and is "unethical because it allows practitioners to refer clients not to the professional most suitable for the client's needs, but to the person who pays the highest fee."[105]

In a community where many private practitioners compete for a limited number of clients, aggressive business practices are likely to exacerbate questions about the ultimate concern of practitioners—whether it is the client's welfare or the clinician's income. Although the question is not ordinarily couched in such crude terms, the behavior of private practitioners may not be lost on the client population. Because clients usually seek services voluntarily, their impressions of practitioners are important; negative perceptions will eventually hurt practitioners as their clients seek services elsewhere. When unfavorable impressions emerge, as a result of the practices described, practitioners would be prudent to take corrective action. While the ethical code of the professional community can be a source for such action, much remains at the discretion of the individual practitioner.

Private practice is literally *private*, and practitioners enjoy "substantial discretion in conducting their activities."[106] Economic and other considerations may encourage private practitioners to engage in unethical or questionable practices. In such instances, other practitioners are obliged to report allegations of violations to the state licensing board or the professional association. Ultimately, it is in the interest of the professional community to address questionable practices of practitioners, and this includes the unethical business practices of private practitioners. When the media report that "routine falsification of insurance billings and other peculiarities of the mental health professions have caused acute anxiety among insurance companies . . . [who] now think they have little control over what they are paying for," more government regulation is probably not far behind.[107] In other instances, the consequences are acutely embarrassing for the professional community, as when a leading proponent of third-party reimbursement for social workers in Kentucky was found guilty of insurance fraud and ordered to return $37,000 to Blue Cross-Blue Shield.[108]

The Future of the Private Sector

In response to the adverse circumstances besetting the profession, many human-service professionals have turned to private practice as a way of securing their economic and professional objectives. Private practice gives program administrators a chance to maintain their direct service skills, educators the opportunity to continue contact with clients, and clinicians with parental responsibilities the freedom to combine professional practice and attention to family needs. More important, private practice may prove an adjunct to agency activities. "By fostering part-time practice," researchers have noted, "the profession can keep its main focus on agency services where there is a commitment to serve persons without regard to their ability to pay and where there can be a basis for social action and reform."[109]

Reconciling economic opportunity with social responsibility will continue to be an issue in private practice. *The New York Times* reported that 82 percent of clinical social workers earned at least $20,000 per year through private practice, while 15 percent earned more than $60,000.[110] These income prospects will continue to attract social workers who are willing to take the risk of going into business for themselves. The primary constraint on private practice has been the rapid expansion of managed care. By the mid–1990s, HMOs had begun to restructure private sector service delivery by making significant incursions into the social markets customarily served by nonprofit agencies and private practitioners. To the extent managed care acquires more of the private market, opportunities in private practice will be curtailed.

As the growth of managed care illustrates, much of private practice is a result of larger social forces. Ellen Dunbar, executive director of the California chapter of NASW, observed that "The major overriding trend that engulfs all others is that social work along with other service professions is becoming more commercial . . . [and] more an integral part of the free enterprise system."[111] In fact, the commercialization of social work attracted wide attention as the profession became more immersed in private practice. "There is concern," reported *Newsweek* magazine, "that too many social workers are turning their backs on their traditional casework among the poor to practice therapy." *Newsweek* wondered at the consequences of "an apparent middle-class therapy explosion at the expense of public welfare and grassroots service."[112] How social work will reconcile its commitment to social justice with the new opportunities presented by private practice remains a central question before the professional community.

Interest in alternative methods of service delivery is implicitly critical of traditional ways in which social agencies provide services. First, traditional agencies place constraints on employee discretion and professional autonomy. Second, rigid agency policies make few allowances for the demands of an employee's family life and community-related obligations. Third, the demands of increasing caseloads compounded by diminishing resources make traditional agencies a less desirable setting in which to practice. Although nonprofit agencies have been superior to governmental programs in the quality of services provided, these traditional auspices of service delivery are beginning to merge. Subsequently, social work in smaller, voluntary agencies is not very different from the "proletarianized" work in larger, public agencies.[113] To the extent traditional agencies become less desirable as contexts in which to practice, innovative models of service delivery surface.

As researchers on private practice have noted, rather than criticize professionals who have opted for the private sector, the social work community should make it a priority to reform the means of service provision through traditional agencies. "The goal should be to make agency practice good for the health and well-being of the practitioner, because the ultimate beneficiary would be the client."[114] Stan Taubman, who has held direct practice and administrative positions and couples county employment with private practice, states the matter succinctly: "Private practice isn't keeping social workers out of public services. Public services are."[115]

One service delivery innovation has been Employee Assistance Programs (EAPs). Since the 1970s, social workers have been involved in EAPs that provide a range of services to workers, a population often neglected by traditional welfare programs.[116] By the late 1980s, occupational social welfare had become a popular specialization within social work, with graduate schools offering special curricula on the subject, a national conference inaugurated for specialists in the field, and a special issue of *Social Work* dedicated to it.[117] Although studies of EAPs are scarce,[118] there is evidence that occupational social work is likely to expand, particularly when located within the corporation. In a modest study of 23 "private-sector, management-sponsored" EAPs, Shulamith Straussner found that those located in-house demonstrated notable advantages over those contracted out. For example, EAPs located within the corporation cost one-third that of contracted-out services. In-house EAPs proved adaptable to management priorities, developing "short-term programs to deal with company reorganization or retrenchment, special health concerns . . . [and] other organizational needs." Significantly, union representatives approved in-house EAPs twice as frequently as they did contracted-out programs.[119] These findings suggest that EAPs that are managed by employers are perceived by management and unions as superior to services provided by an external agency. If corporate executives and labor leaders develop personnel policies consistent with these findings, welfare professionals will find the business community a hospitable setting in which to practice. In that event, occupational social work within the corporation may become as prevalent an auspice of practice as the voluntary and governmental sectors are.

Another service delivery innovation is employee ownership. Curiously, human-service professionals have frequently advocated employee ownership as a method for empowering clients, yet fail to see comparable benefits for themselves. For example, Cooperative Home Care Associates (CHCA) of New York City has been co-owned by some 170 employees since its inception in 1985. CHCA offers above-average wages, health and vacation benefits and has, as a result, proven a vehicle out of poverty for many workers who had been on public assistance.[120]

An as-yet-unexplored innovation for human-service professionals is the Employee Stock Option Plan (ESOP). Through ESOPs, workers gain ownership of a firm by gradually acquiring stock, the acquisition of which is granted certain tax advantages. By 1990, ESOPs had been used to leverage the transfer of 11,000 companies to 12 million employees. Workers had used ESOPs to purchase in part or wholly several large corporations, such as J. C. Penney, Kroger's, Avis, and United Airlines.[121] Inexplicably, human-service professionals had not used ESOPs to gain control over the organizations who employee them. In part this can be explained by the traditional auspices of practice, the nonprofit and governmental sector. While it may seem implausible for Department of Social Service employees to seek ownership of the local welfare department or for professionals hired by the local Family Service Agency to acquire it, recent interest in privatization makes employee-ownership more probable.

State governments have already moved to privatize important public welfare functions. New Jersey announced in 1995 its intent to contract out child welfare; Texas is putting out to bid its entire public welfare function. As states seek to restructure social welfare in order to husband resources and because the 1996 federal welfare reform allows putting welfare activities out to bid with for-profit firms, contracting with health and human-service corporations will accelerate. In response many human-service professionals who now enjoy state civil service protection will find themselves vulnerable employees in a turbulent corporate environment. Historically, such workers have sought more security by establishing unions. Another route, however, is to incorporate a firm that would bid for such state contracts or, if already an employee in one, to organize fellow professionals to acquire the firm through an ESOP. Either way, employee ownership can be an important vehicle for professional empowerment.

◆ ◆ ◆ *Discussion Questions* ◆ ◆ ◆

1. Privatization is a hotly debated issue in social welfare. To what extent are some of the major concerns about privatization (e.g., unfair competition between nonprofit agencies and commercial firms, preferential selection and dumping of clients, superior performance of private providers, the emergence of an oligopoly of private providers) evident in your community? Should human-service professionals practice in for-profit firms?

2. Private practice continues to be a focus of students in schools of social work. How many of your classmates are planning to become private practitioners? What are their motives? Do faculty members in your social work program who also have private practices serve as role models to students? Is there an opportunity in your studies to discuss the implications of private practice for social work?

3. How does your state regulate the practice of social work? What governmental unit is responsible for regulating social work? How is it constituted? Does your state have reciprocity arrangements with other states, honoring licenses granted in other jurisdictions? Has your state's social work licensing unit expelled professionals for unethical practices?

4. What is the position of your state chapter of the National Association of Social Workers on regulating professional practice? Are licensing and vendorship still high on the state chapter's priority list? If so, which social workers in your state remain concerned about the regulation of professional practice? Why?

5. What are the main concerns within your professional community about private practice—fees, misdiagnosis, licensing, image, competition with other professionals, vendorship? How are disagreements arbitrated, formally or informally?

6. The debate between private practice and agency-based practice continues as a heated issue within social work. What are the advantages and disadvantages of each? Is there a common base of social work practice? Can you foresee some ways to resolve the issue and bring private practitioners and agency-based practitioners together?

7. Employee ownership is a way through which human-service professionals can attain control over their practices. Of the prominent social service agencies in your community, which ones might be candidates for employee ownership? If such a transition were accomplished, how would you assure accountability to consumers, the community?

8. In order to attain job security, many human-service professionals join unions. What is the largest union to which social workers belong in your community? Do issues relating to service delivery figure in the union's negotiation with management? Under what conditions would human-service professionals in your community engage in a strike?

Notes

1. John Donahue, *The Privatization Decision* (New York: Basic Books, 1989), p. 216.
2. Harry Specht and Mark Courtney, *Unfaithful Angels* (New York: Free Press, 1994), p. 107.
3. Paul Starr, "The Meaning of Privatization," quoted in American Federation of State, County, and Municipal Employees, *Private Profit, Public Risk: The Contracting Out of Professional Services* (Washington, DC: AFSCME, 1986), pp. 4–5.
4. Charles Schultz, *The Public Use of Private Interest* (Washington, DC: Brookings Institution, 1977); Donald Fisk, Herbert Kiesling, and Thomas Muller, *Private Provision of Public Service* (Washington, DC: Urban Institute, 1978); Harry Hatry, *A Review of Private Approaches for the Delivery of Public Services* (Washington, DC: Urban Institute, 1983).
5. *Privatization: Toward More Effective Government* (Washington, DC: Report of the President's Commission on Privatization, March 1988), p. 230.
6. Ibid., pp. 1–2.
7. See Lawrence S. Lewin, Robert A. Derzon, and Rhea Margulies, "Investor-Owned and Nonprofits Differ in Economic Performance," *Hospitals* (July 1, 1981), pp. 65–69; Robert V. Pattison and Hallie Katz, "Investor-Owned Hospitals and Not-for-Profit Hospitals," *New England Journal of Medicine* (August 11, 1983), pp. 54–65; Robin Eskoz and K. Michael Peddecord, "The Relationship of Hospital Ownership and Service Composition to Hospital Charges," *Health Care Financing Review* (Spring 1985), pp. 125–132; J. Michael Watt et al., "The Comparative Economic Performance of Investor-Owned Chain and Not-for-Profit Hospitals," *New England Journal of Medicine* (January 9, 1986), pp. 356–360; Bradford Gray and Walter McNerney, "For-Profit Enterprise in Health Care: The Institute of Medicine Study," *New England Journal of Medicine* (June 5, 1986), pp. 560–563; Regina Herzlinger and William Kradker, "Who Profits from Nonprofits?" *Harvard Business Review* (January–February 1987), pp. 554–562.
8. Douglas Frantz, "Lobbyists, Interest Groups Begin Costly Health Care Battle," *Los Angeles Times* (May 24, 1993).
9. Patricia Franklin, "The AIDS Business," *Business* (April 1987), p. 44.
10. Richard Titmuss, *The Gift Relationship* (New York: Pantheon, 1971), p. 223.
11. Theodore Marmor, Mark Schlesinger, and Richard Smithey, "A New Look at Nonprofits: Health Care Policy in a Competitive Age," *Yale Journal of Regulation* 3 (Spring 1986): 320.
12. W. Harrison Wellford and Janne Gallagher, *Charity and the Competition Challenge* (Washington, DC:

National Assembly of National Voluntary Health and Social Welfare Organizations, 1987), pp. 13–15.
13. Michael Abramowitz, "Nonprofit Hospitals Venture into New Lines of Business," *Washington Post* (February 15, 1987), p. C5.
14. Todd Gillman, "Health Clubs Hit YMCAs' Tax Breaks," *Washington Post* (June 30, 1987), p. E2.
15. Anne Swardson, "Hill Taking New Look at Nonprofits," *Washington Post* (June 21), 1987, p. F–9.
16. Charles Muntaner et al., "Psychotic Inpatients' Social Class and Their First Admission to State or Private Psychiatric Baltimore Hospitals," *American Journal of Public Health*, vol. 84, no. 2 (February 1994), p. 287.
17. Richard Cloward and Irwin Epstein, "Private Social Welfare's Disengagement from the Poor," in Meyer Zald (Ed.), *Social Welfare Institutions* (New York: John Wiley, 1965), pp. 628–629.
18. Emily Friedman, "The 'Dumping' Dilemma: The Poor Are Always with Some of Us," *Hospitals* (September 1, 1982), p. 52.
19. David Himmelstein, "Patient Transfers: Medical Practice as Social Triage," *American Journal of Public Health* (May 1984), p. 496.
20. Friedman, "The 'Dumping' Dilemma," p. 54.
21. Mark Schlesinger, "The Privatization of Health Care and Physicians' Perceptions of Access to Hospital Services," *The Milbank Quarterly* 65 (1987), p. 40.
22. Marmor et al., "A New Look at Nonprofits," p. 344.
23. Lewin et al., "Investor-Owned and Nonprofits Differ in Economic Performance."
24. Jerry Avorn, "Nursing-Home Infections—The Context," *New England Journal of Medicine* (September 24, 1981), p. 759.
25. Reported in Arnold Relman, "Investor-Owned Hospitals and Health Care Costs," *New England Journal of Medicine* (August 11, 1983), pp. 370–371.
26. Pattison and Katz, "Investor-Owned Hospitals and Not-For-Profit Hospitals," p. 61.
27. Michael McMullan, personal correspondence, March 7, 1988; and "Use of Short-Stay Hospital Services by Medicare Hospital Insurance Beneficiaries by State of Provider and Type of Control: 1985" (Baltimore: Health Care Finance Administration, 1985).
28. Gray and McNerney, "For-Profit Enterprise in Health Care," p. 1525.
29. Robert Kuttner, "Columbia/HCA and the Resurgence of the For-Profit Hospital Business," *New England Journal of Medicine*, vol. 335, no. 5 (August 1, 1996), pp. 365–366.
30. "Hospitals' Medicare Profits Up," *San Diego Union* (March 29, 1987), p. A5.
31. "Competition for Doctors and Patients Increases Hospital Costs," *NCHSR Research Activities* No. 101 (January 1988), p. 3.
32. Richard Buchanan, "Long-Term Care's Pricing Dilemma," *Contemporary Administrator* (February 1981), p. 20.
33. Ann LoLordo, "Life-Care Centers Offer Seniors Worry-Free Living," *Baltimore Sun* (June 4, 1984), p. D4.
34. Carol Olten, "Communities Offering Seniors a Graceful Life," *San Diego Union* (March 13, 1988), p. D5.
35. Anthony Perry, "North County Housing Boom: A Lucrative Shade of Gray," *Los Angeles Times* (March 6, 1988), p. E5.
36. U.S. Senate Special Committee on Aging, *Discrimination Against the Poor and Disabled in Nursing Homes* (Washington, DC: U.S. Government Printing Office, 1984), p. 8.
37. Perry, "North County Housing Boom."
38. U.S. Senate, *Discrimination Against the Poor and Disabled in Nursing Homes*, pp. 6–8.
39. Ibid., p. 36.
40. The most well-known bankruptcy of a life care community was that of Pacific Homes of California in 1979.
41. Sun City—With an Add-On," *Forbes* (November 23, 1981), p. 84.
42. Jesse Glasgow, "Marriott to Test Life-Care" *Baltimore Sun* (June 16, 1984), p. C1.
43. "Merrill-Lynch: Bullish on Health Care," *Contemporary Administrator* (February 1982), p. 16.
44. Anne Somers, "Insurance for Long-Term Care," *New England Journal of Medicine* (July 2, 1987), p. 27.
45. U.S. Senate, *Discrimination Against the Poor and Disabled in Nursing Homes*, p. 25.
46. Ibid., p. 10.
47. Robert Pear, "Lack of Beds Seen in Nursing Homes," *The New York Times* (October 17, 1982), p. 1.
48. Quoted in William Spicer, "The Boom in Building," *Contemporary Administrator* (February 1982), p. 16.

49. Donald Light, "Corporate Medicine for Profit," *Scientific American* (December 1986), p. 42.
50. Arnold Relman, "The New Medical-Industrial Complex," *New England Journal of Medicine* 303, no. 17 (1980), p. 80.
51. Robin Toner, "'Harry and Louise' Ad Campaign Biggest Gun in Health Care Battle," *San Diego Union-Tribune* (April 7, 1994), pp. 1–5.
52. Sandra Boodman, "Health Care's Power Player," *Washington Post Weekly* (February 14–20, 1994), pp. 18–20.
53. Dana Priest, "The Slow Death of Health Reform," *Washington Post Weekly* (September 5–11, 1994), pp. 6–9.
54. Douglas Frantz, "Lobbyists, Interest Groups Begin Costly Health Care Battle," *Los Angeles Times* (May 24, 1993), p A7.
55. Judith Havemann, "Welfare Reform Leader Makes Corporate Move," *Washington Post* (September 17, 1996), p. A13.
56. Paul Starr, "The Limits of Privatization," in Steve Hanke, *Prospects for Privatization* (New York: Proceedings of the Academy of Political Science, 1987), pp. 82–107.
57. Kuttner, "Columbia/HCA", p. 363.
58. Eric Kingson and John Williamson, "Generational Equity or Privatization of Social Security?" *Society* (September/October 1991), p 90.
59. William Gormley, Jr., "Two Cheers for Privatization," in William Gormley, Jr. (Ed.), *Privatization and Its Alternatives* (Madison, WI: University of Wisconsin Press, 1991), pp. 310–311.
60. Reason Foundation, *Privatization 1992* (Los Angeles: Reason Foundation, 1992), p. 17.
61. David Stoesz, "Human-Service Corporations: New Opportunities in Social Work Administration," *Social Work Administration* 12 (1989), pp. 35–43.
62. Mary Adelaide Mendelson, *Tender Loving Greed* (New York: Knopf, 1974).
63. NASW, "'87 Session of Congress Ends in 11th-Hour Win for NASW," *NASW News*, (February 1988), p. 1.
64. Reason Foundation, *Privatization*, p. 251.
65. David Donnison, "The Progressive Potential of Privatisation," in Julian LeGrand and Ray Robinson (Eds.), *Privatisation and the Welfare State* (London: George Allen & Unwin, 1984), pp. 211–231.
66. Milton Tambor, "Unions," *Encyclopedia of Social Work* (19th ed.) (Washington, DC: National Association of Social Workers, 1995), p. 2418–2419.
67. J. Weitzman, *The Scope of Bargaining in Public Employment* (New York: Praeger, 1975), p. 17.
68. Milton Tambor, "The Social Service Union in the Workplace," in H. Karger (Ed.) *Social Work and Labor Unions* (New York: Greenwood, 1988).
69. Dena Fisher, "Problems for Social Work in a Strike Situation," *Social Work* 32 (May–June 1987), pp. 253–254.
70. Jerry Wurf, "Labor Movement, Social Work Fighting Similar Battles," *NASW News*, 25(12) (December 1980), p. 7.
71. Leslie Alexander et al., "Social Workers in Unions," *Social Work* 25 (May 1980), p. 222.
72. Ernie Lightman, "Professionalization, Bureaucratization, and Unionization in Social Work," *Social Service Review* 56(1) (March 1982), p. 130.
73. Gary Shaffer, "Labor Relations and the Unionization of Professional Social Workers," *Journal of Education for Social Work*, 15 (Winter 1979), p. 82.
74. "Public Service Workers' Strikes Disrupts Life in Canada," *Los Angeles Times* (September 10, 1991), p. A8.
75. C. Heckscher, "Beyond Contract Bargaining: Partnership, Persuasion, and Power," *Social Policy* (25)2 (1994), p. 29.
76. Specht and Courtney, *Unfaithful Angels*, p. 8.
77. Gibelman, *Who We Are*, p. 65.
78. Philip Brown and Robert Barker, "Confronting the Threat' of Private Practice," *Journal of Social Work Education* (31)1 (Winter 1995), p. 106.
79. Srinika Jayaratne, Kristine Siefert, and Wayne Chess, "Private and Agency Practitioners: Some Data and Observations," *Social Service Review* 62 (June 1988), p. 331.
80. Margaret Gibelman and Philip Schervish, *What We Earn: 1993 NASW Salary Survey* (Washington, DC: NASW, 1993), pp. 25, 27.
81. Diane Vinokur-Kaplan, Srinika Jayaratne, and Wayne Chess, "Job Satisfaction and Retention of Social Workers in Public Agencies, Non-Profit Agencies and Private Practice," *Administration in Social Work* (18)3 (1994), p. 103.
82. Gibelman, *What We Earn*, p. 32.
83. Vinokur-Kaplan et al., "Job Satisfaction," p. 103.
84. Ibid., p. 329.
85. Ibid.

86. Although Mark Courtney notes that a de facto private practice can be identified much earlier: "Psychiatric Social Workers and the Early Days of Private Practice," *Social Service Review* (June 1992), pp. 95–105.
87. M. A. Golton, "Private Practice in Social Work," *Encyclopedia of Social Work* (Silver Spring, MD: NASW, 1973), p. 949.
88. Walter Trattner, *From Poor Law to Welfare State* (New York: Free Press, 1974), p. 250.
89. Gibelman, *Who We Are*, pp. 65, 73.
90. For details on state licensure and professional certification, see Robert Barker, "Private and Proprietary Services."
91. Srinika Jayaratne, Mary Lou Davis Sacks, and Wayne Chess, "Private Practice May Be Good for Your Health and Well-Being," *Social Work* 36 (May 1991), p. 226–227.
92. Jae-Sung Choi, "Members' Views on the California Licensing System for Social Work Practice" (Sacramento: California Chapter, NASW, 1990), p. 6.
93. Donald Feldstein, "Debate on Private Practice," *Social Work* 22, no. 3 (1977), p. 3.
94. Ibid., p. 4.
95. Patricia Kelley and Paul Alexander, "Part-Time Private Practice," p. 255.
96. N. T. Edwards, "The Survival of Structure and Function in Private Practice," *Journal of the Otto Rank Association* 13 (1979), pp. 12, 15.
97. Jayaratne et al., "Private Practice," *Social Work* 36 (May 1991), pp. 228–229.
98. Franklin Chu and Sharland Trotter, *The Madness Establishment* (New York: Grossman, 1974), p. 61.
99. Robert Barker, *The Business of Psychotherapy* (New York: Columbia University Press, 1982), p. xi.
100. Stuart Kirk and Herb Kutchins, "Deliberate Misdiagnosis in Mental Health Practice," p. 230.
101. Ibid., p. 234.
102. Ibid., pp. 232, 234–235.
103. Ibid., p. 235.
104. Kimberly Strom, "Reimbursement Demands and Treatment Decisions: A Growing Dilemma for Social Workers," *Social Work* 37 (September 1992), p. 18.
105. Robert Barker, *Social Work in Private Practice* (Silver Spring, MD: NASW, 1984), p. 113.
106. Kirk and Kutchins, "Deliberate Misdiagnosis in Mental Health Practice," p. 232.
107. Kathy Sawyer, "Insuring the Bureaucracy's Mental Health," *Washington Post*, (April 10, 1979), p. A8.
108. "'Signing Off' Fraud Charge Warns Kentucky Clinicians," *NASW News* (32)6 (June 1987), p. 1.
109. Patricia Kelley and Paul Alexander, "Part-Time Private Practice," p. 254.
110. Daniel Goleman, "Social Workers Vault into a Leading Role in Psychotherapy," *The New York Times* (April 3, 1985), C1.
111. Ellen Dunbar, "Future of Social Work," *NASW California News* (13)18 (May 1987), p. 3.
112. David Gelman, "Growing Pains for the Shrinks," *Newsweek* (December 14, 1987), p. 71.
113. Michael Fabricant and Steven Burghardt, *The Welfare State Crisis and the Transformation of Social Service Work* (Armonk, NY: M.E. Sharpe, 1992).
114. Srinika Jayaratne, Mary Lou Davis-Sacks, and Wayne Chess, "Private Practice May Be Good for Your Health and Well-Being," *Social Work* 36 (May 1991), p. 229.
115. Stan Taubman, "Private Practice! Oh No!" *NASW California News* (March 1991), p. 8.
116. See Sheila Akabas, Paul Kurzman, and Norman Kolben (Eds.), *Labor and Industrial Settings: Sites for Social Work Practice* (New York: Council on Social Work Education, 1979); Martha Ozawa, "Development of Social Services in Industry: Why and How?" *Social Work* 25 (November 1980), pp. 86–93; and Dale Masi, *Human-Services in Industry* (Lexington, MA: D. C. Heath, 1982).
117. "Social Work in Industrial Settings," *Social Work* 33 (January–February 1988), p. 65.
118. But see J. Decker, R. Starrett, and J. Redhorse, "Evaluating the Cost-Effectiveness of Employee Assistance Programs," *Social Work* 31 (September–October 1986), p. 83.
119. Shulamith Straussner, "Comparison of In-House and Contracted-Out Employee Assistance Programs," *Social Work* 33 (January–February 1988), p. 53.
120. Francis Lappe and P.M. Dubois, *The Quickening of America: Rebuilding Our Nation, Remaking Our Lives* (San Francisco: Jossey Bass, 1994).
121. Ibid.

PART THREE

The Government Sector

CHAPTER 9

The Making of Governmental Policy

This chapter describes the process by which governmental policy is made, examines the influence of various social groups on the policy process, and explores the phases of the policy process with particular attention focused on the role of key organizations. The public policy process is important because many social welfare policies are established by government, and decisions by federal and state agencies have a direct bearing on the administration and funding of social welfare programs that assist millions of Americans.

In an open, democratic society, it is desirable that public policy reflect the interests of all citizens to the greatest extent possible. For a variety of reasons, however, this ideal is not realized in the making of governmental policy. Although many Americans have the right to participate in the establishment of public policy, they often fail to do so. Governmental policy may be perceived as being too far removed from the daily activities of citizens, or too complicated, to warrant the type of coordinated and persistent efforts necessary to alter it. Moreover, many Americans with a direct interest in governmental policy are not in a position to shape it, as in the case of children and the emotionally impaired, who must rely on others to speak on their behalf. Consequently, governmental policy does not necessarily reflect the interests—or, for our purposes, the welfare—of the public even though it is intended to do so. The discrepancy between what is constitutionally prescribed in making public policy and the way decisions are actually made leads to two quite different understandings of the policy process. For welfare professionals concerned with instituting change in social welfare, a technical understanding of how policy is made is essential. It is equally important for them to recognize that the policy process is skewed to favor powerful officials and interests rather than the interests of the uninfluential. Because social workers and their clients tend to be comparatively powerless, a critical analysis of the policy process is all the more important.

TECHNICAL ASPECTS OF THE POLICY PROCESS

In the United States, public policy is made through a deliberative process that involves the two bodies of elected officials that comprise a legislature. This applies both to the federal government and to the states, with the singular exception of Nebraska, which has only one deliberative body, that is, a unicameral legislature.

The concern of a legislator is first developed into a legislative proposal and usually printed in the *Congressional Record*. Because legislators have a party affiliation and a constituency, their proposals tend to reflect these priorities. Usually, several legislators will prepare proposals that are important to similar constituencies, which ensures that all sides of an issue are aired. Through a subtle interaction of ideas, the media, and legislative leadership, one proposal—usually a synthesis of several—is presented as a policy alternative. Other legislators are asked to sign on as cosponsors and the measure is officially introduced. After it is assigned to the appropriate committee, hearings are held, and the committee convenes to "mark up" the legislation so that it incorporates the concerns of committee members who have heard the public testimony. Under propitious circumstances, the legislation is forwarded to the full body of the chamber which must approve it. While being approved by the full body of one chamber, a similar bill is often introduced in the other chamber, where it begins a parallel process. Differences in the legislation approved by each chamber are ironed out in a conference committee. The proposed legislation becomes law after it is signed by the chief executive, or by a two-thirds vote of each legislative chamber if the executive vetoes the bill. This process is always tortuous and usually unsuccessful. The eventual enactment of legislation under these conditions is a true testament to legislative leadership. A third branch of government, the judiciary, assesses legal challenges to existing legislation. In the upper levels of the judiciary, members are usually appointed by the chief executive, and they can hold their posts for life. The primary features of the policy process of the federal government are illustrated in Figure 9.1.

There are several critical junctures in a proposal's tortuous passage into legislation—or oblivion. First, most of the details in any proposal are worked out at the committee or subcommittee level. Differences—an inevitability in virtually every bill—are negotiated and reconciled at a "mark-up" session, during which committee members and staff write their changes onto the draft. This stage offers an important opportunity to inject minor, and sometimes major, changes into

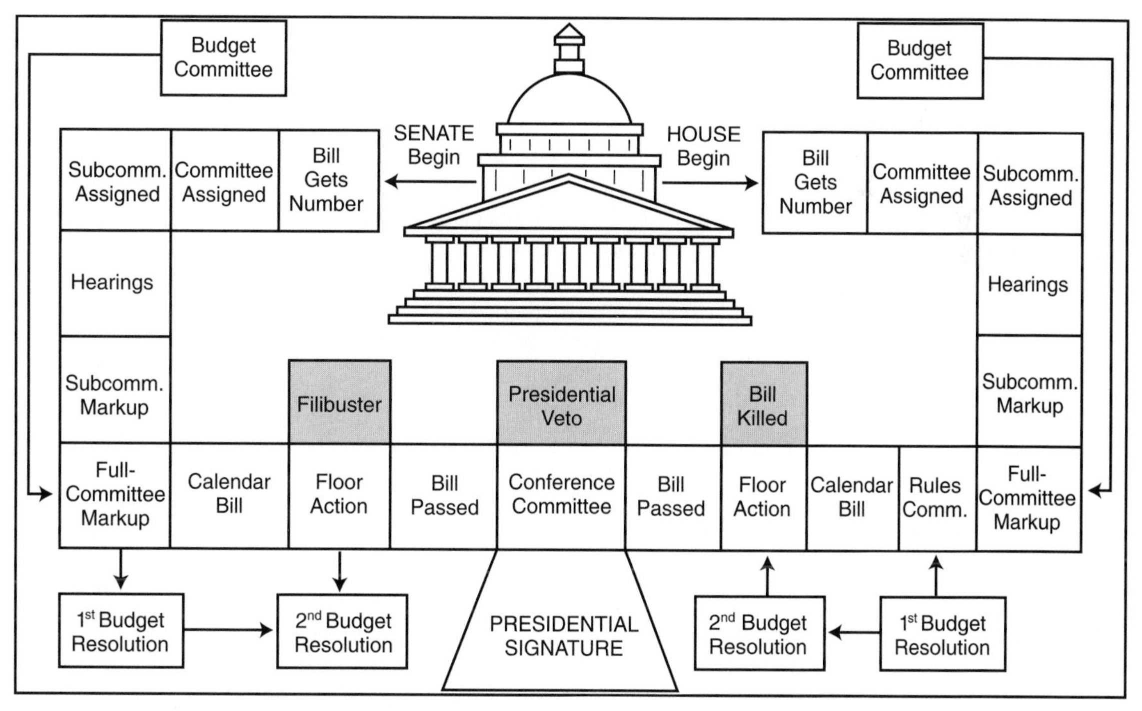

◆ **FIGURE 9.1 The Steps Necessary in Getting a Legislative Proposal Enacted into Law**

the substance of the bill or to alter the intent of the bill's originator(s). Second, the viability of a proposal depends to a large extent on the numbers and weight of the witnesses who testify as to its merits at subcommittee and committee hearings. Obviously, public testimony will work to the advantage of well-financed interests that can afford to pay lobbyists to do this professionally, while advocates of the disadvantaged must rely on volunteers. Nevertheless, the public testimony stage is an important opportunity to clarify "for the record" the position that welfare professionals may take on a given proposal. Third, budget considerations figure heavily in the likelihood of a bill's passage. The federal deficit coupled with the unwillingness of elected officials to raise taxes increases the likelihood that legislation will be underfunded or even passed with no additional funding whatsoever. Innovative revenue "enhancers," such as earmarked taxes or user fees, can make a proposal more acceptable during periods of fiscal belt-tightening. The policy process, then, is not necessarily intended to facilitate the passage of a proposal into law. During the last 20 years, of some 20,000 bills presented to Congress, only 10 percent were reported out of committee and only 5 percent became law.[1]

Beyond this general outline of the public policy process, multiple variations exist depending on historical circumstances. In the federal government, all proposals related to taxation must originate in the House of Representatives, a provision the founders of the nation included in the Constitution in order to locate revenue retrieval in the legislative body most representative of the people. Appointments to key executive posts, such as cabinet secretaries, ambassadors, and judges must be ratified through the advice and consent of the Senate, a body less responsive to popular sentiment. States exhibit countless variations within the general outline of the tripartite balance of powers format. California, for example, has experienced budget gridlock because the state government has been unable to raise sufficient revenue to keep up with mandated expenditures. Since the imposition of Proposition 13 in 1978, a two-thirds majority of the legislature is required not only to raise taxes but also to establish the state budget; this is far beyond the simple majority required in other states. Under these conditions, a small number of recalcitrant representatives can easily block the budget process. As these examples suggest, understanding the intricacies of the policy process is an essential step toward mastering public policy.

A few final points regarding the technical aspects of the policy process warrant mention. The decision-making process itself is defined by *Robert's Rules of Order*,[2] a text that lays out in detail the rules for democratic deliberation. Although *Robert's Rules* can appear obtuse, its value should not be underappreciated. Those who have mastered "the means of deliberation" are one step ahead of the rest of the crowd in seeing their ideas become public policy. Social activists who are optimistic that their proposal is working its way steadily through the legislative minefield may find their hopes exploded by an adroit procedural move on the part of an opponent who sidetracks a bill until the next legislative session. Elaborate rules of decision making, compounded by the traditions of deliberative bodies, may dissuade public citizens from participating more fully in the democratic process. Yet, there are means public policy novices can employ to become better acquainted with the ways in which elected officials go about the public's business. Citizen advocate organizations, particularly the League of Women Voters and Common Cause, can be helpful in explaining how public policy is made. Finally, Congress and the legislatures of the larger states employ staff members as technical experts to aid them in decision making. Legislative staff are frequently the experts most versed in an area of legislative activity simply because they work through policy proposals on a regular basis. Staff reports researched as part of committee deliberations can be valuable in that they often provide the most up-to-date data on particular programs or issues. A good example of this is the "Green Book" used by the U.S. House Ways and Means Committee in its consideration of social programs. Begun in the early 1980s to help committee members comprehend the vast number of programs under their jurisdiction—Social Security, Medicare, Medicaid, AFDC, SSI, and Unemployment Compensation, among others—the volume, *Background Material and Data on Programs within the Jurisdiction of the Committee on Ways and Means*, became essential reading for social program analysts. Because of its convoluted title, the volume became known by its standard-issue green paper cover, hence the Green Book. Fortunately, its popularity led to a (merciful) shortening of its title to *Overview of Entitlement Programs*.[3]

A CRITICAL ANALYSIS OF THE POLICY PROCESS

Experience and sophistication notwithstanding, the public policy process often proves frustrating for social activists. Despite the most urgent of needs, the best of intentions, and the most strategic of proposals, the social welfare program output deriving from the legislative process often appears far short of what is required. Yet, to conclude from this that public policy simply does not work would be an overstatement. A critical approach to public policy helps explain some of the limitations of the technical approach, and offers directions on how to make the legislative process a more effective strategy for those concerned with furthering social justice.

From a critical perspective, the policy process consists of a series of discrete decisions, each heavily conditioned by money and connections—in other words, by "power." The extent to which governmental policy reflects the concerns of one group of citizens while neglecting those of others is ultimately a question of power and influence. Power is derived from several sources and these have attracted the attention of philosophers over the centuries. Plato questioned the organization and execution of the civil authority of the state. Machiavelli focused on the limits of discretionary authority exercised by leaders of the state. During the Enlightenment, the social contract philosophers—Hobbes, Locke, and Rousseau—considered the moral obligations of the state toward its citizens. Later, as the Industrial Revolution proceeded unchecked, Karl Marx attributed inequities in influence to control over the means of production, or capital. Subsequently, as governmental authority expanded to ameliorate the economic and social dislocation brought on by industrial capitalism, Max Weber identified bureaucratic administrators as a pivotal group. As the postindustrial era unfolded, such social critics as Marshall McLuhan and Alvin Toffler emphasized how information can be processed and used as a source of power and influence.

From these general speculations about social organization, other writers have turned to more specific aspects of social policy as subjects of inquiry. Several schools of thought have emerged. According to the elitist orientation, individuals representing a "power structure" control social policy in order to maintain a status quo that advantages themselves and, in the process, excludes marginal groups. In contrast, a pluralist orientation assumes that social policy in a democratic polity is the sum total of trade-offs among different interest groups, all of which have an equal opportunity to participate. At the program level, incrementalists have suggested that the more important questions about social policy are the product of bit-by-bit additions to the public social infrastructure. As counterpoint, other scholars have focused on "paradigm shifts" through which major changes, such as the inception of Social Security in 1935 and devolution of welfare to the states through the Personal Responsibility and Work Opportunity Act of 1996, have altered the very foundation of social policy. With regard to program evaluation, rationalists have used the methods of social science to determine by objective standards to what extent policy changes approximate intended outcomes. By contrast, social activists use the political process as the measure of program performance, assuming that the optimum in program assessment is continued recertification and refunding by public decisionmakers. As might be expected in the investigation of any phenomenon as complex as social policy, a comprehensive explanation is likely to incorporate elements of more than one school of thought.

Underlying these varied approaches to interpreting social policy are assumptions about its very nature. In this regard, three orientations have become prominent. The first orientation might be labeled the *liberal evolutionary perspective*. According to this orientation, social policy reflects steady progress toward a desirable condition of human welfare for all. Most liberal analysts who have promoted the welfare state as an ideal have adopted an evolutionary perspective. Believers in the evolutionary perspective expect that the national government will progressively expand social programs until, eventually, the basic needs of the entire population are guaranteed as rights of citizenship. References to welfare state philosophy appear in many chapters of this book. The liberal evolutionary perspective dominated thinking about the American welfare state from the New Deal until the rise of conservative ideology in the 1980s. The demise of Catastrophic Health Insurance in 1989 and the devolution of AFDC to the states in 1996 raise fundamental questions about the validity of this perspective.

A second orientation is the *systems approach*. Adherents of social systems assume that welfare consists of basic institutions and processes that are related and changed to suit environmental conditions. While reference to "social service delivery systems" was frequent during the 1960s and 1970s when social programs were expanding, this approach commanded less credibility when many public programs were thrown into chaos as a result of budget cuts during the 1980s. What had once been coordinated service delivery systems suddenly became disordered and fragmented clusters of agencies struggling for survival.

Finally, a *conflict perspective* has emphasized the differences between organized groups that compete for social resources, one opportunity for this being the competition for public resources offered through social programs. The conflict perspective views social policy and resultant programs as the product of intense rivalry among various classes and groups. Applied to a capitalist economy and a democratic polity, the conflict approach goes a long way toward explaining the disparate distribution of goods, services, and opportunities within American society. Accordingly, conflict theory is useful in two ways: It accounts for the quite substantial disadvantages experienced by some Americans—the poor, minorities of color, the handicapped, women; and it shows how such groups can be empowered to achieve a measure of social justice. The downside of the conflict perspective is that it fails to offer a unifying vision of future social policy (as does the evolutionary perspective) nor does it help in the management of programs once they have been deployed (as does the systems approach). By definition, any inclusive understanding of social welfare policy will incorporate each of these orientations.

In order to illustrate how assumptions underlying social policy apply to social welfare, consider this question: What is the nature of governmental decision making? Questions of governmental decision making often focus on three aspects: the degree of change in policy represented by a decision, the rationality of the decision, and the extent to which the disadvantaged benefit. Governmental policies vary in the extent to which they depart from the status quo. Although it can be argued that, in the final analysis, there are no new ideas, there *are* new governmental policies that have enormous implications for certain groups. Few could dispute that the Social Security Act and the Civil Rights Act were radical departures from the status quo and substantially changed the circumstances of the aged and African Americans, respectively. On the other hand, such radical departures are dependent on a relatively unique set of circumstances, and occur rarely. As Charles Lindblom has observed, the great bulk of decision making is "incremental," representing only marginal improvements in social policy already in place.[4] From a rational perspective, Amitai Etzioni has suggested the concept of "mixed-scanning" to describe how decisions are reached. According to Etzioni, decision makers take a quick overview of a situation, weigh a range of alternatives—some incremental, some radical—and ultimately select the one that satisfies the most important factors impinging at the moment.[5] Thus, major shifts in public policy are the exception, rather than the rule. Most social policy changes consist of relatively minor technical adjustments in program administration and budgeting.

The rationality of a policy decision refers to how internally coherent or consistent it is and the extent to which it accomplishes its intended objectives. Paradoxically, most governmental policy is irrational when evaluated by these standards. Inevitably, public policy is elaborated to take into account the interests of the various groups that are concerned about its effects. It is not unusual for descriptions of governmental policy to require dozens of pages of text and for its various provisions to be contradictory. For example, the 98-page Immigration Reform and Control Act of 1986 reflected the concerns of three groups: undocumented residents, most of whom are Hispanic; truck farmers, who require migratory laborers to pick the crops; and the Immigration and Naturalization Service (INS), which regulates immigration to the United States.[6] Because the interests of these groups differed greatly, various provisions of the act appeared inconsistent at times. For example, in interpreting the act, the INS initially determined that children of families in which one parent failed to qualify for amnesty faced deportation, although single-parent families in which the parent qualified would be allowed to stay in the United States.[7] Hispanic groups were outraged at this interpretation because it encouraged families to break up in order to qualify for amnesty. Because of the importance of the family in Hispanic culture, this interpretation contributed to the reluctance of undocumented workers to apply for the amnesty program. Meanwhile, some truck farmers watched their crops go unharvested because migrant workers were not coming to the United States owing to the confusion over the provisions of the act.

Despite such irrationality, social policy does order human affairs and, to that extent, the logic of the policy is of great significance. There are two basic forms of rationality that justify social policy: bureaucratic rationality and market rationality.[8] Bureaucratic rationality refers to the ordering of social affairs by governmental agencies. Since Max Weber's work on the modern bureaucracy, this form of rationality has been central to governmental policy and hence to the maintenance of the welfare state. According to bureaucratic rationality, civil servants can objectively define social problems, develop strategies to address them, and deploy programs in an equitable and nonpartisan manner. Bureaucratic rationality takes its authority from power vested in the state, and its bureaucracies have become predominant in social welfare at the federal (through the Department of Health and Human Services) and state levels. A characteristic of bureaucratic rationality is a reliance on social planning. Several social planning methods have been developed to anticipate future problems and deal with existing ones. Generally, these can be classified under two headings: technomethodological and sociopolitical.

Technomethodological planning methods emphasize data bases from which projections about future program needs can be derived. Such methods place a premium on relatively sophisticated social research methods and work best with programs that can be quantified and routinized, as in the case of cash payments through the Social Security program. An illustration of technomethodological planning can be found in the sophisticated research on welfare programs conducted by organizations, such as the Manpower Demonstration Research Corporation, the Institute for Women's Policy Research, and the Institute for Research on Poverty. Sociopolitical approaches to planning are more interactive, involving groups likely to be affected by a program. Community development activities, for example, frequently feature planners bringing together neighborhood residents, businesspeople, and local officials to create a plan that is relevant to the needs of a particular area.[9] Housing programs administered by the federal Department of Housing and Urban Development, for example, frequently require extensive involvement of community groups to facilitate implementation. Regardless of planning method, it is important to recognize the power and influence that governmental agencies have assumed in social welfare policy, much of it by exercise of bureaucratic rationality.

Market rationality refers to a reliance on the supply of and demand for goods and services as a method of ordering social affairs. While on the surface this may appear to be antithetical to the meaning of rationality, a high degree of social ordering in fact occurs within capitalism. Such organization is implicit in the very idea of a market, entailing a large number of prospective consumers that businesses seek to exploit. In a modern market economy, the success of a business depends on the ability of managers to survey the market, merchandise goods and services, shape consumer preferences through advertising, and reduce competition by buying or outmaneuvering competitors. Of course, market rationality is not a panacea for providing social welfare because the marketplace is not particularly responsive to those who do not fully participate in it—such as racial minorities, women, children, the aged, and the handicapped. Yet market rationality cannot be dismissed as a rationale for delivering social welfare benefits. Some 132 million Americans get their health and welfare needs met through employer-provided benefits that are ultimately derived from the market.[10] During the past decade commercial firms have conducted an ambitious campaign to ration health care benefits through "managed care," an idea that has become anathema to health and human service professionals. Another example of the market providing social welfare benefits is the practice by governmental jurisdictions of contracting out particular human services to private sector businesses, usually with the rationale of reducing costs by taking advantage of efficiencies associated with the market.[11] Recent attempts by New Jersey and Texas to privatize major portions of the state social welfare bureaucracy have enormous implications for welfare professionals working in those states.

As a result of differences among policymakers between reliance on government and reliance on the market to ensure social welfare, acrimony frequently accompanies the policy process. If the United States has a serious problem of unemployment among adolescents and young adults, for example, what is the most effective policy response? Proponents of market rationality will prefer a market strategy that eliminates the minimum wage so that employers can hire more young workers for the same amount but at lower wage levels. Proponents of bureaucratic rationality will opt for a governmental public works program that assures constructive activities at an adequate wage. In the absence of definitive data on the most desirable course of action, decisions are often made on the basis of some loosely defined, intended outcome, and rationality—of a bureaucratic or market nature—often features prominently in establishing a policy that intends a particular outcome.

The final aspect of governmental decision making addresses disadvantaged populations. It is entirely possible, of course, for social policy to introduce radical change based on data but that is contrary to the well-being of important groups. The 1996 welfare reform legislation, for example, ended the 60-year entitlement to income for poor families on the basis of evaluations of state welfare demonstrations allegedly showing that states could provide public assistance better if the federal government were not involved. Fearing the consequences of such welfare reform for poor, minority children, advocacy groups, such as the Children's Defense Fund, lobbied ardently against the proposal but to no avail.

In this instance, a welfare advocacy group challenged the veracity of research on state welfare experiments that undergirded a major shift in welfare policy. Of primary concern among children's advocates was the consequence of time-limits on the receipt of welfare for poor children. Analysts from public and private research agencies projected that between one and four million children would be terminated from public assistance if a five-year time limit were imposed on receipt of aid. The 1996 welfare reform legislation did include provisions for chronically welfare dependent families—exempting 20 percent of the AFDC caseload from time limits and allowing a portion of the Title XX Social Services Block Grant to be diverted toward their needs—but children's advocates claimed these were inadequate. The 1996 welfare reform legislation was not welfare "reform," claimed children's advocates, it was welfare "termination." Rather than benefit poor families, the 1996 Personal Responsibility and Work Opportunity Act would eventually kick millions of poor children out of the "safety net" and into the underclass.

Now return to the earlier question: What is the nature of governmental decision making? An appreciation for the dynamic nature of public policy results in the incorporation of elements from several orientations. In certain instances, one orientation may appear clearly applicable, but alone it is incapable of explaining all the factors at play. An integration of orientations is called for, but it must be customized to specific events. While this may appear confusing, it is what makes social policy such a provocative and sometimes volatile area of study.

THE POLICY PROCESS

A critical analysis of the policy process highlights three elements: the social stratification of the society, the phases through which policy is formulated, and the organizational entities that have evolved as instrumental in the decision-making process. These will be described and charted in order to clarify how welfare policy is created in the American context.

Social Stratification

A variety of schemes have been presented to differentiate groups with influence from those lacking it. The most simple of these consists of a dual stratification: for instance, capitalists and the proletariat, such as Marx used. A stratification common to Americans is in three parts: an upper class, a middle class, and a lower class. Placement of individuals in the appropriate class is usually made on the basis of income, education, and occupational status. This three-part stratification is limited in its capacity to explain very much about American social welfare, however. If asked, most Americans identify themselves as middle class, even if by objective criteria they belong to another class. Further, the designation *lower class* is not particularly informative about the social conditions of a large portion of the population about which welfare professionals are concerned.[12] Finally, the term *lower class* is pejorative, connoting a social station that has less value than others.

A more informative stratification was developed by social psychologist Dexter Dunphy, who identified six social groups.[13] Dunphy suggested that these groups differed according to several factors, the most important of which were wealth, internal solidarity, and the control over the environment. This stratification appears in Table 9.1.

As this social stratification illustrates, some groups—executives and organizers—are able to influence the environment, while other groups—erratics and apathetics—have virtually no influence. This has important implications for social welfare because those who are of lower status tend to be the recipients of welfare benefits, which are the product of a social policy process in which they do not participate. The way in which these groups influence the social policy process will be discussed in greater detail.

With these clarifications in mind, the policy process can be divided into four stages: formulation, legislation, implementation, and evaluation. While these terms are somewhat self-explanatory, during the decision-making process different organizational entities exert their influence, making the process an uneven one that is frequently characterized by fits and starts. Organizations correspond to the stratification groups that figure prominently in their organizational activities and thereby in the policy process.

Formulation

Prior to the nineteenth century it would have been accurate to state that policy formulation began with the legislative phase. Clearly, this was intended by the drafters of the Constitution, but theirs was a largely agricultural society with comparatively little institutional specialization. With industrialization, many complexities were injected into the society and, in time, special institutions emerged to assist the legislature in evaluating social conditions and preparing policy options. Eventually, even constitutionally established bodies, such as Congress, lapsed into a reactive role, largely responsive to other entities that formulated policy.[14] Initially, institutions of higher education provided this technical intelligence to assist the legislative branch, and some still do. For example, the University of Wisconsin Institute for Research on Poverty provides analyses on important welfare policies.[15]

That legislators at the federal level, as well as those in the larger states, would rely on experts to assess social conditions and develop policy options is not surprising given the fact that each legislator must attend to multiple committee and subcommittee assignments requiring expertise in particular matters, while at the same time contending with the general concerns of a large constituency. A typical day in the life of a legislator has been reconstructed by Charles Peters, a longtime Washington observer:

> The most striking feature of a congressman's life is its hectic jumble of votes, meetings, appointments, and visits from folks from back home who just drop

◆ TABLE 9.1
Social Stratification of the Population into Six Groups

Name of Group	*Examples*	*Characteristics*
Conservative groups (old wealth)	Upper elites, the independently wealthy, large stockholders	Ownership of resources is the main source of power; control over goals is very high, but control over means is through organizers
Organizer groups (executives)	Top administrators in business, government, the military	Organizational solidarity facilitates effective policy implementation; some control over goals and a high degree of control over means
Cabal groups (professionals)	Middle-level managers, technical experts, private practitioners, community leaders	Environment encourages limited solidarity; control over means is high, and goal setting can be influenced if collective action is undertaken
Strategic groups (organized workers)	Semiskilled workers, civic and political clubs, social action organizations	Environment encourages solidarity, groups have some control over the means by which goals are realized
Erratic groups (working/welfare poor)	Temporary and part-time workers earning minimum wage and who use welfare as a wage supplement	A subjugated position with with no control over the environment; frustration is shared and irrational, explosive behavior results
Apathetic groups (underclass)	Unemployables and illiterates; disabled substance abusers; itinerants, drifters, migrant workers	A subjugated position with no control over the environment; a sense of failure coupled with mobility reduces social interaction and leads to retreatism.

Source: Dexter C. Dunphy, The Primary Group: A Handbook for Analysis and Field Research, © 1972, pp. 42–44. Reprinted by permission of Prentice-Hall, Inc. Englewood Cliffs, NJ.

by. From an 8 A.M. breakfast conference with a group of union leaders, a typical morning will take him to his office around 9, where the waiting room will be filled with people who want to see him. From 9 until 10:30 or so, he will try to give the impression that he is devoting his entire attention to a businessman from his state with a tax problem; to a delegation protesting their town's loss of air or rail service; to a constituent and his three children, who are in town for the day and want to say hello; and to a couple of staff members whose morale will collapse if they don't have five minutes alone to go over essential business with him. As he strives to project one-on-one sincerity to all these people, he is fielding phone calls at the rate of one every five minutes and checking a press release that has to get out in time to make the afternoon papers in his district.

He leaves this madhouse to go to a committee meeting, accompanied by his legislative aide, who tries to brief him on the business before the committee meeting begins. The meeting started at 10, so he struggles to catch the thread of questioning, while a committee staff member whispers in his ear. And so the day continues.

The typical day . . . usually ends around 11:30 P.M., as the congressman leaves an embassy party, at which he has been hustling as if it were a key precinct on election eve. He is too tired to talk about any but the most trivial matters, too tired usually to do anything but fall into bed and go to sleep.[16]

As a result of competing demands, legislators pay somewhat less attention to the policy process than their public image would have you believe, leaving much of the work to their staffs. Even then, public policy tends to get short shrift. Because reelection is a primary concern for legislators, their staffs are frequently assigned to solve the relatively minor problems presented by constituents. In fact, placating unhappy constituents has become so prominent a concern that one legislative observer notes that constituency services—called *casework* by elected officials—have become "more important than issues" for representatives.[17]

Gradually, institutions have begun to specialize in providing the social intelligence necessary for policy formulation. These policy institutes, or think tanks as they are sometimes called, now wield substantial influence in the social policy process. Not unlike prestigious colleges, think tanks maintain multidisciplinary staffs of scholars who prepare position papers on a range of social issues. With multimillion dollar budgets and connections with national and state capitals, think tanks are well positioned to shape social policy. Generally, financial support is derived from wealthy individuals and corporations with a particular ideological inclination, a fact evidenced by the types of think tanks they support. Several prominent policy institutes are located on the ideological continuum in Figure 9.2.

Within policy institutes, prominent scholars, usually identified as senior fellows, hold endowed chairs, having often served in cabinet-level positions within the executive branch. When Republican administrations came into power, large numbers of senior fellows from conservative policy institutes assumed cabinet appointments, while their Democratic counterparts returned to liberal institutes, where senior chairs awaited them. For junior staff, an appointment in a think tank can provide invaluable experience in how the governmental policy process actually works. By way of illustration, Anna Kondratas, a conservative policy scholar, began as an attorney with the Republican National Committee, moved to the Heritage Foundation to become more familiar with social programs, was appointed by HUD Secretary Jack Kemp to manage programs for the homeless, and then, following the Clinton election, retreated to the Hudson Institute, from which she can anticipate a senior appointment by the next Republican president. Despite their influence in public policy, it is important to recognize that think tanks are private, nongovernmental institutions.

Through much of this century, a first generation of largely liberal policy institutes, such as the Brookings Institution, contributed to the formulation of governmental welfare policy. Their role was essentially passive in that they provided technical expertise to legislators and governmental agencies upon request. By the mid–1970s, however, a second generation of conservative policy institutes, such as the American Enterprise Institute and the Heritage Foundation, moved aggressively forward to shape a public philosophy that was more consistent with their own values. The elections of Ronald Reagan and George Bush did much to further the influence of these organizations, and the works of scholars from these policy institutes became important to the implementation and continuation of the "Reagan revolution."[18] A third generation of policy institutes has emerged more recently to promote programs for

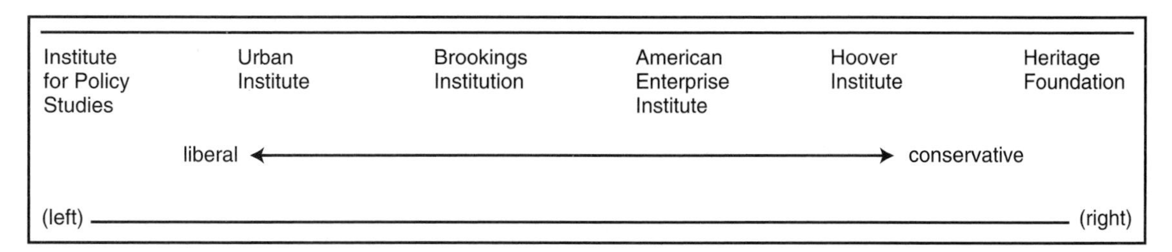

◆ **FIGURE 9.2** Place on the Ideological Continuum of Six Policy Institutes

the poor. The Children's Defense Fund and the Center on Budget and Policy Priorities are efforts to reassert the needs of the disadvantaged in social welfare policy.[19] The election of Bill Clinton to the presidency in 1992 brought to the forefront the Progressive Policy Institute, a think tank responsible for much of the policy research he used during the campaign, and later in establishing domestic policy.

Legislation

The legislative phase involves two primary groups: the legislature and special interest groups that are subclassified as lobbies and political action committees (PACs). The interaction of these groups is frequently intriguing, as Eric Redman's *The Dance of Legislation* portrays so well. Much public policy work is conducted by legislators who are appointed to committees and subcommittees on the basis of their particular interests. An important and often unappreciated component of the legislative phase is the role played by the staffs of committees and subcommittees. Legislative staffers are definitive experts in the subject area of a committee and are highly prized as lobbyists for special interest groups.[20] As a result of the increasing complexity of the policy process, the number of legislative staff has multiplied; 24,000 staff members now serve Congress, more than double the number a decade ago.[21] Committees are the loci of testimony on issues, and legislative hearings provide an opportunity for official and sometimes the only input from the public on some matters. Accordingly, representatives of advocacy groups make it a point to testify before certain committees in order to ensure that their views are heard. At the federal level, the primary committees dealing with social welfare in 1996 are listed below.[22]

Senate

Finance Committee. Subcommittees: Medicaid and Health Care for Low-Income Families; Medicare, Long-Term Care and Health Insurance; Social Security and Family Policy

Agriculture. Subcommittee: Research, Nutrition and General Legislation

Appropriations. Subcommittee: Labor, Health and Human Services, Education

Labor and Human Resources. Subcommittees: Aging; Children and Families; Disability Policy

Special Aging

House of Representatives

Ways and Means. Subcommittees: Health; Human Resources; Social Security

Economic and Educational Opportunities. Subcommittees: Early Childhood, Youth and Families; Employer/Employee Relations; Postsecondary Education, Training, and Life-Long Learning; Workforce Protections

Appropriations. Subcommittee: Labor, Health and Human Service and Education

The procedure by which an idea becomes legislation was described earlier in this chapter in the discussion on technical aspects of the policy process. Throughout the process, "special interests" attempt to shape any given proposal so that it is more congruent with priorities of their members. Special interests can be divided into two groups, according to the nature of their activities: prior to elections, interest groups can influence the composition of legislatures by establishing political action committees (PACs); in between elections, interests can exert pressure strategically through lobbying. Through the somewhat different activities of PACs and lobbying, special interests exert substantial influence on public policy.

Through PACs, campaign contributions are funneled to candidates who reflect the priorities of an interest group—a legal exercise of influence that has increased dramatically over the past two decades. In 1974, 608 PACs contributed $8.5 million to congressional campaigns; but by 1986, 4,157 PACs were showing their muscle by donating $132.2 million.[23] By 1994, PAC contributions exceeded $189 million.[24] Most of these contributions are by business interests. Less well funded are the PACs established by labor and welfare advocacy groups. Regardless of ideological preference, most PACs hedge their bets by endorsing incumbents; more than 90 percent of PAC contributions are given to members of Congress.[25] The way in which PACS influence legislation can be seen in the ill-fated Health Security Act of the Clinton administration. Anticipating a battle over the composition of a national health program, health care PACs were particularly active in funding the 1992 campaigns of officials, contributing $10 million. The largest contributions were made by PACs representing the American Medical Association ($677,969), the American Dental Association ($531,644), and the Independent Insurance Agents of America ($358,718). The largest recipient of health PAC money was Dan Rostenkowski ($162,498), then chair of the House Ways and Means Committee, the committee that would have significant influence on the construction of a national health program.[26] Rostenkowski was later indicted and lost his reelection bid. In contrast to health PAC monies, welfare PACs are small. In conjunction with the National Association of Social Workers, Political Action for Candidate Election (PACE) makes contributions to candidates for national office who profess positions similar to those of the social work professional association. In 1984, PACE distributed more than $250,000 to candidates for national office;[27] yet by 1994, that amount had decreased to $164,370.[28] The 20 largest PACS are listed in Table 9.2.

As Table 9.2 indicates, big labor weighs in heavily as a PAC contributor; however, this obscures the larger total contributions on the part of big business. While labor unions contributed $42.3 million in 1994, businesses contributed $130.2 million. Once single-issue and ideologically oriented PACs are factored in, Democrats received 62 percent of contributions, compared to 38 percent for Republicans.[29] Having won control of Congress as a result of the 1994 midterm elections, Republicans moved swiftly to reverse the revenue flow of PAC contributors. Leading the effort was Representative Dick Armey, House Majority Leader, who, in April 1995 sent a letter to Fortune 500 CEOs complaining that their contributions to such "liberal" charities as the American Cancer Society were contrary to Republican intentions in social reform. In order to clarify his intentions, Armey's staff let PAC contributors know that contributions to Republican ventures was expected and that those to Democrats would also be tallied. Special interests seeking access to the new

◆ TABLE 9.2
Top 20 PACS for 1994

Rank	*PAC Name*	*Total*	*Dem. Pct.*	*Repub. Pct.*
1	United Parcel Service	$2,647,113	52%	48%
2	Teamsters Union	2,546,128	97	3
3	American Medical Association	2,541,856	42	58
4	AFSCME*	2,530,852	98	2
5	National Education Association	2,271,000	99	1
6	Association of Trial Lawyers	2,164,035	94	6
7	United Auto Workers	2,162,190	99	1
8	National Rifle Association	1,853,038	22	78
9	National Association of Realtors	1,851,978	54	46
10	National Auto Dealers	1,832,570	30	70
11	American Institute of CPAs	1,737,520	50	50
12	Machinists Union	1,717,881	99	1
13	IBEW**	1,641,070	99	1
14	American Bankers Association	1,502,667	47	53
15	Marine Engineers Union	1,487,481	72	28
16	Laborers Union	1,468,717	95	4
17	Carpenters Union	1,467,830	96	3
18	FCWU***	1,460,939	98	2
19	Letter Carriers Union	1,443,910	93	7
20	NALU****	1,338,890	48	52

*American Federation of State County and Municipal Employees
**International Brotherhood of Electrical Workers
***Food and Commercial Workers Union
****National Association of Life Underwriters
Source: Joshua Goldstein, *PACS in Profile* (Washington, DC: Center for Responsive Politics, 1995), p. 9.

Republican leadership should be zeroing out their contributions to Democrats. In the annals of special interest politics, Armey's brazen tactics ploughed new ground: "By imposing an ideological test on givers they have introduced a new level of coercion," observed journalist Ken Auletta.[30] Yet, Armey's strategy broke no laws, and the money rolled in. In the first eight months of 1995 the Republican party received $60 million in contributions compared to just $36 million in 1993.[31] Republican leadership of the One-hundred-fourth Congress began to have misgivings about exploiting PACs to advance conservative objectives in social policy when House Speaker Newt Gingrich came under scrutiny from the House ethics committee for his creative use of Gopac, the political action committee he evolved to engineer the Republican takeover of Congress during the early 1990s.

Lest legislators become forgetful of the concerns of specific interest groups, many organizations hire career lobbyists to represent them. By 1987 some 23,011 lobbyists had registered, as required by law, to work the halls of Congress.[32] The top 20 lobbyists are listed in Table 9.3.

As Table 9.3 shows, corporations are just as likely to use lobbying as a policy strategy as PACs. Lobbying allows precisely targeted strikes at specific initiatives or legislative proposals. For example, the disproportionately large amount expended by Philip Morris was to counter federal attempts to classify nicotine as a drug to be regulated by the Food and Drug Administration. Lobbying on the part of the American Medical Association and the Health Insurance Association of America reflects continued concern about the future of Medicare and Medicaid, programs on which the health industry has become dependent. Finally, the Chamber of Commerce invested heavily in the Republican Contract with America initiative to deregulate business.[33]

Limited by meager resources, social welfare advocacy groups usually rely on volunteer lobbyists. In addition to NASW, there are several advocacy groups within social welfare that have been instrumental in advancing legislation to assist vulnerable populations—among them, the American Public Welfare Association, the Child Welfare League of America, the National Association for the Advancement of Colored People, the National Urban

◆ TABLE 9.3
Top 20 Lobbyists

Rank	*Lobby Name*	*Expenditures (millions)*
1	Philip Morris	$11.3
2	American Medical Association	8.5
3	U.S. Chamber of Commerce	7.5
4	General Motors	6.9
5	Christian Coalition	5.9
6	General Electric	5.3
7	Chemical Manufacturers Association	4.5
8	AT&T	4.3
9	Pfizer	4.2
10	Citicorp	4.2
11	Motorola	4.1
12	Ford Motor Company	3.6
13	Lockheed Martin	3.4
14	Health Insurance Association of America	3.3
15	Tenneco	3.2
16	National Association of Realtors	3.2
17	American Association of Retired Persons	3.0
18	Boeing	2.7
19	IBM	2.7
20	BellSouth	2.7

Source: Joshua Goldstein, *PACS in Profile* (Washington, DC: Center for Responsive Politics, 1995), p.12.

League, the National Assembly of Voluntary Health and Welfare Associations, and the National Organization for Women. Of these only one, the American Association of Retired Persons (AARP), has sufficient resources to makes it into the top 20 lobbyists. Despite the number of welfare advocacy organizations and their successful record in evolving more comprehensive social legislation, changes in the policy process are making their work more difficult. Increases in the number of governmental agencies as well as in their staffs make it difficult to track policy developments and whatever changes there are in administrative procedures. Worse, the escalating cost of influencing social policy, evident in the number of paid lobbyists and the contributions lavished by PACs, is simply beyond the means of welfare advocacy organizations. As one Democratic candidate for the Senate lamented, "only the well-heeled have PACs—not the poor, the unemployed, the minorities or even most consumers."[34]

This is not to say that proponents of social justice are ineffectual. Despite their disadvantageous status, welfare advocacy groups were able to mobilize grass-roots support to beat back some of the more regressive proposals of the Reagan administration. In the early 1980s, for example, scholars from the conservative Cato Institute and the Heritage Foundation proposed cutting the Social Security program. They were trounced by an effective lobbying campaign mounted by the AARP under the leadership of the late octogenarian Congressman Claude Pepper. Unfortunately, other social welfare programs did not fare as well. At the same time that Social Security was spared budget cuts, social programs for the poor were reduced by significant margins. Among the newer advocacy organizations, the Children's Defense Fund (CDF) stood to benefit significantly from the election of Bill Clinton because First Lady Hillary Rodham Clinton had been a former chair of its board of directors and Clinton's Health and Human services (HHS) Secretary, Donna Shalala, had succeeded Rodham Clinton at CDF. Although CDF claimed a substantial victory with incorporation of the Children's Initiative in the Clinton 1993 economic package, children's advocates were distraught when Clinton signed a welfare reform plan that they thought was injurious to poor children.

Implementation

Simply because a policy has been enacted does not necessarily mean it will be implemented. Often governmental policy fails to provide for adequate authority, personnel, or funding to accomplish its stated purpose. This is a chronic problem for social welfare programs. Underfunding of children's services has been so chronic that by the early 1990s child welfare agencies in 21 states and the District of Columbia had been placed under in receivership by the courts. It is also possible that governmental policy will not be enforced even after it has been established. Many states have correctional and mental health institutions now operating under court supervision because judges have agreed with social advocates that these institutions are not in compliance with state or federal law. In another instance, full compliance with civil rights and affirmative action policies was not sought during the Reagan presidency because the Justice Department found these policies disagreeable.

Implementation, difficult enough in the normal course of events, is that much more difficult when the public is disaffected from governmental institutions. The episodic nature of public endorsement of governmental institutions has been studied extensively by Albert O. Hirschman. In *Shifting Involvements*, Hirschman investigated the relationship between "private interest and public action." According to Hirschman, public endorsement of governmental institutions is a fundamental problem for industrialized capitalist societies, which emphasize individual competitiveness while generating social and economic dislocations that require collective action. "Western societies," Hirschman observes, "appear to be condemned to long periods of privatization during which they live through an impoverished 'atrophy of public meanings,' followed by spasmodic outbursts of 'publicness' that are hardly likely to be constructive."[35] Disenchantment with governmental solutions to social problems makes public welfare programs vulnerable to their critics, leading to reductions in staff and fiscal support, often followed by an escalation in the social problem for which the social program was initially designed. Thus, the episodic nature of public support for programs designed to alleviate social problems further impedes effective implementation.

The ebb and flow of social policy is evident with respect to immigration. A provision of the 1986 Immigration Reform and Control Act allowed resident aliens who had been in the United States for five years to apply for amnesty, through which they could attain permanent residency status and avoid deportation. To process claims the Immigration and Naturalization Service opened special offices across the nation. But because the window for applications lasted only 12 months, these offices were closed a year later. As a result, some 3 million aliens applied for amnesty, and most of these applicants stopped at having received permanent resident status and did not apply for citizenship. After the amnesty option expired, thousands of immigrants continued their migration to the United States, causing another backlog of resident, illegal immigrants who would not be eligible for amnesty. Many conservatives attributed increasing welfare expenditures to immigrants, legal as well as illegal. As a consequence, by 1996, a conservative Congress restricted public assistance benefits to legal immigrants through the Personal Responsibility and Work Opportunity Act. Fearing that they would lose access to benefits they might need in the future, thousands of legal immigrants who had obtained permanent residency status under the amnesty provisions of the 1986 legislation suddenly decided to become American citizens, a status that would assure their access to welfare benefits. As a result, the INS was deluged with citizenship applications and had to hire additional staff. Eventually, many legal immigrants had become U.S. citizens in order to be able to receive welfare benefits should they need them while thousands of legal immigrants were denied benefits that they had once received, and thousands of illegal immigrants continued to be ineligible for benefits altogether.

Another illustration of problems relating to implementation is the Personal Responsibility and Work Opportunity Act (PRWOA) of 1996, or as it is popularly known, "welfare reform." Subsequent to the previous welfare reform legislation, the Family Support Act of 1988, the federal Department of Health and Human Services granted waivers to states so that they could mount alternative arrangements for providing AFDC and other public assistance benefits. Such welfare "experiments" focused on welfare-to-work, requiring school attendance, denying benefits to additional children born after initial eligibility, preventing teen pregnancy, increasing child support, and instituting time limits to receipt of AFDC. As a result of research required of the waiver experiments, most state innovations produced modest improvements in welfare provision, at best. In several instances, the experimental groups of welfare recipients fared worse after having received the beneficial intervention, compared to the control group. The research evidence notwithstanding, the PRWOA was passed by Congress and signed into law by President Clinton. Welfare policy analysts of liberal and conservative persuasion voiced their misgivings about such welfare reform but to no avail. Of particular concern was a projection of the Congressional Budget Office that between one and four million poor children would be kicked out of the welfare safety net as a result of the imposition of time limits.[36] Under such conditions, it is difficult to be sanguine about the implementation of welfare reform at the state level.

Evaluation

The expansion of governmental welfare policies has spawned a veritable industry in program evaluation. Stung by the abuses of the executive branch during Watergate and the Vietnam War, Congress established additional oversight agencies to review federal programs.[37] As a result, multiple units within the executive and legislative branches of government have the evaluation of programs as their primary mission. At the federal level, the most important of these include the Government Accounting Office (GAO), the Office of Management and Budget (OMB), the Congressional Budget Office (CBO), and the Congressional Research Service (CRS). State governments have similar units. In addition, departments have evaluation units that monitor program activities for which they are responsible. Finally, federal and state levels of government commonly contract with nongovernmental organizations for evaluations of specific programs. As a result, many universities provide important research services to government. The University of Wisconsin's Institute for Research on Poverty is distinguished for its research in social welfare. More recently, private consulting firms, such as the Manpower Demonstration Research Corporation, Abt Associates, Maximus, and Mathematica, have entered the field, often hiring former government officials and capitalizing on their connections in order to secure research contracts. Of course, any politicization of the research process is frowned upon because it raises questions about the impartiality of the evaluation. Is a former government official willing to assess, rigorously and impartially, a program run by an agency in which he or she was employed in the past or would like to be employed in the future? Questions about the validity of evaluation studies generated by the closeness between governmental agencies and research firms have become so common that the consulting firms located near the expressway surrounding Washington, D.C., are often referred to as "the beltway bandits."

Investigations by program evaluation organizations can be characterized as applied research (as opposed to "pure" research), the objective being to optimize program operations. As a result of this emphasis on the function of programs, evaluation studies frequently focus on waste, cost-effectiveness, and goal attainment. Owing to the contradictory objectives of many welfare policies, the constant readjustments in programs, and the limitations in the art of evaluation research, evaluations frequently conclude that any given program has mixed results. Rarely does a program evaluation provide a clear indication for future action. Often the results of program evaluations are used by critics and defenders alike either to dismantle or to advance a program. The very inconclusiveness of program evaluation contributes to the partisan use to which evaluation research can be put. It is not uncommon for decision makers to engage in statistical arguments that have a great influence on social welfare policy. Of the recent "stat wars," several relate directly to social welfare. One example is the question whether underemployed and discouraged workers should be included in the unemployment rate. Currently, the Department of Labor defines as unemployed only those who are out of work and looking for jobs and considers part-time workers as employed. As a result, many African Americans, Hispanic Americans, young adults, and women are not considered unemployed, even though advocates for these groups contend that they are not fully employed. Liberals argue that by including the underemployed and discouraged workers in the unemployment rate, it would become a more accurate measure of the employment experience of disadvantaged groups. Conservatives argue that the employment rate is not a good indicator of employment opportunity, citing the millions of undocumented workers who come to the United States every year illegally to take menial jobs. Further, including underemployed and discouraged workers would increase the unemployment rate by as much as 50 percent and would prove unacceptably expensive because extensions in the number of quarters for which workers are eligible for unemployment compensation are tied to the unemployment rate.

Evaluations of social welfare programs vary considerably. As a result of the research requirement accompanying the welfare reform waivers granted the states, considerable data has been generated about the result of state and local welfare-to-work initiatives. Organizations, such as the Manpower Demonstration Research Corporation, Mathematica, and Abt Associates, have produced volumes of studies on such welfare experiments. By comparison, very little research has been conducted in child welfare, especially the most acute sector of children's services, child protective services. During the 1980s, child welfare professionals believed that family preservation would prove a major innovation in services to abused and neglected children and their families. Often based on rudimentary research, the claims of proponents of family preservation failed to hold up under more rigorous field experiments. Nevertheless, the Family Support and Preservation component of the Children's Initiative of 1993 promised to divert $930 million over 5 years for family preservation. It remains to be seen if this major appropriation in child welfare services will be able to deliver as promised given the weak evidence from field research.[38]

CONCLUSION: IMPLICATIONS FOR SOCIAL WELFARE

If the governmental decision-making process is somewhat irregular and irrational, it is also unrepresentative. As Figure 9.3 illustrates, groups in the upper levels of the social stratification populate the institutions through which policy is made. In the case of welfare policy, welfare beneficiaries must adjust to rules established by other social groups.

The primary players in the social policy game are organizers (executives) and cabals (professionals). Conservatives (old wealth) are able to opt out, leaving their social obligations in the hands of organizers. As one goes down the social stratification scale, the remaining groups have less influence on governmental policy. The interests of these groups are left in the hands of maverick professionals who work through advocacy organizations, although occasional unrest on the part of erratic (working/welfare poor) groups can result in increased welfare benefits. The difficulties that social program advocates can encounter in the policy process are evident in the attempt to legislate Urban Enterprise Zones (UEZs) in order to repair the extensive damage to South Central Los Angeles caused by the 1992 riot. Despite its being the worst civil disturbance in memory, the UEZ provisions of the 1992 Urban Aid Act amounted to a modest $2.5 billion for the creation of 50 enterprise zones. As the result of pressure by special business interests, unrelated tax concessions were added by the House and Senate, which increased appropriations to $28 billion, an amount considered unacceptable by President Bush, who therefore vetoed the measure.[39] President Clinton incorporated aid to the cities in the form of appropriations for Empowerment Zones. In 1993, Congress authorized $3.5 billion for 6 empowerment zones, including a $125 million to Los Angeles as a "supplemental" empowerment zone.[40] The future of the empowerment zone strategy was darkened considerably, however, when Republicans gained control of Congress in 1994. Among their objectives was a reduction in aid to cities.

The lack of influence on the part of lower socioeconomic groups in the social policy process is virtually built into governmental decision making. The term *nondecision making* has been coined to describe this phenomenon—the capacity to keep the interests of some groups off the decision-making agenda.[41] Nondecision making has a long history in the United States; generations of African Americans and women were legally excluded from decision making prior to emancipation and suffrage. More recent attempts to increase the influence of disadvantaged groups in decision making have not been well received. Perhaps the best-known example of this occurred during the War on Poverty when poor people were to be assured of "maximum feasible participation" in the Community Action Program (CAP). Even though this was interpreted to mean that one-third of the members of CAP boards of directors must be poor people—a seemingly reasonable expectation—the militancy of poor people in some cities at the time led to utter chaos in many CAPs. As a result of pressure from mayors and other officials, this requirement was rescinded in order to make CAPs more compliant.[42] Since then, the representation of lower socioeconomic groups in decision making has been limited, for all practical purposes, to an advisory capacity, if it is incorporated at all.

The governmental policy process also poses problems for administrators and practitioners. Policies frequently reflect assumptions about the human condition that may seem reasonable to the upper socioeconomic groups that make them but bear little resemblance to the reality of the lower socioeconomic groups that are supposed to be beneficiaries. For example, child support enforcement policy assumes that fathers of children on the AFDC program have the kind of regular, well-paying jobs that would allow them to meet the amounts of their court orders, when often their jobs are intermittent and low-wage. Consequently, support payments to children who are dependent on welfare have been relatively disappointing. An evaluation of Parents' Fair Share, a program designed to increase the child support of men whose dependents were on AFDC, resulted in reduced child support payments despite the multiple interventions incorporated in the program.[43] To cite another example, welfare-to-work programs assume that youths want to complete their education and gain meaningful employment, when their socialization

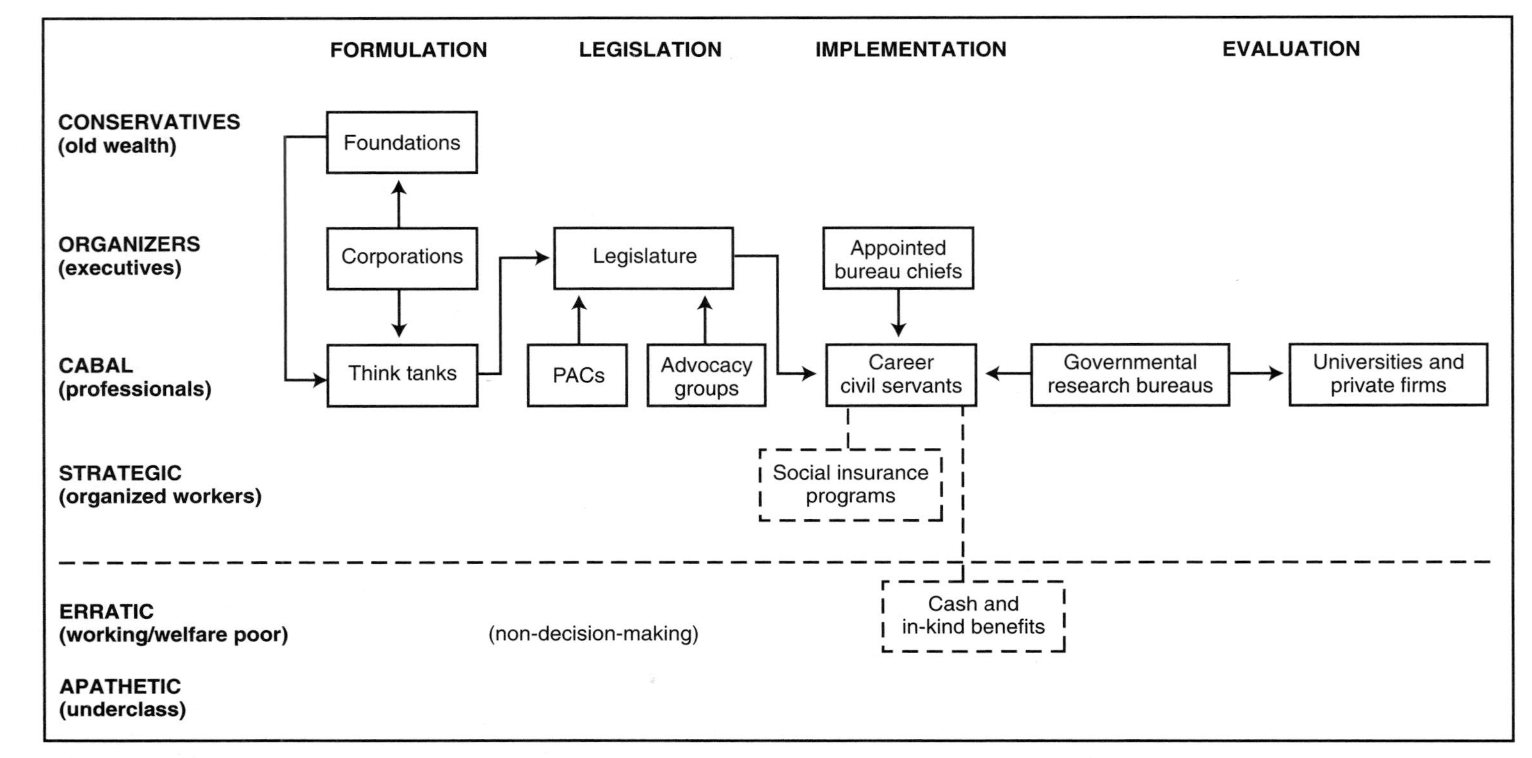

◆ FIGURE 9.3 The Role Played by Six Social Levels in the Governmental Policy Process

often instructs them that school and work are irrelevant and that having a child may be the most meaningful thing they can do. Subsequently, AFDC has provided financial support to poor teenaged mothers, a benefit that many conservatives claim has actually induced girls to become pregnant. An evaluation of New Chance, a teen pregnancy prevention program, resulted in outcomes that were contrary to the intent of the program: young mothers enrolled in New Chance were more likely to become pregnant again and less likely to participate in the labor market than those in the control group.[44] The preliminary studies on child support and teen pregnancy suggest that the poor do not comply with the bourgeois assumptions that are implicit or explicit in social policy.

It is not surprising, then, that welfare programs are not well received by many of the people who depend on them. Instead of being grateful, beneficiaries are frequently resentful. In turn, upper-income taxpayers find this ingratitude offensive and are inclined to make programs more punitive. Ironically, beneficiaries of welfare programs tend to respond to punitive policies with indifference and defiance because, for many of them, welfare programs have never been particularly helpful. The perception that welfare programs are only minimally helpful is occasionally validated when, due to exceptional circumstances, someone from an upper socioeconomic group falls into the social safety net and suddenly appreciates the importance of welfare programs for daily survival.

Not all welfare programs are perceived in such a negative light. Generally, programs that benefit persons solidly in the working class fare better. The social insurance programs, such as Social Security, Unemployment Compensation, and Medicare, are usually regarded more highly by beneficiaries. Of course, the insurance programs require people to first pay into the program in order to claim benefits later, so they are designed to be different from the means-tested programs intended for the poor.

A particular consequence of governmental policy making falls on the shoulders of welfare professionals. "Workers on the front lines of the welfare state find themselves in a corrupted world of service," wrote Michael Lipsky in his award-winning *Street-Level Bureaucracy*. According to Lipsky, "Workers find that the best way to keep demand within manageable proportions is to deliver a consistently inaccessible or inferior product."[45] In response to the irrelevance often characteristic of governmental welfare policies, personnel in public welfare offices consequently deny benefits to people who are eligible for them, a process labeled "bureaucratic disentitlement."[46] It should come as no surprise, then, that public welfare programs mandated by governmental policy have acquired an undesirable reputation within the professional community. The executive director of the California chapter of NASW candidly stated that "Public social services are being abandoned by M.S.W. social workers. It seems to be employment of last resort."[47] Another veteran observer was even more graphic: "To work in a public agency today is to work in a bureaucratic hell."[48] Within the context of public welfare it is not surprising to find that burnout has become pervasive among welfare professionals. The inadequacy of public welfare policies for both beneficiaries and professionals is an unfortunate consequence of the governmental policy process as it is currently structured.

Making the public policy process more representative is a primary concern of welfare advocates. Since the Civil Rights movement, African Americans and the poor have recognized the power of the ballot, and voter registration has become an important strategy for advancing the influence of these groups. The registration of Hispanic Americans in the Southwest has been the mission of the Southwest Voter Research Institute, founded by the late Willie Velasquez. Under the visionary leadership of Velasquez, Latino voter registration grew steadily, reflected in an increase in the number of Chicano elected officials. Fifteen years of voter registration campaigning by the Institute contributed to a doubling of the number of Hispanic elected officials in the Southwest.[49]

The most visible example of the political empowerment of people usually excluded from the decision-making process was Jesse Jackson's 1988 campaign to be the presidential nominee of the Democratic party. Expanding on the grass-roots political base built during his 1984 bid for the nomination, Jackson's 1988 Rainbow Coalition demonstrated the support he commanded from a wide spectrum of disenfranchised Americans. Thus, mobilization of the working- and welfare-poor, as Velasquez and Jackson have shown, can make the policy process more representative. Working to make public policy more democratic in origin is a continuous struggle and one that is supported by welfare advocacy organizations.

◆ ◆ ◆ *Discussion Questions* ◆ ◆ ◆

1. Using a critical approach to welfare policy, select a social welfare program and identify the primary interests that are involved in its creation. To what extent do clients of the program influence the program? To what extent do social workers influence the program? Are there assumptions built into the program that are inconsistent with the assumptions of the clients or social workers who are involved in it? To what extent have classism, racism, sexism, and ageism influenced health and human service programs of interest to you?

2. Politicians elected to the U.S. Congress can be reached through the Capitol Switchboard: (202) 224–3121. Contact your elected representative and one of your two senators and determine which health and human service committee assignments they have. Do your representatives have committee assignments that could make them influential on issues important to you? Do your representatives have position statements available to constituents about specific social programs?

3. Politicians elected to your state legislature have responsibilities similar to those who are elected to Congress. Identify your state representatives. Do they have assignments on health and human-service committees? Do they have position statements they could send to you on health and human-service issues?

4. Select a legislative proposal in a health and human service area of concern to you and follow it through the national or state legislature. Which committees and interest groups supported or fought the proposed legislation? How was the bill changed to make it more acceptable to special interests? Have local interests, such as a major newspaper, endorsed or objected to the proposed legislation? Why?

5. Does your state chapter of the National Association of Social Workers make legislation a high priority for the professional community? What are the legislative priorities for the state NASW chapter? How is that reflected in the resources allocated? How would you prioritize health and human services in your community?

6. If nondecision making leaves many clients of social programs impotent in the public policy process, how could they be made more influential? How could the local professional community assist in empowering beneficiaries of social programs? What could you do?

Notes

1. U.S. Congress, *U.S. Congress Handbook 1992* (McLean, VA: Barbara Pullen, 1992), p. 184.
2. *Robert's Rules of Order* is available from several publishers.
3. The latest annual edition of *Overview of Entitlement Programs* can be obtained through the Government Printing Office in Washington, DC.
4. Charles Lindblom and David Braybrooke, *Strategy of Decision* (New York: Free Press, 1970).
5. Amitai Etzioni, *The Active Society* (New York: Free Press, 1968), pp. 282–288.
6. U.S. Congress, "Conference Report on Immigration Reform and Control Act of 1986," *Congressional Record* (October 14, 1986), pp. H10068–H10095.
7. "An INS Recipe for Family Separation," *San Diego Tribune* (October 24, 1987), p. B3.
8. For a description of these forms of rationality, see Robert Alford, "Health Care Politics," *Politics and Society* 2(Winter 1972), pp. 127–164.
9. Neil Gilbert and Harry Specht, *Dimensions of Social Welfare Policy* (Englewood Cliffs, NJ: Prentice-Hall, 1986), pp. 206–210.

10. "Nuking Employee Benefits," *Wall Street Journal* (August 29, 1988), p. 16.
11. For example, see Harry Hatry, *A Review of Private Approaches for Delivery of Public Services* (Washington, DC: Urban Institute, 1983).
12. Even Marx, who used a two-part classification, conceded the existence of a "lumpen-proletariat," although he did little to develop the concept.
13. Dexter Dunphy, *The Primary Group* (New York: Appleton-Century-Crofts, 1972), pp. 42–44.
14. Charles Peters, *How Washington Really Works*, rev. ed. (Reading, MA: Addison-Wesley, 1983), p. 112.
15. See, for example, Sheldon Danziger and Daniel Weinberg, *Fighting Poverty* (Cambridge, MA: Harvard University Press, 1986).
16. Peters, *How Washington Really Works*, pp. 101–102, 116.
17. Hedrick Smith, *The Power Game: How Washington Works* (New York: Random House, 1988), p. 152.
18. David Stoesz, "Policy Gambit: Conservative Think Tanks Take On the Welfare State," *Journal of Sociology and Social Welfare* 16 (1989), pp. 8–16.
19. David Stoesz, "The New Welfare Policy Institutes." Unpublished manuscript, School of Social Work, San Diego State University, 1988.
20. Peters, *How Washington Really Works*, p. 114.
21. Smith, *The Power Game*, p. 24.
22. *Congress at Your Fingertips* (McLean, VA: Capitol Advantage, 1996).
23. Smith, *The Power Game*, p. 252.
24. Joshua Goldstein, *PACs in Profile* (Washington, DC: Center for Responsive Politics, 1995).
25. Charles Babcock, "At Least the PACs Still Love Those Incumbents in Congress," *Washington Post Weekly* (June 15–21, 1992), p. 32.
26. Dana Priest, "Health Care PACs Pay $10 million for 'Access,'" *Washington Post* (July 22, 1992), p. A17.
27. Steve Burghardt, "Community-Based Social Action," *Encyclopedia of Social Work*, 18th ed. (Silver Spring, MD: NASW, 1987), p. 297.
28. Goldstein, *PACs in Profile*, p. 85.
29. Ibid., p. 3.
30. Ken Auletta, "Pay Per Views," *New Yorker* (June 5, 1995), p. 56.
31. Nancy Gibbs, "Where Power Goes . . . " *Time* (July 17, 1995), p. 21.
32. Smith, *The Power Game*, p. 238.
33. "'Lobbyists spent $400 million in half a year, reports suggest," *Richmond Times-Dispatch* (September 23, 1996), p. A7.
34. Smith, *The Power Game*, p. 254.
35. Albert O. Hirschman, *Shifting Involvements* (Princeton, NJ: Princeton University Press, 1982), p. 132.
36. David Stoesz, "Welfare Behaviorism," *Society* (forthcoming, 1997).
37. Peters, *How Washington Really Works*, p. 111.
38. Lela Costin, Howard Karger, and David Stoesz, *The Politics of Child Abuse in America* (New York: Oxford University Press, 1996).
39. Art Pine, "President Vetoes Urban Aid Measure," *Los Angeles Times* (November 5, 1992), p. A-4.
40. Lori Montgomery, "Feds' Urban Aid Plan Shows Few Triumphs So Far," *Albuquerque Journal* (December 31, 1995), p. B7.
41. Peter Bachrach and Morton S. Baratz, *Power and Poverty* (New York: Oxford University Press, 1979), p. 7.
42. For a review of the CAP experience, see Daniel Patrick Moynihan, *Maximum Feasible Misunderstanding* (New York: Random House, 1973).
43. Dan Bloom and Kay Sherwood, *Matching Opportunities to Obligations: Lessons for Child Support Reform from the Parents' Fair Share Pilot Phase* (New York: Manpower Demonstration Research Corporation, 1994).
44. Janet Quint, Denise Polit, Hans Bos, and George Cave, *New Chance: Interim Findings on a Comprehensive Program for Disadvantaged Young Mothers and Their Children* (New York: Manpower Demonstration Research Corporation, 1994).
45. Michael Lipsky, "Bureaucratic Disentitlement in Social Welfare Programs," *Social Service Review* (33) 4 (March 1984), pp. 81–88.
46. Quoted in Robert Kuttner, *The Economic Illusion* (Boston: Houghton Mifflin, 1984), p. 86.
47. Ellen Dunbar, "Future of Social Work," *NASW California News* 13, no. 18 (May 1987), p. 3.
48. Harris Chaiklin, "The New Homeless and Service Planning on a Professional Campus," University of Maryland, Chancellor's Colloquium, Baltimore, December 4, 1985, p. 7.
49. "Willie's Vision for Chicano Empowerment," *Southwest Voter Research Notes* (2)3 (June 1988), pp. 1.

CHAPTER 10

Social Insurance Programs

This chapter explores the major social insurance. As such, it examines Old Age, Survivors, and Disability Insurance (OASDI), Unemployment Insurance (UI), Workers' Compensation (WC), Earned Income Tax Credit (EITC), and Supplemental Security Income (SSI). In addition, this chapter explores some of the major issues and problems surrounding social insurance programs.

DEFINITION OF SOCIAL INSURANCE

Social insurance is the cornerstone of U.S. social welfare policy. Specifically, it is a system whereby people are compelled—through payroll or other taxes—to insure themselves against the possibility of their own indigence resulting from the loss of a job, the death of the family breadwinner, or physical disability. Based in part on the principles used in private insurance, social insurance sets aside a sum of money that is held in trust by the government and earmarked to be used in the event of the death, disability, or the unemployment of the worker. The major goal of social insurance is to maintain income by replacing lost earnings. It is a pay-as-you-go system in which the workers and employers of today pay for those who have retired, are ill, or have lost their jobs. Although originally designed to replicate a private insurance fund, the Social Security program has been broadened to encompass a series of programs that attempt to provide a socially adequate replacement income. Because the benefits for some retired workers exceed their contributions to the system, Social Security has taken on some of the characteristics of an income redistribution and/or public assistance program.

Public assistance programs are means-tested and based entirely on need. The rationale for public assistance is based on the concept of *safety nets*, which are designed to ensure that citizens receive basic services and that they do not fall below a given poverty level. Social insurance, on the other hand, requires beneficiaries to make contributions to the system **before** they can claim benefits. Moreover, expenditures for social insurance are far greater than they are for public assistance, as can be seen in Figure 10.1. Social insurance is also universal; that is, people receive benefits as legal entitlements regardless of their personal wealth. Table 10.1 illustrates federal spending for major social insurance programs and the number of beneficiaries for each. Because the social insurance benefit structure is linked to occupationally defined productive work, most programs tend to be little or not at all stigmatized. In contrast, public assistance recipients are often highly stigmatized. Perhaps this is because public assistance programs are financed out of

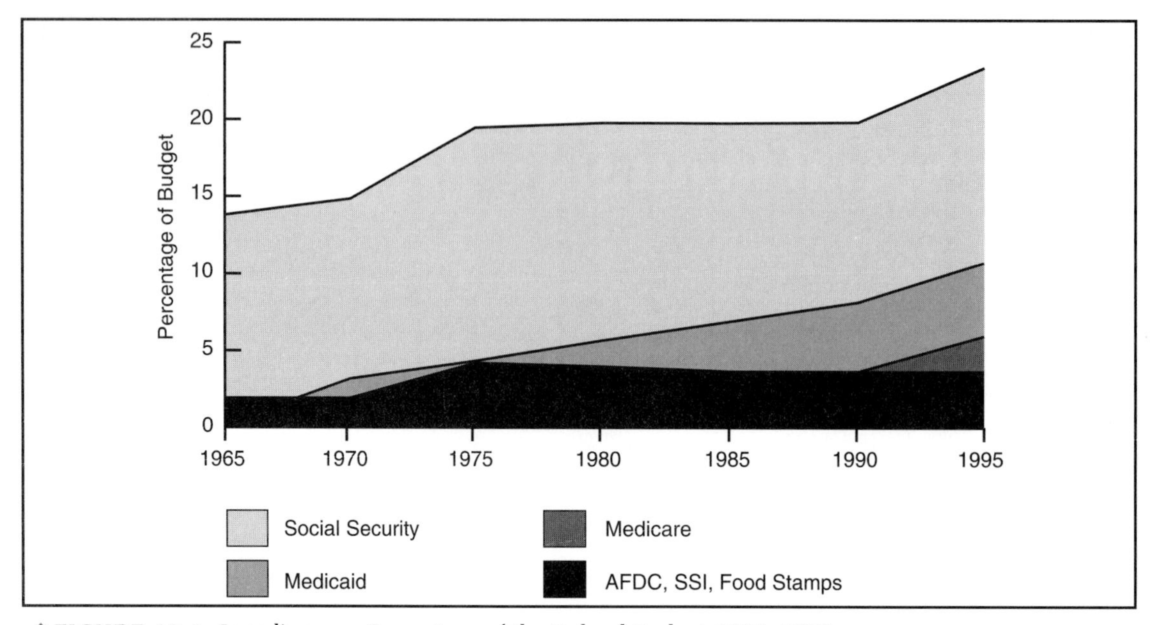

◆ **FIGURE 10.1 Spending as a Percentage of the Federal Budget 1965–1995**

Source: U.S. House of Representatives, House Ways and Mean Committee, Overview of Entitlements, *1994 Green Book* (Washington, DC: US GPO, 1994), p. 1006.

general tax revenues; they are not occupationally linked and not based on a previous work record; and recipients must be determined indigent through means-tests.

Although some people complain about the costs of public assistance programs, social insurance programs are financed at a level roughly four times higher than public welfare is. For example, social insurance programs (OASDI, Workers' Compensation, Medicare, and Unemployment Insurance, among others) cost about $634 billion in 1996 compared with about $190 billion for public assistance programs (AFDC, SSI, food stamps, WIC, and others). Furthermore, social insurance programs accounted for 22.1 percent of the total federal budget in 1993, compared to 3.4 percent for public assistance programs. Finally, the average OASDI beneficiary received $652 a month in

◆ **TABLE 10.1**
Past, Current, and Projected Federal Spending for Major Social Insurance Programs, Selected Years *(Expenditures in billions)*

Programs	*1975*	*1992*	*1996*	*2000*	*2002*
OASDI	$65.8	$284.7	$348.1	$421.3	$463.5
Medicare	$14.1	$128.3	$174.7	$252.8	$300.7
Unemployment Insurance	$ 8.2	$ 34.6	$ 23.7	$ 27.0	$ 29.2
Total	$90.3	$450.5	$546.5	$701.1	$793.4

Sources: Compiled from various tables in U.S. Bureau of the Census, *Statistical Abstract*, 1990 (Washington, DC: U.S. Government Printing Office, 1990); and Committee on Ways and Means, U.S. House of Representatives, *Overview of Entitlement Programs: 1992 Green Book* (Washington, DC: U.S. Government Printing Office, 1992); US Budget, FY 1997, Analytic Perspectives, Review of Direct Spending and Reports. On-line: http://www.doc.gov/BudgetFY97/spectoc.html

1995 compared with a little over $420 for a mother with two children on AFDC.

THE BACKGROUND OF SOCIAL INSURANCE

The first old-age insurance program was introduced in Germany in 1889 by Chancellor Otto von Bismarck. Although originally intended as a means of curbing the growing socialist trend in Germany, by the onset of World War I nearly all European nations had old-age assistance programs of one sort or another. In 1920 the U.S. government began its own Federal Employees Retirement program. By 1931, 17 states had enacted their own old-age assistance programs, although these often had stringent eligibility requirements. For example, in some cases where relatives were capable of supporting an elderly person, benefits were denied. Often the elderly who applied for assistance had to sign over all their assets to the state when they died. These state-administered retirement programs were restrictive and often punitive.[1] Nevertheless, the concept of governmental responsibility for welfare grew during the early part of the twentieth century and, by 1935, all states—with the exception of Georgia and South Carolina—had programs that provided financial assistance to widows and children.[2]

Spurred on by the Great Depression of the 1930s and the growing rebellion inspired by a California physician named Francis Townsend (who advocated a flat $200 per month for each retired worker), President Franklin Roosevelt championed a government assistance program that would cover both unemployed and retired workers.[3] The result of Roosevelt's efforts was the Social Security Act of 1935, through which the federal government established the basic framework for the modern social welfare state.

The 1935 Social Security Act was relatively modest compared with its present orientation. It established categorical assistance to the elderly poor, dependent children, the blind, and some handicapped children. Money was earmarked for vocational rehabilitation, rural public health, and training for public experts under Title IV. Two titles covered eligibility and financing for old-age retirement; two others established UI under joint state and federal government auspices. Title VII established a Social Security Board, whose job it was to monitor the fund. Title XI provided the right to alter any part of the act.[4]

As amended, the Social Security Act provides for: (1) OASDI; (2) UI programs under joint federal and state partnership; (3) federal assistance to the aged, blind, and disabled under the SSI program; (4) public assistance to families with dependent children under the AFDC program; (5) federal health insurance for the aged (Medicare); and (6) federal and state health assistance for the poor (Medicaid). Although all these programs fit under the rubric of the Social Security Act of 1935, not all are social insurance programs (e.g., Medicaid, AFDC, and SSI).

The insurance feature of Social Security emerged as the result of an intense debate: Progressives wanted Social Security funded out of general revenue taxes whereas conservatives wanted it funded solely out of employee contributions. The compromise reached was that old-age insurance would be financed by employer and employee contributions of 1 percent on a base wage of $3,000, with a maximum cap for worker contributions set at $30 per year. At age 65, single workers would receive $22 per month, while married workers would get $36. In order to allow the trust fund to accumulate reserves, no benefits were paid out until 1940.

The Social Security Act of 1935 has been modified repeatedly, almost always in the direction of increasing its coverage. The original Social Security Act of 1935 afforded retirement and survivor benefits to only about 40 percent of the labor force. Farm and domestic workers, mariners, bank employees, the self-employed, and state and local government employees were excluded. In 1950 farmers and self-employed persons were added, thereby bringing the coverage to more than 90 percent of the labor force. Congress made survivors and dependents of insured workers eligible for benefits in 1939, and in 1956 disability insurance was added to include totally and permanently disabled workers. In 1965, Health Insurance for the Aged (Medicare)—a prepaid health insurance plan—was incorporated into the law. In later years, the act was amended to allow workers to retire as early as age 62, provided they agreed to accept only 80 percent of their benefits. In 1977 an automatic cost-of-living index was affixed to benefit payments.

With the amendments of 1939 (extending coverage to widows, elderly wives, surviving children, etc.) the Social Security technically became bankrupt because it was no longer entirely self-financed. As such, the federal government assumed responsibility for any financial shortfalls and thus implicitly assumed responsibility for promoting the general welfare. By 1996, more than 43 million Americans and more than one-quarter of all U.S. households depended on a monthly Social Security check.[5] As Figure 10.2 illustrates, by 1996 only 61.5 percent of Social Security beneficiaries were retired workers.

KEY SOCIAL INSURANCE PROGRAMS

OASDI

OASDI is a combination of old-age and survivors' insurance (OASI) and disability insurance (DI). OASDI, or what most people refer to as Social Security, is currently the largest social program in the nation, covering approximately nine out of ten workers. OASDI is a federal program administered by the Social Security Administration, which in 1994 became an independent agency headed by a commissioner and a board appointed by the U.S. president for a six-year term.

In many ways, Social Security is a stellar example of a program that has worked. For example, the poverty rate for the elderly in 1995 was 10.3 percent, lower than the poverty rate for the general population (13.8 percent). As recently as 1969, before the Social Security cost-of-living adjustments (COLAs) took effect, the poverty rate for the elderly was double that of the general population, 25 versus 12 percent.[6] According to the Social Security Administration, in 1996 the poverty rate for the elderly would have been 52 percent without Social Security.[7] In that sense, Social Security has a strong redistributive effect by transferring resources from those with high lifetime earnings to those with low lifetime earnings.

Social Security relies on pay-as-you-go financing. In other words, unlike pre-funded private annuity plans in which a worker draws off money already invested, Social Security benefits are paid by today's workers. Benefits under OASDI are entitlement-based; that is, they are based on the beneficiaries

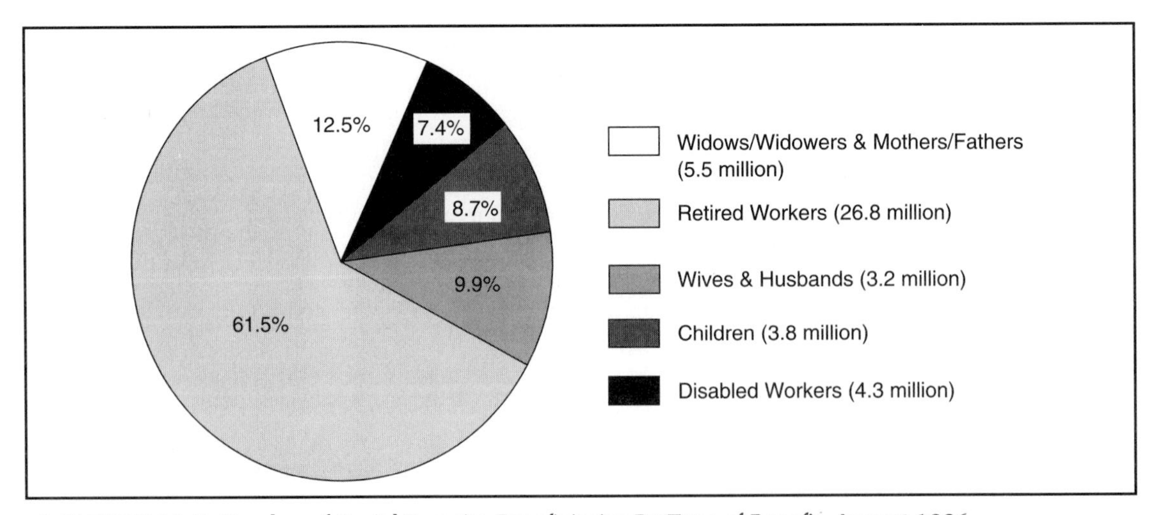

◆ **FIGURE 10.2 Number of Social Security Beneficiaries By Type of Benefit, August 1996**
Source: Social Security Administration, "Number of Social Security Beneficiaries." On-line: http://www.ssa.gov/research

earnings, not on the amount of the revenue in the trust fund. If benefits exceed the funds, the difference is made up by using the reserves in the trust funds. OASDI operates in the following manner:

- In 1996 the employer and the employee each paid an OASDI tax equal to 6.20 percent of the first $62,700 in earnings and a Medicare Hospital Insurance (HI) tax equal to 1.45 percent of earnings. Employees therefore paid a total of 7.65 percent. Self-employed persons paid 15.3 percent. In general, increases in the wage base are automatic and are based on the increase in average wages in the economy each year. The highest Social Security tax a worker could pay in 1996 was $3,887 (not including the HI tax), with a joint employer/employee tax of $7,785. Self-employed persons had their taxes computed on a lower base (net earnings from self-employment less 7.65 percent), and half of that tax was deductible for income tax purposes.
- Based on their age at retirement and the amount earned during their working years, workers receive a monthly benefit payment. Retired workers aged 62 receive a reduction of 5/9 of 1 percent for each month of entitlement before age 65, with a maximum reduction of 20 percent. Benefits are modest, with the average retired worker receiving $652 a month in 1996.[8] The maximum benefit in 1996 for a retired worker at age 65 was $1,249 per month, and for a couple, $1,720.
- Under the OASI program, a monthly payment is made to an unmarried child or eligible dependent grandchild of a retired worker or a deceased worker who was fully insured at the time of death, if the child or grandchild is: (1) under age 18; (2) a full-time elementary or secondary school student under age 19; and (3) a dependent or disabled person aged 18 or over whose disability began before age 22. A grandchild is eligible only if the child was adopted by the insured grandparent.
- A lump sum benefit of $255 is payable to a spouse who was living with an insured worker at the time of his or her death.
- Under the Disability Insurance Program (DI), monthly cash benefits are paid to disabled workers under age 65 and to their dependents. The purpose of the DI program is to replace lost income when a wage earner is no longer able to work. Monthly cash benefits are paid and computed generally on the same basis as they are in the OASI program; that is, they are calculated on the basis of past earnings. Medicare benefits are provided to disabled workers, widows or widowers, or adult children after they have been entitled to disability benefits for 24 months.
- Almost all people, whether or not they paid into Social Security, are eligible for Medicare benefits. (Medicare is treated in depth in Chapter 12).
- Social Security beneficiaries are required to have completed at least 40 quarters of work (10 years) before they are eligible to draw benefits.

Social Security, especially OASDI, has been a heated topic for much of its relatively short history. Political conservatives and laissez-faire economists are troubled because social security basically socializes a portion of the national income. Other critics claim that Social Security will lead to moral and economic ruin because it discourages savings and causes retired people to become dependent on a supposedly fragile governmental system. The Social Security system, on the other hand, is popular with the elderly, who rely on it for much of their income, and with their grown children, for whom it helps to provide peace of mind.

Problems in Social Security

The criticism leveled at the Social Security system has been particularly pointed during the 1980s and 1990s. Adversaries argue that Social Security is depressing private savings (thereby providing less capital for investment) by giving people a retirement check that is financed by the working population rather than interest on accumulated savings. In 1996, the average Social Security recipient would need a savings account of over $150,000 (paying 5 percent interest) to collect the average benefit

($7,700) in interest. Social Security has also been accused of overpaying the elderly, slighting younger workers (who could get a better return if they invested privately), and leading the nation to financial collapse.

Problems endemic to Social Security are helping to exacerbate intergenerational tensions. Specifically, younger workers are skeptical about the ability of the Social Security system to support them when they retire. They are frightened that a poorly structured and underfinanced system will buckle when the baby boomers begin to retire around 2010. Moreover, they are anxious because many are saving less than their parents. In short, some fear they will be excluded from receiving Social Security checks despite having made enormous contributions. Ted Dimig sums up the dilemma: "So, where does this leave my generation? First of all, it leaves us with a huge resentment over the idea that our elders might saddle us with the debt for their retirement; Social Security's "unfunded liability" currently stands at $2.7 trillion, while shortchanging us on our own retirement."[9] Despite these criticisms, the support for Social Security has been consistent, probably because of its widespread public support.

Merton and Joan Bernstein challenge the criticisms leveled at Social Security. They claim that rather than discouraging private savings, Social Security actually stimulates financial planning for retirement and thus encourages savings.[10] Moreover, the overpayment argument is countered by noting that 60 percent of family households over age 65 had total annual incomes of under $30,000 in 1990, while only 16.8 percent had annual incomes exceeding $50,000. Almost 50 percent of elderly nonfamily households (persons living alone or with relatives) had annual incomes below $10,000.[11] These statistics do not suggest an aged population that has become wealthy by exploiting an overly generous Social Security system.

Although OASDI has become an important component of economic security for many of the nation's elderly, there are problems that threaten its future viability. The original strategy of the Social Security Act of 1935 was to create a self-perpetuating insurance fund with benefits for the elderly being in proportion to their contribution. That scenario did not materialize. For example, in 1992 a single worker retiring at age 65 would have received a *maximum* Social Security (OASDI) benefit of $13,056 per year, plus an additional $1,756 yearly in Medicare reimbursements. If that worker had started contributing to the Social Security fund in 1950, and regularly contributed at the maximum level until he or she retired in 1992, the total contribution would have been about $52,000. Yet in three and a half years this worker will have received his or her entire contribution back in benefits. If the worker survives to age 72 (the average life expectancy for a male), the benefit level realized would be more than $51,300 in excess of contributions. That amount does not include any cost-of-living increases. Put another way, a man who retired in 1980 could expect to receive Social Security benefits 3.7 times more than his contribution would have generated had he invested in low-risk government securities. For a similar woman, this ratio was even higher—4.4 times—given her longer life expectancy.[12] This situation has led some observers to doubt the long-term viability of Social Security.

Social Security began to show signs of being in trouble by the mid–1970s. Between 1975 and 1981, the Old Age and Survivors Fund suffered a net decrease in funds and a deficit in the reserve of between $790 million and $4.9 billion a year. This imbalance between incoming and outgoing funds threatened to deplete the reserve by 1983. Moreover, the prospects for Social Security seemed bleak in other ways. Whereas the ratio of workers to supported beneficiaries (the dependency ratio) was then three to one, by the end of the century (with the retirement of the baby boom generation) that ratio was expected to be only two to one. In short, the long-term costs of the program would have exceeded its projected revenues. The crisis in Social Security was fueled by demographic changes (a dropping birthrate plus an increase in life expectancy), more liberal benefits paid to retiring workers, high inflation, high unemployment, and the COLAs passed by Congress in the mid–1970s.

Facing these short- and long-term problems, Congress moved quickly to pass P.L. 98–21, the Social

Security Amendments of 1983. Among the newly legislated changes were a delay in the cost-of-living adjustments and a stabilizer placed on future COLAs. In other words, if trust funds fall below a certain level, future benefits will be keyed to the consumer price index (CPI) or the average wage increase, whichever is lower. Another change was that Social Security benefits became taxable if taxable income plus Social Security benefits exceeded $25,000 for an individual or $32,000 for a couple. A third change will increase the retirement age in 2027 to 67 for those wanting to collect full benefits. Although people could still retire at age 62, they would receive only 70 percent of their benefits instead of the current 80 percent. Finally, coverage was extended: New federal employees were covered for the first time, as well as members of Congress, the president and vice president, federal judges, and employees of nonprofit corporations.

In the middle 1990s, the Social Security rules were again changed, this time easing the historic Social Security penalty for about one million people aged 65 to 67 who are still working. Previously, any earnings that exceeded $11,250 a year would result in $1.00 lost for every $2.00 earned. The new rules gradually raise the limit to $14,000 and to $30,000 by the year 2002. The new rules also allow those over 70 to continue working without losing Social Security benefits.[13]

The Long-Term Prospects for Social Security

Despite these Social Security reforms, the fiscal viability of the system continues to remain in question. Some analysts suggest that Social Security is on a sound footing. They point to the fact that the income and assets reserve in the combined OASDI trust funds reached $842 billion in 1995. By 2021 that amount is projected to peak at $4.96 trillion.[14] Proponents maintain that the finances of the system will be in close actuarial balance for the next 75 years, with no more than a 5 percent difference between incoming and outgoing revenues.[15] Other analysts point to the Congressional Budget Office (CBO) projections that by 2015 (when the post-World War II baby boomers retire), OASDI taxes will fall short of expenditures. Beginning in 2012 expenditures will exceed tax incomes. Moreover, the OASDI trust fund (the largest fund) is expected to be exhausted by 2029[16] (see Figure 10.3).

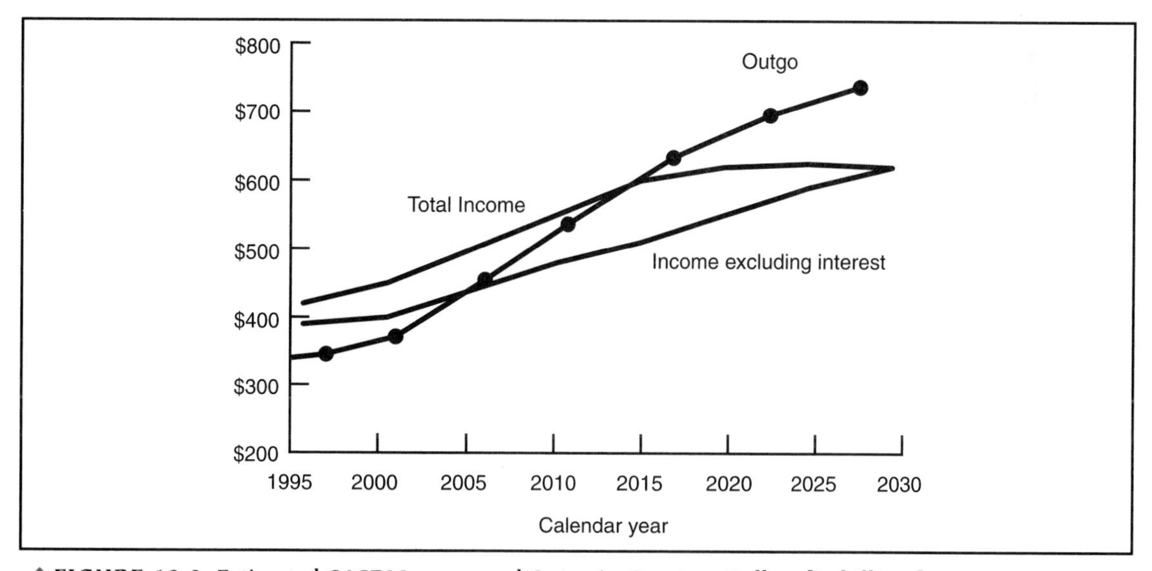

◆ **FIGURE 10.3 Estimated OASDI Income and Outgo in Constant Dollars [In billions]**
Source: Social Security Administration. On-line: http://www.ssa.gov/OACT/TRSUM/trsummary.html

Apart from the expected shortfalls in OASDI, severe problems exist in other funds. For example, the projected year of exhaustion for the HI Trust Fund is early 2001; under more adverse conditions it could be as soon as mid–2000. In addition, the DI part of OASDI is also problematic, as can be seen from Table 10.2.

Other critics complain that the federal government is borrowing from the current Social Security surplus to fund other programs and is thereby hiding the real extent of the deficit. For all intents and purposes, money in the Social Security trust fund was intended to be invested and to be set aside for future years, not to be used to finance other government spending. When OASDI funds are received, they are deposited into the Federal Treasury like any other tax. The taxes then become part of a general pool of funds that finance government activities. When OASDI funds are received by the Treasury, the fund is presented IOUs. The problem arises when OASDI tax funds fall below expenditures and the IOUs must be reclaimed. At that point, the federal government will be required to cut back on expenditures, raise taxes, or borrow from the public. For example, in 1990, $65 billion in Social Security surpluses went for non–Social Security spending. As a result, part of every federal program is paid for by the Social Security payroll tax. In that sense, the *real* budget deficit—and the absence of a *real* Social Security surplus to pay for future benefits—has been hidden from the public.[17]

Although some Social Security reforms have provided a short-term solution, structural problems continue to plague the system. For example, one problem is the "graying of America." Since 1900 the percentage of Americans 65 years and older has tripled (from 4.1 percent in 1900 to 12.6 percent in 1990), and the absolute number has increased 10 times (from 3.1 million to 31.2 million). Demographic projections suggest that by 2030 the number of persons over age 65 will increase to 65.6 million. In other words, the percentage of elderly is expected to climb from the current rate of 12.6 percent to more than 21 percent by 2030. Furthermore, the elderly are living longer. Between 1900 and 1990 the 75- to 84-year-old group increased 13 times while the 85-and-over group was 24 times larger.[18] These demographic trends suggest that the dependency ratio will significantly increase, as will the pressures on the Social Security system. For example, in 1960 the worker/beneficiary ratio was 5 to 1; by 1980 it had dropped to 3.2 to 1. By 2040 the worker/beneficiary is expected to be 2 to 1.[19] Therefore, a question remains as to whether two workers in 2040 will be able to support one retired person, and whether the Social Security system—at least as it is presently structured—can support more than 20 percent of the American population.

Another problem facing Social Security is the increasing tax burden. Social Security taxes on working families grew more rapidly in the 1980s than at any time since the passage of the Social Security Act in 1935. From 1983 to 1990 the Social Security tax rate was raised six times, and the income level subject to the tax almost doubled from 1981 to 1992. As a result, a worker's maximum payroll tax jumped from

◆ TABLE 10.2
Is the Test of Financial Adequacy for the Social Security System Met?

Trust Fund	*Short Range (10 Years)*	*Long Range (75 Years)*	*Years Until Exhaustion*
OASI	Yes	No	35
DI	Yes	No	19
OASDI (Combined)	Yes	No	33
HI	No	No	5
The SMI Trust Fund is financed on a year-to-year basis.			

Source: Social Security Administration. On-line: http://www.ssa.gov/OACT/TRSUM/trsummary.html

$1,502 in 1981 to more than $4,000 (including the Medicare portion of the tax) in 1996, more than a 66 percent increase allowing for inflation. From 1937 to 1990 the maximum Social Security tax increased 100 times.[20] Social Security taxes now represent the second largest revenue producer for the federal government. The tax burden of Social Security rests on the shoulders of workers and employers and results in a net decrease in both consumption and production.

Several solutions have been proposed to remedy the impending crisis in Social Security. In 1994 President Bill Clinton appointed a Social Security Advisory Council. The goal of the council was focus on the fund's future viability. Three distinct proposals emerged from this group, all of which envisioned investing some Social Security funds in private financial markets. Two of the three recommendations proposed the creation of individual investment accounts (over which the beneficiary would have some control) financed with Social Security payroll taxes. The first, proposed by former Social Security Commissioner Robert Ball, calls for raising Social Security taxes. In addition, Ball's plan also calls for investing up to 40 percent of trust fund reserves in private capital markets. The second solution, offered by Edward Gramlich, trims benefits and adds revenues. Gramlich calls for creating a "double deck" plan in which workers would receive a basic benefit based on the number of years they worked. On top of that, workers would get a "second deck," which is an add-on to their benefits equal to 15 percent of their average wages earned over their lifetime. Benefits for low-income workers would remain the same, while benefits for high-income workers would be cut. Under Gramlich's proposal, the retirement age would be raised to age 67 in 2027. In addition, Gramlich proposes to exclude benefits awarded to spouses of future retirees. To compensate, workers would be allowed to purchase annuities from the government. This would be done by setting up defined contribution accounts established within the Social Security system and funded by an increase of 1.6 percent in the payroll tax. Participants would have limited investment discretion over these accounts. Lastly, Gramlich proposes that the Social Security fund be forced to invest 25 percent of its funds in stocks, which would yield a higher return than investing in government bonds.[21] The third option, proposed by businessman Sylvester Shieber, would replace Social Security with flat benefits independent of earnings and large mandatory personal retirement accounts. These accounts would be funded by diverting a part of the current payroll tax, and would be held and managed by individuals.[22] There is clearly increasing pressure for at least a partial privatization of the Social Security system.

Projections about the future of Social Security are predicated on the belief that certain economic and demographic factors will be in play for the next 50 years, but economic and demographic shifts could easily invalidate the most earnest predictions, and Social Security could again go into crisis. For example, stagnant industrial productivity, changing demographic trends, an oil crisis, and major changes in immigration patterns would all have profound consequences for the future of Social Security. However, there is nothing inviolate about the way Social Security is currently funded. An act of Congress could easily eliminate the insurance feature of Social Security and replace it with general revenue taxation. Given the widespread dependence on Social Security, it seems highly unlikely that policymakers and the public will allow the system to go bankrupt.

Another issue in Social Security involves the competition between public (compulsory) and private (voluntary) pension plans. Some critics argue that private pension plans are preferable to public schemes because they are based on less dependence on the government and have the potential for yielding higher returns. Private pensions originated as a means of encouraging employee loyalty and as a way of easing out aging workers. However, only about one-third of all workers and one-fourth of current employees are covered under private pension plans. Moreover, only a small fraction of these plans are indexed for inflation.

Critics of private pension plans argue that they are basically unreliable. Employees can switch jobs and thus lose their pension rights, companies may go bankrupt, corporations may attempt to raid pension funds, and corrupt or incompetent managers can wreak havoc on well-endowed pension plans. U.S. pension reserves are currently worth well over one trillion dollars and form a major source for investment capital. Despite federal tax subsidies to private pension plans, totaling more than $64 billion in 1988, coverage under these plans has actually decreased since 1980. Supporters of Social Security argue that unlike the riskier private pension plans, OASDI benefits are portable and indexed for inflation, workers are immediately vested, and benefits are not contingent on the financial condition of the employer.[23]

While originally intended to supplement private pension funds and to operate as a pay-as-you-go insurance scheme, OASDI has taken on many characteristics of a public welfare program in the past 60 years. For example, some workers receive high benefit levels even though their fiscal contributions to the system have not justified them. Almost all current retirees are realizing benefits far in excess of what they contributed over the course of their working lives in Social Security taxes. (Those retiring in 1993 were the first group of workers to receive less in benefits than they paid in taxes.) The bill for those benefits is paid by the young workers of today.

Given this scenario, should social insurance be modified so as more clearly to reflect social assistance and income redistribution goals? If the answer is yes, then benefits must be structured to reflect the current needs of retired workers rather than their past contributions. Furthermore, if Social Security is viewed as a public welfare program, then its regressive tax structure must be modified to reflect a more progressive framework. For example, Social Security is the single largest tax paid by a low-income worker; yet that same worker receives the lowest benefits when he or she retires. Thus, workers hurt most by the tax receive the fewest benefits. Using that same line of reasoning, if Social Security is designed for social assistance, then should everyone, regardless of income, be eligible? More particularly, should the wealthy be allowed to be beneficiaries? The answers to these questions are obviously rooted in the values of the inquirer.

UNEMPLOYMENT INSURANCE

The first line of defense for workers fired or laid off from their jobs is Unemployment Insurance (UI). Coming out of the Social Security Act of 1935, UI is a federal/state program whose objectives are: (1) to provide temporary and partial wage replacement to involuntarily and recently unemployed workers, and (2) to help stabilize the economy during recessions. Although the U.S. Department of Labor oversees the general program, each state administers its own UI program.[24] The current guidelines of the UI program require employers to contribute to a trust fund, which is then activated if an employee loses his or her job.

The UI system consists of two basic parts: (1) regular state-funded benefits generally provided for a maximum of 26 weeks, and (2) a federal/state extended benefits program. The second part provides an additional 13 weeks of benefits to unemployed workers who have used up their regular benefits and are still searching for a job. Extended benefits in the UI system are activated when the level of unemployment insurance claims in a state rises above a specified threshold. The extended benefits program is based on the assumption that when a state's unemployment rate is high, it usually takes longer to find a new job.[25] States pay 50 percent of the benefits provided by the UI extended benefits program.

To be eligible for UI benefits, a worker must be ready and willing to work, be unemployed, be registered for work with the state employment service, and have been working in covered employment during a base eligibility period. Conversely, a worker who is fired for misconduct, quits a job without a legally acceptable reason, fails to register with the state employment service, refuses a job equal to or better than the one previously held, or goes on strike is ineligible for unemployment benefits. States cannot, however, deny benefits to workers who refuse to be strikebreakers or who refuse to work for less than the prevailing wage rate.[26]

Basic decisions concerning the amount of benefits, eligibility, and length of benefit time are determined by the states. In all states, unemployment benefits are temporary and usually last no more than 26 weeks. Benefits are not equal to previously earned income, and average unemployed workers in 1991 received around 36 percent of their previous wage. Normal state unemployment benefits vary widely, and in 1991 they ranged from a weekly low of $110 in Louisiana to a high of $218 in New Jersey. In 1991 the mean benefit was $155 per week.[27]

Problems in Unemployment Insurance

The UI program is rife with difficulties and inequities. For example, UI was predicated on the assumption that layoffs are temporary and that in most cases employers will recall workers. Because of deepening recessions, corporate downsizing (the number of workers laid off due to corporate downsizing doubled from 1984 to 1995), and increasing numbers of plant closures resulting in permanent displacement (1.5 million factory workers were displaced from 1991 to 1993), the UI system is strained. As a result, the average duration of unemployment has increased over the past two decades, and growing numbers of people have applied for extended benefits. In response, Congress passed the Unemployment Compensation Amendments of 1993, which required new claimants to be profiled according to their demographic characteristics and work history. Those considered high risk were then targeted for special job search assistance.[28]

UI is based in the belief that individuals will find suitable reemployment if given the opportunity to find a job that matches their skills and experience, but those who receive assistance longer than the norm question the underlying assumption that an appropriate fit will be found. In effect, the same principles that apply to the short-term unemployed are extended to the long-term unemployed, which may in fact be a different population. For example, most people laid off find reemployment within 27 weeks. However, one study found that among the long-term unemployed, more than 33 percent were unemployed for more than 53 weeks; 38 percent from 27 to 40 weeks; 28 percent from 41 to 52 weeks; and 34 percent from 53 to 100 weeks. In contrast, 41 percent of the short-term unemployed were unemployed from 1 to 5 weeks; 37 percent from 6 to 14 weeks; and 22 percent from 15 to 26 weeks. To complicate matters, the percentage of those considered long-term unemployed rose from 6 percent in 1970 to 19 percent in 1995.[29]

Many states in recent years have tightened UI eligibility requirements. In addition, the UI program often fails to help the states with the most severe unemployment problems. For example, the calculation of unemployment rates is based on a study conducted by the Department of Labor in which 60,000 households (individuals 16 years or older are included in the survey) are interviewed each month. Part-time workers in this study are counted as employed, and discouraged workers who have dropped out of the labor force are not counted at all. Although the UI program includes mechanisms that allow states to receive more federal reimbursement when unemployment rates are unusually high, the official state rate is lowered because many of the unemployed are not counted. The consequence is that this artificially low rate of unemployment may not set off the extended benefits mechanism.[30] Furthermore, states with "pockets of poverty" receive no additional help when the overall state unemployment rate is not high enough to set off the triggers.

Another problem with the UI program involves coverage. In 1967 the unemployment rate was 3.8 percent, with 43 percent of all unemployed workers covered under the UI program. By 1975, the unemployment rate had soared to 8.5 percent with a record 75 percent of the unemployed being covered. From 1984 to 1989, the share of unemployed workers receiving benefits ranged from a low of 31.5 percent in 1987 to 51 percent in 1992. By mid–1994, only 32.5 percent of unemployed workers received benefits in a given month.[31] In 1991 there were only 14 states in which more than half of the unemployed received benefits. In that same year, ten states gave benefits to less than one in four unemployed workers.[32]

Equity problems also plague in the UI program. For example, the federal unemployment insurance tax rate has been raised only three times since it was initially set at $3,000 in 1935. In 1940, the taxable wage base encompassed 98 percent of a worker's wages; by 1988 it covered just 32 percent. But this is not the only inequity involving the UI taxation. For instance, an employer pays the same federal unemployment insurance tax on an employee who earns $100,000 a year as for an employee who earns only $7,000. Yet, the worker with a higher income is eligible for higher unemployment benefits. This tax and benefit structure effectively discriminates against low wage earners who are at or near the taxable wage base.[33]

Oren Levin-Waldman argues that policy reform of the UI system must be two-tiered. The first tier should reduce the incidence of layoffs; the second tier should help the long-term unemployed develop skills which would make them marketable in today's economy. Among other options, Waldman-Levin suggests implementing work-sharing, which involves paying UI benefits to workers as partial compensation for the loss of hours worked. So instead of laying off workers in bad economic times, employers simply reduce the numbers of hours each employee works. Work sharing averts layoffs by redistributing unemployment within a firm rather than laying off workers. In better economic times, work-sharing would be discontinued. In addition, Waldman-Levin also suggests the development of coordinated job-retraining programs. Lastly, bonuses (e.g., $500) could be offered to unemployed workers who found reemployment and/or to companies that employed them.[34]

WORKERS' COMPENSATION

Workers' Compensation (WC) programs began in Wisconsin and New Jersey in 1911. By 1948 every state operated some form of WC program. WC programs provide cash, medical assistance, rehabilitation services, and disability and death benefits to persons (or their dependents) who are victims of industrial accidents or occupational diseases. In 1990, WC laws protected more than 97 million workers or 87 percent of the labor force.[35] While laws vary from state to state, the basic principle is that employers should assume the costs of occupational disabilities without regard to fault.[36]

The specific laws governing Workers' Compensation vary from state to state, and there is little consistency either in benefit levels or in the administration of the programs. For example, some states require employers to carry insurance, other states provide a state-sponsored insurance fund, others allow employers to act as self-insurers, and still others do not require compulsory WC coverage. Some state programs exempt employees of nonprofit, charitable, or religious institutions. Nevertheless, because of the potential for large claims, most employers transfer their responsibility by purchasing insurance from private companies that specialize in Workers' Compensation.

WC programs are problematic in several ways. First, benefit levels are established on the basis of state formulas and are usually calculated as a percentage of weekly earnings (generally about 66.5 percent). As such, each state sets its own annually adjusted benefit level, which varies widely across states. For example, the benefit level in 1990 ranged from $175 a week in Georgia to $1,094 in Alaska, with the median at $340.50. Second, the cost to employers for providing Workers' Compensation insurance has been rising rapidly. Employers paid $43 billion to insure their workers in 1990, a 12.6 percent increase over the 1987 figure of $38.1 billion. The bulk of that money—$28.5 billion—was paid to private insurance carriers.[37] Third, there is great variability among states in the way claims are handled. Workers are often encouraged to settle out of court for an attractive lump sum, even though that amount may not equal their lost wages. Often, benefits are uneven. For example, the price attached to the loss of a body part has been interpreted differently from state to state. Prigmore and Atherton note that in Hawaii the loss of a finger was valued at $5,175 in 1978, more than the courts in the state of Wyoming allowed for the loss of an eye.[38] In addition, there are often long delays between the time an injury occurred and the period in which benefits start. Finally, in some states employers are exempt from the Workers' Compensation tax if they can demonstrate that they are covered by private insurance. Unfortunately, private insurance coverage may prove inadequate after a disability benefit is determined. Even though injured workers or their survivors received $34 billion in benefits and medical payments in 1990, Workers' Compensation may not provide adequate protection for many disabled workers.[39]

THE EARNED INCOME TAX CREDIT

A program that crosses the increasingly vague boundary between social insurance and public assistance is the Earned Income Tax Credit (EITC) program. Specifically, while the EITC is limited to those participating in the workforce, it is also means-tested. The EITC can be described as tax reform, public assistance, and social insurance. It is tax reform in that it moderates the regressive social security tax for low-income workers. It is a public assistance program in that it supplements the wages of low-income households.[40] It is social insurance in that only people actively participating in the workplace are eligible. Because the EITC is linked to workplace participation, we have included it under the umbrella of social insurance.

Created by Congress and signed into law by President Gerald Ford in 1975, the EITC was designed to provide a minimum income for low-wage workers by providing them with a tax rebate. The goals of EITC were to (1) offset the burden of social security payroll taxes on poor working families, (2) supplement low wages, and (3) promote work as a viable alternative to welfare.[41] The original EITC was available only to working families (including unmarried heads of households) with at least one child who filed a joint or a "head of household" return. EITC was expanded three different times since 1995: first under the Reagan administration; then under the Bush administration; and finally under the Clinton administration when EITC was enlarged to include low-income workers without children, and benefits were raised for families with more than one child. These changes were expected to reduce the number of people in poverty by more than 2 million in 1994. The cost of EITC was approximately $23.3 billion in 1995; it is expected to reach almost $31 billion by the year 2000.[42]

The EITC functions like a negative income tax. Under the EITC program all eligible workers receive a basic tax credit that increases with family size (up to two children). In addition, there is a maximum dollar benefit that an individual or family can receive. For eligible families, the maximum benefit is slowly reduced (phaseout) as income rises. Tax credits vanish altogether above a given yearly income. The amount by which the credit exceeds the taxes owed is paid as a refund[43] (see Table 10.3).

In 1995, some 18.4 million people received EITC benefits with an average credit of $1,265. By 1996, a family of four with an income below $11,610 a year was eligible for the maximum tax credit of $3,556. Single female-headed families with children make up half of all working families eligible for EITC. Sixty percent of all young married couples (age 20–24) with children are eligible. Forty-seven percent of Hispanic American, 30 percent of African American, and 15 percent of white married couples are eligible. Approximately 29 percent of EITC eligible families have less than a high school

◆ TABLE 10.3
EITC Amounts and Eligibility, 1996

	Filing Unit With:		
EITC factor	*No children*	*One child*	*Two or more children*
Child Percentage	7.65%	34.00%	40.00%
Max. Creditable earnings	$4,220	$6,330	$8,890
Max. EITC amount	$323	$2,152	$3,556
Phaseout rate	7.65%	15.98%	21.06%
Income above which phaseout occurs	$5,280	$11,610	$11,610
Income above which EITC disappears	$9,500	$25,078	$28,495

Source: J.R. Storey, "The Earned Income Tax Credit: Benefit Amounts," *CRS Report for Congress*, (94–399 EPW) (Washington, DC: February 15, 1996).

diploma; 44 percent have attained a high school degree. The typical EITC family had low to moderate income, placing it above the poverty line.[44]

The EITC program has generally not been as stigmatized as other income maintenance programs such as AFDC or food stamps. Perhaps this is because the middle class can generally understand EITC because they have a closer proximity to the working poor than to AFDC beneficiaries.[45] Secondly, the middle class see the EITC as promoting work, family life, and job creation.[46] The EITC also fit squarely within the Reagan administration's philosophy of substituting tax policy for welfare policy. In fact, Regan referred to the EITC as "the best anti-poverty program, the best pro-family, the best job-creation measure to come out of Congress."[47] Indeed, when direct public welfare expenditures for the poor were under assault in the 1980s, indirect payments under EITC actually increased. It was not until the One-hundred-fourth Congress in 1994 that neoconservatives turned against EITC.

Economists Saul Hoffman and Lawrence Seidman summarize the weaknesses of the EITC program:

> . . . [The EITC program] provides benefits to one-third of all poor families and one-quarter of all African-American families. The EIC [EITC] population is, however, predominantly white and non-poor. The typical EIC family has a low-to-moderate income that places it above the poverty line. . . . Finally, the average credits were quite low, so the contributions of the EIC program to the economic well-being of low- and moderate-income families is certainly quite modest.[48]

The EITC suffers from several weaknesses. First, low-income families will not receive EITC unless they file federal income tax returns. Many poor families fall below the income level for which they are required to file returns.[49] It is estimated that in 1990 only 80 to 86 percent of those eligible filed for the EITC credit. This means that about 2.1 million eligible people did not receive EITC.[50] Second, EITC has not received the publicity of other programs such as food stamps. Therefore, many poor families may not know of its existence. Third, the EITC is also less useful for large families since the credit amount is not adjusted to family size after the second child. Finally, it is difficult to imagine that the modest benefits of EITC will make a profound difference in the economic lives of the majority of low-income working families.

SUPPLEMENTAL SECURITY INCOME

Supplemental Security Income (SSI) is perhaps one of the more confusing social programs in America. In essence, SSI is designed to provide cash assistance to the elderly and disabled poor, including children. Although generally a public assistance program, SSI is administered entirely by the Social Security Administration. It is because of SSI's organizational auspice that it is included under the social insurances.

In 1994 the SSI program served about 6.3 million people and cost the federal government $23 billion. Unlike OASDI, SSI is a means-tested, federally administered public assistance program funded through general revenue taxes. The basic SSI payment level is adjusted annually for inflation. A portion of the elderly receive SSI in conjunction with Social Security. Age is not an eligibility criterion for SSI, and children may receive benefits under the disabled or blind portion of the act. Among others, the following people are eligible for SSI: (1) the mentally retarded, (2) the aged who are at least 65 years old and have little or no income, (3) those considered legally blind, (4) adults (at least 18 years old) who qualify as disabled because of a physical or mental impairment expected to last for at least 12 months, (5) visually impaired persons who do not meet the criteria for blindness, (6) drug addicts and alcoholics who enter treatment, and (7) children under 18 who have an impairment of comparable severity with that of an adult. In 1993, 25 percent of the SSI rolls were made up of eligible low-income seniors; 75 percent of SSI recipients were disabled; and 33 percent were age 65 or older.[51]

To qualify for SSI, an applicant must have limited resources. In 1996, SSI applicants were allowed to own resources valued at less than $2,000 for an individual and $3,000 for a couple (excluding a house, a car valued at less than $4,500, burial plots, certain forms of insurance, etc.). SSI benefits are not generous, although they can be higher than AFDC benefits. For an individual living alone in 1994, the maximum SSI benefit was $436 per month; for a couple, it was $669. About 30 percent of an SSI payment is deducted if the person lives in the home of someone who is contributing to his or her support.

The SSI program began during the Nixon administration. When President Richard Nixon took office in 1972, he attempted to streamline the welfare system by proposing a Family Assistance Plan (FAP). In this plan, Nixon proposed a guaranteed annual income that would replace AFDC, Old Age Assistance (OAA), Aid to the Blind (AB), and Aid to the Permanently and Totally Disabled (APTD). Although the overall plan was rejected by Congress, the OAA, AB, and APTD programs were federalized in 1972 under a new program called Supplemental Security Income (SSI). Basically, the federal government took over the operation of those programs from the state governments. No longer would state governments set eligibility levels, establish minimum payment levels, or administer the programs.

In 1994, there were 3.25 million SSI recipients. By 1994, that number had doubled to 6.3 million. Concomitantly, SSI expenditures increased from $5 billion in 1974 to more than $25 billion in 1996. By 1993, the number of SSI recipients were up nearly one-half since 1980 and one-quarter since 1990. In large part, these increases resulted from the rapid growth in the numbers of disabled persons receiving SSI, a population that doubled from 2.4 million in 1984 to 4.4 million in 1993.[52] Some analysts predict that SSI spending will outpace every social welfare program with the exception of Medicaid. At its current rate of growth, in 1999 SSI will cost $35 billion, more than food stamps, AFDC, and EITC.[53]

Two groups of SSI recipients that have shown dramatic growth in their numbers are children with disabilities and adults with disabilities relating to drug addiction and alcoholism. One reason for this growth was the Supreme Court's decision in the *Sullivan v. Zebley* case, which made children eligible for SSI if they had a disability that was comparable to that of an adult. As a result, new SSI revisions expanded the group of qualifying disorders to include attention deficit disorders, and it elevated the importance given in eligibility hearings to testimonials by friends, teachers, and family members. Children are now the fastest growing population on SSI, and by 1994, almost 1 million children were recipients. Of those children, more than 60 percent either have an emotional/mental disorder or are mentally retarded. Moreover, more than 50 percent of adults on SSI have either a mental/emotional disorder or are mentally retarded.[54]

The other group of SSI recipients that have drawn attention are those individuals whose drug or alcohol addiction (DAA) is the primary contributing factor in their disability. Between 1980 and 1994, the number of DAA recipients on SSI rose from 23,000 to 86,000, bringing the number to more than 250,000. This group cost the federal government $1.4 billion in 1994.[55]

As a response to SSI's rapid growth, Congress passed the Social Security Independence and Program Improvements Act in 1994, which among other things, restricted SSI and DI benefits to individuals disabled by drug and alcohol addiction. The new restrictions required SSI beneficiaries with a DAA diagnosis to participate in a substance abuse program. In addition, they would receive benefits for only 36 months (except for those for whom treatment was not available). Those beneficiaries removed from the SSI rolls would continue to receive Medicare or Medicaid unless they failed to comply with their treatment program for 12 successive months.[56] In addition, the law also established a Commission on Childhood Disabilities to reevaluate the SSI definition for childhood disability and to look into possible alternative definitions.[57] In addition, the Immigration and National Interest Act of 1995 further curtailed SSI by limiting the eligibility of noncitizens for SSI benefits.

A major concern regarding SSI involves the low level of income and the requirements for eligibility. In fact, 27 states (and Washington, D.C.) supplement SSI payments with an additional grant, and some states have opted to let the federal government administer that stipend. States may also choose to set their own requirements for supplementary SSI payments, thereby including only certain beneficiaries or limiting disabilities. In any case, the median state supplement was $36 a month for an elderly individual and $49 a month for an elderly couple in 1991.[58] In addition, stringent eligibility requirements and complex red tape have kept many people off the SSI rolls. For example, the cases of recipients are reviewed every three years (usually involving a medical review) and "continuing disability reviews" may be required. Some critics believe that the federal government has purposely made entrance and continued maintenance in SSI difficult in order to discourage participation.

The majority of individuals and couples receiving SSI benefits remain below the poverty line. The 1994 benefit for an individual on SSI was about $470 a month, or approximately three-quarters of the federal poverty line. Historically, only those couples receiving a combination of SSI, Social Security, and food stamps were raised to or above the poverty line. In 1994, an individual SSI recipient who received both food stamps and Social Security benefits was raised to only 86.3 percent of the poverty threshold (see Table 10.4).

CONCLUSION

Social insurance programs are replete with both contradictions and difficulties. Nevertheless, social insurance programs, especially OASDI, have become a mainstay of the American social welfare state. Despite the original intent of its architects, Social Security has become a primary source of financial support for America's elderly. Moreover, OASDI has demonstrated the ability not only to arrest the poverty rate for its constituents, but actually to reduce it. A majority of Americans have come to view Social Security as a right and to count on its benefits.

Social insurance programs represent a major source of security for both America's elderly and its present-day workers. In the past 50 years, Americans have come to believe that regardless of the ebb and flow of economic life, Social Security and Unemployment Insurance embody a firm governmental commitment to care for workers and the elderly. Economic gains made by the elderly since the mid–1960s have validated this belief.

EITC is one of the newer programs that currently make up America's safety net. EITC is clearly less stigmatized than public assistance programs. Perhaps this is because those helped by EITC's tax rebate are currently in the workforce and are generally families with children. In short, EITC beneficiaries are the *working* poor, rather than those who are unattached to the workforce. Because Social Security is clearly linked to past contributions, beneficiaries experience little stigma. This is not true for the highly stigmatized beneficiaries of public assistance programs. It is to this population that we will now turn.

◆ TABLE 10.4
Supplemental Security Income: Expenditures, Benefits, Growth Rate, and Percentage of Poverty Threshold, Selected Years

	1975	*1980*	*1990*	*1994*
*Expenditures	$14.9	$13.5	$17.8	$23.8
**Population	4.0	4.1	4.8	6.0 (1992)
Yearly Benefits (Individuals)	$1,822	$2,677	$4,632	$5,592
Percent of Poverty Line	70.8	72.3	73.9	75.2
Yearly Benefits (Couples)	$2,734	$4,016	$6,948	$8,028
Percent of Poverty Line	84.6	81.1	87.9	89.4

* Expenditure in billions
** Population in millions
Source: Table compiled from U.S. House of Representatives, House Ways and Means Committee, *Overview of Entitlements, Green Book, 1994* (Washington, DC: US GPO, 1994)

◆ ◆ ◆ *Discussion Questions* ◆ ◆ ◆

1. The social insurances, especially Social Security, are among the most popular social welfare programs in the nation. Part of the reason for this popularity is that unlike income maintenance programs, the social insurances are not stigmatized. What are other reasons for the popularity of the social insurance programs?

2. There are serious questions about the future of the Social Security system. Some critics argue that Social Security is doomed because the trust funds are expected to be depleted by the middle of the next century. Other observers argue that Social Security is sound because the federal government is backing it. Is the Social Security system currently on solid ground and can we expect it to be healthy in the future? If so, why? If not, why? What can be done to make the system more stable?

3. The Social Security is currently plagued by a number of problems. What is the most important problem facing the system?

4. The EITC has components of both a social insurance program and an income maintenance program. Nevertheless, it is a relatively popular (if little understood) part of the social welfare state. What are some reasons for the popularity of the EITC program? What elements of the EITC could lead some critics to argue that it is basically an income maintenance program? What components of the EITC could lead other analysts to argue that it is basically a social insurance program?

5. Although administered by the Social Security Administration, the SSI program has a stigma similar to public assistance programs like food stamps or the AFDC program. Why does this stigma exist? What can be done to diminish it?

Notes

1. Frances Fox Piven and Richard A. Cloward, *Regulating the Poor: The Functions of Public Welfare* (New York: Vintage Books, 1971).
2. David P. Beverly and Edward A. McSweeney, *Social Welfare and Social Justice* (Englewood Cliffs, NJ: Prentice-Hall, 1987).
3. Piven and Cloward, *Regulating the Poor,* p. 100.
4. W. Andrew Achenbaum, "Social Security: Yesterday, Today and Tomorrow," The Leon and Josephine Winkelman Lecture, School of Social Work, University of Michigan, March 12, 1996.
5. Achenbaum, "Social Security."
6. Department of the Census, *Current Population Reports, 1981,* Series P–60, No. 125 (Washington, DC: U.S. Government Printing Office, 1981).
7. Social Security Administration, "Fast Facts: SSI." On-line: http://www.ssa.gov:80/statistics/fastfacts/pageii.html
8. Committee on Ways and Means, U.S. House of Representatives, *Overview of Entitlement Programs: 1992 Green Book* (Washington, DC: U.S. Government Printing Office, 1992), p. 4.
9. Ted Dimig, "Social Security on the Brink," *Houston Chronicle* (August 4, 1996), pp. 1F and 4F.
10. C. Merton and Joan Broadshaug Bernstein, *Social Security: The System That Works* (New York: Basic Books, 1987).
11. AARP, "A Profile of Older Americans" (Washington, DC: American Association of Retired Persons, 1991), pp. 9–10.
12. Joseph F. Quinn and Olivia S. Mitchell, "Social Security on the Table," *The American Prospect* 26 (May–June 1996), pp. 76–81.
13. Michael Doerflein, Angela Garner, Niki Gober, and Stacy Lochala, "Social Insurance." Unpublished paper, Graduate School of Social Work, University of Houston, Houston, TX, May 1996.
14. Spenser Rich, "Plan Deepens Cuts for Future Retirees," *Washington Post* (May 22, 1995), p. A1.
15. Bernard Gavzer, "How Secure is Your Social Security?" *Parade* (Oct. 18, 1987), p. 9.
16. Social Security Administration. On-line: http://www.ssa.gov/OACT/TRSUM/trsummary.html
17. Robert J. Shapiro, "The Right Idea for 1990: Cut Social Security Taxes," *Economic Outlook,* 4 (January 29, 1990), n.p.

18. AARP, "A Profile of Older Americans" (1991), p. 1.
19. U.S. House of Representatives, *1992 Green Book*, p. 109.
20. Social Security Administration, *Social Security Bulletin, Annual Statistical Supplement, 1984–85* (Baltimore, MD: Social Security Administration, April 1986); and Shapiro, "The Right Idea for 1990."
21. Doerflein et al., "Social Insurance."
22. Quinn and Mitchell, "Social Security on the Table."
23. Bernstein and Bernstein, *Social Security*.
24. U.S. House of Representatives, *1992 Green Book*, p. 485.
25. Isaac Shapiro and Marion Nichols, *Far From Fixed: An Analysis of the Unemployment Insurance System* (Washington, DC: Center on Budget and Policy Priorities, Mar. 1992), p. viii.
26. Diana M. DiNitto, *Social Welfare: Politics and Public Policy* (Englewood Cliffs, NJ: Prentice Hall, 1991), p. 87.
27. U.S. House of Representatives, *1992 Green Book*, pp. 520 and 513–514.
28. Oren Levin-Waldman, "Reforming Unemployment Insurance: Toward Greater Employment," Working Paper No. 152, The Jerome Levy Economics Institute, Annandale-on-Hudson, NY, December 1995.
29. Ibid.
30. Ibid.
31. Marion Nichols and Isaac Shapiro, *Unemployment Insurance Protection in 1994* (Washington, DC: Center on Budget and Policy Priorities, 1995).
32. Shapiro and Nichols, *Far From Fixed*, pp. viii and 16.
33. Isaac Shapiro and Robert Greenstein, *A Painless Recession* (Washington, DC: Center on Budget and Policy Priorities, February 1991), p. xiii.
34. Levin-Waldman, "Reforming Unemployment Insurance."
35. Diana M. DiNitto, *Social Welfare: Politics and Public Policy* (Boston: Allyn and Bacon, 1995).
36. U.S. House of Representatives, *1992 Green Book*, pp. 1707–1709.
37. Ibid.
38. Prigmore and Atherton, *Social Welfare Policy*, pp. 66–67.
39. W. Joseph Heffernan, *Introduction to Social Welfare Policy* (Itasca, IL: F. E. Peacock, 1979), p. 138.
40. "The Increasing Role of the Earned Income Tax Credit," *Focus* (13)1 (Spring 1991), p 19.
41. Frederick Hutchinson, Iris J. Lav, and Robert Greenstein, *A Hand Up: How State Earned Income Credits Help Working Families Escape Poverty* (Washington, DC: Center on Budget and Policy Priorities, April 1992), p. vii.
42. Oren M. Levin-Waldman, *The Consolidated Assistance Program* (The Jerome Levy Economics Institute, 1995).
43. Ibid., p. ix.
44. Saul Hoffman and Laurence Seidelman, *The Earned Income Tax Credit: Antipoverty Effectiveness and Labor Market Effects* (Kalamazoo, MI: The Upjohn Institute for Employment Research, 1990).
45. Doerflein et al., "Social Insurance."
46. D. S. Cloud, "Clinton Looking to Tax Credit to Rescue Working Poor," *Economics and Finance* (March 13, 1993), pp. 583–587.
47. "A Slap in the Face of the Working Poor," *The Economist* (July 8, 1995), pp. 23–24.
48. Saul D. Hoffman and Lawrence S. Seidman, *The Earned Income Tax Credit* (Kalamazoo, MI: W. E. Upjohn Institute for Employment Research, 1990), p. 34.
49. Ibid., p. 82.
50. John Karl Scholz, "The Earned Income Tax Credit: Participation, Compliance, and Antipoverty Effectiveness," *National Tax Journal* (47)1 (1994), pp. 63–87.
51. Social Security Administration, "Fast Facts: SSI."
52. Carolyn L. Weaver, "Welfare Payment to the Disabled: Making America Sick?" *The American Enterprise* (January/February 1995), pp. 61–64.
53. Ibid.
54. Ibid.
55. Ibid.
56. Jeffrey Katz, "Social Security, Conference OKs Bill Creating Independent Agency," *Social Policy* (July 23, 1994), pp. 6–9.
57. Ibid.
58. Ibid., pp. 25–30.

CHAPTER 11

Public Assistance Programs

This chapter examines key public assistance programs, including the former Aid to Families with Dependent Children (AFDC), Temporary Assistance to Needy Families (TANF) (AFDC's replacement), and General Assistance (GA). This chapter also investigates and analyzes the inherent problems and issues in public assistance programs.

The American social welfare state is a complex brew of programs, policies, and services. Perhaps few people, including many policymakers, fully appreciate the complexity of the welfare system. One reason is that unlike many European countries, which operate under a comprehensive and integrated welfare plan, the American system of social welfare is a patchwork quilt of programs and policies. Because of the nation's historical ambivalence about providing public relief, most welfare legislation has resulted from compromises and adroit political maneuvering rather than from a systematic plan. In short, public assistance in the United States is not a coordinated, comprehensive, integrated and nonredundant system of social welfare services; instead, it is a helter-skelter mix of programs and policies.

Public assistance programs are one of the most misunderstood parts of the American welfare state. Although expenditures for public assistance programs are far less than for social insurance programs, they tend to be more controversial. Unlike social insurance, public assistance programs are based entirely on need and are therefore means-tested. Figure 11.1 lists the major federal governmental spending areas and the relative expenditures on each.

The rationale for public assistance programs that offer cash, medical, and other forms of assistance, is grounded in the concept of *safety nets* designed to ensure that citizens receive basic services and that they do not fall below a certain poverty level. There are, however, actually 51 separate safety nets—one in each state and one in the District of Columbia. Although federal guidelines help determine the level of aid for the poor, individual states have extensive freedom to fashion their own safety nets. States differ as to benefit levels, and one national study found that the vast majority lack an adequate safety net to help the poor and the jobless.[1] Nevertheless, a major component of the safety net consists of programs designed to ensure that families and individuals receive the resources necessary for survival.

SOME ASSUMPTIONS THAT UNDERLIE PUBLIC ASSISTANCE

American attitudes toward public assistance are characterized by a mixture of compassion and hostility. This ambivalence plays out in a series of harsh and often conflicting assumptions about public assistance recipients. Moreover, the struggle around

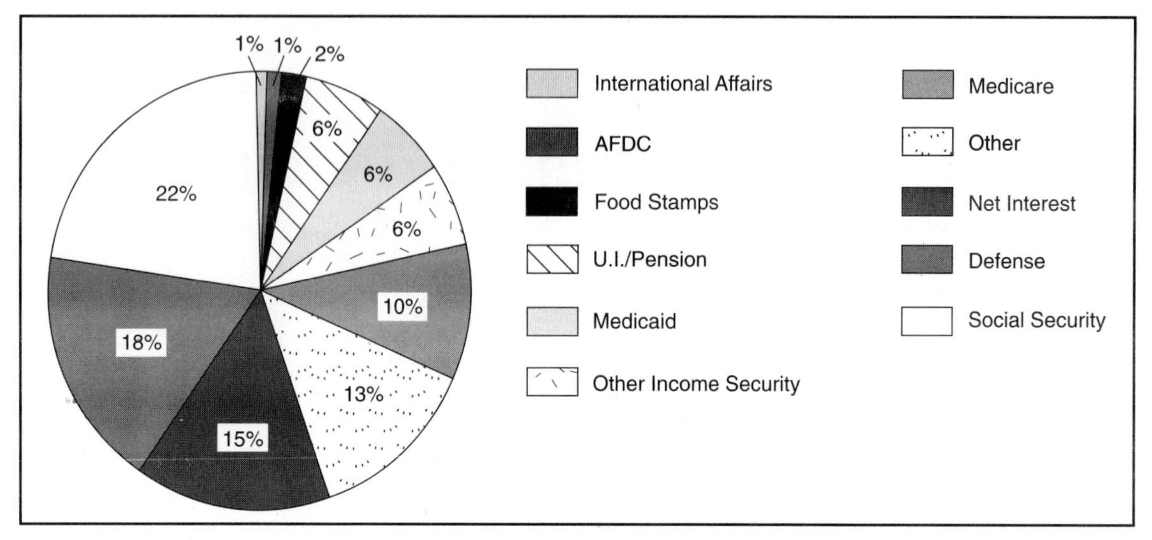

◆ **FIGURE 11.1 Where Federal Dollars Go**
Source: *Economic Report of the President, February 1995* (Washington, DC: U.S. GPO, 1995).

AFDC is a symbolic one, reflecting the tension surrounding American ideas about wealth, opportunity, privilege, and the American dream.

The argument goes like this: If privilege in America is earned by application and hard work, then people are poor because they lack the desire to elevate themselves out of poverty. In effect, the poor do not apply themselves because they are lazy. The refusal of the poor to compete appears as a serious character flaw to those driven by the intense competition in American society. On the other hand, only a few paychecks separates the welfare recipient from the average citizen—thus the compassion. While democratic capitalism implies that hard work guarantees success, the reality of people's lives often tells a different story. The tensions and contradictions that characterize contemporary life color people's views about public assistance. The following assumptions, among others, underlie public assistance: (1) Generous benefits create a disincentive to work (therefore recipients must always get fewer benefits than they would under the minimum wage); (2) welfare recipients need prodding to work because they lack internal motivation; (3) recipients must be forced to economic opportunities; (4) work is the best antipoverty program; (5) public assistance programs must be highly stigmatized otherwise people will turn to them too readily; and (6) women receiving public assistance should work and poor children should not have the luxury of being raised by a full-time homemaker. These assumptions about public assistance—many of which are remarkably similar to those that formed the basis of the Elizabethan Poor Laws—lead to numerous myths and fears.

Myths about Public Assistance

Because of so many commonly held myths about public assistance, it is important to discriminate between fact and fiction. (AFDC is used here as a descriptor of public assistance because it continues to have the same clientele as TANF):

Myth 1. The public assistance rolls are composed of many families containing an able-bodied father who refuses to work.

Fact. The former Aid to Families with Dependent Children-Unemployed Parent (AFDC-UP) program (322,000 families) accounted for only 12 percent of the total 4.7 million families on AFDC in 1992. About 90 percent of TANF families are headed by one parent—mostly mothers who are either single, divorced, widowed, or separated—with only 10 percent of public assistance households being two-parent families.[2] Ninety percent of AFDC children lived with their mothers and 10 percent with their fathers. Sixty-six percent of AFDC recipients were children, the remaining recipients being mothers (18.6 percent) and the aged (15.6 percent). Less than 1 percent of all welfare recipients are able-bodied males. Among children who were AFDC recipients, almost 60 percent have parents who are not married to each other.[3] Forty-one percent of the fathers of these children cannot be found.[4]

Myth 2. Most poor people are on public assistance and the number is growing.

Fact. The percentage of poor people receiving welfare has declined since the early 1970s. Although the number of poor people with children rose 50 percent between 1973 and 1989, the number of AFDC families grew by only 20 percent.[5] The AFDC rolls decreased from 1992 to 1995 by about 10 percent. Moreover, two-thirds of the poor (21.2 million of the 33.6 million poor people in 1991) received *no* money from AFDC, and more than a third do not receive food stamps or Medicaid. AFDC rolls have historically gone up or down depending upon the economic conditions in a particular state or locality.

Myth 3. Recipient mothers have more children in order to collect greater benefits; therefore families on public assistance are large and steadily growing in size.

Fact. In 1991, 72 percent of AFDC families had 2 or fewer children, and 42 percent had only one child. The average welfare family was composed of 2.9 persons. Only 10 percent of AFDC families had four or more children.[6] Moreover, the average size of AFDC families has steadily decreased, from a high of 4 in 1969 to 2.9 in 1990. Furthermore, having additional children to increase public assistance benefits hardly seems worth the effort. In 1991 the difference in gross AFDC benefits for a family of three and a family of four in Louisiana was $44 per month. As the family size increased, the benefit was lowered; for example, the difference in benefits between a Louisiana family of five and a family of six was $39 per month in 1991.[7] This may explain why mothers on AFDC gave birth to only one-fourth the number of babies as nonwelfare mothers.[8] Finally, some of the lowest benefit states, including Mississippi, Arkansas, Louisiana, and Alabama, had the highest out-of-wedlock birthrates.[9]

Myth 4. Once on welfare, always on welfare.

Fact. The truth is that more than half of all AFDC recipients left the rolls within their first year of welfare receipt; by the end of two years, the percentage increased to 70 percent. However, many of those who left welfare cycled back on. Within the first year after leaving welfare, 45 percent returned; almost 66 percent returned by the end of three years. By the end of seven years, more than 75 percent of those who left the welfare system returned at some point. About 40 percent of women who used AFDC were short-term users, about 33 percent were episodic users, and 25 percent were long-term users. From 1968 to 1989, the average time on welfare was 6.2 years. Half of all welfare spells ended when a recipient became employed.[10] Therefore, long-term recipients were generally those with the fewest market opportunities. Although long-term users accounted for a small percentage of caseloads, they consumed a disproportionate portion of the welfare budget.

Myth 5. Welfare programs create dependency, which is transmitted intergenerationally.

Fact. Although the vast majority of people who started on AFDC stayed less than four years, people who stayed eight years or more accounted for half the number of people on welfare at any given point in time. People who stayed for an extended period of time tended to accumulate in the system, thereby representing a significant portion of caseloads and expenditures, even if they only represented only a small fraction of those who started on welfare at any given time.[11]

Research regarding dependency is inconclusive. Robert Moffitt found that length of welfare spells varied with demographic characteristics, the generosity of the state's public assistance program, and local labor market conditions.[12] Leahy, Buss, and Quane found that previous work experience, age at entry to welfare, and number of children were the best predictors of long-term welfare use.[13] Bane and Ellwood found that race, education, marital status, work experience, and disability status influenced first-spell durations. These same variables influenced recidivism. Bane and Ellwood also point out that many of the long-term users cycled in and out of welfare, apparently trying to leave but unable to do so permanently.[14]

According to Greg Duncan and Saul Hoffman, the total income package received by AFDC families often contained more income from other sources than it did from welfare, with labor income being mixed with welfare income.[15] Moreover, roughly 25 percent of the U.S. population lived in families in which some form of welfare was received between 1969 and 1978, but fewer than 44 percent of those families received income from welfare sources for at least 8 of those 10 years. The question of welfare receipt across generations is complex and not yet fully understood. According to Greg Duncan and Saul Hoffman, only 19 percent of African American and 26 percent of white women coming from heavily dependent welfare homes were observed to be heavily dependent on welfare themselves. The 19 percent of African American women heavily dependent on welfare was the same percentage as black women heavily dependent on welfare who did not come from heavily dependent welfare households. The researchers found that African American men who came from heavily dependent welfare households showed no decrease in the average number of working hours, while white men from heavily dependent welfare homes averaged fewer hours of work per week than did otherwise similar white men.[16]

On the other hand, Peter Gottschalk found a positive intergenerational relationship between the use of welfare by mothers and the use of it by daughters.[17] M. Ann Hill and June O'Neill also found persistence in welfare receipt across generations. Looking at data from the National Longitudinal Survey of Youth (NLSY), the authors found that young white women from welfare families had a 24 percent chance of being on welfare compared with a 2 percent chance for white women coming from nonwelfare families. Comparable figures for African Americans were 42 percent and 15 percent; for Hispanic Americans, 34 percent and 8 percent.[18] In their study of men's earnings, Mary Corcoran, Roger Gordon, Deborah Laren, and Gary Solon found that "One of our strongest results is the large negative association between a son's outcomes and welfare receipt in his family of origin."[19] Although some correlation may exist between welfare receipt and family of origin, the question remains as to whether parental receipt of AFDC was the *cause* of the children's behavior. Because receiving AFDC was a manifestation of poverty, it makes sense to analyze how low-income status is transmitted intergenerationally rather than to focus on intergenerational welfare receipt.

Myth 6. Most welfare recipients are African American and Hispanic Americans.

Fact. Close to the same number of whites as African Americans received AFDC. In 1992 whites constituted 38 percent of recipients, African Americans 39 percent, and Hispanics 16 percent. Of the remaining, 2.8 percent were Asians, 1.3 percent Native Americans, and 1.6 were of another race or ethnicity.[20] Clearly, the percentage of African American and Hispanics on the welfare rolls was larger than their total representation in the population. However, this is not surprising given that people of color are generally poorer than whites.

Myth 7. Kathryn Edin's research shows that this is not correct—most public assistance recipients have significant unreported income.

Facts. Both individual states and the federal government had quality control systems to monitor the error rate in public assistance programs. In 1990 the national overpayment dollar error rate for AFDC was only 6 percent and states that exceeded that rate were penalized by the federal government. According to Elizabeth Huttman, a 1977 study concluded that 51 percent of AFDC errors were made by welfare agencies or social workers. Specifically, 5.3 percent of the 11.2 million AFDC recipients were ineligible, 13 percent were overpaid, and 4.9 percent were underpaid. According to the study, there was fraud or misrepresentation in less than 0.4 percent of the total national caseload.[21] According to the *Washington Post*, "USDA officials note that the most costly scams in the Food Stamp program have originated or involved the federal employees assigned to minotor and distribute the coupons, not the people who receive them."[22]

On the other hand, Kathryn Edin found that none of the recipient families that she studied lived solely by the income provided by AFDC. All of the recipient families found a way to cover their expenses: "Every single mother supplemented her check in some way, either by doing unreported work, by getting money from friends and relatives, or by persuading someone else to pay a lot of her expenses. Not one of these fifty mothers reported all her extra income to the welfare department, and only four reported any of it."[23]

Myth 8. Public assistance benefits provide a disincentive to work; people on welfare either don't want to work or are too lazy to work.

Fact. In 1994 there were only three states in which the AFDC cash benefit for a family of three reached 75 percent of the poverty line. In 45 states, AFDC benefits were below 50 percent of the poverty threshold. Eight states provided a single parent with two children less than $250 per month in AFDC benefits in 1993; five out of those states provided $200 or less. In the typical or median state, AFDC benefits in 1992 for a three-person family equaled $372 per month, or 41 percent of the poverty line. Even with the inclusion of food stamps, in every state the combined benefits fell below the poverty line, and in over half the states the combined benefits of food stamps and AFDC did not equal two-thirds of the poverty line.

A report by the Congressional Budget Office noted that all growth spurts in the AFDC program occurred around recessions. For example, between 1983 and 1989 the number of AFDC families grew by less than 1 percent a year. In 1988, AFDC caseloads actually declined in 22 states. However, because of the recession that began in 1989, only three states registered such declines in 1990.[24] Most of the poor either work or desire a job, although their employment frequently does not allow them to overcome poverty. In 1990 nearly two out of every three poor families with children (63 percent) included at least one worker; 25 percent of poor people lived in families with at least one year-round full-time worker.[25] Compulsory experiments in workfare suggested that AFDC recipients believed they *ought* to work for their checks.[26]

Myth 9. Public Assistance recipients are doing better than ever.

Fact. The reverse is true. Public assistance recipients are actually doing worse than ever. AFDC benefit levels did not keep pace with inflation, having fell 43 percent (after adjusting for inflation) in the typical state from 1972 to 1992. This reflected a benefit loss of $279 per month, or more than $3,300 a year in 1992 dollars.[27]

Myth 10. Unmarried mothers constitute the bulk of welfare recipients.

Fact. According to Duncan and Hoffman, the most important causes for beginning AFDC spells were (1) divorce or separation (45 percent), (2) an unmarried woman becoming a pregnant household head (30 percent), and (3) a drop in earnings of the female head of the household (12 percent). Conversely, the predominant reasons for terminating AFDC spells were (1) remarriage (35 percent), (2) an increase in the earnings of a female householder (21 percent), and (3) children leaving the parental home (11 percent).[28]

Myth 11. It is easy to get on public assistance; hence too many undeserving people are receiving benefits.

Fact. In addition to meeting stringent income and asset guidelines, potential food stamp and public assistance recipients must provide extensive documentation and meet verification requirements. Almost 97 percent of Food Stamp Program benefits go to households with incomes at or below the poverty line. More than half those benefits go to households with gross incomes at or below *half* of the poverty line.[29] Moreover, 63 percent of all applications for AFDC assistance were denied in 1990.[30]

Myth 12. AFDC recipients migrate to states where benefits are high.

Fact. A Wisconsin study showed that only 10 percent of AFDC recipients who had entered the state in a given period were motivated primarily by the availability of higher benefits.[31] Other studies indicate that poor people migrate for a variety of reasons, including proximity to family and friends, the desire for a better life, and the hope of finding a job. However, research by the Wisconsin Policy Research Institute concluded that poor people do migrate across state lines to receive higher benefits.[32] The study failed to show that it is high benefits per se that cause migration. According to Henry Freedman of the Center for Social Policy, "Census data on migration show that poor people move in the same direction as those who are not poor, usually toward states with jobs and booming economies rather than those offering higher welfare benefits."[33] At best, the question of whether poor people migrate for higher welfare benefits remains unresolved.

Myth 13. Welfare spending consumes a large portion of state budgets.

Fact. In 1991, states spent an average of 3.4 percent of their total budgets on AFDC. However, 1.5 percent of that sum came from the federal government. Thus, states spent only about 2 percent of their budgets on AFDC.[34]

Myth 14. AFDC benefits influence decisions having to do with family structure (i.e., childbearing, marriage, divorce, and living arrangements) by encouraging women to head their own households.

Fact. Although some empirical studies have found a small correlation between AFDC benefits and the number of women who chose to head households or remarry, most researchers believe that the available evidence does not support the hypothesis that the generosity of the welfare system is responsible for the trends in illegitimacy or the growth of single female-headed households. For example, although total welfare benefits have declined since 1975, the number of single female-headed households and the illegitimacy rate has remained relatively constant.[35]

Myth 15. Public Assistance caseloads are composed mainly of unwed teenage mothers.

Fact. Although half of recipient mothers began their receipt of AFDC as teenagers (i.e., under age 20), teenage mothers made up only a small portion of the public assistance caseload at any one time. In 1992, 8.1 percent of the AFDC caseload was headed by a teenage mother. Almost half (47.2 percent) of AFDC mothers were in their twenties, a third (32.6 percent) were in their thirties, and 12.1 percent in their forties.[36]

AID TO FAMILIES WITH DEPENDENT CHILDREN

AFDC was the most controversial program in the American welfare system. The ostensible purpose of AFDC was to maintain and strengthen family life by providing financial assistance and care to needy dependent children in their own homes or in the homes of responsible caretakers. Despite these modest goals, the AFDC program has often been used as a symbol in the ideological battle between liberals and conservatives. This has caused AFDC recipients to be victimized in two ways: (1) by their own poverty and (2) by ideologically motivated assaults against their character and motives.

Actually AFDC was the fourth largest public assistance program behind Medicaid, SSI, and Food Stamps. The requirements for receiving AFDC were the deprivation of the parental care of one parent because of death, desertion, separation, or divorce. (In the case of AFDC-Unemployed Parent, it was deprivation of parental economic support through unemployment or illness.) In 1992, AFDC served 4.8 million families (about 13.6 million individuals) at a cost of $22.2 billion. Of the 13.5 million recipients about 67 percent, or 9.2 million, were children. Total AFDC monthly benefits in 1992 averaged $388 per month, per family, but benefits varied widely across states. In 1992, AFDC recipients totaled about 5 percent of the U.S. population, and 13 percent of all children in the United States were covered. In 1990, about 60 percent of all children in poverty received AFDC benefits, a significant reduction from the 81 percent of poor children who received them in 1973.[37]

THE EVOLUTION AND TRANSFORMATION OF THE AFDC PROGRAM

Welfare reform has been a heated topic in the United States for several decades. Most presidents since John F. Kennedy have either offered welfare reform proposals or at least given lip service to the need for reform. It is also a concept that has a relatively narrow meaning in the United States because it was primarily associated with the AFDC program. However, to understand the broader debate around welfare reform, it is important to examine the history of the AFDC program.

Originally called Aid to Dependent Children (ADC), the AFDC program was part of the Social Security Act of 1935 and was designed to provide support for children by dispensing aid to their mothers. In 1950 the adult caretaker (usually the mother) was made eligible for ADC benefits.[38] Also in the 1950s, medical services that were paid in part by the federal government were made available for ADC recipients. In the late 1950s and early 1960s, some critics began to believe that ADC rules led to the desertion of fathers because only families without an able-bodied father were eligible for relief. In 1961 a new component was added that allowed families to receive assistance in the event of a father's incapacity or unemployment. The new program, Aid to Families with Dependent Children-Unemployed Parent (AFDC-UP), was not made mandatory for the states, and until the welfare reform act of 1988, only 25 states and the District of Columbia had adopted it. In 1962 ADC was changed to AFDC to emphasize the family unit.

By 1962 the focus of the AFDC program had shifted to rehabilitating the poor. Policies were enacted that mandated massive casework and treatment services. To increase the chances for success, the social service amendments of 1962 limited the caseloads of social workers to a maximum of 60. By 1967 the service requirement was transformed into job assistance. Before 1967 all services provided to AFDC recipients were delivered by one worker who was responsible for financial as well as social services. By 1972, federal policy has dictated that the AFDC program be divided into social services and income maintenance. The new policy separating social services from income maintenance required that one worker be assigned the AFDC paperwork, while the other was responsible for social services.

Despite intensive social services, the number of AFDC recipients grew rapidly throughout the 1960s. The number of recipients tripled in the 10-year period from 1960 to 1970, from 3 million to 9.6 million. From 1971 to 1981 that figure rose 50 percent, and in 1992 it reached an all-time high of 13.6 million recipients (an increase of 2.6 million since 1990). While in 1950 the number of AFDC recipients accounted for 1.5 percent of the population, by 1992 that proportion had reached 5 percent.

The growth in the AFDC rolls (and the reaction of public and welfare officials to that growth) also gave rise to a grass-roots protest organization started by a former chemistry professor, George A. Wiley. Under the leadership of Wiley, by 1967 the National Welfare Rights Organization (NWRO), a direct-action advocacy group of welfare recipients, had grown to encompass more than 100,000 dues-paying members representing some 350 local groups.[39] Although at its height the NWRO had a sizable constituency—and received a grant of $400,000 from the outgoing Johnson administration in 1968—its lasting effects remain unclear.

One of the more egregious chapters in AFDC history involved the man-in-the-house rule. This policy mandated that any woman who had an able-bodied man in the house would be cut off from

AFDC because, regardless of whether he was the father of her children, it was thought to be his responsibility to support the family. This policy was manifested in "midnight raids," in which social workers made late-night calls to determine if a man was present. Even a piece of male clothing found on the premises could be used as an excuse for cutting off aid. In some states the man-in-the-house rule was extended to include rules on dating. In 1968 the U.S. Supreme Court struck down the rule in Alabama and later reinforced its decision in a California case.[40]

During President Ronald Reagan's term in office, several changes were made in the AFDC rules, including making many expectant mothers ineligible for Medicaid and thus denying them early access to prenatal care; counting stepparent income in determining a child's eligibility; and improving the efforts of states to collect child-support payments. By the mid–1980s, almost 450,000 families were removed from the welfare rolls because of these and other AFDC changes.[41]

Until the recent TANF program, the Family Support Act (FSA) of 1988 was one of the most important pieces of welfare legislation to emerge in the United States since the New Deal. Touted by Thomas Downey, former chairman of the House Subcommittee on Public Assistance, as the first "significant change in our welfare system in 53 years,"[42] the welfare reform bill (which was budgeted at only $3.3 billion over a five-year period) contained several important components. For one, the bill attempted to change AFDC from an income support to a mandatory work and training program. The stated objective of the Job Opportunities and Basic Skills (JOBS) part of the bill was to encourage self-sufficiency among welfare recipients. To carry out this goal, the bill required women on welfare with children under age three (at state option, age one) to participate in a work or training program. By 1990 each state was required to enroll at least 7 percent of its recipients in a state basic education program, job training, a work experience program, or a job search program. By 1993 that requirement was to rise to 20 percent. As a further incentive, recipients who became employed were to get 12 months of child care assistance and Medicaid benefits after they terminated AFDC.[43]

Adoption of the AFDC-UP program became mandatory for all states, although they could decide to limit enrollment for two-parent families to 6 out of 12 calendar months in a year. Moreover, one family member of an AFDC-UP household was required to participate at least 16 hours per week in a make-work job in return for benefits. By 1994, 40 percent of AFDC-UP recipients were expected to be in a make-work program, and by 1997 that number was to increase to 70 percent. In addition, the AFDC reform bill called for mandatory child support payments to be automatically deducted from an absent parent's paycheck, even though that payment might not be in arrears. Finally, the bill allowed states to require a welfare recipient under age 18 to live with a parent or in a "supervised environment" to be eligible to receive benefits.[44] Dan Rostenkowski, former chairman of the House Ways and Means Committee, which oversees most welfare legislation, estimated that an additional 65,000 two-parent families would receive benefits, that 400,000 people would participate in workfare by 1993, and that 475,000 people would be eligible for transitional Medicaid benefits under provisions of the bill.[45]

The promise of the FSA soon faded. Instead of reducing the number of recipients, AFDC caseloads actually rose by 2.1 million from 1990 to 1992. Federal matching funds to states for the JOBS component of the FSA was capped at $1.1 billion in 1994. Sar Levitan and Frank Gallo wrote that "even if the program expends all the available federal funds, the total work/welfare investment will remain below the peak level of $3 billion (1992 dollars) in 1980. The most serious deficiency of JOBS is its failure to create jobs for recipients unable to find work in the regular economy. JOBS permits subsidized employment, but less than 5 percent of enrollees have been placed in such jobs, and federal regulators banned public service employment, provided during the 1970s."[46] By the end of 1991, the states had spent less than half of the available federal JOBS funds.[47] "The effect of the JOBS program on the number of AFDC recipients or on spending on benefits in welfare programs is thus expected to be modest," concluded the House Ways and Means Committee.[48] Only 9 percent of the 4.6 million families then receiving AFDC were enrolled in JOBS programs by late 1991. Part of this failure reflected a lack of state interest, the other part reflected loopholes in the law that exempted almost two-thirds of AFDC adults from participation in the JOBS program. By the early 1990s, many policymakers viewed the FSA as yet another example of failed welfare reform.[49]

Nevertheless, the most significant reforms in the FSA were the extension of child day care and Medicaid for one year after the recipient found employment and the mandatory inclusion of two-parent households in the AFDC program. With limited exceptions, welfare reform in 1988 was a conservative triumph. "By replacing liberal tenets of entitlement, self-determination and federal responsibility with more conservative notions of contract, compulsion, and states' rights," observed Mimi Abramovitz, "welfare reform erodes some of the fundamental principles that support the U.S. welfare state."[50] Underappreciated at the time, was the component of the FSA that allowed states to request waivers to existing AFDC rules. In part, it was this section that opened the door for the radical welfare reforms that emerged in 1996.

In his 1992 presidential campaign, Bill Clinton promised to "end welfare as we know it" by instituting a two-year cap on AFDC benefits. In May 1993, Clinton appointed a Working Group on Welfare Reform, headed by well-known poverty researchers David Ellwood and Mary Jo Bane, and White House Advisor Bruce Reed. The Clinton administration welfare reform bill, The Work and Responsibility Act, was completed in June 1994. Among other things, the bill called for expanding the JOBS program to help recipients move from welfare to work. Developing a personal plan, each AFDC recipient would enter into an agreement with a public assistance agency in return for subsidized child care, health care benefits, and other supportive services. Incorporated into this plan was a two-year time limit for parents to receive cash assistance, after which they would be expected to become employed (preferably in the private sector). Parents unable to find employment after two years would leave the JOBS program and enter the WORK program, a subsidized employment program. The WORK program would offer subsidies to public or private employers to employ recipients in "work-like" positions. Employers would offer a paycheck in the amount that equaled the former welfare check in return for the number of hours of work that the paycheck would have bought at the minimum wage. Participants would have to change jobs every 12 months and be reassessed every two years. In addition, WORK participants would be eligible to receive AFDC benefits if their wages were low enough. Participants would also continue to receive Medicaid and subsidized child care. The Clinton bill attempted to fight teenage pregnancy by providing grants to up to 1,000 high-risk high schools that proposed innovative teenage pregnancy prevention programs. Lastly, the Clinton bill would have made time limits and work requirements national, but states would have had considerable flexibility for innovation.[51]

While some political insiders believe that the Clinton administration got the policy right, they also believe that the administration introduced welfare reform far too late in the game and with far too little focused effort.[52] Specifically, the Clinton welfare reform bill was introduced in the summer of 1994, when it was forced to compete with a faltering health care bill and a struggling crime bill. In effect, welfare reform took a back seat to these other bills. By November 1994, the ultraconservative One-hundred-fourth Congress was in place, thereby obviating the chances for passage of any welfare reform bill that included liberal components such as subsidized employment.

The Personal Responsibility and Work Opportunity Reconciliation Act of 1996

On August 22, 1996, President Bill Clinton signed the Personal Responsibility and Work Opportunity Reconciliation Act of 1996 (PRWOA) (H.R. 3734), a 900-page document that confused even seasoned welfare administrators.[53] The PRWOA was one of the most important pieces of welfare legislation to emerge since the Social Security act of 1935. Specifically, the act included deep cuts in basic programs for low-income children, families, and elderly and disabled people. It also fundamentally changed the social welfare system by replacing AFDC, JOBS, and the Emergency Assistance Programs with the Temporary Assistance to Needy Families (TANF) program. The PRWOA was touted as reducing federal AFDC costs by $55 billion over a six-year period.

One of the most radical features of the PRWOA was among the least understood. Under the PRWOA there is no federal "entitlement" to assistance. In contrast, the former AFDC Program operated under the principle of entitlement. This meant that states had a duty to provide assistance to persons who were eligible under the law. This did not mean that states were required to provide something for nothing. In fact, states could have required the vast majority of those receiving assistance to participate in work, education, training, or job search programs as a condition of receiving aid. The principle of entitlement does mean, however, that states were not permitted to turn away those who qualified under the rules. Under TANF, no family or child is *entitled* to assistance.[54] As such, each state is free to determine which families receive assistance, and under what circumstances. In effect, enactment of the TANF program rescinded the 60-year old federal entitlement to support for poor children and families. TANF operates in the following manner:

- In order to receive a TANF grant, a state must submit a state plan to HHS. In turn, HHS determines whether the plan contains the information required by law. Generally, the plan requirements are very limited, and much of the operational detail for a state program may be omitted in the plan.
- TANF provides a lump-sum federal block to states to run their own welfare and work programs. Each state receives a block grant representing recent federal spending (generally, the higher of 1992–1995 spending) for that state for the AFDC Program, the JOBS Program, and the Emergency Assistance Program. A minority of states will receive annual 2.5 percent adjustments in the form of supplemental grants, but for most states, the TANF block grant amount will be frozen through FY 2002, except for any adjustments due to bonuses or penalties. Under limited circumstances, a state experiencing an economic downturn may qualify for additional federal funding through a contingency fund ($2 billion for 1997–2001). To be eligible to receive funds from the contingency fund in an economic downturn, the state needs to maintain 100 percent of its historic spending level in the year in which contingency funds are requested. A state may also apply for a Rainy Day Loan Fund, which provides a $1.7 billion federal revolving loan fund. To be eligible, a state may not have incurred any penalties under the cash block grant. The maximum loan is 10 percent of a state's grant for up to 3 years, after which the loan must be repaid with interest.
- Maintenance of effort requires that in order to receive a full block assistance grant, the state must spend nonfederal funds at no less than 80 percent of a historic spending level based on 1994 spending. This requirement is reduced to 75 percent for a state that meets the act's work participation rate requirements. A state that does not maintain the required spending level will risk a dollar-for-dollar reduction in its block grant funding.
- States are prohibited from using TANF funds to assist certain categories of families and individuals. The most important prohibition involves using TANF funds to assist families in which an adult has received assistance for 60 months or more. States may provide exceptions for up to 20 percent of their caseloads. (While the PRWOA mandates a five-year lifetime limit on cash assistance, it allows states to set a shorter time limit. States can decide to pay beneficiaries with their own monies.) Other restrictions include a prohibition on assisting minor parents unless they are attending school and living at home or in an adult-supervised living arrangement (subject to limited exceptions); and a requirement to reduce or eliminate assistance to a family if an individual in the family does not cooperate with child support-related requirements (e.g., not identifying the father).
- The TANF Block Grant has four specific work requirements. For one, unless a state opts out, it must require nonexempt parents or caretakers

not engaged in work to participate in community service after receiving assistance for two months. Second, states must outline how they will require a parent or caretaker receiving benefits to engage in work not later than 24 months after they receive assistance. Third, a state must meet a participation rate for all families, beginning at 25 percent in 1997 and increasing to 50 percent by 2002. (See Table 11.1) Fourth, states must meet different participation rates for two-parent families, with the rate set at 75 percent in 1997–1998, and at 90 percent in 1999. Failure to comply with the last two work requirements results in the state paying a penalty of 5 percent the first year and 2 percent thereafter (capped at 21 percent). Detailed and complex, the rules determining which activities count toward work participation sharply limits the opportunities adults can count toward the participation rate through their involvement in education, training programs, or job searches.

- States can spend their block grants on cash assistance, noncash assistance, services, and administrative costs in connection with assistance to needy families with children. The states can also choose to spend up to 30 percent of their TANF funds to operate programs under the Child Care and Development Block Grant and the Title XX Social Services Block Grant (which was cut by 15 percent in 1996). Not more than one-third of that amount can be used for programs under Title XX, and the funds must be spent on programs for children or families whose incomes fall below 200 percent of the poverty line. Existing child care provider standards for health and safety are maintained.
- When parents participate in required work activities, the state may (but is not required to) provide child care assistance. However, a state may not reduce or terminate a family's assistance if a single parent of a child under age six refuses to comply with work requirements based on a demonstrated inability to obtain needed child care.
- In contrast to AFDC, TANF recipients are not automatically eligible for Medicaid. However, states are required to provide Medicaid coverage for single-parent families and qualifying two-parent families with children if they meet the income and resource eligibility guidelines that were in effect in the state's AFDC Program on July 16, 1996 (states may modify these guidelines to a limited extent).
- When PRWOA was enacted, most states were in the midst of welfare reform activities through the AFDC waiver process. The PRWOA provides that if a state had a waiver in place at the time of enactment, it can continue that waiver and will not be required to comply with inconsistent provisions of the act.[55]
- The TANF program has tried to address the dramatic increase in nonmarital births (especially teen births). First, state TANF plans must demonstrate how they intend to establish goals and take action to prevent and reduce out-of-wedlock births, especially teenage pregnancies. Second, states must establish actual numerical goals for reducing their "illegitimacy ratio" for fiscal years 1996–2005. Third, the act provides financial incentives to states to reduce their out-of-wedlock birth rates and provides methods for embarrassing states that don't comply. On the incentive side, the act authorizes HHS to give the five states with the greatest success in reducing their nonmarital birth rate—while lowering their abortion rate below its 1995 level—$20 million apiece.[56]

◆ TABLE 11.1
TANF Work Participation Rates for All Families

FY 1997 — 25%
FY 1998 — 30%
FY 1999 — 35%
FY 2000 — 40%
FY 2001 — 45%
FY 2002 and beyond — 50%

Work Participation for Two-Parent Families:
FY 1997 — 75%
FY 1998 — 75%;
FY 1999 and beyond — 90%

Source: American Public Welfare Association, "The Personal Responsibility and Work Opportunity Reconciliation Act of 1996 (Conference agreement for H.R. 3734)." Analysis prepared by the American Public Welfare Association, the National Governors' Association, and the National Conference of State Legislatures, August 22, 1996.

- The PRWOA also allows states to impose a "family cap," which denies assistance to children born into families who are receiving public assistance.
- States must permanently deny all Title IV-A cash assistance and Food Stamp Program benefits to individuals convicted of felony drug possession, use, or distribution. Other members of the family can continue to receive benefits. States may opt out of this provision or limit the period of prohibition by passing legislation.

In addition to TANF, the PRWOA included other reforms:

- Newly arriving legal immigrants are barred from all means-tested, federally funded public benefits for the first five years they are in the country. Current and future legal immigrants are barred from receiving SSI and food stamps until they become citizens. Legal immigrants losing SSI benefits also lose Medicaid coverage. States have the option of denying Medicaid coverage to persons who are legal residents but not citizens. Accordingly, aged, blind, and disabled immigrants are not categorically eligible for Medicaid. New immigrants are automatically barred for five years after entry. After that, the state may offer Medicaid coverage. There are exceptions made for persons who worked for 40 quarters in covered employment or who served in the military. No state can deny coverage of emergency medical services to either illegal or legal aliens.
- Illegal immigrants are barred from the following federal public benefits: (a) grants, contracts, loans, licenses and (b) retirement, welfare, health, disability, public or assisted housing, post secondary education, food assistance, and unemployment benefits.
- SSI eligibility was tightened for children. The new standard eliminates the comparable severity standard, the individual functional assessment, and references to maladaptive behavior.
- The Food Stamp Program retained its structure as an uncapped, individual entitlement. States were not given the option to choose a Food Stamp Program block grant and alter the structure of the program. However, PRWOA included $27.7 billion in food stamp cuts, accounting for more than half of all non-Medicaid savings. The 1995 Urban Institute report on the effect of the PRWOA noted that the food stamp cuts were a main factor behind its estimate that the bill would push 1.1 million children (2.6 million people overall) into poverty. Under the PRWOA, Food Stamp Program benefits would be cut almost 20 percent in 2002, with average benefits falling from about 80 to 66 cents per person per meal. A substantial portion of these benefit savings would come from across-the-board reductions affecting nearly all recipient households, including families with children, the working poor, the elderly, and the disabled. In addition, Food Stamp Program benefits were limited to three months every three years for unemployed able-bodied single adults age 18–50. An additional three months of eligibility was granted to adults laid off their jobs.
- Child collection support efforts were strengthened through a number of provisions. First, one condition for receiving assistance is that families must assign child support rights to the state.[57] Second, states will have to operate automated centralized collection and disbursement units. Third, noncustodial parents who are in arrears of $5,000 or more are subject to passport revocation. Fourthly, states must accord full faith and credit to out-of-state child support orders and liens. Federal income withholding, liens, and subpoena forms must be used for interstate cases. Fifth, states must have laws in effect that establish authority to withhold, suspend or restrict driver's, professional, occupational and recreational licenses of individuals who owe over due support or fail, after notification, to comply with subpoenas or warrants. Other provisions include: automated state directories of new hires; expansion of income withholding requirements; access to locator information networks such as law enforcement; use of social security numbers on licenses and other government issued documents; and expedited paternity establishment.[58]

Why was such a radical welfare reform bill passed in 1996? The conservatism of the One-hundred-fourth Congress clearly spurred on the bill. In addition, the rapidly approaching presidential election may have also played a role, especially because Clinton had already vetoed a welfare reform bill in January 1996 that was almost identical to the one he later signed. Furthermore, the rhetorical slogans used by Clinton in his 1992 presidential campaign, calling for "an end to welfare as we know it" and "two years and off to work," may have been viewed by the public as an incitement toward the popular dislike of AFDC, not as an opportunity to relieve poverty. Frances Fox Piven argues that Clinton's rhetoric created a maelstrom of which he eventually lost control. Moreover, by the time Clinton signed the PRWOA, he had already approved draconian state waivers that were in some cases more punitive than TANF. These factors made it relatively easy for the One-hundred-fourth Congress to snatch the welfare issue that the Clinton administration had already heated up.[59] After signing the PRWOA, Clinton had promised to revisit the bill if a Democratic Congress were elected in 1996. He specifically wanted to remove measures that eliminated aid to legal immigrants and cut benefits to disabled groups. Because control of the Congress in 1996 remained in Republican hands, it is questionable whether parts of the bill will be reexamined.

State Welfare Reform Waivers

Radical welfare reform was well underway through the waiver process even before President Clinton singed the PRWOA into law. In fact, Clinton had granted waivers to more states than all the previous administrations combined. By mid–1996, 43 of the 50 states already had approved or pending AFDC waivers that incorporated many of the "reforms" contained in TANF. Pointing to the flood of AFDC waivers signed by the Clinton administration, the American Enterprise Institute's Douglas Besharov observed, "Based on what happened in the last year, President Clinton can justifiably claim that he has ended welfare as we know it." Besharov pointed to the waiver requests as "welfare reform on the cheap" without an increase in spending for child care or a "penny for job training," the "revolutionary result" is an "end to personal entitlement."[60] By 1996, state waivers which included time limits, benefit cuts, and widespread sanctions for disapproved behaviors had already resulted in a 10 percent drop in the AFDC rolls.

Many of the state waivers incorporate several components, including:

- Time limited benefits (often a two-year cap).
- Enforcement of parental responsibility, including: child support; family caps (the denial of benefits to children born while the parent(s) is on public assistance); requiring the immunization of children as part of the benefit process; linking benefits to school attendance and grades; and discouraging teenage pregnancy by requiring teen mothers who are recipients to live at home or in an approved setting and/or to finish high school in order to continuing receiving benefits.
- Simplification and efficiency in the delivery of benefits, including: the use of electronic benefit transfers (EBT) for delivering public assistance benefits; fraud deterrent measures such as using debit cards for food stamps instead of coupons which can be sold on the street; and privatization through subcontracting out to the private sector the delivery and management of public assistance programs.
- Moving people quickly from work to welfare, including: encouraging the private sector to hire recipients (often with tax breaks); permitting higher earnings and raising the limit on assets (e.g., the value of a vehicle); and job placement and training.
- Increasing personal responsibility by providing cash-out incentives that offer beneficiaries the cash equivalent of food stamps; offering one-time lump-sum payments (equaling total benefits for three months to a year) instead of monthly grants; aiding in the development of asset accounts; cutting off cash benefits to those who fail to comply with state welfare rules and regulations; the required performance of community service; and the mentoring of recipients.

Because the TANF program allows states with AFDC waivers to continue to function under them until the waiver expires, the vast majority of the states will be free to continue with their welfare demonstration projects. Table 11.2. summarizes some of the states' welfare demonstration programs.

GENERAL ASSISTANCE

Although not formally connected to SSI or TANF, General Assistance (GA) often serves a similar clientele. GA is a term applied to a variety of state and local programs designed to provide cash or in-kind benefits to needy families and individuals who are, generally speaking, not within the eligibility categories for either TANF or SSI. In short, GA is the program of last resort for people who fall through the cracks in the federally funded safety net. The program commonly serves nonelderly individuals or childless couples, including individuals who are disabled for a year or less and are awaiting determination of their eligibility for SSI.In some cases, GA may be used when AFDC or SSI recipients have benefits that are too low to cover an emergency.[61] GA programs are entirely financed and administered by state, county, or local governmental units (or some combination thereof). No federal funds are used for GA and several states have no such program.

A 1992 study found that 21 states (and the District of Columbia) operated statewide GA programs. These states, however, may not have full fiscal responsibility for the program.) Ten more states have some involvement in GA (e.g., requiring that counties operate programs), although in most of these county governments have control over eligibility and payment levels. The remaining 18 states do not impose a GA program on counties, although in 10 of these states some counties have chosen to operate programs.[62] Although several states have some form of GA, it does not mean that there are uniform standards across the state or even that there is any state role in administration. Because no federal standards apply to GA, the total discretion that states or localities have in this area has led to a wide variety of programs, some of which are funded solely by counties or towns, others of which are funded totally or partially by the state. GA programs can be administered differently from state to state or even by county by county. As a result, states and localities have the ability to easily scale back or even eliminate GA programs.

Seven of the statewide uniform programs and five of the nonuniform statewide programs are "comprehensive" in that they cover all needy families and individuals who do not fit within the categories of persons eligible for TANF or SSI. The other statewide programs cover only limited groups of people that are ineligible for federally subsidized cash assistance. Some statewide programs provide aid for an extended period if needed, while others limit aid to a fixed period regardless of need. Other states pay only if there is an emergency, and some states treat all eligible individuals the same as far as the type and duration of the benefits are concerned.[63] In addition, some GA programs provide cash assistance, others rely on in-kind assistance such as medical vouchers. Other programs use acombination of the two. In many ways, the GA program represents a holdover from the days of county welfare. For example, in San Diego, California, GA is given as a loan that must be repaid.

Because no federal funds or federal standards apply to GA, it is difficult to find reliable data or even to draw a national picture as to the extent and comprehensiveness of General Assistance programs.[64] Nevertheless, the overall cost of GA is estimated to be in the vicinity of $4 billion, and in 1991 some 1.4 million households were beneficiaries. GA benefits are often lower than the state's TANF benefits, but in a few places they are the same or higher. In the typical state with a statewide GA program, the maximum monthly benefit for an individual was $215 in 1993, or just 36 percent of the federal poverty line for 1992. Overall, GA benefits have been declining since 1982. Between 1982 and 1989, the maximum GA benefit fell (in real dollars) in 28 programs and increased in only seven. In 1992, GA benefits were reduced or eliminated entirely in eight states. This came on the heels of an elimination or reduction of GA benefits in 14 states in 1991. From 1991 to 1993, GA reductions affected more than a half-million recipients in 17 of the 28 states that operated statewide GA programs in 1991.[65] In particular, the real value of GA benefits declined in the six states with the largest number of GA recipients: New York (−13 percent); Pennsylvania (−12 percent); Ohio (−1 percent); Michigan (−20 percent);

◆ **TABLE 11.2**
Selected State Welfare Demonstration Projects, 1995

Arizona	EMPOWER (Employing and Moving People Off Welfare and Encouraging Responsibility) establishes a time limit on adult AFDC benefits of 24 months in any 60-month period. Additional AFDC benefits will not be provided to families for children conceived while on AFDC or conceived within 12 months after leaving AFDC if the family later reapplies for benefits. Families can put aside $100 a month in Individual Development Accounts, up to $9,000, for training and education. Transitional Child Care and Medicaid will be extended from 12 months (as currently allowed) to 24 months after leaving AFDC. An additional three-year pilot project will operate in limited areas and will provide work experience by placing participants in subsidized jobs for 9 to 12 months, funded by AFDC grants and cashed-out food stamp allotments.
Arkansas	AFDC parents age 16 or younger will be required to attend school regularly or face reductions in benefits. If appropriate, teenage parents can meet the requirement by attending an alternative educational program. Arkansas will also implement a family cap. Family planning and group counseling services focusing on the responsibilities of parenthood will be included in the demonstration.
California	This demonstration will encourage teenage AFDC parents to attend school regularly by paying them a $100 cash bonus for maintaining a C average and $500 for ultimately graduating from high school. Teenage parents who fail to maintain a D average can have their AFDC payments reduced by up to $50 a month for two months. The demonstration will also permit AFDC families to accumulate $2,000 in assets and have $4,500 equity in a car. Families will be able to deposit $5,000 into savings as long as the funds are used to purchase a home, start a business, or finance a child's postsecondary education or training. Finally, the demonstration will allow recipients who work—but who have low AFDC benefits—to opt out of the program. They will remain eligible for health care under Medi-Cal as well as other services, such as child care, which are available to AFDC recipients. Participants in both programs will also be able to exclude college assistance and work-study funds from the resource limit and up to $100 in gift income each quarter. AFDC participants are able to deduct $4,500 from the equity value of a vehicle when figuring resources, and California counties now have more flexibility in determining the method of setting the equity value.
Colorado	The Personal Responsibility and Employment Program includes a number of major revisions to the state's AFDC program. Under the demonstration, parents who are able to work or able to participate in a training program must do so after receiving AFDC benefits for two years. Individuals who refuse to perform the assignments face a loss of AFDC benefits. The demonstration will "cash out" food stamps for participants, meaning that the value of the coupons will be added to the monthly AFDC payment. Participants will be encouraged to work through a new formula that will enable families to keep more of the money they earn. Asset levels and rules pertaining to ownership of an automobile will be changed so that participants will be permitted to own a car regardless of its value or their equity in it. Finally, the demonstration provides for payment of financial bonuses when participants stay in school and graduate from a secondary school or GED program, and permits financial penalties to be assessed when parents fail to have their children immunized.
Connecticut	The Fair Chance initiative is designed to increase supports, incentives, and work expectations for AFDC recipients. There are two components: Pathways and Family Strength. Pathways requires AFDC recipients to work a minimum of 15 hours a week after two years of AFDC, 25 hours a week after three years, and 35 hours a week after four years. Pathways will help families leaving welfare increase their incomes by paying the difference between the noncustodial parent's child support payments and a state-established minimum. Family Strength provisions raise the resource limit for AFDC eligibility from $1,000 to $3,000 and extend transitional child care and medical benefits an additional year, to a total of two years. Family Strength will be implemented statewide, and Pathways will be implemented in the New Haven and Manchester areas. *(continued)*

◆ Table 11.2 ***(continued)***

Delaware	Under "A Better Chance," all AFDC participants will be required to sign and comply with a Contract of Mutual Responsibility. The contract will specify employment-related activities as well as those leading to self-sufficiency. The demonstration sets a time limit of 24 months on cash benefits for able-bodied adults over 19 years old. It also requires teen parents to live in an adult supervised setting, attend school, participate in parenting and family planning education, and immunize their children. Incentives include a $50 bonus for teens who graduate from high school and the receipt of an additional 12 months of transitional child care and Medicaid benefits to help parents move to work. Gradual sanctions can lead to the family losing benefits if participants fail to meet education and employment requirements. There is a family cap. Participants who do not cooperate with child support enforcement will be denied benefits.
Florida	In the Family Transition Program, most AFDC families will be limited to collecting benefits for a maximum of 24 months in any five-year period. Individuals who exhaust their transitional AFDC benefits but are unable to find employment will be guaranteed the opportunity to work at a job paying more than their AFDC grant. The demonstration also provides a longer period of eligibility—36 months in any six-year period—for families at a highrisk of becoming welfare dependent. Medicaid and child care benefits will be available in the demonstration. Local community boards will play a large role in overseeing the program. Other elements of the demonstration include an increase in the earnings disregard formula and asset ceilings, as well as a statewide requirement that AFDC parents must ensure that their children have been immunized.
Georgia	The Personal Accountability and Responsibility Project (PAR) strengthens federal work requirements that must be met in order to receive cash benefits. Georgia's welfare agency will now be able to exclude from an AFDC grant any able-bodied recipient between the age of 18 to 60 who has no children under the age of 14 and who willfully refuses to work or who leaves employment without good cause. The rest of the family will continue to be eligible for AFDC benefits. The plan also includes a family cap. However, PAR would allow recipients to "learn back" the denied benefits through the receipt of child support payments or earnings. Medicaid and food stamps eligibility will continue for all family members. In addition, Georgia will offer family planning services and instruction in parental skills to AFDC recipients.
Hawaii	Under Creating Work Opportunities for the Job Opportunity and Basic Skills (JOBS) Families programs, job-ready JOBS recipients who would otherwise expect to wait at least three months to be placed in a regular education or training activity are required to pursue job leads developed by JOBS program specialist. The positions are part-time (up to 18 hours per week), private sector jobs at minimum wage and will allow participants to gain work experience, develop their skills, and better target training needs. The demonstration will operate for five years.
Illinois	The Work Pays component, added to the previously approved Project Fresh Start, encourages employment and thereby self-sufficiency by enabling recipients to keep more of their earnings than is normally allowed. The state will disregard two of each three dollars earned for as long as recipients continue working.
Indiana	Under the Indiana Manpower Placement and Comprehensive Training Program (IMPACT), up to 12,000 job-ready individuals will be assigned to a "Placement Track" and will receive help in job search and placement. Once on this track, AFDC benefits will be limited to 24 consecutive months. The time limit applies to adult benefits only; children's benefits will not be affected. Case management and supportive services will continue for a period after AFDC benefits end. For all recipients who become employed, earnings will be disregarded in determining food stamp benefits for the first six months. There will be increased sanctions for quitting a job or for failure to comply with program requirements. There will also be fewer exemptions from current JOBS participation requirements. Another provision will extend subsidies to employers who hire welfare recipients for a maximum of 24 months. A family benefit cap will be in effect. Children will be required to attend school and be immunized. IMPACT will operate for seven years. *(continued)*

◆ Table 11.2 *(continued)*

Iowa	This plan encourages AFDC and food stamp recipients to take jobs and accumulate assets through a program of Individual Development Accounts. Funds deposited in an account can only be withdrawn to pay for education, training, home ownership, business start-up or family emergencies. The current law that limits each family's assets to $1,000 will be changed to allow each applicant to have up to $2,000 in assets and each AFDC family to possess up to $5,000 in assets. Additionally, the vehicle asset ceiling will rise from $1,500 to $3,000. Recipients will also be encouraged to work under a new formula that disregards 50 percent of their earnings in the calculation of benefits. For recipients lacking in significant work histories, all income will be disregarded during the first four months on AFDC. A Family Investment Program will be created for most AFDC parents, requiring them to participate in training and support services as a condition of AFDC receipt. Only parents with a child under 6 months old at home, those working at least 30 hours per week, and the disabled are exempt. Individuals who choose not to participate in the Family Investment Agreement will have their AFDC benefits phased out over six months and will not be able to reapply for another six months.
Michigan	This expansion of Michigan's "To Strengthen Michigan Families" welfare demonstration requires AFDC recipients to participate in either the (JOBS) Training Program or Michigan's "Social Contract" activities that encourage work and self-sufficiency. Michigan is also testing the requirement that AFDC applicants participate in job searches, by actively seeking employment while eligibility for AFDC is being determined. The demonstration requires that preschool-age children be immunized and disregards the value of one vehicle in determining eligibility. On a limited scale, Michigan will evaluate mediation services to determine if this increases compliance with child support.
Mississippi	This plan promotes health and education for children receiving welfare assistance and supports work efforts by their parents. The demonstration includes a wide component and two projects, The wide component requires all children aged 6 through 17 to attend school and all children under 6 to be immunized and receive regular health checkups. It extends AFDC eligibility for two-parent families by allowing mothers or fathers to work more than 100 hours a month. The Work First component provides subsidized, private-sector employment for job-ready participants. A special fund created from participants' AFDC and food stamp benefits will reimburse employers' wages. The state will provide supplemental payments to recipients when their total income is less than the combined AFDC and food stamp benefits they would otherwise receive. Each Work First participant will have an individual development account for family savings, to which employers will contribute one dollar per hour of work. The state will pass on to the family all the child support payments it collects on its behalf. Under both the Work First and Work Encouragement components, courts may require unemployed, noncustodial fathers to participate in the JOBS program to meet child support obligations.
Missouri	Missouri Families-Mutual Responsibility Plan requires AFDC recipients to sign and fulfill a self-sufficiency agreement that establishes a plan for work and places a two-year time limit on benefits. An additional two years may be allowed, if necessary, to achieve self-sufficiency. Individuals who are not self-sufficient by the end of the time limit must participate in job search or work experience programs. Those who have received AFDC benefits for 36 months or more and have completed their agreement by leaving AFDC will not be eligible for further benefits, with certain good cause exceptions. Children's benefits will not be affected. Minor parents must live with their parents or guardians to receive benefits. If they attend school full-time and work, they may keep all employment income. In some counties, non-custodial parents who volunteer for the state's JOBS program can receive credit against past-due child support. For two-parent families with at least one parent under 21, the limit will be waived on the number of hours the principal wage earner can work. The resource limits will be increased for all families, and they may own one automobile, without regard to its value.

(continued)

◆ **Table 11.2 *(continued)***

Montana	Families Achieving Independence has three components: the Job Supplement program, AFDC Pathways program, and Community Services program. The Job Supplement program helps at-risk families avoid becoming welfare dependent by providing a one-time payment of as much as three times the monthly AFDC payment the family would otherwise be eligible to receive. Child support collections will also be passed directly on to the custodial parent. Other AFDC applicants must enroll in the AFDC Pathways component and sign a Family Investment Agreement that limits its benefits to 24 months for one-parent families and 18 months for two-parent families, with some exceptions. Income disregards and asset limits will be raised, and recipients must participate in JOBS, comply with child support enforcement provisions, and obtain medical screenings and immunizations for their children. Adults who do not leave AFDC by the end of the time limit must enroll in the Community Services program and perform 20 hours of community work per week. Children's AFDC benefits will not be time-limited, and they will continue to be eligible for Medicaid and food stamps. All participants must also choose between a reduced Medicaid benefit package and a partial premium payment toward a private health insurance policy. Full Medicaid coverage will be provided on an emergency basis if certain services are needed for employment purposes.
Nebraska	Under this demonstration project, most welfare recipients will be given a choice between two time-limited welfare plans. One will offer slightly lower benefits but will enable recipients to retain more benefits when they begin to earn income from work. An alternative benefit program will offer slightly higher benefits, but the level of benefits will decrease more quickly when recipients begin to earn employment income. A nontime-limited program will remain in place but can only be chosen by recipients exempted by the state from enrolling in one of the time-limited programs. Under all three programs, a recipient must develop a self-sufficiency contract with a caseworker. There will be a family cap; resource limits will be raised to $5,000; benefits will be reduced by $50 for each minor child who fails to attend school; and minor parents who live at home will be expected to receive support from their parent(s) if the parent's income exceeds 300 percent of the federal poverty rate. Under the two time-limited programs, cash assistance will be provided for a total of 24 months in a 48-month period; food stamps will be cashed out; AFDC payments will be slightly reduced; and all adult wage earners must work or participate in job search, education, or training. Two years of transitional Medicaid and child care will be available for recipients who leave welfare for work.
New York	A Jobs First Strategy gives applicants alternatives to welfare, provides new incentives for recipients to find work and create businesses, and encourages the formation and preservation of two-parent families. The demonstration allows applicants otherwise eligible for Aid to Families with Dependent Children the option to receive child care or JOBS Training program services in place of AFDC. The program will also provide one-time cash assistance or other services necessary to remedy a temporary emergency that has resulted, or may result, in job loss or impoverishment. The demonstration allows children in AFDC families to receive AFDC for up to two years after a caretaker parent marries and the new spouse's income makes the family ineligible as long as the household's income does not exceed 150 percent of the federal poverty guidelines. It extends to a full-year transitional child care benefits for employed recipients who leave the rolls because of child support payments. In addition, clients are encouraged to develop their own business enterprises by excluding certain business income and resources, including vehicles.
North Dakota	This demonstration will provide federal AFDC matching funds to the state for low-income women during the initial six months of pregnancy with their first child. Such payments are usually not available until the last trimester of the pregnancy. In addition, the demonstration links AFDC to a requirement that individuals enroll in the state's welfare-to-work program and pursue education or training activities both during the first six months of pregnancy and after their child is three months of age.

(continued)

◆ Table 11.2 ***(continued)***

Ohio	The Ohio demonstration has three components: Families of Opportunity, Children of Opportunity, and Communities of Opportunity. Communities of Opportunity will operate in up to five sites, primarily in Empowerment Zone/Enterprise Community areas. In these sites, the state will work with local business, industry and community leaders to generate up to 2,500 wage-supplemented jobs during the five-year life of the demonstration. These jobs are expected to pay at least $8 per hour and provide the economic stability for a family to leave welfare permanently. Wages will be supplemented with food stamp allotments and AFDC grants. Families of Opportunity expands eligibility for two-parent families, extends transitional child care for up to 18 months, and increases the amount of earnings a family can retain before losing AFDC eligibility. It will operate in ten counties. Children of Opportunity will operate in two counties and will focus on education. Under this component, dependent children between 6 and 18 will be required to attend school regularly. Case management services will be available for families with attendance problems, and there will be financial penalties for failure to comply.
Oklahoma	This demonstration seeks to encourage welfare recipients to regularly attend school and ultimately graduate from a high school or an equivalent educational program. The demonstration provides that AFDC recipients between the ages of 13 and 18 need to remain in school or face a reduction in benefits if they drop out. The plan applies to teenage parents as well as children. Under Mutual Agreement—A Plan for Success (MAAPS) work incentives are increased by allowing recipients to keep some of their earnings without losing AFDC benefits. MAAPS also waives the requirement that the principal wage earner in a two-parent family work fewer than 100 hours per month to qualify for AFDC, and it raises the allowance for an automobile, from $1,500 to $5,000. After receiving AFDC benefits for three years in any five-year period, recipients still unable to find a job are required to work at least 24 hours a week in a subsidized job. MAAPS also provides intensive case management for three targeted groups: teen parents, long-term recipients, and those with a continuing cycle of dependence on welfare. An agreement between the recipient and the state assesses abilities and outline rights, responsibilities, and consequences.
Oregon	The JOBS Plus demonstration provides individuals with short-term (up to nine months) subsidized public or private employment at minimum wage or better. The state will provide supplemental payments if an individual's income is less than the combined Aid to Families with Dependent Children and food stamp benefits. Participants will continue to be eligible for Medicaid and will receive workplace mentoring and support services. The state also will pass on to the family all the child support payments it collects on the family's behalf. Each JOBS Plus participant will also have an Individual Education Account (IEA), to which employers will contribute one dollar per hour of work. After a participant begins working in a nonsubsidized position, the state will transfer the IEA to the State Scholarship Commission. The commission will then make funds available to the participant or the immediate family for continuing education and training at any state community college or institution of higher learning.
Pennsylvania	The Pathways to Independence project provides incentives and support for single and two-parent families moving from welfare to self-sufficiency. It increases earned income disregards so that recipients can keep more of what they earn before they become eligible for public assistance. Additionally, it raises AFDC resource limits, including the value of a family's vehicle, and increases the time that a family is eligible for transitional child care and Medicaid after the family leaves welfare due to earnings. To further aid the transition to work, Pathways extends case management counseling and referral services to up to one year after the family leaves welfare. Families will be able to deposit money into retirement savings and education accounts without penalty. Furthermore, after two months of employment, recipient families can also choose to receive cash payment of their monthly food stamp benefit. *(continued)*

◆ **Table 11.2 *(continued)***

South Carolina	The Self-Sufficiency and Personal Responsibility Program sets work requirements and provides transitional assistance for program participants. After completing Individual Self-Sufficiency Plans (ISSPs) to help prepare them to become self-sufficient, AFDC recipients have 30 days to find a job in a designated vocational area. If they fail to secure such employment, recipients receive an additional 30 days on AFDC to find any private sector job, after which time they must participate in a community work experience program in order to continue to receive AFDC benefits. Progressive sanctions for noncompliance, up to and including removal of the entire family from assistance, are components of this program. To aid in the transition to work, recipients who would otherwise no longer be eligible for AFDC because of employment can receive reduced benefits for up to 12 months. Families remain eligible for Medicaid and child care during this phase-down period, and regular transitional Medicaid and child care benefits begin at the end of this period. The program also raises resource limits to $3,000 and exempts the cash value of life insurance policies, one vehicle, and interest and dividend payments. Children of recipients are required to attend school regularly and obtain appropriate immunizations.
South Dakota	The Strengthening of South Dakota Families Initiative encourages welfare recipients to undertake either employment or education activities. The program assigns AFDC participants to either an employment or education track that enables them to move from dependency to self-sufficiency. Individuals enrolled in the employment track will receive up to 24 months of AFDC benefits; those participating in the education track will receive up to 60 months of AFDC benefits. Upon completion of either track, participants will be expected to find employment or, failing that, will be enrolled in approved community service activities. Individuals who refuse to perform the required community service without good cause will have their benefits reduced until they comply. In addition, in conformance with the food stamp program, AFDC benefits can be denied to any family in which an adult parent quits a job without good cause. The sanction period will last three months or until the parent acquires a comparable job. The demonstration also enacts new rules pertaining to the employment and earnings of children receiving AFDC. Under current law, income earned by children can reduce the family's overall AFDC payment. The South Dakota demonstration will disregard such earnings for children who are attending school at least part-time. Children will be permitted to have a savings account of up to $1,000.
Texas	The Texas plan has a three-tiered system for establishing the length of time for which people will receive benefits. Recipients are eligible for either one, two, or three years depending on their work history and level of functional literacy. Time limits begin when a family gets into a work program. The Texas plan has a five-year cap after which recipients cannot receive funds. The five-year cap only applies to adults; children can continue to receive benefits. The state can opt to continue to provide assistance to families who reach the cap. Parents are required to sign a Personal Responsibility Agreement stating that they will keep their children in school and off drugs and commit to providing regular checkups and immunizations for their children. Parents/caretakers will lose benefits if they fail to comply with the Agreement. The Texas plan also creates a system of local Workforce Development Boards to oversee all welfare and job training programs. Lastly, the Texas plan allows for the full privatization of the service delivery system for public assistance.
Vermont	Vermont's Family Independence Project (FIP) promotes work by enabling AFDC recipients to retain more income and accumulate more assets than is normally allowed. FIP also requires AFDC recipients to participate in community or public service jobs after they have received AFDC for 30 months for most AFDC families, 15 months for families participating in the unemployed parent component of AFDC. Current child support payments will now go directly to families entitled to them.

(continued)

◆ Table 11.2 *(continued)*

Virginia	The "Welfare Reform Project" will encourage employment by identifying employers who hire AFDC recipients for jobs that pay between $15,000 and $18,000 a year and by providing additional months of transitional child care and health care benefits. A second statewide project will: enable AFDC families to save for education or home purchases by allowing the accumulation of up to $5,000 for such purposes; encourage family formation by changing the way a stepparent 's income is counted; and allow full-time high school students to continue to receive AFDC benefits until age 21. AFDC recipients who successfully leave welfare for work may be eligible to receive transitional benefits for child and health care for an additional 24 months, for a total of 36 months.
Wisconsin	The Work Not Welfare project will require that most AFDC recipients either work or look for jobs. The plan provides case management, employment activities, and work experience to facilitate employment. Receipt of AFDC benefits will be limited to 24 months in a 4-year period, except under certain conditions, such as an inability to find employment in the local area due to a lack of appropriate jobs. Upon exhaustion of benefits, recipients become ineligible for 36 months. With exceptions, a family cap is in effect, although additional children will remain eligible for Medicaid benefits and food stamps. Child support will be paid directly to the AFDC custodial parent in cases where the funds are collected by the state. All AFDC recipients will be offered family planning services and instructions on parenting skills.
Wyoming	This reform plan will encourage AFDC recipients to enroll in school, undertake a training program, or enter the workforce. Wyoming's plan will allow AFDC families with an employed parent to accumulate $2,500 in assets, rather than the current ceiling of $1,000. Wyoming will promote compliance with work and school requirements with tough penalties: AFDC minor children who refuse to stay in school or accept suitable employment could have their monthly benefit reduced by $40; and adult AFDC recipients who are required to work or perform community service but refuse to do so face a $100 cut in their monthly benefit. Wyoming will severely restrict eligibility for adults who have completed a postsecondary educational program while on welfare and will deny payment to recipients who have confessed to or been convicted of program fraud until full restitution is made to the state. Unemployed, noncustodial parents of AFDC children who are not paying child support can now be ordered by the courts into Wyoming's JOBS program.

Source: Compiled with information from the Department of Health and Human Services, "State Welfare Demonstrations" (Washington, DC: DHHS, June 1995); and "Speak Out Sheet," Fax Alert for Child Advocates, Children at Risk, Houston, TX, October, 29, 1996.

California (−3 percent); and Illinois (−17 percent).[66]

Perhaps the most dramatic example of GA cuts occurred in Michigan where the program was eliminated on October 1, 1991, leaving approximately 82,000 beneficiaries without any federal, state, or local help to face the winter. These people faced a bleak job market in a state with an unemployment rate of 9 percent.[67] A follow-up study done in eight Michigan counties where almost two-thirds (55,000) of the former recipients lived revealed that nearly 20,000, or about 36 percent of the former recipients, had been evicted because they could not pay the rent. At the time of the study, more than 20,000 of the former 55,000 recipients surveyed had no regular place to live.[68] For example, homeless shelter service capacity doubled in Detroit after GA ended, but demand still outstripped available beds. Shelter providers reported that virtually all single homeless clients formerly had GA income, and that without this income, single homeless adults had the most difficulty finding permanent housing.[69] The correlation between homelessness and the unavailability of GA benefits was also shown by Martha Burt, who examined homelessness in 147 cities from 1981 to 1989. Burt found that the highest rates of homelessness were in cities where no GA program existed. The next highest incidence of homelessness was in cities where GA benefits were provided only to the disabled and to families. Conversely, the lowest rates of homelessness were found in cities where GA benefits were extended to "able-bodied" individuals.[70] The elimination of even minimal GA safety nets puts large numbers of poor people at grave risk.

ISSUES IN WELFARE REFORM

The new PRWOA incorporates a number of ideological and programmatic perspectives. Specifically, the act was designed to transfer authority for the design and management of social programs from Washington to the states. Promoted early by the Reagan administration, this ideological perspective has been labeled the "devolution revolution" or the "new federalism."[71] Energized by the omnipresent cry of "states rights," this new federalism trades off long-term and stable federal funding for increased state control in the form of block grants.

The use of social service block grants are not new. The last social program that was block granted and devolved to the states, the Title XX Social Services Block Grant, has been so mismanaged that it is implicated in the 2,000 American children who die of abuse and neglect annually—almost half of such child deaths are cases known to state children's agencies that are unable or unwilling to protect them.[72] States have proven so inept at protecting children that courts have assumed management of child welfare agencies in 21 states and the District of Columbia.[73]

The responsibility of states to care for their poor is also not new. In part, it was the failure of states to care for their poor that originally led to the creation of the 1935 Social Security Act, legislation which federalized most public assistance and social insurance programs. Devolving welfare responsibility to the states is neither new nor novel. It is retrograde welfare reform. Nevertheless, the question remains: If states were unable to mount compassionate social welfare programs prior to 1935, what is the evidence that they will do so today?

The Race to the Bottom

Devolving federal responsibility for welfare to the states helps set the stage for a "race to the bottom." Under TANF, states have no duty to operate a program of cash assistance for poor families, no duty to maintain prescribed levels of benefit payments for needy families, and no duty to provide aid to needy families for longer than five years. In addition, states will be able to withdraw or divert approximately $40 billion between 1997 and 2002 without such action affecting the amount of federal block grant funds they receive. If state funding is reduced and federal funds are diverted to other purposes (to the extent the bill allows), basic benefits for needy families and resources for work programs will fall short of need. Given this, some observers believe that the combination of a lack of minimum federal standards, restricted federal funding, and incentives to withdraw state funding will encourage a race to the bottom, in which states sharply reduce the availability of assistance to needy families. In response, block grant proponents argue that this concern is unwarranted and that states can be counted on to develop thoughtful, moderate responses to a welfare block grant.[74]

The race to the bottom will be influenced by other factors, including funding shortfalls. Federal funding for most states is frozen through FY 2002, regardless of whether there is a recession or a high level of unemployment. George Miller, Director of Oklahoma's Department of Human Services observed that: "As along as our economy is good and as long as our caseloads are going down, we're in good shape. But if we get into another recession, our block grant is fixed."[75] The Congressional Budget Office estimates that the federal funding under the TANF grant will be $1.2 billion lower over the next six years compared to what states would have received under AFDC and other assistance programs. By 1999 federal funding is projected to fall short of what would have been provided under AFDC guidelines. By 2002, the funding shortfall is expected to reach more than $1 billion a year. Although federal funding is frozen, TANF still requires states to expand their work programs, thereby adding new costs. These problems will intensify during economic downturns when poverty rises and the number of families applying for aid increases and may well cause states to cut back on benefits just when they are needed the most.

States also generate much larger savings by cutting aid under the TANF block grant than under the previous AFDC program. Under AFDC, if a state with a 50 percent match reduced aid by $1, it saved $.50 and the federal government $.50. In TANF, states retain federal funds regardless of how sharply the state reduces benefits or eligibility, and each $1 reduction in aid generates $1 in state savings. The incentive to reduce aid is therefore doubled. In poorer states, where the current federal match rate may reach 75 percent or 80 percent, the return to the state by cutting aid may be quadrupled or quintupled. Where federal matches are no longer available, states may employ grant reductions or eligibility restrictions to avoid long waiting lists and the depletion of funds in midyear.[76] Lastly, some states will be encouraged to race to the bottom as a strategy to discourage welfare migration.

Welfare Behaviorism

The TANF program is predicated on a kind of "welfare behaviorism" that is intended to change the behaviors of the poor. However, as an attempt to reprogram the behavior of the poor, current welfare reform efforts are unlikely to deliver on its promises. Evidence accumulating from the multitude of state welfare demonstrations indicates that the imposition of conditions for receipt of welfare yields modest results at best, at worst, the consequences are antithetical to the purposes of the demonstration. Despite data demonstrating the marginal economic benefits of making welfare conditional, conservatives effectively leveraged a moral argument that public policy should change the behavior of the welfare poor. In so doing, welfare behaviorism represented a change in the way that conservatives had come to understand poverty. On the eve of passage of the 1988 Family Support Act (FSA), conservative theorists had arrived at a new consensus on poverty: although the liberally-inspired public assistance programs, such as AFDC, may have once been appropriate for the "cash poor," they were counterproductive with the "behaviorally poor."[77] Rather than alleviate problems of the behaviorally poor, public welfare exacerbated the culture of poverty. As poverty programs expanded, conservatives contended, the social dysfunctions of the behaviorally poor metasticized: beginning as teen mothers, women dominated family life, ultimately becoming generationally dependent on welfare; young men dropped out of school, failed to pursue legitimate employment, and resorted to sexual escapades and repetitive crime to demonstrate prowess; children, lacking adult role models of effective parents at home and capable workers on the job, promised to further populate the underclass.

Conservatives, however, differed in how to respond to behavioral poverty. In *Losing Ground*, Charles Murray suggested "scrapping the entire federal welfare and income support structure for working-aged persons."[78] Not long thereafter Lawrence Mead offered a less draconian measure in *Beyond Entitlement:* make receipt of public aid contingent on conventional behaviors, particularly work.[79] Eventually, both prescriptions were to be incorporated in welfare policy. Following Mead's admonition, the TANF required recipients to participate in work-related activities. As states secured federal waivers for "experiments," welfare mothers often had to meet a number of other requirements or risk losing aid: through "learnfare" children on public assistance had to demonstrate regular school attendance; through the "family cap," additional assistance for children born after a mother became eligible for assistance would be denied, inducing family planning; in order to pursue child support, the establishment of paternity was required for a child to receive benefits; as a method for protecting public health, recipient children were required to have immunizations in order to attend school; to dissuade teenagers from becoming pregnant, teen mothers would have to live with their parents in order to get welfare. In seeking waivers, some states pursued Murray's contention that public assistance be terminated for the able-bodied. As momentum for welfare reform snowballed, time-limiting welfare benefits was incorporated into newer congressional proposals.[80]

The ending of the 60-year federal entitlement to an income floor for poor families has had extensive political fallout. Die-hard conservatives justified termination of welfare with George Gilder's contention that what the poor needed most was "the spur of their own poverty,"[81] while "bleeding heart" conservatives found a rationale in "tough love." Either way, welfare reformers conceded that terminating benefits would probably worsen deprivation, but that was necessary too. If making welfare conditional worsened poverty, that was the price for combating the underclass. As a manifestation of public policy, welfare behaviorism might not be pretty, but it was no less essential to restore social order. Liberals were aghast. Following Marian Wright Edelman's earlier demand that the president veto welfare reform crafted by the One-hundred-fourth Congress,[82] the *Washington Post* weighed in with an editorial declaring that Clinton's signing the welfare reform plan would be "the low point of his presidency."[83] Citing conservative analysts, such as James Q. Wilson, Lawrence Mead, John DiIulio, and William Bennett who had trepidations about the welfare reform plan, Senator Daniel Patrick Moynihan castigated President Clinton for endorsing a bill that was premised on the belief "that the behavior of certain adults can be changed by making the lives of their children as miserable as possible."[84] Liberal advocacy groups scrambled to convince the president to veto the legislation, but they failed.[85] Cleverly, Clinton had preempted their condemnation by announcing his intention to sign the plan before the conference proposal was voted on by either chamber of Congress. But heat from liberal activists intensified, leading Clinton to promise ameliorative action on the most controversial features of the welfare reform plan—elimination of benefits for the handicapped and legal immigrants—through the incoming One-hundred-fifth Congress.

If the politics of welfare reform were hyperbolic, the research on various welfare waivers scarcely mattered. By mid–1996 evaluation research revealed that the results of state welfare demonstrations were at best problematic. Yet, regardless of what both liberal and conservative policy analysts were coming to conclude about making receipt of welfare contingent on specific behaviors, this seemed to accelerate the momentum behind welfare reform. Indeed, the contradictory evidence may well have fueled the palpable urgency that propelled welfare reform through the One-hundred-fourth Congress and on to the White House. Accumulating research on a range of welfare reform experiments—welfare-to-work, learnfare, teen pregnancy, paternity, and time limits—suggested caution in proceeding with major changes in public assistance programs. But despite the data, Congress and the White House were determined to reform welfare in anticipation of the upcoming election.

Time Limits

The ultimate in welfare behaviorism is time-limiting public assistance benefits. During the presidential campaign, Bill Clinton won voters' approval for his pledge to end welfare. As conceived during the campaign, Clinton's prescription for welfare reform included a two-year time limit on receipt of AFDC followed by government-provided employment in the event a private sector job could not be found. In the presidency, however, Clinton was confronted with the cost of his proposal: while the provision of a job for welfare recipients would increase welfare costs (perhaps $10 billion), the price tag on making similar opportunities available to the working poor was simply unacceptable (between $45 billion and $60 billion).[86] The president's working group on welfare reform finally resolved the matter by applying the two-year time limit after which public employment would be available only to those AFDC recipients born after 1971 (at that time those under age 25).

Under the leadership of Speaker Newt Gingrich, the Republican One-hundred-fouth Congress presented a much stricter time limit through the Personal Responsibility Act (PRA). In addition to a two-year time limit for any given episode of receipt of welfare, the PRA imposed a five-year lifetime limit on receipt of public assistance. It was clear that Clinton and Gingrich had tapped deep public resentment about welfare. As recently as 1996, Public Agenda, a nonprofit public opinion research organization, surveyed sentiment about welfare. In response to a series of vignettes about families on welfare, respondents approved time limits in the 80- and 90-percentile ranges. (The only exception was the vignette for a physically and mentally handicapped young man whose family could not support him.) Significantly, even respondents who were welfare recipients approved of time limits, although at just slightly lower percentages.[87]

One of the most concise examinations of time-limiting welfare was done by the Urban Institute's LaDonna Pavetti. Using a computer simulation, Pavetti programmed a number of scenarios constructed from the primary features of welfare reform proposals before Congress. Both two- and five-year time-limits were simulated; in addition, a series of exemptions were incorporated, including having a child under 18-months of age, being disabled, and already having a job. Pavetti then projected the consequences for families who were newly eligible for AFDC as well as those who were long-term dependents on public assistance. As might be expected, there are many permutations generated by so complex an analysis; however, the major findings were: (a) overall, 58 percent of families receive AFDC longer than two years; more than one-third for longer than five years; (b) because welfare roles are populated by families who have been on AFDC for a long period, at any given time about 70 percent have already received AFDC for longer than two years, and 48 percent for longer than five years; by exempting a recipient because of a very young child at home, the number of families hitting a two-year time limit drops from 37 percent to 10 percent; and by exempting a recipient who has a young or disabled child, or who is already working, the number of families reaching a two-year time limit falls to 5 percent.

The implementation of time limits without exemptions would cut a swath through public assistance. If exemptions were granted for young children under Pavetti's scenarios, the AFDC termination rate for a two-year time limit would eliminate 207,000 families, including 307,000 children.[88] Yet, Pavetti's numbers may underestimate the casualty rate. Before passage of the PRWOA, the Center on Budget and Policy Priorities cited a Congressional Budget Office (CBO) report stating that "if all states were to adopt a two-year time limit, 5.5 million children would be denied aid by 2006, even assuming that states exempted 20 percent of their caseloads from these state time limits."[89]

Time-limiting welfare is troubling in several respects. Because no state welfare experiment has yet reached that point (although several will in the near future), the consequences for poor families can only be speculated upon. When Michigan terminated its General Assistance (GA) program in 1991, only 20 percent of former recipients held formal jobs two years later.[90] If AFDC mothers are similar to Michigan GA recipients, only a minority will make the transition to employment; a substantial—yet unknown—number will be ejected from the safety net. There will be little incentives for states to track the casualties of time limits because they will only highlight the more conspicuous failure of welfare reform.[91] On the other hand, operationalizing time limits will be problematic, particularly the five-year lifetime limit. A nationwide, integrated data system necessary to record the on-again, off-again cycles of welfare experienced by many families does not exist; and given the states' difficulties in fielding their own computer systems, it is unlikely anytime soon. States may have more valid information about the experiences of families within their borders, but even then, data systems are often inadequate to defend against a legal challenge.

Personal and Parental Responsibility

The welfare behaviorism in TANF reflects a belief in the value of personal and parental responsibility. This harkens back to America's supposedly traditional "main street" values of self-reliance, independence, and individual responsibility. It is based on the idea that in America there is a level playing replete with abundant economic and social opportunities. It is also a philosophy that also includes a de facto belief in the limited role of government. For liberals who have advocated expanded social programs, these welfare reforms embody a world that seems at odds with the realities of modern civilization. For liberals, postindustrial capitalism is marked by an interdependence between individuals and government, with human and market needs being inextricably linked. From this perspective, the PRWOA is not only out of sync with the requirements of a postindustrial economy, but it also serves to condemn individuals for their own impoverishment, to "blame the victim," and to aggravate social injustice.

The view of parental responsibility reflected in the PRWOA focuses on several fronts: (1) fathers who conceive children have a responsibility to financially support them; (2) mothers requesting public aid have a responsibility to establish paternity for the purpose of collecting child support; (3) mothers who have physical custody of children have a responsibility to provide for them financially through work efforts; (4) custodial parents have a responsibility to ensure that their children receive and appropriately respond to educational opportunities; and (5) custodial parents have a responsibility to provide basic public health protection for their children, including immunizations. These tenets of parenthood are neither extreme nor especially controversial. In fact, they are part the glue that holds society together. Controversy arises, then, not on the correctness of these values but in their operationalization. More specifically, significant controversy surrounds the question of whether attempts at engineering appropriate social behaviors are successful or whether they simply function as punishment. Examples of this form of social punishment abound.

Introduced in Wisconsin in the fall of 1988, Learnfare targeted teenagers who had more than two unexcused absences from school. Under Learnfare sanctions, the family's AFDC benefits for a dependent teen were reduced by $77 a month; for an independent teen with a child, the penalty was $190 a month. Wisconsin officials contended that such sanctions would result in the return of 80 percent of teens on AFDC who had dropped out of school. Rhetoric notwithstanding, subsequent evaluation of the Milwaukee demonstration conducted by an independent agency "did not show improvement in student attendance that could be attributed to the Learnfare requirement." Undeterred, state officials wrote to the evaluators demanding that they suppress parts of the study that detailed the failure of Learnfare to enhance teen school attendance. When the researchers refused, Wisconsin officials canceled the contract, in the process impugning the professionalism of the evaluators.[92]

Meanwhile, Ohio promised teens a $62-a-month carrot for good school attendance, coupled with a $62-a-month stick for truancy through LEAP (Learning, Earning, and Parenting). Three years after program's inception, LEAP was heralded as a major victory in the battle against teen truancy. Pundits such as William Raspberry trumpeted LEAP's 20 percent increase in the rate that teens completed high school and a 40 percent increase in employment. A closer examination of the LEAP evaluation is less sanguine. The glowing results were reported only for those teens currently enrolled in school and excluded those who had dropped out, even though both groups were part of the study's population. Including dropouts, LEAP's outcomes plummet: the number completing high school is not 20 percent, but 6.5 percent; the number employed is not 40 percent, but 20 percent. By comparative measures, LEAP *does* improve teen behavior but only modestly, and, if LEAP generated outcomes that were positive, it also produced negative results. For teens who had already dropped out of school—arguably, those most likely to join the underclass—LEAP produced no discernable effect. However, because of the benefit reduction sanction levied against all truant teens, a significant number of all mothers in the study reported "diminished spending on essentials for their families, especially clothing and food."[93] In their concluding observations, evaluators conceded that changing adolescent behavior is difficult and admitted that LEAP produced some "perverse effects."[94]

As Learnfare and LEAP demonstrated the difficulty of altering the apparent intransigent behavior of the poor, conservatives began to target teen mothers. Research had identified a number of welfare-related problems that were correlated with single parenthood; among the most welfare dependent were women who had entered AFDC as teenagers. This led conservatives to attribute much of the underclass to teen parenthood. Clearly, substantial welfare savings could be achieved by dissuading teenage girls from becoming pregnant. Furthermore, because teenagers who had been on welfare were more than twice as likely to be welfare reliant themselves,[95] reducing teen motherhood would lower the likelihood of future welfare dependence. As discussed in Chapter 5, the results of Project Redirection (designed to provide AFDC-eligible mothers age 17 or younger with intensive services to optimize educational, employment, and life-management skills) were mixed, but generally inconclusive. Project Redirection teens fared no better than the control group in obtaining a high school diploma or GED certificate, their weekly earnings five years later were only $23 more than those in the control group. Moreover, five years after participation, 10 percent fewer of the control group were on welfare than the Project Redirection teens. The live birth rate of Project Redirection teens exceeded the control group five years after the study."[96] Modeled after Project Redirection, New Chance program graduates fared *worse* than the control group in two important respects: they were more likely to get pregnant again, and they were participating less in the labor market.[97]

Findings from research on programs designed to divert young people from welfare are, at best, vexing. When Learnfare seemed a wash, Wisconsin officials attempted to suppress research findings. In response to LEAP, proponents have exaggerated benefits, gleaning for public dissemination the positive results of participants remaining in high school but conveniently omitting the negligible impact on dropouts, the most likely candidates for the underclass. Those conservatives who decided to target teens for the evils of welfare dependence and to show the positive impact of behavioral corrective measures could not have chosen a more troublesome scapegoat.

Another issue underlying the new welfare reforms involves (re)marriage. According to a number of studies, no more than a fifth of mothers left the AFDC program as a result of earnings increases; most exits resulted from a change in marital status.[98] Yet, public assistance programs punish marriage in two ways: (1) by how they treat a married couple with children in common, and (2) by how they treats families with stepparents. First, a needy two-parent family with children is less likely to be eligible for aid than a one-parent family. Although the nonincapacitated two-parent family can apply for TANF, the restrictions involving work expectation and time limits imposed by many states make the program inaccessible to many poor families. Second, a stepparent has no legal obligation to support the children of his or her spouse in most states. Nevertheless, AFDC cut or limited benefits when a woman remarried by counting much of the stepparent's income when calculating the family's countable income, thus jeopardizing the mother's eligibility status.[99] In effect, there is a strong economic disincentive for a low-income woman to marry a man with low earnings.

For many welfare mothers the decision to marry a man with a low income is often financially based. The Congressional Research Service calculated that an AFDC recipient in Texas (capitalizing on AFDC, food stamps, and Medicaid) who married a man earning $10,000 a year would lose 24 percent of her disposable income; if he earned $15,000 per year, she would lose 25 percent; and if the man earned $20,000, she would lose 29 percent. That same recipient in New York who married would have had disposable income reduced by 10 percent, 41 percent, and 42 percent, respectively.[100] A poor female-headed four-person family in New Jersey in 1988 that fully capitalized on their potential benefits could have realized $12,070. Thus, the yearly per capita income would have been $3,018. If that same mother married a man earning $15,000 a year, the annual *gross* per capita income of that now five-person family would shrink to $3,000 a year. That gross income would be further diminished by the Social Security tax, the federal income tax, work expenses, and so on. Perhaps more important, the former recipient would risk losing her valuable Medicaid perk. According to the conservative Heritage Foundation's Robert Rector:

> The current welfare system has made marriage economically irrational for most low-income parents. Welfare has converted the low-income working husband from a necessary breadwinner into a net financial handicap. It has transformed marriage from

> a legal institution designed to protect and nurture children into an institution which financially penalizes nearly all low-income parents who enter into it. Across the nation, the current welfare system has all but destroyed family structure in the inner-city. Welfare establishes strong financial disincentives, effectively blocking the formation of intact, two-parent families.[101]

Welfare-to-Work

TANF is predicated on the belief that recipients should be moved off public welfare and into private employment as quickly as possible, a theme that has permeated welfare reform since the 1960s. While conservatives argue that work is the best antipoverty program, some liberals have asserted that child rearing is also a productive form of work. Moreover, these liberals have contended that while it is socially acceptable for middle-class mothers to stay at home with young children, poor mothers are considered lazy and unmotivated if they try to do the same.

Workfare programs have been a constant feature of the welfare landscape since 1967 when new AFDC amendments were added that pressured recipient mothers into working. As part of those new rules, work requirements became mandatory for unemployed fathers, mothers, and certain teenagers. AFDC recipients who were deemed employable and yet refused to work could be terminated.[102] A work incentive program (WIN) was developed to provide training and employment for all welfare mothers considered employable (recipients with preschool age children were exempt). Day care was made available to facilitate the WIN program. Owing in part to a lackluster federal commitment (in 1985 the total federal contribution to WIN was only $258 million), the performance of work programs have generally been disappointing. In addition, many states were reluctant to enact mandatory job requirements because they believed that enforcing them would cost more than simply maintaining families on AFDC. Workfare was again resurrected in 1988, when it formed the backbone of the Family Support Act.

By the early 1990s, the Manpower Demonstration Research Corporation (MDRC) had amassed considerable evidence about the performance of state welfare-to-work programs, and the results fell far short of what conservatives had promised in converting AFDC to an employment-based program. In the best of all welfare worlds, state welfare-to-work programs would show positive outcomes in three ways: earnings of welfare participants would improve, optimally enough for them to become economically self-sufficient; welfare expenditures through AFDC would decrease; and states would recover the costs of putting in place welfare-to-work programs. Of 13 welfare-to-work programs evaluated in 1991, most boosted participants' earnings little more than $700 per year. While most programs also experienced reductions in AFDC payments, these were modest, typically less than $400 per year. Significantly, in only two programs were AFDC payment reductions greater than the cost per welfare-to-work participant. In other words, in 11 of 13 welfare-to-work programs, the cost of mounting the welfare-to-work program was not recovered initially in welfare savings.[103]

As in most field research, there are important caveats to these findings. First, the welfare-to-work program that met the three requirements noted above most efficiently was Arkansas; for the first year of the program, earnings increased on average $167, and AFDC payments were reduced $145, enough to recover the additional cost of Arkansas's WORK program, $118 per participant. This explains much of presidential candidate Clinton's enthusiasm about "ending welfare as we know it." Second, two programs were noted for significantly higher annual earnings ($2,000 plus) as well as welfare savings (more than $700), but in both cases the cost per participant was also high ($5,000 plus). Thus, independence from welfare carries with it an acute case of "sticker shock".

Yet, such modest accomplishments were not to dampen the fervor of welfare-to-work zealots. Quickly, they pointed to the Riverside County, California, Greater Avenues for Independence (GAIN) program as an exemplar. Culminating an eight-year investigation of California's GAIN program, the nation's largest welfare-to-work effort, Judith Gueron, head of MDRC, chronicled Riverside County's achievements: a 26 percent increase in AFDC parents working, an average earnings increase of 49 percent, and a 15 percent savings of welfare payments. Over three years, Riverside County GAIN participants' income increased $3,113; welfare savings for the same period were $1,983. In Gueron's words, these were "the most impressive [outcomes] measured to date anywhere."[104] On an annual basis, of course, such figures diminish in significance. Earnings increases on the order of $1,000 a year are unlikely to vault the typical AFDC family off of the program; welfare savings of little more than $600 a year do not raise the specter of cashiering the welfare bureaucracy, either. Indeed, the Riverside experience led Randall Eberts of the Upjohn Institute for Employment Research to observe that only 23 percent of participants were still employed and off AFDC three years after beginning GAIN.[105] Riverside County's vibrant economy probably accounted for much of this superior performance, raising the question of how representative it is of other American communities.

To welfare reform researchers, the welfare-to-work bandwagon was less the star-spangled apparatus that its proponents had made it out to be. Before his assignment to the Clinton working panel on welfare reform, Harvard's David Ellwood admitted as much, writing that the typical welfare-to-work program increased earnings between $250 and $750 per year. "Most work-welfare programs look like decent investments," he concluded, "but no carefully evaluated work-welfare programs have done more than put a tiny dent in the welfare caseloads, even though they have been received with enthusiasm."[106] A similar sentiment was expressed by workfare expert Judith Gueron:

> [While] welfare-to-work programs have paid off by increasing the employment and earnings of single mothers and reducing their receipt of public assistance . . . MDRC's research also reveals the limits of past interventions. Whether the targeted group were welfare mothers, low-income youth who dropped out of high school, teenage parents with limited prospects, or unemployed adult men, the programs had little success in boosting people out of poverty. . . . Often, welfare recipients who get jobs join the ranks of the working poor.[107]

But, perhaps the modest returns in welfare-to-work programs would be amplified over a longer period, welfare reform proponents averred. If many AFDC recipients have been out of the labor force for so long, they suggested, a two- or three-year assessment of a welfare-to-work program's performance might not reveal more substantial, longer-term benefits. Fortunately, a five-year assessment of welfare-to-work programs in Virginia, Arkansas, Baltimore, and San Diego examines this possibility. At the end of 5 years, Virginia and Arkansas participants increased earnings a little more than $1,000, while those in Baltimore and San Diego experienced an earnings increase of a little more than $2,000. Welfare savings, on the other hand, varied widely; Baltimore reduced welfare costs $62, while San Diego reported the greatest savings, $1,930. Net program costs varied as well, from $118 a participant in Arkansas to $953 a participant in Baltimore.[108] Once annualized, these figures confirm the shorter-term experience of welfare-to-work programs in other locales. Again, earnings increases are modest, welfare programs savings somewhat less, and the recovery of set-up costs questionable.

The long-term study of welfare-to-work provides additional insight that had not been available in previous research. Earnings of participants do not continue to increase with each additional year; rather, earnings tend to peak during the second or third year and then fall back toward the range prior to enrollment in welfare-to-work. The only program in which earnings did not fall was in Baltimore, the program with the highest cost per participant.[109] By definition, higher cost per participant is inconsistent with welfare savings; hence, a trade-off appears: the objectives of increasing earnings in order to make families independent of welfare and reducing government welfare payments are contradictory.

If the reality of welfare-to-work diverges from the rhetoric of welfare reform, it is because of the assumption that AFDC mothers are so welfare dependent that they have no experience with the labor market. In fact, many mothers have worked and have, as a result, come to see welfare benefits as a form of unemployment or underemployment assistance. To explain the relationship between work and welfare, labor economist Michael Piore split workers into primary and secondary labor markets. Workers in the primary labor market hold down salaried jobs that include health and vacation benefits, are full-time, and incorporate a career track. Workers in the secondary labor market work for hourly wages—often at the minimum wage—without benefits in jobs that are part-time or seasonal and are not part of a career track. Welfare program analysts, by way of illustration, hold jobs in the primary labor market, while working welfare recipients populate the secondary labor market.

Recent research has captured the erratic relationship between work and welfare for many mothers on AFDC. Findings of the Institute for Women's Policy Research reveal that 43 percent of AFDC mothers are either peripherally attached to the labor market, augmenting welfare with wages, or drifting on and off of welfare depending on the availability of work. Once AFDC mothers who are seeking work are coupled to those above, 66 percent of welfare mothers are either participating in the labor market or are trying to.[110] But conditions of the secondary labor market, to say nothing of the machinations of the welfare bureaucracy, make this problematic.[111]

Given the reality of the secondary labor market, the trick of welfare reform is to catapult AFDC mothers beyond the secondary labor market and into the primary labor market. If this could be done, earnings would increase enough to assure economic self-sufficiency, and welfare savings would be substantial because families would be unlikely to revert to public assistance in the future. The sticking point is that substantial investments are necessary to achieve such welfare-to-work program performance. But to do so creates two problems: First, a "moral hazard" emerges as welfare beneficiaries become recipients of benefits that are not available to the working poor not on welfare. While working people often grumble about the welfare dependent obtaining benefits not available to them, they also suspect that ample benefits induce those who should be working to apply for public assistance. Second, a "political hazard" is created for any elected or appointed official who states a willingness to support welfare recipients over the working poor. In such circumstances, the prudent politician favors the least costly and most expedient option—push welfare recipients into the labor market and celebrate doing so with paeans to the work ethic. These moral and political hazards thus prescribe the boundaries of plausibility: perforce, welfare reform is limited to elevating the welfare poor up to the strata of the working poor.

If welfare reform means modest work opportunities for TANF recipients, it has come to mean something else for welfare program managers. Confronted with static, if not declining, revenues, welfare officials—both elected officials and appointed department heads—have come under increasing pressure to reform welfare by whatever means possible. Exactly how this has come about is revealed in the five-year study noted above. From the perspective of welfare administrators, there are three primary ways to reduce welfare costs: trim monthly benefits to TANF recipients who have found work (but who are not earning enough to escape reliance on welfare completely), sanction families who are not complying with work or other conditions attached to receipt of benefits, or simply terminate cases. Regarding these options, researchers found that reducing benefits in relation to earnings accounted for no more than 2 percent of savings, while sanctioning noncompliant recipients only produced a "very small direct effect."[112] Most of the savings in welfare costs were generated by terminating cases, closing them as soon as possible. In Arkansas case closings reduced receipt of AFDC three months on average, in San Diego almost four months.[113] Yet, case closings did not alter recidivism (frequent cycling on and off welfare). Even those AFDC recipients who had found work and were terminated from public assistance were soon back on welfare. Why is this situation going on?

The likely answer to this question can be found in the way welfare programs are administered. Welfare programs such as AFDC require a significant amount of paperwork to establish and maintain eligibility. Yet, welfare departments are rarely adequately staffed to process the mountains of paperwork that program management dictates. The resulting quagmire is familiar to anyone who has spent time in a welfare department: Applicants for assistance spend hours waiting to be seen by eligibility workers, often only to be sent off in search of additional documentation to support an application. Until the application is complete, no aid will be forthcoming. Facing a lobby full of anxious and resentful applicants, eligibility workers exercise latitude in making decisions about the fate of those applying for benefits, occasionally expediting the application of someone in dire straits, often impeding the applications of those more troublesome. Sociologist Michael Lipsky coined the term "bureaucratic disentitlement" to describe those instances in which eligibility workers decline valid applications for capricious reasons.[114] The prevalence of outright denial of benefits to those who are entitled is unknown, but may approach one in four cases in some welfare offices. Recognizing that administrative caprice is routine in public assistance, it requires little imagination for the ambitious welfare administrator to use welfare reform as an opportunity to accelerate the denial of benefits, thereby achieving significant welfare savings. Given the difficulty in reestablishing eligibility, any case termination realizes a three-to-four month dividend in benefit reductions simply because it takes that long for a recipient to reactivate a claim on public assistance. Thus, purging and churning the AFDC caseload generates savings but not necessarily for the reasons claimed by proponents of welfare reform.

Lastly, work-to-welfare programs are flawed in another way. In 1996 the unemployment rate exceeded 5 percent nationally; there were about 5 million unemployed workers, of which almost 1 million were long-term unemployed. In addition, there were 2 million working adults who, even though they were working full-time, did not earn enough to escape poverty. If these people are unable to find work or to earn enough from the work they have, how can welfare recipients be expected to become self-sufficient?

The Inadequacy of Public Assistance Benefits

The TANF program is characterized by dramatically different state benefit levels. Unlike federal programs such as Social Security and SSI, AFDC benefits levels in most states were not automatically adjusted for inflation. In 1992, the combined benefits of AFDC and Food Stamp Program were below the poverty level in all 50 states. In 41 of the 50 states the benefits were below 75 percent of the poverty line, less than $8,700 for a family of three. The median AFDC benefit level for a family of three was $367 a month in 1992. The highest monthly benefits were $924 in Alaska, $693 in Hawaii, $633 in California, and $629 in Vermont. The lowest were $120 in Mississippi, $164 in Alabama, $181 in Texas, and $285 in Tennessee. In 36 states, the AFDC benefit level in 1992 for a three-person family was less than $434, the same benefit as for one recipient in the SSI program. In half of these states the benefit level was below $335. AFDC and Food Stamps Program benefits combined were less than 31 percent of state median income in all states and less than 25 percent of median income in 42 states. AFDC benefits alone were below 15 percent of state median income in 31 states.[115]

Families receiving AFDC in 1992 were worse off than those receiving assistance in 1975. Alaska was the only state which had increased the value of AFDC benefits from 1975 to 1992; in 18 states benefits were more than $100 less than in 1975. From 1988 to 1992 there was a loss in purchasing of 10 percent or more in 35 states. Between 1972 and 1991, the value of combined AFDC and Food Stamp Program benefits decreased 26 percent (from $847 to $623), measured in 1991 dollars.[116] It is this benefit structure that forms the basis for the TANF funding formula. Ellwood sums up the funding dilemma for the TANF program:

> Few people realize just how small the block grants are and how much they will vary by state. Arkansas will have less than $600 per poor child per year in federal dollars for cash support, work and training, and child care! That is less than $12 per week. But somehow, the state is going to place tens of thousands of mothers in jobs. In contrast, many of the wealthier northeastern states will get more than $2,000 per poor child per year. That still amounts to just $40 per week per poor child. Simultaneously, states will have to cope with dramatic cuts in support for disabled children, immigrants, and Medicaid, not to mention the impact of any recession. . . . States cannot and will not do the impossible, but they will do the possible. The possible is to cut people off, to offer less service, and to provide less child care for the working poor not on welfare. Because the block grant will reduce federally

> required state spending and eliminate federal laws regarding eligibility, some states will find it much easier to cut people off than to move them to work. And so the race to the bottom will begin. Even governors and legislators who want to focus on work-based reform may find it too costly if nearby states threaten to dump their poor by simply cutting benefits.[117]

The low funding base for TANF coupled with an estimated $1 billion shortfall projected for 2002, promises to exacerbate the plight of America's poor. In July 1996, the Urban Institute released a study, based on conservative assumptions, showing that the PRWOA would push 1.1 million children—and 2.6 million people overall—into poverty. The Urban Institute study also found that the bill would make large numbers of families who are already poor still poorer. Specifically, the report found that the PRWOA would increase the depth and severity of child poverty by 20 percent. Most children who would be pushed below the poverty line are in families that are already working; in most cases, their families would be pushed into poverty by the Food Stamp Program cuts or a loss of benefits because they are legal immigrants. Finally, the Urban Institute researchers found that one in every five U.S. families with children—or 8.2 million families—would see their incomes fall an average of $1,300 a year as a result of the PROWA.[118]

The assumptions employed by the Urban Institute are conservative and hence are more likely to underestimate rather than overestimate the extent to which the bill increases the number of children living in poverty. Specifically, the Urban Institute analysis is based on current economic conditions, and if a state were to suffer a recession, the impact of the PRWOA on poverty would be larger. In addition, the Urban Institute assumed all states would adopt a five-year time limit on assistance, the maximum the bill allows. A number of states are planning to institute shorter time limits. The PRWOA was passed based on political expediency rather than empirical estimates of the its effects. Hence, researchers are uncertain as to its real long-term effects. In that sense, a generation of children have become guinea pigs in a risky, politically motivated social experiment.

Privatizing Public Welfare

The PRWOA allows states to buy welfare services and gatekeepers to determine eligibility and benefits. Faced with a financial crush, states may opt to reduce costs by privatizing the delivery of public assistance benefits, an option that Texas has recently adopted. While privatization has been going on in child support enforcement and in some sectors of child welfare, it has not been tried in public assistance until recently. Not surprisingly, some corporations stand to make considerable profits from the privatization of public assistance. According to Nina Bernstein, "The new welfare bill is still a matter of confusion in statehouses and city streets. But to some companies it looks like the business opportunity of a lifetime."[119]

Proponents argue that allowing private companies to run public welfare will prove to be the most cost-effective and humane way for states to face the fiscal demands of the new law. For these supporters, privatization promises technological efficiency by cutting administrative costs and detecting fraud. Meanwhile, these privatized operations will help recipients by offering a one-stop shopping approach for benefits and enrollment. Supporters believe that a profit-making company has the flexibility to reward employees for positive results and to change the welfare system from one that dispenses checks to one that quickly moves people into jobs. Moreover, states that are able to reduce administrative costs will have more money available for child care, transportation, and job-training programs. If states overspend, they have no recourse for going to the federal government for a match; if they underspend, it frees up money for other purposes. For state welfare administrators faced with capped block grants and substantial penalties if they fail to move recipients into jobs, a private fixed-price contract has strong appeal.

Driven by a vision of cutting administrative expenses by 20 to 40 percent (mostly by closing offices and eliminating state jobs),[120] Texas was the first state to experiment with letting a private company create and run a system to screen applicants for welfare benefits. In Texas, corporations bid to manage the more than $8 billion public welfare system made up of AFDC, Food Stamps, Medicaid, and more than 25 other programs. The corporate players in this privatization scenario had substantial assets and involved such companies as IBM, Lockheed Information Management Services (a nonmilitary division of the $30 billion Lockheed Martin), Electronic Data Systems (a $12.4 billion company formerly owned by Ross Perot), Andersen Consulting (a $4.2 billion company), and Unisys.[121] Even while Texas was the stalking horse for the multibillion welfare operations in the rest of the nation, similar discussions were underway in states ranging from Wisconsin to Maryland.[122] Moreover, as a testimony to their commitment to the vast public welfare market, Lockheed hired Gerald Miller, the former director of the Michigan Family Independence Agency and president of the influential American Public Welfare Association. According to Miller, "I see this as the future of welfare reform. The private sector will ultimately run these programs. The era of big government is over."[123] In addition to Miller, Lockheed hired welfare officials from both the states and the federal government to lead its efforts to manage privatized welfare programs.

Opponents argue that if a corporation's profits are linked to reducing the welfare rolls, the incentive to deny aid will be overwhelming. According to Henry Freedman of the Center for Social Welfare Policy and Law, "No company can be expected to protect the interests of the needy at the expense of its bottom line, least of all a publicly traded corporation with a fiduciary duty to maximize shareholder profits."[124] Clearly, corporations will have strong incentives to use the letter of the law to cut people off in an effort to improve their profits and performance.[125] Much of this fiscal incentive will be based on the fixed price nature of contracts, which will include penalties for a failure to perform. For example, Texas may require a corporation to put up a $250 million performance bond. Given this, states will prefer larger corporations because they have deeper pockets into which to reach if there is a problem.

Other problems exist with privatizing public welfare. For one, administrative costs for public welfare are already low, overseen to some degree by federal government regulations. To make money managing public welfare, corporations will have to use several strategies. For one, they may have to cut staff and replace long-term welfare workers and managers with inexperienced, lower-wage workers. One Texas union estimated that "at least half of the 13,000 state employees who now determine welfare eligibility will be cut out of the new system."[126] Secondly, as a way to control salaries, corporations may try to dislodge public sector unions where they exist, and to prohibit them where they do not. A third strategy for saving money would be to replace welfare offices and state workers in rural areas with automated kiosks and highly sophisticated voice mail systems, similar to automated banking. All of these corporate strategies would have a major impact on the quality of services delivered. For instance, it is questionable whether automated screening and services coupled with inexperienced welfare workers will be able to provide the same level of service asface-to-face interviews. What of dealing with people of diverse languages and cultural backgrounds? These and other questions remain unanswered.

Corporations have an established precedent for bailing out of projects they ultimately find to be nonprofitable. This is illustrated in IBM's desertion of its OS2 operating system after an initial investment of billions and in the breakup of AT&T. What will happen if managing the public welfare system proves to be unprofitable or ultimately impossible to administer? Will corporations break their contract? Even if they complete the contract, will the state be able to find another corporation to run their operations if a company begs out of renewing its contract? This will be especially problematic because states will have disbanded their public welfare bureaucracies and will thus be dependent on corporations to administer public welfare. Indeed, this will put states in a tenuous bargaining position in terms of renegotiating corporate contracts. Moreover, what will happen to needy people if a contractor fails to deliver as promised? Will these people be held hostage as the time-consuming process of litigation is begun? Lastly, there is a long precedent involving private corporations who bid on defense contracts, only to come back again and again to ask for more money.

Corporations have a long history of establishing monopolistic pricing once they gain a large share of the market. It is conceivable that the bidding process in public welfare will initially produce low bids. In fact, corporations may even underbid—knowing that they will lose money—in order to gain a foothold in a state. If public welfare services were privatized nationally, with only a small group of corporations running it, these companies would be in a strong position to determine their rates of reimbursement. Despite the short-term savings, privatizing public assistance entails significant long-term risks to both recipients and government.

CONCLUSION: FUTURE PROSPECTS FOR WELFARE REFORM

Research on various welfare reform projects indicates the tentative progress made by states vis-à-vis important factors related to poverty: employment, education, and family life. At best, welfare reform demonstrations generate positive program outcomes on the order of 20 percent. While this may be a noteworthy accomplishment, it should be placed in context. For a half-century, AFDC had been a program that did little more than dispense checks; not until relatively recently has recipient behavior been a target for systematic intervention. Because of its lack of direction, AFDC became the source for a number of diminishing colloquialisms, from "welfare mess" to "welfare queen." Instilling some order in welfare is bound to produce some desirable outcomes, and these seem to be about 20 percent.

But what of the remaining 80 percent? Welfare analysts suspect that most of the improvement in welfare program performance is attributable to those recipients who are relatively well educated, have employment experience, and are upwardly mobile. Such welfare beneficiaries are good candidates for integration with the secondary labor market, and some of them will even find secure employment in the primary labor market, an accomplishment that will inoculate them against future poverty. Of the remaining welfare families, most may be socially mainstreamed with adequate inducements and supports. The welfare behaviorism articulated through initiatives such as welfare-to-work has been assessing the malleability of this population. Some of this group will respond positively to incentives and sanctions; some will not. In all likelihood, many—perhaps another 20 percent—will fail to negotiate the procedural thicket imposed by recent welfare reforms. While the PRWOA allows states to exempt 20 percent of families from time limits, there is no requirement that those on the lowest social register be allowed to stay on aid indefinitely. Actually, there is no assurance that states will exempt the most troubled families from time limits. It is just as plausible that the savvy state welfare administrator would exempt those mothers who are in lengthy educational/training programs on the basis that they represent a better, long-term investment of public resources. Even some conservatives are opposed to the institution of arbitrary time limits. At a recent conference on welfare reform, Lawrence Mead stated his opposition to time limits, primarily on the basis that virtually no research has been done to determine the consequences of terminating poor families from public assistance.[127]

Several features of TANF make its full implementation unlikely. A fundamental question is the extent to which states can be expected to comply with the federal work requirements: states must have 25 percent of single parents working at least 20 hours per week by 1997, and 50 percent working at least 30 hours per week by 2002. To date, only a few states/localities have even approached the first target, and by their performance the second seems unreachable. The CBO projects that over six years PRWOA falls $12 billion short of that necessary to provide the services and opportunities necessary to meet work requirements; yet, the legislation penalizes states—from 5 percent up to 21 percent of federal funds—for noncompliance. This will produce an enormous compression effect on the states. Squeezed between static resources and increasing demands for job placement, the initial response will be to remove families on welfare. Whenever possible, states will attempt to transfer the most troubled families to SSI, a program that is entirely federally funded. This, however, will require certification of disability, and the federal government will resist becoming a dumping ground for the states' welfare reform failures. Indeed, PRWOA tightens the eligibility requirements for SSI in a manner that makes transfers from welfare more difficult. Without the SSI transfer option, states will be induced to reduce the number of cases out of compliance with work requirements. Given difficulties in operationalizing the federal five-year lifetime limit, states will be induced to consider ever shorter limits. Terminating families as soon as possible on the basis of noncompliance will ultimately screen out those families least likely to become employed. Eventually, such families will cease seeking aid; to the extent large numbers of more disorganized families disappear from state welfare rolls, states will avoid federal penalties for failing to meet employment requirements. Because disentitlement is a zero-sum game, many members of those families may show up on other rolls, including criminal court dockets.

What will happen to the families dumped from state welfare programs is open to conjecture. Conservative scholars, such as Marvin Olasky, have promised that private, especially religious agencies will pick up the slack,[128] but this is doubtful. Contributions to nonprofit agencies, such as the United Way, have stagnated during the past few years. Ineligible for state aid and unable to get necessary assistance from the nonprofit sector, former welfare families will turn to metropolitan government as the last resort. Big-city mayors are already dreading the impact that such families will have on their precarious budgets. Rudolph Giuliani has projected the costs of PRWOA for New York City at $900 million per year;[129] the costs for Los Angeles have been pegged at $500 million annually.[130]

Aside from the impending problems accompanying its implementation, specific incremental benefits must be acknowledged. For example, the welfare reform plan includes $22 billion over seven years for child care in the form of a capped block grant to the states. This goes some distance toward meeting the child care requirements if so many welfare parents must enter the workforce; yet, the amount is $1.8 billion short of what the CBO estimates is required. PRWOA allows states to establish Individual Development Accounts (IDAs), a strategy to increase the assets of poor families, the most effective method for vaulting them out of poverty. Unfortunately, the welfare reform plan makes no specific allocations for IDAs, leaving funding the option of state and local government or philanthropy. PRWOA, for example, denies for life benefits to parents convicted of felony drug offenses unless they are participating in a drug treatment program. The absence of family-oriented drug treatment for addicts who are also mothers makes it unlikely that many exemptions will be forthcoming. Several of the provisions of PRWOA target teenagers on welfare: teen mothers are required to live with their parents and stay in school to receive benefits; HHS is mandated to mount a teen pregnancy prevention initiative; and the Justice Department is required to conduct research on older men who impregnate female teenagers and prosecute them for statutory rape. Several provisions address child support, including the requirement that states establish registries for child support and streamlining the process for establishing paternity. States are encouraged to be more aggressive in pursuing income withholding for noncustodial parents in arrears for child support. Furthermore, more vigorous penalties will be directed at noncustodial parents to encourage them to pay up, such as revocation of professional, drivers, occupational, and recreational licenses.[131]

Given the track record of demonstration programs designed to prevent teen pregnancy and increase child support, stiff penalties directed at adolescents and deadbeat dads would seem to be of more rhetorical value to elected officials than they are to save the public revenues now allocated to welfare programs. Regarding a larger issue, no one seems to have taken the trouble to calculate the ultimate cost of deploying a state-administered welfare apparatus with the sort of tracking, surveillance, and sanction capacity designed to reprogram the behavior of the 5 million or so families now on welfare. In this respect, it is probably just a matter of time until some pundit relabels PRWOA as the "Social Workers' Full-Employment Act."

Finally, PRWOA includes funding for further research on welfare reform, most of it for the benefit of children. From 1996 to 2002, $6 million will be allocated annually to study a random sample of children who have been abused and neglected. The focus of this longitudinal research will be child protection and out-of-home placements. An additional $15 million annually will be allocated from 1997 to 2002 to track child poverty rates. If the child poverty rate increases by 5 percent or more for a given year, HHS must prepare a plan for corrective action. Significantly, there are no specific requirements that states study the consequences of deleting families from welfare as a result of time-limits, particularly as this affects children.

Recipients of public assistance programs do not fare as well as those covered under the social insurances. Public assistance programs contain a large dose of stigma, with the character of recipients being maligned because of their need. Moreover, the relative success of Social Security in arresting poverty among the elderly has not been replicated in public assistance programs. In fact, the reverse is true; public assistance recipients have endured greater levels of poverty during the 1980s and early 1990s than in earlier decades. Indeed, the legacy of welfare reform engineered by the One-hundred-fourth Congress and signed by President Clinton does not bode well for the future prospects of America's poor.

This is clearly a difficult time for the American welfare state. Even after huge expenditures on social welfare services, according to Richard Estes, the United States ranks only twenty-third internationally in terms of the adequacy of its social provisions.[132] Given the present economic trend in which vast numbers of service jobs are produced—many of which are part-time, have few, if any, benefits, and pay the minimum wage—long-term welfare benefit packages will likely be required for an increasing number of citizens. How much these income benefit packages will contain, and at what cost, will be a matter for future discourse in public policy.

◆ ◆ ◆ *Discussion Questions* ◆ ◆ ◆

1. Public assistance is arguably the most controversial set of programs in the American welfare state. It is frequently lambasted by critics for encouraging everything from welfare dependency to teenage pregnancy. Supporters argue that it is a poorly funded program that barely allows its recipients to survive. Why is public assistance so controversial? What, if anything, can be done to make the TANF program less controversial?

2. A number of myths have arisen around the TANF program. In your opinion, what myths have been the most harmful to the program and to recipients? Why?

3. GA is often the hardest hit when states decide to implement social welfare funding cuts. What accounts for the relative unpopularity of GA? Is the GA budget the most logical place to cut when states are faced with fiscal crises? What, if anything, can be done to strengthen the image of GA?

4. Since the 1970s, most strategies for reforming public assistance have revolved around implementing a mandatory work requirement for recipients. This strategy was evident in the programs of Presidents Carter and Reagan and was the centerpiece of the 1988 Family Support Act. More recently, the TANF program mandated that benefits should last for a maximum of five years, after which a recipient would be terminated from assistance. Is establishing a mandatory work requirement a viable strategy for reforming public assistance? If so, why? If not, why not? What would be a better strategy for reforming public assistance?

5. TANF benefit levels vary widely from state to state. This situation exists because the federal government has refused to establish a national minimum benefit level. Moreover, there is little federal pressure on states to increase benefit levels and thereby curtail the erosion of public assistance benefits that has taken place since the 1970s. Should the federal government establish a minimum national benefit level for TANF and compel states to meet that level? If not, why? If you agree, what should that level be?

6. Public assistance programs are increasingly being designed to change the behavior of poor recipients. Can and should the behavior of poor people be changed through social policy legislation? Will this legislation work? If not, why?

Notes

1. Isaac Shapiro and Robert Greenstein, *Holes in the Safety Nets* (Washington, DC: Center on Budget and Policy Priorities, 1988).
2. Ibid., pp. 669–671.
3. Department of Health, Education, and Welfare, *Aid to Families with Dependent Children* (Washington, DC: Social Security Administration, Office of Research and Statistics, 1979), p. 1.
4. Children's Defense Fund, *A Children's Defense Budget* (Washington, DC: Children's Defense Fund, 1986), p. 43; and Department of Health, Education, and Welfare, *Welfare Myths and Facts* (Washington, DC: Social and Rehabilitation Service, ca. 1972), p.1.
5. U.S. House of Representatives, Select Committee on Hunger, "Myths and Realities: Food Stamp and AFDC Recipients" (Washington, DC: U.S. Government Printing Office, April 9, 1992), p. 59.
6. Ibid.
7. League of Women Voters of Louisiana, "1991 Welfare Fact Sheet" (Baton Rouge, LA: League of Women Voters, October 1991), n.p.
8. See Children's Defense Fund, *A Children's Defense Budget, 1986*.
9. Children's Defense Fund, *The State of America's Children, 1991* (Washington, DC: Children's Defense Fund, 1991), p. 156.
10. "Welfare Reform Issue Paper," Working Group on Welfare Reform, Family Support and Independence, U.S. Department of Health and Human Services, February 26, 1994; Peter Gottschalk, "Achieving Self-Sufficiency for Welfare Recipients—The Good and Bad News." In Select Committee on Hunger, *Beyond Public Assistance: Where Do We Go From Here?* Serial No. 102–123 (Washington, DC: U.S. Government Printing Office, 1992), p. 56.
11. Mary Jo Bane and David T. Ellwood, *Welfare Realities: From Rhetoric to Reform* (Cambridge, MA: Harvard University Press, 1994).
12. Quoted in Hillary Hoynes and T. McCurdy, "Has the Decline in Benefits Shortened Welfare Spells," *AEA Papers and Proceedings* (84)2 (May 1994), pp. 43–48.
13. P.J. Leahy, T.F. Buss, and J.M. Quane, "Time on Welfare: Why Do People Enter and Leave the System," *American Journal of Economics and Sociology* 54 (January 1995), pp. 33–46.
14. Bane and Ellwood, *Welfare Realities: From Rhetoric to Reform*.
15. Greg J. Duncan and Saul D. Hoffman, "Welfare Dynamics and Welfare Policy." Unpublished paper, Institute for Social Research, Ann Arbor, MI, 1985.
16. Ibid.
17. Peter Gottschalk, "Is Intergenerational Correlation in Welfare Participation Across Generations Spurious?" Boston College, November 1990, Conference Papers, 1990 ASPE-JCPES Conference on the Underclass (Washington, DC: U.S. Department of Health and Human Services).
18. M. Ann Hill and June O'Neill, "Underclass Behaviors in the United States: Measurement and Analysis of Determinants," City College of New York, March 1990, Conference Papers, 1990 ASPE-JCPES Conference on the Underclass (Washington, DC: U.S. Department of Health and Human Services).
19. Mary Corcoran, Roger Gordon, Deborah Laren, and Gary Solon, "Problems of the Underclass: Underclass Neighborhoods and Intergenerational Poverty and Dependency," University of Michigan, 1991, Conference Papers, 1990 ASPE-JCPES Conference on the Underclass (Washington, DC: U.S. Department of Health and Human Services).
20. U.S. House of Representatives, Committee on Ways and Means, *Overview of Entitlement Programs, 1992 Green Book* (Washington, DC: US GPO, 1992), p. 670.
21. Elizabeth D. Huttman, *Introduction to Social Policy* (New York: McGraw-Hill, 1981), p. 179.
22. Quoted in Select Committee on Hunger, "Myths and Realities," p. 58.
23. Kathryn Edin and Christopher Jencks, "Reforming Welfare," in Christopher Jencks, *Rethinking Social Policy* (Cambridge, MA: Harvard University Press, 1992), pp. 206–207.
24. Quoted in Select Committee on Hunger "Myths and Realities," p. 59.
25. Ibid.
26. Michael Harrington, with the assistance of Robert Greenstein and Eleanor Holmes Norton, *Who Are the Poor?* (Washington, DC: Justice for All, 1987), p. 21.
27. Iris Lav and Steven Gold, *The States and the Poor* (Washington, DC: Center on Budget and Policy Priorities, 1993), p. 11.
28. Duncan and Hoffman, "Welfare Dynamics."
29. Select Committee on Hunger, "Myths and Realities," p. 57.

30. U.S. House of Representatives, *1992 Green Book*, p. 1606.
31. Select Committee on Hunger, "Myths and Realities," p. 58.
32. Thomas Corbett, "The Wisconsin Welfare Magnet: What Is an Ordinary Member of the Tribe to Do When the Witch Doctors Disagree?" *Focus (13)*3 (Fall/Winter 1991), pp. 2–4.
33. Quoted in Diane Rose, Terri Sachnik, Josie Salazar, Eunice Sealey, and Virginia Wall, "Welfare Reform II." Unpublished paper, Graduate School of Social Work, University of Houston, Houston, TX, 1996.
34. Select Committee on Hunger, "Myths and Realities," p. 58.
35. Robert Moffitt, "Incentive Effects of the U.S. Welfare System: A Review," *Journal of Economic Literature* 30 (March 1992), pp. 1–61; see also Barbara Vobejda, "Decline in Birth Rates for Teens May Reflect Major Social Changes," *Houston Chronicle* (October 29, 1996), p. 13A.
36. "Welfare Reform Issue Paper."
37. U.S. House of Representatives, *1992 Green Book*, pp. 653–687.
38. W. Joseph Heffernan, *Introduction to Social Welfare Policy* (Itasca, IL: F. E. Peacock, 1979).
39. Frances Fox Piven and Richard A. Cloward, *Regulating the Poor: The Functions of Public Welfare* (New York: Vintage Books, 1971).
40. Huttman, *Introduction to Social Policy*, p. 168.
41. Diana DiNitto and Thomas Dye, *Social Welfare: Politics and Public Policy* (Englewood Cliffs, NJ: Prentice-Hall, 1987), p. 124; Children's Defense Fund, *A Children's Defense Budget, 1986*, p. 145.
42. William Eaton, "Major Welfare Reform Compromise Reached," *Los Angeles Times* (September 27, 1988), p. 15.
43. American Public Welfare Association, *Conference Agreement on Welfare Reform* (Washington, DC: American Public Welfare Association, September 28, 1988) pp. 1–3.
44. David Stoesz and Howard Karger, "Welfare Reform: From Illusion to Reality," *Social Work* (35)2 (March 1990), pp. 141–147.
45. Spencer Rich, "Panel Clears Welfare Bill," *Washington Post* (September 28, 1988), p. A6.
46. Sar Levitan and Frank Gallo, *Jobs for JOBS: Toward a Work-Based Welfare System* (Washington, DC: Center for Social Policy Studies, March 1993).
47. Ibid.
48. Committee on Ways and Means, U.S. House of Representatives, *Overview of Entitlement Programs, 1990 Green Book* (Washington, DC: U.S. Government Printing Office, 1990), p. 618.
49. See David T. Ellwood, "Welfare Reform as I Knew It: When Bad Things Happen to Good Policies," *The American Prospect* 26 (May–June, 1996), pp. 22–29.
50. Ibid., p. 240.
51. Ellwood, "Welfare Reform as I Knew It."
52. Ibid.
53. "Legal Immigrants to Carry Burden of Welfare Reform," *El Paso Times* (August 3, 1996), p. B1.
54. Mark H. Greenberg,"No Duty, No Floor: The Real Meaning of 'Ending Entitlements'" (Washington, DC: Center for Law and Social Policy, 1996). On-line: http://epn.org/clasp/clduty-2.html
55. Mark Greenberg and Steve Savner, "The Temporary Assistance for Needy Families Block Grant," (Washington, DC: Center for Law and Social Policy, August 1996). Online: http://epn.org/clasp/clsummry.html
56. Paula Roberts, "Relationship between TANF and Child Support Requirements," (Washington, DC: Center for Law and Social Policy, September 1996). On-line: http://epn.org/clasp/cltcsr.html
57. "Welfare Reform," *NASW News* (September, 1996), pp. 1, 12.
58. NACo Legislative Priority Fact Sheet, New Welfare Reform Law, "The Personal Responsibility and Work Opportunity Reconciliation Act of 1996" (Washington, DC: NACo, 1996).
59. Frances Fox Piven, "Was Welfare Reform Worthwhile?" *The American Prospect* 27 (July–August 1996), pp. 14–15.
60. Quoted in Ibid., p. 14.
61. Center on Social Welfare Policy and Law, "Compilation of Information About 1992 State Cutbacks in AFDC, GA and EAF," Washington, DC: Center on Social Policy and the Law, pp. 2–3.
62. Marion Nichols, Jon Dunlap, and Scott Barkin, *National General Assistance Survey, 1992* (Washington, DC: Center on Budget and Policy Priorities and the National Conference of State Legislators, December 1992); see also Diana M. DiNitto, *Social Welfare: Politics and Public Policy*, 4th ed. (Boston: Allyn and Bacon, 1995).
63. Ibid.

64. Center on Social Welfare Policy and Law, "Compilation of Information About 1992 State Cutbacks in AFDC, GA and EAF."
65. Lav and Gold, *The States and the Poor*, p. 36.
66. Center on Social Welfare Policy and the Law, "1991: The Poor Got Poorer as Welfare Programs Were Slashed," Publication No. 165 (Washington, DC: Center on Social Welfare Policy and the Law, February 1992), pp. 5–6.
67. Isaac Shapiro, Mark Sheft, Julie Strawn, Laura Summer, Robert Greenstein, Steven D. Gold, *The States and the Poor: How Budget Decisions in 1991 Affected Low-Income People* (Washington, DC: Center on Budget and Policy Priorities, December 1991), p. 23.
68. Knud Hansen, "The Impact of the Elimination of General Assistance Programs in Michigan, Interim Report," Center for Urban Studies, Wayne State University, August 29, 1992.
69. Sandra Danziger and Sherrie Kossoudji, "When Welfare Ends: Subsistence Strategies of Former GA Recipients," University of Michigan School of Social Work, Ann Arbor, MI, 1994.
70. Martha Burt, "Over the Edge" (Washington, DC: The Urban Institute, 1992).
71. Thomas Corbett, "The New Federalism: Monitoring Consequences," *Focus* (18)1 (1996), pp. 3–6.
72. Lela Costin, Howard Karger, and David Stoesz, *The Politics of Child Abuse in America* (New York: Oxford University Press, 1996).
73. Joe Sexton, "Child Welfare Chief Provides A Glimpse at Decentralization," *The New York Times* (September 8, 1996), p. 5.
74. Mark Greenberg, "Racing to the Bottom? Recent State Welfare Initiatives Present Cause for Concern," (Washington, DC: Center for Law and Social Policy, 1996).
75. Quoted in Helen O'Neill, "States Scramble to Understand Effect of Coming Welfare Shift," *The Star Ledger* (Newark, NJ, August 12, 1996), p. A3.
76. Ibid.
77. Michael Novak, *The New Consensus on Family and Welfare* (Washington, DC: American Enterprise Institute, 1987).
78. Charles Murray, *Losing Ground* (New York: Basic Books, 1984), pp. 227–228.
79. Lawrence Mead, *Beyond Entitlement* (New York: Free Press, 1986).
80. Center on Budget and Policy Priorities, *The New Welfare Law* (Washington, DC: Center on Budget and Policy Priorities, 1996).
81. George Gilder, *Wealth and Poverty* (New York: Basic Books, 1981), p. 118.
82. Marian Wright Edelman, "Say No to This Welfare Reform'," *Washington Post* (November 3, 1995), p. A23.
83. "A Children's Veto," *Washington Post* (July 25, 1996), p. A28.
84. Daniel P. Moynihan, "When Principle Is at Issue," *Washington Post* (August 4, 1996), p. C7.
85. Barbara Vobejda and Dan Balz, "President Seeks Balm for Anger Over Welfare Bill," *Washington Post* (August 22, 1996), p. B3.
86. Mickey Kaus, *The End of Equality* (New York: Basic Books, 1992), p. 135.
87. Steve Jarkas, *The Values We Live By: What Americans Want from Welfare Reform* (New York: Public Agenda, 1996).
88. LaDonna Pavetti, "Policies to Time-Limit AFDC Benefits," (Washington, DC: Urban Institute, 1994).
89. Center on Budget and Policy Priorities, *The New Welfare Law*, p. 6.
90. Anthony Halter, "State Welfare Reform for Employable General Assistance Recipients," *Social Work* (January 1996), p. 65–69.
91. Paul Peterson and Mark Rom, "State Welfare Policy: A Race to the Bottom?" (School of Public Health: University of California, Berkeley, 1995).
92. Lois Quinn and Robert Magill, "Politics versus Research in Social Policy," *Social Service Review* (December 1994), pp. 83–90.
93. David Long, Judith Gueron, Robert Wood, Rebecca Fisher, and Veronica Fellerath, *LEAP* (New York: MDRC, 1996), p. ES6.
94. Ibid., p. ES13.
95. U.S. House of Representatives, *Overview of Entitlement Programs* (Washington, DC: U.S. GPO, 1994), p. 448.
96. Denise Polit, Janet Quint, and James Riccio, *The Challenge of Serving Teenage Mothers* (New York: MDRC, 1988), Tables 2 and 3, p. 17.
97. Janet Quint, Denise Polit, Hans Bos, and George Cave, *New Chance* (New York: MDRC, 1994), Tables 5 and 6.
98. Moffitt, "Incentive Effects of the U.S. Welfare System," p. 30.
99. Mark Greenberg, testimony before the Domestic Task Force, Select Committee on Hunger, U.S.

House of Representatives, April 9, 1992, in *Federal Policy Perspectives on Welfare Reform: Rhetoric, Reality and Opportunities*, Serial No. 102–25 (Washington, DC: U.S. Government Printing Office, 1992), pp. 52–53.

100. U.S. House of Representatives, *1992 Green Book*, pp. 1216–1220.
101. Robert Rector, "Strategies for Welfare Reform," Testimony before the Domestic Task Force, Select Committee on Hunger, U.S. House of Representatives, April 9, 1992, in *Federal Policy Perspectives on Welfare Reform: Rhetoric, Reality and Opportunities*, Serial No. 102–25 (Washington, DC: U.S. Government Printing Office, 1992), pp. 67–68.
102. Huttman, *Introduction to Social Policy*.
103. Judith Gueron and Edward Pally, *From Welfare to Work* (New York: Russell Sage Foundation, 1991).
104. Judith Gueron, "Work Programs and Welfare Reform," *Public Welfare* (Summer 1995), p. 10.
105. Randall Eberts, "Welfare to Work," *Upjohn Employment Research* (Fall 1995), p. 4.
106. David Ellwood, *Poor Support* (New York: Basic Books, 1988), p. 153.
107. Judith M. Gueron, "Statement by the President," *Manpower Demonstration Research Corporation, 1991 Annual Report* (New York: MDRC, 1991), p. 2.
108. Daniel Friedlander and Gary Burtless, *Five Years After* (New York: Russell Sage Foundation, 1995), Chap. 1, pp. 4–25.
109. Ibid., p. 17.
110. Roberta Spalter-Roth, Beverly Burr, Heidi Hartmann, and Lois Shaw, *Welfare that Works: The Working Lives of AFDC Recipients* (Washington, DC: Institute for Women's Policy Research, 1995), p. 18.
111. LaDonna Pavetti, "Questions and Answers on Welfare Dynamics," (Washington, DC: Urban Institute, 1995).
112. Friedlander, *Five Years After*, p. 27.
113. Ibid., p. 28.
114. Michael Lipsky, *Street-level Bureaucracy* (New York: Russell Sage Foundation, 1980).
115. Center on Social Policy and the Law, "Living at the Bottom: An Analysis of AFDC Benefit Levels" (Washington, DC: Center on Social Policy and the Law, July 1993).
116. Ibid.
117. Ellwood, "Welfare Reform as I Knew It," p. 28.
118. Results quoted in David A. Super, Sharon Parrott, Susan Steinmetz, and Cindy Mann, "The New Welfare Law"(Washington, DC: Center on Budget and Policy Priorities, August 13, 1996).
119. Nina Bernstein, "Giant Companies Entering Race to Run State Welfare Programs," *The New York Times* (September 15, 1996), p. 1.
120. Polly Ross Hughes, "Stakes are High as State Rushes to Privatize System," *Houston Chronicle* (October 29, 1996), pp. 1A and 10A.
121. Ibid.
122. Judith Havemann, "Welfare Reform Leader Makes Corporate Move," *The Washington Post* (September 17, 1996), p. B6.
123. Ibid.
124. Quoted in Bernstein, "Giant Companies Entering Race to Run State Welfare Programs," p. 1.
125. Ibid.
126. Quoted in Ibid., p. 10A.
127. Personal discussion at a conference on welfare reform, the Jerome Levy Economics Institute, Bard College, Annandale-on-Hudson, New York, July 12, 1996.
128. Marvin Olasky, "Beyond the Stingy Welfare State," *Policy Review* (Fall 1990), p. 14.
129. Robert Pear, "Giuliani Battles Congress on Welfare Bill," *The New York Times* (July 27, 1996), p. A7.
130. William Claiborne, "Welfare Limits Could Cost California $7 Billion in Aid," *Washington Post* (October 23, 1995), p. C9.
131. "Personal Responsibility and Work Opportunity Reconciliation Act of 1996," (Washington, DC: National Association of Social Workers, 1996).
132. Richard J. Estes. *The Social Progress of Nations* (New York: Praeger, 1984), p. 109.

CHAPTER 12

The American Health Care System

This chapter examines the American health care system—specifically, the organization of medical services, key governmental health programs such as Medicare and Medicaid, the crisis in health care, including attempts to curb health care costs, the large numbers of uninsured people, the impact of the American Medical Association on health care, the growing role of managed care, and the ramifications of AIDS on the health care system. In addition, the chapter examines various health care proposals designed to ameliorate the problems in American health care. Finally, the chapter examines how medical services are organized in Great Britain, Israel, and Canada.

American health care is marked by several contradictions. While the vast majority of Americans have easy access to a wide range of health care services through employment-based or public insurance programs, 40.6 million people (15.4 percent of the population) are totally without coverage. The rate for poor people without health care coverage is 30.2 percent, double that for the general population.[1] Thus, while uninsured people *may* be admitted to a hospital emergency room if they are in acute crisis (by way of legal prohibitions against turning them away), in less life-threatening situations they may not be so lucky. A chronic ear infection in a child may go untreated in a rural area that has no free clinics, with the child suffering pain and possibly permanent hearing loss. A pregnant woman may not get prenatal care in a county that lacks a public health clinic, thereby giving birth to a low birth-weight baby. A homeless man may be turned away if he seeks a preventive checkup or treatment for a cough or other "noncritical" illness. Approximately one million Americans seeking health care are turned away each year because they cannot pay, and millions more forgo preventive services.[2] This situation exists even though every major city has at least one major medical center with an annual budget of $100 to $200 million.[3]

THE ORGANIZATION OF MEDICAL SERVICES

Most health care costs in the United States are paid for by private insurers, public plans, and the direct public provision of health care. Only about 25 percent of health care costs are paid for directly by consumers. The dominant form of health care coverage in the United States is private insurance, which covers about 80 percent of the population (two-thirds are covered by employer-based plans). Many elderly people use private health insurance plans to supplement the coverage offered by Medicare. Medical services in the United States is made up of five major components:

1. Physicians in solo practice. This is typically the traditional physician who may employ a nurse

and receptionist. This form of medical organization is increasingly becoming rare in the era of group practices and managed care.

2. Group outpatient settings, including groups of physicians sharing facilities. This setting is becoming more common as physicians are forced to pool resources such as capital, equipment, office staff, and so forth in order to compete in an increasingly difficult health care marketplace. Group outpatient settings may also include HMOs (health maintenance organizations), physicians in industrial EAP (Employee Assistance Plan) settings, or doctors operating under university auspices. During the past few decades, physicians have increasingly worked in group practices or other organized settings. In 1984 this segment accounted for about half of all patient-physician services).[4] The federal government has strongly supported the development of HMOs.
3. Hospitals—private, nonprofit, or public.
4. Public health services delivered on the state, local, regional, national, or international level. This includes health counseling, family planning, prenatal and postnatal care, school health services, disease prevention and control, immunization, referral agencies, STD (sexually transmitted diseases) services, environmental sanitation, health education, and maintenance of indexes on births, deaths, and communicable diseases. Government-sponsored health services include the Veterans Administration Hospitals (the largest network of hospitals in America); Community and Migrant Health Centers; services provided under Title V, Maternal and Child Health Block Grant; and the Title X Family Planning Program.
5. Sundry and corollary health services. This includes home health services, physical rehabilitation, group homes, nursing homes, and so forth.

THE MAJOR PUBLIC HEALTH CARE PROGRAMS: MEDICARE AND MEDICAID

Health care spending is the fastest-growing component of the federal budget. Overall, health care spending accounts for at least 14 percent of total governmental expenditures at the state and federal levels. Eighteen percent of the population are covered by Medicare and Medicaid, which accounts for 7 about percent of all health care provided in the United States.[5]

Medicare

Medicare, Public Law 89–79, was added to the Social Security Act on July 30, 1965. This program was designed to provide prepaid hospital insurance for the aged, as well as voluntary medical insurance. Medicare is composed of two parts: compulsory Hospital Insurance (HI), known as Part A; and Supplemental Medical Insurance (SMI), known as Part B. After two years, people under age 65 who receive disability benefits are eligible for Part B.

Part A is a compulsory hospital insurance (it also includes some nursing home care) plan for the aged, with the premiums coming out of a payroll tax that is part of the Social Security deductions. Most Americans 65 or older are automatically entitled to Part A. Medicare Part A covers a portion of the costs of inpatient hospital care, home health care and 100 days in a skilled nursing facility. Benefits are provided at no premium cost to the beneficiary; however, they do involve deductibles and copayment. Medicare generally pays 80 percent of the cost of goods and services, leaving a 20 percent copayment for beneficiaries.

Part B is a voluntary supplemental medical insurance plan for any senior who is eligible for Part A benefits. An estimated 96 percent of senior enrollees in Part A also enroll in Part B. Each enrollee pays a monthly Part B premium ($46.10 per person in 1996). This plan covers a portion of physician services, outpatient hospital services, lab and diagnostic costs, and medical supplies including durable medical equipment. Like Part A, Part B also involves a deductible and a copayment. Medicare reimbursement to health care providers is subject to maximum rate of payment by level of service. The relatively modest costs of SMI are paid for by the beneficiary; the remainder is subsidized by general tax revenues. The SMI premium is paid by the federal government only if the beneficiary is on public assistance. When Medicare was created in 1965, premiums paid by the elderly covered 50 percent of Part B program costs; today, premiums cover only 25 percent. Despite the umbrella provided by Parts A and B, Medicare contains extensive gaps in coverage. For example, Medicare does not cover long-term custodial nursing home care, most dental care, private-duty nurses, eyeglasses, eye exams, most prescription drugs, routine physical exams, and hearing tests and devices. This has led many elderly recipients to purchase supplemental private health insurance policies to cover the gaps in Medicare.

With an enrollment of 37 million and costing almost $200 billion a year, Medicare costs have risen at an average of 10 percent yearly since the 1970s. Total Medicare spending more than doubled from 1984 to 1996. In 1970, Medicare spending represented less than 1 percent of the GDP, by 1994 it had increased to 2.7 percent. In fact, expenditures under Part A are growing so rapidly that the Social Security trust fund that pays hospital bills for the elderly and disabled is expected to be depleted by 2000 and run a $53 billion deficit in 2001 (see Figure 12.1.). The Medicare program is expected to experience even greater hardships when the baby boom generation begins retiring around 2010.[6] Both political parties clearly recognize the need for Medicare reform.

Medicaid

Before 1965, medical care for those who could not afford to pay for it was primarily a responsibility of charitable institutions and state and local governments. In 1950 the federal government authorized states to use federal/state funds under the Social Security Act of 1935 to provide medical care for the indigent. By 1957, the Kerr-Mills Act provided for a federal/state matching program to provide health care for the elderly and the poor. However, Kerr-Mills was not mandatory, and many states chose not to participate. Designed as a compromise to ward off more far-reaching health policies, President Lyndon Johnson signed the Medicaid and Medicare programs into law in 1965.[7] Replacing all previous governmental health programs, Medicaid became the largest public assistance program in the nation, covering about 13 percent of the population, including more than 15 percent of all children. In 1996, Medicaid served more than 35 million people at a total federal/state cost of $166 billion. Expenditures on Medicaid grew by nearly 700 percent from 1980 ($25.7 billion) to 1993 ($166 billion).[8]

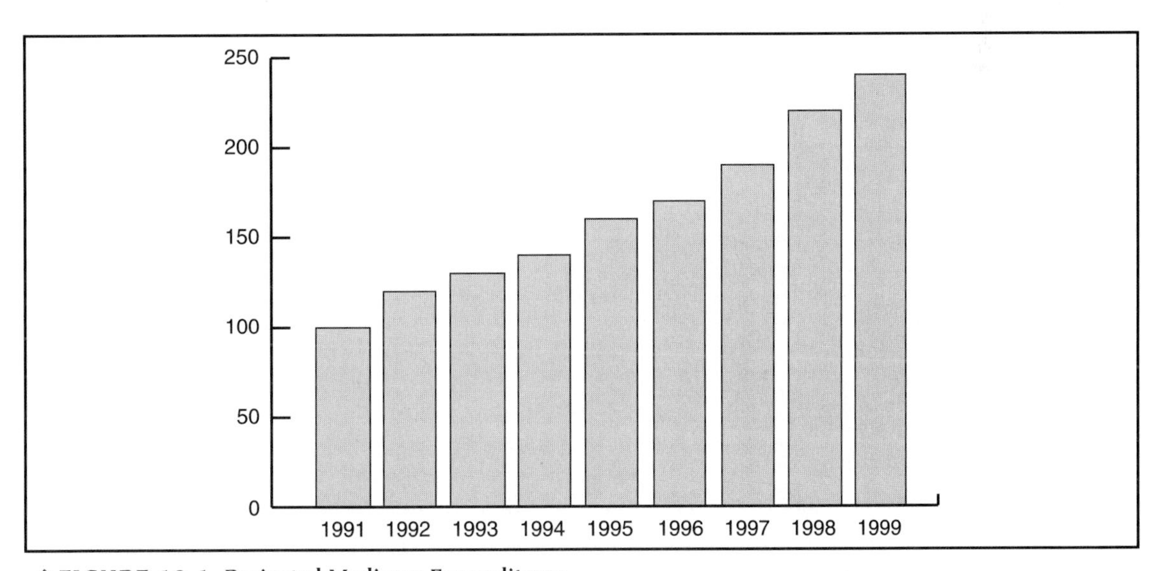

◆ **FIGURE 12.1 Projected Medicare Expenditures**

Source: Alex F. Brown and Sons, Inc. *Medicare: Where Do We Go From Here?* Baltimore, MD, February 16, 1996.

Medicaid is a means-tested public assistance program. Eligible persons receive services from physicians who accept Medicaid patients (in many places a minority of the physicians) and other health care providers. These providers are then reimbursed by the federal government on a per-patient basis. Medicaid is also a federal/state program. States determine eligibility within broad federal guidelines. As such, states make many of the key decisions as to where to set income eligibility limits, which groups to cover, what services to cover, and how much to pay for these services. In general, Medicaid serves the following groups: (1) all families on public assistance; (2) first-time pregnant women if they would qualify for TANF upon the birth of their child; (3) pregnant women in qualifying two-parent families in which the breadwinner is unemployed; (4) children who were born before 1983 and who live in families below the poverty line; and (5) most SSI recipients (see Table 12.1). The majority of states also extend coverage to the medically indigent—those people ineligible for public assistance but who cannot obtain medical care or pay a medical bill. More than half the states extend coverage to families in which the breadwinner is receiving unemployment compensation.

Because Medicaid is funded by federal/state matching funds (on average states pay 43 percent of their Medicaid costs), states help to set Medicaid benefit levels. While all states are required to provide inpatient and outpatient hospital care, physicians' services, laboratory and X-ray services, skilled nursing home services for adults, home health care, family planning services and supplies, nurse and midwife services, and early periodic screening for children, they also have the option of further extending Medicaid benefits to include drugs, eyeglasses, inpatient psychiatric care for individuals under age 21 or over age 65, and so forth. In addition, states have broad administrative powers over Medicaid, including the determination of reimbursement rates. As a result, individual states can discourage Medicaid participation by establishing low reimbursement rates and low state-defined income standards.

States may also restrict the content, scope, and duration of various services. For example, the state of Oregon received a Medicaid waiver from the Clinton administration that allowed the state to move away from the goal of providing all possible health services to a limited number of Medicaid recipients. Instead, Oregon opted to provide coverage to a greater number of persons by establishing a list of medical priorities and then allocating a specific level of dollars according to that priority list. Other care was not provided under the Oregon Medicaid

◆TABLE 12.1
Medicaid Recipients by Category, 1972–1993, Selected Years
(In thousands)

					Families With Dependent Children	
Year	*Total*	*Age 65 or Older*	*Blindness*	*Total Disability*	*Children*	*Other*
1972	17,606	3,318	108	1,625	7,841	1,576
1975	22,013	3,643	106	2,355	9,598	1,800
1977	22,831	3,636	92	2,710	9,651	1,959
1980	21,605	3,440	92	2,819	9,333	1,499
1982	21,603	3,240	84	2,806	9,563	1,434
1984	21,365	3,165	80	2,870	9,771	1,185
1990	25,255	3,202	83	3,635	11,220	990
1993	33,432	3,863	84	4,932	16,285	642

Sources: Social Security Administration, *Social Security Bulletin, Annual Statistical Supplement, 1984–85* (Baltimore, MD: Social Security Administration, 1986), pp. 219–22; and Committee on Ways and Means, U.S. House of Representatives, *Overview of Entitlement Programs, 1992 Green Book* (Washington, DC: U.S. Government Printing Office, 1992), p. 1653.

plan.[9] Under Oregon's plan, 120,000 more people were covered under Medicaid (almost everyone under the poverty line), but certain procedures were disallowed, including experimental forms of cancer and AIDS treatment. Other states have modified Medicaid by placing a limit on the number of days of hospital care a patient can receive or by limiting the number of physician visits covered in a year. States are also free to impose limited copayments for some Medicaid services.[10]

Federal law allows states to provide Medicaid benefits to poor children and pregnant women who are ineligible for public assistance. One such option involves the establishment of a Medically Needy component under the state Medicaid program. Under this option, a family whose countable income is greater than the state's Medicaid income eligibility limits but whose medical expenses are so large that the remaining income places the family below the poverty line is eligible for Medicaid. The Medically Needy component allows states to set Medicaid income limits that are up to one-third higher than the state's maximum TANF benefit. This option is particularly important for self-sufficient families who face a medical catastrophe that will deplete their economic resources. Families whose health insurance limits are exhausted or who have no insurance may also be eligible. Thirty-six states had adopted a Medically Needy program by 1988.[11]

Medicaid was designed as a federal/state program to pay for health care for low-income and disabled citizens. Two-thirds of Medicaid recipients are low-income people who are covered for doctor's visits and hospital stays. Medicaid also pays for one-third of all births, which costs about $1,300 per person annually. Despite this, the greatest outlay of Medicaid funds goes to the elderly. In 1995, Medicaid paid for more than two-thirds of all people in nursing home (excluding care for the mentally retarded), with an average annual cost of $18,000 per person.[12] As a result, close to three-fifths of all nursing home expenditures are paid for by the federal government. Not surprisingly, the growth of the nursing home industry parallels the creation of Medicaid. From 1965 (the year Medicaid was created) to 1970, the number of nursing home residents rose by 18 percent. From 1970 to 1975 that number rose another 17 percent; from 1975 to 1980, 14 percent; and from 1980 to 1985, about 12 percent. Because four-fifths of nursing homes are for-profit facilities, Medicaid functions as a de facto subsidy for the nursing home industry.

Despite federal guidelines, four important gaps exist in Medicaid coverage: (1) the low eligibility limits set for Medicaid; (2) the refusal of many states to adopt most or all of the Medicaid options; (3) the gaps in coverage for the elderly and disabled; and (4) the general ineligibility of single poor persons and childless couples for Medicaid unless they are elderly or disabled. The Children's Defense Fund observed that there was no increase in the percentage of pregnant women receiving early prenatal care from 1986 to 1991. The Robert Wood Johnson Foundation noted that Medicaid reached 19 percent fewer poor and near-poor families in 1986 than it did in 1976.[13] While Medicaid covered 12 percent of the population in 1994, only 46 percent of those with incomes below the poverty line were covered.[14] Of those eligible, children up to age 5 are the most likely to be covered (64 percent), while young adults age 11–18 are the least likely (52.4 percent).[15]

Despite these shortcomings, the Medicaid program has led to important gains in the nation's health. In 1963, 54 percent of the poor did not see a physician. In that same year, only 63 percent of pregnant women received prenatal care; by 1976 that number had increased to 76 percent. Between 1964 and 1975, the use of physicians' services by poor children increased 74 percent. In part, this increased health care utilization resulted in a 49 percent drop in infant mortality between 1965 and 1988. For African American infants, the drop in mortality was even sharper: Infant mortality dropped by only 5 percent in the 15 years before Medicaid, but by 49 percent in the 15 years after the program began. Ongoing preventive care also cut program costs for Medicaid-eligible children by 10 percent.[16] As such, Medicaid is one of the most important governmental health programs in the United States. In 1986,

Medicaid payments represented 55 cents of every public health dollar spent on children; 26 cents out of every dollar (public or private) spent on hospitalization for children under age six; 30 cents of every dollar spent on delivery services for pregnant teens; and 10 cents out of every dollar spent on ambulatory pediatric services.[17]

Despite these successes, Medicaid has been under constant attack by Congress, most presidential administrations, and a range of state governments. Cuts in federal funds and rule changes has led many states to reduce eligibility and to provide fewer services. For example, roughly 800 Medicaid-related cost-containment measures were adopted in the vast majority of states between 1984 and 1988. These measures included limiting the number of hospital days and reimbursable visits to physicians, reducing or freezing Medicaid provider rates, imposing copayments and deductibles, requiring preadmission screening, and mandating second opinions for elective surgery.[18]

THE HEALTH CARE CRISIS

Health care in America is plagued with problems that include medical eroding coverage, rising costs, cost shifting, chaos, and nervous citizens. The following section explores some parameters of the health care crisis, including health care spending and cost efficiency, the effectiveness of the American health care system, attempts at cost cutting, the growing importance of managed care, and the effect of AIDS on the health care budget.

Health Care Expenditures

The United States has the highest per capita medical care expenditures in the world. In 1993, the United States spent 14.1 percent of its gross domestic product (GDP) on health care. As such, health care in the United States costs 40 percent more than in any other industrialized nation.[19] The United States also provides the least social protection against health care costs of all the major industrialized nations; in other words, the United States has the smallest percentage of people covered under publicly subsidized health care programs. (See Table 12.2.) Furthermore, the United States provides the least social protection against ambulatory medical care costs, and it covers only 25 percent of the population for outpatient physician visits compared with between 90 and 100 percent for most other nations. Finally, social protection against the cost of medical goods (pharmaceuticals) is provided to only 10 percent of the U.S. population, again a low figure when compared with the 90 to 100 percent for other industrialized nations.[20] Hence, despite large U.S. health care expenditures, the net benefit appears questionable. The life expectancy for U.S. males and females is in the midrange of many industrial nations (see Table 12.2). In short, Americans are neither healthier nor do they live longer than in similar industrial nations where health care spending is lower.[21]

Accounting for the enormous costs of the U.S. health care system is problematic. Some policy analysts attribute these high costs to:

- The increasing costs of malpractice suits against health care providers are passed along directly to consumers by higher medical costs and indirectly through the practice of defensive medicine. Fearful of malpractice suits, some physicians behave overcautiously and order the use of overly aggressive diagnostic and treatment methods. Some policy analysts estimate that as much as 30 percent of current health care costs goes toward services that are not needed, much of this under the guise of defensive medicine.[22] The Congressional Budget Office put the cost of practicing defensive medicine at 5 percent of total health care spending, while the American Medical Association has estimated that it may account for as much as 14 percent.[23] In 1991, the cost of practicing defensive medicine was conservatively estimated at $25 billion. Nevertheless, annual malpractice insurance premiums for general surgeons rose from $9,900 in 1982 to $22,500 in 1991. In 1991, malpractice insurance for physicians cost $5.1 billion.[24]

◆ TABLE 12.2
International Comparison of Health Care: Per Capita Health Care Expenditures, Health Care Expenditures as a Percentage of Gross Domestic Product (GDP), the Percentage of Health Care Expenditures Covered by a Public Insurance Scheme, and Life Expectancy at Birth, Selected Countries, 1993.

Country	*Per Capita Expenditure*	*Percentage of GDP*	*Percentage Covered by Public Insurance*	*Life Expectancy at Birth 1980*	
				Females	*Males*
Australia	US $1,493	8.5%	67.7%	78.0	70.9
Austria	1,777	9.3	66.2	76.1	69.0
Belgium	1,601	8.3	88.9	75.5	69.8
Canada	1,971	10.2	71.9	79.0	71.0
Denmark	1,296	6.7	82.6	77.6	71.4
Finland	1,363	8.8	79.3	77.6	69.2
France	1,835	9.8	74.4	78.3	70.1
Germany	1,815	8.6	70.2	76.5	69.7
Ireland	922	6.7	76.7	75.0	69.5
Italy	1,523	8.5	73.1	77.4	70.4
Japan	1,495	7.3	71.8	79.3	73.7
Norway	1,592	8.2	93.3	79.0	72.2
Spain	972	7.3	78.6	78.0	71.5
Sweden	1,266	7.5	82.9	78.9	72.6
Switzerland	2,283	9.9	69.0	79.1	72.4
United Kingdom	1,213	7.1	83.0	75.9	70.2
United States	3,299	14.1	43.9	76.7	69.6
OECD average	1,537	8.3	75.4	NA	NA

Source: Table adapted from Committee on Ways and Means, U.S. House of Representatives, *1996 Green Book* (Washington, DC: US GPO, 1996), p. 1037; and OECD, *Measuring Health Care, 1960–1983* (Paris: Organization for Economic Cooperation and Development, 1985), p. 131.

- While the United States leads the world in the development and use of medical technology, many of these advances have come at a high price. Between 1980 and 1991, the number of coronary bypass operations for men increased from 108,000 to 206,000; diagnostic ultrasounds for women rose from 114,000 to 652,000; and the use of CAT scans increased from 306,000 to more than 1.4 million.[25] Overall, treatment is now available for some diseases that were formerly untreatable, albeit at a high price. In addition, some technologies are introduced before being sufficiently tested to determine their cost effectiveness and superiority to existing technologies.
- The administrative costs involved in processing millions of insurance claims also adds to rising health care expenditures. It is estimated that as much as 25 percent of every health care dollar goes for managing the mountains of paperwork required to run the system.[26] Despite the paperwork, the U.S. General Accounting Office estimated that in 1991 fraud cost $70 billion, or 10 percent every health care dollar.
- The treatment of people with AIDS has led to increasing fiscal strains on the health care system.[27] While spending on HIV and AIDS victims has grown faster than all other health care spending, it is still relatively small. Overall expenditures on HIV-positive individuals increased from 1.3 to 1.4 percent of the total health care budget between 1992 and 1995.[28]
- Increased longevity has led to growing numbers of elderly people. Many of these elderly have chronic diseases that are often expensive to treat. While it is easy to blame rising health care

costs on the elderly, the Congressional Budget Office maintains that increases in the aged population accounted for only 5 percent of the increase in per capita health care spending between 1965 and 1990. Increases in the numbers of elderly are expected to add only modestly to the growth of health care spending throughout the 1990s.

The cost of providing health care has risen dramatically in the past 25 years. In constant dollars, per capita health care expenditures were $706 in 1960; by 1994, that amount had risen to $3,510. Adjusting for inflation, health care expenditures rose from $194 billion in 1965 (the year prior to the enactment of Medicaid and Medicare) to $950 billion in 1994. Put another way, health care expenditures rose from 5.1 percent of the GDP in 1960 to 13.7 percent in 1994.[29] In comparison, education was only 7.3 percent of the GNP in 1992 and military spending had actually decreased to less than 6 percent.[30] Moreover, the costs of providing health care has risen faster than the rate of inflation. From 1980 to 1992 per capita expenditures on health care were approximately 5 points above the rate of inflation. Beginning in 1992, the growth in health care expenditures decelerated somewhat, registering less than 3 points above the rate of inflation,[31] but even if health-related expenditures continue to decline, the United States will spend at least 18 percent of its GNP on health care by the year 2005.[32] In other words, without wide-ranging health care reform, health care spending is expected to reach $1.7 trillion by the year 2000.[33] Figure 12.2 illustrates the phenomenal growth in health care expenditures.

When health care expenditures are broken down (see Figure 12.3), the largest share goes to hospitals; in 1994 hospital care alone cost $338.5 billion.[34] Increases in the cost of hospital care have been a key factor in driving up health care costs. In 1965 the average daily hospital room charge was $41; by 1994 it had risen to $1,127. In 1965 the average cost per hospital stay was $315; by 1994 the cost had risen to $6,427.[35] Without comprehensive health care reform, health care

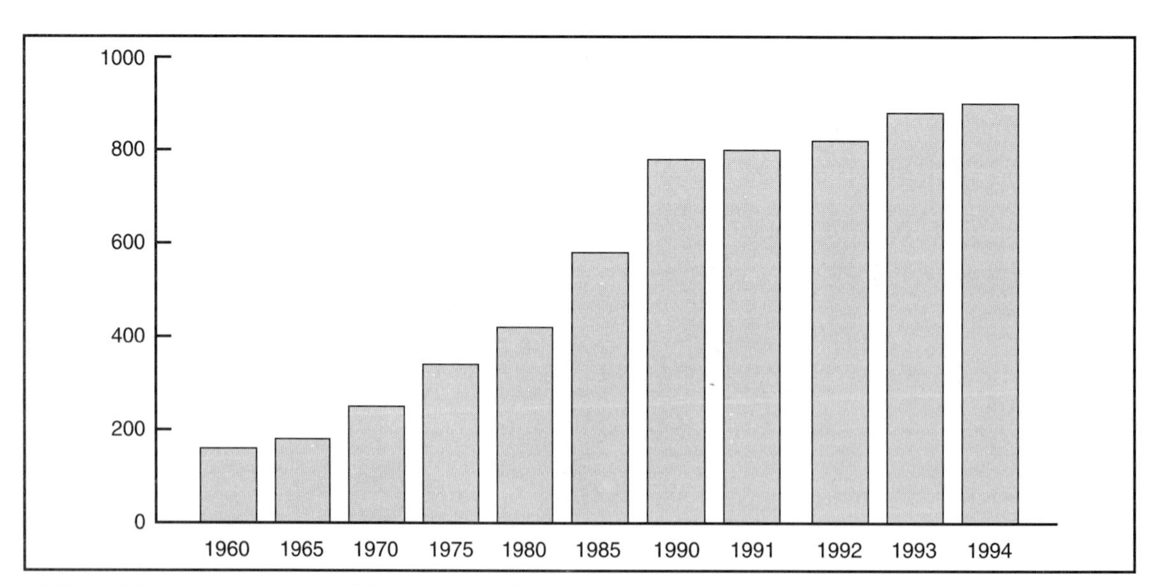

◆ **FIGURE 12.2 National Health Care Expenditures in Constant 1994 Dollars Selected Years, 1960–1994 (Dollar Amounts in Billions)**

Source: Figure Adapted from U.S. House of Representatives, Committee on Ways and Means, *1996 Green Book* (Washington, DC: US GPO, 1996), P. 995.

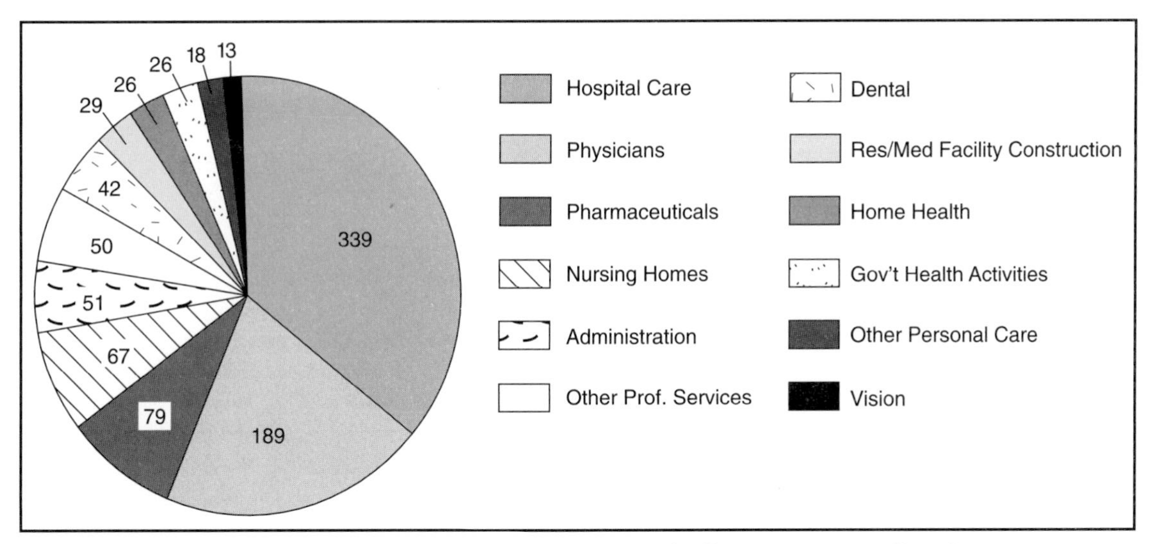

◆ **FIGURE 12.3 National Health Cared Expenditures, 1994 (Dollar Amounts in Billions)**
Source: Figure Adapted from U.S. House of Representatives, Committee on Ways and Means, *1996 Green Book* (Washington, DC: US GPO, 1996), p. 994.

expenditures are expected to reach almost $2 trillion by 2005.[36]

Hospital Costs and Physicians' Salaries

Hospital costs account for 36 percent of all health care expenditures. The total expenses of these hospitals reached $308 billion in 1995. After growing at a rate of 10 percent a year in the 1980s, per diem hospital costs grew more slowly in 1994 and 1995 than in any two years since the data has been compiled. The increased costs per case grew by only 1.9 percent a year in 1994 and 1995, compared with 14 percent a year during the period from 1975 to 1982. This deceleration of hospital costs is explained by several factors, including a modest increase in admissions rates between 1992 and 1995, shortened hospital stays, a lower inpatient hospital occupancy rate, a downsizing of hospital personnel, and lower rates of general inflation.[37]

Apart from hospital care, the second largest health care expenditure is for physicians' services, which accounted for approximately 20 percent of all health care costs, totaling almost $190 billion in 1994. Until recently, increases in physicians' incomes have grown alongside the general increases in medical costs. From 1984 to 1994, the income of physicians rose by 5 percent annually, with inflation and population growth accounting for only 40 percent of this increase.[38] By 1993 the average medical doctor had a yearly net income (before taxes) of $189,300. However, by 1994 the average income of physicians began to decline, the first decrease ever recorded by the AMA. After expenses (but before taxes) the average physician's income in 1994 was $182,400, a 3.6 percent decrease from 1993. Table 12.3. lists physicians' salaries by specialities in 1994 and 1984, and examines the percent change from 1993 to 1994.

Physician organizations argue that high salaries are necessary to repay the high debts accrued by medical students. They point out that the average medical school debt was $55,859 in 1993. The median cost of a four-year private medical school for the class of 1995 was $79,160. At public institutions, the total cost of medical education in 1993 was $27,500 for in-state students and $65,572 for out-of-state students.[39] The problem of high physician salaries is aggravated by the growth in the number of expensive medical specialists. For example, in 1994 only 34 percent of the nation's physicians were in primary care specialities (e.g., family practice, internal medicine, obstetrics/gynecology,

◆ **TABLE 12.3**
Physicians' Average Net Income After Expenses & Before Taxes, 1984 and 1994
(Salaries in Thousands)

Category	1984 Salary	1993 Salary	1994 Salary	Salary Change 1993–4 (in percent)
All physicians	$108.4	$189.3	182.4	–3.6
Speciality:				
General/family practice	71.1	116.8	121.8	3.9
Internal Medicine	103.2	180.8	174.9	–3.3
Surgery	151.8	262.7	255.2	–2.9
Pediatrics	74.5	135.4	126.2	–6.8
OB/GYN	116.2	221.9	200.4	–9.6
Radiology	139.8	259.8	237.4	–8.6
Psychiatry	85.5	131.3	128.5	–2.1
Anesthesiology	145.4	224.1	218.1	–2.7
Employment Status:				
Self-employed	118.6	218.0	210.2	–3.6
Employee	80.4	150.7	148.2	–1.7

Source: American Medical Association, *Physician Marketplace Statistics* (Chicago: AMA, 1995); and American Medical Association, *Socioeconomic Characteristics of Medical Practice* (Chicago: AMA, 1995)

and pediatrics). Roughly 65 percent of current medical school graduates are specialists, which is a reversal of the ratio that existed 30 years ago.[40] Not unexpectedly, the average doctor visit went from $30 in 1986 to $46 in 1992.[41]

The high costs of prescription medication is another engine driving up health care costs. Older Americans unprotected by Medicaid spend 10 percent of their total income on prescription drugs. Many of these people are exposed to financial catastrophe as a result of highly inflated drug prices. In fact, the drug manufacturers of the top 20 drugs have increase their profits at 5 times the average of the Fortune 500 companies.[42] In short, while health care costs almost doubled in the last decade, prescription drug prices increased by a huge 152 percent.[43]

Cutting Health Care Costs

The substantial rise in health care costs during the past three decades has put increasing pressure on federal and state governments to subsidize more of the nation's health care budget, as shown in Table 12.4. From 1960 to 1994, the percentage of health care costs paid for by federal and state governments rose from 22 to 51 percent. In 1994, federal/state governments spent approximately $362 billion on health care.[44] Partly as a result of federal spending, the proportion of personal health care expenditures paid for directly by consumers decreased from 55 percent in 1960 to 21 percent in 1994. By 1994 federal/state governments had become the single largest payer of medical bills, paying for some 44 percent of health care expenditures, compared with 32 percent for private insurance companies.[45]

There are two aspects to cutting health care costs, both of which are interconnected. The first involves cutting costs for governmental health care programs; the second involves lowering overall medical costs.

Medicare grew from 20 million enrollees in 1968 to 37 million by 1994. With it, Medicare's budget rose from $15.8 billion in 1975 to $162 billion in 1994. Both the scope and costs of Medicare have grown since its inception: In 1967, Medicare accounted for 2 percent of the federal budget; by 1994 it consumed 10 percent. By 1993, the federal government was paying almost 30 percent of all hospital costs. This fiscal burden led the federal government to seek alternative ways to lower hospital costs, including the Diagnostic Related Group system (DRG). In 1983 Congress enacted the DRG form of medical payment. Although earlier Medicare rules had restricted the fees hospitals could charge, the government generally reimbursed them for the entire bill. This style of reimbursement was called retrospective (after-the-fact) payment. By contrast, DRGs are a form of prospective (before-the-fact) payment; the federal government specifies in advance what it will pay for the treatment of 468 classified illness- or diagnosis-related groups.[46]

Developed by health researchers at the Yale–New Haven Hospital, the DRG system was designed to enforce economy by defining expected lengths of hospital stays. This system—which only applies to the HI part of Medicare—provides a treatment and diagnostic classification scheme, using the patient's medical diagnosis, prescribed treatment, and age as a means for categorizing and defining hospital services. In other words, the DRG system determines the length of a typical patient's hospital stay and reimburses hospitals only for that period of time. (Exceptions to the DRG classification system are made for long hospital stays, certain kinds of hospital facilities, hospitals that are the only facility in a community, and hospitals that serve large numbers of poor people.) Additional costs beyond the DRG allotment must be borne by the hospital. Conversely, if a patient requires less hospitalization than the maximum DRG allocation, the difference is kept by the hospital. Hospitals may not charge the patient more than the DRG allotment. Hence, patients not yet ready for discharge (e.g., those patients who do not have appropriate aftercare services available) may be discharged—a situation that can result in patient dumping.

Proponents of DRGs argue that hospital costs must be curbed and that there is no painless way to accomplish this. Supporters contend that because DRGs require physicians to be designated as the primary professional responsible for cost containment, they are relieved of some of the financial incentives for ordering unnecessary hospital admissions and longer stays. In addition, there is less incentive for physicians to overuse medical tests, ancillary services, surgery, and so forth. Often removed from the economics of cost containment, physicians are forced to acknowledge that "maximum efficiency

◆ TABLE 12.4
Sources of Payment for Personal Health Care in Selected Years, 1929–1994
(In percentages)

				Governmental		
Year	*Direct Payment*	*Private Health Insurance*	*Philanthropy and Industry*	*Total*	*Federal*	*State and Local*
1929	88.4	NA	2.6	9.0	2.7	6.3
1940	81.3	NA	2.6	16.1	4.1	12.0
1950	65.5	9.1	2.9	22.4	10.4	12.0
1960	54.9	21.1	2.3	21.8	9.3	12.5
1965	51.6	24.2	2.2	22.0	10.1	11.9
1970	40.5	23.4	1.7	34.3	22.2	12.1
1975	32.5	26.7	1.3	39.5	26.8	12.7
1980	28.7	30.7	1.2	39.4	28.4	10.9
1982	27.8	31.4	1.2	39.6	29.3	10.3
1984	28.8	30.7	1.2	39.3	29.5	9.8
1986	28.7	30.4	1.2	39.4	30.2	9.4
1990	24.1	32.8	3.5	39.5	29.0	10.6
1994	21.0	32.1	3.4	43.5	33.7	9.8

Sources: Table adapted from U.S. Department of Health and Human Services, *Health, United States–1987*. DHHS Pub. No. (PHS) 88–1232, Table 102 (Washington, DC: U.S. Government Printing Office, 1988), p. 158; and Committee on Ways and Means, U.S. House of Representatives, *1996 Green Book* (Washington, DC: US GPO, 1996), p. 998.

leads to maximum reimbursement in the DRG system."[47] On the other hand, critics argue that patient care suffers when it is subordinated to the economies imposed by the DRG system. Erring on the side of cost containment, doctors often curtail necessary medical tests and ancillary services. Moreover, the DRG system supports the dominance of the medical model in that it emphasizes the physiological causes of disease at the expense of the psychological correlates of health and illness. The second strategy to cut costs in the public and private health care market is managed care.

The Growing Influence of Managed Care

Managed care is a term that is used extensively in reference to health care. Schmolling, Youkeles, and Burger define *managed care* as "an umbrella for health care insurance systems that contract with a network of hospitals, clinics, and doctors who agree to accept fees for each service of flat payments per patient. The advantage to providers is that they are given a ready source of referrals."[48] The primary purpose of managed care is to curb escalating health care costs.

Managed care plans can take several different forms. First, they can take the form of Preferred Provider Organizations (PPOs), which are groups of doctors and hospitals that provide health care services at a fixed rate. The enrollee is given a list of providers from which they can choose a primary physician. Typically, the enrollee pays a modest copayment. The second is a Point-of-Service (POS) plan that also includes a list of health care providers. However, patients may seek care outside of the network if they are willing to pay a higher share of the cost. This has become an increasingly popular option because it affords patients more choice than the PPO or Health Maintenance Organization (HMO) plans.[49] The third option is an HMO that typically provides comprehensive health care for enrolled members. Members usually pay a fixed fee and are entitled to free (or heavily subsidized) physician and hospital care. Under the Health Maintenance Organization Act passed in 1973, an HMO must have four characteristics: (1) an organized system for providing health care in a geographic area, (2) a set of basic and supplemental medical services, (3) a voluntarily enrolled group of people, and (4) a community rating. Some HMOs have their own clinics, while others rely on network of independent doctors. Care in an HMO is coordinated by a primary care physician, who functions as a gatekeeper for restricting access to physician specialists.[50]

Proponents of managed care argue that the system has effectively lowered health care costs while not reducing the quality of health care services. Advocates maintain that managed care encourages more-efficient and less-expensive medical care and that it can stress prevention over treatment. Because doctors reimbursed by managed care operations have little incentive to "overtreat" patients and recommend unnecessary medical care, the health care system is expected to be more efficient. On the first point, there is evidence to strongly suggest that managed care systems have indeed lowered health care costs. For example:

- The per capita growth in health care expenditures was 2.7 percent in 1994, dropping from an average of 5 percent throughout the 1980s and 1990s. Moreover, the per capita national expenditure on health care was $3,510 in 1994, only $100 more than in 1993 and half the increase of $200 from 1992 to 1993.
- Community hospital expenses grew only 2.9 percent in 1994 and 3.2 percent in 1995. This was a two-thirds drop from 9 percent in 1990 and a drop of five times from the 18 percent growth rate in 1981.
- For the first time, hospital costs per case in 1994 rose more slowly than the rate of inflation.
- The average length of stay in a hospital (5.7 days) dropped 4.2 percent from 1994 to 1995. For those 65 and over, the average length of a hospital stay (7.1 days) dropped by 6.6 percent. Moreover, the occupancy rate of hospitals dropped from 73.7 percent in 1978 to 59.7 percent by 1995.
- After increasing an average of 6.4 percent between 1978 and 1983, hospital employment decreased by 0.5 percent from 1993 to 1995.

- As noted earlier, physicians' salaries dropped on average 3.6 percent from 1993 to 1994 (the first recorded drop in physicians' salaries in the AMA's history).[51] In areas of California where managed care dominates the market, some medical specialists have reported declines of 30 percent in their income over the past two years.[52]

Managed care is clearly having an important impact in shaping American medicine. On average, physicians received 83 percent of their 1992 gross practice incomes from third party (e.g., governmental and private insurers) sources. Of that amount, more than 40 percent came specifically from private managed care operations. In fact, broadly defined private managed plans now cover two-thirds of all privately insured Americans. Jumping on the boat, the federal and many state governments are encouraging (and in some states, requiring) Medicare and Medicaid beneficiaries to join managed care plans. In 1992 there were 96 Medicare HMOs covering 1.6 million members. By 1995, that number had risen to 165 with 2.6 million members.[53]

Not surprisingly, the AMA has taken a position against managed care. AMA Vice President James Todd noted that: "Whoever would have imagined that the noble practice of medicine would be shoved around by cutthroat competition in a rough and tumble marketplace? . . . Physicians want to be treated as professionals, not as commodities, not as medical merchandise to be bought and sold . . . by market traders who are more concerned with profits than patients."[54] Also not surprisingly, managed care's emphasis on primary care may result in a glut of 165,000 specialists by the year 2000.[55]

Critics of managed care operations (including HMOs) maintain that they are plagued with serious problems.[56] For one, managed care operations often make access to specialists difficult for consumers. This is done by pressuring primary physicians not to refer or by limiting specialist care to one or two visits. Some managed care plans are reluctant to cover costly procedures as well as experimental ones, especially those relating to cancer. A portion of managed care plans refuse to pay for medical care gotten while out of state, even if it was required in an emergency. Other enrollees complain that managed care forces them to use only primary care physicians, hospitals, and specialists that are on an approved list, which restricts their freedom of choice. Still other managed care operations do not provide the same level of benefits as Medicare, especially when it comes to home health care, physical therapy, and nursing home care.[57] Critics also note that the presumed administrative advantages of managed care plans has led to greater bureaucratization and impersonality.[58]

The Under- and Uninsured

The American medical system provides good care for much of the upper-middle and upper classes who are protected by adequate health insurance policies. More than 70 percent of Americans are covered by private insurance plans. While a large proportion of Americans receive the best and most advanced medical care in the world, a growing percentage of the population receive little or no health care. Of the 40.5 million people without health care coverage (15.4 percent of the population) in 1995, almost 10 million were children under age 18.[59]

Despite the existence of Medicaid, the poor are the most likely group to have no health insurance. In 1995, 30.2 percent of the poor (11 million) had no health insurance of any kind. According to the Census Bureau, noncoverage is also higher among minorities and women. The noncoverage rate among whites was 14 percent compared to 21 and 33 percent for African Americans and Hispanics, respectively. In 1993 more than 9.5 million women in the United States of childbearing age had no health insurance; 6.8 million of them were in the workforce. Young adults aged 18 to 24 were the least likely to have coverage (28 percent). Of workers between ages 18 and 64, 22 percent of part-time workers had no health insurance coverage. Surprisingly, poor workers had a higher uninsured rate than nonworkers. Almost a quarter of all households with incomes less than $25,000 a year were uninsured in 1995.[60]

Leaving a large proportion of Americans without any form of health insurance affects all of society. For instance, when the uninsured receive medical care, they may not be able to pay for it; this results in uncompensated care, which includes both bad-debt and charity or free care. Hospitals have traditionally offset the costs of uncompensated care by shifting these costs to patients who had private insurance, Medicare, or Medicaid. The American Hospital Association estimated that 6,438 nonprofit and state and local government hospitals provided a total of $14.6 billion worth of uncompensated care in 1988, a rise from $2.8 billion in 1980.[61] Later estimates suggest that cost shifting was valued at $21 billion in 1991.[62] In addition to cost shifting, some hospitals engage in patient dumping, thereby leaving public hospitals (and those with a historical commitment to serve the poor) with the job of providing health care for those unable to pay. The net result is an increased health risk for the uninsured or underinsured.[63]

Inadequate care for those relying on the American health care system is exacerbated by gaps in medical coverage even for those who are fully insured. Gaps in private health insurance may include high co-payments, limits placed on the length of hospital stays, dollar limits on payments to hospitals and physicians, exclusion of certain laboratory tests, refusal to cover office visits and routine health care, noncoverage for mental health services, declaring ineligible individuals who are found to be in poor health when applying for insurance, and a lack of coverage for dental and eye care. Because privately purchased health insurance has become almost unaffordable, the availability of health insurance may be a major factor in an employee's job search or decision to continue in a job.[64] Moreover, employers may be reluctant to hire individuals with high-risk conditions because of the negative effect on their insurance premiums. Lastly, one of the most dramatic gaps is the frequent failure of private health insurance to cover catastrophic medical costs—those costs that could reduce a middle-class family to the status of "medically indigent" within only a few months.

AIDS AND HEALTH CARE

The U.S. health care crisis is aggravated by the AIDS epidemic, which surfaced during the presidency of Ronald Reagan. The Reagan administration initially saw the AIDS problem as being of little consequence. Indeed, expressing public concern for the suffering of homosexuals was a political liability, especially because the Republican Party was actively courting the religious Right, most of whose leaders saw AIDS as a divine punishment for the sin of homosexuality. As a result, the Reagan administration did not make an AIDS-related budget request to Congress until FY 1985, by which time 20,000 Americans had already died from the disease. Furthermore, this budget request came three years after the alarms had sounded and after Congress had already allocated $34 million between 1982 and 1983.[65] Unlike the Reagan and Bush administrations, Clinton was not afraid to talk directly about AIDS. As such, Clinton pushed for full funding for the Ryan White Care Act, created the National Task Force on AIDS Drug Development, strengthened the Office of AIDS Research at the National Institutes of Health, and placed people with HIV/AIDS under the protection of the Americans with Disabilities Act.

The current epidemiological data on AIDS is striking. Through June 1996, 548,102 cases of AIDS in the United States were reported to the Centers for Disease Control (CDC); 343,000 AIDS-related deaths were reported. Another 275,000 persons were reported living with HIV infection (not AIDS). Five states—New York, California, Florida, Texas, and New Jersey account for more than half of the cumulative AIDS cases. Among adults and adolescents with AIDS, three HIV exposure categories account for almost 85 percent of AIDS cases: men who have sex with men (51 percent), injecting drug users (25 percent), and heterosexual contact with a person who is in a high-risk group or who has HIV/AIDS (8 percent). (See Table 12.5) Of the 7,296 reported cases of pediatric AIDS, 30 percent resulted from transmission from mother to child.[66]

Recent CDC data suggest that the overall rate of growth of the AIDS epidemic is slowing. AIDS cases increased at a rate of 5 percent from 1995 to 1996, considerably lower than the higher rates of increase from 1990 to 1992. While the incidence of AIDS is leveling among whites, it is increasing among blacks and Hispanics. The relative stabilizing of AIDS cases is generally attributable to its leveling

◆ TABLE 12.5
U.S. Male and Female Adult/Adolescent Cumulative AIDS Cases by Major Exposure Category and Race/Ethnicity (Major Population Groups), 1996

		White (not Hispanic)		*Black (not Hispanic)*		*Hispanic*
Exposure Category	*Male*	*Female*	*Male*	*Female*	*Male*	*Female*
Men who have sex with men	180,294	NA	55,327	NA	34,906	NA
Injecting drug use	20,664	8,050	51,143	20,745	29,410	7,026
Men who have sex with men and inject drugs	18,670	NA	10,869	NA	5,337	NA
Hemophiliac/ Coagulation disorder	3,259	87	430	47	346	21
Heterosexual contact:	3,234	7,169	8,527	15,054	3,396	7,197
Sex with injecting drug user	1,351	3,162	3,591	7,005	1,167	3,881
Sex with HIV-infected person, risk not specified	1,739	2,415	4,822	6,986	2,152	2,836

Source: Table adapted from Centers for Disease Control, "HIV Surveillance Report," Vol. 8, No. 1, June 1996. Atlanta, GA: Centers for Disease Control, pp. 8–9.

off among men who have sex with men and pediatric AIDS cases. Conversely, there is an upward trend among women who were infected with HIV through sexual contact, principally with drug-using partners.[67] Despite its relative slowing, AIDS has become the second leading cause of death in men of age 25 to 44 and one of the top five causes of death in women of the same age group.[68]

AIDS is maldistributed within racial groupings (see Table 12.5). Of the 548,102 AIDS cases reported in 1996, 237,206 occurred in while males and 143,587 in African American men. Thus, while African American males make up about 6 percent of the total U.S. population, they account for more than 25 percent of AIDS cases. This same overrepresentation occurs in pediatric AIDS cases and among women: African American women face three times the risk of contracting AIDS compared to white women; black children face four times the risk of white children.[69] Of the 7,296 children with AIDS in 1996, 4,201 were black, 1,703 were Hispanic, and 1,314 were white.

The scope of the AIDS problem extends beyond the borders of the United States. Globally, HIV/AIDS is spreading most rapidly in developing countries. The World Health Organization (WHO) estimates that about 20 million people are infected worldwide, of whom at least 4 million have died. The cumulative total could reach 26.6 million by the year 2000. Asian and African countries have been hit the hardest; in South and Southeast Asia, the number of HIV infections rose from 1.5 to 2.5 million from 1993 to 1995.[70] Overall, the estimated number of African adults infected with the HIV virus has surpassed 11 million. The vast majority of these cases are in Sub-Saharan Africa.[71] Moreover, WHO estimates that in many developing countries, more than 60 percent of all new HIV infections occur in people under 25 years of age. Sixty percent of these new cases are females under the age of 21.[72]

The AIDS problem is exacerbated by the fiscal inability of poorer nations to treat AIDS cases adequately. For example, the typical treatment for AIDS in most of Sub-Saharan Africa is bed rest and aspirin. The total budget of Zaire's largest hospital is equivalent to the cost of treating 10 AIDS patients in the United States. Moreover, the U.S. military spent $43 million in 1990 to identify 5,890 infected soldiers, a sum greater than Central Africa's total health budget.[73]

The AIDS epidemic is having a dramatic effect on public policy and society at large. For example, at least 10 percent of the U.S. population is somehow affected by AIDS through contacts with friends, family members, or colleagues. There are also significant costs in treating the AIDS epidemic. Fred Hellinger estimated that in 1991 the average cost of treating an HIV-positive (without AIDS) person was $5,150 per year; the average cost of an AIDS case was $32,000 a year. The lifetime cost of medical care for a person with AIDS was estimated at $85,333 in 1991—the cost of treating all HIV-infected persons was roughly $5.8 billion.[74] While high, these health care costs are not out of line with the costs of treating other serious traumas. For example, the lifetime health care expenses of someone suffering a major heart attack are $66,837; for cancer of the digestive system, $47,542; and for paraplegia resulting from an auto accident, $68,700.[75]

The AIDS epidemic is costly to American society in other ways. Health care economist Anne Scitovsky estimated that in 1991 the U.S. economy absorbed $55 billion in annual losses in productivity due to illness and premature deaths caused by AIDS.[76] These costs are especially high because the incidence of AIDS is greatest in the group that is the most productive, the 20- to 44-year-old age group. AIDS is also having a major impact on health insurance. It is estimated that private insurers paid $15 billion in AIDS-related health and death claims in 1994.[77] As a result, the cost of private health insurance is likely to rise as AIDS-related increases are passed on to employers and policyholders.

AIDS has other important implications for public policy. For one, the health care system will likely to be strained as it tries to meet the enormous medical needs of AIDS victims, many who are indigent and may live five or more years with proper care. This fiscal tension may help promote health care reforms, such as a universal health care system, or a cap on the profits of medical facilities and pharmaceutical companies. On the other hand, escalating costs may force the adoption of draconian measures such as health care rationing. In the end, the AIDS epidemic may help force society to decide what and how many resources it will allocate to the care of terminally ill patients. The AIDS epidemic is clearly helping to shape the important public debate around health care and public priorities.

REFORMING AMERICAN HEALTH CARE

The American health care system is driven by ideological as well as fiscal concerns. Primary among these ideological considerations is whether access to health care should be a right or privilege. Conservatives generally believe that health is not a right but a privilege that must be earned through past or present labor force participation. Neoliberals, in turn, believe that health care should be a right that is somehow tied to labor force participation, except in instances where people are not linked to the workforce. Grounded in a European context, democratic socialists argue that health care is right that must be bestowed upon each individual at birth.

A second ideological engine that drives health care is the role of the private marketplace in the provision of medical care. Both conservatives and (neo)liberals agree that the provision of health care services must be lodged squarely in the private marketplace. More specifically, health care should be provided by independent or quasi-independent medical facilities and by physicians who are either self-employed or employed by companies/organizations. As such, conservatives argue that medical institutions and drug companies should be free to regulate the price of health care and medical goods. Their belief is that medical care is like other commodities in which increased competition lowers the price of goods and increases quality. Government regulation of the health care market is therefore seen as leading to more inefficiencies, lower quality or service, and higher prices. On the other hand, while some conservatives and (neo)liberals believe that the private marketplace is the proper venue for the delivery of health care, they also recognize that it is a commodity that does not respond to market conditions in the same way as other commodities. For example, when a person is immobilized by cardiac arrest, it is unlikely that the person is in a position to shop around for the best cardiac care prices. Likewise, if facing serious surgery, most patients will not choose a surgeon based only on price considerations. Thus, while some conservatives and (neo)liberals believe that the private marketplace is the right place to provide health care, they also recognize that it must be regulated (at least somewhat) by government to ensure quality, price, and access.

Democratic socialists argue that health care is too important to be left to the vicissitudes of the marketplace. For them, health care must be removed from the context of a market in which decisions are made purely on economic terms. As such, they believe that the marketplace is not designed to meet the needs of people but to maximize profits. Health care must therefore be socialized, that is, free or heavily subsidized at the point of access, universal in its coverage, and administered and controlled by government. In short, democratic socialists see a fundamental incompatibility between the needs of the market to maximize profits by raising prices and cutting costs, and the needs of citizens to receive high quality medical care.

In the past 30 years, most proposals designed to reform or transform American health care have been either directly or indirectly linked to the political economy that makes up American society. Consequently, proposals for improving American health care fit into three basic categories: (1) removing health care from the marketplace through socialized medicine; (2) maintaining the private health care marketplace while providing universal coverage through national health insurance; and (3) the institution of incremental reforms designed to eliminate the more egregious features or gaps in the American health care system.

Socialized Medicine

The most radical proposal for reforming the American health care system involves the creation of a National Health Service (NHS). During the mid–1970s, Left-wing health planners had worked with certain members of Congress to draft proposals for a NHS. Proposed by Congressman Ronald Dellums (a social worker) in the late 1970s, the NHS would establish health care as a right of citizenship. Similar to the British model, it would provide free (no fee at the point of access and no payments from third-party vendors) and comprehensive health care coverage, including diagnostic, therapeutic, preventive, rehabilitative, environmental, and occupational health services. Also included would be free dental and eye care, emergency and routine transportation to medical facilities, child care, homemaking, social work, and counseling. To improve the maldistribution of medical services, the NHS would provide free medical education in return for required periods of service in medically underserved areas. Poor communities would receive extra resources for funding, personnel, and equipment needs.[78]

NHS would be financed by progressive taxation on individual and corporate income, supplemented by a gifts and estate tax. The goal of the NHS would be the elimination of private profit in the health care system, and a national commission would be responsible for establishing a formulary of drugs, equipment, and supplies, with regional branches purchasing these goods in their inexpensive generic forms. Although private insurance companies would have no role in the NHS, the Dellums bill was vague as to whether private medical practice would be abolished.[79]

Another proposal for restructuring the health care system on a single-payer basis was Senate Bill 2817 (The National Health Care Act of 1992). Supported by the National Association of Social Workers and modeled after the Canadian system, this bill called for a single-payer national health care system. As with the Canadian model, states would have responsibility for ensuring delivery of health services, for paying all providers, and for planning in accordance with federal guidelines. Although this plan would have allowed the practice of private medicine, private health insurance coverage would be discontinued.[80] Supporters of this bill claimed that it would immediately reduce health care spending by 18 percent. Moreover, they argued that a "single-spigot" would reduce the fraud that is endemic to a multiple payer system.[81]

Proponents argue that socialized health care would allow for the coordination of health services and reduce profiteering by professionals and corporations. Moreover, they contend that the experience of other countries illustrates that strict budgeting, nationalization, and the elimination of the profit motive arrests the growth of health care costs, and in the end, it will prove less expensive than the current privatized system. Although an NHS plan appears unlikely to be adopted in the near future, the reality of the present does not always dictate the future. As illustrated by the New Deal programs of the 1930s, Americans can make abrupt changes in a short period of time; naysayers who predict more of the same are wrong as often as they are right.

National Health Insurance

Another strategy to restructure America's health care system is National Health Insurance (NHI). NHI proposals date back to the turn of the century. According to Paul Starr, the United States was on the brink of establishing national health insurance a number of times during the twentieth century, but each time factors unique to the political and social institutions of America prevented its adoption.[82] In the 1930s, NHI plans began to proliferate as part of Roosevelt's New Deal, but the idea was abandoned because of the strident opposition of the AMA—originally a supporter of NHI—and the fear that its inclusion would jeopardize passage of the 1935 Social Security Act. President Harry Truman took up the NHI banner in the days following World War II, but by that time most middle-class and unionized workers were covered by private insurance plans. Moreover, the AMA again set its powerful lobbying machine into motion, this time equating national health insurance with socialized medicine and with Communism, a tactic that proved successful during the "red hysteria" of the late 1940s and early 1950s. NHI bills were introduced in Congress every year between 1935 and 1965, and every year they failed.[83]

Of the several national health insurance plans advanced, the most comprehensive was proposed in the 1970s by Senator Edward Kennedy (and a number of successive co-authors). The Kennedy plan, supported by large segments of organized labor, included a National Health Board that would be appointed by the president to develop policy guidelines, manage the program, and plan and direct the yearly federal health budget. In addition, a national health insurance corporation would be developed to collect tax premiums from workers and disperse them to private insurance companies, which would process all claims. Under this system every American would have compulsory health insurance: Workers would be insured through their employers, the poor through a special federal insurance fund. Based on its broad coverage, the Kennedy plan would have eliminated the need for Medicare and Medicaid.[84]

The Clinton National Health Plan

The Health Security Act (HSA) proposed by President Bill Clinton in 1993. Although the HSA was not a NHI plan in the strictest sense, it contained important components of national insurance. Clinton's bill was in part based on the ideas of the Jackson Hole Group, whose professionals reiterated the need for cost consciousness in health care and the need for substantial investment in outcome and evaluation research. The Jackson Hole Group proposed a plan called the 21st Century American Health System, which would establish a health care system based on universal access (all individuals would have health benefits from some source) and cost consciousness.[85]

Health care reform was one of the major goals of the first Clinton administration. To accomplish this goal, Hillary Clinton and Ira Magaziner led a 500-person task force charged with: (1) extending medical insurance to the uninsured at a reasonable cost, (2) guaranteeing continued coverage when workers change jobs or get sick, (3) curbing and controlling steadily rising national health care costs by developing health care networks, (4) addressing the problems of the insurance industry, (5) stopping drug companies from overinflating drug prices, (6) developing a basic core benefits package for every American, and (7) providing universal health care coverage. The result of this task force was the 1,342 page Health Security Act.

The HSA would have worked in the following manner. All citizens and legal immigrants were to get a card guaranteeing them a comprehensive lifelong package of health care benefits. This package would include in- and out-patient medical care, prescription drugs, dental and vision care, long-term care, mental health services, and substance abuse treatment. Coverage would be continuous regardless of employment status. Competition marked the Clinton plan. All participants were to buy into large purchasing pools, called Health Care Alliances. Each alliance would offer three separate plans from which consumers could choose: (1) a fee-for-service option allowing consumers to choose their doctors; (2) a plan based on joining a network of doctors and hospitals; (3) and the choice of an HMO. Consumers would then select from three levels of cost-based benefit packages, although all plans would have a yearly out-of-pocket limit of $1,500 for an individual and $3,000 for a family. Low-income self-insurers would be charged based on a sliding scale. Those on public assistance would have their fees paid by Medicaid. Employers would have been compelled to pay 80 percent of the premium of the standard benefit package; workers would pay the additional 20 percent. Employers would not be charged more than 7.9 percent of their payroll costs for insuring their workers.[86]

Alliances would be run by boards of directors made up of consumers and employers with limited federal oversight. Premiums would be paid to the alliances, who would then stimulate competition by the increased purchasing power of individual consumers and small businesses. Regional Alliances would be used by small employers (less than 5,000 workers), self-employed individuals, and those not in the labor force. Alliances would solicit and accept bids from providers, process claims, and determine consumer eligibility. Businesses with 5,000 or more employees would have the option of forming their own Corporate Alliance or joining Regional Alliances. Eligibility would be universal (no bans on preexisting conditions) and everyone would receive the same level of service at the same rate. National cost targets would be established to curb inflation in health care, and all alliances would be required to meet that target. Medicare would have remained intact, with recipients having the choice of whether to stay on Medicare or join an alliance. In addition, the HSA would have limited malpractice suits by requiring participation in dispute resolution before a suit is filed, limiting the percent that lawyers can make from an award, and requiring evidence of malpractice before a suit is actually filed. Finally, funding would have come from employer and individual fees and from Medicaid and Medicare program payments.[87]

Despite a promising start, the HSA bill faltered almost from the moment it was announced. Opposition to the plan came from several quarters. Smaller health insurers incapable of launching Health Alliances understood they were being maneuvered out of the industry and took to the airways. Immediately, the Health Insurance Association of America (HIAA) broadcast $2 million worth of "Harry and Louise" ads, attacking the HSA as rationing health care under socialized medicine.[88] Within days of the ad's play, HIAA claimed that more than 40,000 callers had called the 800-number televised in the ad to register their concerns about health reform.[89] On the congressional front, small business lobbyists argued that the costs of the "employer mandate" that businesses must provide health insurance to workers would bankrupt thousands. Within weeks, dozens of lobbyists ranging from pharmaceutical companies to tobacco companies to restaurants and labor unions besieged Congress. Anticipating the 1994 elections, health industry interest groups contributed $26 million to congressional campaigns.[90] Health care reform was the biggest domestic policy initiative before Congress in decades, and its provisions would not go unchallenged by interested parties. Observers put the total price tag on influence peddling around the Health Security Act at $100 million.[91] By late summer of 1993 the HSA was stopped dead in its tracks. The inauguration of the conservative One-hundred-fourth Congress in 1994 further precluded the possibility of comprehensive health care reform bill.

Critics of NHI

Critics of NHI plans charge that they would modify payment mechanisms rather than encourage major changes in the health care system. They claim that the nature of private medical practice would remain intact, as would the organization of hospitals and other health institutions. Although NHI schemes would equalize the ability of patients to pay, they would not improve the accessibility or quality of services. Furthermore, most NHI proposals call for coinsurance (co-payments), a sum that many poor people would not find affordable.[92] Contrary to what some critics claim, NHI schemes are not socialized medicine: Hospitals would remain private, doctors would continue to be private practitioners, and most plans preserve a major role for private insurance companies. Although coverage would be extended to the entire population, the general profitability of the health care industry would remain in the hands of those who prosper most from the current arrangement.

Incremental Reform

The incremental reform of health care policy has generally been a more acceptable alternative to the American public and policymakers than sweeping reforms. Incremental reform of the health care system has generally focused on remedying the more egregious and troubling aspects of the private health care marketplace and on fine-tuning the public health care programs. One example of incremental reform that bordered on wider reform was the Catastrophic Health Act of 1988.

Former President Ronald Reagan signed the Catastrophic Health Insurance Act in 1988, then the most sweeping reform of Medicare ever attempted. This legislation was designed to provide 33 million elderly and disabled Medicare beneficiaries with protection from catastrophic hospital, doctor, and outpatient drug costs. The new Medicare benefits were to be financed by two premiums. The first was applicable to all Medicare enrollees and would have been $4 per month in 1989, rising to $10.20 in 1993. (This amount was to be paid in addition to the regular 1988 premium of $24.80 per month.) The second, income-related premium was to be paid each year in conjunction with the federal income taxes paid by the 40 percent of Medicare enrollees with the highest incomes. Everyone eligible for Medicare hospital benefits would have been required to pay the supplemental premium if their incomes were high enough to meet the taxation threshold.[93] Because of consumer pressure (i.e., the elderly refused to support the self-financing part of the reforms) and the rising deficit, the Catastrophic Insurance Act was repealed by Congress even before it was implemented.[94]

With the defeat of Clinton's HSA, the only politically viable alternative to current health care policy was seen in incremental reform. One of these took the form of the Kennedy-Kassebaum bill (the Health Care Coverage Availability and Affordability Act of 1996). While federal tax law subsidizes employer-based health insurance, it does not provide the same subsidy for insurance purchased by individuals. Hence, almost 90 percent of people who have private health insurance obtain it through their employers. To address this problem, Congress passed the Consolidated Budget Reconciliation Act (COBRA) in 1985, which permitted individuals leaving a company of 20 or more employees to continue their health insurance benefits for up to 18 months by paying 102 percent of the premium their employer had been paying. While this helped some people, others remained trapped in "job lock," fearing that they would not be insurable because of a preexisting condition.

Passage of the Kennedy-Kassebaum bill marked the first time any legislation had been adopted to protect people with preexisting medical conditions—including HIV—from total exclusion from health insurance coverage. This bill was expected to help an estimated 25 percent of Americans caught in job lock—afraid to change jobs or start their own businesses because they had preexisting conditions that prevented them from obtaining new insurance coverage. Among other things, the new law did the following:

- It prohibited insurance companies from refusing coverage to people with preexisting medical conditions who move from one job to another. In short, it assured the availability of individual policies for those who leave jobs voluntarily or involuntarily and for their dependents.
- This protection applies only to those who had maintained continuous private coverage for the preceding 18 months and who were ineligible for further coverage under COBRA. If a person changes jobs, the person cannot be denied medical coverage in the new job for a preexisting condition, except for a one-time, 12-month exclusion for any such condition that was diagnosed or treated in the preceding six months.

After the 12-month period, the condition is covered. The 12-month exclusion is a lifetime limit so long as an individual maintains continuous coverage (i.e., no more than a 63-day gap in coverage).

- It prohibited insurers from denying coverage or charging higher premiums to individuals in group plans who are in poor health. It also prohibits insurance companies from refusing to sell policies to small employers (those with 2 to 50 employees).[95]

While the Kassebaum-Kennedy bill was an important first step, it failed to address the critical issue of making health care insurance both accessible and affordable for all Americans. Nor did it address the fact that millions of Americans have no health coverage at all. In addition, the bill contained some conservative features. For one, it allowed the creation of 750,000 Medical Savings Accounts (MSAs). These MSAs would be limited to the self-employed, the uninsured, and workers in businesses with fewer than 50 employees. Under the MSA demonstration project, specified individuals are able to purchase high-deductible health insurance plans while setting aside pre-tax dollars to pay for medical expenses. Opponents of MSAs fear they would appeal only to the healthy and wealthy, leaving those with less money and more health problems behind in an increasingly costly insurance pool. After four years, there would be no further expansion of MSAs unless Congress voted to extend and expand the program. Finally, the bill criminalizes transfers of assets and imposes fines of up to $10,000 and jail sentences of up to one year for anyone who knowingly and willingly transfer assets to qualify for Medicaid. This provision may have a chilling effect on people needing nursing home care because it may discourage many from applying for Medicaid assistance.[96]

Congress also passed legislation that would require insurers to pay for a 48-hour hospital stay following a vaginal birth and a 96-hour stay after a C-section. In addition, Congress passed an amendment that would create some level of parity between mental health and physical health benefits. The amendment would required insurers to set the same level for lifetime and annual caps for mental health benefits as for physical health benefits. Specifically, the amendment stated that health insurance plans will not impose limitations or financial requirements on the coverage of mental health services if similar limitations or requirements are not imposed on coverage for services for other conditions. However, the bill also stipulates that plans are not prohibited from requiring preadmission screening prior to authorization of services nor are they prohibited from restricting coverage for mental health services to those services that are medically necessary.[97]

On the national level, it is likely that future health care reforms will be enacted to reduce Medicare costs, thereby making the future of the program more viable. Other incremental reforms may also involve the limitation of malpractice awards, extending some form of coverage to the uninsured, and instituting some limitations on the power of managed care operations to shape American health care.

Other health care reforms have been enacted on state levels. In Hawaii, employers are required to insure employees who work more than 20 hours a week.[98] A Health Rights program in Minnesota extends health care coverage to all noncovered low-income residents and charges them on a sliding-scale basis.[99] Given the escalating costs of Medicaid, it is likely that within the next several years there will also be significant state by state changes to Medicaid program eligibility. It is also likely that many states will try to implement substantial cuts to the Medicaid program.

COMPARATIVE ANALYSIS: HEALTH CARE IN CANADA, BRITAIN, AND ISRAEL

Americans often overlook what is happening in other parts of the world. The following section briefly explores medical systems in three countries: Canada (a single-payer system), Great Britain (socialized medicine), and Israel (an HMO-based system).

The Canadian Health Care System

The current Canadian health care system began more than 30 years ago when a hospital insurance plan in Saskatchewan evolved into a network of plans developed by each of Canada's ten provinces and two territories.[100] In 1966, Canada passed the Medical Care Act (Medicare), which instituted a nationwide, federal/provincial health insurance system that is publicly funded, privately delivered, and free at the point of access.[101] Each province is responsible for administering its own health care plan.[102] Although the insurance plans of the ten provinces and two territories are unique, all are essentially universal and comprehensive, covering all residents for inpatient and outpatient hospital and physician services. To receive federal funds, the plans must meet basic national eligibility standards:

1. *Universal coverage:* Every provincial resident must be covered under uniform terms and conditions.
2. *Portability:* Services must be portable in that they must cover residents who are temporarily away from home or who have moved to another province.
3. *Comprehensiveness:* All approved hospital and physicians' services must be covered. This includes medical and hospital care, mental health services, and prescription drugs for those over 65 and for those with catastrophic illnesses.
4. *Free at Point of Access:* Services must be free at point of access and include no financial barriers to care.
5. *Nonprofit Administration:* Plans must be nonprofit and publicly administered.
6. *Freedom of Choice:* Each Canadian is free to choose their provider.[103]

Unlike the U.S. system, health care coverage in Canada is grounded in universal entitlement rather than employment. As such, all of Canada's 25 million residents are eligible for provincial health insurance (regardless of their employment status), except for segments covered by other federal programs such as the military.[104] Questions arose in the 1980s about direct charges made to patients beyond the level paid by the provincial health care plan. The 1984 Canada Health Act eliminated all extra billing and user charges. Today, virtually every Canadian is covered by a comprehensive medical and hospital plan with no co-payment.[105]

General practitioners (GPs) make up the majority of physicians and provide most of Canada's health care. Specialists can only be used if a referral is received from the GP. Although patients may choose their primary-care physician, the choice is contingent upon whether the physician has openings for new patients. Patients also use the hospital in which the physician has admitting privileges. Besides providing free physician and hospital care, most provinces also cover the cost of travel and medical services if the treatment cannot be obtained in the area where the patient resides. While health care is free at the point of access, some services not covered include out-of-hospital drugs, dental services, eyeglasses, physical therapy, and chiropractic care not ordered by a medical doctor.[106]

Contrary to some misconceptions, the Canadian health care system is not based on socialized medicine; instead, it is a social insurance model that mixes public funds with private health care delivery. Canada's single-payer model is based on the idea that provincial governments function as single-source payers of health care with a centralized locus of control. As such, Canada's provincial governments reimburse both hospitals and physicians on a prospective budgeting basis. Specifically, private physicians' fees are negotiated between the provincial governments and the medical associations. Reimbursements for physicians are on a fee-for-service basis. The salaries of physicians in Canada are generally lower than their American counterparts. Because of budgetary problems, several provinces have limited the earnings of physicians who earn above a certain income by lowering the reimbursement rates. In addition, some provinces are currently considering placing a limit on the number of doctors to be licensed and ending the fee-for-service policy.[107]

There are about 1,250 hospitals in Canada, of which 57 percent are run by religious orders or nonprofit organizations. Hospital reimbursements are made on a global prospective basis. In other words, hospitals operate on a negotiated but fixed yearly budget. As such, they must stay within the budgetary allotment granted by the province regardless of the number of patients seen in a year.[108]

Funding for Canada's Medicare system is based on a mixture of federal and provincial funds. Federal funds are transferred to the provinces through block grants and transfer payments. Provincial funds to operate the medical system are derived from general revenue taxes and, in the case of Alberta and British Columbia, from insurance premiums paid for by employers. In provinces where premiums are charged, exemptions or subsidies are provided for the aged, the unemployed, and the indigent.[109]

Critics of the Canadian health care system point to numerous problems facing the system. One of the most important is the question of funding. Cutbacks in government spending (from 1981 to 1992 the Canadian government cut transfer payments to the provinces by almost $8 billion), an ongoing recession, increasing demands for services, and the high cost of technology have made controlling costs the number one issue facing the Canadian health care system. The "cure" being discussed for these problems has the replacement of federal support to the provinces with block grant transfers; a downsizing of the Canadian health care system, particularly the hospital sector (e.g., closing or merging hospitals, cutting staff, and shortening in-patient stays); and an increasing reliance on paraprofessional staff (e.g., replacing nurses with nursing attendants).[110]

Some critics have charged that Canada's prospective hospital global budgeting system has caused health care rationing. These critics argue that Canadian hospitals have coped with budgetary constraints by closing down hospital wards during certain times of the year, by filling up one-third of hospital beds with long-term elderly patients to keep high-volume (and expensive) traffic down, by using cheaper medical materials, by rushing medical procedures and thus curtailing accuracy, by providing substandard hospital care, by not investing in technology or capital improvements, and by prioritizing illnesses into "urgent," "emergent," and "elective" cases, thereby causing artificial queues for treatment.[111] According to these critics, health care rationing is having a dramatic effect on Canada's medical system.[112]

Some health care analysts have suggested that the United States adopt a health care reform plan similar to the Canadian model.[113] They argue that a single-payer system allows for greater control of systemwide health care capacity—that is, supply, distribution, and costs—than a fragmented insurance system in which no party has the overall authority for controlling the production and distribution of medical goods and services. Health care analysts also point to the uneven coverage provided to Americans under the current patchwork of private and public health insurance plans. In comparison to the universal, comprehensive, and publicly funded health care system that Canadians enjoy, most Americans are forced to purchase employer-based health insurance offering coverage that ranges from minimal to comprehensive, depending upon the type of policy. Moreover, a significant number of Americans fall through the cracks in health insurance; they receive no employment-based health insurance and they are ineligible for Medicaid or Medicare. Critics claim that a Canadian-style universal health care policy would ensure all Americans adequate medical care without regard to their ability to pay or the generosity of their employers.

Perhaps the most formidable argument for the United States to adopt a Canadian-style health care system is provided by an examination of leading health indicators and per capita health care spending. Before Canada's Medicare system became operational in 1971, it lagged behind the United States in the important indicators of infant mortality and life expectancy. Impressive gains now place Canada ahead of the United States on both health indicators. Moreover, Canada is able to achieve those gains by spending less of its GNP on health care than the United States. While health care costs are rising in Canada, they are doing so at a slower rate than in the United States.[114]

Factors that influence lower health care costs in Canada include lower physician and administrative costs and less concern with malpractice litigation. In 1985 the per capita physician expenditure in

Canada was $202 (calculated in U.S. dollars) compared with $347 in the United States. According to the *Journal of the American Medical Association*, the higher per capita expenditure in the United States is explained entirely by higher fees because the quantity of physician visits per capita is actually lower in the United States than in Canada. Fees for procedures in the United States are more than three times as high as they are in Canada; the difference in fees for evaluation and management services are about 80 percent lower in Canada. Part of the difference in fee structures may be related to the lower rates of malpractice litigation in Canada. For example, fewer malpractice suits may place less pressure on Canadian doctors to practice the defensive (and costlier) medicine that their American counterparts frequently practice.

Because Canadian health care is based on a single-payer system, overhead costs run at about 3 percent per annum compared with the 24 percent of all U.S. health care spending that goes toward administration.[115] In part, this is due to the significant portion of America's health care budget that is spent on advertising and billing.[116] The single-payer system also lessens the paperwork load on physicians, thereby freeing them up to see more patients. One indicator of the success of Canada's health care system is that the majority of Canadians are generally satisfied with it and show no inclination of giving it up.[117]

Britain's National Health Service

The National Health Service (NHS) is the most enduring pillar of the British Labour Party's postwar welfare state. The direct inspiration for the NHS was a 1944 white paper written by Sir William Beveridge for the wartime coalition government. The Beveridge Report maintained that a "comprehensive system of health care was essential to any scheme for improving living standards."[118]

After initial resistance from the British Medical Association, the National Health Service Act was passed in 1946 and took effect in 1948. In the words of the act establishing it, the aim was to promote "the establishment of a comprehensive health service designed to secure improvement in the physical and mental health of the people . . . and the prevention, diagnosis and treatment of illness."[119] The principle of freedom of choice was upheld in that people could either use the NHS or seek outside doctors. Doctors were guaranteed that there would be no interference in their clinical judgment, and they were free to take private patients while participating in the service. The main goal of the NHS was to provide free medical service to anyone in need. The NHS Act called for a tripartite system: (1) hospital service with specialists; (2) general medical doctors, dentists, and eye doctors, maintained on a contractual basis; and (3) prevention and support systems, provided by local health departments.

Under the leadership of Britain's Minister of Health Anuerin Bevan, all hospitals were nationalized. Because most hospitals were owned by local governments or were heavily subsidized nonprofit hospitals, nationalization was not difficult. General medical practitioners were brought into a new governmentally subsidized plan that provided universal and basic medical care that was free at the point of access. This was also not a major change because physicians' services had been subsidized for industrial workers since before WWII. The NHS Act simply extended this coverage to the whole population. British physicians generally came to support the act because it guaranteed a steady income.

The NHS Act did not eliminate private medicine, and a small percentage of NHS beds were reserved for private patients. General practitioners (GPs) and specialists were (and continue to be) permitted to treat private patients while working in the NHS. Moreover, affluent patients were (and still are) permitted to purchase private health insurance and therefore private care. The major advantages of private care are more attractive hospital rooms and quicker service for elective surgery. About 15 percent of the British currently have private health insurance, which is often provided as a fringe benefit for upper-level management employees.

The backbone of the NHS is the GP. Patients in Britain are registered with a GP who provides family care. Patients may change their GPs except if they are diagnosed with a chronic illness such as AIDS. GPs are paid by the NHS on the basis of an annual capitation fee for each registered patient. Roughly half of a GP's income comes from capitation payments, with the rest made up by allowances for services such as contraceptive advice and immunization. The role of the GP is to provide primary medical care; they are forbidden to restrict their practice to any special client group. Individuals can register with any GP provided he or she is willing to accept them. GPs see almost 75 percent of their registered patients at least once a year and, because mobility is low in Britain, many people retain the same GP for a considerable length of time.[120]

The GP has considerable professional latitude and equips his or her own office, hires staff, and may choose to work singly, in pairs, in groups, or in a government health center. Close to 50 percent of all GPs practice in groups of three or more. Health centers, part of the original Health Service Act, mushroomed in the late 1960s and 1970s, and by 1975 there were 600 nationally. Sweeping changes in 1967 gave GPs increased benefits, including a higher capitation rate if they had a patient load of between 2,500 and 3,500. In addition, extra remuneration was provided for each person on their list who was over 65, for night calls, for transients, for maternity care, for family planning services, and for certain preventive measures. GPs also receive partial reimbursement for secretaries, receptionists, and nurses, as well as for the rental costs of their offices. Extra payments are also provided for seniority, postgraduate education, vocational training, for working in groups of three or more, and for practicing in underdoctored areas.[121]

The second tier of the British health care system is the physician consultant (specialist). Most referrals to consultants—except for accidents and emergency care—are made through GPs. While employed by the government and under contract to a public hospital, physician specialists are allowed a small private practice. In effect, patients in the community are served by GPs, whereas in the hospital they are under the care of specialists. As in the U.S. health care system, physician specialists are accorded greater prestige and remuneration.[122]

The NHS is funded from general taxes, with the proceeds divided among regional health authorities that plan local health services. The regions, in turn, divide their money among districts that pay for hospitals through global prospective budgets.[123] Health services under the NHS are relatively comprehensive, with hospital and primary medical care being free. However, there are significant patient charges for adult dentistry and eyeglasses and a charge for prescriptions that in 1996 cost between $5 and $6. Drug prices are agreed upon between the health department and the pharmaceutical industry according to a specific pricing formula based on company profits. In addition, the government subsidizes medical education so that the direct cost to the student is low.[124]

The NHS faces serious problems despite its high rate of utilization. For one, critics complain that NHS hospital funds are doled out in a haphazard manner. For instance, considerable monies are spent on health care facilities in fast-emptying city centers rather than in burgeoning population centers. One of the reforms suggested to remedy this problem was the creation of "internal markets," whereby the distribution of NHS money would follow patients rather than the other way around. An even more important problem was that hospitals received nothing extra for efficiently treating more patients at less cost, which resulted in less incentive to improve efficiency.[125]

Under the original NHS Act, Parliament allocated money and power to local health authorities who managed the hospitals and contracted with specialists for services.[126] Passed in 1990, the National Health and Community Care Act was designed to reduce the long queues for the treatment of nonacute illnesses and procedures by introducing market efficiencies. Loosening the knot between funders and providers, this bill permitted some hospitals (called trust hospitals) to operate independently of the local health authority in setting fees, managing budgets, developing personnel packages, and purchasing goods. The theory was that independently managed hospitals would be more efficient that centrally planned ones. To further encourage efficiency, these trust hospitals were allowed to sell their services to any local health authority, private patients, or to private insurance companies. In addition, GPs with large practices were permitted to become fundholders of NHS grants from which they could purchase hospital or specialized services for their clients. It was expected that GPs would refer their patients to those hospitals or specialists that were the most efficient. Inefficient hospitals would get fewer referrals, thereby forcing them to increase their quality of care while reducing costs.[127]

Another criticism of the NHS is that its funding is not based on the medical needs of consumers, but rather on how much the British treasury believes it can afford to spend on health care. The result is de facto health care rationing and long waiting lists for elective procedures that are not based on inefficiencies in the system but on limited resources. For example, dialysis is not provided through the NHS for those over age 62. In addition, consumers complain of long waits in GP offices and hospital buildings are often in poor repair. There are also long waiting lists for elective surgeries such as hip replacements, routine treatment of varicose veins, and repairs of hernias. (There is believed to be little wait for urgent surgery.) Research illustrates, however, that long waiting lists are misleading because they can include people who have died, moved, already had their operations, or who have been kept waiting by consultants who want to secure more resources or private patients.[128]

Other critics charge that despite government efforts, there are serious shortages of doctors in certain parts of Britain. In addition, expenditures and resources under the NHS seem to be slanted toward hospitalization rather than primary, first-level care. Critics also complain about the lack of accountability of doctors and about strong unions that have supported restrictive practices and fought attempts to privatize support services.[129] Finally, other critics charge that the inequality in the British health system has resulted in higher disease and mortality rates for lower socioeconomic groups.

Much of the American reporting on the NHS has tended to emphasize its flaws. Although some GPs express dissatisfaction with the system, the public continues to use it in large numbers. For example, while 15 percent of Britons have private insurance, most use it as a supplement rather than as a substitute for the NHS.[130] Despite the criticisms, the NHS appears to be serving the majority of the British population as well as, and in some ways better than, the American health care system. For instance, per capita health care expenditures in Britain are only 6 percent of its GDP compared to more than 14 percent for the United States. (Much of this lower cost is attributable to the success of GPs in keeping down hospital admission rates and to the relatively low administrative costs of the NHS.) Notwithstanding the lower cost of the British health care system, most health indicators such as life expectancy and infant mortality rates are equivalent to or better than those found in the costlier U.S. health care system. Enoch Powell, a former health minister, summed up the contradictions of the NHS: "One of the most striking features of the NHS is the continual, deafening chorus of complaints which rises day and night from every part of it, a chorus only interrupted when someone suggests that a different system altogether might be preferable . . . it presents what must be a unique spectacle of an undertaking that is run down by everyone engaged in it."[131]

The Israeli Health Care System

The Israeli health care system was chosen as an example because it represents a unique blend of private and public health care provision. Specifically, the social organization of Israeli health care functions somewhat like a large governmentally subsidized HMO.

The Israeli health care system is based on voluntary or semivoluntary health insurance in public nonprofit sick funds, known as Kupat Holim. Most of the sick funds have a long-standing political identity or are somehow affiliated with political groups. The largest of these sick funds, the General Kupat Holim, is run by the Histadrut (the General Federation of Labor) and is politically affiliated with the Israeli labor movement. In recent years there has been a significant change in the membership of the various sick funds. For example, the General Kupat Holim covered 85 percent of the employee population and about 70 percent of the nonworking population in the mid-1980s; by the 1990s membership in the General Kupat Holim had declined with a corresponding growth in the smaller sick funds. The Israeli system provides health insurance coverage to about 94 percent of the country's population.[132]

The General Kupat Holim system operates in the following way. Employees who belong to the Histadrut (the labor union) can join the General Kupat Holim, with employers and employees sharing the cost of coverage. Insured individuals and their families receive service through clinics that are scattered throughout the country or from private doctors under contract to the General Kupat Holim system. Most medical care is free at the point of access and throughout the entire process of treatment. In addition, most drugs are subsidized by the Kupat Holim. Similar to the NHS, specialist services in the Kupat Holim require a referral through a primary care physician. Hospital care is provided through governmental, for-profit, or private nonprofit hospitals. Finally, all General Kupat Holim doctors have the option of establishing a private practice in their off-hours. Given the relatively low income of doctors employed by Kupat Holim (about $1,300 a month in 1992), many take advantage of this option. Apart from the General Kupat Holim, there are other smaller HMOs available that do not require labor union or political party affiliation. All Israeli HMOs offer similar coverage.

The Kupat Holim system has experienced severe difficulties in the past decade, including (1) increased strains in its relationship with doctors, (2) the growing cost of medical care, (3) the changing attitudes of the Israeli government toward the Kupat Holim system, and (4) the negative impact of increased bureaucratization on its consumer-members. First, the medical profession has become a powerful organization that militantly promotes the interests of its members. As a result, doctors' strikes grew in frequency throughout the 1980s and regularly undermined the delivery of medical care. Second, the cost of medical care in Israel has risen sharply over the last two decades. This increase is attributable to several factors. For one, the rapid growth in the elderly population has led to higher costs. Second, the effect of the "global medical economy" is being felt in Israel. In particular, the growth of medical technology in the Western world has dramatically raised consumers' expectations of medical care, especially among the middle classes. No longer content with an emphasis on primary care, consumers expect state-of-the-art medical care replete with the newest and most sophisticated technology. This problem is exacerbated as doctors returning from postgraduate training in North America and Western Europe demand that Israeli hospitals and medical schools provide the same level of facilities, laboratories, and medical equipment as the places in which they were trained. Their expectations result in higher medical costs, especially in the areas of hospital and specialist services.

Third, the main sources of income for the sick funds are based on the contributions paid by insured members and employers. While medical costs have rapidly increased in the past decade, the wages and incomes to which these contributions are linked has remained steady, if not static. The fiscal resources of the sick funds has lagged behind health care costs, especially for the General Kupat Holim, which covers most of the low-income population. Finally, the direct contribution of the government to the sick funds decreased sharply during the 1980s. For instance, government contributions fell from 7 percent of the total sick fund expenditure in 1984 to only 2 percent in 1988.[133]

Several changes to the Israeli system have occurred in the past few years. For example, new private health insurance plans are being launched to cover medical services that were once covered by the existing sick fund arrangements. Also, private medical practice is spreading within government-owned and nonprofit health care facilities. Both these measures are basically indirect or hidden forms of privatization, and they have significant effects on access to medical care, especially for poorer population groups.[134]

Most Israelis want the Kupat Holim system to continue because it has served them well. This health care system ensures reasonable access to most medical services at no cost at the point of access. In addition, experience has shown that private medical care is beyond the means of the majority of the people. At the same time, there are widespread desires to rid the Kupat Holim of some of the more cumbersome bureaucratic features it has acquired.[135]

It is difficult to compare the quality of the Canadian, British, and Israeli health care systems with that in the United States. For affluent or middle-class Americans with good health insurance, the U.S. system of health care may well provide the best medical care in the world, and for complex medical procedures involving sophisticated equipment and technology, the American health care system is probably unequaled. Moreover, unlike the long queues characteristic of the systems previously discussed, the waiting period for surgery, tests, and other procedures is relatively short in the United States. Finally, American physicians are among the best trained in the world. However, the American emphasis on costly equipment and technology is not without a price. Medical care that emphasizes specific diseases over primary care and preventive medicine usually results in good care, but for fewer people. Health care systems that emphasize personal and primary care, accessibility, and involve free or inexpensive out-of-pocket expenses for consumers often reach more people. Given that, the health care systems of Canada, Britain, and Israel appear to more equitably distribute health resources than does the American health care system.

CONCLUSION

The examination of health care in America raises important questions. What is America's responsibility for providing health care to all its members? How much technological medicine can American society realistically afford? How should U.S. medical resources be allocated? What, if any, limitations on personal freedom are permissible in the name of promoting health and preventing disease? These and other questions urgently require answers.

The American health care system is facing an acute crisis. Much of this crisis is based on runaway medical costs. It is grounded in the failure of the marketplace and the federal government to curb health care expenditures, an overreliance on medical technology at the expense of providing primary health care services, the failure of cost containment measures in Medicaid and Medicare, the growth in health care administrative costs, and an upsurge in the number of employed workers and their families who cannot afford any form of health care coverage. Moreover, huge expenditures on health care in the United States are not reflected in greater longevity, lower rates of infant mortality, or in any other indicator of a healthier nation.

The United States is one of the few industrialized countries that does not have a comprehensive plan for national health insurance or socialized medicine. Moreover, the United States is one of the few industrialized nations where medical expenses can cause poverty. Terri Combs-Orme suggests that a progressive reconstruction of the health care system must be grounded in the following principles:

1. Accessible health care should be a universal right of all Americans, not a privilege to be purchased or earned.
2. The quantity, quality, and accessibility of health care should be equal for all, not dependent on income or categorical status. No health care system should result in differential quantity, quality, or accessibility of care based on income, gender, age, or any other criterion.
3. Health care should not be linked to employment. A majority of Americans purchase health care insurance through their place of employment, but the fear of job loss or other issues not under their control undermines the security of this arrangement and limits their job mobility.
4. The quality, quantity, and accessibility of health care should not vary on a state-by-state basis.
5. A progressive health care system must balance the needs and rights of children and the elderly in a fair and rational way.
6. A comprehensive health care system should include coverage for and accessibility to long-term care for the elderly.[136]

Left unchecked and convulsed by wildly escalating costs, health care in America may someday be out of reach for the majority of citizens. Moreover, the increasing share of the GNP and the federal budget currently allocated to health care may soon reach a saturation point, making it unaffordable for all but the most well-off Americans. Although the likely outcome of the American health care crisis is unknown, left solely to the caprice of the marketplace, the situation will undoubtedly worsen.

◆ ◆ ◆ *Discussion Questions* ◆ ◆ ◆

1. The American health care system currently costs close to $1 trillion a year. Its cost has risen dramatically over the past 25 years in terms of the amount spent, the percentage of the GNP used for health care, and the per capita costs of health care. What are the main factors that have driven up health care costs? Can these factors be controlled? If so, how?

2. Some of the most striking increases in health care costs have occurred in the area of Medicaid and Medicare. What are the major factors contributing to the steep rise in Medicaid and Medicare costs? What can be done to stabilize these costs?

3. Some critics charge that Medicare and Medicaid costs cannot be brought under control without radically reforming the entire health care system. They argue that incremental reforms in the Medicare and Medicaid programs will have only a minuscule impact on the steep increase in federal and state expenditures for health care. Are these critics correct?

4. Evidence of the effectiveness of cost-cutting mechanisms such as DRGs has been mixed, although generally negative. Critics charge that not only has the DRG system failed to substantially reduce health care costs, but it has also led to a reduced level of patient care. Is the DRG system successful? If so, should it be a model for future health care reforms?

5. Many critics argue that there is a serious health care crisis in the United States. Describe the main characteristics of that crisis (e.g., health care costs, accessibility issues, noncovered populations, U.S. health indicators compared with those of other nations, etc.).

6. The AIDS epidemic is one of the most important public health issues facing the global community in the coming decades. Some critics insist that more money should be spent on basic AIDS research, outreach, and treatment. Other critics argue that AIDS is only one of many health care problems facing the United States and other countries around the world. They argue that the money spent on AIDS research should be in proportion to the numbers affected by the disease, which are relatively small when compared to those suffering from cancer and heart disease. Is AIDS a significantly more important public health problem than cancer, heart disease, or the effects of drugs, alcohol, and tobacco? Should the federal governmental spend proportionally more on AIDS research than on other diseases? If so, why?

7. Some health care analysts are calling for radical reform in the U.S. health care system. Many of these analysts insist that America's free market system of health care must be replaced by a more cost-effective and comprehensive system of health care. Assuming that these health care analysts are correct, which of the health care systems described in this chapter would be the best model for the United States to emulate and why?

8. Why has America not developed a health care system (similar to its industrial counterparts) that is universal and publicly funded? Identify the forces and interests that have (and are continuing) to shape health care policy in the United States. What, if anything, can be done to reform or radically transform American health care?

Notes

1. Daniel Weinberg, "Press Briefing on 1995 Income, Poverty, and Health Insurance Estimates," Washington, DC: U.S. Bureau of the Census, Household Economic Statistics Division, September 26, 1996.
2. Terri Combs-Orme, "Should the Federal Government Finance Health Care for All Americans?: Yes." In Howard Jacob Karger and James Midgley (Eds.), *Controversial Issues in Social Policy* (New York: Allyn and Bacon, 1993).
3. Irving J. Lewis and Cecil G. Sheps, *The Sick Citadel* (Boston: Oelgeschlager, Gunn, and Hain, 1983), p. 16.
4. Sumner A. Rosen, David Fanshel, and Mary E. Lutz (Eds.), *Face of the Nation* 1987 (Silver Spring, MD: NASW, 1987), p. 75.
5. Barbara Wolfe, "Changing the U.S. Health Care System: How Difficult Will It Be?" *Focus* (14)2 (Summer 1992) p. 16.
6. David E. Rosenbaum, "Gloomy Forecast Touches Off Feud on Medicare Fund," *The New York Times* (June 6, 1996), pp. A1 and B14.
7. For a good historical analysis of the Medicare program, see Theodore R. Marmor, *The Politics of Medicare* (Chicago: Aldine, 1973).
8. Committee on Ways and Means, U.S. House of Representatives, *1996 Green Book* (Washington, DC: US GPO, 1996), p. 896.
9. Ibid., p. 19.
10. Isaac Shapiro, Mark Sheft, Julie Strawn, Laura Summer, and Robert Greenstein, *The States and the Poor* (Washington, DC: Center on Budget and Policy Priorities, December 1991), p. 37.
11. Ibid., p. 17.
12. See S. Dentzer, "The War Over that Other M Program," *U.S. News and World Report* (October 9, 1995), p. 71.
13. Children's Defense Fund, *The State of America's Children* (Washington, DC: Children's Defense Fund, 1987), pp. 110–118.
14. U.S. House of Representatives, *1996 Green Book*, p. 886.
15. Ibid., p. 886.
16. See Children's Defense Fund, *A Children's Defense Budget*, p. 109; and Barbara Wolfe, "A Medicaid Primer," *Focus* (17)3 (Spring 1996), pp. 1–6.
17. Ibid., p. 107.
18. Rosen et al., *Face of the Nation*, p. 76.
19. G.J. Schieber and J.P. Poullier, "International Health Care Spending: Issues and Trends," *Health Affairs*, 10 (1991), p. 110.
20. OECD, *Measuring Health Care, 1960–1983* (Paris: OECD, 1985), p. 68.
21. Ibid.
22. R. Brook, C. J. Kamberg, and A. Meyer-Okaes, *Appropriateness of Acute Medical Care for the Elderly: Analysis of the Literature* (R3717) (Santa Monica, CA: Rand Corporation, 1989).
23. See U.S. Congressional Budget Office, *Projections of National Health Care Expenditures*. See also American Medical Association, *Trends in Health Care* (Chicago: American Medical Association, 1987).
24. Randolph D. Smoak, "Costs Hurt Doctors, Patients Alike," *USA Today* (May 5, 1993), p. A13.
25. Clemens, "Rising Costs Reflect Many Instances, " p. B2.
26. Thomas A. Daschle, Rima J. Cohen, and Charles L. Rice, "Health Care Reform: Single-Payer Models," *American Psychologist* (48)3 (March 1993), pp. 265–267.
27. See Paul Schmolling, Merrill Youkeles, and William Burger, *Human Services in Contemporary America* (Pacific Grove, CA: Brooks/Cole, 1997); and "Doctors Under the Knife," p. 29. See also Leon Ginsberg, *Social Work Almanac* (Washington, DC: National Association of Social Workers, 1992), p. 123.
28. U.S. Congressional Budget Office, *Projections of National Health Care Expenditures* (Washington, DC: U.S. Congressional Budget Office, 1992).
29. U.S. House of Representatives, *Overview of Entitlement Programs: 1996 Green Book*.
30. Starr, *The Logic of Health-Care Reform*, p. 45.
31. U.S. House of Representatives, *Overview of Entitlement Programs: 1996 Green Book*.
32. U.S. General Accounting Office, *U.S. Health Care Spending Trends, Contributing Factors, and Proposals for Reform* (GAO/HRD-91-102), (Washington, DC: U.S. General Accounting Office, 1991).
33. Clemens, "Rising Costs Reflect Many Influences," p. B2.
34. U.S. House of Representatives, *1996 Green Book*, p. 995.
35. See Ibid.; and U.S. Department of the Census, *Statistical Abstract of the United States, 1991*

(Washington, DC: U.S. Government Printing Office, 1991), p. 107.
36. See U.S. House of Representatives, *1996 Green Book*, p. 994; and Robert G. Frank, "Health-Care Reform: An Introduction," *American Psychologist*, (48)3 (March 1993), pp. 258–260.
37. U.S. House of Representatives, *1996 Green Book* (Washington, DC: US GPO, 1996).
38. See *Methods of Technology Assessment* (Washington, DC: National Academy Press, 1991), p. 32; and U.S. House of Representatives, *1996 Green Book*, p. 1009.
39. "Doctors Under the Knife," *Newsweek* (April 5, 1993), p. 31.
40. J. M. Colwill, "Where Have all the Primary Care Applicants Gone?" *The New England Journal of Medicine* 326 (1992), pp. 387–392.
41. Clemens, "Rising Costs Reflect Many Influences," p. B2.
42. Katherine van Wormer, *Social Welfare: A World View* (Chicago: Nelson-Hall Publishers, 1997), p. 412.
43. "Doctors Under the Knife," p. 31.
44. See Bob Kerry and Philip J. Hofschire, "Hidden Problems in Current Health-Care Financing and Potential Changes" *American Psychologist* (48)3 (March 1993), p. 262; and U.S. House of Representatives, *1996 Green Book*.
45. John H. Goddeeris and Andrew J. Hogan, "Nature and Dimensions of the Problem." In John H. Goddeeris and Andrew J. Hogan (Eds.), *Improving Access to Health Care: What Can the States Do?* (Kalamazoo, MI: W. E. Upjohn Institute for Employment Research, 1992), pp. 14–15.
46. Quoted in Marie A. Caputi and William A. Heiss, "The DRG Revolution," *Health and Social Work* (3)6 (June 1984), p. 5.
47. Ibid., p. 9.
48. Paul Schmolling, Jr., Merrill Youkeles, and Willima R. Burger, *Human Services in Contemporary America* (Pacific Grove, CA: Brooks/Cole Publishing Co., 1997), p. 54.
49. Ibid.
50. See Ibid.; and U.S. Department of the Census, *Statistical Abstract of the United States, 1991*, p. 100.
51. U.S. House of Representatives, *1996 Green Book*.
52. Stuart Schear, "The Ultimate Self-Referral: Medicare Reform, AMA-Style," *The American Prospect* 25 (March–April, 1996), pp. 68–72.
53. Ellyn E. Spragins, "Simon Says, Join Us," *Newsweek* (June 19, 1995), pp. 55–58.
54. Ibid., p. 68.
55. Ibid.
56. Howard Waitzkin, *The Second Sickness: Contradictions of Capitalist Health Care* (New York: Free Press, 1983), p. 220.
57. Spragins, "Simon Says, Join Us."
58. Thomas H. Ainsworth, *Live or Die* (New York: Macmillan, 1983), p. 89.
59. U.S. Census Bureau, "Health Insurance Coverage: 1995 (September 26, 1996). On-line: http://www.census.gov/hhes/hlthins/cover95/c95tabb.html
60. U.S. Census Bureau, "Health Insurance Coverage: 1995, Who Goes Without Health Insurance (September 26, 1996). On-line: http://www.census.gov/hhes/hlthins/cover95/cov95asc.html
61. John M. Herrick and Joseph Papsidero, "Uncompensated Care: What States are Doing." In Goddeeris and Hogan (Eds.), *Improving Access to Health Care*, pp. 139–140.
62. D. Moran and J. Shields, *Employer Cost-Shifting Expenditures* (Washington, DC: Lewin-ICF, 1991), p. 453.
63. John M. Herrick and Joseph Papsidero, "Uncompensated Care: What States are Doing." In Goddeeris and Hogan (Eds.), *Improving Access to Health Care*, pp. 139–140.
64. W. Greenberg, "Elimination of Employer-Based Health Insurance." In R. B. Helms (Ed.), *American Health Policy: Critical Issues for Reform* (Washington, DC: AEI Press, October 1992), pp. 1–4.
65. Robert Searles Walker, *AIDS: Today, Tomorrow* (New Jersey: Humanities Press International, 1992), p. 134.
66. Centers for Disease Control, "HIV Surveillance Report," Vol. 8, No. 1 (June 1996), Atlanta, GA: Centers for Disease Control.
67. Ibid.
68. Walker, *AIDS*, p. 134.
69. Centers for Disease Control, "HIV Surveillance Report."
70. World Health Report, "Executive Summary, 1995." On-line: www.who.ch/programmes/whr/xsum95_e.htm
71. Quoted in Glendolyn Alex, Amy Ambler, Lisa Amundson, Nanette Biersdorfer, Tracy Milan, and

Laila Narsi, "Social Issues III: Homosexuality and AIDS." Unpublished paper. Graduate School of Social Work, University of Houston, Houston, TX, Spring 1996.
72. Ibid.
73. Eric Ekholm and Jon Tierney, "AIDS in Africa," *The New York Times* (September 16, 1990), p. A1.
74. Fred J. Hellinger, "Forecasting the Medical Care Costs of the HIV Epidemic: 1991–1994," *Inquiry* 28 (Fall 1991), p. 213.
75. Walker, *AIDS*, p. 128.
76. Anne A. Scitovsky, "Estimates of the Direct and Indirect Costs of AIDS in the United States." In Alan F. Fleming, (Ed.), *The Global Impact of AIDS* (New York: Alan R. Liss, 1988), p. 156.
77. Walker, *AIDS*, p. 125.
78. Ronald V. Dellums et al., *Health Services Act* (H.R. 2969) (Washington, DC: U.S. Government Printing Office, 1979). For a good summary of the act, see Waitzkin, *The Second Sickness*, pp. 222–226.
79. Dellums et al., *Health Services Act*.
80. "Summary of S. 2817, The National Health Care Act of 1992," *NASW-LA News* (16) 5 (September/October 1992), p. 2.
81. Daschle et al., "Health-Care Reform," p. 267.
82. Paul Starr, *The Social Transformation of American Medicine* (New York: Basic Books, 1984).
83. Ibid.
84. Ibid.
85. Jeff Bingaman, Robert G. Frank, and Carrie L. Billy, "Combining a Global Health Budget With a Market-Driven Delivery System," *American Psychologist* (48)3 (March 1993), pp. 271–272.
86. Diane M. DiNitto, *Social Welfare: Politics and Public Policy* (Boston: Allyn and Bacon, 1995), pp. 270–272.
87. Ibid.
88. Robin Toner, "'Harry and Louise' Ad Campaign Biggest Gun in Health Care Battle," *San Diego Union-Tribune* (April 7, 1994), p. A7.
89. Sara Fritz, "Ads Are Designed to Counter Health Care Proposals," *Los Angeles Times* (May 15, 1993), p. A16.
90. Dana Priest, "The Slow Death of Health Reform," *Washington Post Weekly* (September 5–11, 1994), p. 11.
91. Douglas Frantz, "Lobbyists, Interest Groups Begin Costly Health Care Battle," *Los Angeles Times* (May 24, 1993).
92. Waitzkin, *The Second Sickness*, p. 218.
93. Spencer Rich, "Provisions of 'Catastrophic' Insurance Act," *Washington Post* (July 1, 1988), p. A21.
94. Ibid.
95. National Center for Policy Analysis, "Health Care Policy Brief," Dallas, TX, 1996.
96. Ibid.
97. C. Sabatino, "Kassebaum-Kennedy Health Insurance Bill Clears Congress: Medical Savings Accounts Limited to Demonstration Program," Families USA (Washington, DC: Families USA).
98. Wolfe, "Changing the U.S. Health Care System," p. 17.
99. DiNitto, *Social Welfare*, p. 270.
100. W. Barnhill, "Canadian Health Care: Would it Work Here?" *Arthritis Today* (6) 6 (November–December 1992), p. 8.
101. Elaine Vayda and R. B. Deber, "The Canadian Health Care System: An Overview," *Social Science and Medicine* (18)3 (1984), pp. 191–197.
102. I. Callaway, "Canadian Health Care: The Good, the Bad, and the Ugly," *Health Insurance Underwriter* (October 1991), pp. 18–35.
103. See Tracy Falwell, Suzy Carter, Jodie Daigle, Renee Mills, Lissa Cameron and Leticia Gonzalez-Castro, "International Health Care Systems Analysis: Canada, Britain, Germany, Sweden, France, Mexico and South Africa." Unpublished paper. Graduate School of Social Work, University of Houston, Houston, TX, April 30, 1996; and T. Mizrahi, R. Fasan, and S. Dooha, "National Health Line," *Health and Social Work* (18)1 (1993), pp. 7–12.
104. Jonathan S. Rakich, "The Canadian and U.S. Health Care Systems: Profiles and Policies," *Hospital and Health Services Administration* (36)1 (Spring 1991), pp. 26–27.
105. Falwell et al., "International Health Care Systems Analysis."
106. Barnhill, "Canadian Health Care," p. 19.
107. Ibid.
108. Ibid.
109. Rakich, "The Canadian and U.S. Health Care Systems," p. 32.
110. See Cynthia Crosson, "Canadian Health Care is in Critical Condition," *National Underwriter* (January 20, 1992), p. 12; and van Wormer, *Social Welfare*, p. 419.

111. See Barnhill, "Canadian Health Care"; I. Munro, "How Not to Improve Health Care," *Reader's Digest* (September 1992), p. 21; and B. Gilray, "Standing Up for American Health Care," *Health Insurance Underwriter* (February 1992), p. 10.
112. Robert E. Moffitt, "Should the Federal Government Finance Health Care for All Americans?: No." In Howard Jacob Karger and James Midgley (Eds.), *Controversial Issues in Social Policy* (New York: Allyn and Bacon, 1993).
113. For example, David Himmelstein and Steffie Woolhandler, "A National Health Care Program for the United States: A Physicians' Proposal," *The New England Journal of Medicine* 320 (January 12, 1989), pp. 102–108; and Terri Combs-Orme, "Should the Federal Government Finance Health Care for All Americans?"
114. Combs-Orme, "Should the Federal Government Finance Health Care for All Americans?"
115. van Wormer, *Social Welfare*, p. 419.
116. See Combs-Orme, "Should the Federal Government Finance Health Care for All Americans?"; and "How Does Canada Do It?: A Comparison of Expenditures for Physicians' Services in the United States and Canada," *Journal of the American Medical Association* (265)19 (May 15, 1991), p. 2474.
117. W. Caragata, "Medicare Wars," *Maclean's* (108)14 (1995), p. 4.
118. Ruth Levitt, *The Reorganised National Health Service* (London: Croom Helm, 1979), p. 15.
119. Quoted in Levitt, p. 17.
120. Victor W. Sidel and Ruth Sidel, *A Healthy State* (New York: Pantheon Books, 1983), p. 144.
121. Ibid., pp. 144, 157–159.
122. Ibid., p. 172.
123. Ibid.
124. Sidel and Sidel, *A Healthy State*, p. 172.
125. "Nye Bevan's Legacy," *The Economist* (July 6, 1992), p. 12.
126. Levitt, *The Reorganised National Health Service*, p. 27.
127. "Nye Bevan's Legacy."
128. Ibid.
129. Ibid.
130. "Nye Bevan's Legacy," p. 12.
131. Quoted in "Nye Bevan's Legacy," p. 12.
132. Most of this section is drawn from Abraham Doron, "The Future of the Israeli Health Care System." Unpublished paper, the Paul Baerwald School of Social Work, The Hebrew University of Jerusalem, 1992.
133. Ibid.
134. Ibid.
135. Ibid.
136. Combs-Orme, "Should the Federal Government Finance Health Care for All Americans?"

CHAPTER 13

Mental Health and Substance Abuse Policy

This chapter reviews the provision of mental health services to the seriously mentally impaired. Prior to the community mental health movement, states were solely responsible for the care of the mentally disturbed. When the movement to improve mental health services through federal assistance to the states stalled, many who suffered from serious mental illness were left without care. This lack of adequate care was made worse by a series of legal decisions that reinforced the civil rights of mental patients while requiring the states to provide adequate services. As a result of these developments, many former mental patients are now living on the streets or in squalid single-room-occupancy hotels. Added to this mental health crisis, problems associated with alcohol and drug abuse are becoming more prevalent. The failure to support substance abuse prevention and treatment efforts adequately, coupled with the economic collapse of inner-city neighborhoods, has left many urban areas subject to unprecedented levels of street violence and social deterioration.

Throughout the history of American social welfare, states have played a prominent role in mental health services. During the nineteenth century, social problems attributable to immigration, urbanization, and industrialization overwhelmed the local poorhouses established during the colonial era. In the United States, Dorothea Dix championed the humane treatment of the mentally disturbed and, by the 1840s, she was instrumental in convincing many states to construct special institutions to provide asylum to the emotionally deranged. In fact, Dix's leadership was so persuasive that Congress passed legislation authorizing federal aid to the states for mental institutions. However, because President Franklin Pierce thought that the federal government should not interfere with the responsibility of the states to ensure social welfare, he vetoed the legislation in 1854.[1] It would not be until more than a century later that the federal government would assume a central role in determining mental health policy through the Community Mental Health Centers Act.

Consequently, mental health policy in the United States was articulated through the various states that operated their own mental hospitals. Originally, state mental hospitals were intended to be self-sufficient communities offering good air, clean water, nutritious food, and healthful activities consistent with the dictates of "moral treatment." Considering the quality of life experienced by many Americans at that time, such refuges were sorely needed. Conditions in rural America were no less dire than the conditions of urban America in the nineteenth century. Some newspaper clippings from an immigrant community in Wisconsin, circa 1890, reveal the fate of many residents who failed to negotiate dispiriting social conditions.

> The naked body of the wife of Fritz Armbruster, a woman who had worked in Best's Butcher Shop, was found frozen by the roadside near Albion, 6 miles from Black River Falls. She and her husband had separated, he living in town, she living alone in the house. Although no one had noticed that she had been suffering from any physical or mental disorder, 2 years ago, the loss of a child is said to have affected her very deeply and may have led to her becoming partially demented. The probability is that she rose in a fit of delirium and wandered away. . . .
>
> Mr. Axel, a farmer living about 6 miles east of Kiel, Manitowoc County, cut his wife's throat a few days ago so that she might not recover and then killed himself. There were various rumors as to the cause of the tragedy such as domestic infelicity etc., but a few who had dealings with Axel of late attributed the act to an aberration of mind. . . .
>
> Milo L. Nichols, sent to the insane hospital a year or two ago after committing arson on Mrs. Nichols' farm is now at large . . . and was seen near the old place early last week. . . . He has proven himself a revengeful firebug.
>
> A woman who gave her name as Wilson died at Chippewa Falls from a criminal operation performed upon herself. Her parents live near Eau Claire . . . her brother took charge of her remains. The woman was young and pretty and visited every physician in Chippewa Falls to accomplish her object, but without success.[2]

In response to these casualties, the state hospital served as a haven for the disturbed as well as protection for the community.

> Admitted July 19, 1893. Town of Black River Falls. Norwegian. Married. Age 29. Seven children. Youngest 8 months. Housewife. Poor. First symptoms were manifested . . . when patient became afraid of everything and particularly of mediums. She is also deranged in religion and thinks everyone is disposed to persecute her and to injure her husband. . . .
>
> Admitted January 20th, 1896. Town of Garfield. Age 52. Norwegian. Married. Two children, youngest 19 yrs old. Farmer. Poor. Illness began 10 months ago. Cause said to be his unfortunate pecuniary condition. Deluded on the subject of religion. Is afraid of injury being done to him. Relations say he has tried to hang himself . . . September 29, 1896: Discharged . . . improved . . . Readmitted May 4, 1898: Delusion that he and his family are to be hanged or destroyed.[3]

An adverse social climate, coupled with the absence of welfare programs to cushion people against poverty, joblessness, inadequate housing, and illness, served to swell the population of state hospitals. By the 1920s the state hospital was an asylum in name only, and much of the care amounted to merely warehousing patients. In this milieu, some of the scientifically minded reformers of the Progressive Era found in the ideas of the Eugenics Movement a straightforward and surgically precise solution to the problem of state institutions being inundated by "mental defectives." Proponents of the Eugenics Movement who believed that the human race could be improved by selective breeding argued that mental patients often suffered from hereditary deficiencies and that generational patterns of mental impairment should be eliminated by sterilization. In that adherents of eugenics were less concerned about the civil rights of individual mental patients than they were about the future of civilization, the fact that some patients might object was merely an inconvenience. In such instances, eugenicists obtained court permission to sterilize patients involuntarily. Many patients, of course, lacked the mental capacity to comprehend sterilization and had no idea that the surgical procedures to which they were subjected would terminate their reproductive lives. By the 1930s, 30 states had passed laws authorizing involuntary sterilization, and by 1935, 20,000 patients had been sterilized, almost half of them in California. Involuntary sterilization of the feebleminded generated great controversy, eventually culminating in a Supreme Court decision, written by Oliver Wendell Holmes, that validated the practice. Tragically, the case on which the decision was based involved a young woman in Virginia who was sterilized, only to be judged psychologically normal years later. The case record upon which Holmes based his decision had been prepared by a social worker.[4]

MENTAL HEALTH REFORM

More humane efforts to reform state institutions invariably involved the National Association for Mental Health (NAMH). Begun early in the century as an extension of the work of Clifford Beers, who had himself recovered after being hospitalized for mental illness, NAMH became critical of the custodial institutions operated by state governments. The issue of mental health attracted wide public attention during World War II, when approximately one in every four draftees was rejected for military service owing to psychiatric and neurological problems.[5] In response to the public outcry about mental health problems immediately after the war, Congress passed the Mental Health Act, which established the National Institute of Mental Health (NIMH). Accompanying the Mental Health Act of 1946 was an appropriation for an exhaustive examination of the mental health needs of the nation. In 1961, NIMH released *Action for Mental Health*, a report that called for an ambitious national effort to modernize the U.S. system of psychiatric care.[6]

As David Mechanic observed, *Action for Mental Health* was a utopian vision of mental health care, the idealism of which conformed perfectly with a set of extraordinarily propitious circumstances. First, the postwar economy was booming and, with cutbacks in military expenditures, a surplus existed that could be tapped for domestic programs. Second, a new generation of drugs—psychotropic medication—showed promise of being able to stabilize severely psychotic patients who before had been unmanageable. Third, a literature emerged that was critical of the "total institution" concept of the state hospital and implied that noninstitutional—and presumably community—care was better. Finally, because of his experience with mental retardation as a family problem, President John F. Kennedy was supportive of programs that promised to improve mental health care.[7] These political and social circumstances did not go unnoticed by Dr. Robert H. Felix, a physician who had grown up with the Menninger family in Kansas and had developed a sharp critique of the state mental hospital as an institution for the care of the emotionally disturbed. Felix was later to become director of NIMH. A primary architect of the community mental health movement, Felix was able to draw on his extensive experience in the Mental Hygiene Division of the U.S. Public Health Service as well as on the breadth of professional and political contacts that three decades of public service afforded.[8] Felix's objective was as simple as it was radical. He intended to pick up the banner last advanced by Dorothea Dix and reassert the role of the federal government in the nation's mental health policy. Through the community mental health movement, Felix would use federal legislation to reform the archaic state mental hospitals. The legislation that enabled NIMH to reform mental health care was the Community Mental Health Centers Acts of 1963 and 1965.

THE COMMUNITY MENTAL HEALTH CENTERS ACT

Under the unusually advantageous circumstances of the postwar era, the Community Mental Health Centers (CMHC) Act was passed by Congress and signed by President Kennedy on October 31, 1963. The enactment of CMHC legislation was not, however, without obstacles. To allay the American Medical Association's fears that the act represented socialized medicine, the CMHC Act of 1963 appropriated funds only for construction purposes. It was not until 1965, when the AMA was reeling from governmental proposals to institute federal health care programs for the aged and the poor, that funds were authorized for staffing CMHCs. Advocates of the CMHC acts of 1963 and 1965 maintained that a constant target of the legislation was "to eliminate, within the next generation, the state mental hospital, as it then existed."

> The strategy of the mental health leadership and their allies was to "demonopolize" the state role in the provision of mental health services and attempt to establish a triad of federal, state, and local support for mental health services. At this time, federal bureaucrats planned to blanket the whole country with comprehensive community mental health services. Their intention was not to federalize the total program through its financing, but to obtain a degree of control through the resulting federal regulations and standards.[9]

The philosophical basis for transferring mental health care from the state hospital to the community was borrowed from public health, which had developed the concept of prevention. In adopting this formulation, proponents of community mental health presumed that services provided in the community would be superior to the warehousing of patients in state institutions. Prevention, according to the public health model, was of three types. *Primary prevention* efforts were designed to eliminate the onslaught of mental health problems. Certain psychiatric disturbances, such as depression and anxiety disorders, seemed to be caused by stress, which could be reduced by eliminating the source of stress. *Secondary prevention* consisted of early detection and intervention to keep incipient problems from becoming more debilitating. For example, screening school children for attention deficit disorders and providing corrective treatment could enhance a child's educational career and, thereby, enhance development throughout adolescence. *Tertiary prevention* consisted of "limiting the disability associated with a particular disorder, after the disorder had run its course." Typically, tertiary prevention activities sought to stabilize, maintain, and—when possible—rehabilitate those with relatively severe impairments.[10] It was clear to the community mental health activists that the state hospital addressed only tertiary prevention (and then poorly), whereas community mental health offered the prospect of combining primary and secondary intervention with a more adequate effort at tertiary prevention. The structure through which prevention would be operationalized was the community mental health center (CMHC).

According to the CMHC acts, the United States was to be divided into catchment areas, each with a population of from 75,000 to 200,000 persons.[11] Eventually, NIMH planned a CMHC for each catchment area, some 2,000 in all.[12] Programmatically, each CMHC was to provide all essential psychiatric services to the catchment area: inpatient hospitalization, partial hospitalization, outpatient services, 24-hour emergency services, and consultation and education for other service providers in the community. Soon after passage of the CMHC Act, child mental health as well as drug abuse and alcoholism services were added to the array of services provided. To make sure that patients were not lost between programs within the CMHC network, a "case manager" role was defined, whereby every case was assigned to one professional who monitored the patient's progress throughout treatment. Financially, NIMH provided funding to disadvantaged catchment areas through matching grants over an eight-year cycle. At the end of the cycle, the catchment area was supposed to assume financial responsibility for the CMHC.[13] With this framework, mental health reformers believed that the CMHC was an effective alternative to the state hospital.

DEINSTITUTIONALIZATION

Enthusiasm for community mental health reform ebbed when a series of circumstances, beyond the control of the CMHC architects, began to subvert the movement. Despite promising growth in the number of CMHCs during Johnson's presidency, the Nixon administration did not look favorably on CMHCs and impounded funds appropriated for mental health programs. Although funds were later released, the Nixon administration had clearly stated its disapproval of governmental mental health initiatives. Subsequent legislation to restore momentum to the flagging CMHC movement was crushed by a veto from President Ford. By the time a more sympathetic Carter administration assumed office, economic problems were so serious that additional appropriations for mental health were constrained.[14] Still, at the end of Carter's term, 691 CMHCs continued to receive federal assistance. With the Omnibus Budget and Reconciliation Act of 1981, however, the Reagan administration collapsed all mental health funding into a block grant available to states for any mental health services they deemed fundable. As a result, the designation of CMHCs in direct receipt of federal funds ceased in 1981.[15]

In the meantime, many states planned to shift responsibility for the mentally ill to the CMHCs. In fact, the community mental health movement had proved a timely blessing for officials in states where the maintenance of archaic state hospitals was an increasing economic burden. As the states discharged patients from state institutions, immediate savings were realized; moreover, "the continuing fall in the numbers of patients to be housed provided state governments with plausible reasons for abandoning expensive schemes of capital investment designed to extend and (or) renovate their existing state hospital systems."[16] Subsequently, 14 state hospitals were closed between 1970 and 1973. The prospect of substantial cost savings through the "deinstitutionalization" of patients received wide support. As governor of California, Ronald Reagan proposed closing all state hospitals by 1980.[17] Unfortunately, the transfer of patients from state institutions to those in the community was not well planned. Through the mid–1970s, the deinstitutionalization movement was characterized by "severe fragmentation of effort and distribution of activity broadly throughout government with little effective coordination at the state or national level."[18] For purely economic reasons, then, state officials were strongly encouraged to facilitate deinstitutionalization regardless of whether or not alternative forms of care were available for those discharged from state hospitals.

Deinstitutionalization was further confounded by a series of judicial decisions in the mid–1970s that enhanced the civil rights of mental patients while at the same time requiring states to provide them with treatment. In *Wyatt v. Stickney*, Alabama District Court Judge Frank Johnson ruled that the state of Alabama was obliged to provide treatment to patients in state hospitals and ordered Governor Wallace and the state to appropriate millions of dollars for that purpose—a judgment with which the state subsequently failed to comply. Shortly thereafter, in *Donaldson v. O'Connor*, the Supreme Court determined that "the state could not continue to confine a mentally ill person who was not dangerous to himself or others, who was not being treated, and who could survive outside the hospital." Finally, in *Halderman v. Pennhurst*, the Third District Court established that institutionalized patients deserved treatment in the "least restrictive alternative."

As a group, these rulings had a profound effect on institutional care for the mentally impaired. Only persons dangerous to themselves or others could be hospitalized involuntarily. For those hospitalized, involuntarily or otherwise, states were obliged to provide adequate treatment in a manner that was least restrictive to the patient. These decisions promised to be enormously costly to state officials who were trying to curb mental health expenditures. To comply with the court decisions, states would have to pump millions of dollars into the renovation of institutions that had been slated to be closed. The solution, in many instances, was to use a narrow interpretation of *Donaldson* to keep the emotionally disturbed out of state institutions. Judicial decisions, coupled with the fiscal concerns of state officials, provided a convoluted logic that served as the justification for first emptying state hospitals of seriously disturbed patients and then requiring the manifestation of life-threatening behavior for their rehospitalization. If people were not hospitalized in the first place, the states bore no obligation to provide the adequate, but expensive, treatment demanded by *Wyatt v. Stickney*. The criteria for hospitalization specified the most serious self-destructive behaviors, but once admitted, patients were stabilized as quickly as possible and then discharged. As a result, those in greatest need of mental health services, the seriously mentally ill, were often denied the intensive care they needed. The consequences for the mentally ill were substantial. In his interpretation of the legal decisions influencing mental health services, Alan Stone, psychiatrist and professor in the Harvard University School of Law, observed that the true symbol of the Supreme Court *Donaldson* decision was a bag lady.[19] Thus, legal decisions favoring the mentally ill often proved illusory; in the name of enhancing the human rights of the mentally ill—but with no corresponding improvement in services—they offered nothing more than the right to be insane.[20]

THE REVOLVING DOOR

The shortfall of the community mental health movement, state transfers of patients from mental hospitals, judicial decisions assuring patients of their civil rights, and the deinstitutionalization movement in mental health all combined to leave tens of thousands of former mental patients adrift. Although some former mental hospital patients were able to deal with community agencies in order to obtain mental health care, many of the seriously mentally ill were left to themselves.[21] By the late 1970s, some 40,000 poor, chronic mental patients had been "dumped" in New York City. The 7,000 on the Upper West Side of Manhattan represented "the greatest concentration of deinstitutionalized mental patients in the United States."[22] Reporting in *Scientific American*, two mental health researchers described their experiences with deinstitutionalized patients.

> Time and time again we see patients who were released from state hospitals after months or years of custodial care; who then survive precariously on welfare payments for a few months on the fringe of the community, perhaps attending a clinic to receive medication or intermittent counseling; who voluntarily returned to a hospital or were recommitted . . . who were maintained in the hospital on an antipsychotic medication and seemed to improve; who were released again to an isolated "community" life and who, having again become unbearably despondent, disorganized, or violent, either present themselves at the emergency room or are brought to it by a police officer. Then the cycle begins anew.[23]

The high incidence of readmissions for psychiatric patients—the "revolving door"—had become an unavoidable problem in mental health. In 1970 the ratio of readmissions per resident of a mental hospital was 1.4; in 1974 the ratio was 1.74; but by 1981 it had reached 2.83, double that of a decade earlier.[24] Through the mid-1980s, the ratio of admissions per resident continued to edge up so that by 1986 it stood at 2.98.[25] By 1991, the ratio had fallen slightly to 2.88.[26]

Meanwhile, resources for state mental hospitals dwindled, leaving patient care uncertain. In an attempt to manage patients more cost-effectively, state mental institutions relied more heavily on psychoactive medication, sometimes with disastrous consequences. In California, for example, a federally funded group that oversees mental health care complained of unnecessary deaths of mental patients who had been left unsupervised after receiving medication:

> The 28-year-old . . . patient died December 26, 1989, while he was locked in his dorm room . . . for 3 and one-half hours, the report charges. In addition to lithium and Valium, he was given Cogentin, which can cause vomiting, and Thorazine, which can suppress the body's natural coughing reflex. He suffocated on his own vomit and a piece of Christmas candy, the report said.
>
> The [other deaths] involved a 24-year-old patient who collapsed and died after he was given five different medications, and a 21-year-old man who had a fatal heart attack after he was given an injection of the psychiatric drug Haldol, the report said.[27]

A coherent mental health policy had ceased to exist in the United States in the 1980s. By 1990, psychiatrist E. Fuller Torrey and his associates observed that, "services for individuals with serious mental illness in the United States are a disaster by any measure used. Not since the 1820s have so many mentally ill individuals lived untreated in public shelters, on the streets, and in jails."[28] State hospitals had been divested of much of their responsibility for patients with serious psychiatric problems, but a complete system of CMHCs was not in place to care for many of those who had been deinstitutionalized.

As state hospitals converted from long-term custodial care to short-term patient stabilization, psychotropic medication came to be a routine form of treatment. But the psychopharmacological revolution, though consistent with the relatively orderly movement toward deinstitutionalization in the late 1960s, seemed incongruent with the psychiatric chaos of two decades later. Shown to stabilize psychotic patients until interpersonal treatment methods could be employed, the major tranquilizers—Prolixin, Thorazine, Haldol, Stelazine, to name a few—seemed clinically indicated within the controlled environment of the hospital. In a community setting, however, psychotropic medication became problematic. Once stabilized on major tranquilizers, patients frequently found the side effects of the medication—dry mouth, nervousness, torpor, lactation in women, impotence in men—unacceptable and stopped taking the medication.

Yet, without medication, such patients frequently decompensated, and without the regular supervision of psychiatric personnel, patients disappeared into inner-city ghettos or rural backwaters, adding to an already growing homeless population. Definitive data on the psychological condition of the homeless are difficult to generate, but a study of the homeless in Fresno, California, revealed that

"34 percent were rated severely impaired and urgently in need of [psychiatric] treatment. An additional 33 percent were rated moderately impaired so that treatment would be of substantial benefit."[29] A Baltimore study found that 80 percent of the homeless were mentally ill, and most of these were also abusing illicit drugs and alcohol.[30] In the absence of mental health care, increasingly desperate former mental hospital patients turned to petty crime to gain income, thus clogging local courts. Commenting on the surge in arrests of the mentally ill, one mental health worker became exasperated: "These people are forced to commit crimes to come to the attention of the police and get help."[31]

CMHCS UNDER SIEGE

The discharge of patients from state mental hospitals eventually imposed an enormous burden on the CMHCs. Because the seriously mentally ill were often unable to get care from hospitals, the CMHCs provided the only service these people received. A Philadelphia CMHC reported that 44 percent of its patients were chronically disturbed and that these patients consumed 70 percent of the mental health services provided.[32] CMHCs had to restructure their activities so as to focus on immediate care for the seriously disturbed, with the result that "indirect" services, such as prevention and evaluation, were cut back, as shown in Table 13.1. A study of 94 CMHCs showed that increasing demand for direct services to the seriously mentally disturbed began to skew mental health service delivery.[33] Thus, rather than being a mental health agency that provided a comprehensive range of services to all persons in a catchment area, the CMHC rapidly became an outpost for the seriously mentally disturbed, a population that it was not intended to serve, at least exclusively.

While client demand escalated, CMHCs faced significant cuts in federal funding. The Reagan administration moved to consolidate mental health funding in the form of a block grant that was devolved to the state, but in the process reduced federal funding 21 percent.[34] As funding from the federal government diminished, CMHCs became more dependent on the states, which had historically defined

◆TABLE 13.1
Percent of CMHCs Reporting Changes in Services, 1975-1985

Service	*Percent*
Community residential services	+75
Services for young chronic adults	+72
Day treatment/partial care services	+68
Case management	+63
Outpatient services	+49
Consultation and education	−57
Prevention	−48
Evaluation	−36

Source: Judith Larsen, "Community Mental Health Services in Transition," Community Mental Health Journal (Winter 1987), pp. 19, 20.

mental health care in the United States. CMHCs were able to compensate for federal reductions to some extent by obtaining more funding from government assistance programs. Significantly, nongovernmental sources, such as client fees and private insurance, continued to account for a relatively minor portion of CMHC operating expenses. Precisely how this reduction in federal assistance affected the CMHC effort varied, of course, with individual programs. CMHCs in wealthier states, for example, were better able to weather the fiscal turmoil than were those in poorer states. Generally, however, CMHCs reduced staffing and programming through such strategies as layoffs and hiring freezes, staff reassignments, and internal reorganization.[35]

By the mid–1980s, CMHCs seemed to have made the necessary organizational adjustments to funding changes, but these were at the expense of staffing and programming needs that had been increasing. CMHCs were able to hire some new staff to make up for earlier reductions, but programming had stagnated completely. Eventually, the morale of CMHC staff suffered as mental health professionals could no longer see any relief from their inability to provide even minimal care to the seriously mentally ill. In San Diego, for example, county officials decided to target scarce resources for only the most seriously disturbed, which drew this editorial response from a CMHC staff member:

> In the future . . . the community mental health clinics will provide little or no talking therapy to their thousands of clients. Instead, most patients

will find their treatment limited to a 15-minute visit with a psychiatrist and a prescription for expensive psychotropic medications—bought, incidentally, at taxpayer expense.[36]

A decade after devolving the mental health block grant to the states, CMHCs had adjusted by reducing professional staff, increasing caseloads, reorganizing and targeting services for the chronically mentally impaired and the insured, and reducing services to children, adolescents, and the elderly who were uninsured.[37]

By 1990, mental health service delivery was diversifying. CMHCs maintained an important institutional role; yet no longer served as the focus of mental health reform as was the case during the late 1960s and 1970s. As Table 13.2 shows, CMHCs failed to replace the state hospital system, although state hospitals faced several competitors in providing inpatient services. With respect to outpatient services, the role of CMHCs had also been diminished, as indicated by Table 13.3.

PREVENTIVE COMMITMENT

By the early 1990s, governmental mental health policy was in disarray. Deinstitutionalization had contributed to the homelessness problem, with as many as 50 percent of the homeless being former mental hospital patients.[38] When winter threatened the safety of some homeless people in New York City, a team of mental health workers was authorized to pick up those who posed a danger to themselves and to commit them to Bellevue Hospital for a three-week observation period, a policy referred to as "preventive commitment." The first person picked up was Joyce Brown, who "was dirty, malodorous and abusive to passersby and defecated on herself."[39] To the chagrin of then-Mayor Ed Koch, Brown had been stabilized in Bellevue when attorneys from the American Civil Liberties Union challenged her involuntary commitment. The prospect that pending litigation might cancel the program led one supporter to observe that "for the severely mentally ill, liberty is not just an empty word but a cruel hoax."[40]

Despite initial setbacks in preventive commitment, 26 states and the District of Columbia have laws authorizing the practice. The high number of treatment dropouts from outpatient therapy and the revolving door of hospitalization served to encourage local authorities to find some method for ensuring that the seriously mentally ill would not deteriorate owing to lack of intervention by mental health professionals. Preventive commitment provides for commitment of individuals who do not meet the statutory standard for involuntary hospitalization but who, it is asserted, are mentally ill, are unable to voluntarily seek or comply with treatment, and who need treatment in order to prevent deterioration that would predictably result in dangerousness to self or others or grave disability.[41]

◆ TABLE 13.2
Distribution of Persons Treated in Inpatient Settings *(In thousands)*

Setting	*Number of persons*	*Percent*
General hospitals	696	43.3
State and county hospitals	566	35.2
CMHC	68	4.2
Private mental hospitals	174	10.8
VA hospitals	114	7.1
Alcohol/drug unit	116	7.2
Nursing home	53	3.3
Total	1,608	100.0

Source: Ronald Manderscheid and Mary Sonnenschein, (Eds.), Mental Health, United States, 1994 (Rockville, MD: Substance Abuse and Mental Health Services Administration, 1994), p. 38.

◆ **TABLE 13.3**
Distribution of Persons and Visits to Ambulatory Settings
(In thousands)

Setting	*No. of Persons*	*Percent*	*No. of Visits*	*Percent*	*Visits/Person*
Psychiatric hospital outpatient clinic	409	3.6	4,711	3.3	11.5
CMHC	1,591	14.1	21,768	15.5	13.7
General hospital	901	8.0	7,454	5.4	8.3
VA hospital	562	5.1	4,108	2.9	7.3
Alcohol/drug unit	682	6.1	15,945	11.4	23.4
Mental health clinic specialist	1,839	16.3	15,219	10.8	8.3
Mental health private practice	5,099	45.3	70,745	50.4	13.9
Crisis center	174	1.5	455	0.3	2.6
Total	11,257	100.0	140,405	100.0	12.6

Source: Derived from Ronald Manderscheid and Mary Sonnenschein (Eds.), *Mental Health, United States, 1994* (Rockville: Substance Abuse and Mental Health Services Administration, 1994), p. 37.

A seemingly humane policy, preventive commitment nevertheless presents serious problems when there are inadequate mental health services to see that it is used properly. Without adequate staff resources, preventive commitment can become a form of social control—as opposed to therapy—in which treatment "consists of mandatory medication and little else."[42] One authority on preventive commitment speculated that mental health professionals would have little choice but to use "forced medication" as "the treatment of choice" for those in preventive commitment and that they would have to "actually track down noncompliant patients at their place of residence or elsewhere and administer medication as part of a mobile outreach team."[43]

For those concerned with the civil rights of the mentally impaired, such an eventuality is nothing less than ghoulish, an exercise in tyranny on the part of the state in the name of social welfare.[44] Even under conditions of adequate staffing, preventive commitment remains problematic. The side effects of psychoactive medication are so pronounced for many patients that they simply refuse to take it, even under duress. Among the contraindications of psychoactive medication is tardive dyskinesia, permanent damage to the central nervous system resulting from long-term use of medications such as Prolixin and Stelazine. Because tardive dyskinesia is irreversible and is manifested by obvious symptoms—"protrusion of tongue, puffing of cheeks, puckering of mouth, chewing movements"[45]—the disorder raises a haunting specter: In an attempt to control psychological disturbances, psychiatry has created a host of physiological aberrations. Because tardive dyskinesia appears after long-term use and sometimes after medication is discontinued, the number of mental patients with the disorder promises only to grow. In fact, one observer has prophesied that the mental health problem "of the next decade is tardive dyskinesia."[46] Unfortunately, the critics of preventive commitment who cite the danger of tardive dyskinesia offer no alternative for the care of the seriously mentally ill that is economically or politically plausible. As a result, preventive commitment is likely to be an increasingly prominent feature—however troublesome—of future mental health policy.

STATE INNOVATIONS IN MENTAL HEALTH

By the 1990s several states were exploring innovative methods for delivery of mental health services.[47] One approach involved the integration of services and payment through a capitation method, a strategy developed in several localities. Under a capitation method of payment, agencies are awarded a predetermined amount per client with which they must provide a range of services. Agencies are funded the capitation amount regardless of the actual cost of serving an individual client. Capitation in mental health care would mimic health maintenance organizations (HMOs), which have a successful track record in providing preventive and primary health care. "Mental health HMOs would centralize financing and delivery system responsibility, create financial incentives to reallocate resources from inpatient to outpatient settings, and reduce system fragmentation, as perceived by patients."[48] Such an arrangement has the advantage of being easy to administer, and it builds into the reimbursement scheme certain incentives that do not exist in other arrangements. Under a capitation reimbursement method, for example, agencies are encouraged to cut down on expensive services, such as hospitalization, because a surplus can be realized when the actual cost of care is below the capitation amount. "Money can be used to develop walk-in crisis centers, step-down units that provide intermediate care after an acute hospitalization, special case management programs for coordinating services and rehabilitation or special housing services."[49] In addition, agencies are penalized for neglecting to serve clients, because every capitated client represents a resource base for the agency.

An example of how a capitation method of payment could be used in mental health service delivery is the integrated mental health (IMH) concept being developed in New York State and Philadelphia. Capitated mental health care under IMH would have three major features. First, current categorical funding—Medicaid, Supplemental Security Income, Food Stamps Programs, local funding—would be aggregated into a common fund from which capitation "premiums" would be paid. Second, a nonprofit planning and coordination agency would be established to oversee mental health care and in so doing negotiate contracts with providers, monitor performance, and evolve innovative programs. Third, particularly high-usage clients would be targeted for provision of less costly services in order to generate surpluses for less intensive services.[50]

The magnitude of cost savings that can be realized through IMH is illustrated by the deployment of a capitated system in two New York counties. In order to induce CMHCs to participate in the capitation arrangement, payment rates were established for levels of service for three types of patients: "continuous patients" who had been hospitalized for some time, $39,000; "intermittent patients" who generally required intermediate care (two rates), $18,000 and $13,000; and "outpatients" who needed the least intensive care, $5,000. State officials calculated that such payments would realize savings because state hospital care exceeded $100,000 per patient annually. By 1991–1992 the continuous patient rate was reduced to $28,000, the intermittent rate was combined and lowered to $15,600, and the outpatient rate was increased to $11,600. Initial assessment of the program indicated cost savings and improved patient functioning. Participating CMHCs planned to used their revenue surpluses to extend mental health services to children and the elderly.[51]

The idea of integrating services through an arrangement such as the IMH is likely to become an important source of innovation in future mental health policy. Such an eventuality has significant implications for human service professionals, who may miss an important opportunity to shape mental health programs unless they are willing to sharpen their administrative skills. The capitation of mental health services, as might be suspected, places a premium on fiscal analysis, cost accounting, and strategic planning skills. In a policy environment in which capitation is an increasingly prevalent method of ensuring access to service while containing program costs, mental health administrators who are not knowledgeable about fiscal management may well lose control of programs to professionals from business and public administration. Unfortunately, there is a precedent for such a loss of program control. When Medicare and Medicaid subsidized long-term care for the elderly, human service professionals were slow to take advantage of administrative opportunities in the emerging nursing home industry. Eventually, long-term care came under the control of business executives who were not particularly sensitive to the psychological and social problems of patients in nursing homes. Outside the nursing home industry, human service professionals have had to lobby aggressively for the inclusion of advocacy services for the hospitalized elderly, a struggle that continues today. The prospect of a similar development in mental health policy is as troubling as it is plausible. Social workers have been reluctant to become managers in human-service corporations;[52] yet case management services for the seriously mentally ill "have enjoyed a rapid increase in prominence within the mental health system."[53] Unless mental health professionals increase their understanding of capitalism, they may find themselves working under the direction of business executives—or outside mental health services altogether. Such a development is unlikely to be in the best interests of the seriously emotionally disturbed.

In addition to the role that mental health professionals might play if mental health services are restructured, other issues emerge. If capitated services becomes a primary vehicle for reimbursing providers, should government prefer nonprofit providers, ordinarily CMHCs, or for-profit providers, usually HMOs? As the commercialization of health care demonstrates, HMOs are quick to exploit new markets, and mental health delivery is no exception. But would HMOs continue to provide services to the chronically mentally ill, or would more disturbed patients become "refugees" from the HMOs that were once eager to recruit them?[54] Under either arrangement, is it reasonable to expect mentally impaired consumers to make wise choices in selecting a mental health provider? "Many clients receiving services in managed mental health care," cautioned one observer, "may have difficulty understanding and processing" the type of information necessary to make a prudent choice in service provider.[55]

PARITY FOR MENTAL HEALTH CARE

Although managed care defined much of the parameters of mental health care during the late 1980s and early 1990s, a reaction was building. Under aggressive managed care plans, many who had received mental health services in the past found their options attenuated or eliminated altogether.[56] Accompanying the rationing of mental health services under managed care, a group of parents and relatives of the mentally ill organized the National Alliance for the Mentally Ill (NAMI) and fought for extended mental health coverage.[57]

Advocates of extended mental health coverage were encouraged by the Clinton administration's Health Security Act, a health care reform that might have placed mental health provision on a par with physical health services. The demise of health care reform left mental health advocates searching for a vehicle for obtaining parity in mental health care. Health insurers opposed parity in mental health care because it would increase the cost of premiums. The Congressional Budget Office projected that mental health parity would raise premiums by 4 percent, or about $12 billion.[58] Given its aversion to increased health costs, to say nothing of objecting to government meddling in health care, few expected the conservative One-hundred-fourth Congress would move toward parity.

Yet, smarting from negative ratings associated with an overzealous conservative agenda, the One-hundred-fourth Congress suddenly reversed field in the closing days of the legislative session and delighted mental health advocates by agreeing on legislation establishing parity for mental health care. Effective January 1, 1998, employers with more than 50 employees who offer health insurance must include mental health benefits that are comparable to health benefits.[59] The consequences of legislatively mandating parity in mental health coverage were immediately disputed. Opponents warned of significant increases in health insurance premiums and the likelihood that employers would eliminate mental health coverage in order to dodge the parity mandate.[60] Defenders, on the other hand, minimized the implications for premium increases, noting that mental illness was, for the first time, being interpreted as a physiological disorder.

Parity for mental health care marked the end of the downsizing of mental health care. The devolution of mental health care to the states beginning in the early 1980s and the rationing of resources for mental health through managed care through the remainder of the decade, had effectively checked the expansion of mental health care. Although important questions remained regarding implementation, parity in mental health represented a long-awaited and prospectively sizable increase in resources for the mentally ill.

SUBSTANCE ABUSE

Mental health services are often associated with substance abuse. Human-service professionals in direct services are familiar with clients who have chosen to anesthetize themselves from stress or misery with alcohol and other substances. Individual psychological problems are of course compounded by reliance on such substances, and these problems not only affect the families of substance abusers but also become more severe when addiction is manifested. Ordinarily, addiction is associated with alcohol and drugs, less often with tobacco. Substance abuse has become an important area of public policy not only because of appropriations for treatment programs but also because of the enormous costs that substance abuse extracts from society. As these costs have escalated, substance abuse policy has attained a higher profile in domestic affairs.

The interaction of emotional difficulties, alcoholism, and substance abuse is reflected in social welfare policy and has been institutionalized in the Alcohol, Drug Abuse, and Mental Health Administration (ADAMHA) of the Department of Health and Human Services. ADAMHA oversees the federal Alcohol, Drug Abuse, and Mental Health block grant, which consolidates several separate or "categorical" programs established earlier, such as the CMHC Act. Since 1981 all mental health expenditures have been in block grants to states. By using a block grant strategy, the federal government removed the power from federal agencies and transferred it to the individual states. The federal ADAMHA budget (see Table 13.4) has increased, but many critics would argue that it is still insufficient to address the mounting demands for substance abuse programs.

A block grant enables states to apportion funds on the basis of what they deem most important. As a result, some states invest more in mental health services, other states prefer to fund drug abuse programs, while still others favor alcoholism programs. Although the block grant method of funding provides states with the flexibility to tailor programs to suit their needs, it also raises the risk of defunding programs that are no longer topical. For example, the recent concern about cocaine use may well lead to increased funding for substance abuse programs that could come at the expense of alcohol and mental health programs unless additional money is budgeted for the ADAMHA block grant. Because increased funding is unlikely, new cocaine treatment programs will probably be developed to the detriment of long-standing alcoholism and mental health programs.

The consolidation of categorical grants into a block grant reflects the preference of many human-service professionals for preventive programs that apply generically to all forms of substance abuse. This approach has been argued persuasively by Mathea Falco:

> An estimated 18 million Americans are alcoholics and 55 million are regular smokers, compared to 5.5 million serious drug abusers. Each year alcohol causes 200,000 deaths from disease and accidents,

◆ TABLE 13.4
Expenditures in the Federal Alcohol, Drug Abuse, and Mental Health Administration
(In thousands of dollars)

Program	Allocations by year 1994	1995*	1996*
Mental health	139,176	163,711	164,049
Mental health block grant to states	290,237	275,420	275,420
Substance abuse prevention	253,469	238,559	216,080
Substance abuse treatment	240,102	222,405	236,694
Substance abuse block grant to states	1,164,741	1,234,107	1,294,107
Program management	61,152	61,128	61,042
Buildings and facilities	158	—	—
Total	2,149,035	2,195,330	2,247,392

*estimated
Source: *Budget of the U.S. Government: Fiscal Year 1996* (Washington, DC: U.S. GPO, 1995), p. 477.

> while more than 400,000 Americans die from smoking. By contrast, deaths from all illicit drugs range from 5,000 to 10,000. The costs of health care and lost productivity caused by tobacco-related illnesses are estimated at $60 billion a year, and those attributed to alcoholism exceed $100 billion. For all illegal drugs, the National Institute of Drug Abuse sets the annual bill to society at $40 billion.[61]

What is the logic in having separate preventive programs for tobacco, alcohol, and illegal drugs when effective prevention programs can be developed for all of them? In the light of diminishing resources for social programs, Falco's book, *The Making of a Drug-Free America: Programs That Work*—a call for integrating prevention efforts—is compelling.

History of Substance Abuse

Although most societies have incorporated addictive substances into their religions or social conventions, their use is ordinarily circumscribed. For historical and demographic reasons, American culture has been accepting of certain substances, ambivalent about some, and phobic about others. Tobacco, a crop the colonists were encouraged to cultivate by their European sponsors, has been a legal commodity since Europeans first settled in North America. Alcoholic beverages appear in most agrarian societies, and these are a fixture in American folklore. Still, the consequences of excessive consumption on family life led some religiously inspired Progressives to call for the prohibition of alcohol. From 1919 to 1933, the Eighteenth Amendment to the Constitution prohibited the manufacture and sale of alcoholic beverages in the United States. Cocaine was a common ingredient in many early patent medicines and popular beverages like Coca-Cola. Concern about quality in production, however, led to the Pure Food and Drug Act of 1906, which required that ingredients be listed on product labels. When the public learned that there was cocaine in some products, local jurisdictions prohibited their sale. Imported with the Chinese laborers who built the western rail system, opium was initially ignored until reports surfaced that women from upright families were frequenting "opium dens." The Hague Opium Convention of 1912, of which the United States was a leader, controlled the production and sale of opium internationally. In the United States, restrictions on the manufacture and sale of cocaine, heroin, and marijuana were first established through the 1914 Harrison Narcotic Act. Marijuana was effectively made illegal through the Marijuana Tax Act of 1937.[62]

Despite this legacy, governmental control of mind-altering substances is anything but consistent. Although the federal government wages a "drug war," some states, for all practical purposes, disregard marijuana possession. The sale and use of cocaine and heroin have become so essential to the economy of many poor, inner-city communities that the police are ineffectual in controlling trade, able at best only to harass users. During the 1980s, cocaine was commonly used by young urban professionals (YUPPIES) as the drug of choice and glamorized by Hollywood. Meanwhile, a substantial market emerged in prescription drugs, such as Valium, which were as available as there were corrupt physicians willing to prescribe them.

Public intolerance of drug abuse escalated because of several factors. Continued carnage on the nation's highways because of drunk drivers led to the founding of Mothers Against Drunk Drivers (MADD), a voluntary group that fought aggressively for stiffer penalties for drivers under the influence of alcohol. The alcohol- and drug-related deaths of entertainers—Janis Joplin, Jimi Hendrix, and Elvis Presley—were sobering experiences for many young people. When sports stars Len Bias and Don Rogers died from cocaine overdoses, drug abuse took center stage in America. In the meantime, an ominous development served to underscore drug abuse as a public health problem, not simply as an individual moral problem. AIDS, initially associated with male homosexuals, was increasingly prevalent among inner-city intravenous drug users (IDUs). Needle sharing among cocaine and heroin addicts was identified as a primary means of transmitting HIV. Indiscriminate injections by IDUs quickly transmitted AIDS within the African American and Hispanic communities in major urban centers. When IDUs practiced unsafe sex, AIDS was passed to minority heterosexuals. As women who had contracted AIDS became pregnant, they bore infants who were HIV-positive. By the early 1990s, concerns about substance abuse drew together diverse groups in America. The anguish of white, suburban mothers of MADD was shared by black, inner-city mothers with AIDS.

Alcohol Abuse

Americans steadily increased their consumption of alcohol from the end of World War II until the 1980s, when drinking began to decrease. By 1987, the average American drank a little more than 2.5 gallons of alcoholic beverages a year.[63] However, that amount was not evenly distributed throughout the population. One-third of the population abstains from alcohol consumption; one-third considers its consumption as light; and the remaining third are considered moderate to heavy drinkers. In 1987, the National Institute of Health estimated that approximately 18 million adults in the United States have problems attributable to alcohol use.[64]

These problems are directly related to serious social problems. Forty-eight percent of all convicted offenders used alcohol just prior to committing a crime, and 64 percent of public order offenses are alcohol related.[65] In 1980, almost 100,000 deaths were related to alcohol consumption.[66] The cost of alcohol abuse and dependence was estimated at $136.3 billion in 1990.[67] Perhaps the most significant adverse consequence of alcohol consumption is highway accidents: approximately 23,000 people died in 1987 in traffic accidents in which alcohol was implicated. The tragic death toll on American highways provoked the establishment of MADD and cries to increase penalties for drunk drivers as well as public education campaigns to dissuade people from drinking while driving. This combination of motivators seemed to have a positive effect. Between 1982 and 1986 the percent of inebriated drivers involved in fatal accidents dropped significantly, as is shown in Table 13.5.

Among the most pernicious effects of alcohol consumption is fetal alcohol syndrome (FAS), a physiological and mental deformation in infants caused by their mothers' ingestion of alcohol during pregnancy. FAS children exhibit behaviors that make them extraordinarily difficult to manage growing up: limited attention span, slow response to stimuli, and an inability to incorporate a moral code. Because of these deficiencies, FAS children tend to have difficulty in the early socialization experiences of elementary school. Children with FAS frequently fail to understand complicated instructions, wander about, and take the property of classmates without understanding the inappropriateness of such behavior. FAS is particularly difficult to diagnose in that its milder form, fetal alcohol effect (FAE), does not cause any physiological abnormality in facial structure. The National Institute of Health estimated that the incidence of FAS among heavy-drinking women was as high as 25 per 1,000 births and that the cost of the disorder was almost one-third of a billion dollars.[68]

Although FAS has been recognized by pediatric researchers since 1973,[69] the syndrome was not widely known to the public until Michael Dorris's account of his adopted son's FAS condition was published in *The Broken Cord.* A novelist and the husband of award-winning author Louise Erdrich, Dorris

◆TABLE 13.5
Percent of Drunk Drivers* Involved in Fatal Accidents, 1982 and 1986

Vehicle Type	*1982*	*1986*	*Change*
Motorcycles	40.7	41.0	+1
Passenger cars	36.7	27.5	–25
Light trucks and vans	36.3	30.9	–15
Medium trucks	7.2	6.2	–14
Heavy trucks	4.2	2.6	–38

* Drivers with a blood alcohol content of 0.10 percent or higher.
Source: Adapted from *Alcohol and Health, Seventh Special Report to the U.S. Congress* (Washington, DC: U.S. Government Printing Office, 1990), p. 165.

wrote poignantly about his adoption of Adam, a Native American infant with FAS. Ignorant of Adam's condition, Dorris spent years consulting with teachers, having his son tested by psychologists, and transferring Adam to special schools. It was not until he visited an Indian reservation and a special education bus discharged a group of FAS children for school that Dorris learned about FAS from a friend. Suddenly, Dorris understood that Adam was suffering from a permanent disorder brought about by his birthmother's drinking.

In *The Broken Cord,* Dorris and Erdrich write movingly about the consequences of FAS. Because both are Native Americans themselves, their observations are as acute as they are controversial. Noting that as many as 25 percent of the children born on the Sioux Pine Ridge Reservation suffer from FAS, Dorris contends that alcohol consumption during pregnancy represents genocide among Indian peoples. In order to contain FAS, Dorris suggests that women who have given birth to FAS children and who demonstrate an inability to control their drinking during pregnancy be incarcerated until they give birth. Erdrich concurs, her rationale being that the health of the fetus has primacy over the mother's freedom to consume alcohol:

> Knowing what I know now, I am sure that even when I drank hard, I would rather have been incarcerated for nine months and produce a normal child than bear a human being who would, for the rest of his or her life, be imprisoned by what I had done. And for those so sure, so secure, I say the same thing I say to those who would not allow a poor woman a safe abortion and yet have not themselves gone to adoption agencies and taken in the unplaceable children, the troubled, the unwanted: If you don't agree with me, then please, go and sit beside the alcohol-affected while they try to learn how to add.[70]

The idea of restraining women during pregnancy to prevent fetal damage surged in the popular media. This controversy was fueled by two related issues. First, a rapid increase in the number of infants who tested positive for cocaine at birth raised the specter of a "bio-underclass" consisting of a generation of minority children condemned to disability by maternal substance abuse.[71] Second, arrests of women for exposing their infants to substance abuse in utero enraged feminists who had watched the cutbacks in maternal health and social services during the 1980s. "It has become trendy," columnist Ellen Goodman observed acidly, "to arrest pregnant women for endangering their fetuses."[72] By the early 1990s an unstable truce had evolved between proponents of fetal health and women's rights. Clearly, both camps favored aggressive public education and early treatment for substance abuse before, during, and after pregnancy, but lack of funding made such initiatives unlikely.

As a result, the question of how to manage substance-abusing women during pregnancy has been passed down to program managers and clinical staff. As the number of infants testing positive for substance abuse increased, opposition to social control intervention on the basis that it violated women's rights became less tenable for human-service professionals. Indeed, the possibility of compulsory treatment for pregnant drug abusers became an unavoidable issue when drug abuse was associated with the transmission of AIDS.[73] Compulsory treatment, of course, runs contrary to the individual liberties guaranteed by the Constitution because it is possible only through some commitment procedure. Proponents of compulsory treatment and preventive commitment have argued that it is the only way to protect potential victims against the uncontrolled and hazardous behavior of addicts. Critics, on the other hand, insist that effective public education and treatment would make such draconian measures unnecessary.

The issue of alcohol abuse and pregnancy was highlighted in 1996 when a 35-year-old Wisconsin woman was charged with attempted murder for going on a drinking binge shortly before giving birth. Delivered by Caesarean section, the infant appeared to suffer from FAS and was placed in foster care. In prosecuting the case, the district attorney presented witnesses to the mother's having stated her intent to kill the fetus by drinking. By the trial date, the mother had been in recovery, pleaded innocent to the murder charge, and was trying to regain custody of her child. The case broke new ground in the legal status of an unborn child and a woman's maternal responsibility during pregnancy.[74]

This dilemma has serious implications for clients of substance abuse programs, as it does also for practitioners. Compulsory treatment is likely to deter some people from seeking treatment for problems that they might have sought voluntarily, though perhaps at a later date. Compulsory treatment also places the practitioner in the role of social control agent, a role not conducive to building a client's trust. Compulsory treatment is likely to drive the problem underground, further exacerbating the very problem it is intended to remedy. Without adequate investments in education and treatment, the future of substance abuse policy appears likely to be plagued by a series of such negatively reinforcing decisions.

Drug Abuse

By contrast with alcohol abuse, the prevalence of drug abuse is more difficult to ascertain because the use of controlled substances—the focus of drug abuse—is illegal. It now appears that general drug abuse has begun to decline after peaking during the period 1979–1980. Still, by the late 1980s as many as 30 million Americans used drugs illegally. "During each of the last few years," reported one analyst, "police made about 750,000 arrests for violations of the drug laws."[75] But even while drug abuse was stabilizing, the use of cocaine—or its popular derivative, crack—mushroomed. The sale and use of cocaine among residents of poor urban communities as well as among professionals in middle-income communities had become epidemic by the late 1980s. Between 1976 and 1985, the number of emergency room episodes attributed to cocaine use rose by a factor of 10, to almost 10,000.[76] The cocaine epidemic proved extremely costly for the governmental agencies that bore the primary responsibility for interdiction of controlled substances as well as for the incarceration and treatment of substance abusers. One analyst placed these costs at about $10 billion per year, although this does not include the costs associated with loss of employment or productivity.[77] The National Institute on Drug Abuse pegs the annual cost of drug abuse due to lost productivity at $33 billion.[78] But the rise in cocaine use became of urgent concern to public health officials when it was discovered that as many as 25 percent of the persons who had contracted AIDS were intravenous (IV) drug users.[79] A haunting scenario began to take shape: IV drug users were no longer tortured souls in the slow process of self-destruction; they had become transmitters of an epidemic that promised to be as costly as it was deadly.

The federal response to illicit drug use has been twofold, involving both interdicting the supply of illegal substances and reducing the demand through treatment and public education. Government strategies toward containing drug abuse have oscillated wildly between interdiction and prevention. Before Reagan came to power, federal policy emphasized treatment and public education, assuming that these strategies would diminish demand. During the early 1970s, for example, two-thirds of the federal appropriations for drug abuse were for treatment and education. A decade later, however, supply interdiction had superseded demand reduction as the prime strategy, consuming 80 percent of federal drug funds. Illegal drug use is considered in greater detail in chapter 14.

For human-service professionals, the emphasis on treatment over interdiction is a positive development in drug abuse policy; yet resources targeted at prevention have been available only recently. The $500 million for school drug abuse prevention programs through the Drug Free Schools Act was not available until the early 1990s. Applying the prevention trinity used in public health to drug abuse, it is evident that most funding has been directed toward rehabilitating addicts (tertiary prevention) or treatment of abusers (secondary prevention). Limited primary prevention efforts have been field tested, but these are only now being widely adopted. Falco notes that all have not been equally effective. Life Skills Training (LST) developed in New York City and STAR (Students Taught Awareness and Resistance) deployed in Kansas City have been superior to DARE (Drug Abuse Resistant Education). But the real test of school prevention programs comes in poor neighborhoods where drug abuse is part of the community fabric. Programs such as the Westchester Student Assistance Program in New York, Smart Moves of the Boys and Girls Clubs, and the Seattle Social Development Project show promise; yet, upon evaluation, program graduates tend to report resistance to "soft" drugs—tobacco, alcohol, marijuana—while avoidance of "hard" drugs has not been clearly demonstrated.[80] This inability of prevention programs to produce resistance to hard drugs in high-risk neighborhoods may be due to methodological problems. Those high-risk youth susceptible to hard drug use are probably unlikely to complete a prevention program, nor are they good candidates to report hard drug usage through an outcome instrument. Instead, they are likely to be casualties of the research process for the same reasons they are casualties of substance abuse. For these reasons, some researchers have contended that substance abuse prevention efforts will not be successful until a much more expansive definition of primary prevention—including social, economic, and institutional factors—is adopted.[81]

In the absence of major prevention initiatives, intervention strategies focus on treatment. Generally, employees with generous health insurance have been able to gain ready admission to drug abuse treatment programs. The poor, by contrast, have found treatment available irregularly, if at all. In response to the pervasive use of alcohol and drugs, treatment facilities expanded rapidly. From 1978 to 1984, the number of hospital units treating alcohol and drug abusers increased 78 percent (from 465 to 829) and the number of beds in these facilities increased 62 percent (from 16,005 to 25,981). However, inpatient facilities provided only a fraction of treatment services to substance abusers. Of the 540,411 persons in treatment for alcohol and drug abuse in 1984, 8 percent were in an inpatient facility and 10 percent were in residential facilities, but 82 percent were under outpatient care.[82] Treatment is virtually nonexistent for the abusers who are incarcerated. For those in the community, drug abuse programs are too few in number. Perhaps half of the 5.5 million currently using drugs would elect treatment if it were available, but that number is one million more than the number of available treatment slots.[83]

Although treatment lags behind demand, research continues to demonstrate the wisdom of investing in rehabilitation. Columbia University's Center on Addiction and Substance Abuse has reported that 32.3 percent of Medicaid hospitalization days were due to neonatal complications attributed to substance abuse. Cardiovascular and respiratory disorders associated with substance abuse accounted for 31.4 percent of Medicaid hospitalization days. Significantly, when substance abuse was noted as a secondary diagnosis, the length of hospitalization doubled.[84] A comprehensive investigation of substance abuse treatment programs in California claimed savings of $7 for every $1 dollar in program costs. "Treatment is a good investment!" affirmed the California director of alcohol and drug programs.

The extent to which substance abuse services will benefit from 1996 legislation establishing parity of mental health services with health care remains to be seen. A major expansion of substance abuse treatment through employer insurance plans would inject substantial private resources into a service area that has been dominated by governmental programs and self-help groups. Yet, because such insurance is connected to employment, it will not influence the treatment of abusers who are marginal to the labor market, those most impaired and in need of intensive rehabilitation.

◆ ◆ ◆ *Discussion Questions* ◆ ◆ ◆

1. In the early 1980s, funding for community mental health centers (CMHCs) was converted to a mental health block grant. To what extent did your community evolve complete community mental health centers? What happened to them during the 1980s? What priorities have been established through the mental health block grant? How has this changed mental health services in your community?

2. The misuse of psychoactive medication has been implicated in several undesirable consequences. Has tardive dyskenisia become a significant problem among mental health patients in your community? If so, what is being done to prevent it? Are more or fewer mental patients going through the "revolving door"?

3. The effect of substance abuse on innocent people presents several difficult policy dilemmas for decision makers. What policies could be put in place to prevent the birth of infants with FAS or AIDS? How could the rights of mothers be protected? What should be the role of human-service professionals in such circumstances?

4. Prevention and treatment of substance abuse vary from locality to locality. What has your community done to dissuade young people from substance abuse? Have these initiatives been successful? According to what indicators?

5. What resources has your community committed to deal with substance abuse? Is this adequate? Which organizations support or oppose increasing treatment for substance abuse?

Notes

1. Jean Quam, "Dorothea Dix," *Encyclopedia of Social Work*, 18th Ed. (Silver Spring, MD: NASW, 1987), p. 921.
2. Michael Lesy, *Wisconsin Death Trip* (New York: Pantheon, 1973), p. 33.
3. Ibid.
4. Stephen Gould, "Carrie Buck's Daughter," *Natural History* (July 1984), pp. 85–92.
5. Walter Trattner, *From Poor Law to Welfare State* (New York: Free Press, 1974), p. 175.
6. Joint Commission on Mental Illness and Health, *Action for Mental Health* (New York: Basic Books, 1961).
7. David Mechanic, *Mental Health and Social Policy* (Englewood Cliffs, NJ: Prentice-Hall, 1969), pp. 59–60.
8. Henry Foley, *Community Mental Health Legislation* (Lexington, MA: D. C. Heath, 1975), pp. 13–14.
9. Ibid., pp. 39, 40.
10. Bernard Bloom, *Community Mental Health* (Monterey, CA: Brooks/Cole, 1977), pp. 74–75.
11. National Institute of Mental Health, *Community Mental Health Center Program Operating Handbook* (Washington, DC: U.S. Department of Health, Education, and Welfare, 1971), pp. 2–6.
12. Foley, *Community Mental Health Legislation*, p. 126.
13. The description of CMHCs is derived from the *Community Mental Health Centers Policy and Standards Manual*, 1988; see *Community Mental Health Centers Program Operating Handbook*, 1989.
14. Bloom, *Community Mental Health*, pp. 46–56.
15. *Statistical Abstract of the United States, 108th Edition* (Washington, DC: U.S. Government Printing Office, 1987), p. 104.
16. Andrew Scull, *Decarceration* (Englewood Cliffs, NJ: Prentice-Hall, 1977), p. 71.
17. Ibid., p. 69.
18. Donald Stedman, "Politics, Political Structures, and Advocacy Activities." In James Paul, Donald Stedman, and G. Ronald Neufeld (Eds.), *Deinstitutionalization* (Syracuse, NY: Syracuse University Press. 1977), p. 57.
19. Alan Stone, *Law, Psychiatry, and Morality* (Washington, DC: American Psychiatry Press, 1984), pp. 116, 117.
20. Jean Isaac Rael, "'Right' to Madness: a Cruel Hoax," *Los Angeles Times* (December 14, 1990), p. E5.
21. Uri Aviram, "Community Care of the Seriously Mentally Ill," *Community Mental Health Journal* (26)1 (February 1990), pp. 23–31.
22. Peter Koenig, "The Problem That Can't Be Tranquilized," *The New York Times Magazine*, (May 21, 1978), p. 15.
23. Ellen Bassuk and Samuel Gerson, "Deinstitutionalization and Mental Health Services," *Scientific American* (238)2 (February 1978), p. 18.
24. Steven Segal, "Deinstitutionalization," *Encyclopedia of Social Work*, 18th Ed. (Silver Spring, MD: NASW, 1987), p. 378.
25. Per conversation with Joanne Atay on September 22, 1988. Source: Division of Biometry and Applied Sciences, *Additions and Resident Patients at End of Year, State and County Mental Hospitals, by Diagnosis and State* (Rockville, MD: National Institute of Mental Health, 1988).
26. Steven Segal, "Deinstitutionalization," *Encyclopedia of Social Work*, 19th Ed. (Washington, DC: NASW, 1995), p. 706.
27. "State Blamed for 3 Deaths at Mental Hospitals," *Los Angeles Times* (October 2, 1991), p. A4.
28. Cited in Glenn Yank, David Hargrove, and King Davis, "Toward the Financial Integration of Public Mental Health Services," *Community Mental Health Journal* (8)2 (April 1992), p. 99.

29. Joseph Sacks, John Phillips, and Gordon Cappelletty, "Characteristics of the Homeless Mentally Disordered Population in Fresno County," *Community Mental Health Journal* Summer 1987), p. 114.
30. "Survey of Homeless Shows Mental Illness and Addiction," *The New York Times*, (September 10, 1989), p. 16.
31. Hector Tobar, "Mentally Ill Turn to Crime in a Painful Call for Help," *Los Angeles Times* (August 26, 1991), p. A1.
32. A. Anthony Arce and Michael Vergare, "Homelessness, the Chronic Mentally Ill and Community Mental Health Centers," *Community Mental Health Journal* (Winter 1987), p. 9.
33. Judith Larsen, "Community Mental Health Services in Transition," *Community Mental Health Journal* (Winter 1987), pp. 19, 20.
34. Trevor Hadley and Dennis Chulhane, "The Status of Community Mental Health Centers Ten Years into Block Grant Financing," *Community Mental Health Journal*, (April 1993), p. 96.
35. Judith Larsen, "Community Mental Health Services in Transition," p. 22.
36. Donald Woolson, "Policy Makes Short Shrift of Mentally Ill," *Los Angeles Times*, (November 2, 1986), p. C4.
37. Trevor Hadley, "The Status of Community Mental Health Centers," p. 97.
38. Community for Creative Non-violence, *Homelessness in America* (Washington, DC: CCNV, 1987).
39. Josh Barbanel, "Homeless Woman to be Released after Being Forcibly Hospitalized," *The New York Times* (January 19, 1988), p. 8.
40. Charles Krauthammer, "How to Save the Homeless Mentally Ill," *The New Republic*, (February 8, 1988), p. 23.
41. "Developments in Mental Disability Law: 1986," *Clearinghouse Review* 20 January 1987: 1148. Quoted in Ruta Wilk, "Involuntary Outpatient Commitment of the Mentally Ill," *Social Work* (March–April 1988), p. 133.
42. Ibid., p. 133.
43. Ibid., p. 136.
44. See, for example, Thomas Szasz, *The Myth of Mental Illness* (New York: Harper and Row, 1961); David Ingleby (Ed.), *Critical Psychiatry: The Politics of Mental Health* (New York: Pantheon, 1980).
45. *Physician's Desk Reference* (Oradell, NJ: Medical Economics Company, 1986), p. 2014.
46. Harris Chaiklin, "The New Homeless and Service Planning on a Professional Campus," 53. Chancellor's Colloquium (Baltimore, MD: University of Maryland, December 4, 1985), p. 10.
47. Glenn Yank, David Hargrove, and King Davis, "Toward the Financial Integration of Public Mental Health Services," *Community Mental Health Journal*, (28)2 (April 1992), pp. 2–12.
48. Jon Christianson and Muriel Linehan, "Capitated Payments for Mental Health Care: The Rhode Island Programs," *Community Mental Health Journal* (25)2 (Summer 1989), p. 122.
49. A. P. Schinnar, A. B. Rothbard, and T. R. Hadley, "Opportunities and Risks in Philadelphia's Capitation Financing of Public Psychiatric Services," *Community Mental Health Journal* (25)4 (Winter 1989), p. 256.
50. Schinnar et al., "Opportunities," pp. 257–258.
51. Phyllis Marshall, "The Mental Health HMO: Capitation Funding for the Chronically Mentally Ill. Why an HMO?" *Community Mental Health Journal* (28)2 (April 1992), pp. 9–14.
52. David Stoesz, "Human Service Corporations: New Opportunities for Administration in Social Work," *Administration in Social Work* (Fall 1993), pp. 8–16.
53. Charles Rapp and Ronna Chamberlain, "Case Management Services for the Chronically Mentally Ill," *Social Work* (September–October 1985), p. 417.
54. R. Thomas Riggs, "HMOs and the Seriously Mentally Ill—A View from the Trenches," *Community Mental Health Journal* (32)3 (June 1966), p. 214.
55. Patricia Backlar, "Managed Mental Health Care: Conflicts of Interest in the Provider/Client Relationship," *Community Mental Health Journal*, (32)2 (April 1996), p. 104.
56. Charles Hall, "What Price Peace of Mind?" *Washington Post* (April 23, 1996), p. A7.
57. Agnes Hatfield, "The National Alliance for the Mentally Ill: A Decade Later," *Community Mental Health Journal* (27)2 (April 1991), pp. 89–106.
58. Robert Samuelson, "Mental Health's Gray Areas," *Washington Post Weekly* (June 10–16, 1996), p. 5.

59. Helen Dewar and Judith Havemann, "Conferees Expand Insurance for New Mothers, Mentally Ill," *Washington Post* (September 20, 1996), p. A1.
60. Stuart Auerbach, "The Cost of Increased Coverage," *Washington Post Weekly* (September 30–October 6, 1996), p. 19.
61. Mathea Falco, *The Making of a Drug-Free America* (New York: Times Books, 1992), p. 24.
62. Mathea Falco, *Winning the Drug War* (New York: Priority Press, 1989), pp. 19–20.
63. U.S. Congress, *Alcohol and Health, Seventh Special Report to the U.S. Congress* (Washington, DC: U.S. Government Printing Office, 1990), p. 14.
64. *Alcohol and Health: Sixth Special Report to the U. S. Congress* (Washington, DC: Department of Health and Human Services 1987), pp. 2, 12.
65. Ibid., p. 13.
66. Ibid., p. 6.
67. *Alcohol and Health, Seventh Special Report to the U.S. Congress*, p. 163.
68. Ibid., pp. 140, 139.
69. Ibid., p. 139.
70. Louise Erdrich, "Foreword" to Michael Dorris, *The Broken Cord* (New York: Harper and Row, 1989), p. xviii.
71. Charles Krauthammer, "The Horror of Addicted Newborns," *San Diego Tribune* (July 31, 1992), p. B7.
72. Ellen Goodman, "Community Begs Off, But Prosecutes Mom," *Los Angeles Times* (February 9, 1992), p. B9.
73. Department of Health and Human Services, *Compulsory Treatment of Drug Abuse* (Washington, DC: U.S. Government Printing Office, 1989).
74. Edward Walsh, "In Case Against Alcoholic Mother, Underlying Issue Is Fetal Rights," *Washington Post* (October 7, 1996), p. A4.
75. Ethan Nadelmann, "The Case for Legalization," *The Public Interest* (Summer 1988), p. 14.
76. C. Schuster, "Initiatives at the National Institute on Drug Abuse," in *Problems of Drug Dependence 1987* (Rockville MD: Department of Health and Human Services, 1987), pp. 1–2.
77. Nadelmann, "The Case for Legalization," pp. 14–16.
78. Falco, *Winning the Drug War*, p. 6.
79. Carl Leukefeld and Frank Tims, "An Introduction to Compulsory Treatment for Drug Abuse: Clinical Practice and Research." In *Compulsory Treatment of Drug Abuse: Research and Clinical Practice* (Rockville MD: Department of Health and Human Services, 1988), p. 2.
80. Falco, *The Making of a Drug-Free America*, Chap. 3 and 4.
81. Derek Mason, Mark Lusk, and Michael Gintzler, "Beyond Ideology in Drug Policy: The Primary Prevention Model," *Journal of Drug Issues* (22)4 (Fall 1992), pp. 81–89.
82. *Alcohol and Health*, Seventh Special Report, pp. 120–121.
83. Barry Bearak, "Road to Detox: Do Not Enter," *Los Angeles Times* (September 30, 1992), p. A1.
84. Center on Addiction and Substance Abuse, *The Cost of Substance Abuse to America's Health Care System* (New York: Center on Addiction and Substance Abuse, 1993), pp. 33, 42.

CHAPTER 14

Criminal Justice

This chapter provides an overview of crime and corrections in the United States. The history of criminal justice is summarized. The roles of various governmental jurisdictions in criminal justice are considered as well as recent data on crime and justice expenditures. Important developments and issues in American criminal justice are explored, including deinstitutionalization, the War on Drugs, the underclass and crime, and the "new penology."

All societies respond to norm defying behavior through sanctions, though there is considerable variation as to which penalties are applied to specific behaviors. In Western cultures, irrational deviance is usually understood as a mental health matter, while anormative behavior on the part of a rational actor falls under the purview of law enforcement. In either case, deviance is of interest to human service professionals because clients often present anormative activity. Deviance is also an issue of social justice because the poor and minorities of color are disproportionately represented among those incarcerated in mental or correctional institutions.

HISTORY OF CRIMINAL JUSTICE

Modern criminal justice can be traced to the faith in social science that originated in the eighteenth century. Prior to the advent of classical criminology, justice was predicated on vengeance: illegal acts brought the wrath of authority on the deviant. In premodern societies where deviance was understood to be a product of evil influences, the most vicious and barbaric methods were justified to excise Satan or maintain archaic social structures. Thus, mutilation, torture, and capital punishment were often employed, sometimes in grotesque public displays, in order to rid society of malevolent influences.

Modern criminology dates from the Enlightenment, and the notion that humankind was capable of producing the methods for its own perfectibility. The radical philosopher, Jeremy Bentham (1748–1832), contended that scientific methods could be the vehicle for "the rational improvement of the condition of men." Accordingly, Bentham successfully advocated a series of reform laws in Great Britain including several pertinent to penal institutions.[1] In the United States, Cesare Beccaria applied Bentham's utilitarian philosophy to corrections, arguing that crime could be measured in its severity, that prevention was more important than punishment, that the purpose of punishment is deterrence (not revenge), and that incarceration should be to segregate prisoners so as not to exacerbate lawlessness.[2] Thus, liberal, humanistic values in criminal justice can be traced to the earliest thinkers in criminology.

American colonists imported European thinking about crime and its control. Jails were a fixture of all settlements of any size, and justice was often swift and uncompromising. In response to the dungeonlike facilities that typified colonial America, the Quakers established the Philadelphia Society for Alleviating the Miseries of Public Prisons in 1776.[3] During the following decades, institutional reformers, such as Dorothea Dix, sought to make jails and almshouses more humane. Unfortunately, their accomplishments were often subverted. An influx of immigrants, many of whom were unable to adjust to the American experience, became incarcerated in mental and correctional institutions. An American ethos of rugged individualism left little room for compassion, particularly when adults were concerned. Finally, in 1854 President Franklin Pierce vetoed legislation that would have involved the federal government in institutional care for the mentally ill, effectively leaving institutional control of deviants in the hands of the states.

Midway through a relatively bleak nineteenth century, an unlikely pioneer in American corrections emerged. In 1841 a Boston shoemaker, John Augustus, agreed to supervise petty criminals, post bail, and report to the courts his progress in their rehabilitation. The services provided by Augustus were less expensive than prison and many of his charges seemed to benefit from rehabilitation—all the more so because Augustus used his own money. Thus, a modest shoemaker began what was to become a nationwide system of probation.[4]

Some early criminologists sought more direct applications of the emerging sciences to the study of crime. The Italian psychiatrist, Cesare Lombroso, for example, proposed the existence of a "criminal type," a construct of inferior intelligence, exaggerated physical features, and a taste for amoral activities, including tattooing. The idea that a criminal could be physiologically identifiable and criminal behavior genetically transmitted has preoccupied some criminologists since Lombroso's assertions. For example, in 1913 Charles Goring studied English convicts, and Earnest Hooton evaluated American criminals during the 1920s, both concluding that prisoners were "organically inferior" compared to their law-abiding compatriots.

The genetic origin of deviant behavior was popularized by the Eugenics Movement shortly after the turn of the century. Proponents of natural selection, some of them esteemed scientists and jurists, convinced state legislators to pass legislation allowing for involuntary sterilization of "mental defectives". By the mid–1950s, more than 58,000 mental patients and convicts had been forcibly sterilized.[5] The practice of involuntary sterilization abated during the Civil Rights movement when it became apparent that many of the victims were women and minorities of color. That most victims of the Eugenics Movement were disadvantaged populations was not coincidental. Race suffused the thinking of eugenicists, as Lombroso illustrated when he wrote in 1871 that "Only we White people have reached the most perfect symmetry of bodily form."[6]

The suggestion that crime was organically determined generated a firestorm of criticism during the 1960s when an increasing number of criminals were minorities of color, the same populations that had been victimized by oppressive social policies. Despite this recognition, the contention that criminogenic behavior is hereditary continues to surface in the popular literature. The most recent popularization of genetically transmitted deviance is *The Bell Curve* by Richard Herrnstein and Charles Murray. The authors contend that, to a significant extent, poverty is hereditary, resulting in wasteful social program expenditures. Herrnstein and Murray argue that American society is becoming stratified by intellectual ability, a "cognitive elite" overseeing a degenerative underclass.[7] A subsequent review of research on genetically transmitted crime revealed that heredity had a slightly positive influence on criminal behavior; however, the researcher suspected that future research would be more productive by focusing on the interaction between environment and genetic attributes.[8]

THE CRIMINAL JUSTICE SYSTEM

The American justice system is similar to education and mental health in that states and localities provide a significantly larger portion of services compared to the federal government. The Constitution, of course, reserves public functions to the states unless they are ceded to the federal government; in the case of criminal justice, this means that state and local government expenditures exceed those of the federal government by a factor of four. Table 14.1

◆ **TABLE 14.1**
Justice System Direct and Intergovernmental Expenditures, Selected Years by Level of Government, United States, Fiscal Years 1982–1992
(Dollar amounts in millions)

					Local		
Fiscal year	*Total all governments*	*Federal*	*Total state and local*	*State*	*Total*	*Counties*	*Muni-cipalities*
1982	$35,842	$4,458	$31,573	$11,802	$20,968	$8,636	$12,455
1983	39,680	4,944	38,836	12,785	23,186	9,792	13,550
1985	46,563	6,416	42,284	16,252	27,462	11,610	16,011
1987	58,871	7,496	51,640	20,157	33,265	14,530	18,973
1989	70,949	9,674	61,745	25,269	38,825	17,503	21,579
1991	87,867	15,231	75,461	31,484	47,075	21,913	25,599
1992	93,777	17,423	80,248	33,755	50,115	23,820	26,771
Percent change							
1982–7	64.3%	66.1 %	63.6%	73.7%	58.6%	68.3%	
52.3%							
1982–92	161.6	290.8	154.2	190.9	139.0	175.8	114.9

Source: U.S. Department of Justice, Bureau of Justice Statistics, *Justice Expenditure and Employment Abstracts: 1992* (Washington, DC: 1993).

shows changes in justice expenditures for different levels of government.

As the data indicate, expenditures for criminal justice more than doubled between 1982 and 1992, a fact that warrants clarification. Much of the increase is attributable to corrections (as opposed to police protection and judicial and legal costs) which, on a per capita basis, increased from $30.34 in 1980 to $123.40 in 1992, an increase of 306 percent. Moreover, there is considerable variation in state expenditures. In 1992, for example, the per capita cost of criminal justice in the District of Columbia was $1,184.60 while that of nearby West Virginia was $117.30.[9] In other words, more resources are allocated to locking up inmates than police protection and legal services; and wealthier jurisdictions spend substantially more than poorer ones in criminal justice.

Similarly, the rate of crime varies with the type of offense as well as over time. From 1983 to 1993 crime increased 16.8 percent, as shown in Table 14.2.

Significantly, violent crime increased 52.9 percent, four times more than property crime. On a per population basis, however, the rate of increase is modulated somewhat, and in recent years the crime rate has fallen for all categories of offenses, save murder. The reasons for this are unclear. Demographers note that more crime-prone, younger adults are aging and less likely to be violent as a result; the Clinton administration cites its crime policies. In all likelihood, the proliferation of a drug economy in inner cities, the easy availability of firearms, and escalating gang violence contribute to an increasing murder rate.

But how accurate are these figures? Traditionally, crime data have been aggregated by the FBI from the reports of state and local law enforcement agencies in the form of the Uniform Crime Report (UCR). These are the basis for Table 14.2. Since 1973, however, an annual National Crime Survey (NCS) has been conducted as an alternative to the UCR. By 1990, it was evident that quite different portraits of crime were emerging from the two methods. With regard to burglary and auto theft, shortly after its inception the NCS reported significantly higher rates than the UCR, but the path of both surveys merged by the late 1980s. With regard to larceny and assault, the NCS and UCR diverged significantly over time, failing to merge.

In the case of rape, the results were even more perplexing. In 1973 the UCR rape rate was 24 per 100,000 population, while the NCS rate was more than 50 percent higher at 38. By 1990, the surveys had reversed; the UCR reported more than 105 rapes per 100,000 population while the NCS had dropped to 24. According to the UCR, rape had increased fourfold in 17 years, but the NCS documented a reduction of 50 percent. The data indicated that law enforcement was escalating its offense against sexual assault; at the same time, households were reporting a significant decline in rape. In their attempt to sort out the differences in UCR and NCS rape rates, Gary Jensen and Maryaltani Karpos speculated that an escalating UCR documented law enforcement taking rape more seriously, the result eventually yielding a suppression in the rape rate reported by the NCS.[10] If this explanation endures, it is rather dramatic evidence of the deterrence of crime when victims, in this case women, press upon law enforcement, primarily men, the import of gender-related crimes.

The Jensen and Karpos interpretation of the sharp downturn in rape has policy implications as well. In 1994 the Violence Against Women Act (VAWA) was passed, and in the following year $26 million was allocated to the states, the first of $800 million over a five-year period.[11] During the period that the UCR documented reductions in rape, the incidence of child abuse—a different indicator of domestic violence—continued to climb. Thus, while domestic violence against women seemed to be diminishing, violence directed at children escalated. If law enforcement *is* being diligent at containing rape, then a case can be made for diverting funding to reduce domestic violence targeted at abused children.[12]

Juvenile Justice and the Massachusetts Experiment

Juvenile justice is a prominent feature of American criminal justice for several reasons. Young deviants are good candidates for becoming adult deviants, in which case they become subject to the adult criminal justice system. Because the majority of adult offenders were also known to the juvenile justice system, it stands to reason that diverting youngsters away from juvenile justice may well divert them from the adult criminal justice system. From a crime prevention standpoint, reaching youngsters early, when their understanding of themselves in relation to social norms is still formative, is a more plausible strategy than attempting to intervene with adult offenders who have a less malleable sense of themselves vis-à-vis social institutions.

The first institution for juvenile delinquency was the New York City House of Refuge established in 1825. Massachusetts followed suit with a boys facility established in 1847 and one for girls in 1854.[13] These institutions paralleled other institutions designed to care for neglected children, such as Charles

◆ TABLE 14.2
Crimes and Crime Rates, by Type, Selected Years: 1983 to 1993

		Violent Crime					*Property Crime*			
Item and Year	*Total*	*Total*	*Murder*	*Forcible rape*	*Robbery*	*Aggravated assault*	*Total*	*Burglary*	*Larceny theft*	*Motor veh. theft*
Number of offenses (1,000s)										
1983	12,109	1,258	19.3	78.9	507	653	10,851	3,130	6,713	1,008
1985	12,431	1,329	19.0	88.7	498	723	11,103	3,073	6,926	1,103
1987	13,509	1,484	20.1	91.1	518	855	12,025	3,236	7,500	1,289
1989	14,251	1,646	21.5	94.5	578	952	12,605	3,168	7,872	1,565
1991	14,873	1,912	24.7	106.6	688	1,093	12,961	3,157	8,142	1,662
1993	14,141	1,924	24.5	105.0	660	1,135	12,217	2,835	7,821	1,561
Percent change, number of offenses:										
1983–93	16.8%	52.9%	26.9%	33.1%	30.2%	73.8%	12.6%	–9.4%	16.5%	54.9%
Percent change, rate per 100,00 population:										
1983–93	6.0%	38.7%	14.5%	20.5%	18.0%	57.7%	2.2%	–17.9%	5.7%	40.4%

Source: U.S. Department of Commerce, *Statistical Abstract*, 1995 (Washington, DC: Department of Commerce, 1995).

Loring Brace's New York Children's Aid Society, established in 1853. Such institutions were not known for indulging children; furnishings were Spartan, the discipline harsh, and escapes common. The orphanage/asylum for children became the subject of scathing parody under the pen of Charles Dickens.

Institutional care for adolescent deviants remained virtually unchanged until the 1960s when critics of warehousing children advocated for community alternatives. In 1972 the Juvenile Justice and Delinquency Prevention Act was passed, a measure that intended, in part, to remove children who were "status offenders" from the more serious deviants who had actually committed felonies or violent crimes. According to Jerome Miller, a youth service advocate, the act ultimately failed. However, it gave impetus to those who were proponents of noninstitutional care for delinquents.

In 1969 Miller assumed the directorship of the Massachusetts Division of Youth Services (DYS), a position that was to become symbolic of correctional reform in the United States. A social worker, Miller had been an officer in the Air Force, trained in the Menninger Clinic, and earned a doctorate at Catholic University. His initial plan to seek incremental reforms in Massachusetts faded as the structural flaws of state juvenile justice became more apparent. All of the personnel positions were filled through political patronage and very few human service professionals could be found at DYS. Staff routinely resorted to cruel and inhumane treatment, such as breaking fingers of escapees, smearing feces on incorrigibles, and placing miscreants in solitary confinement, that would have been unconstitutional in an adult institution. As Miller learned during his first months on the job, rather than institute reforms, staff and administration subverted attempts to make DYS more amenable to treatment. As the institutional conspiracy of DYS was becoming as evident as it was implacable, Miller became aware of a compelling research finding: the longer children were institutionalized at DYS the *more* likely they were to become more serious, adult offenders. As Miller saw it, not only were his reforms being disregarded, but he was also managing an institution that made youth *worse*. This seemed unwarranted when it became evident that the vast majority of adolescents in DYS institutions were not violent felons, but teens who had a knack for getting into trouble.

Miller's solution to the intransigence of DYS staff resulted in the most radical of plausible outcomes: if DYS was not amenable to reform and continued to damage adolescents, the most conscionable act would be to simply close it down. Thus, over a period of months, Miller and a hand-picked staff discharged the children to community-based, alternative care programs. With the exception of a handful of violent-prone adolescents, all of the youth were removed from DYS by the end of Miller's tenure.

The consequences of such an abrupt transformation were predictable. Legislator's objected to closing DYS facilities, particularly when an institution was in the legislator's district and thereby an employer of constituents. Law-and-order activists condemned Miller for letting loose the next generation of felons on the Massachusetts public. Researchers recorded a different experience. Using recidivism as an outcome measure, Lloyd Ohlin and Bob Coates of Harvard's Center for Criminal Justice, found that districts of the state in which strong, community-based alternatives had been deployed were those in which recidivism was markedly lower.[14]

Eventually, the Massachusetts experiment was to become a benchmark in American juvenile justice, a case study used by several prominent professional schools. In writing a postscript on the experience, Miller targeted the indiscriminate labeling of youthful deviants by human service professionals who were oblivious of the fate their judgment brought on young offenders: "our prisons and reform schools are filled with fabricated aliens made yet more alien by those who should know better, but who insufficiently understand the subjects of their research beyond narrow methodological parameters or highly controlled settings which demean and impoverish human experience."[15]

Incarceration as the intervention of choice for youthful offenders continues to be a source of disagreement within juvenile justice. Research on existing as well an innovative programs yields mixed outcomes. An analysis of Maryland youth detention facilities that were closed revealed that youth who were not institutionalized had higher recidivism rates, although this only held for crimes against property, not for crimes against persons or involving drugs.[16] Proponents of a more recent initiative, boot camps, has promised that discipline, exercise, and routine would deter adolescents from future offending. At boot camp: "inmates would receive physical training, military discipline, and drug abuse treatment, all under the direction of military personnel and with the aim of preparing them for a life that would combine . . . the requirement of regular drug tests and the opportunity for gainful employment."[17]

By 1993 boot camps had been established in 25 states, but just as rapidly enthusiasm faded. A study of Georgia facilities commissioned by the Justice Department concluded that boot camps failed to deter young offenders.[18] Not long thereafter, Connecticut closed its National Guard boot camp citing "rampant gang activity, assaults on weaker inmates, marijuana use, sexual activity, and gambling."[19] An analysis of boot camps in eight states concluded that alumni of boot camps were neither more nor less likely to commit future offenses.[20]

THE WAR ON DRUGS

By the 1980s, events had propelled the control of drug abuse to a top priority in American criminal justice. The deterioration of inner cities had been accompanied by an alarming degree of social dysfunction. Illegal drugs were not only prevalent in the poorest minority neighborhoods but had also become an essential, if not the predominant, part of the local economy. As gangs vied over turf and ever more profitable drug peddling, violence exploded. Drive-by shootings became commonplace in larger cities; gang-bangers invaded previously neutral territory—hospitals, mortuaries, cemeteries—in pursuit of enemies. Innocent people became victims of a rash of holdups, car-jackings, and seemingly random shootings. In response, President Reagan declared war on drugs.

Logically, two strategies dominated the War on Drugs: government interdicted supplies, thus eliminating the substance, or treatment programs were deployed to diminish the demand for illegal drugs. While appropriations for criminal justice increased substantially during the 1980s, much of the funding was allocated for interdiction and comparatively less for drug treatment. For example, federal funds for law enforcement increased from $800 million in 1981 to $1.9 billion in 1986; yet, funding for prevention, education, and treatment decreased from $404 million in 1981 to $338 million in 1985, a 40 percent drop when adjusted for inflation.[21]

Despite massive infusions of funds for the Drug Enforcement Administration (DEA) and the Coast Guard, by the end of the 1980s, most analysts agreed that supply interdiction had failed. Experts contended that emphasizing law enforcement would not solve the nation's drug problem. "It would be naive to assume that this well-meant legislative effort will be an end to our drug dilemma," concluded the late Sidney Cohen, former director of the Division of Narcotic Addiction and Drug Abuse of the National Institute of Mental Health:

> We have not yet come to understand the resolute, determined, amoral nature of the major traffickers or their enormous power. Perhaps we do not even recognize that, for tens of hundreds of thousands of field workers, collecting coca leaves or opium gum is a matter of survival. At the other end of the pipeline is the swarm of sellers who could not possibly earn a fraction of their current income from legitimate pursuits. If they are arrested, they are out after a short detention. If not, many are waiting to take their place.[22]

If efforts to reduce the propagation of cocoa in South and Central America proved futile, attempts to reduce street trafficking were similarly unsuccessful. A kilogram of cocaine wholesaled in Miami for $60,000 in 1981; by the late 1980s, the cost had plummeted to $10,000.[23] The price of cocaine was so low that crack houses were able to offer cocaine free to new customers, charging regulars as little as $2.[24]

To compound the problem, the application of interdiction at the street level, where drugs were sold, led to arrests of users and petty distributors, swelling already overcrowded prisons. Between 1980 and 1990 the number of federal prisoners incarcerated for the violation of drug laws increased from 1,945 to 9,804.[25] Thus, the focus on interdiction proved perverse. To contain drug use through law enforcement, thousands of addicts were imprisoned at enormous cost. Meanwhile, funds for prevention and treatment were held in check. Most ironic, drug treatment for incarcerated addicts was virtually nonexistent. With the passage of the Anti-Drug Abuse Act of 1988, the emphasis shifted back to prevention, education, and treatment. Yet under the Bush administration, when appropriations for drug abuse swelled to $12 billion, supply interdiction once again became the focus of policy, consuming 70 percent of federal funding.[26]

The mismatch between the needs of drug addicts and the eligibility requirements of social programs was captured by journalist Barry Bearak, who followed a group of junkies in New York City. Scavenging what funds he had left, one junkie decided to have himself admitted to a detox program. After a full day's bouncing from one welfare agency to another seeking eligibility to "special" Medicaid, which would pay for the detox services, Georgie, a middle-aged Hispanic, found himself in a line for public assistance only a few minutes before closing time. While Georgie waited, a friend who had come with him also to get into detox was shooting up in the rest room:

> The line moved slowly. Georgie's turn finally came a few minutes before 5 p.m. It was a short discussion. He had been in the wrong spot. He needed to be at the Application Desk, back over by Table Five where he had started.
>
> He hurried across the big room. "Can I ask you a question?" he said to a clerk.
>
> "I'm sorry," she answered, her fingers busy in a file drawer. "I need to get this out of the way."
>
> Georgie spoke up with more urgency: "I want to get into detox."
>
> The woman turned to face him now. "You came too late," she said, shaking her head. "We're not giving out any more appointments."
>
> "We've been getting the runaround all day."
>
> She eyed him more carefully, looking over his sweaty face. She spoke slowly and distinctly for the junkie's benefit. "When you come back in, all they'll give you is an appointment," she said. "You won't get emergency Medicaid. Then, with an appointment, you have to come back in a week or so and see an interviewer. Then, after they have reviewed the case, the client is contacted by mail, and that takes three weeks or a month."
>
> Georgie took this in and was stunned. "So the mumbo jumbo about getting on Medicaid the same day is bull—?" he said without anger, but with resignation.
>
> "That's right. The only way to get on is with HIV [the AIDS virus]." At last, good news. His face brightened. "Well, I'm HIV," he said.
>
> The clerk took a step back from him. "You'd have to be able to prove it with a certified letter from your doctor," she said.
>
> With that, Georgie was beaten. His shoulders sagged. And the clerk knew she could shift her attention back to the end-of-the-day filing.[27]

How Georgie came to drug addiction is speculative, of course; yet many social observers cite social and economic conditions in the poorest, inner city neighborhoods that conspire to make self-administered anaesthesia desirable for many adolescents. John Kasarda, for example, has charted the number of young blacks who are not in school nor in the labor market, as shown in Table 14.3. By the early 1990s, for the first time the number of young African Americans who were not in school nor unemployed exceeded 50 percent in every section of the United States.

During the 1980s the combination of reductions in governmental assistance to cities through social programs and the prevalence of drug trafficking was to have a pronounced effect on inner-city neighborhoods. Gradually, once squalid but quiet urban neighborhoods began to echo with gunfire as rival gangs fought over turf. By the 1990s, areas in many industrial cities had virtually imploded.[28] The "wilding" of New York City teenagers who savagely beat a female jogger was replicated when a gang of Boston youth raped and murdered a young mother.[29] Gang killings in Los Angeles soared 69 percent during the first eight months of 1990.[30] In 1992, Los Angeles reported more than 800 drug-related homicides for the year.[31] Gang-related murders in the nation's capital reached a three-year high, leading the police department's spokesperson to quip, "At the rate we're going the next generation is going to be extinct."[32]

Observers of urban poverty described a serious deterioration in inner-city communities of the 1980s contrasted with those of the 1960s. When Claude

◆ **TABLE 14.3**
Percent of Out-of-School Males Age 16–64 Not Working and Residing in the Central City, by Race, Education, and Region for Selected Metropolitan Areas: 1968–70, 1980–82, and 1990–92

REGION/Race & Education Level	*1968–1970*	*1980–1982*	*1990–1992*
NORTHEAST			
White			
Less than High School	15	34	37
High School Graduate Only*	7	17	24
Black			
Less than High School	19	44	57
High School Graduate Only	11	27	31
MIDWEST			
White			
Less than High School	12	29	34
High School Graduate Only	5	16	18
Black			
Less than High School	24	52	63
High School Graduate Only	10	30	41
SOUTH			
White			
Less than High School	7	15	18
High School Graduate Only	3	9	19
Black			
Less than High School	13	29	52
High School Graduate Only	1	19	22
WEST			
White			
Less than High School	18	20	26
High School Graduate Only	10	16	19
Black			
Less than High School	26	44	57
High School Graduate Only	13	14	43

*Completed high school, but no higher education completed.
Northeast includes Boston, Newark, New York, Philadelphia, and Pittsburgh; Midwest includes Cleveland, Chicago, Detroit, Milwaukee, and St. Louis; South includes Atlanta, Dallas, Houston, Miami, and New Orleans; West includes Denver, Long Beach, Los Angeles, Oakland, Phoenix, San Francisco, and Seattle
Source: John Kasarda, "Industrial Restructuring and the Consequences of Changing Job Locations." In Reynolds Farley (Ed), *Changes and Challenges: America 1990* (New York: Russell Sage Foundation, 1995), Table 5.15.

Brown returned to Harlem 20 years after the publication of his *Manchild in the Promised Land*, he was shocked by the casual viciousness of gang members toward their victims.[33] "In many if not most of our major cities, we are facing something very like social regression," wrote New York's Senator Daniel Patrick Moynihan. "It is defined by extraordinary levels of self-destructive behavior, interpersonal violence, and social class separation intensive in some groups, extensive in others."[34] In the socioeconomic vacuum that had developed in the poorest urban neighborhoods, the sale and consumption of drugs became central to community life. The toll this conversion was to take on young African Americans proved astonishing. As of 1988, 43 percent of those convicted of drug trafficking were African American. In New York, Hispanics and African Americans accounted for 92 percent of arrests for drug offenses in 1989. In 1990, a criminal justice reform organization, the Sentencing Project, reported that one-fourth of all African Americans between the ages of 20 and 29 were incarcerated, on parole, or on probation. Yet, the Sentencing Project data scraped only the top of what was a very large statistical iceberg.

In *Search and Destroy: African-American Males in the Criminal Justice System*, Jerome Miller identifies the frequency with which young, African American males are likely to run afoul of the law:

> *on an average day in 1991, more than four in ten (42%) of all the 18-35-year-old African-American males who lived in the District of Columbia were in jail, in prison, on probation/parole, or being sought on arrest warrants; on an average day in Baltimore, 56% of all its young African-American males were in prison, jail, on probation/parole, on bail, or being sought on arrest* [original emphasis].[35]

According to Miller, incarceration is damaging enough, but substantial harm is inflicted by simply being arrested; most employment applications inquire about an arrest record, and research demonstrates that employers avoid candidates with arrest records.

For Miller, the War on Drugs is just another "moral panic," the sort of melodrama that an insecure, middle-class creates in order to retain its social standing. A moral panic is manifested by policies and professionals that seek to reestablish social control over a phantom threat. In the case of the War on Drugs, conservative politicians and law enforcement officers have convinced the public that the nation suffers from a new generation of violent minority youth that must be held in check. The evidence presented for the law-and-order agenda consists largely of the arrest rates for violent and repeat offenders; yet Miller contends that most of "violent" offenses are the result of overzealous police overcharging miscreants, and most "repeat" offenders are rearrested for drug-related offenses. Not coincidentally, Miller contends, blacks are the target of the War on Drugs. For 1991, he notes that "the national incarceration rate in state and federal prisons was 310 per 100,000. For white males it was 352 per 100,000. For black males ages 25–29 it stood at an incredible 6,301."[36] Many of the arrests were drug related, a category that was increasing dramatically among African American youth. Per 100,000 population, drug arrests for black youth increased from 683 in 1985, to 1,200 in 1989, to 1,415 in 1991.[37] The racial disparity in juvenile drug arrests is shown in Figure 14.1.

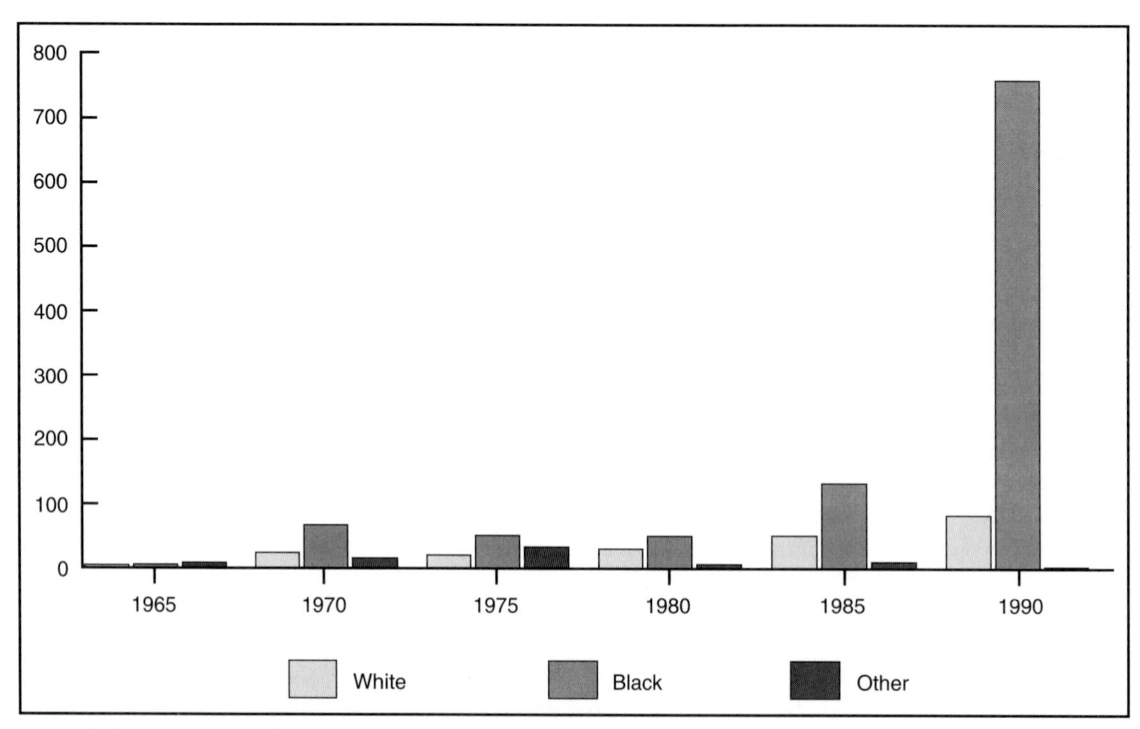

◆ **FIGURE 14.1 Tracking Racial Bias**

Source: Adopted from Jerome Miller, *Search and Destroy* (New York: Cambridge University Press, 1996).

The social consequences of arrest and incarceration for so many black youth, Miller alleges, is the cultivation of an oppositional culture, replete with rap music, personal strutting, dissing opponents, and reckless, often gun-related, violence. For youngsters brought up in an urban environment where conventional rewards through school or work are rare or nonexistent, engaging the criminal justice system is "something of a puberty rite, a transition to manhood."[38] In drawing an Orwellian conclusion, Miller predicts that jails will soon morphologize into "simple internment camps" for minority youth who are refugees from an alienating American culture.

Other observers have documented the grim circumstances of poor, minority families in urban America. A common denominator of their portrayals was drug-related violence that seemed to metastasize throughout inner-city communities, extracting a horrifying toll on minority populations. The effect on African American family life was depicted poignantly by Alex Kotlowitz, who followed the daily activities of two youngsters, Lafayette and Pharaoh Rivers. The boys ventured out of their mother's apartment in one of Chicago's housing projects at risk of being shot by drug dealers.[39] In New York City, a popular elementary school principal, Patrick Daly, was shot to death while walking through a drug-infested neighborhood searching for a nine-year-old who had left school in tears after a fight.[40] During the summer of 1992, drug-related street violence in Baltimore reached the point where the state chapter of the National Association for the Advancement of Colored People formally requested the governor of Maryland to declare a state of civil emergency and call out the National Guard to restore order in the city.

The Underclass and "Moral Poverty"

The liberal contention that crime was largely a bourgeois contrivance to maintain control over hostile, minority youth was challenged by conservatives crime theorists. Since the 1980s conservatives had argued that the chronic poor suffered from problems qualitatively different than the temporarily poor. The latter lacked basic resources, and the provision of cash benefits was a prudent response to their circumstances. The chronic poor, however, evidenced a "behavioral" poverty that differentiated from the transient poor. The behaviorally poor engaged in habits—teen pregnancy, drug abuse, petty theft, unmarried parenthood, and welfare dependency—that not only assured continual destitution, but also subverted the intent of social programs designed to help them.[41] Behavioral poverty precipitated and maintained the underclass.

In similar fashion, William Bennett, John DiIulio, Jr., and John Walters have suggested that the recent upsurge in crime can be attributed to "moral poverty". According to these conservative thinkers, moral poverty is

> the poverty of being without loving, capable, responsible adults who teach right from wrong; the poverty of being without parents and other authorities who habituate you to feel joy at others' joy, pain at others' pain, satisfaction when you do right, remorse when you do wrong; the poverty of growing up in the virtual absence of people who teach morality by their own everyday example and who insist that you follow suit. In the extreme, moral poverty is the poverty of growing up severely abused and neglected at the hands of deviant, delinquent, or criminal adults.[42]

According to the authors, moral poverty is the cause of recent increases in crime. In substantiating their argument, Bennet, DiIulio, and Walters cite data on the behavior of state prisoners in 1991. For that year 45 percent of prisoners were on probation or parole when they committed their latest conviction offense. During community supervision in the previous 17 months, the 162,000 probation violators committed some 6,400 murders, 7,400 rapes, 10,400 assaults, and 17,000 robberies. During community supervision of the previous 13 months, the 156,000 parole violators committed some 6,800 murders, 5,500 rapes, 8,800 assaults, and 22,500 robberies. "Together, probation and parole violators committed 90,639 violent crimes while 'under supervision' in the community."[43]

> At the core of the crime wave is a new category of "super-predators"—radically impulsive, brutally remorseless youngsters, including ever more preteenage boys, who murder, assault rape, rob,

> burglarize, deal deadly drugs, join gun-toting gangs, and create serious communal disorders. They do not fear the stigma of arrest, the pains of imprisonment, or the pangs of conscience. They perceive hardly any relationship between doing right (or wrong) now and being rewarded (or punished) for it later.[44]

Bennett, DiIulio, and Walters aver that much of the increase in crime can be attributed to a proliferation of drugs that has become so extensive as to represent de facto normalization of drug abuse. The severe damage associated with heroin and cocaine justifies increasing drug interdiction efforts and getting tough with street criminals who peddle drugs. Regarding treatment, Bennett, DiIulio, and Walters note that recent funding increases for treatment have not been accompanied by a significant decrease in the number of addicts seeking rehabilitation, as shown in Figure 14.2.

Although existing treatment capacity can serve only half the number of addicts, the authors of *Body Count* advocate eliminating bureaucratic waste in order to extend treatment resources. Beyond that, little can be done given the poor track record of treatment programs in getting addicts into recovery. For many addicts treatment is a cyclical experience, not an end to their substance abuse. The California Civil Addict Program reported that more addicts eventually died (27.7 percent) after receiving treatment than had become drug free (25 percent).[45]

The conservative prescription for moral poverty is as extensive as it is sometimes implausible. Bennett, DiIulio, and Walters advocate reinforcing work as opposed to receipt of unconditional welfare, removing young children from dysfunctional homes, and encouraging adoption as an alternative to foster care. Although public policy may prove instrumental in reducing such "criminogenic" influences, it is less apropos, if not irrelevant, for other suggestions, such as limiting children's TV time and reasserting the importance of religious values in daily life.[46]

Legalization of Drugs

If Bennett, DiIulio, and Walters appear to have liberal tendencies in support of social programs that support family life, they are inalterably opposed to

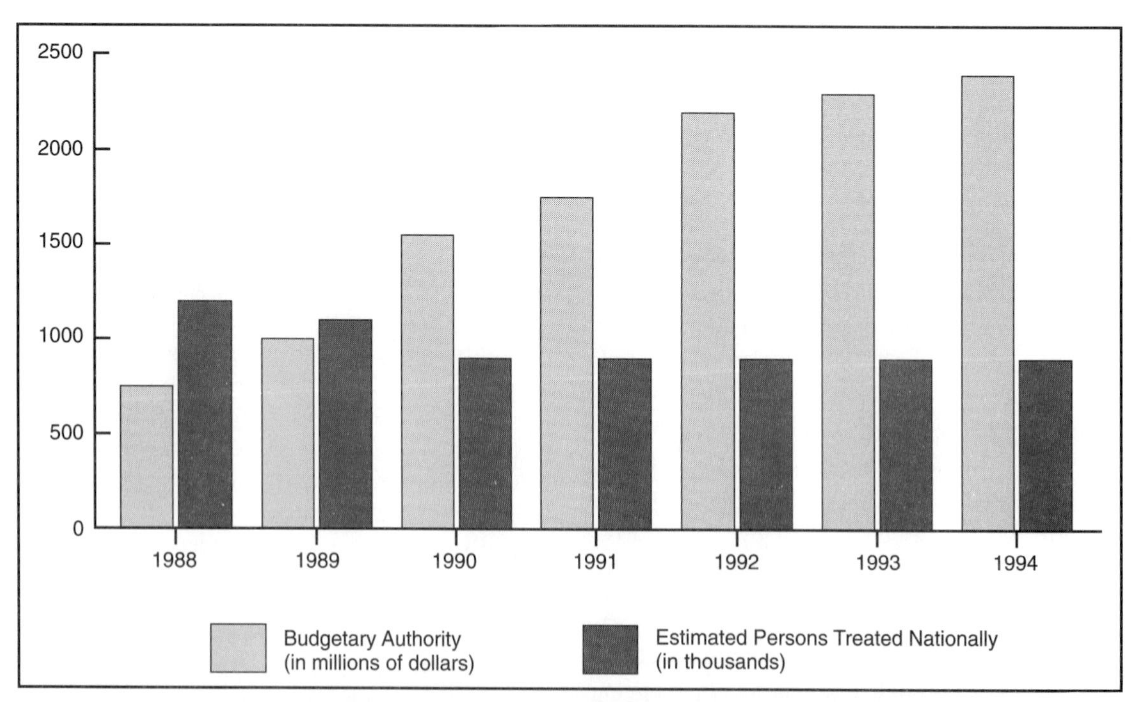

◆ **FIGURE 14.2 Federal Drug Treatment Spending and Number of Persons Treated, 1988–1994**
Source: Table adapted from William Bennett, John DiIullio, Jr., and John Walters, *Body Count* (New York: Simon and Schuster, 1996), p. 174.

legalization of drugs. During the 1980s, seemingly endless retreats in the war on drugs led some analysts to propose legalizing controlled substances.[47] Drug legalization had been a standard demand among libertarians, who argued that individuals should have the freedom to engage in any activity so long as it does not harm others. Then, during the Reagan presidency, a small number of leaders representing law, economics, and politics complemented the libertarian position, calling for the legalization of controlled substances. Noting the massive sums pumped into law enforcement and the meager results demonstrated by interdiction and treatment, proponents of legalization argued that American substance abuse policy was at best naive and at worst counterproductive. Those favoring drug legalization argued that the current policy was little more than a replication of Prohibition, a futile effort to ban alcohol from American culture. A more mature and pragmatic policy would be to admit that certain substances were part of contemporary lifestyles and simply to regulate them, much as tobacco and alcohol are regulated. By legalizing drugs, substantial sums would be freed from law enforcement and put toward abuse prevention and treatment programs. Legalization would decriminalize drug abuse, thereby cutting the prison population significantly, and by destigmatizing abusers make it more likely that they would enter treatment. Additional revenues could be raised by government because illegal substances would be available legitimately and taxed accordingly. Advocates of legalization questioned the claims of defenders of the status quo, arguing that prevention, treatment, and interdiction were effective strategies that would show positive results in the long run. Legalization of drugs, claimed its adherents, could produce substantial results immediately.

Momentum toward legalizing drugs reached its peak during the mid–1980s and then flagged. Public policy scholars raised a number of questions for which there were no ready answers. Should all drugs be legalized, or should legalization be limited to soft drugs, such as marijuana and minor tranquilizers, while restrictions on hard drugs were maintained? Should availability be unlimited, or should age restrictions apply, as they do now with tobacco and alcohol? If there are taxes on drugs and restrictions on their purchase, would not the government still have to fund law enforcement, regulate product safety, and maintain a taxing authority in order to contain an illicit market? If the government were to attempt to counter a black market by supplying drugs directly, it would be in the contradictory position of supplying drugs while also treating abusers of those same drugs.[48]

Further confounding the issue of drug legalization was the firestorm of controversy over crack cocaine. Proponents of legalization visualized drugs as relatively benign substances, similar to tobacco and alcohol. Marijuana, heroin, and many psychedelics could be used discreetly, they contended, without disrupting society or drawing public attention to users. The proliferation of crack cocaine, however, presented a completely different picture. Crack had not only been implicated in violent incidents, but the craving for it by intravenous drug addicts was so intense that many failed to practice the needle hygiene necessary to prevent the transmission of HIV. The prospect of legalizing a substance over which users seemed to have so little control and which, moreover, was connected to homicides, addicted infants, and community destruction seemed inconsistent with the vision implied by drug legalization.

By the 1990s the legalization of drugs had drifted to the margin of the substance abuse debate. Despite obvious contradictions represented by the status of tobacco and alcohol, few suggested that other substances should be legalized. In fact, pressure increased to contain the use of tobacco and alcohol. Municipalities expanded the areas they designated as smoke-free, and stricter standards and fines were established for driving under the influence of alcohol. Increasingly, authorities came to believe that soft drugs served a "gateway" function, introducing young users to more addictive substances. Rather than loosen the regulation of such substances, continued restrictions were called for.[49] Finally, the most limited form of legalization—allowing physicians to prescribe certain substances for addicts—faltered when the country that had pioneered this strategy, Great Britain, halted the practice.[50]

If a consensus began to emerge about not legalizing controlled substances, there was far less unanimity about reclaiming neighborhoods in which drugs had become central to social and economic life. Aggressive action by law enforcement officers appeared to have reached an apex, then degenerated into a lawless netherworld when, as an example, DEA agents raided the wrong house and critically wounded a San Diego man in a drug bust gone wrong. The practice of handing down severe sentences for even first-time offenders began to lose its luster as a strategy when the cost of incarceration proved to far exceed the value of taking small-time drug traffickers off the street. The seizure of property belonging to persons who had been implicated in drug transactions became a small scandal when newspapers reported that innocent people had lost belongings to overzealous law enforcement officers.[51] The promise of paramilitary boot camps for first-time offenders who had been convicted of drug-related crimes, while an appealing solution to a public frustrated by increasing numbers of crime-prone youth, failed to demonstrate any long-term changes in behavior.[52]

In the last decade of the century, many inner-city neighborhoods were more lethal for minority Americans than they had been at any time in the nation's history. Children learned that they could make hundreds of dollars a day carrying crack between dealers, easily eclipsing the income of conventionally employed adults in the community. This made a joke of the work ethic; no one with any self-respect would consider a dead-end job paying the minimum wage. Young men who had little hope of finding a good job traded their future for quick wealth and community notoriety in the drug trade. Many did not expect to live to the age of 30 and impregnated girlfriends as the only way they knew to ensure posterity. Drug-related violence made a mockery of already fragile community institutions. Gang members were shot to death in funeral homes, schools, even hospitals. Most tragically, infants born of crack-addicted mothers writhed and screamed at birth as they experienced withdrawal, only to be diagnosed later with HIV. Unwanted, they suffered in group homes and died at an early age.

While academics debated the finer points of drug legalization, the quality of life for the urban poor grew increasingly desperate. What had once been a grim struggle to reconcile meager income with daily living requirements had become a frantic scramble for safety. At best, the drug scourge forced inner-city residents to sharply curtail their expectations. At worst, it abruptly terminated expectations altogether. Eventually, the degradation of life attributed to the proliferation of drugs entered the popular media, clashing with cherished images of America. For too many of the urban poor, the American dream had not just faded from memory; it had been replaced by an image that was perversely antithetical—the American nightmare.

THE "NEW PENOLOGY"

While academics debated the merits of the legalization of drugs, the public was growing increasingly intolerant of crime. Since the mid–1980s, the nation has seen a significant increase in prison construction, the passage of laws to incarcerate repeat offenders, and the reinstitution of capital punishment. Approaching the end of the century, the United States boasted an incarcerated population that exceeded one million. In 1970 the number of inmates in state and federal correctional facilities was 96.7 per 100,000 population; by 1993 the rate had more than tripled at 352.9.[53] In 1994, the Violent Crime Control and Law Enforcement Act introduced the "three strikes" penalties for repeat offenders and increased the number of federal crimes to which the death penalty applies.[54] In little more than a decade the number of prisoners under the death sentence had tripled. In 1980, 688 inmates were on death row; by 1993, that number had increased to 2,716. Of these, 42 percent were black;[55] the number of African Americans with death sentences thus exceeded their proportion of the general population by a factor of three.

The rapid expansion in correctional facilities has led criminologists Malcolm Feeley and Jonathan Simon to suggest the advent of a "new penology." In contrast to the old penology that focused in individual rehabilitation (probation or parole) or deterrence (incarceration), the new penology eschews these for the efficient management of large populations of high-risk offenders. The mission of criminal justice, contend Feeley and Simon, is "managerial, not transformative";[56] the social function of criminal justice is "rabble management,"[57] or controlling "unruly groups."[58]

As a managerial phenomenon, the new penology requires a method for classification and incarceration, and the federal sentencing guidelines incorporated in the 1984 Comprehensive Crime Control Act (implemented on November 1, 1987) serves just that purpose. The U.S. Sentencing Commission has established an elaborate system of 258 categories for determining the punishment for an offense according to its severity and the offender's previous convictions.[59] The guidelines generated controversy when it became evident that drug sentences varied considerably according to the type of substance and the race of the offender. For example, regular cocaine is considered less serious than crack cocaine; yet crack cocaine is used most widely by African Americans; thus drug offenses by black offenders yields longer sentences. An appellate judge in Minnesota determined that the average sentence for African Americans was more than twice as long as that of whites.[60] Racial disparities in sentencing have infuriated some federal judges because the guidelines provide little latitude to tailor the punishment to fit the crime.

The use of the sentencing guidelines is consistent with the new penology, contend Feeley and Simon. In its new configuration, the purpose of criminal justice is not to arbitrate punishment in relation to lawlessness, but to incapacitate large numbers of high-risk offenders selectively. Accordingly, prisons become warehouses for offenders who are determined to be of highest risk. Because high-risk is positively associated with race and indigence, the new penology functions to regulate the most troublesome—and allegedly dangerous—elements of the underclass, and drug abuse is the catalyst for ascertaining those among the underclass who are at the highest-risk. Thus, within the contemporary urban milieu, the new penology serves as the instrument of racial and class oppression.

It could be argued that prisons have historically served as institutions of last resort for incorrigible populations that have proven difficult to socialize. In that respect the large numbers of African Americans who dominate the prisons today are little different from the Irish or Italian immigrant inmates who disproportionately populated correctional facilities decades ago. If there is a qualitatively different aspect to contemporary corrections, however, it would be the merging of systems management with the rapid expansion of the correctional corporations. The fundamental difference between the government-maintained, old penology and the corporate managed, new penology is that the latter has a financial stake in an expanding correctional market, while the incentives under the old penology were such that the state attempted to limit criminal justice expenditures.

Thus, an analysis produced by Steven Donziger for the National Criminal Justice Commission targets the emerging "prison-industrial complex" as an issue in corrections. According to Donziger, the prison-industrial complex consists of an "iron triangle" of "government bureaucrats, private industry leaders, and politicians who work together to expand the criminal justice system."[61] In the United States there are 21 companies with annual revenues exceeding $250 million, managing some 88 prisons in which 50,000 inmates are incarcerated, a twentyfold increase in the number of inmates managed by for-profit correctional firms since 1984.[62] The passage of the "three strikes" legislation targeting repeat offenders, the War on Drugs, and the consequences of the Sentencing Guidelines assure the prison-industrial complex with a more-than-adequate supply of inmates. Because most inmates are nonviolent offenders, the minimum- and medium-security facilities that are favored by for-profit firms are ideal for incarceration purposes. Contrasted to the archaic prisons typical of the old penology, the facilities managed by for-profit firms are not only more adequate with regard to basic amenities, but they are also more likely to provide educational and other services as methods to maintain a compliant population. A staunch critic of for-profit corrections are the prison guard unions because a primary means by which for-profit firms reduce their costs is by hiring staff who are less expensive than state correctional officers who benefit from state civil service regulations and higher pay. Although prisoners tend to benefit from correctional facilities managed by for-profit firms, the new penology brings with it a classic conflict between labor (prison guards) and management (CEOs).

CONCLUSION: THE FUTURE OF CRIMINAL JUSTICE

American criminal justice presents a paradox. Despite reductions in adult and juvenile crime,[63] the federal government has redoubled efforts at law enforcement. During the 1996 presidential campaign, President Clinton was criticized for increases in cocaine abuse among adolescents, even though the incidence data were below one percent. The federal drug czar, four-star general Barry McCaffrey, promised an all-out campaign in the continuing War on Drugs.[64] In response to increased security at more heavily trafficked routes along the Mexican border, drug smugglers resorted to inland caravans, in the process terrorizing American ranchers along the Texas-Mexico border.[65] Little noticed, the U.S. Army was being brought into the War on Drugs, providing training, equipment, and intelligence for state and federal law enforcement agencies.[66]

In many cities, community policing was introduced as a reform. Conceived in Houston, community policing reassigned law enforcement officers from patrol cars and specialty units that had isolated them from the public to beats on the streets of high-crime areas. As mayors and the public noted the benefits of community policing,[67] the reform spread, eventually becoming a prominent feature of federal crime policy. In one of the few refrains that captured public attention, President Clinton promised federal funding to deploy 100,000 more police officers to combat crime. In 1995, the attorney general boasted that the Clinton administration had placed more than 25,000 police officers in the Community Oriented Policing Services (COPS) program.[68]

Yet, neither the War on Drugs nor community policing promised to alleviate the conditions that spawn and exacerbate crime. To the extent social and economic factors are associated with crime, particularly the skewing of opportunities of minority youth who become adult offenders, an argument can be made for preventive strategies in criminal justice. This is the logic that John Hagan has adopted in developing the concept of the "social embeddedness" of crime. In reviewing research on juvenile delinquency and adult offenders, Hagan noted the interaction of family and environment in the transmission of criminal behavior. Poor neighborhoods generate delinquents, often from families in which a parent has been an offender. Such intergenerational transmission of crime can be attributed to heredity, but as noted earlier in the chapter, the relationship is too weak to be anywhere near conclusive. Consequently, Hagan takes a more direct, and more useful, route in explaining how poor communities harbor crime-prone families that produce delinquents, many of whom become adult criminals. In poor communities, Hagan contends that two developmental paths evolve for children. Kids from working families with effective adult supervision are socialized in school and through early employment into a world in which there is the likelihood of success. By contrast, children from families in which an adult is an offender are more likely to encounter a juvenile justice system that not only labels them as delinquent, but the punishment of juvenile offenders—incarceration or its surrogates—also interferes with completion of school or building a sound foundation for future employment. Essentially, kids from families with adult offenders are doubly burdened:

> involvements of parents in crime likely provide youths with more promising connections to illegal than legal labor markets. As well, contacts with criminal friends are more likely to integrate youths into the criminal underworld than into referral networks for legal employment. And youthful delinquent acts are likely to distance actors further from the job contacts that initiate and sustain legitimate occupational careers.[69]

So oriented, it is understandable how delinquent-prone youth could find gang involvement a natural progression in socialization. Drug-related gang activities, frequently targeted by law enforcement, yield arrests and sentences that label youngsters and disrupt education and employment. Before the end of high school, a delinquent has accumulated sufficient negative attributes to subvert conventional awards. In place of education and employment, gang activity alternates with incarceration, producing a vicious circle. Measures of the intractability of the delinquent's circumstance can be found in the "oppositional culture" that flourishes among poor, minority youth. The popularization of a vulgar gangsta' rap, claiming the loyalty of young women through impregnating them, and "dissing" enemies (including authority figures)—even at the risk of bodily harm—are all part of the capitulation that young, minority males make in the face of overwhelming odds militating against traditional means of success. Oppositional culture reproduces itself through births by young, minority women whose aspirations have been sabotaged. Infants experience little that is nurturing or dependable, least of all a father who, given the tentativeness of life on the streets, expects to be dead or incarcerated well before his child reaches adolescence. The scenario is as tragic as it is "embedded" in the social reality of its perpetrators and victims.

The solution to this problem is straightforward, if also complex. With regard to social embeddedness, it is necessary to construct plausible alternatives for delinquent-prone young men and women. Alternative education for young welfare recipients, as described by Sapphire in *Push*, could convince minority women of more meaningful, and less brutal, futures than welfare dependence.[70] On the other hand, welfare reforms that simply force young women into a labor market for which they are unprepared, under threat of terminating benefits, is unlikely to suggest a more compelling future. Mentoring programs for young men can increase the chances of completion of school and getting a job, while providing essential modeling by a capable adult. By contrast, drug sweeps alone will continue to marginalize young men, increasing the likelihood that they will become resolute, adult offenders. That future has been portrayed aptly in Spike Lee's movie *Clockers*.

The evolution of policies that divert youth from delinquency and subsequently prevent adult lawlessness has been advocated eloquently by William Julius Wilson. Mainstreaming the underclass requires enhanced educational opportunity, the realization of educational standards in inner-city schools, an increase in the Earned Income Tax Credit for poor working families, and, in the end, a WPA-type public employment program. Eventually, the restitution of education and employment opportunity will overcome current inducements to engage in lawlessness.

> As more people become employed, crime, including violent crime, and drug use will subside; families will be strengthened and welfare receipt will decline significantly; ghetto-related culture and behavior, no longer sustained and nourished by persistent joblessness, will gradually fade.[71]

Thus, Wilson reiterates a major finding from the research on opportunity and crime: lawlessness declines in relationship to employment and marriage.

Unfortunately, the prospect that the federal government will assume leadership in such an endeavor is dim. The One-hundred-fifth Congress is firmly in the hands of conservatives who prefer canards to law-and-order than programs that contend with the realities of inner city life. The Clinton presidency has been unwilling to propose a major initiative that would be a viable alternative to welfare and gangs, pursuing instead punitive legislation on both fronts. Meanwhile the prison-industrial complex metamorphoses as it expands to process and capitalize on the legions of young, black men sentenced and placed in their care. Thus, criminal justice remains one of the greatest institutional challenges facing American social policy.

◆ ◆ ◆ *Discussion Questions* ◆ ◆ ◆

1. Crime varies considerably with regard to the nature of offense as well as offenders. How prevalent is crime in your community? What are the primary offenses? Who are the offenders?

2. State and local governments vary regarding the management of juvenile delinquency. Does your community have a juvenile court? Are its deliberations open to the public? What are the usual offenses that bring a youth to juvenile court?

3. Many communities are building new correctional facilities. Is your community up-grading corrections? To what extent do new facilities reflect the new penology? Are for-profit correctional firms active in your state? If not, should they be? Should they be allowed to contract for probation and parole?

4. Legalization of drugs has become a heated issue. What are the implications of drug legalization for substance abuse programs? How could drug legalization be structured in your state? How would substances be taxed? How would tax revenues from legalization be allocated?

5. In many poor urban communities, drug-related street violence has escalated to unprecedented heights. How has your community balanced resource allocations for supply interdiction versus resources for demand reduction? To what extent is substance abuse treatment available to inmates in local correctional facilities? Have specific neighborhoods in your community organized to contain and reduce drug trafficking? Which agencies have supported such initiatives?

6. As the War on Drugs program failed to live up to its promise, more attention has been focused on prevention, particularly among children. What models have agencies in your community adopted to prevent substance abuse among kids? How much money has been allocated for prevention programs? What is the track record of the prevention programs adopted in your community?

Notes

1. *Encyclopedia of Sociology* (Guilford, CT: Dushkin Publishing Group, 1974).
2. D. Stanley Eitzen and Doug Timmer, *Criminology* (New York: John Wiley, 1985), pp. 15–16.
3. Phyllis Day, *A New History of Social Welfare* (Englewood Cliffs, NJ: Prentice Hall, 1989), p. 181.
4. Ibid., p. 182.
5. Jerome Miller, *Search and Destroy: African-American Males in the Criminal Justice System* (New York: Cambridge University Press, 1996), p. 207.
6. Ibid., p. 185.
7. Richard Herrnstein and Charles Murray, *The Bell Curve* (New York: Free Press, 1994).
8. Glenn Walters, "A Meta-Analysis of the Gene-Crime Relationship," *Criminology* (30)4 (1992), pp. 8–16.
9. *Sourcebook of Criminal Justice Statistics, 1994* (Washington, DC: Congressional Information Services, 1995), Tables 1.7 and 1.8.
10. Gary Jensen and Maryaltani Karpos, "Research on the Behavior of Rape Statistics," *Criminology* (31)4 (1993), p. 382.
11. *Annual Report, Attorney General of the U.S.* (Washington, DC: Department of Justice, 1995), p. 4.
12. Lela Costin, Howard Karger, and David Stoesz, *The Politics of Child Abuse in America* (New York: Oxford University Press, 1996).
13. Day, *A New History of Social Welfare*, p. 180.
14. Jerome Miller, *Last One Over the Wall* (Columbus, OH: Ohio State University, 1991), p. 222.
15. Ibid., p. 243.
16. Denise Gottfredson and William Barton, "Deinstitutionalization of Juvenile Offenders," *Criminology* (31)4 (1993), pp. 98–117.
17. James Q. Wilson and John DiIulio, Jr., "Crackdown," *The New Republic* (July 10, 1989), p. 54.
18. Rhonda Cook, "Georgia's Prison Boot Camps Don't Work, Study Says," *San Diego Union Tribune* (May 8, 1994), p. A32.
19. "Connecticut Suspends Gang-Riddled Youth Boot Camp," *San Diego Union Tribune* (June 12, 1994), p. A6.
20. Doris Mackenzie et al., "Boot Camp Prisons and Recidivism in Eight States," *Criminology*, 33, 3 (1995), p. 78.
21. Falco, *Winning the Drug War*, pp. 26–27.
22. Sidney Cohen, "The Drug-Free America Act of 1986," *Drug Abuse and Alcoholism Newsletter* (San Diego, CA: Vista Hill Foundation, 1987), pp. 1–3.
23. Falco, *Winning the Drug War*, p. 29.
24. Barry Bearak, "A Room for Heroin and HIV," *Los Angeles Times* (September 27, 1992), p. A18.
25. "Drug Policy: It's Time to Try Something Very Different," *Los Angeles Times* (January 4, 1993), p. B6.
26. Barry Bearak, "In War on Drugs, Battle Against AIDS Falls Behind," *Los Angeles Times* (September 28, 1992), p. A16.
27. Bearak, "Road to Detox," p. A18.
28. Christopher Jencks, "Deadly Neighborhoods," *The New Republic* (June 13, 1988), p. 18; Juan Williams,

"Hard Times, Harder Hearts," *Washington Post* (October 2, 1988), p. C4.

29. "Eight Boston Teenagers Charged in Savage Slaying of Young Mother," *Los Angeles Times* (November 21, 1990), p. A4.
30. Louis Sahagun, "Gang Killings Increase 69%, Violent Crime Up 20% in L.A. County Areas," *Los Angeles Times* (August 21, 1990), p. B8.
31. Jesse Katz, "County's Yearly Death Toll Reaches 800," *Los Angeles Times* (January 19, 1993), p. A23.
32. Gabriel Escobar, "Slayings in Washington Hit New High, 436, for 3rd Year," *Los Angeles Times* (November 24, 1990), p. A26.
33. Claude Brown, *Manchild in the Promised Land* (New York: Macmillan, 1965); Claude Brown, "Manchild in Harlem," *The New York Times* (September 16, 1984), p. 16.
34. Daniel Patrick Moynihan, *Came the Revolution* (San Diego: Harcourt Brace Jovanovich, 1988), p. 291.
35. Miller, *Search and Destroy*, pp. 7–8.
36. Ibid., p. 54.
37. Ibid., p. 85.
38. Ibid., p. 99.
39. Alex Kotlowitz, *There Are No Children Here* (New York: Doubleday, 1991).
40. Barry Bearak, "Brooklyn Neighborhood Grieves for Its Mr. Chips," *Los Angeles Times* (December 19, 1992), p. A6.
41. Michael Novak, *The New Consensus on Poverty and the Family* (Washington, DC: American Enterprise Institute, 1987).
42. William Bennett, John DiIulio, Jr., and John Walters, *Body Count* (New York: Simon and Schuster, 1996), p. 56.
43. Ibid., p. 105.
44. Ibid., p. 27.
45. Ibid., pp. 175–176.
46. Ibid., Chap. 5.
47. Nadelmann, "The Case for Legalization."
48. James Jacobs, "Imagining Drug Legalization," *The Public Interest*, 101 (Fall 1990), pp. 27–34.
49. Falco, *The Making of a Drug-free America*, p. 100.
50. Jacobs, "Imagining Drug Legalization," p. 30.
51. Jim Newton, "Seizure of Assets Leaves Casualties in War on Drugs," *Los Angeles Times* (October 14, 1992), p. A1; David Savage, "Drug-Case Forfeitures Will be Reviewed," *Los Angeles Times* (January 16, 1993), p. A2.
52. David Lamb, "Last Shot to Salvage Their Lives," *Los Angeles Times* (January 17, 1993), p. A1.
53. *Statistical Summary of the United States* (Washington, DC: U.S. Census Bureau, 1995), Table 349.
54. *Annual Report of the Attorney General of the U.S.* (Washington, DC: U.S. Department of Justice, 1995).
55. *Statistical Abstract of the United States, 1995*, Table 354.
56. Malcolm Feeley and Jonathan Simon, "The New Penology," *Criminology* (30)4 (1992), p. 452.
57. Miller, *Last One Over the Wall*, p. 76.
58. Freeley, "New Penology," p. 455.
59. Mary Flaherty and Joan Biskupic, "Justice by the Numbers," *Washington Post Weekly* (October 14–20, 1996), p. 88.
60. Mary Flaherty and Joan Biskupic, "Rules Often Impose Toughest Penalties on Poor, Minorities," *Washington Post* (October 9, 1996), p. A26.
61. Steven Donziger, "The Prison-Industrial Complex," *Washington Post* (March 17, 1996), p. C3.
62. Ibid., p. C3.
63. Pierre Thomas, "Crime Rate in U.S. Falls to 10-Year Low," *Washington Post* (October 13, 1996), p. A1; Roberto Suro, "Violent Crime Drops Among Young Teens," *Washington Post* (December 13, 1996), p. A1.
64. Weston Kosova and Daniel Klaidman, "A Reluctant Campaigner," *Newsweek* (October 21, 1996), pp. 36–37.
65. William Branigin, "Drug Gangs Terrorize the Texas Border," *Washington Post* (September 25, 1996), p. A1.
66. Jim McGee, "At War Against Drugs," *Washington Post Weekly* (December 9–15, 1996), p. 6.
67. Janet Vinzant and Lane Crothers, "Street-Level Leadership: The Role of Patrol Officers in Community Policing," *Criminal Justice Review*, (19)2 (Autumn 1994), pp. 56–71.
68. *Annual Report, Attorney General, 1995*.
69. John Hagan, "The Social Embededness of Crime and Unemployment," *Criminology*, (31)4 (1993), p. 469.
70. Sapphire, *Push* (New York: Knopf, 1996).
71. William Julius Wilson, *When Work Disappears* (New York: Knopf, 1996), p. 238.

CHAPTER 15

Child Welfare Policy

This chapter examines the evolution of child welfare policy in the United States. Child protective services, foster care, adoption, and Head Start have been the focus of child welfare policy since the 1960s. The devolution of welfare to the states through the Personal Responsibility and Work Opportunity Act of 1996 increases the likelihood that the circumstances of children will worsen and that demands for child welfare will increase in the future.

In American social welfare, the condition of children is inextricably linked to the status of their families. Because the United States has failed to establish a family policy that ensures basic income, employment, and social service supports to parents, they frequently have difficulty in caring for their children. As families are less able to care for their children, the demand for child welfare services escalates. The commitment that national governments make toward reducing poverty among children varies considerably. Among industrialized nations, the United States fares poorly, indeed. The Luxembourg Study, which rated the extent to which nations deploy income assistance to lift children out of poverty, found the U.S. ranked last, as indicated in Table 15.1.

In recent years, the proportion of children living in poverty, the proportion of children in single-parent households, the percentage of mothers in the workforce, and the birthrate of women in minority groups have all increased. By 1994, 5.6 million American children were living in working-poor families, a significant increase from the 4.3 million poor children in 1989.[1] While an increase in a broad range of family and child welfare services might be expected as a result of these trends, the societal response has been extremely varied. As Jeanne Giovannoni notes, "at best we have a hodgepodge of funding and regulatory mechanisms, and we rely predominantly on market mechanisms dictating both the amount and variety of care available."[2] A classification of child welfare services completed by the Child Welfare League of America identified nine diverse components: services in the home, day care, a homemaker service, foster care, adoption, group home care, institutional care, protective services, and services to an unmarried parent.[3] Of these, protective services, foster care, and adoption are most frequently identified as being exclusively related to child welfare and, therefore, are the focus here.

Child welfare services are often controversial because they sanction the intervention of human-service professionals in family affairs that are ordinarily assumed to be private matters relating to parental rights. This dilemma places extraordinary demands on child welfare professionals, who are mandated to protect the best interests of the child while not intruding on the privacy of the family. Recently, this conundrum has become more pronounced as advocates for child welfare services

◆ **TABLE 15.1**
Child Poverty in 17 Developed Countries Before and After Government Assistance

Country	*Before Assistance*	*After Assistance*	*Percent of Children Lifted out of Poverty*
United States	26%	22%	17%
Australia	20	14	29
Canada	23	14	40
Ireland	30	12	60
Israel	24	11	54
United Kingdom	30	10	67
Italy	12	10	17
Germany	9	7	24
France	25	7	74
Netherlands	14	6	55
Norway	13	5	64
Luxembourg	12	4	65
Belgium	16	4	77
Denmark	16	3	79
Switzerland	5	3	35
Sweden	19	3	86
Finland	12	3	78

Source: *Kids Count 1996* (Baltimore: Annie E. Casey Foundation, 1996), p. 17.

demand more programs, while traditionalist groups attempt to cut programs which they perceive as designed to subvert the family. Ironically, much of this argument could be defused if the United States adopted a family policy that assisted parents in caring for children more adequately, thus reducing the need for the more intrusive child welfare interventions. For the moment, any family policy is unlikely, and child welfare policy remains among the more controversial in American social welfare.

HISTORY OF CHILD WELFARE POLICY

Although many states established orphanages during the eighteenth century, current child welfare policy has its origins in the 1870s.[4] The large number of child paupers led Charles Loring Brace, founder of New York's Children's Aid Society, to remove thousands of children from deleterious urban conditions in New York City to farm families in the Midwest. Eventually, criticism of Brace's methods, which were divisive of family and community, contributed to more preventive approaches to children's problems.

By the beginning of the twentieth century, most large cities had children's aid societies that practiced the "boarding-out" of children (the payment of a fee for child rearing) to a sponsor in the community.[5] The boarding-out of children until adoption (or, in the case of children with handicaps, those who were unlikely to be adopted) was the beginning of foster care and adoption programs in the United States.

Protective services for children began with one of the more unusual incidents in American social welfare. In 1874, a New York church worker, Etta Wheeler, discovered that a nine-year-old child, Mary Ellen, was being tied to a bed, whipped, and stabbed with scissors. On investigating what could be done for Mary Ellen, Wheeler spoke with the director of the New York Society for the Prevention of Cruelty to Animals (NYSPCA) on behalf of the indentured child. Although it was subsequently believed that intervention on behalf of Mary Ellen was predicated on her status as an animal warranting protection, rather than as a child, a careful review of the case indicated that Mary Ellen's case was adjudicated consistently with legal precedents involving abused children.[6] The following year, the New York Society for the Prevention of Cruelty to Children was established.[7] By 1922, 57 societies for the prevention of cruelty to children had been established to protect abused youngsters.[8]

Child welfare proved an effective rallying issue for Progressives, who advocated intervention on the part of the federal government. In 1909, James E. West, a friend of President Theodore Roosevelt and later head of the Boy Scouts of America, convinced Jane Addams and other welfare leaders to attend a two-day meeting on child welfare. This first White House Conference on Children focused attention on the plight of destitute families, agency problems with the boarding out of children, and the importance of home care. The conference proved so successful that it was repeated every ten years—with the exception of 1981, when the conference was canceled by the Reagan administration. Still, the White House Conference on Children served as a model for legitimating and attracting attention to social welfare needs. One significant product of the White House Conference on Children was the call to establish a federal agency to "collect and exchange ideas and information on child welfare." With an initial appropriation of $25,640, the U.S. Children's Bureau was established in 1912 under the auspices of the Department of Commerce and Labor.[9] Instrumental in the early years of the Children's Bureau were Lillian Wald, of New York's Henry Street Settlement House, and Florence Kelley, an alumna of both the Henry Street Settlement and Hull House. Julia Lathrop, a former resident of Hull House, was the bureau's first director.[10]

Because of the economic circumstances of poor families, child labor emerged as a primary concern of early child welfare advocates. The absence of public relief meant that families were compelled to work at whatever employment might be available, however wearing and demeaning. Children worked full shifts in coal mines and textile mills; women labored in sweatshops. Neither were protected from dangerous or unhygienic working conditions. Under the guidance of Florence Kelley, the National Consumer League fought for children and women using a dual strategy. First, the league lobbied for reform in the working conditions of women through regulating sweatshops and factories, and for ending the exploitation of children through prohibiting child labor. Second, it advocated ameliorating the grinding poverty of many families by means of a family subsidy that would make such deplorable work less necessary. For Kelley, the family subsidy was a preventive measure with which she was quite familiar; she had successfully lobbied for passage of the Funds for Parents Act in 1911 in Illinois. This act was a precursor of the Aid to Dependent Children program, part of the original Social Security Act of 1935.[11]

Before the Great Depression, welfare advocates could boast of a series of unprecedented initiatives designed to improve the conditions of America's poor families. The Children's Bureau Act of 1912 established a national agency to collect information on children. The Child Labor Act of 1916 prohibited the interstate transportation of goods manufactured by children. The Maternity and Infancy Act of 1921 assisted states in establishing programs that dramatically reduced the nation's infant and maternal mortality rates. Yet these successes, however hard-won, were constantly at risk of being subverted. The Supreme Court ruled the Child Labor Act unconstitutional in 1918, and the Maternity and Infancy Act was terminated in 1929, when Herbert Hoover and Congress refused further appropriations.[12] Child and family welfare initiatives remained unsuccessful until the Social Security Act of 1935 ushered in a complete set of welfare policies.

The Social Security Act addressed child welfare in two of its provisions. Title IV introduced the Aid to Dependent Children program, which provided public relief to needy children through cash grants to their families. Title V reestablished Maternal and Child Welfare Services (which had expired in 1929) and expanded the mandate of the Children's Bureau, whose goal was to oversee a new set of child welfare services "for the protection and care of homeless, dependent, and neglected children, and children in danger of becoming delinquent."[13] Significantly, both family relief and child welfare services were to be administered by the states through public welfare departments. As a result, as of 1935 the provision of child welfare services shifted largely from the private, voluntary sector to the public, governmental sector.

Within public welfare, the responsibility for child welfare has shifted between the federal and state governments. Since 1935 the state and federal governments have shared responsibility for social services provided to families, but the role of the federal government has changed with respect to income maintenance benefits to poor families. From 1935 until 1996, federal and state government shared the funding and administration of the AFDC program. With devolution of public assistance to the states through the Personal Responsibility and Work Responsibility Act (PRWOA), however, the federal government limited its role to one of funding and limited oversight. PRWOA instituted a block grant, Temporary Assistance to Needy Families, that is primarily under the control of state government. Thus, while the federal government continues to shape child welfare services, its role in welfare to poor families has been circumscribed.

PROTECTIVE SERVICES FOR CHILDREN

Through the Social Security Act, states proceeded to develop services to children independently of one another and within the relatively loose specifications of the act. Free of a centralized authority that would ensure standardized care throughout the United States, child welfare services varied greatly from state to state and even within states. In the two decades following the passage of the Social Security Act, child welfare services had become established within American social welfare, but with a high degree of fragmentation.

By the 1960s, the status quo in child welfare was upset by reports of increasing incidents of child abuse and neglect. A pediatrician, C. Henry Kempe, identified nonaccidental injuries to children as the "battered child syndrome." As more states began to address the problem, child welfare advocates built a compelling case for a national standard for child protective services. This lobbying led to the passage of the Child Abuse Prevention and Treatment Act of 1974, which established the National Center for Child Abuse and Neglect within the Department of Health and Human Services, as well as a model statute for state child protective programs. All 50 states eventually enacted the model statute, which, among its provisions, specified the following:

- A standard definition of child abuse and neglect
- Methods for reporting and investigating abuse and neglect
- Immunity for those reporting suspected injuries to children
- Prevention and public education efforts to reduce incidents of abuse and neglect

As a result of these national standards, the National Center for Child Abuse and Neglect was able to report—for the first time—trends in child abuse and the need for protective services for children. Alarmingly, the data collected by the National Center revealed a dramatic increase in reports of child abuse, which more than doubled between 1976 and 1986, when reports of child abuse numbered 2 million.[14] In 1991, Chicago's National Committee for the Prevention of Child Abuse reported that 1,383 children died as a result of abuse, 50 percent more than the number reported in 1986.[15] Most troubling was that reports of child abuse continued to climb through the mid–1980s, while at the same time expenditures for child protective services were decreasing.[16]

Increases in child abuse reports and decreases in expenditures led to a crisis in child welfare services. The magnitude of this crisis was mapped by Douglas Besharov, an authority on child welfare policy:

> Of the 1,000 children who die under circumstances suggestive of parental maltreatment each year, between 30 and 50 percent were previously reported to child protective agencies. Many thousands of other children suffer serious injuries after their plight becomes known to authorities. . . . *Each year, about 50,000 children with observable injuries severe enough to require hospitalization are not reported* [original emphasis].[17]

Stories of child abuse fatalities began to appear with greater frequency in the media. Shortly before Thanksgiving of 1987, the report of the beating death of a six-year-old girl under the care of a middle-class couple in Greenwich Village in New York City became a feature story in *Newsweek*.[18] Unfortunately, incidents of child abuse were too often associated with child welfare programs mandated to protect children. In Kansas City, 25 percent of the children in foster care were found to have been abused.[19] During the spring of 1988, National Public Radio broadcast a report of two Illinois state "social workers" who had been dismissed for failure to make home visits and falsification of records that were associated with the deaths of two children who had been reported as victims of child abuse.[20] In Baltimore, a group of current and former foster children won a decision in the Fourth District Court of Appeals after charging that 20 administrators and caseworkers of the Baltimore City Department of Social Services had failed "to adequately monitor and protect children in foster care."[21] Such litigation placed child welfare personnel in a double bind: being faced with increasing demands for services, yet not having adequate staff resources to respond effectively. "If you take children out of the home, you're snatching them. If you leave them in the home [and they're abused], you didn't protect them," complained Jim Bell of the Massachusetts Department of Social Services. "We try to deal the best we can in that environment and protect the [case]workers. We don't want them hanging out there all alone."[22]

One consequence of this disintegration of children's services was a volatile debate over the definition of *child abuse and neglect*. One solution to the widening disparity between resources for children's services and increasing reports of abuse and neglect, of course, would be to redefine the criteria in accordance with which emergency services for children were deployed. If conservatives could promulgate a more restrictive definition of *abuse and neglect*, they would benefit directly in that such a change would effectively subvert demands for greater funding for children's services and parents would retain wider latitude for their behavior in the home. Contending that confirmed reports of child abuse had consistently declined since implementation of the Child Abuse Prevention and Treatment Act, Besharov argued for a more restrictive definition.[23] Countering this claim, David Finkelhor of the University of New Hampshire's Family Research Laboratory noted that annual data from the American Humane Association indicated fairly steady rates of validated abuse and neglect, from 40 to 43 percent of all reports. Because more specific research on the nature of general abuse and sexual abuse suggested increasing incidence, Finkelhor argued for more resources for child protection.[24]

The rapid deterioration of child welfare services led children's advocates to call for more funding of social services. But proposals for increased support for child welfare services did not go unchallenged. Ambiguity in the definition of what constituted child abuse and neglect had contributed to incidents in which child welfare workers appeared to disregard parental rights in their eagerness to protect children. Perhaps the most notorious instance of such overzealousness occurred during the summer of 1984, when social workers from the Vermont Department of Social and Rehabilitation Services and the state police rounded up 112 children from "a radical Christian sect" and detained them for three days to search for indications of abuse. When the American Civil Liberties Union threatened to sue the state on behalf of the religious community, state officials reconsidered, and the children were returned to their parents.[25] Similar but less newsworthy incidents enraged parents who, feeling unjustly accused, formed VOCAL (Victims of Child Abuse Laws) in an attempt to restore traditional parental rights in the face of what they perceived to be the intrusiveness of the state.

Conservative scholars contributed to the grassroots indignation that fueled VOCAL. Sociologists Bridgitte and Peter Berger contended that social services, such as child welfare, were the vehicle through which middle-class professionals evangelized among lower-class clients. When disputes over parents' versus children's rights surface between professionals and parents, the Bergers' recommendation was to "trust parents over against experts."[26] With momentum building during the 1980s, the 3,000 members of VOCAL took their complaints into the public arena. In Arizona, for example, VOCAL held up a $5.4-million appropriation to improve child protective services.[27]

Further distracting public attention from child maltreatment, during the 1980s some family therapists suggested that childhood abuse could be retrieved by "recovering memories" through therapy. By the end of the decade, showcase trials of child day-care providers, teachers, the clergy, and parents resulted in a series of convictions, all based on incidents that had been previously forgotten but were later recovered during clinical treatment. Later, as appeals raised questions about the veracity of allegations, the "recovered memory" movement came under scrutiny. By the time a Wenatchee, Washington, minister and his wife were found innocent in 1996 of charges they had run a satanic cult that abused children, judgments for most of the perpetrators convicted in earlier trials had been reversed on appeal.[28]

While academics, policy wonks, and therapists debated definitional, ideological, and clinical aspects of child maltreatment, child protective services continued to deteriorate. New York City's child welfare services became the focus of a series of children who had died despite having been active child protection cases. In 1992, five-year-old Jeffrey Harden died from broken ribs and burns caused by scalding water. Known to child welfare authorities for 18 months, intervention by four different caseworkers failed to identify the risk to Jeffrey. By the time of his death, all four workers had left the agency.[29]

During Thanksgiving 1995, young Elisa Izquierdo was beaten to death by her demented mother. Despite repeated calls by neighbors and school officials, the city's child protection workers failed to prevent her murder. Within a year, four-year-old Nadine Lockwood had starved to death. Again, child welfare workers failed to confirm Nadine's deteriorating health even though neighbors had complained about her neglect. An investigation into the Child Welfare Administration showed the magnitude of agency failure: in a fifth of reported cases, workers failed to interview all of the children in the family; in two of five cases, workers ignored previous reports of child abuse; almost one fifth of cases were closed despite the risk of future abuse. Subsequent to the exposé, Mayor Rudolph Giuliani announced plans to restructure child welfare in the city.[30]

Although New York City provided the headlines, the child fatality scandal was nationwide. By the mid–1990s, the U.S. Advisory Commission on Child Abuse and Neglect concluded that some 2,000 children died of abuse and neglect annually,[31] far above the 1,111 deaths counted by the National Center on Child Abuse and Neglect.[32] In rating the child homicide rates for industrial nations, a British researcher concluded that the child fatality rate of the United States was double that of the second most lethal nation for children, Australia.[33] By 1996, the management of child welfare was so inadequate that agencies in 21 states and the District of Columbia were placed under court supervision.

Regardless of increases in injury and death to children due to abuse and neglect, child welfare professionals were fancying a new orientation to serving at-risk families, family preservation. Initially demonstrated in the late 1970s through the Homebuilders program, family preservation called for the provision of intensive services for a brief period, usually six weeks, by a worker assigned four to six cases. Services provided included a range of activities, from crisis intervention, to home repair, to child day care, all intended to stabilize the family and prevent out-of-home placement of a child.

Family preservation was greeted enthusiastically by child welfare professionals because of the multiple benefits it offered. Foremost, by keeping a family intact, out-of-home placement of a child who had been abused or neglected was avoided. Because of the high cost of out-of-home placement, family preservation thus offered financial benefits: the cost of mounting a family preservation program was quickly recovered by savings from reduced out-of-home placements. Finally, in valuing family unity over child removal, family preservation allied child welfare with conservative traditionalists who placed family rights over those of children.

The relationship between family preservation and child protective services was oblique but no less consequential. Child welfare professionals understood family preservation as a preventive strategy that precluded the most dramatic disposition of child protective services, out-of-home placement. As family preservation captured the allegiance of child welfare professionals, the focus on child protection began to lapse. Even as fatalities mounted due to child abuse, children's advocates pressed for policy changes focusing on family preservation. Consequently, when the Clinton 1993 economic package was passed, it included $930 million for family support and preservation services over five years, but only a footnote to child protective services.[34]

Despite policies intended to ameliorate child abuse, the number of maltreated children continued to climb. In 1994 the number of children who had been victimized by abuse and neglect exceeded one million, an increase of 27 percent since 1990. Of the 2.9 million reports of maltreatment in 1994, 56 percent were unsubstantiated, while 38 percent were substantiated.[35] Between 1986 and 1993, the number of children who were seriously injured increased from 143,000 to 570,000. Yet, despite increased injuries to children, fewer cases were investigated; while 44 percent of cases were investigated in 1986, only 28 percent were so disposed in 1993.[36] The types of maltreatment inflicted on children are shown in Table 15.2. Girls, 52.3 percent of victims, were more likely to be maltreated than boys, 46.7 percent. Although the majority of abused children were white, 56.4 percent, African American children were disproportionately overrepresented at 26.4 percent of victims. The vast majority of perpetrators were parents, as shown in Table 15.3.

◆ TABLE 15.3
Perpetrators 1994

Type of perpetrator	*Percent*
Parents	79.2
Other relatives	9.9
Noncaretakers	4.7
Child care providers	1.3
Foster parents	0.6
Facility staff	0.4
Unknown	3.8

NOTE: Total is less than 100 percent due to rounding.
Source: U.S. Department of Health and Human Services, *Child Maltreatment, 1994*, pp. 2–10.

FOSTER CARE FOR CHILDREN

When parents are unable to care for their children, foster care is often used to provide alternative care. As an extension of the practice of boarding out children, most foster care in the United States is at no cost to the parents, and children are placed in the homes of other families. There is an important relationship between child protective services and foster care in American social welfare. Foster care is a primary service for victims of child abuse; more than half of children in foster care were placed there by child protective service workers. The second most prevalent reason for child foster care is the "condition or absence of the parent," accounting for about 20 percent of foster care placements.[37]

◆ TABLE 15.2
Victims by Type of Maltreatment

Type of Maltreatment	*Percentage of Victims*
Neglect	52.9
Physical	25.5
Other	14.8
Sexual	13.8
Emotional	4.7
Unknown	4.1
Medical	2.5

NOTE: Total exceeds 100 percent because some states report multiple types of maltreatment.
Source: U.S. Department of Health and Human Services, *Child Maltreatment 1994*, pp. 2–5.

As in the case of protective services, foster care for children was not coordinated under the provisions of the Social Security Act. States adopted separate policies and, unfortunately, took few measures to monitor children in foster care. During the early 1960s, a series of studies began to document a disturbing development. Rather than being a temporary arrangement for child care, foster care had become a long-term experience for many youngsters: 70 percent of children had been in foster care for more than one year.[38] Not only had states planned poorly for the reunification of children with their original families, but in many instances child welfare agencies had lost track of foster care children altogether. During the summer of 1992, the District of Columbia's Department of Human Services (DHS) was rocked by a foster care scandal when it was reported that the department had literally no idea of the location of one out of every four children it had placed in foster care.[39] As a result of mismanagement of child welfare in the District, Jerome Miller was appointed receiver by the courts to reform the agency.

In response to the deterioration of children's services, several demonstration projects were begun that offered intensive services to families in order to prevent their children from being placed in foster care and to effectively reunite children with their biological parents. The demonstrations seemed to be cost-effective. In Virginia, 14 prefoster care placement service projects concluded that family functioning improved in 69 percent of the families receiving intensive support services. Moreover, the cost of support services was $1,214 per child, substantially less than the cost of foster care ($11,173) or residential care ($22,025) for the average length of time (4.6 years) a child was in these more intensive forms of treatment.[40] As a result of these field experiments, "permanency planning" became a central feature of the Adoption Assistance and Child Welfare Act of 1980.

Permanency planning is "the systematic process of carrying out, within a brief time-limited period, a set of goal-directed activities designed to help children live in families that offer continuity of relationships with nurturing parents or caretakers and the opportunity to establish lifetime relationships."[41] The Adoption Assistance and Child Welfare Act was an ambitious effort, and one expert heralded it as making it "possible to implement at state and local levels a comprehensive service delivery system for children."[42] As a result of permanency planning, the number of children in foster care plummeted. In 1977, 500,000 children were in foster care; by 1983 the number had dropped to 251,000. Welfare workers swiftly removed children from foster care and reunited them with their biological families under the rationale that community support services would assist parents. Early research on family preservation services indicated cost savings, but some families needed extensive service, as much as $2,600. As caseloads expanded, public agencies struggled to pay for necessary services. An analysis of a model family reunification program found that deficits in agency resources—gaps in service, large caseload and worker turnover, inadequate family preparation, among others—presented problems in more than half of all cases. The researchers were "unaware of any reported successful permanency planning program that has high caseloads as a program component."[43]

Tragically, inadequate resources sometimes created a vicious circle: When biological parents received few support services, they were less able to care for their children, thereby contributing to the need for child protective services. In the absence of intensive support services, permanency planning for many children meant a revolving-door placement in foster care, reunification with the biological parent(s), and then a return to foster care. In 1982, 43 percent of children had been in multiple placements, but by 1983, 53.1 percent had been in more than one placement. Of this number, 20.1 percent had been placed twice, 24.2 percent three to five times, and 8.8 percent six or more times.[44] The National Association of Social Workers newsletter reported the instance of a 4-year-old New York boy who was placed in 37 different homes in 2 months and another who had been placed in 17 homes in 25 days.[45]

In large measure, the permanency planning movement faltered due to lack of support services to families. Not long after passage of the Adoption Assistance and Child Welfare Act of 1980, Ronald Rooney observed prophetically that "if the promise of permanency planning is to be realized, those who allocate funds must provide money for a continuum of services that are delivered from the point of entry into foster care and include programs designed to prevent the removal of children from their homes."[46] Yet in 1981, an important source of family support services, Title XX, was cut 21 percent. For 1992 the Title XX appropriation, $2.8 billion, was $100 million less than the amount funded in 1981, despite a 58 percent increase in reports of child abuse and neglect since that time.[47] Yet, gross appropriations for Title XX reveal only a small part of the defunding of the program. Once inflation is factored into the appropriations, it can be seen that between 1977 and 1992, Title XX actually lost $3.2 billion, or 55.4 percent of its funding.[48] A decade after the early permanency planning demonstration projects, Theodore Stein feared that the movement was being subverted by budget cuts and a reliance on crisis services in child welfare.[49]

Limited funding under Title XX for child welfare induced states to become more dependent on other federal sources of revenue. Because it was funded completely by the federal government and did not require any state matching funds, Title XX was the optimal funding source for child welfare program administrators, but it had one important flaw: Revenues were capped. Other federal assistance, such as Title IV-B of the Social Security Act, allocated a fixed amount of funds for children's services but required a 25 percent state matching contribution. In addition, though Title IV-E of the Social Security Act was not capped, federal funds did require a matching contribution on the part of the state ranging from 25 to 50 percent. Moreover, the two programs that child welfare program administrators looked to under Title IV-E, foster care and adoption assistance, were reserved for poor children who would have been eligible for AFDC had they stayed at home. In other words, beyond Title XX, child welfare administrators could try to address increases in service demand through other federal programs, but Title IV-B funds were capped and required a state match, while open-ended Title IV-E funds were earmarked for AFDC children in addition to requiring a state match.

Under these circumstances, Byzantine patterns of service funding evolved during the 1980s as child welfare officials strove for matching formulae that optimized federal reimbursement. Imaginative program managers from affluent states first matched federal requirements for AFDC children in order to capture Title IV-E funds, then fronted the state match for IV-B funds, to the extent possible reserving Title XX funds for non-AFDC children. Program managers from states unwilling to meet the federal matching requirements had little choice but to use scarce Title XX funds, sometimes for AFDC children. Three sources of federal revenues for children's services are found in Table 15.4. The rapid expansion of funds for foster care of AFDC children under Title IV-E, an open-ended entitlement, contrasts with capped funding under Title IV-B and Title XX,[50] raising the specter that states may be induced to place poor, and disproportionately minority, children in foster care rather than to help them stay at home by funding in-home support services.

To compound the problems faced by foster care workers, quality foster care placements became scarce. A declining standard of living forced many women into the job market, thus restricting the pool of families with a parent at home to supervise children[51]—a requisite for desirable foster care. Soon the shortage of foster homes became critical. The director of the Illinois Department of Children and Family Services pleaded for 1,000 new foster parents to prevent the collapse of the state's foster care program.[52] In an investigation into the death of one foster care child, a Virginia grand jury cited "the acute shortage of suitable shelter for the 6,000 neglected, abused, and disabled children" in the state as a factor contributing to the child's death.[53] Thus, by the late 1980s, permanency planning was beset with multiple problems, leaving foster care as an unreliable way of serving many of the most troubled children in the United States.

◆ TABLE 15.4
Federal Funding for Child Welfare, Foster Care, and Adoption
(In millions of dollars)

Year	*Title IV-B Child Welfare*	*Title IV-E Foster Care*	*Title IV-E Adoption*
1983	156.3	394.8	12.6
1985	200.0	546.2	41.8
1987	222.5	792.6	73.7
1989	246.7	1,153.1	110.5
1991	273.9	1,819.2	175.3
1993	294.6	2,547.0	272.4
1995*	294.6	2,914.0	378.0
1997*	294.6	3,647.0	457.0
1999*	294.6	4,378.0	528.0

*Estimated
Source: U.S. House of Representatives, House Ways and Means Committee, *Overview of Entitlement Programs* (Washington, DC: U.S. GPO, 1994), p. 597.

Reversing the decline of the early 1980s, some 442,000 children were in foster care by 1992. Table 15.5 depicts changes in attributes of the foster care population during this period. Of children in foster care, most—33 percent—were placed less than one year, 24 percent for one to two years, 16 percent from two to three years, and 27 percent longer than three years.[54] In 1990, 54 percent of children in foster care were moved from one placement to another. Paralleling the younger age of children in foster care, family reunification is an increasingly frequent disposition for them; in 1982 reunification was the

◆ **TABLE 15.5**
Characteristics of the Foster Care Population
(percentage)

Characteristics	*1982*	*1988*	*1990*
Type of substitute care			
Family foster care	72.0	71.4	74.5
Nonfinalized adoptive home	—	2.3	2.7
Group home	21.5	18.6	16.4
Living independently	0.6	0.7	0.5
Other	5.2	5.7	5.6
Unknown	0.7	1.3	0.3
Age			
Under one year	2.7	5.0	4.9
One to five years	19.8	27.4	31.1
Six to 12 years	29.0	31.1	32.3
13 to 18 years	45.3	34.1	29.7
19 and over	2.9	2.3	1.7
Unknown	0.4	0.1	0.3
Race/ethnicity			
White	52.7	45.5	39.3
African American	34.2	36.5	40.4
Hispanic	6.7	10.1	11.8
Other	4.6	4.2	4.3
Unknown	1.8	3.7	4.2

Source: Joyce Everett, "Child Foster Care," *Encyclopedia of Social Work, 19th ed.* (Washington, DC: National Association of Social Workers, 1995), p. 383.

objective in 39.2 percent of cases, and in 1988 that had increased to 60 percent.[55]

ADOPTION

From the standpoint of permanency planning, adoption has become an important child welfare service. In the early 1980s, the Children's Bureau noted that 50,000 "hard to adopt" children were waiting for homes. Many of these children were of minority origin, handicapped, or older and had been in foster care for several years.[56] Because such children posed a financial burden for adoptive parents, the Adoption Assistance and Child Welfare Act of 1980 provided subsidies to adoptive parents. In 1983, 6,320 children were being subsidized each month at a cost of $12 million.[57] By 1996, the adoption assistance program had mushroomed to 113,000 cases, with maintenance payments totaling $302 million.[58] Providing incentives for parents to adopt hard-to-adopt children clearly supported the concept of permanency planning: "90 percent of subsidized adoptions involve foster parents whom the subsidy has enabled to adopt children with whom they had formed a relationship . . . and most of these are minorities or have special needs."[59] Moreover, subsidized adoption proved cost-effective, costing 37 percent less than foster care.

Still, adoption is not without controversy. Because children come from a variety of racial and cultural groups, the issue of transcultural adoption is raised. Should consideration be given to maintaining the cultural identity of children placed for adoption by finding them homes in their "native" culture? This question is at the heart of the Indian Child Welfare Act of 1978. Native Americans were disturbed that "25 to 35 percent of all American Indian children [were] separated from their families and placed in foster homes, adoptive homes, or institutions."[60] However, the fact that 85 percent of such placements were in non-Indian families and the children "without access to their tribal homes and relationships" raised the specter of cultural genocide.[61] To reinforce the cultural identity of Native American children, the Indian Child Welfare Act established:

> Minimal Federal standards for the removal of Indian children from their families and the placement of such children in foster or adoptive homes which will reflect the unique values of Indian culture, and for assistance to Indian tribes in the operation of child and family service programs.[62]

Equally important, the Indian Child Welfare Act established tribes, rather than state courts, as the governing bodies for Indian foster children.

A similar argument for culturally appropriate placement of children was advanced by the National Association of Black Social Workers (NABSW) during the 1980s. Noting an unacceptably high percentage of black children placed with white families, NABSW contended that cross-racial adoptions deprived individual children their racial identity and would eventually result in cultural genocide for the black community. Research on cross-racial adoption, however, consistently found that African American children did not suffer adverse consequences from growing up in white families. In 1996 President Clinton signed legislation forbidding interference in child placement for reasons based on race, exempting Indian tribes.[63]

While provisions to reinforce the cultural identity of children are unquestionably valid for a pluralistic society, the circumstances of many racial and cultural minorities leave the implementation of such policies in doubt.[64] Without basic health, education, and employment supports, minority families are likely to have difficulty in considering the adoption of children. For example, the number of African American children available for adoption far outstrips the number of African American families recruited to adopt children, despite the fact that "black families adopt at a rate 4.5 times greater than white or Hispanic families."[65]

Changes in family composition further cloud the picture. The pool of adoptive families has diminished with the increase in the number of female-headed households. The combination of low wages for women and a shortage of marriageable men means that mothers are encouraged to maintain small families, not to expand them through adoption. Esther Wattenberg of the University of Minnesota Center for Urban and Regional Affairs suspected that:

> the remainder of the [century] will be dominated by a sorting out of "the best interests of the child" in the extraordinary complex family relationships that develop out of extending family boundaries to stepparents, several sets of grandparents, and an assortment of new siblings from remarried families that join and unjoin family compositions.[66]

Compounding the circumstances surrounding adoption is the welfare reform legislation enacted in 1996. In requiring unrealistic labor market participation rates on the part of welfare recipients of 50 percent by 2002 and allowing states to institute time limits of less than two years, hundreds of thousands of welfare-poor families will be deleted from public assistance rolls in the next few years. The Congressional Budget Office projects that 2 to 4 million children will be kicked out of the social safety net if the federal five-year lifetime limit on receipt of welfare is instituted.[67] Termination of public aid will leave poor parents unable to care for children and induce many to consider foster care as a regrettable but no less necessary option for caring for their children. Thus, welfare reform will probably increase the number of children in foster care.

HEAD START

In response to concerns about the lack of educational preparation of poor children, Head Start was incorporated in the Economic Opportunity Act of 1964. A year later, the first Head Start programs were established in poor communities. Intended to compensate for a range of deficits displayed by poor children, Head Start offered health and dental screening, nutrition, and socialization experiences in addition to preschool academic preparation. Of the War on Poverty programs, Head Start was one of a few that captured the imagination of the nation. Despite wide public support, however, official support of Head Start was somewhat uneven, as Table 15.6 shows.

Although funding for Head Start has grown significantly since its founding, current appropriations, when adjusted for inflation, are actually lower than when the program first began. Moreover, the number of children now enrolled is lower than when the

◆ TABLE 15.6
Head Start: Participation and Federal Funding, Selected Years
(Dollars in millions)

Fiscal Year	*Enrollment*	*Budget Authority*
1965 (summer only)	561,000	$ 96.4
1970	477,400	325.7
1975	349,000	403.9
1980	376,300	735.0
1985	452,080	1,075.0
1990	548,470	1,552.0

Source: House Ways and Means Committee, U.S. House of Representatives, *Overview of Entitlement Programs, 1992 Green Book*, pp. 1695–1696.

program was established 25 years earlier; by the early 1990s, only 27 percent of eligible children participated in the program.[68]

During the 1980s, when government assistance to the poor was restrained, many poor families dispatched both parents to the labor market to stabilize family income, and this increased the need for Head Start. Even the Deficit Reduction Act of 1990, which held spending for most social programs in check, provided for modest increases in Head Start.[69] In large measure, this reflected a growing appreciation that Head Start was a proven investment in human capital. Award-winning author Sylvia Ann Hewlett noted that "Head Start ($3,000 a year per child) is much less expensive than prison ($20,000 a year per inmate)."[70] Such agreement notwithstanding, the federal fiscal crisis makes it unlikely that Head Start's allocation will be dramatically increased.

EMERGING ISSUES IN CHILD WELFARE

Changes in the economic and social circumstances of American families have broadened the scope of issues that have defined child welfare policy in the past. Of these changes, three are likely to shape child welfare in the future: day care, maternal and child health, and teenage pregnancy. Day care for children has risen in importance as more and more parents with children work. The need for child day care is felt both by middle-income families, in which both parents work in order to meet the income requirements of a middle-class lifestyle, and by low-income families, in which a parent is encouraged or required to participate in an AFDC workfare program. The child care available for these families is often unreliable, expensive, and of questionable quality. Furthermore, available child care does not often conform to the work schedules of parents. A study of New York City families found that half had to patch together day care from multiple providers. Low wages fail to attract the more skilled providers to the field, leading the Children's Defense Fund to observe ruefully that "despite their higher levels of education, child care providers are paid less than animal caretakers, bartenders, or parking lot and amusement park attendants."[71]

The crisis in child day care received nationwide attention in 1986 when two Miami children, unsupervised because their mother had to work and could not locate child care, climbed into a clothes dryer in which they "tumbled and burned to death."[72] This incident was cited in the introductory remarks to the proposed $375 million Child Care Services Improvement Act. An indicator of the severity of the day care crisis was that the legislation was sponsored by Orrin Hatch, a conservative senator noted for his prior opposition to social welfare legislation.[73]

Before 1990, the primary policies assisting parents with child care were the Federal Dependent Care Tax Credit and Title XX, neither of which has expanded child care for low-income families. The Dependent Care Tax Credit allows families to deduct up to 30 percent of $2,400 spent on child day care for a given year. As a "tax expenditure"—a de facto allocation through the Internal Revenue Service by not taxing income spent for a specific purpose—the Dependent Care Tax Credit is the largest form of federal assistance for child care.[74] For 1993 this tax credited is expected to cost the treasury $2.8 billion.[75] Unfortunately, this tax expenditure is nonrefundable, requiring poor families to pay the out-of-pocket expenses before they receive a partial rebate at a later date. Few poor families can afford this; as a result, the Dependent Care Tax Credit is virtually useless for them. Under Title XX, states were able to purchase day care for poor families, but few appropriated significant funds for that purpose.

As part of the 1990 Deficit Reduction Act, the Child Care and Development Block Grant program was established. The Child Care Block Grant provided $750 million in 1991, $825 million in 1992, and $925 million in 1993 to states through a complicated matching formula based on the number of children below five years of age and the number participating in the federal school lunch program. Of these funds, 75 percent are to be spent on direct assistance to families for child care services, and 25 percent for grants and contracts to child care providers. While the Child Care Block Grant represented a triumph for children's advocates, it contained an important flaw. Because federal allocations were predicated on state matching funds, the poor fiscal situation of many state governments led federal analysts to anticipate that only $715 million will actually be used out of the $1.5 billion made available during the first half of the 1990s for child care through the block grant.[76]

Maternal and child health has emerged as an issue among child welfare advocates as younger poor women give birth to low birth-weight babies for which they have received inadequate prenatal care. Low birth weight is a concern because such infants have a higher incidence of developmental disabilities, some of which are permanent and eventually require institutional care. The relationship between low birth weight and developmental disabilities, long recognized by public health officials, resurfaced in *Hunger in America*, a 1985 report by the Physician Task Force on Hunger in America funded through the Harvard University School of Public Health. In this report, researchers noted that "low birth-weight is the eighth leading cause of death in the United States." Efforts to sustain premature and low birth-weight infants are expensive and, even when successful, the consequence is often "long-term growth and developmental problems." Infants born small and premature suffer 25 percent more major neurological problems and 117 percent more minor neurological problems compared with normal infants.[77] Despite such documentation, the incidence of low birth weight among infants in the United States is relatively high, as indicated in Table 15.7. Moreover, the percentage of low birth-weight infants born to nonwhite teenagers is alarming, ranging from a low of 15.3 percent in Hawaii to a high of 32.9 percent in Mississippi.[78] Given the relatively high number of teen pregnancies in the nonwhite population, these figures show a disturbing reality: Substantial numbers of nonwhite infants in the United States are born with serious neurological deficits.

The primary federal program to enhance prenatal care for low-income families is WIC, the special supplemental food program for women, infants, and children. Under WIC, poor women who are pregnant and those who are breast-feeding youngsters are eligible for food coupons through which they may obtain especially nutritious foods. While the WIC program would seem a logical method for addressing the low birth-weight problem of infants born to poor women, participation in the WIC program is not at desirable levels. Nationwide, only 40.4 percent of the population financially eligible to participate in WIC did so in 1986. In 44 states, fewer than half of eligible women and children were served through WIC.[79]

The consequences of poor prenatal care are devastating. In 1986, twice as many African American infants died as did white infants, a disparity that has widened since 1940.[80] This difference is depicted in Figure 13.1. By 1990 the first-year cost of extensive medical care for low birth-weight infants rose to $2.1 billion, most of which could have been saved had the nation promoted maternal and child health more aggressively.[81]

Problems relating to maternal and infant health are exacerbated by the sharp rise in the numbers of adolescent females having children. Out-of-wedlock births became an important family issue in the 1980s when the incidence of unwed motherhood increased so rapidly that by 1983 half of all nonwhite births were outside of marriage.[82] Most troubling about this development was that the percentage of unmarried teenage mothers was rising so rapidly that by 1984 it was triple what it had been 25 years before.[83] By the mid–1980s, more than half of all teenage births were outside of marriage.[84] This increase in very young women having children on their own poses a serious problem for public policy for two basic reasons. First, teenage mothers are more likely to drop out of school and thus fail to gain those skills that would make them self-sufficient. As Figure 13.2 illustrates, adolescent mothers, particularly those who are African American or Hispanic, are apt to have less command

◆ **TABLE 15.7**
Percentage of Infants Born at Low Birth Weight, Selected Countries, 1990

Rank	*Nation*	*Percent*
1	Spain	1
2	Norway	4
2	Sweden	4
2	Ireland	4
2	Finland	4
6	Kuwait	5
6	Jordan	5
6	New Zealand	5
6	Switzerland	5
6	Portugal	5
6	Japan	5
6	Belgium	5
6	Hong Kong	5
6	Egypt	5
6	Iran	5
6	France	5
17	Romania	6
17	Greece	6
17	Germany	6
17	Saudi Arabia	6
17	UAE	6
17	Soviet Union	6
17	Singapore	6
17	Bulgaria	6
17	Austria	6
17	Australia	6
17	Canada	6
17	Denmark	6
17	Czech/Slovakia	6
17	Costa Rica	6
31	U.K.	7
31	Turkey	7
31	Yugoslavia	7
31	**United States**	**7**
31	Paraguay	7
31	Chile	7
31	Albania	7
31	Oman	7
31	Israel	7
40	Panama	8
40	Jamaica	8
40	Poland	8
40	Uruguay	8
40	Tunisia	8
40	Botswana	8
40	Benin	8
40	Colombia	8
40	Ethiopia	8
40	Cuba	8
50	Peru	9
50	Mauritius	9
50	Venezuela	9
50	South Korea	9
50	Burundi	9
50	Algeria	9
50	Iraq	9
50	China	9
58	Malaysia	10
58	Mongolia	10
58	Madagascar	10
58	Hungary	10
58	Lebanon	10
63	Senegal	11
63	Syria	11
63	Lesotho	11
63	Mauritania	11
67	South Africa	12
67	Thailand	12
67	Bolivia	12
67	Mexico	12
71	Zaire	13
71	Guinea-Bissau	13
71	Cameroon	13
74	Guatemala	14
74	Tanzania	14
74	Indonesia	14
74	Coast d'Ivoire	14
	U.S. black population	**14**
78	Niger	15
78	Sudan	15
78	Kenya	15
78	Central Afr. Republic	15
78	El Salvador	15
83	Sri Lanka	25

Source: Children's Defense Fund, *The Health of America's Children* (Washington, DC: Children's Defense Fund, 1992), Table 7, p. 8.

of basic skills. Poor skill development poses a critical problem when these skills are parenting skills. Second, teenage mothers are more likely to have to depend on welfare for assistance, the benefits of which are at levels lower than the actual cost of raising children. This combination of poor skill development and dependence on public welfare programs presents the specter of poor children bearing more poor children in an endless cycle of hopelessness. The consequences are particularly tragic for poor children, who have little prospect of escaping the poverty trap. Reductions in the numbers of working males who are marriageable means that these children have little hope that their mother's marriage will pull them out of poverty, although this is the most prevalent way for mothers to become independent of public welfare.[85] The loss of earning power through the Aid to Families with Dependent Children program means that public assistance will not provide an adequate economic base for poor children.[86] Moreover, the interaction of these factors has devastating implications for African American children: 30 percent of all African American children are "persistently poor." Approximately 90 percent of children who are poor for 10 or more years of their childhood are African American.[87] Unfortunately, the prevalence of teenage motherhood is likely to worsen the life opportunities of poor children, particularly those who are minorities. For these reasons, Thompson and Peebles-Wilkins reinforce the importance of interventions that incorporate societal supports while distancing friends in order to elevate the self-esteem of African American adolescent mothers.[88]

CONCLUSION: THE FUTURE OF CHILD WELFARE

After a half-century of federal legislation, child welfare advocates cannot be hopeful about the care provided to American youngsters. The prospect of using the family as the primary institution for child welfare has diminished because of the absence of economic and social supports to keep the family intact. Without a coherent family policy, families have been less able to care for children, and child welfare services—such as protective services, foster care and adoption—have been deployed to ameliorate the most serious problems experienced by children. During the 1980s, however, even these programs became subject to budget rescissions, further exposing youngsters to economic and social insecurity as well as physical danger. By the 1990s, children's services resembled a tangle of categorical programs more closely connected to vital, but diminishing, funding streams than to the actual troubles that children and their families experienced.

At the national level, child welfare advocates found that the plight of troubled children might prove to be a compelling justification for reassessing the neglect of children's programs. In promoting its welfare reform proposal, the American Public Welfare Association highlighted (in its publication of that title) that "one child in four" was poor in the United States.[89] In May 1991, the National Commission on Children presented its comprehensive report on at-risk children and their families. The report called for an extensive expansion of federal efforts in several areas: income support, health, education, job training, employment, service collaboration, and moral development. Several suggestions departed from the traditional methods of supporting poor children. First, the commission recommended that "welfare be reoriented as short-term relief in periods of unanticipated unemployment, disability, or other economic hardship,"[90] as opposed to an indefinite entitlement. Limiting AFDC to a fixed period would, of course, require additional income supports for the poor. The commission addressed this by suggesting an expansion of the Earned Income Tax Credit (EITC) and the creation of a $1,000 refundable Child Tax Credit. Finally, the commission recommended the deployment of a demonstration program to test an enhanced child support enforcement and insurance scheme.

A Child Support Enforcement and Assurance Program (CSEAP) to replace AFDC had been proposed by Irwin Garfinkel. CSEAP would reform child support in three ways: (1) The amount of child support would be calculated as a percentage of the absent parent's income; (2) support payments would be automatically withheld from paychecks; and (3) a minimum benefit to children would be assured by the federal government.[91] A federal CSEAP initiative with these components, Garfinkel reasoned, could replace most of the highly stigmatized AFDC program. CSEAP is not without its critics, however. One critic, Mickey Kaus, opposed the idea because it placed the federal government in the same awkward position it has had with respect to AFDC, namely, subsidizing broken families. For that reason, Kaus favors an enhanced EITC, an increased minimum wage, and a federal jobs program in which any AFDC beneficiary would have to participate after two years, or lose benefits.[92]

Child welfare advocates had much to choose from given the relative neglect of children's issues on the part of the Reagan and Bush administrations. Perhaps the best-positioned among child welfare advocates, the Children's Defense Fund (CDF) had, during the 1980s, brought to the nation's attention a new set of child welfare problems—teen pregnancy, homeless and runaway youth, malnutrition among mothers and infants, and unemployment and school absence among adolescents. Child welfare advocates were particularly pleased when President Clinton selected Donna Shalala to head the Department of Health and Human Services because Shalala had succeeded Hillary Clinton as chair of the CDF board.[93]

Meanwhile, states were experimenting with various methods for stretching their dollars to do more for children. Gradually, these efforts evolved into a potent critique of the traditional ways in which children's services had been delivered. "What's needed is a complete overhaul of children's services, bringing together public and private organizations to meet the comprehensive needs of children, adolescents, and parents," stated Stanford University's Michael Kirst.[94] Noting that many children from problem families were known to several, separate health and human agencies—none with sufficient resources to substantively help any one child—children's advocate Sid Gardner called for collaborative efforts among service providers: "In fact, we are ultimately failing our children not only because we haven't invested in them, but also because as communities we have failed to work together to hold ourselves accountable for the substantial resources we do invest—and for the outcomes of our most vulnerable residents."[95]

Social worker Bonnie Bernard of the Far West Laboratory for Educational Research and Development observed that, however defined, collaboration or restructuring targets power relations. "True restructuring means the redistribution of policymaking power, not only from the central office administration to the local school," but to professionals and ultimately to consumers and their communities.[96]

The restructuring movement has enormous implications for child welfare. Since the Social Security Act of 1935, child welfare has been integrally connected to federal funding for categorical programs that serve children with specific problems. If categorical programs are consolidated through restructuring, how will services be assured for children who are most at risk—the homeless, the disabled, those with AIDS? Giving parents vouchers to choose their service providers is one way to empower them, but who will see to it that they make prudent choices for their dependent children? Also, what will happen to the identity of social workers when they are assigned to interdisciplinary teams that include nurses, counselors, and educators? Perhaps most provocatively, does service collaboration around children presage the development of a new, postindustrial profession, the "human-service professional," who will effectively replace social work as an activity properly retired with the industrial era?

◆ ◆ ◆ *Discussion Questions* ◆ ◆ ◆

1. Much of child welfare—protective services, foster care, adoptions—is funded through a complex arrangement of categorical funding. How does your welfare department optimize reimbursement through these funding sources? As a result of this, what are the priorities for children's services? How would you reconcile discrepancies between categorical funding priorities and community needs?

2. Maintaining the cultural identity of minority children who receive foster care and adoption services is a heated issue in child welfare. When there are too few minority families for the children needing foster care and adoption services, what should the policy of the welfare department be in placing minority children? How consistent is this with current child welfare policy in your community?

3. Providing preschool programs for children is an increasingly important issue as more mothers enter the work force. How adequate are day care provisions in your community? Who is responsible for the oversight of day care? To what extent are the needs of low-income families considered in planning day care? What percentage of families eligible for Head Start actually participate in this program in your community?

4. Among the health-related child welfare concerns is infant mortality and low birth weight. How do the statistics in your community compare with the state and national incidence of these two important indicators of child welfare? What are the incidences of infant mortality and low birth weight for teenage and minority mothers in your community? What plans does your community have for improving the health status of infants of minority and low-income families?

5. AFDC (now TANF) is arguably the most unpopular of social programs. What are the advantages and disadvantages of replacing it either by expanding the Earned Income Tax Credit or by a Child Support Enforcement and Assurance program? If you favor one of these, how would you convince the public that it constitutes *real* welfare reform?

Notes

1. *Kids Count 1996* (Baltimore: Annie E. Casey Foundation, 1996), p. 5.
2. Jeanne Giovannoni, "Children," *Encyclopedia of Social Work*, 18th Ed. (Silver Spring, MD: NASW, 1987), p. 247.
3. Alfred Kadushin, "Child Welfare Services," *Encyclopedia of Social Work*, 18th Ed. (Silver Spring, MD: NASW, 1987), p. 268.
4. Walter Trattner, *From Poor Law to Welfare State* (New York: Free Press, 1974), p. 100.
5. Ibid., pp. 106–107.
6. Sallie Watkins, "The Mary Ellen Myth," *Social Work*, 35 (November 1990), p. 503.
7. Diana DiNitto and Thomas Dye, *Social Welfare* (Englewood Cliffs, NJ: Prentice-Hall, 1987), p. 153.
8. Kathleen Faller, "Protective Services for Children," *Encyclopedia of Social Work*, 18th Ed. (Silver Spring, MD: NASW, 1987). p. 386.
9. Trattner, *From Poor Law to Welfare State*, pp. 181, 183.
10. James Leiby, *A History of Social Welfare and Social Work in the United States* (New York: Columbia University Press, 1978), pp. 148–149.
11. June Axinn and Herman Levin, *Social Welfare* (New York: Harper and Row, 1982), p. 159.
12. Trattner, *From Poor Law to Welfare State*, p. 186
13. Axinn and Levin, *Social Welfare*, pp. 224–228.
14. Barbara Kantrowitz et al., "How to Protect Abused Children," *Newsweek* (November 23, 1987), p. 68.
15. Sandra Evans, "Increase in Baby Killings Attributed to Family Stress," *Washington Post* (June 23, 1992), p. A1.
16. Faller, "Protective Services for Children," pp. 387, 389.
17. Douglas Besharov, "Contending with Overblown Expectations," *Public Welfare* (Winter 1987), pp. 7, 8.
18. Kantrowitz et al., "How to Protect Abused Children," p. 68.
19. "Foster Care: Duty v. Legal Vulnerability," *NASW News* (July 1988), p. 3.
20. "Social Workers' Neglect," *All Things Considered* (Washington, DC: National Public Radio, April 15, 1988). *NASW News* later reported that the employees cited in this broadcast were not professional social workers but, rather, employees of the state (see n. 18).
21. "High Court Review Urged on Foster Care Liability," *NASW News* (July 1988), p. 3.
22. Ibid.
23. Douglas Besharov, "Right versus Rights: The Dilemma of Child Protection," *Public Welfare*, 43 (1985), pp. 19–46.
24. David Finkelhor, "Is Child Abuse Overprotected?" *Public Welfare*, 48 (1990), pp. 22–29.
25. Fox Butterfield, "Sect Members Assert They Are Misunderstood," *The New York Times*, (June 24, 1984), p. 16.
26. Bridgitte Berger and Peter Berger, *The War Over the Family* (Garden City, NY: Anchor, 1983), p. 213.
27. Besharov, "Contending with Overblown Expectations," p. 8.
28. William Claiborne, "Child Sex Ring or Witch Hunt: Charges Divide Town," *Washington Post* (November 14, 1995), p. A1; "A Northwest Town's Nightmare Continues," *Washington Post Weekly* (June 24–30, 1995), p. 31; Lela Costin, Howard Karger, and David Stoesz, *The Politics of Child Abuse*

in *America*(New York: Oxford University Press, 1996).

29. Douglas Besharov with Lisa Laumann, "Child Abuse Reporting," *Society* (May/June 1996), p. 43.
30. David Stoesz and Howard Karger, "Suffer the Children," *Washington Monthly* (June 1996), p. 20.
31. Costin et al., *The Politics of Child Abuse in America*.
32. U.S. Department of Health and Human Services, National Center on Child Abuse and Neglect, *Child Maltreatment 1994: Reports from the States to the National Center on Child Abuse and Neglect* (Washington, DC: U.S. GPO, 1996).
33. Costin et al., *The Politics of Child Abuse in America*.
34. Ibid.
35. U.S. Department of Health and Human Services, *Child Maltreatment 1994*, p. ix.
36. Barbara Vobejda, "HHS Study Finds Sharp Rise in Child Abuse," *Washington Post* (September 19, 1996), p. A8.
37. Theodore Stein, "Foster Care for Children," *Encyclopedia of Social Work*, 18th Ed. (Silver Spring, MD: NASW, 1987), pp. 641–642.
38. Ibid., p. 643.
39. Keith Harriston, "D.C. Foster Children Are Missing," *Washington Post* (August 6, 1992), p. C1.
40. *A Children's Defense Budget* (Washington, DC: Children's Defense Fund, 1988), p. 179.
41. Anthony Maluccio and Edith Fein, "Permanency Planning: A Redefinition," *Child Welfare* (May–June 1983), p. 197.
42. Duncan Lindsey, "Achievements for Children in Foster Care," *Social Work* (November 1982), p. 495.
43. Peg Hess, Gail Folaron, and Ann Jefferson, "Effectiveness of Family Reunification Services," *Social Work*, 37 (July 1992), pp. 306, 310.
44. Stein, "Foster Care for Children," p. 641.
45. "Foster Care vs. Legal Vulnerability," p. 3.
46. Ronald Rooney, "Permanency Planning for All Children?" *Social Work* (March 1982), p. 157.
47. *A Children's Defense Budget*, p. 54.
48. U.S. House of Representatives, *1992 Green Book* (Washington, DC: U.S. Government Printing Office, 1992), p. 830.
49. Stein, "Foster Care for Children," p. 649.
50. Revenues for Title XX are not included in the table because the federal government does not collect data on how much is expended by states for child welfare.
51. Esther Wattenberg, "The Fate of Baby Boomers and Their Children," *Social Work* (January–February 1986), pp. 85–93.
52. Kantrowitz et al., "How to Protect Abused Children," p. 71.
53. Mary Jordan, "Foster Parent Scarcity Causing Crisis in Care," *Washington Post* (July 20, 1986), p. A9.
54. Patrick Curtis et al., *Child Abuse and Neglect: A Look at the States* (Washington, DC: Child Welfare League of America, 1995), p. 67.
55. Everett, "Child Foster Care," p. 385.
56. Elizabeth Cole, "Adoption," *Encyclopedia of Social Work*, 18th Ed. (Silver Spring, MD: NASW, 1987), p. 70.
57. Committee on Ways and Means, U.S. House of Representatives, *Background Material and Data on Programs within the Jurisdiction of the Committee on Ways and Means* (Washington, DC: U.S. Government Printing Office, 1985), p. 494.
58. Committee on Ways and Means, U.S. House of Representatives, *Overview of Entitlement Programs* (Washington, DC: U.S. GPO, 1994), p. 599.
59. Cole, "Adoption," p. 71.
60. Ronald Fischler, "Protecting American Indian Children," *Social Work* (September 1980), p. 341.
61. Evelyn Lance Blanchard and Russell Lawrence Barsh, "What Is Best for Tribal Children?" *Social Work* (September 1980), p. 350.
62. Fischler, "Protecting American Indian Children," p. 341.
63. Spencer Rich, "Wage Bill Includes Provisions Intended to Increase Adoptions," *Washington Post* (August 10, 1996), p. A4.
64. Patricia Hogan and Sau-Fong Siu, "Minority Children and the Child Welfare System," *Social Work* (November–December 1988), pp. 312–317.
65. Cole, "Adoption," p. 70.
66. Wattenberg, "The Fate of Baby Boomers and Their Children," p. 24.
67. David Stoesz, "Welfare Behaviorism," *Society* (Spring, 1997), p. 33.
68. Children's Defense Fund, *The State of America's Children, 1991* (Washington, DC: Children's Defense Fund, 1991), p. 44.
69. Paul Leonard and Robert Greenstein, *One Step Forward: The Deficit Reduction Package of 1990* (Washington, DC: Center on Budget and Policy Priorities, 1990), p. 34.

70. Sylvia Ann Hewlett, *When the Bough Breaks* (New York: HarperCollins, 1992), p. 300.
71. Children's Defense Fund, *The State of America's Children, 1988*, p. 207.
72. Ibid., p. 214.
73. Ibid., p. 32; also National Association of Social Workers, "1986 Voting Record" (Silver Spring, MD: NASW, 1987).
74. U.S. House of Representatives, *1992 Green Book*, p. 948.
75. Ibid., p. 984.
76. Leonard and Greenstein, *One Step Forward*, pp. 33–34.
77. Physician Task Force on Hunger in America, *Hunger in America* (Cambridge, MA: Harvard University Press, 1985), p. 65.
78. Children's Defense Fund, *The Health of America's Children* (Washington, DC: Children's Defense Fund, 1987), p. 72.
79. Ibid., p. 84.
80. Ibid., p. 195.
81. Ibid., p. 25.
82. Michael Novak (Ed.), *The New Consensus on Family and Welfare* (Washington, DC: American Enterprise Institute, 1987), p. 135.
83. Lisbeth Schorr, *Within Our Reach* (Garden City, NY: Anchor Books, 1988), p. 13.
84. Novak, *The New Consensus on Family and Welfare*, p. 48.
85. William Julius Wilson, "American Social Policy and the Ghetto Underclass," *Dissent* (Winter 1988), pp 80–91.
86. David Ellwood, *Poor Support: Poverty and the American Family* (New York: Basic Books, 1988), p. 58.
87. Committee on Ways and Means, U.S. House of Representatives, *Children in Poverty* (Washington, DC: U.S. Government Printing Office, 1985), p. 44.
88. Maxine Seaborn Thompson and Wilma Peebles-Wilkins, "The Impact of Formal, Informal, and Societal Support Networks on the Psychological Well-being of Black Adolescent Mothers," *Social Work*, 37 (July 1992), pp. 65–71.
89. American Public Welfare Association, *One Child in Four* (Washington, DC: American Public Welfare Association, 1987).
90. National Commission on Children, *Beyond Rhetoric: A New American Agenda for Children and Families (Final Report)* (Washington, DC: National Commission on Children, 1991), p. 34.
91. Irwin Garfinkel, "Bringing Fathers Back In: The Child Support Assurance Strategy," *The American Prospect* (Spring 1992), p. 75.
92. Mickey Kaus, *The End of Equality* (New York: Basic Books, 1992).
93. Marlene Cimons, "Shifting toward a Mainstream Approach to Children's Issues," *Los Angeles Times* (December 24, 1992), p. A5.
94. Michael Kirst, "Improving Children's Services," *Phi Delta Kappan* (April 1991), p. 616.
95. Sid Gardner, "Failure by Fragmentation," *California Tomorrow* (Fall 1989), p. 19.
96. Bonnie Benard, "School Restructuring Can Promote Prevention," *Western Center News* (December 1991), p. 8

CHAPTER 16

Housing Policies

Problems associated with housing have entered the news by way of the national focus on homelessness. Although homelessness is undoubtedly an important social problem, finding and maintaining adequate and affordable housing is also problematic for those on public assistance, the working poor, and for a large section of the middle class. This chapter examines the problems in housing, with particular emphasis on problems related to low-income housing, housing affordability, homelessness, and proposals for housing reform.

OVERVIEW OF HOUSING LEGISLATION

Federal housing legislation began in 1937. As Table 16.1 illustrates, this tangle of legislation often evolved in conflicting directions.

In 1990, Congress passed the Cranston-Gonzales National Affordable Housing Act, the first new piece of legislation in more than a decade to address the housing needs of low- and moderate-income people. This act authorized a new, indirect approach to housing in the form of block grants to state and local governments. The 1990 act had six specific goals: (1) to decentralize housing policy by allowing states to design and administer their own housing programs; (2) to use nonprofit sponsors to help develop and implement housing services; (3) to link housing assistance more closely with social services; (4) to facilitate home ownership for low- and moderate-income people; (5) to preserve existing federally subsidized housing units; and (6) to initiate cost sharing among federal, state, and local governments and nonprofit organizations.[1]

The 1990 act required applicants to prepare a comprehensive housing affordability strategy (CHAS), which outlined a state or jurisdiction's housing needs. HUD required the plan to be updated annually in order to determine whether state and local jurisdictions were utilizing federal housing money to meet the goals enumerated in the CHAS document. Federal housing funds were to flow directly to the government agencies that drew up the plans. In addition, the act called for citizen input into preparation of CHAS documents.[2] The 1990 act also introduced the HOME investment partnerships block grant program, the Homeownership and Opportunity for People Everywhere (HOPE) program, and the national homeownership trust demonstration.

The centerpiece of the National Affordable Housing Act is the HOME program, which was designed to increase the supply of affordable housing for low-income families by providing federal grants to state and local governments. All states and more than 300 local jurisdictions receive HOME funds. Ninety

◆TABLE 16.1
Historical Highlights of Pre-1990 Housing Legislation

The Housing Act of 1937	The United States had no national housing policy prior to the Housing Act of 1937. The objective of the act was to: "provide financial assistance to the states and political subdivisions thereof for the elimination of unsafe and unsanitary housing conditions, for the eradication of slums, for the provision of decent, safe and sanitary dwellings for families of low income, and for the reduction of unemployment and the stimulation of business activity, to create a United States Housing Authority and for other purposes."[3]
The Housing Act of 1949 (amended 1937 act)	This amendment called for federal money for slum clearance and urban redevelopment and for the creation of a public authority charged with building and administering 135,000 low-income housing units annually for six years. In addition, the Housing Act of 1949 included the goal of providing a decent home and a suitable living environment for every American family.[4] Specifically, this bill required each locality to develop a plan for urban redevelopment that contained provisions for "predominantly residential dwellings." The wording of this bill was interpreted by localities to mean that only one-half of new construction was to be devoted to low-income housing. Inadvertently, the federal government created a policy that encouraged urban redevelopment at the expense of existing low-income housing.
Housing Act of 1954 (amended the 1949 act).	"Urban development" was changed to urban renewal, and localities were required to submit a master plan for removing urban blight and for community development. The act removed the requirement that new federally subsidized urban construction be "predominantly residential," clearing the way for massive slum clearance projects. It also allowed localities to more easily lease or sell land and to avoid the construction of public housing. This led to charges that cities were insensitive to the needs of poor long-term residents. Using renewal projects, localities tried to revitalize inner cities by attracting middle- and upper-income families at the expense of displaced poor families. From 1949 to 1963, urban renewal projects removed about 243,000 housing units and replaced them with 68,000 units, of which only 20,000 were for low-income families.[5]
The Demonstration Cities and Metropolitan Development Act (Model Cities)	This act was passed in 1966 and was part of President Lyndon Johnson's War on Poverty. In large part, it focused on issues of deteriorated housing and blighted neighborhoods. The Model Cities legislation promised to "concentrate public and private resources in a comprehensive five-year attack on social, economic, and physical problems of slums and blighted neighborhoods."[6] In 1974 the Model Cities Act and virtually all neighborhood development acts were superseded by the Housing and Community Development Act of 1974. *(continued)*

percent of HOME-assisted units must be affordable for families with incomes below 60 percent of the area median, and the remaining units must be affordable for families with incomes at 80 percent of the median. The HOME program allows states and entitlement communities a large measure of flexibility in addressing their local housing needs. Funds under the matching federal/state HOME program can be used for tenant-based rental assistance, property acquisition, or rehabilitation and, in some cases, for new construction. The HOME program also includes an opportunity for local innovation. For example, at least 15 percent of HOME funds must be used for projects sponsored by Community Housing Development Organizations (CHDOs) or neighborhood-based nonprofit groups.[10]

A second major component is the HOPE program, which was designed to facilitate homeownership by low-income families through the sale of publicly owned or held homes to current residents or other low-income households. The HOPE program has four components: (1) HOPE I finances the sales

◆ **TABLE 16.1** ***(continued)***

The Housing and Community Development Act of 1974	This was a wide-ranging bill that included provisions for urban renewal, neighborhood development, model cities, water and sewer projects, neighborhood and facility grants, public facilities and rehabilitation loans, and urban beautification and historic preservation grants.[7] Although spending priorities were determined at the national level, communities were required to submit a master plan, including specific reference to their low-income housing needs. The amount allocated for fiscal years 1978 to 1980 was almost $11 billion, and more than 1,800 communities received entitlement grants in the first two years of the program.[8]
Home Mortgage Disclosure Act	This act was concerned with the problem of mortgage redlining. Housing observers had argued that a major cause of community deterioration was a "lending strike," or redlining, by financial institutions. Redlining is defined as "an outright refusal of an insurance company, bank, or other financial institution to provide its services solely on the basis of the location of the property in question. The term is derived from the practice of marking in red the area on a map that is to be avoided by those responsible for the distribution of the services of that institution."[9] As a result of this policy, families seeking to purchase a home in a redlined neighborhood might be denied a mortgage loan, insurance, or other necessary services. In 1976, President Gerald Ford signed the Home Mortgage Disclosure Act, which required virtually every bank or savings and loan association to annually disclose where it made its loans. Although useful for community groups trying to pressure local banks into greater neighborhood involvement, in cities without active community organizations the law was rendered almost useless.
Community Reinvestment Act of 1977	Significantly broader than the HMDA, the CRA established the principle that each bank and savings institution has an obligation to make loans in every neighborhood of its service area. Virtually all lending institutions are covered under the CRA, and the law requires the federal government to evaluate annually the performance of each lending institution. Primary enforcement involves the control by federal regulatory agencies over new charters, bank growth and mergers, relocations, and acquisitions. Although CRA works well in theory, only a handful of the estimated 250 or more CRA challenges resulted in punitive action against lenders. In the main, the power of the Community Reinvestment Act rests with the ability of community groups to win commitments directly from lending institutions, usually in the form of negotiated settlements. It is estimated that $7.5 billion has been committed by banks and savings associations to low income communities as the result of negotiated CRA agreements.

of public housing apartments to residents; (2) HOPE II finances the sales of other apartment buildings held by the federal government (such as property acquired from failed savings-and-loan associations) to low-income persons; (3) HOPE III finances the sale of single-family homes owned by federal, state, or local governments; and (4) HOPE IV represents an effort to combine social services with housing assistance for elderly and disabled households that would otherwise be unable to live independently. Nearly $1 billion was authorized for HOPE I, II, and III in the 1990 act.[11]

Title VI of the 1990 act, the Low Income Housing Preservation and Resident Homeownership Act, was an effort to protect hundreds of thousands of residents in privately owned federally subsidized apartment buildings from displacement through the sale or conversion of their buildings. Under some federal housing programs enacted during the 1960s, private owners received mortgage insurance and subsidies to finance rental housing for low- and moderate-income families. In many cases, the Department of Housing and Urban Development (HUD) offered these owners an option to prepay or pay off their mortgages after 20 years. Upon payment of their mortgages, owners were freed of any obligation to reserve their units for low- and moderate-income residents (i.e., the landlords could raise the rents and evict poor tenants). The Congressional Budget Office estimated that in 1989 as many as 300,000 rental units would be jeopardized unless Congress acted quickly. At a cost of $400 million in 1996, Title VI requires HUD to limit the approval of prepayments, and it creates incentives for owners to remain in the program or to sell to new owners who will maintain the project's low-income financial restrictions.[12]

The linkage between housing and social services was further strengthened by the Family Sufficiency program of the 1990 Housing Act. Specifically, this component called for public housing authorities to offer programs that allow residents access to coordinated social services designed to assist them in gaining employment. Participating families must complete these programs or risk losing their housing assistance. In return, as a participant's income increases, the money normally contributed toward a higher rent (calculated at 30 percent of income) is set aside in a special escrow account to be used for the purchase of a home. The act also includes modest funds to create Family Investment Centers in or near public housing projects, where social services will be provided.[13]

THE FEDERAL GOVERNMENT AND LOW-INCOME HOUSING PROGRAMS

For many families, housing costs represents the single largest expenditure in the household budget. It is a fixed cost that is often paid before food, clothing, and health care bills. For poor families, the precious little that remains after rent or mortgage payments are made is used to buy necessities for the rest of the month. The important impact of housing costs on family finances has helped encourage the federal government's involvement with low- and non–low-income housing programs. Table 16.2 provides an overview of key HUD and FmHA programs relating to the housing problems of low-income households.

Despite its importance, governmental assistance for housing was never provided as an entitlement to all households that qualify for aid. Hence, unlike income-maintenance programs such as SSI and the former AFDC program, housing programs are not automatically provided to all eligible applicants. In contrast to entitlement-based funding, Congress appropriates funds yearly for a number of new commitments, most of which run for from 5 to 50 years. Because funding levels are usually low, only a portion of eligible applicants actually receive assistance. The 1993 American Housing Survey found that out of the 15 million poor households eligible for housing assistance, only 4.5 million actually received it. (An additional 17.6 million near-poor households also received no housing assistance.) Out of the poor households that did receive housing assistance, about one-third lived in government-run projects; two-thirds rented from private landlords under Section 8.[14] Moreover, contrary to popular myth, fewer than one quarter of all AFDC families receive any form of housing assistance.[15]

This funding scheme has resulted in waiting lists for public housing and rent subsidies that are in some cases multiyear. The Council of Large Public Housing estimated that, nationwide, waiting lists for public housing include 2.35 million households, many of whom will wait two or more years before getting a unit. In its 1995 study on the status of hunger and homelessness in 29 cities, the U.S. Conference of Mayors found that requests for housing assistance increased in 19 of the survey cities. Applicants for public housing in the survey cities were forced to wait an average of 17 months from the time they applied until the time they received assistance. The average wait for Section 8 housing was 40 months; for vouchers, it was 39 months. In 20 of the cities surveyed, the waiting list for at least one assisted housing program was so long the cities stopped accepting applications for that program. For example, in Cleveland, family public housing and Section 8 certificates and vouchers were closed; in Nashville, Section 8 applicants waited up to nine or ten years for housing. Many cities found it especially difficult to locate housing for large families and those suffering from mental illness.[16]

Despite the overwhelming need for housing assistance, federal housing programs were cut back sharply in the 1980s and 1990s. For example, during the mid–1970s, housing assistance was extended to as many as 400,000 new families a year. Under the Reagan administration, that number was slashed to 40,000. For the first time since the federal government became involved in housing, the FY 1997 budget reduced the number of new families receiving housing assistance to zero.[17] Moreover, in 1993 HUD had a staff of 13,294 and a budget of $25 billion. By 1996, the staff was cut to 11,628 and the budget reduced to $19.5 billion.

Notwithstanding the severity of housing problems for poor families, most federal housing subsidies continue to benefit the upper and middle classes. These housing subsidies provide billions of dollars in benefits each year to homeowners through mortgage interest and property tax deductions. Subsidies to those who are better off far outstrip assistance provided to the poor. For example, the entire HUD budget was $19 billion in 1996—the amount that mortgage deductions cost the federal government was $100 billion. Moreover, this federal expenditure predominantly benefits households in the top fifth of the income distribution, and more than two-thirds of that money went to families with incomes above $75,000 a year. In fact, the higher the income, the greater the benefit—up to a cap of $1 million in mortgage principal. While more than 80 percent of homeowners with incomes of more than $90,000 receive these tax breaks, only 10 percent of homeowners earning between $10,000 and $20,000 get any benefit from homeowner deductions.[18] Cushing Dolbeare sums up

◆ TABLE 16.2
Overview of HUD and Farmers Home Administration Programs

Section 8	Less-known than public housing, this important HUD program provides subsidized rental payments for more than 2.9 million families. Section 8 is based on a voucher system that allows low-income tenants to occupy existing and privately owned housing stock. The voucher is a subsidy that covers the difference between a fixed percentage of a tenant's income (30 percent) and the fair market rent of a housing unit. The HUD subsidy goes directly to the local public housing authority, which then pays the landlord, provided that the unit meets quality standards. Contract terms for subsidies last for from 5 to 15 years. About half of Section 8 is project-based, meaning that tenants have to live in specific apartments. The other half is tenant-based, allowing tenants to take their subsidies and move. Section 8 also provides funds for new construction and for substantial and moderate rehabilitation of existing units.[19]
Public Housing	Public Housing was established by the U.S. Housing Act of 1937. It is restricted to households whose incomes are too low to afford decent housing on the private market. Public housing is owned—or in some cases leased—by local public housing authorities. In 1993, 1.4 million public housing units were occupied by 3.3 million residents.[20] One-half are families with children, one-third are elderly households without children, and the remainder are households headed by people with disabilities. Sixty-three percent are households headed by people of color; 75 percent of these are headed by women and one-third by single parents. The median income of families with children in public housing was $6,190 in 1995. For elderly families, the median income was $7,010. The income of most families in public housing is less than 25 percent of the area median income. About one-half of the households rely primarily upon public assistance (AFDC, SSI, and General Assistance) for their income; the other half rely on earned incomes, pensions, or Social Security. Residents pay 30 percent of their monthly adjusted income on rent, 10 percent of monthly gross income or the welfare shelter allowance, whichever is higher. The average rent payment, as of 1995, was $169 per month. There are more than 15,000 public housing developments (most are low-rise) in 3,400 localities.[21] *(continued)*

TABLE 16.2 (*continued*)

Section 202: Housing for the Elderly and Handicapped	This program provides financing to nonprofit organizations wishing to build housing for elderly or handicapped people. In 1974, Section 202 was tied to Section 8 so that instead of providing only low-interest loans to build apartments, it also provides rental subsidies. By 1988, 210,000 units had been produced under Section 202.[22]
Section 236: Below-Market Interest Rate Program	Provides developers with low-interest loans in return for construction of moderately priced rental housing. This program was intended to provide housing for people whose incomes were too high to qualify for public housing but too low to meet the rental costs of unsubsidized housing. Finally, Section 235 provides low-income families with subsidized and low-interest mortgages to enable them to purchase a home. In 1988, almost 150,000 units were subsidized under this program; an additional 400,000 units existed where the mortgages were paid off, where the purchasers had graduated to unsubsidized interest rates as their incomes rose, or where the owners had defaulted.[23]
FmHA Section 502	This is the largest FmHA program. It makes low-interest loans available for home purchases in rural areas. By 1985, some 1.6 million rural families had borrowed under the Section 502 program.
FmHA Section 504	Section 504 provides grants or low-interest loans to low-income families for home repairs.
Other FmHA Programs	FmHA operates a rental housing program much like Section 236 and a rural rental assistance program that provides subsidies to tenants. The FmHA also has a number of smaller, special-purpose programs, such as Sections 514 and 515, which provide housing for migrant workers.
The Low-Income Housing Tax Credit (LIHTC)	The LIHTC dispenses more than the equivalent of $3 billion to subsidize the construction or rehabilitation of housing for low-income families. Support is given to private investors in the form of a tax credit which is cashed in over a ten-year period. In exchange, rents must be maintained at affordable levels. Under the supervision of the U.S. Internal Revenue Service, 54 state and local housing finance agencies administer the LIHTC program. Because of this decentralized administration, little national data is available.

the problem: "Benefits from federal programs are so skewed that *the total of all the assisted housing payments ever made under all HUD assisted housing programs, from the inception of public housing in 1937 through 1980, was less than the costs to the federal government of housing related tax expenditures in 1980 alone* [original emphasis]."[24]

Low-income housing has historically been one of the most unpopular issues on the domestic policy agenda. Because of its close association with public housing, HUD has become one of the more unpopular federal agencies.[25] Apart from the public's skepticism, HUD suffers from other problems. First, housing poor people is expensive. In 1996 HUD spent more than $6,000 a year to house a poor family. By comparison, it cost Medicare $5,000 a year to provide health care to an elderly person. Second, HUD insures the mortgages on roughly 700,000 financially troubled private apartments. If the owners default, the bailout could cost HUD $18 billion over the next few years. Even a fraction of such losses (which seem inevitable) could plunge the department into deeper political and financial turmoil. Moreover, HUD is responsible for funding the Section 8 housing program. In 1996, Section 8 subsidized 800,000 apartments at a cost of $3.6 billion. By the year 2000 HUD will have to resubsidize 2.5 million apartments at a cost of $17 billion, the department's whole budget.[26] By 1993, HUD was in danger of being abolished. Only by adroit political maneuvering was Henry Cisneros, then the director of HUD, able to rally with a plan to "reinvent" the agency.

ISSUES IN HOUSING POLICY

On first examination the American housing situation has a patina of success.[27] For example, homeownership rates were relatively high in 1995. In fact, these rates had climbed from 44 percent in 1940 to over 64 percent by 1995. From 1981 to 1991, more than 18 million housing units were started, a number far greater than the 11.6 million units completed between 1960 and 1970. This phenomenon encompassed all sectors of the American population. For example, 23.6 percent of African American- and minority-occupied units were owner-occupied in 1940; by 1995 that number had climbed to 44 percent for both groups.[28] The quality of the housing stock also increased dramatically in the post–World War II period. For instance, more than 45 percent of U.S. housing units lacked some or all plumbing facilities in 1940; by 1976 that percentage had declined to 3.4 percent. Moreover, 17.8 percent of all housing units were considered dilapidated or in need of major repairs in 1940; by 1989 that number was only 3.4 percent.[29]

The size and comfort of new owner-occupied homes are a positive development. More than 60 percent of the housing units built in 1988 had three or more bedrooms, two or more bathrooms, and central air-conditioning. By 1991, the median square footage for a new single-family house was 1,890 square feet. Apart from significant regional variations, almost 16 percent of the total U.S. housing stock was constructed post–1970. In the South and West, one out of every five units was constructed between 1970 and 1976. Seven out of ten new housing starts were single-family houses, underscoring the dramatic shift in home ownership.[30] These statistics can easily lead to the conclusion that the majority of Americans are purchasing good-quality, large, and relatively new homes. The true housing situation emerges only when the veneer of success is rubbed off.

Problems in Homeownership

Beginning in the 1970s, many people were forced to spend a higher percentage of their income on housing than they could reasonably afford. Some of these people became so financially overextended that they became vulnerable to mortgage default or eviction, or lacked the necessary cash for purchasing other necessities.

Between 1967 and 1991, the median income for homeowners rose slightly (in constant 1989 dollars) from $28,011 to $32,320, while the median home price went from $56,466 to $67,672. During that same period, the total annual cost of homeownership rose from $4,727 to $7,806. Although this increase is high, it is also geographically sensitive. For example, while the annual costs of homeownership rose from $4,502 to $6,545 in the southeastern United States between 1967 and 1991, these costs jumped from $4,549 to $12,686 in the Northeast. In 1967, the median annual mortgage payment was $3,400; by 1991, it had risen to $5,245. Perhaps more important, the total cost of homeownership as a percentage of income for first-time buyers rose from 17.1 to 31.3 percent between 1967 and 1991.[31]

The increase in the price of single-family homes is even sharper when dollar costs are not adjusted for inflation. In 1970, the average new single-family home sold for $26,600; in 1996, it sold for $158,700. For existing single-family homes the price went from $25,700 to $139,000 (see Table 16.3). While in the past the price of new homes was moderated by consumers' ability to purchase existing stock, the relatively low levels of new construction (1.3 million completed units in 1995 compared to 2.1 million in 1973), high rates of new household formation, and increased investment and speculation have caused the median price of a used home to be only slightly lower than a new one. The median price of housing also varies widely by city and region. From 1985 to 1989, the median price of an existing single-family home in Los Angeles went from $118,700 to $218,000; in New York and Boston it rose from $134,000 to $186,000; and in Providence, Rhode Island, it rose from $67,500 to $131,000.[32] Although home prices have dropped in many areas since 1989, this drop has been marginal compared to the increases in the 1980s.

As a result of these and other factors, homeownership rates for very-low-income families with

◆ **TABLE 16.3**
Average U.S. Housing Prices, Mortgage Rates, and Median Family Income in Noninflation Adjusted Dollars: Selected Years

Period	*$ New SF Homes**	*$ Existing SF Homes*	*Mortgage Rates*	*Median Income*
1970	$ 26,600	$ 25,700	8.35%	$ 9,867
1975	42,600	39,000	9.21	13,719
1980	76,400	72,800	12.95	21,023
1985	100,800	86,000	11.74	27,735
1990	149,800	118,600	10.04	35,353
1995	158,700	139,000	7.85	39,558

*SF=Single Family
Source: Table adapted from U.S. Department of Housing and Urban Development, *U.S. Housing Market Conditions* (Washington, DC: HUD, Office of Policy Development and Research, 2nd Quarter, August 1996).

children dropped by more than 20 percent in the last 15 years.[33] Moreover, 43 percent (1.8 million households) of poor homeowners spent a minimum of 50 percent of their income on housing costs in 1989. More than two-thirds of poor homeowners (2.8 million households) spent 30 percent or more of their income on housing. The housing problems of poor homeowners are also exacerbated by additional housing-related costs. For example, the median expenses for electricity, gas, property insurance, property taxes, and water bills totaled about $160 per month in 1989, an amount that equaled 38 percent of the median income of poor homeowners. Although the effects of the affordable housing shortage are hardest on poor homeowners, moderate-income homeowners also suffer. Almost one-third (32 percent) of moderate-income homeowners spent at least 30 percent of their income on housing in 1989; almost 20 percent spent at least 50 percent.[34]

Families with householders under age 25 experience especially severe housing problems. The median income of these families is low and has declined since the 1970s. Moreover, homeownership rates among young families has been declining since the 1980s. In 1982, more than 19 percent of those under age 25 owned their own homes; by 1995 that number had dropped to 16 percent.[35] In 1989, 50 percent of householders under age 25 spent at least 30 percent of their income on housing, thereby exceeding the federal affordability standard.[36]

Factors such as mortgage instruments also play an important role in determining housing affordability for poor and moderate-income homeowners. Specifically, many poor, moderate-income, and first-time home buyers lack adequate credit, have a sketchy credit history, or do not have the required down payment or qualifying income necessary for a conventional mortgage. During the high inflation of the late 1970s and early 1980s, a variety of inflation-sensitive mortgage instruments were introduced, including variable or adjustable rate mortgages (ARM). These ARM mortgages often include a low initial interest rate, sometimes four or more percentage points below fixed rates. Although most ARM mortgages are capped, they often fluctuate seven or more percentage points above the initial loan rate, depending on the rate of inflation. Thus, a family with an ARM-based home loan may originate a mortgage at 4 percent, but by the fifth year of an inflationary spiral, the interest rate could climb to 11 percent, resulting in a huge increase in mortgage payments. While ARMs protect lending institutions against inflation, they make homeownership more tenuous in that the homeowner no longer has the security of predictable fixed payments for the life of the mortgage.[37]

Problems in Rental Housing

The poorer the household, the more likely it is to experience housing problems. While 33 percent of all households experience housing problems, 80 percent of poor families live in problem housing. Households with housing problems cut across several lines. Roughly 12 million (more than 40 percent) of the 30 million households with housing problems have children. More than nine million (32 percent) of these households are single; 40 percent are married; and 23 percent (6.7 million) are elderly. Renters are more likely to experience housing problems than owners—25 percent of all homeowners and 47 percent of renters report housing problems. According to the most recent American Housing Survey, housing problems include:

- Cost burdens—spending more than 30 percent of household income on housing.
- Physically inadequate housing which includes incomplete plumbing or kitchens, inadequate heating, structural or maintenance problems, and/or adequate electricity.
- Overcrowding—more than one person per room.[38]

One of the most common housing problems involves affordability.

Problems in Finding Affordable Housing. If finding affordable housing is difficult for poor and moderate-income homeowners, it has reached crisis proportions for low-income renters. There are four major reasons for the affordability gap in rental housing: (1) Real incomes of renter households have been dropping; (2) the number of renter households has been increasing; (3) the number of low-cost unsubsidized rental units is dropping, and governmental housing assistance has not compensated for these losses; and (4) rents have increased.

The standard benchmark for affordability is that households should pay no more than 30 percent of their income for housing. Households paying between 30 and 50 percent for housing have moderate cost burdens; households paying more than 50 percent have severe cost burdens. Almost 30 million household pay more than 30 percent of their income for housing.[39]

About 24 million (one in every four) households experience housing cost burdens. More than 1 out of every 10 households spends more than 50 percent of its income on housing. Roughly 9.2 million households with children pay more than 30 percent of their income for housing; of these, almost 3.8 million pay more than half their income for housing, and more than 2.2 million pay more than 70 percent of their incomes for housing.[40] Renters are more likely to have affordability problems than owners. Almost 40 percent of renter households face affordability problems compared to 20 percent of homeowners. Almost three out of every four poor households experiences housing cost burdens; more than half have severe cost burdens; and more than one out of every three households spends 70 percent or more of its income on housing. According to the 1993 American Housing Survey, more than 25 percent of renters live below the poverty line; an additional 25 percent live near the poverty line. Nearly 50 percent of all renter families cannot afford a two-bedroom apartment.[41]

Black and Hispanic households face particularly severe housing problems. In 1989, 39 percent of all black households and 42 percent of all Hispanic households paid at least 30 percent of their income for housing. In contrast, only 25 percent of white households paid that amount. Moreover, 18 percent of African American and Hispanic households paid at least 50 percent of their income for housing, compared with 9 percent of white households.[42]

Evidence of the crisis in affordable rental housing is illustrated by examining Fair Market Rents (FMR) as a ratio of monthly minimum wage income and public assistance benefits. (*Fair Market Rent [FMR]* is a HUD designation, which is the amount equal to or more than what is paid for rent by 45 percent of recent movers. As such, the FMR is the monthly amount needed to rent privately owned, decent, safe, and sanitary rental housing of a modest [nonluxury] nature with suitable amenities.) In every state, a full-time minimum wage job does not cover the costs of a one-bedroom unit at FMR.[43] Moreover, 2 million out of the 5 million household heads with *severe* rent burdens are employed, and 1.2 million are working full-time.[44] A 1995 survey of 29 U.S. cities found that one in five homeless persons is employed in a full- or part-time job.[45] According to the National Low Income Housing Coalition, in every state except Alaska and Vermont, a family of three would have to spend more than their total monthly public assistance benefits to pay the FMR for a two-bedroom housing unit.[46] A 1994 report by the Center on Social Welfare Policy and Law found that in 78 out of 95 sample localities nationwide, a family of three would have to spend more than their total monthly

AFDC benefits to pay the FMR for a two-bedroom apartment; in more than half of these, the AFDC benefit level was below the FMR for a one bedroom unit.[47] Similarly, SSI grants fail to provide the necessary resources for adequate housing. Current SSI grants would have to double in every state in order to meet HUD's recommendation that only 30 percent of household income be used for housing.[48] As a result of this affordability crisis, many low-income workers and public assistance recipients are forced to rely on boyfriends or unreported income. In other cases, two or more families are forced to double up in order to afford rental apartments.

When poor households live in adequate housing, they usually pay for it by spending an excessive percentage of their income on rent. Hence, many of these households have little left over for other necessities such as heat, food, clothing, and health care. Some of these families find themselves in a "heat or eat" situation. While little research has been done on rent burdens, Dr. Alan Meyers, a pediatrician at Boston Medical Center, found in studying 200 poor children that only 3 percent of children whose families received rent subsidies were underweight for their age. For those children whose families were on the subsidized housing wait list, 22 percent were underweight for their age. After examining the records of 11,000 poor children, Meyers found they were most likely to be underweight in the 90 days after the coldest month of the year, thus bolstering his theory that families make the choice of whether to "heat or eat."[49]

Perhaps the most dramatic development in the rental housing market has been the decrease in the number of low-cost rental units. Between 1973 and 1993, 2.2 million low-rent units disappeared from the market; these units were abandoned, converted into condominiums or expensive apartments, or became unaffordable because of cost increases. Thus, the number of low-rent housing units in 1993 totaled 6.5 million. During the same period (1970–1993), the number of low-income renters increased from 7.4 million to 11.2 million. The resulting shortage of 4.7 million affordable housing units is the largest shortage on record. It also translates into two low-income households competing for every available low income housing unit. This shortage of affordable housing is not only restricted to urban centers. In 1970, there were 500,000 more low-cost units in rural areas than there were rural households needing them; by 1985 that ratio was reversed.[50]

Several other factors have converged since the 1970s to deplete the stock of low-income housing. According to Sternlieb and Hughes, there is evidence that "a new town may be evolving in town."[51] This new town, or "gentrified" neighborhood, is a major component of an urban renaissance taking place in many American cities. Attracted by unique houses amenable to restoration, good transportation facilities, and close proximity to employment and artistic, cultural, and social opportunities, young, professional, white-collar workers have begun to resettle the poor, aging, and usually heavily minority sections of central cities in a process called gentrification.

Although the renovation of central-city areas, such as New York's Soho district, often makes a neighborhood more attractive (and potentially a tourist attraction), the effect on the indigenous—and often poor—population can be devastating. As homes become renovated, the prices of surrounding homes may increase. Although low-income homeowners may be able to command a high resale price for their homes, they may find few other suitable places to move to. Furthermore, as neighborhoods become affluent, property taxes are likely to increase, thus creating a burden on low-income homeowners. Previously affordable rental housing may undergo huge rent increases as neighborhoods become more desirable, thereby driving out older and poorer tenants and precluding the possibility of new low-income residents. Although gentrification has been selective, with the main demographic movement continuing to be suburban, it has had a striking impact on some central-city neighborhoods.

The conversion of apartment buildings into condominiums represents another threat to the poor. As a consequence of tax breaks and income shelters, previously affordable rental housing is rapidly being turned into condominiums. Initiated by either tenants or developers, these condominiums represent a serious depletion of good-quality rental stock. Because apartments in these conversions may cost $50,000 or more, low-income tenants can rarely afford the benefits of condominium living, and although renters are often offered a separation fee when a building undergoes conversion, this amount may barely cover the costs of moving, much less make up for the difference between the current rent and a higher alternative rent.

The commercial renovation of central-city downtown areas is another problem for the poor. The development of new office buildings, large apartment complexes, shopping areas, and parking lots often replace low-income housing bordering on downtown areas. Traditionally affordable (and often rundown) apartment buildings, cheap single-room-occupancy (SRO) hotels, rooming houses, and bed-and-boards are razed as new office buildings and shopping complexes are erected. Displaced longtime residents are forced to find housing in more expensive neighborhoods, to double up with family or friends, or, in some cases, to become homeless. According to HUD, demolition, arson, abandonment, condominium conversion, or conversion to nonresidential use removed some 2.8 million rental units between 1970 and 1977. The federal government estimates that 2.8 million families are displaced by private or governmental action each year.[52]

Lastly, the crisis in affordable housing has been exacerbated by federal and state policies designed to upgrade housing stock. For example, HUD has demolished 22,000 scarcely inhabitable apartments and replaced them with smaller, mixed-income developments. While this upgrades the housing stock, the new complexes are also smaller and contain fewer units, which further reduces the low-income housing stock. Also, in an attempt to enforce housing standards, many localities employ housing inspectors to force landlords to repair rundown apartments. Faced with high repair bills, some landlords simply abandon their property and allow it to be condemned. Others may choose arson as a way to realize a final profit on the building.

Overcrowded and Deficient Housing. HUD considers a housing unit overcrowded if it is occupied by more than one person per room. More than 1.9 million (2 percent of all households) live in severely overcrowded conditions of more than 1.5 persons per room, an increase from 1.4 percent (1.1 million) in 1980.[53] The problem of overcrowding is particularly acute among Hispanic Americans, where 26 percent of all households lived in overcrowded quarters in 1989. Renters are twice as likely as owners to live in overcrowded housing.

According to 1993 American Housing Survey, 6.1 million households live in homes needing rehabilitation. The housing problems experienced by these low income households include a lack of complete plumbing or a complete kitchen, insufficient heating, structural problems, and a lack of adequate electricity. Although poor households accounted for only 13 percent of all households in 1989, they occupied 36 percent of the units with holes in the floor, 33 percent of the units with evidence of rats, and 32 percent of the units lacking kitchen facilities such as a stove or refrigerator.[54] HUD defines a unit as having "severe" physical problems if it has one or more of the following deficiencies:

- It lacks hot or cold water or a flush toilet or both a bathtub and a shower.
- The heating equipment has broken down at least three times in the previous winter for periods of six hours or more, resulting in the unit being uncomfortably cold for 24 hours or more.
- The unit has no electricity, or it has exposed wiring *and* a room with no working wall outlet *and* it has had three blown fuses or tripped circuit breakers within the past 90 days.
- In public areas such as hallways and staircases, it has no working light fixtures *and* loose or missing steps *and* loose or missing railings *and* no elevator.
- The unit has at least five basic maintenance problems such as water leaks, holes in the floors or ceilings, peeling paint or broken plaster, or evidence of rats during the previous 90 days.[55]

Lead paint is one of the principal problems in units that need rehabilitation. The Centers for Disease Control and Prevention notes that lead poisoning is one of the most common and devastating environmental diseases that affects young children, leading to developmental and behavior problems. Children are exposed to lead poisoning by living in older homes with peeling, chipping and flaking paint. Friction around windows and doors, renovation and remodeling of older homes can also cause lead-based paint and dust hazards. According to the National Low Income Housing Coalition, almost 9 percent of all children under the age of 6—1.7 million children—suffer from lead poisoning. Rates of lead poisoning for children between ages one and two is more than 11.5 percent. In many poor urban communities, very many more than half the children are affected by exposure to lead hazards. Because low income people often occupy older homes, poor children are four times more likely to have lead poisoning than high income children. While lead was banned from residential paint in 1978, more than half of the housing stock in the United States contains some lead paint.[56]

Other Factors Affecting Housing

Another problem affecting affordable housing is property taxes—the heart of local revenue gathering. The escalating costs of providing governmental services has resulted in significant increases in homeowner property taxes, which landlords generally pass along to renters in the form of higher rents. In response, a number of states have tried to reduce property tax burdens for low-income households. The most common form of property tax relief occurs through a "circuit breaker" program. A typical circuit breaker program is activated when taxes exceed a specified proportion of a homeowner's income, and in most programs, low-income households are sent a yearly benefit check in which all or part of the property tax is refunded. Circuit breaker programs for low-income renters operate in a similar manner. Typically, a portion of the rent paid by a low-income household is considered to represent the property tax passed on by the landlord and is thus refunded by the state or local government. Although circuit breaker programs can provide some relief, they are often restricted to the elderly or disabled. For example, while 31 states and the District of Columbia have circuit breaker programs, 21 states restrict eligibility to elderly and disabled households. Twenty-seven of these 31 states cover both renters and homeowners; six states restrict eligibility to homeowners.[57]

Housing costs are aggravated by high utility rates. In many parts of the country, especially the Northeast and the Midwest, the average family pays thousands of dollars a year in utility bills. According to the National Consumer Law Center, in 1984 families in 21 states had average annual heating bills that exceeded $1,000. In 1986, the average low-income household eligible for energy assistance spent over 15 percent of its income on utility bills, nearly four times the average (3.9 percent) spent by all other U.S. households. Increases in home energy bills disproportionately affect the poor, and, in some cases, they result in utility shutoffs. For example, it is estimated that in 1984 more than 1.4 million households had their natural gas shut off because of delinquent payments.[58]

To mitigate the effects of the federal deregulation of oil prices and the large oil price increases in the 1970s, Congress passed the Low Income Home Energy Assistance Program (LIHEAP) in 1981. This act permits states to offer three types of assistance to low-income households: (1) funds to help eligible households pay their home heating or cooling bills; (2) allotments for low-income weatherization; and (3) assistance to households during energy-related emergencies. States are required to target LIHEAP benefits to households with the lowest incomes and highest energy costs relative to their income and family size. About $1.3 billion was appropriated for LIHEAP in 1997, considerably less than the $2.2 billion in 1992. LIHEAP serves roughly 6 million households.[59]

Housing discrimination is another barrier facing the poor. This discrimination takes two forms: racial discrimination and discrimination against families with children. Although illegal, racially based discrimination in housing is still prevalent. In addition, many landlords and real estate agents refuse to rent to families with children. Often, these families are required to pay higher rents, provide exorbitant security deposits, or meet qualifications not required of renters without children.[60] Discrimination against families with children continues, even though Congress has banned such discrimination since 1988.[61]

HOMELESSNESS

Homelessness can be defined simply as a lack of housing. Homeless people include those living in streets, parks, transportation terminals, abandoned buildings, automobiles, and campgrounds. It also includes people whose primary nighttime residence is a public or private shelter or an emergency housing placement (such as those used by welfare departments). Less visible are the homeless who move from one temporary setting to another, doubling up with friends and relatives and using emergency shelters only when necessary.

Homelessness represents both a simple and a complex problem. Specifically, homeless people are not a homogeneous group. For some, homelessness is a life choice, the freedom to roam without being tied down to one place. For others, particularly the mentally ill and chronic alcoholics, homelessness reflects the deterioration of an overburdened public mental health system. This breakdown in the mental health system is aggravated by an influx of previously healthy people who, when forced into economic deprivation and homelessness, develop symptoms of mental disturbance. For other people, homelessness is rooted in cuts in federally subsidized housing programs and the cost-income squeeze of the housing market. Finally, large numbers of people experience homelessness as a result of the inability of public assistance benefits to keep pace with the cost of living, especially in the area of housing and utilities. Despite the variety of causes, almost all forms of homelessness are tied to poverty. In that sense, homelessness is a manifestation of poverty.

The actual number of homeless people in the United States is unknown for several reasons: (1) people who lack permanent addresses are not easily counted; (2) definitions of homelessness vary from study to study; and (3) different methods for counting homeless people yield different results. In addition, the homeless population tends to be undercounted in federal surveys for political reasons. Specifically, if the true extent of homelessness is acknowledged, financially strapped local, state, and federal authorities will have to target more services and funds for the homeless. For example, the U.S. Census Bureau estimated the homeless population was only 228,000 in 1990.[62] In contrast, the social worker Joel Blau (using figures from the National Alliance to End Homelessness), maintains that on any given night some 735,000 Americans are homeless; over the course of a year, between 1.3 and 2 million people experience homelessness.[63] Other advocacy organizations claim that 3 million people are homeless.[64] These numbers, however, do not include the several million people estimated to be doubled up—staying temporarily with family and friends but with no housing of their own. Although the exact number of homeless people is unknown, the population appears to be growing rapidly. For example, overall requests for emergency shelter jumped 10 percent from 1992 to 1993. While the resources allocated to fight homelessness increased since the late 1980s, between 25 and 29 percent of emergency requests still went unheeded in 1993.[65]

Although homelessness has been a long-standing problem in most large urban areas, it has recently been propelled onto center stage by media images of "bag ladies," the mentally ill, chronic alcoholics, "street people," and uprooted families. While these images make for interesting copy, popular stereotypes obscure the extent of homelessness and the true nature of the problem. Homeless people are the poorest of the poor. They include single-parent families and, occasionally, dual-parent families. They are people who work but who earn too little to afford housing. They are women and children escaping from domestic violence. They are runaway youngsters or those who have been thrown out. They are the unemployed—those looking for work, and those who have never worked. The homeless include retired people on small fixed incomes, many of whom lost their cheap SRO hotel rooms to gentrification; school dropouts; drug addicts; disabled and mentally ill people lost in a maze of outpatient services; people who have worn out their welcome with family or friends; young mothers on welfare who remain on long waiting lists for public housing; families who lost their overcrowded quarters; and "street people."

Families constitute the fastest-growing sector of homeless people. In 1978, 21 percent of homeless people in shelters were families; by the early 1990s, that number had risen to 38 percent. Nine out of 10 homeless families are female-headed, with an average of two children per family. The median age of homeless mothers is in the late twenties; approximately one-half of homeless mothers never marry and one-half never finish high school. Most homeless families receive some form of public assistance.[66] One estimate suggests that between 40 and 70 percent of homeless women have suffered physical or sexual

◆ TABLE 16.4
Who Are the Homeless?

Single men	43%
Single women	11%
Families with children	38%
Children with families	4%
African Americans	56%
Whites	31%
Hispanics	13%
Native Americans	3%
Asians	1%
Substance abusers	43%
Mentally ill	26%
Vietnam veterans	36%
Employed full- or part-time	19%
Have AIDS or related illnesses	25%

Source: Table compiled from Katherine van Wormer, *Social Welfare: A World View* (Chicago: Nelson-Hall Publishers, 1997), p. 439; U.S. Conference on Mayors, *A Status Report on Hunger and Homelessness in America's Cities: A 26 City Survey* (Washington, DC: U.S. Conference of Mayors, 1993); and CNN News, November 8, 1996.

abuse.[67] Vietnam veterans also make up a sizable portion of the homeless, and their number rose from 21 percent in 1992 to 36 percent in 1996. Table 16.4 illustrates the breakdown of the homeless population.

An Urban Institute study of 1,704 homeless people found that 79 percent of the sample had been homeless for more than three months, and 19 percent had been homeless for more than two years. Almost half the sample had not graduated from high school. Moreover, only 5 percent had any income from the former AFDC program, only 12 percent from General Assistance, only 4 percent from SSI, and only 18 percent received food stamps. In addition, only 25 percent of the sample ate more than twice daily, and 36 percent went one day or more per week with nothing to eat. Seventeen percent had no food for two days a week.[68]

According to the sociologist Ellen Bassuk, children who were living in a Boston shelters experienced acute effects from homelessness: 47 percent of them showed at least one developmental lag on the Denver Developmental Screening Test; one-third had difficulty with language skills, fine and gross motor coordination, and social and personal development; almost half the school-age children were depressed and anxious, with one-third showing signs of clinical depression; 43 percent had failed a grade, 24 percent were in special education classes, and nearly half were failing or doing below-average work in school.[69]

Attempts to Address Homelessness

On July 22, 1987, President Ronald Reagan signed the Stewart B. McKinney Homeless Assistance Act into law. The McKinney Act created more than 20 separate programs to be administered by nine federal agencies. Some of the services provided by the McKinney Act included emergency food and shelter, job training, mental health care, transitional and permanent housing, education, health care services, substance abuse treatment, and veteran's assistance services. In 1990, Congress amended the act to remove barriers that kept homeless children from attending school, including proof of immunization, former school records, and proof of residency. The federal government spent close to $1 billion in 1996 on programs to help the homeless.[70]

Over the past few years, much of the activity on homelessness has taken place at HUD, which has expanded its funding for homelessness. During the first Clinton administration, homelessness was a high priority and HUD sought increased funding to address it. At the same time, then–HUD Secretary Henry Cisneros sought to consolidate the various HUD McKinney programs (Shelter Plus Care, Supportive Housing, Emergency Shelter Grants, Section 8 SRO, Rural Homeless Grants and Safe Havens) into a formula allocation to states and localities. Under this plan, comprehensive assistance was supposed to lead to a "continuum of care" that would take the form of a separate block grant or "performance fund" for homeless assistance. The distribution formula would be based on need, with funds distributed to states and localities who set their own performance measures and benchmarks through a HUD-approved plan.[71]

Most HUD homeless assistance has historically gone directly from the federal government to nonprofit organizations. However, some housing advocates are concerned about block grant proposals to turn over control of these funds to state and local governments, especially because they have not always been supportive of efforts to help the homeless. These advocates argue that any block granting of homeless funds should include a formal procedure through which local nonprofits groups can participate in deciding how the funds are spent.[72]

Apart from the McKinney Act, several broader proposals have emerged for alleviating the problem of homelessness. The "Federal Plan to Help End the Tragedy of Homelessness," prepared under the auspices of the Interagency Council for the Homeless, provides a set of objectives to reduce homelessness.

- Increase the participation of homeless families and individuals in mainstream programs that provide income support, social services, health care, education, employment, and housing. In addition, these programs should be monitored to gauge their impact on homelessness.
- Improve the efficiency and effectiveness of homelessness-targeted programs in addressing the multiple needs of homeless persons.
- Increase the availability of support services in combination with appropriate housing. Improve access to quality, affordable, and permanent housing for homeless families and individuals.
- Develop strategies for preventing homelessness by improving the methods for identifying families and individuals at risk of imminent homelessness, change current policies that may contribute to homelessness, and propose other initiatives to prevent people from becoming homeless.[73]

Chester Hartman proposes a nine-point solution for ending homelessness: (1) Massively increase the number of new and rehabilitated units offered to lower-income households; (2) lower the required rent/income ratio in government housing from 30 to 25 percent; (3) arrest the depletion of low-income housing that is occurring through neglect, abandonment, conversion, and sale; (4) preserve the SRO hotels; (5) establish a national "right to shelter"; (6) require local governments to make available properties that can be used as shelters and second-stage housing; (7) create legislation that gives tenants reasonable protection from eviction; (8) provide governmental assistance to homeowners facing foreclosure; and (9) provide suitable residential alternatives for mentally ill people.[74]

Homelessness cannot be eradicated unless basic changes are made in federal housing, income support, social services, health care, education, and employment programs. Benefit levels for these programs must be made more adequate, the erosion of welfare benefits must be stopped, residency and other requirements that exclude homeless persons must be changed, and programs (including outreach) must be made freely available to the homeless and the potentially homeless. Moreover, a real solution to the homeless problem must involve the provision of permanent housing for those who are currently or potentially homeless. Federal programs and legislation must be coordinated and expanded to provide decent, affordable housing, coupled with needed services for *all* poor families. Finally, both the states and the federal government must intervene directly in the housing market by controlling rents, increasing the overall housing stock, limiting speculation, and providing income supports.

HOUSING REFORM

The housing crisis faced by low-income people has led to numerous suggestions for housing reform. Some conservative critics argue that low-income housing assistance should be abolished, thus allowing the law of supply and demand to regulate rents and, eventually, to drive down prices. Free market philosophy suggests that as rents increase, demand slackens, and eventually rents will drop. Other critics contend that government intervention in housing should occur only through the supply side. In other words, the government should stimulate production in rental housing by offering financial incentives such as tax breaks to builders, entrepreneurs, and investors. If rental housing is made more profitable, more units will be built, and the increase in the housing stock will lower prices.

Some liberal critics contend that because housing is a necessity, and the demand is relatively inelastic, marketplace laws should not be allowed to dominate. For example, the National Low Income Housing Coalition has called for:

- Guaranteeing housing assistance to people who need it
- Ending homelessness in America by linking housing with services to support recovery and self-sufficiency
- Providing a permanent and adequate supply of affordable housing
- Preserving and improving federally assisted affordable homes for people with low incomes
- Providing the opportunity for resident control of housing
- Preserving neighborhoods and ending displacement
- Ending economic and racial segregation through affirmative housing programs and the enforcement of Fair Housing Laws
- Reforming federal tax laws to reflect priority for aiding people with the greatest housing needs
- Providing the financing needed to preserve, build, and rehabilitate housing[75]

Several housing reforms have either been tried or proposed in recent years. The first involves the Clinton administration's plan to collapse and convert all HUD funds into state block grants. Known as the "blueprint," this approach calls for the conversion of the public housing program into a voucher system. In effect, HUD would provide local authorities with block granted funds from which to provide vouchers to public housing tenants. The tenants would then be free to stay in public housing, or to use their vouchers to rent private apartments. These vouchers would be worth the difference between 30 percent of a tenant's income and the total rent, up to a predetermined ceiling.[76]

In theory, these changes would enhance a tenant's housing choices, deconcentrate very low income neighborhoods, and reduce HUD's program costs. If a tenant uses their voucher to move from public housing, the housing authority would then be free to rent that apartment to an unsubsidized family. Public housing prices could be priced competitively, with new unsubsidized families having higher incomes than previous tenants. In effect, HUD believes that at least some new residents entering public housing would be working class families (with less social problems), who could function as a role model for those families who stayed.[77]

Critics argue that public housing was never designed to be competitive in the private real estate market. Instead, it was developed to provide cheap housing for those people who lack other alternatives. As such, it is unlikely to attract people who do not require subsidization.[78] In addition, the residential mobility that HUD claims will result from privatizing public housing is predicated on the belief that affordable, private rental housing is available, housing antidiscrimination laws are respected in the private market, landlords are willing to rent to low income families of color who have children, and landlords are willing to participate in a governmental program.[79] The Clinton administration hopes that the creation of vouchers coupled with the deregulation of public housing will provide low income renters with the option of moving out of public housing and into the private market. In turn, block grants will provide the flexibility for local public housing authorities to administer funds effectively in needed areas. This strategy puts considerable trust in local officials, something which housing advocates warn against.[80]

Much of the innovation in housing in recent years has come from the nonprofit sector. There are now more than 2,000 nonprofit housing groups that have built or renovated more than 450,000 housing units, most of them in the past decade. These nonprofits operate with a combination of government subsidies and private contributions. They also get help from two important foundations—the Local Initiatives Support Corporation and the Enterprise Foundation. According to the journalist Jason De Parle, "Their impressive track records address the fear that more subsidized housing would mean more Government-financed slums."[81]

One of the largest of these nonprofit foundations is the Enterprise Foundation. Started by Jim and Patty Rouse in 1982, the Enterprise Foundation is a national, nonprofit housing and community development organization. Comprised of distinguished national business and community development leaders, its goal is "to see that all low-income people in

America have the opportunity for fit and affordable housing, and to move up and out of poverty into the mainstream of American life."[82] Specifically, the Enterprise Foundation assists community-based nonprofit organizations and state and local governments in developing affordable housing and community services by providing low-interest loans, grants and equity to finance affordable housing; help with linking residents to human services; and training people to be effective community leaders. Enterprise works with more than 550 nonprofit organizations in more than 150 locations across the nation. It has helped develop 61,000 new and renovated homes by raising and committing more than $1.7 billion in loans, grants, and equity investments. Through their job placement network, 26,000 hard-to-employ people were placed in entry level jobs.[83]

Although nonprofit housing organizations like the Enterprise Foundation are making a significant impact on America's housing problem, they have limitations. For example, many of the housing groups focus their attention on less needy people—those with incomes at 50 percent of the median. In part, this occurs because the less needy are generally easier to serve. Moreover, no one group knows how to house large numbers of the poorest people, especially those on public assistance. If they are grouped together too tightly, neighborhoods may collapse. If they are spread out in the suburbs, the new neighbors complain. Perhaps more important, the pace of building or renovating under nonprofits is inadequate to meet the need. Although nonprofits are building or renovating about 50,000 units a year, at the current rate it would take a century to house the 5 million families with rent burdens.[84]

CONCLUSION

Ninety-two percent of households with children who have housing problems receive no housing assistance. After 60 years of federal housing efforts, the instance of very-low-income renters who receive no assistance and experience "worst case" housing problems continues to rise. According to HUD, there were 5.3 million such households in 1991, not counting the homeless. These households spent more than half their incomes on housing and/or lived in housing stock with serious physical problems. The problem is clearly getting worse.[85]

The housing crisis is grounded in issues of availability and affordability. It is a structural problem that is based on the failure of incomes to keep pace with housing costs; an overdependence on credit to build and buy houses; a profit-making system that drives homeownership, development, and management; and the failure of states and the federal government to actively intervene in the housing market through higher subsidies or stricter regulation. Driven by speculation, the profit motive has forced up the price of rental and residential property faster than income growth. As a profit is made by each succeeding link in the housing chain (real estate developers, lenders, builders, materials producers, investors, speculators, landlords, and homeowners), renters and homeowners are forced to pay the costs. In that sense, the cost of every rental unit or home reflects the profits made by all the parties who directly and indirectly came into contact with the property.

The provision of adequate low- and moderate-income housing is an important challenge facing modern society. The poor have difficulty finding decent and affordable housing, while blue collar workers and the lower middle class are caught in the cost/income squeeze and are having a difficult time buying and holding onto their homes. This "affordability squeeze" may eventually result in increased mortgage foreclosures, higher rates of property tax and delinquency defaults, more evictions and homelessness, more overcrowding and doubling up of families, decreases in the consumption of other important necessities, deteriorating neighborhoods, increased business failures, higher rates of unemployment in the building trades, and the collapse of some financial institutions.

Past and current government programs have had minimal impact on the crisis in affordable housing. Current housing programs are seriously underfunded, fragmentary, and without clear and focused goals. Because the federal government has often been viewed as an arbiter of last resort, some housing advocates contend that the government has the responsibility to ensure that adequate housing becomes a right rather than a privilege, and that healthy, sound, and safe neighborhoods become a reality.

An adequate housing policy for the United States must address cost burden, overcrowding, and housing quality. It must also provide opportunities for true housing choice, ending the discriminatory patterns that have led to the de facto housing segregation in American society. The nation will not have achieved the 1949 housing goal of "a decent home and suitable living environment for every American family" until all households have the opportunity to live in adequate housing located in safe neighborhoods.

◆ ◆ ◆ *Discussion Questions* ◆ ◆ ◆

1. From 1937 until the present, the history of federal housing policy has been marked by evolving priorities and programmatic shifts. Describe the dominant trends in federal housing policy since 1937, and show how those trends led to the creation of current housing policies. Specifically, what, if any, ideas and programs in current housing policies have their roots in earlier federal policies? In what direction has federal housing policy evolved? What is the current emphasis in federal housing policy?

2. According to some critics, federal low-income housing policy is marked by severe inadequacies. Describe the more serious shortcomings in federal low-income housing policy, and discuss alternative policies to rectify those shortcomings.

3. Homeownership is an important variable in American society because it is equated with the growth of assets. For example, a poor family has nothing to show after paying rent for 30 years except 360 rental receipts. By contrast, another poor family will at least have its home as a major asset after paying off a 30-year mortgage. What are some of the more serious obstacles standing in the way of homeownership for poor people? What policies can be developed to help poor families overcome these barriers?

4. There are serious barriers to finding affordable and decent rental housing. What are some of the most significant problems facing poor people in finding affordable and decent-quality rental housing? What federal or state policies can be implemented to assist poor families to find such housing?

5. HUD has created a series of guidelines by which to evaluate whether a particular housing unit has "severe" physical deficiencies. Are HUD's criteria for determining physical deficiencies in housing adequate? If not, what other criteria should be added to HUD's guidelines?

6. Homelessness has been described by some commentators as just another housing problem. Others argue that homelessness is another manifestation of poverty. Still others contend that homelessness has deeper psychological roots and should be seen as a social or human-service problem. Where do you stand on the issue? Will the homeless problem essentially be solved if people are simply given adequate shelter and decent jobs, or is homelessness for many a manifestation of deeper psychosocial problems? If so, what programs, if any, should be developed for the homeless?

7. Several proposals have been offered to eradicate the problem of homelessness. Which of these programs (or combination of programs) has the best chance of eradicating homelessness?

8. Many experts argue that the housing situation for low-income renters and homeowners has reached crisis proportions. Do you agree? If so, why? Moreover, what kinds of housing policies are needed to defuse this crisis and stabilize the housing market for low-income families? Should housing be considered a right and thus be removed from the grip of the marketplace?

Notes

1. Edward B. Lazere, Paul A. Leonard, Cushing N. Dolbeare, and Barry Zigas, *A Place to Call Home: The Low Income Housing Crisis Continues* (Center on Budget and Policy Priorities and Low-Income Housing Information Service: Washington, DC: December 1991), pp. 45–47.
2. Ibid., pp. 48–50.
3. Quoted in Charles S. Prigmore and Charles R. Atherton, *Social Welfare Policy: Analysis and Formulation* (Lexington, MA: D. C. Heath and Company, 1979), pp. 146–147.
4. Robert Morris, *Social Policy of the American Welfare State*, 2nd Ed. (New York: Longman, 1985), p. 131.
5. Ibid., p. 132.
6. Barbara Habenstreit, *The Making of America* (New York: Julian Messner, 1971), p. 46.
7. Richard Geruson and Dennis McGrath, *Cities and Urbanization* (New York: Praeger, 1977), pp. 6–7.
8. Ibid., p. 40.
9. National Training and Information Center, *Insurance Redlining: Profits v. Policyholders* (Chicago: NTIC, 1973), p. 1.
10. Quoted in Charles S. Prigmore and Charles R. Atherton, *Social Welfare Policy: Analysis and Formulation* (Lexington, MA: D. C. Heath and Company, 1979), pp. 48–50.
11. Ibid.
12. Ibid., pp. 51–52.
13. Ibid., pp. 52–53.
14. U.S. Census Bureau, "1993 American Housing Survey." On-line: http://www.census.gov/ftp/pub/hhes/www/ahs.html
15. Sharon Parrott, *The Cato Institute Report on Welfare Benefits: Do Cato's Numbers Add Up?* (Washington, DC: Center on Budget and Policy Priorities, 1996).
16. See Laura Waxman, *A Status Report on Hunger and Homelessness in America's Cities: 1995* (Washington, DC: U.S. Conference of Mayors, 1995); and Children's Defense Fund, *The State of America's Children, 1991* (Washington, DC: Children's Defense Fund, 1991).
17. Ibid.
18. NLIHC Background on Housing Issues. On-line: http://www.handsnet.org/nlihc/backgrd1.htm#needs
19. Paul A. Leonard, Cushing N. Dolbeare, and Edward B. Lazere, *A Place to Call Home: The Crisis in Housing for the Poor* (Center on Budget and Policy Priorities and Low-Income Housing Information Service: Washington, DC: April 1989), pp. 76–80.
20. Ibid.
21. National Low-Income Housing Coalition. NLIHC Background on Housing Issues. On-line: http://www.handsnet.org/nlihc/backgrd2.htm#pubhsg
22. Ibid.
23. Ibid.
24. Quoted in Lazere et al., *A Place to Call Home: The Low Income Housing Crisis Continues*, p. 69.
25. National Academy of Public Administration, "Renewing HUD: Study Recommends Major Changes in Housing Agency," *Journal of Housing* (1994), pp. 22–28.
26. Jason De Parle, "Slamming the Door," *The New York Times Magazine* (October 20, 1996), pp. 52–58; 94; 105–106.
27. See, for example, Chester Hartman (ed.), *America's Housing Crisis* (Boston: Routledge and Kegan Paul, 1983).
28. See George Sternlieb and James W. Hughes, "Housing in the United States: An Overview." In George Sternlieb, James W. Hughes, Robert W. Burchell, Stephen C. Casey, Robert W. Lake, and David Listokin (eds.), *America's Housing* (New Brunswick, NJ: Rutgers University, Center for Urban Policy Research, 1980), pp. 5–7; and Sumner M. Rosen, David Fanshel, and Mary E. Lutz (eds.), *Face of the Nation*, 1987 (Silver Spring, MD: NASW, 1987), p. 68; and Joint Center for Housing Studies of Harvard University, *The State of the Nation's Housing, 1992* (Boston: Joint Center for Housing Studies of Harvard University, 1992), p. 12.
29. Sternlieb and Hughes, "Housing in the United States," pp. 5–7; and Cushing N. Dolbeare, *The Widening Gap* (Washington, DC: Low Income Housing Information Service, June 1992), p. 14.
30. Ibid; and U.S. Bureau of the Census, *Statistical Abstract of the United States, 1991* (Washington, DC: U.S. Government Printing Office, 1991), p. 715.
31. Joint Center for Housing Studies of Harvard University, *The State of the Nation's Housing*, 1992, pp. 28–31.
32. U.S. Bureau of the Census, *Statistical Abstract of the United States, 1991*, pp. 715–717.

33. Habitat for Humanity, "Poverty Housing Defeats Families." On-line: http://www.habitat.org/Why/HW_Articles/Poverty_Housing.html
34. Lazere et al., *A Place to Call Home: The Low Income Housing Crisis Continues*, pp. 9–12.
35. Children's Defense Fund, *The State of America's Children, 1992* (Washington, DC: Children's Defense Fund, 1992), p. 35; see also U.S. Department of Housing and Urban Development, *U.S. Housing Market Conditions* (Washington, DC: HUD, August 1996).
36. Lazere et al., *A Place to Call Home: The Low Income Housing Crisis Continues*, pp. 72–73; see also Cushing N. Dolbeare, *Out of Reach: Why Everyday People Can't Find Affordable Housing* (Washington, DC: Low Income Housing Information Service, September 1991), pp. 1–2.
37. U.S. Department of Housing and Urban Development, *U.S. Housing Market Conditions*, August 1996.
38. Quoted in NLIHC Background on Housing Issues.
39. NLIHC Background on Housing Issues.
40. Habitat for Humanity, "Poverty Housing Defeats Families."
41. U.S. Census Bureau, "1993 American Housing Survey."
42. Lazere et al., *A Place to Call Home: The Low Income Housing Crisis Continues*, p. 63.
43. Tracy L. Kaufman, *Out of Reach: Can America Pay the Rent?* (Washington, DC: National Low Income Housing Coalition, 1996).
44. Ibid.
45. Waxman, *A Status Report on Hunger and Homelessness in America's Cities: 1995*.
46. Kaufman, *Out of Reach: Can America Pay the Rent?*
47. Adele Blong and Barbara Leyser, *Living at the Bottom: An Analysis of 1994 AFDC Benefit Levels, 1994* (New York: Center on Social Welfare Policy and Law, 1994).
48. Kaufman, *Out of Reach: Can America Pay the Rent?*
49. Quoted in ibid., p. 57.
50. See Edward Lazere, *In Short Supply: The Growing Affordable Housing Gap* (Washington, DC: Center on Budget and Policy Priorities, 1995); Lazere et al., *A Place to Call Home: The Low Income Housing Crisis Continues*, p. xii; and Paul A. Leonard and Edward A. Lazere, *A Place to Call Home: The Low Income Housing Crisis in 44 Metropolitan Areas* (Washington, DC: Center on Budget and Policy Priorities, 1992), p. xiii.
51. George Sternlieb and James W. Hughes, "Back to the Central City: Myths and Realities," in Sternlieb et al., *America's Housing*, p. 173.
52. Children's Defense Fund, *The State of America's Children, 1989* (Washington, DC: Children's Defense Fund, 1989), p. 196; seel also Joint Center for Housing Studies of Harvard University, *The State of the Nation's Housing, 1992*, p. 30.
53. U.S. Census Bureau, "1993 Census of Housing: Crowding." On-line: http://www.gov/hhes/housing/census/crowding.html
54. Lazere et al., *A Place to Call Home: The Low Income Housing Crisis Continues*, p. 23.
55. Ibid., p. 22.
56. National Low-Income Housing Coalition. NLIHC Background on Housing Issues.
57. Ibid., pp. 43–44.
58. Center on Budget and Policy Priorities, *Smaller Slices of the Pie* (Washington, DC: Center on Budget and Policy Priorities, November 1985), p. 33.
59. Committee on Ways and Means, U.S. House of Representatives, *Overview of Entitlement Programs: 1992 Green Book* (Washington, DC: U.S. Government Printing Office, 1992), pp. 1697–1702.
60. Ibid.
61. Children's Defense Fund, *The State of America's Children, 1992*, p. 38.
62. Quoted in Diana M. DiNitto, *Social Welfare: Politics and Public Policy* (Boston: Allyn and Bacon, 1995), p. 87.
63. Joel Blau, *The Visible Poor: Homelessness in the United States* (New York: Oxford University Press, 1992), p. 124.
64. Ibid.
65. Brent McCarthy, Heather McClellan, Terry Moore, Jorge Morales, and Andrea Pucciarello, "Social Welfare in the Clinton Era." Unpublished paper, Graduate School of Social Work, University of Houston, Houston, TX, April 25, 1996.
66. E. Anderson and S. Koblinsky, "Homeless Policy: The Need to Speak to Families," *Family Relations*, 44 (1995), pp. 13–18.
67. K. Grimm and J. Maldonado, "No Home of Her Own: Gender and Homelessness," *Family Relations*, 2(14) (1995), pp. 20–22.
68. Urban Institute, *America's Homeless* (Washington, DC: Urban Institute, 1990).

69. Ellen Bassuk, "Homeless Families: Single Mothers and Their Families in Boston Shelters." In Ellen Bassuk (Ed.), *The Mental Health Needs of Homeless Persons* (San Francisco: Jossey-Bass, 1987).
70. National Low Income Housing Coalition, *1996 Advocate's Resource Book* (Washington, DC: National Low Income Housing Coalition, 1996).
71. Ibid.
72. Ibid; see also R. Stanfield, "Vouching for the Poor," *National Journal*, 18(27) (1995), pp. 1094–1098.
73. Ibid., p. 10.
74. Chester Hartman, "The Housing Part of the Homelessness Problem," in Boston Foundation, *Homelessness: Critical Issues for Policy and Practice* (Boston: Boston Foundation, 1987), pp. 17–19.
75. See National Low-Income Housing Coalition. NLIHC Background on Housing Issues; and National Low Income Housing Coalition, *1995 Advocate's Resource Book*.
76. McCarthy et al., "Social Welfare in the Clinton Era," pp. 23–25.
77. Ibid.
78. Stanfield, "Vouching for the Poor."
79. E. Mulroy and P. Ewalt, "Is Shelter a Private Problem," *Social Work* 41 (1996), pp. 125–128.
80. Stanfield, "Vouching for the Poor."
81. De Parle, "Slamming the Door," p. 94.
82. The Enterprise Foundation. On-line: http://www.entrprisefdn.org/
83. Ibid.
84. De Parle, Slamming the Door."
85. National Low-Income Housing Coalition. NLIHC Background on Housing Issues.

CHAPTER 17

The Politics of Food Policy and Rural Life

The policies related to the production and distribution of food form an important component of the American welfare state. This chapter examines the federal response to hunger and the subsequent attempts to distribute foodstuffs to the poor. As part of that examination, this chapter explores the Food Stamps Program, WIC and other food programs, U.S. farm policy, the plight of America's farmworkers, and the overall problems of food production and distribution. Although these issues around food may initially seem disparate, they are tied together in a complex mosaic that forms an important component of the well-being of the nation.

The terms *hunger* and *malnutrition* conjure up images of highly emaciated Third World children with bloated bellies, skinny arms, and protruding eyes. The problem of hunger is viewed as distant and remote, something which pertains mainly to the Southern Hemisphere. Hunger in America, however, often exhibits itself in more subtle ways. This ranges from eating only once a day or skipping meals for several days, to chronic malnutrition, low birth-weight babies, and high infant mortality rates. Crossing age, race, and gender lines, hunger in America affects children, the elderly, the unemployed and the underemployed, the homeless, the handicapped, and single- and dual-parent families. The single common thread connecting these diverse groups to the problem of hunger is poverty.

GOVERNMENTAL FOOD PROGRAMS

The politics of food—or the way food is distributed in American society—is a complex phenomenon. Like all resources in a capitalist society, food is a commodity that is bought and sold. In a pure market sense, those who cannot afford to purchase food are unable to consume it. Left to the caprice of the marketplace, many poor people would face malnutrition or even starvation. This problem is particularly acute in an urban society, where many people lack the necessary gardening skills and have little access to land. Providing the poor with access to food is a redistributive function of the welfare state. The obligation of the government to provide food to the poor is similar to that of providing economic opportunity: When both are unavailable in adequate quantities, it is the responsibility of the welfare state to respond.

The federal government's response to hunger and malnutrition has consisted of several major programs: (1) the Food Stamps Program, (2) the Commodity Distribution program, (3) the National School Lunch and Breakfast programs, (4) the Special Milk program, (5) the Special Supplemental

Nutrition Program for Women, Infants, and Children (WIC), (6) the Child Care Food program, (7) the Summer Food program, and (8) the Meals on Wheels and Congregate Dining programs.

A Short History of Food Stamps and a Description of the Program

In 1933, Congress established the Federal Surplus Relief Corporation, an agency designed to distribute surplus commodity foods, as well as coal, mattresses, and blankets. In 1939, Congress established the Food Stamp Program. This was terminated in 1943, at which time a commodity food distribution program was reestablished. A pilot Food Stamp Program began during the presidency of John F. Kennedy, and in 1964 the current Food Stamp (FS) Act was passed.

Although the Food Stamp Program is a federal program administered by the United States Department of Agriculture (USDA), it is state and local welfare agencies that qualify applicants and provide them with stamps. Recipients are given an allotment of stamps based on family size and income, with eligibility requirements and benefits determined at the federal level. Food stamp eligibility is based on a means test. Recipients originally had to pay a set price (depending on family size and income) for their stamps, with the amount to be paid always being less than the face value of the stamps. This enabled some people to purchase $75 worth of food stamps for $35. The difference between the amount paid and the face value of the stamps was called a "bonus." However, this system proved unwieldy because many poor people could not afford to purchase any stamps. In 1977, purchase requirements were dropped, and, not surprisingly, national participation rates rose by 30 percent.

While the 1996 PRWOA did not allow states to convert the FS Program into a block grant (something originally proposed), it did include almost $28 billion in food stamp cuts over a 6-year period. When these cuts are fully implemented, they will reduce FS benefits by almost 20 percent, the equivalent of reducing the average benefit from its current level of 80 cents per person per meal to 66 cents per person per meal.[1] These reductions will affect all FS recipients, including children, the working poor, legal immigrants, and the elderly and disabled.

FS reductions are based on several reforms. First, until they become citizens, most legal immigrants and their families are not entitled to FS benefits and assistance provided under smaller programs such as Meals-On-Wheels and prenatal care for pregnant women. Second, the PRWOA limits FS benefits to just three months in any three-year period to unemployed individuals between the ages of 18 and 50 who are not raising children. (Some unemployed workers may be able to receive FS for six months while unemployed in a three-year period.) Although states may be granted waivers to this provision, it will likely be difficult to secure. The Congressional Budget Office estimates that this rule change will deny FS benefits to about one million unemployed workers a month. Many of these people are ineligible for any government assistance except food stamps. As such, denying these individuals food stamps eliminates their only safety net. Third, the welfare bill includes $2.9 billion in reductions in child nutrition programs. More than 85 percent of these cuts would come in the Child and Adult Care Food Program, which primarily supports meals provided to children in child care centers and family day care homes. The bulk of these reductions will result from reduced federal support for meals served in family day care homes that are not located in a low-income area or operated by a low-income provider. To stem fraud in the FS system, states are required to implement Electronic Benefit Transfer (EBT) systems for by October 1, 2002, unless waived.[2] Under EBT systems, FS recipients would present benefit identification cards for payments at food stores, and then funds would be transferred to the retailer's account. This would allow FS purchases to be tracked, and would discourage trading FS coupons for cash, noneligible goods, and services.[3]

Because children and very poor families are the primary beneficiaries of FS, they are among those hurt most by the cuts. About 66 percent of the FS reductions are borne by families with children. In 1998, close to 7 million FS families with children will lose an average of $435 in benefits. Working poor families also will be affected. The 2.3 million FS households with a worker will lose about $465 a year by 2002. Hardest hit are the poorest of the poor—those with incomes below half of the poverty line. This group will absorb 50 percent of the FS cuts. In 1998, they will lose about $655 a year in food stamp benefits; by 2002, that amount will rise to about $790 per year. The elderly will also be adversely affected. The 1.75 million low-income elderly households receiving food stamps will lose about 20 percent of their food stamp benefits.[4]

Food Stamps: Who Is in the Program and What Does It Cost?

Some 27 million people, or about 9 percent of the total U.S. population, received FS benefits in 1996. Of that number, 46 percent were white, 33 percent were African American, and 17 percent were Hispanic American.[5] Virtually all FS benefits (92 percent) go to households with incomes at or below the poverty line, and 82 percent of the benefits go to families with children.[6] In 1994, some 2.3 million food stamp households included at least one worker.[7]

Eligibility guidelines and FS benefits are set by the federal government and are uniform throughout the continental United States. Benefits are based on 100 percent of the USDA's Thrifty Food Plan. AFDC families are automatically eligible for FS. Households must meet a gross and a net income test. As such, gross monthly household income must be at or below 133 percent of the federal poverty line. Households with a member over age 60 or with a disabled person are exempt from the gross means test. All households must meet the net income test. After allowable program deductions, household net income must be at or below the federal poverty level. Benefits are prorated according to net monthly income. To be eligible for FS, total assets generally cannot exceed $2,000 dollars, with a maximum cap of $4,500 for an automobile. Households with an elderly person over age 60 can have up to $3,000 in assets.[8] Table 17.1 illustrates the FS income guidelines. FS program costs tend to be relatively high because of heavy utilization. In 1996 the total cost of operating the FS program stood at $24 billion[9] (see Table 17.2).

Special Supplemental Nutrition Program for Women, Infants, and Children (WIC)

The WIC program was enacted on September 26, 1972. This program originally began as a two-year pilot program to provide nutritional counseling and supplemental foods to pregnant and breast-feeding women, infants, and young children at nutritional risk. The goal of the program is to address areas of child development that are most affected by poor health and inadequate nutrition, including impaired learning.[10] Specifically, the twin goals of WIC are to: (1) enrich the food intake of participants by providing them with coupons or food cards that they redeem at local grocery stores, and (2) to educate mothers on how to prevent nutritional difficulties using individual and group classes.

WIC is administered through the Food and Nutrition Service of the USDA, in conjunction with 1,500 local agencies (mainly health departments). Each state receives cash grants and is responsible for developing, implementing, and monitoring its WIC program.[11] Income eligibility is less restrictive than public assistance programs, and federal guidelines target families who fall between 100 to 185 percent of the poverty line. Eligibility is limited to low-income pregnant women (Medicaid recipients are automatically eligible for WIC),

◆TABLE 17.1
Income Guideline for Food Stamps, 1995

Household Size	*Maximum Allowable GROSS Countable Income/month*	*Maximum Monthly FS Allotment (for ZERO Net Income)*
1	$ 810	$119
2	1087	218
3	1364	313
4	1642	397
5	1919	472
6	2196	566
7	2474	626
8	2751	716
9	3029	806
10	3307	896

Source: Texas Department of Human Services, "Program Information Sheets—Gulf Coast Region 6," Texas Department of Human Services, Community Relations Department, 5425 Polk St., Houston, TX, n.d., n.p.

◆ **TABLE 17.2**
Food Stamps Statistics: Total Federal Expenditures for FS, Participation Rates, Percent of Population Using FS Benefits, and Average Monthly Benefits, Selected Years, 1975–1995
(Participants and dollars in millions)

Year	*Cost*	*Number of Participants*	*% of Population*	*Average Monthly Benefits Per Person*
1975	$ 4,624	16.3	7.6	$21.40
1978	5,573	14.4	6.5	26.80
1981	11,812	20.6	9.0	39.50
1984	13,275	20.9	8.8	42.70
1987	13,535	19.1	7.8	45.80
1990	17,686	20.0	8.0	59.00
1991	21,012	22.6	9.0	63.90
1993	23,653	26.9	9.3	67.97
1995	20,500	26.7	8.9	71.50

Source: Compiled from various tables in Committee on Ways and Means, U.S. House of Representatives, *Overview of Entitlement Programs, 1992 Green Book* (Washington, DC: U.S. Government Printing Office, 1992), Table 4., p. 1616; Table 9., p. 1629; and Table 12., p. 1639; and NDB5 Production Sys, U.S. Summary, USDA, Washington, DC, October 17, 1995, SR #4.

mothers who breast-feed their infants, and children up to age five. Qualified beneficiaries receive supplemental foods each month in the form of actual food items or, more often, are given vouchers for the purchase of specific items in retail stores. Items that may be included in a food package include milk, cheese, eggs, infant formula, cereals, and fruits and vegetables. The USDA requires food packages that provide specific types and amounts of food appropriate for six categories of participants: (1) infants from birth to 3 months; (2) infants from 4 to 12 months; (3) women and children with special dietary needs; (4) children from 1 to 5 years of age; (5) pregnant and nursing mothers; and (6) postpartum nursing mothers. In addition to receiving food benefits, WIC participants also receive nutritional counseling.[12] About $3.7 billion was spent on WIC in 1996 and it served roughly 6.2 million women and children.

Other Food Programs

Other food programs include the Child and Adult Care Food Program (CACFP), which provides funds and USDA-donated foods to nonresidential child care and adult care facilities. CACFP generally operates in child care centers, outside-school-hours care centers, family day care homes, and certain adult day care centers. Operated by the USDA, CACFP funded 614 million meals and cost $1.2 billion in 1995.[13] The federal government also funds the Commodity Donations Program, which distribute food directly to needy people.

In 1946 the National School Lunch Act was passed. This bill provided school-age children with hot lunches at reduced rates or with free lunches if their parents were unable to pay. After research studies found a positive correlation between poor school performance and the failure of school-age children to eat a nutritious breakfast, the federal government instituted the School Breakfast Program. Each program has a three-tiered reimbursement system that allows children from households with incomes at or below 130 percent of the poverty line to receive free meals, permits children from households with incomes between 130 and 185 percent of the poverty line to receive meals at a reduced price, and provides a small subsidy for children whose family income does not qualify them for free or reduced meals.[14] Table 17.3 examines the income guidelines for free and reduced school lunches.

The National School Lunch Program (NSLP) provides subsidized lunches to students in most

◆ TABLE 17.3
Annual Income Guidelines for the School Lunch Program, 1995-96

Family Size	*Free*	*Reduced*
1	$ 9,711	$3,820
2	13,039	18,556
3	16,367	23,292
4	19,695	28,028
5	23,023	32,764
6	26,351	37,500
7	29,679	42,236
8	33,007	46,972
9	36,335	51,708
10	39,663	56,444
11	42,991	61,180
12	46,319	65,916

Source: USDA, "National School Lunch and Child Nutrition Programs," Washington, DC USDA, n.d., n.p.

schools. In 1995 the average daily participation rate was 23.7 million students, and just under 4 billion meals were served at a total federal cost of $4.4 billion (down from $5 billion in 1994). Roughly half the subsidized NSLP meals go to children from lower-income families, and 90 percent of federal funding is used for these children. In 1991, 42 percent of the children who received NSLP meals received free lunches, 8 percent received reduced-price lunches, and the remaining 50 percent paid full price for their meals. Overall, 52 percent of U.S. students in 92,200 schools benefited from the school lunch program.[15]

Smaller than the NSLP, the School Breakfast Program (SBP) serves only about 15 percent of those served by the School Lunch program. In 1995 the SBP served almost 6 million students at a cost of $901 million. In 1991, the SBP operated in 46,100 schools, or about half of the schools participating in the NSLP. Of the 22 million children enrolled in these schools, only 20 percent participated in this program. The SBP differs from the NSLP in that most of the participating schools are in low-income areas, and the children who participate are mainly from low- or moderate-income families.[16]

Although some of the low-income elderly receive food stamps, they can also be served by Meals on Wheels and the Congregate Meal Dining program. Meals on Wheels was begun in 1972 and was designed to improve nutrition for the elderly. Various community agencies arrange the daily delivery of meals to elderly persons living at home, and aged persons who receive food stamps can use them to purchase the meals (for others a donation is requested). The Congregate Meal Dining program provides meals at such places as senior citizen centers.

Other federal food programs include the Emergency Food Assistance Program, which provides funds to local agencies through a national board of charitable organizations. This national charitable board, in part consisting of the United Way, the Salvation Army, and Catholic Charities, distributes funds to local charities, soup kitchens, shelters, and other organizations that deal with hunger and homelessness. The federal government also provides funding to help subsidize emergency food agencies and to help pay for the storage and distribution of federal surplus food commodities.

Have the Food Programs Worked?

Evidence on the effectiveness of federal food policies is inconclusive. For example, the American Dietary Association found little hard evidence that the WIC program was effective.[17] A report by the Government Accounting Office (GAO) to the Committee on Agriculture, Nutrition, and Forestry, stated that "no group of studies provided the kind of evidence to refute or confirm the claims that WIC is effective."[18] The GAO report did affirm, however, that WIC was responsible for decreasing the proportion of low birth-weight babies of eligible mothers by 16 to 20 percent.[19] Moreover, WIC's effect on mean birth weights also appears to be positive. The report tentatively concluded that African American and teenage mothers who participated in WIC had better birth outcomes than comparable women. Another study found that children 6 to 11 years old who participated in WIC had higher intakes of calcium; vitamins C, A, and B6; riboflavin; and iron.[20] According to Michael Harrington et al., studies by the USDA and others show that WIC has: (1) improved the diets of low-income women, infants, and children; (2) increased the proportion of low-income pregnant women who utilize prenatal care; and (3) reduced anemia among WIC recipients.[21] A 1994 study commissioned by the

USDA found that for every $1.00 spent prenatally in WIC, $1.77 to $3.13 was saved in Medicaid costs in the first 60 days after birth. Prenatal WIC enrollment is estimated to have saved $1.2 billion in 1992 in first year medical costs for infants.[22]

WIC was one of the few social programs that escaped deep budgetary cuts between 1980 and 1993, but by 1995 WIC's program budget was $400 million less than in 1994, even though it served about 400,000 more people. Because WIC is a discretionary rather than entitlement program, it can only serve as many people as its budget allows. As such, it is estimated that only 46 percent of those eligible receive benefits.[23] Moreover, many counties have no WIC program, while others turn away people or have long waiting lists.[24] Although states *may* provide additional funds for WIC, only a minority of them do so.[25]

The Food Stamp Program fails to reach millions of eligible people because of excessive red tape and inadequate outreach services. A USDA study estimated that only 66 percent of eligible individuals and 60 percent of eligible families participated in FS in 1984. A CBO study estimated that only 50 to 66 percent of the 30.4 million people eligible for FS participated in the program in 1994. In addition, participation rates differed among subgroups. For example, eligible elderly households had a participation rate of between 34 and 44 percent; eligible households without children or elderly members had participation rates of from 24 to 39 percent.[26] Although the causes for nonparticipation are complex, one University of Michigan study found that more than half of all eligible persons who fail to participate either mistakenly believe they are ineligible or don't know of their eligibility.[27] Modest government efforts to alleviate this problem were hindered when Congress required a 50 percent state match for outreach efforts. Nevertheless, even the most conservative estimates reveal that at least one-third of those eligible for food stamps receive no benefits from the program.

Hunger in the U.S. The late Michael Harrington maintained that USDA surveys indicated that food stamps had been effective in improving the nutrition of millions of Americans.[28] Despite this, hunger in the United States continues to be problematic. According to one 1993 study, every ninth citizen in the United States suffers from hunger.[29] In addition, over 30 million Americans are at risk of being unable to meet their basic nutritional needs. Of these people, 12 million are children and 3 million are elderly.[30] According to David Beckman, director of Bread for the World Institute, "World-wide hunger is going down, in Africa and ironically, in America it's going up."[31] The number of hungry people in the United States increased by 50 percent between 1985 and 1990.[32]

Children are the hardest hit by hunger. A 3-year study released in 1995 found that an estimated 4 million children under age 12 were hungry during at least part of a year; an additional 10 million under the age of 12 were at risk of being hungry. This is double the rate of any other industrialized nation.[33] The USDA relies on poverty statistics to determine the extent of hunger in America. USDA data shows that only 12 percent of households with incomes below the poverty line have an adequate levels of basic nutrition.[34] Moreover, hunger and malnutrition are exacerbated by the low level of FS benefits. For example, the current average FS benefit of 80 cents a meal (expected to drop to 66 cents as a result of recent FS changes) is inadequate. Studies by the USDA reveal that most families whose food expenditures equal the maximum FS benefit lack adequate diets, and only one-tenth of those families receive adequate nutrition.[35]

Because most USDA food programs function as a form of indirect income support for farmers, the relationship among food prices, governmental supports, and food subsidization forms a complex web involving both consumers and producers.

FARMING IN AMERICA

The 1980s were a tumultuous time for American farmers, and in many places the crisis rivaled that of the 1930s.[36] Agricultural members of the American Bankers Association estimated that 3.8 percent of all farmers had filed for bankruptcy in 1985 alone.[37] A 1985 USDA study of 1.7 million farms indicated that

214,000 were in serious financial difficulty, with 38,000 classified as technically insolvent.[38]

Other farm indicators were equally bleak. In 1981, the total asset value of U.S. agriculture was $1 trillion; by 1985 it had shrunk to $692 billion, a 30 percent drop and the steepest fall since the Great Depression. Although the prices of U.S. farmland peaked at an average of $823 an acre in 1982, they plunged to $599 an acre over the next five years (a loss of one-third of the value of the nation's farmland). Some states experienced even steeper declines. For example, the total value of farmland (including buildings) in Iowa fell from $67.4 billion in 1981 to $25.1 billion in 1987. In at least five other states, the total value of farmland was more than halved in that six-year period. Although U.S. farms had declined in number by a modest 16,000 between 1978 and 1982, from 1982 until 1987 they declined by 151,000, or at a rate of about 30,000 annually. Moreover, while the United States exported 163 million tons of farm products in 1980, by 1986 that number was reduced to only 110 million.[39]

In spite of these dire predictions, U.S. farmers made a relative comeback in the late 1980s. This comeback was due in part to the 1987–1988 worldwide drought, which depleted the grain reserves of many nations. Nevertheless, by early 1990, farmland prices in the United States had risen to $693 per acre, and farm exports increased to 148.5 million tons. Real net cash farm income went up from $48.5 billion in 1987 to about the same level as had prevailed in the mid–1970s. More important, the farm debt stabilized.[40]

Despite this improvement, American farmers are by no means out of danger. Although positive farm income was reported by 89 percent of farms in 1989 (up from 64 percent in 1988), economists warn that the future prospects for a healthy farm income are shaky at best. Moreover, the farming sector has not fully recovered from the crisis of the mid–1980s, and the growth in farm equity is still trailing the 3 to 4 percent rate of general inflation.[41]

The Ongoing Farming Crisis

American agriculture has historically never been a stable enterprise. Since the nineteenth century, farmers have ridden an economic roller coaster of good and bad times, with much of this instability attributable to factors outside their control, such as weather, international trade and monetary policy, and government farming policies.

American agriculture was heavily influenced by large-scale operations from the early days of European colonization. Early agriculture was characterized by the slave plantations of the South, the Spanish haciendas of the Southwest, and the large wheat and cattle farms of the West. Much of agricultural production was in the hands of wealthy individuals or foreign investors.

By the mid–1800s, federal government policies began to encourage the growth of small family farms. The development of small-scale agriculture was aided by the defeat of slavery, the institution of the Homestead Acts, and the general movement westward. Despite the new agricultural opportunities, farmers found themselves caught in the classic cost/price squeeze. High prices for seeds, credit, and transportation (costs) often exceeded the crop prices offered by the large grain monopolies. This situation resulted in a series of rural depressions in the late nineteenth and early twentieth centuries.[42]

Angry farmers responded to these injustices by demanding protection from the railroads, banks, and grain monopolies. Through political organizing, they created the Farmers Alliance, the Populist Party, the Greenback Party, and the Non-Partisan League.[43] Although the World War I period brought some relief, it was quickly followed by a major farming disaster almost a decade before the Great Depression of the 1930s.

Coupled with severe droughts, the Depression of the 1930s seriously crippled rural America. Outraged by years of poor farming and inadequate or nonexistent governmental policies, farmers began to engage in direct action. In the plains states, they barricaded highways to stop foreclosures, insisted that local lenders exercise leniency, called farm strikes, and, in some instances, rioted.[44] Legislatures in farm states tried to curb this insurgency by enacting moratoriums on foreclosures, while the federal government moved to set prices at parity levels (the ratio between farm prices and input/output costs).[45] In the 1930s, Congress passed the Farm Parity Program, an innovative bill that contained three central features:

1. The Commodity Credit Corporation (CCC) was established to set a minimum floor under farm prices. The CCC was designed to make loans to farmers whenever the prices offered by the grain companies were lower than the cost of production. Crops were used as collateral, and when prices returned to normal, farmers repaid the loans with interest.
2. Farm production was managed in order to maintain a balance between supply and demand, thus preventing surpluses. Managing supply and demand would also reduce the government's responsibility for storing and purchasing surpluses.
3. A national grain reserve was created to stabilize consumer prices in the event of droughts or natural disasters.[46]

In 1942, Congress established the price support levels at 90 percent of parity. From 1942 to 1953, the average prices paid to farmers were at 90 to 100 percent of parity, thereby raising market prices, ensuring a secure income for farmers, reducing the need for excessive debt, and encouraging stabilization in the price of grain.

However, by the end of World War II, powerful corporations, academics, "free traders," and others began to wage war on the Farm Parity Program. Soil conservation, supply management, and parity were characterized as socialist programs that interfered with a free market economy. Grain companies called for lower prices in order to sell abroad, arguing that expanded exports and food-aid programs would compensate farmers for lower commodity prices. Industrialists maintained that lower food prices would translate into cheaper labor costs, and agribusiness believed that lowered commodity prices would result in more production, thereby increasing the use of their products. The small farmer inevitably lost to this powerful coalition, and President Eisenhower and Secretary of Agriculture Ezra Taft Benson helped defeat the Farm Parity Program in 1953.

The optimism of the corporate sector proved ill founded, at least with respect to the small farmer. The purchasing power of net farm income decreased even as exports rose. Held constant in 1967 dollars, the purchasing power of net farm income dropped from an annual average of $25 billion from 1942 to 1952 (the years of farm parity) to an average of $13.3 billion from 1953 to 1972. In 1952, net farm income was greater than total farm debt; by 1983 net farm income was less than farm interest payments.[47]

All farmers were not affected equally by the farming crisis of the mid–1980s. For instance, almost one-sixth of all U.S. farming households suffered net income losses in 1984.[48] Many farmers with middle-sized operations (in the 80- to 500-acre range) were forced to abandon farming, while at the same time large and small farms were growing. In 1984, more than two-fifths of all U.S. farms had total annual sales of less than $10,000, accounting for only 2 percent of all farm sales. These farms experienced an overall net loss of income. By contrast, farms with sales exceeding $500,000 a year earned an average income of $219,000. Three-fifths of the total income of farming families (a figure that is growing) came from nonfarm employment in 1984.[49]

Family farming embodies many of America's most cherished traditional values—hard work, independence, strong family life, close-knit communities, and democratic institutions. Farming for many rural families is not a vocation but a way of life. The connection to the land, often a legacy from parents or grandparents, creates a commitment to a specific place and to the family heritage.[50] This psychological connection to farming means that many farmers see themselves as farmer-caretakers. Financial failure may therefore leave farmers not only with a sense of personal failure but with feelings of shame for having failed both their families and their heritage. This situation can result in emotional disturbances ranging from stress and depression to self-destructive or aggressive behavior.[51] The Reverend Paul Tidemann, a Lutheran minister who studied the farm crisis of the 1980s, reported that "The loss of a farm . . . is not the same as a loss of a job. It signals the loss of a personal and family connection to the land. It prompts a sense of betrayal, in many cases, of generations of farmers, past, present, and future."[52]

Although the pace of farm foreclosures had slowed by the late 1980s, a decline in the number of family farms continues to plague the agricultural sector. Approximately 2 percent of the nation's population lives on approximately 1.93 million family farms. Sixty-two percent of these farms are small with annual sales of less than $20,000. The vast majority of farms are family owned, and farms with less than annual sales of $50,000 are unable to generate enough income to support a family. Despite the high number of small family farms, only 18 percent of farms are responsible for 75 percent of farm commodity production.[53] Perhaps most troubling, though, is that the largest decline in new entries into farming has occurred among the youngest farmers. Entries into farming fell 50 percent for those under age 25, and 35 percent for those 25 to 34. This problem troubles rural communities and farm advocates who worry about the "graying" of America's rural communities.[54]

Some critics maintain that traders and the grain monopolies lay at the heart of the farming problem. For example, while farm exports increased by 143 percent from 1973 to 1983, net farm income dropped by 40 percent.[55] On the other hand, grain traders profited from the renewed price instability, which allowed them to reap enormous profits through speculation and, therefore, to increase their control over agricultural, transportation, and food processing industries.[56] The ideological tool used by these large multinational corporations was the concept of free trade that suggested that the market will regulate price and demand. In reality, free trade worked to the advantage of powerful multinational corporations by encouraging high-volume production at lower profit margins, thereby making it difficult to use sound soil, water, and conservation practices.[57]

The U.S. commodities trade is dominated by a few large corporations such as Cargill, Louis Dreyfus, Bunge and Born, Mutsui/Cook, and Andre/Garnac. These corporations handle 96 percent of all U.S. wheat exports, 95 percent of corn, and 80 percent of oats and sorghum. According to critics, these powerful corporations lobbied for lower price supports, further exposing farmers to a predatory marketplace stacked against them. When farm debt rose, multinationals argued that the solution lay in increased exports, a move that required cutting price support levels even further. Thus, instead of ushering in prosperity, the export expansionists brought the farming community a 1930s style depression.[58]

The concentration of agricultural production into the hands of a few large farmers has profound consequences for many rural communities. A 1986 congressional study of counties dominated by superfarms found that they were populated by a few wealthy elites, a large majority of poor laborers, and virtually no middle class. This trend in agricultural concentration is being driven by a federal farm policy that targets large subsidies—estimated at $13 billion in 1992—toward the nations's largest farms. According to Osha Davidson, 73 cents of every federal farm program dollar ends up with 15 percent of the nation's superfarms.[59] Although the worst of the 1980s farm crisis has passed—at least temporarily—many of the structural problems that originally led to the crisis continue. Crunched between the "hobby farms" and the superfarms, the midsized family farms are in danger of being squeezed out.

U.S. FARM POLICIES

President Ronald Reagan signed into law the Food and Security Act of 1985. This legislation was distinctive in three ways: (1) It was the most complicated farm bill ever passed; (2) it cost the federal government more than previous farm bills had (about $80 billion from 1986 to 1990); and (3) the price supports, at least in terms of parity, were lower than they had been in previous bills.[60] The 1985 farm bill operated in the following manner: A target price was set by Congress and the Secretary of Agriculture; if prices fell below that level, participating farmers received a subsidy from the government. This system was connected to the CCC loan rates. For example, in 1986 the CCC loan rate for a bushel of corn was $1.92, while the target price was $3.03. Because the market price was roughly the CCC loan rate, the federal government made up the deficiency of $1.10 per bushel of corn. On 7 billion bushels of corn, this cost almost $8 billion in subsidies. Despite the high target price of $3.03 for a bushel of corn, the USDA estimated that it was 17 cents less per bushel than it actually cost to raise it.[61] This meant that farmers were losing money on every bushel harvested, forcing them to borrow more money to cover their losses. Grain corporations and foreign buyers were therefore allowed to purchase grain at prices more than $1.00 below the cost of production. In other words, federal policy was subsidizing the grain corporations at the expense of farmers, taxpayers, and the general public.

In 1990, Congress passed a five-year farm bill that made important changes in policies affecting farmers, consumers, and the environment. Specifically, the 1990 farm bill cut down on the number of acres for which farmers could receive deficiency payments, permitted planting flexibility, and maintained the market-oriented loan rates contained in the 1985 farm bill. In addition, the bill contained features that improved the quality of U.S. grain, continued the protection of fragile wetlands, created new incentives to help farmers prevent contamination of ground and surface water on 10 million acres, created incentives to help farmers use fewer pesticides and required farmers who used hazardous chemicals to keep records of their use, helped farmers meet environmental laws, established the first-ever national "organically grown" label, and provided a significant rural development aid package.[62] This bill was estimated to cost $40 billion over five years as opposed to the $80 billion price tag on the 1985 farm bill.

On April 4, 1996 President Bill Clinton signed the Federal Agricultural Improvement and Reform (FAIR) Act into law, which replaced the 1990 Farm Bill. Otherwise known as the 1996 Farm Bill, this legislation enjoyed broad support from Republicans who wanted an agricultural free market and from urban liberals who wanted to end farm subsidies. The heart of the bill contained the "Freedom to Farm" commodity program, which replaced traditional farm subsidies (i.e., those that reimburse farmers when market prices drop) with a system of fixed payments that decline over seven years. The amount a farmer receives under the Freedom to Farm program is based on past program participation. Moreover, under this new program farmers have the option whether to plant commodity crops. Restrictions on fruit, vegetable, hay, and forage crops were continued so as to restrict planting flexibility. New farmers receive subsidies if they are farming land that been in the program and has received payments in the past. Freedom to Farm went from a program that was supposed to save taxpayers money, to one that cost more than the legislation it replaced. In fiscal 1996, Freedom to Farm is estimated to have cost $5 billion more than would have been spent under the 1990 Farm Bill. The U.S. Department of Agriculture estimates the higher cost will continue for the seven-year life of the program.[63]

Sustainable Agriculture

The environmental challenges facing the world are greater than at any time in the nation's history. Global environmental threats such as climate change; stratospheric ozone depletion; and the loss of biological diversity (i.e., different species of animals), forests, and fish stocks, affect all countries regardless of their stage of development.

In June 1993, President Clinton appointed 25 leaders from business, government, environmental, civil rights and Native American organizations to the Council on Sustainable Development. Their charge was to transform the idea of sustainable development into a concrete plan of action. As a benchmark, the council adopted the definition of sustainable development proposed by the United Nations Brundtland Commission in 1987. This stated that sustainable development must "meet the needs of the present without compromising the ability of future generations to meet their own needs." The final vision statement of the council noted that: "Our vision is of a life-sustaining earth. We are committed to the achievement of a dignified, peaceful, and equitable existence. We believe a sustainable United States will have an economy that equitably provides opportunities for satisfying livelihoods and a safe, healthy, high quality of life for current and future generations. Our nation will protect its environment, its natural resource base, and the functions and viability of natural systems on which all life depends."[64] Sustainable development theories also address the crisis of farmland mismanagement in the United States and abroad.

Farming and related activities serve as the foundation for the U.S. food and fiber industry, an industry that provides jobs for 20 percent of the workforce and contributes $820 billion to the GNP. Moreover, the nearly 1 billion acres of land in agricultural production is responsible for feeding, clothing, and housing 250 million people in the United States and millions more abroad. Yet, every minute, the United States loses three acres of productive farmland to urban sprawl—shopping malls, housing subdivisions and the like. Since the first Earth Day in 1970, the United States has lost more than 40 million acres of farmland to development. In North Carolina and Florida, 283,000 acres of cropland disappear each year. In California 100,000 acres disappear. Net cropland losses in the United States between 1982 and 1992 covered an area the size of New Jersey.[65]

Urbanization is a leading cause of cropland loss. The spread of roads, buildings, and industrial parks consumes precious farmland. Cropland is also being lost because of the depletion or diversion of irrigation water. In many water-scarce areas, water is supplied from nonrenewable aquifers. If farmers deplete the water stock or if it is siphoned off by large cities, agricultural land will either be abandoned or become less productive. Although irrigated land accounts for only 16 percent of all cropland, its supplies 40 percent of the world's grain.[66]

Each year, the United States loses 2 billion tons of topsoil to wind and water erosion. As many as 1 billion tons wash into nearby waterways, carrying away natural nutrients and the fertilizers and pesticides contained in the soil. This erosion damages water quality, fish and wildlife habitat, and recreational opportunities. Farmers spend an estimated $8 billion on fertilizers and $6 billion on fuel each year. As such, the use of fertilizers, pesticides and fuel are straining already tight farm budgets and are threatening the environment. The overuse and misapplication of fertilizers and fuel threatens both the land and the farmers profitability.[67]

The impressive success of intensified agriculture that began in the 1960s has led to a complacent attitude toward cropland loss. Specifically, it was believed that since farm yields were rising so quickly they more than compensated for the loss of arable land. By 1984 the growth in crop yields had slowed down. This trend was intensified in the 1990s as the amount of cropland per person fell to less than one-sixth the size of a soccer field. With global grain production falling, the world has consumed half its grain reserves since 1987, dropping them to an all-time low.[68] Moreover, the shrinking supply of cropland and slow yield increases comes on the brink of the largest projected increase in food demand in history. In 25 years, farmers will be required to feed 2.2 billion more people than they do today; yet, most governments continue to allow land that could be used to grow food to be developed or washed away by erosion.[69]

Sustainable development is seen by many as an alternative to environmental degradation. According to the social worker Richard Estes, the concept of sustainable development has succeeded in uniting differing theoretical and ideological perspectives into a single conceptual framework.[70] In an ecological context, sustainable development promotes a process whereby natural resources are replenished and future generations continue to have adequate resources to meet their needs.[71] While sustainable development remains an important concept, its wide use by different actors in the development process gives some pause for concern. For example, some actors use it to designate a radical restructuring of society with regard to environmental development and economic growth. Others simply use the idea of sustainable development to signal a change in attitudes and emphasis. Such different approaches are sometimes labeled *dark green strategies* versus *light green strategies*. Although some policy analysts claim that sustainable development is the basis for a new developmental and ecological paradigm, others caution that it is a concept not yet fully developed.[72]

Farmworkers

Without the efforts of farmworkers, it would be impossible to support the multibillion dollar U.S. fruit and vegetable industry. Because agricultural production depends on the influx of seasonal labor, each year anywhere from 3 to 5 million families leave their homes to follow the crops. While some parts of the American agricultural industry rely heavily on undocumented workers, most migrant farmworkers are either American citizens or are working in the country legally.

The conditions faced by migrant and seasonal farm workers (a group heavily composed of Mexican Americans and among the most impoverished group in America) are in many ways scandalous. Working six to eight months a year, migrants travel in family groups, and virtually all family members—including children—work in the fields. Laboring under extremely arduous and hazardous conditions, migrants face dangers from both powerful pesticides and complicated farm equipment, thus making them highly vulnerable to accidents and health problems. The following represents some of the hardships faced by America's farmworkers:

- The majority of farmworkers earn annual wages of less than $7,500. Although wage rates for farmworkers have risen over the last decade, when adjusted for inflation farmworkers' real wages have decreased 5 percent. Nearly one-third of the migrant farmworkers surveyed in 1989 reported running out of food or not having enough to eat during a year. Most migrant farmworkers earn annual incomes below the federal poverty level, but few receive benefits such as Medicaid, Social Security or Workers' Compensation. Because many agricultural employers do not report the wages of farm laborers, if they become disabled or reach retirement age, they are often unable to prove their claims for Social Security benefits.
- Housing is a problem for farmworkers. More than 35 percent of farmworker housing in eight major agricultural labor states (California, Florida, Texas, Washington, Colorado, Michigan, New York, and Ohio) lacked inside running water. The number of farmworkers needing housing exceeds the available housing units. In addition, migrant farmworkers face barriers in obtaining private housing. For example, rural communities may not have enough rental units available, or they may be unwilling to rent to migrant farmworkers because they cannot provide deposits, qualify for credit checks, or make long-term rental commitments.
- Forty-eight out of every 100,000 agricultural workers died of unintentional work-related injuries in 1988. This compares unfavorably to the national industrial average of 9 workers per 100,000.
- Health statistics for farmworkers are scandalous. Up to 78 percent of all farmworkers suffer from parasitic infections compared to 2-3 percent of the general population. Mostly water-related parasitic infections afflict migrant farmworker adults and children an average of 20 times more often than the general population. Farmworkers suffer from the highest rate of toxic chemical injuries of any group of workers in the United States. More than any other working group, farmworkers suffer and die from heat stress and dehydration. Health centers rank alcohol and drug abuse as the fourth-largest health problem among adult patients of migrant health centers. A 1987 study conducted by the Centers for Disease Control (CDC) indicated that the percentage of migrant farmworkers testing positive for the HIV virus was 0.5 percent. A similar study conducted in 1992 found that the average had risen to 5 percent, 10 times greater than it was 5 years before. Death rates for farmworkers from influenza and pneumonia are as much as 20 percent and 200 percent higher, respectively, than the national average. In a study conducted by the CDC, 44 percent of farmworkers screened had positive TB tests. The Environmental Protection Agency estimates that 300,000 farmworkers suffer acute pesticide poisoning each year. A 1988 study of 460 farmworkers in Washington state found that 89 percent did not know the name of a single pesticide to which they had been exposed; 76 percent had never received any information on appropriate protection measures. Many of the illnesses afflicting farmworkers are preventable through vaccines. In addition, the majority of preschool age farmworker children are not appropriately vaccinated for their age level. It is estimated that as few as 33 percent of female farmworkers receive prenatal care during the first trimester of pregnancy, even many migrant pregnancies are classified as high-risk with multiple indicators. Studies have found the infant mortality rate among children of farmworkers to be more than twice the national average.
- Education is also problematic for the families of migrant farmworkers. Constant mobility makes it hard for the children of farmworkers to complete their education. The median educational level for the head of a migrant household was 6 years in 1986. Moreover, children who move often are two and a half times more likely to

repeat a grade than children who do not move. Changing schools is emotionally difficult for children and they are more likely to drop out of school if they change schools four or more times. Educators who work with migrant children say that 55 percent of these children graduate nationwide. Migrant children face intense economic pressure to drop out of school.

- Child labor is yet another problem. The Department of Labor has found that most seasonal agricultural workers are married and/or have children. The family's poverty requires that all able family members work. In fact, agriculture is the only industry that allows workers under the age of 16. In fact, the Fair Labor Standards Act sets age 12 as the legal limit for farm work, with exemptions available for children as young as 10 or 11. Studies have shown that children under 12 frequently engage in farm work. A 1988 survey of farmworker parents in six states found that about a third of those interviewed had children working in the fields. When children work in the fields, occupational injury presents an even more significant risk than for adults because of their lack of experience. A 1990 study of migrant children working on farms in western New York found that one third of the children had been injured while working during that past year.[73]

In the 1960s the difficult conditions faced by farmworkers led to the emergence of the United Farm Workers Association (UFW) in California, a movement led by the charismatic César Chávez. Initiating a grape and lettuce boycott, the UFW was able to raise the wages of farm workers and lobby for protective legislation. Despite the limited victories of the UFW the plight of many migrant farmworkers remains desperate at best.

RURAL POVERTY

Difficulties related to American farming have helped to create widespread rural problems, including increased levels of poverty. Although tourism, recreation, and retirement developments have helped stem the tide of the "brain drain" from rural areas that occurred during the 1980s, poverty rates remain higher in rural areas than in metropolitan centers. In 1993, the poverty rate for nonmetropolitan areas was 17.3 percent compared to 14.6 percent for urban areas. On the other hand, the poverty gap between these areas is slightly narrowing.[74]

Rural poverty has a significant impact on traditionally vulnerable groups, including children and minorities. From 47 to 55 percent of the rural poor live in the South, which is home to 34 percent of the U.S. population. Nearly 97 percent of the rural African American poor lived in the South in 1990. In 1993, the nonmetro poverty rate for African Americans was 40.6, significantly higher than the black metro poverty rate of 31.7 percent. While the rural poverty rate for African Americans living in the South remains high, the rate of growth in rural poverty was more significant in the West and Central regions. Moreover, while poverty rates for nonmetro blacks and Hispanics (33 percent) remains high, almost 71 percent of the rural poor are white.[75] Large number of rural children are also severely affected by poverty. In 1993, almost 25 percent of rural children—3.7 million—under the age of 18 were poor. Of those children, 50 percent lived in single-female-headed families.[76]

The rural poor tend to differ somewhat from the urban poor. First, most rural families have at least one family member who is working full-time. Second, the rural poor are more often married and living with a spouse. Third, the rural poor are less likely to be minorities than the urban poor. Fourth, the rural poor are more likely than the urban poor to own land or houses, although they may have a negative income. Last, the rural poor appear to be more resistant to accepting public assistance than the urban poor.[77]

The number of poor, rural communities has dropped since 1960, when 2,083 counties had a poverty rate of 20 percent or more. By 1993, the number of persistently poor counties (designated by the USDA as having poverty rates of 20 percent or more) had dropped to 500. Although the average poverty rate for persistently poor counties was 29 percent, rates ranged from a low of 20 to a high of 63 percent. Traditionally poor areas include the Colonias of the Southwest, the Mississippi Delta, Appalachia, and Indian reservations.[78] Most of the low-income counties were in the South, and half were located in just three states—Kentucky, Mississippi, and Tennessee.[79]

A multitude of factors contribute to chronic rural poverty, including high levels of illiteracy and low levels of education, a shortage of highly trained workers, high numbers of low-skill and low-paying jobs, high levels of under-employment and unemployment, an inadequate infrastructure, limited access to credit opportunities, and inexperienced county and city managers who find it difficult to attract large manufacturing projects. As a result, the dearth of economic opportunity and restricted social mobility has resulted in the outmigration of rural families to urban areas, especially when the primary breadwinner possesses higher level skills and education. The lure of better-paying jobs in urban areas is also a powerful enticement for younger workers. As the pool of rural professional and skilled workers begins to evaporate, fewer industries are attracted to the area and the economic conditions deteriorate. Consequently, poor rural counties begin to experience the same social and economic desperation as poor urban areas. Drug and alcohol abuse climbs, as does theft, high rates of school dropouts, and teenage pregnancies. The increased need for mental health and economic development services can create a fertile ground for rural social work activities.

CONCLUSION

The production, distribution, and consumption of food have historically been political issues. Thus, the federal government has traditionally responded to the needs of diverse groups that have an interest in food—farmers, consumers, the poor or their advocates, food distributors, grain traders, Third World countries that depend on America for food, and wealthier nations that depend on U.S. food—through various forms of legislation.

The federal government has responded to these interests by creating a patchwork quilt of policies and programs. One of the most important of these is the Food Stamp program, an ingenious strategy that helps keep food affordable for low-income consumers, helps stabilize farm prices, slows down agricultural surpluses by subsidizing consumption, and allows food merchants and distributors to increase their profits by ensuring a volume of subsidized consumers. While America's food problems are serious for many poor people and farmers, for others—including the very poor, farmworkers, and marginal farmers—it has reached crisis proportions. Tragically, many American farmers now profit from food stamps not because the program helps them control surplus farm goods, but because it provides them with coupons. It is a sad commentary when the producers of food are unable to purchase what they grow.

◆ ◆ ◆ *Discussion Questions* ◆ ◆ ◆

1. The Food Stamps (FS) Program is currently the single most important federal program for combating hunger. Nevertheless, there are serious questions as to why close to 40 percent of those eligible for food stamps are not enrolled. Why has the federal government not been more aggressive in promoting food stamps? What changes, if any, could be made in the FS Program to make it more accessible to greater numbers of eligible people?

2. The WIC and FS programs are similar in many respects. What are the specific differences between these programs? Is it necessary for WIC to be a distinct program? If so, why?

3. There are serious questions as to the effectiveness of U.S. food programs for the poor. What alternatives, if any, are there to the matrix of food programs that currently make up the nutritional safety net?

4. The farming situation in America has historically been an economic roller coaster. Farming was reasonably good in the 1970s, after which it spun into a depression during the early and mid–1980s; by the late 1980s, however, it had recovered somewhat. What programs and policies, if any, should be implemented to stabilize the situation in farming?

5. Some claim that sustainable development is the basis for a new developmental and ecological paradigm.

6. Is sustainable development a theory viable enough to develop a series of policies around? If so, why?

7. The problem of how to deal fairly with America's farmworkers is both difficult and chronic. What are some possible solutions for promoting equity and fairness for American farmworkers?

8. Poverty continues to be a persistent part of America's rural landscape. Describe the most important causes of rural poverty. What, if anything, can be done to lower the rates of rural poverty?

Notes

1. David A. Super, Sharon Parrott, Susan Steinmetz, and Cindy Mann, "The New Welfare Law" (Washington, DC: Center on Budget and Policy Priorities, August 13, 1996. On-line: http://epn.org/cbpp/wconfbl2.html
2. Ibid.
3. Angela Bartlett, Karen Newman, Carolyn Olivent, Annette Rhiner, and Kim Unger, "Hunger, Poverty and Farming in the 90s," unpublished paper, Graduate School of Social Work, University of Houston, Houston, TX, April 25, 1996.
4. Ibid.
5. Committee on Ways and Means, U.S. House of Representatives, *Overview of Entitlement Programs, 1992 Green Book* (Washington, DC: U.S. Government Printing Office, 1992), pp. 1636, 1639; and Isaac Shapiro, *White Poverty in America* (Washington, DC: Center on Budget and Policy Priorities, October 1992), p. 35.
6. U.S. House of Representatives, *1992 Green Book*, p. 1627.
7. Super et al., "The New Welfare Law."
8. See Texas Department of Human Services, "Program Information Sheets—Gulf Coast Region 6," Texas Department of Human Services, Community Relations Department, 5425 Polk St., Houston, TX, n.d.; and Children's Defense Fund, *The State of America's Children, 1991* (Washington, DC: Children's Defense Fund, 1991), p. 27.
9. U.S. House of Representatives, *1992 Green Book*, p. 1616.
10. Illa Tennison, "WIC Policy Analysis," unpublished paper, School of Social Work, University of Missouri-Columbia, 1987, p. 5.
11. Ibid.
12. U.S. House of Representatives, *1992 Green Book*, p. 1687.
13. Food and Nutrition Service, U.S. Department of Agriculture, "Food Program Facts," USDA, Washington, DC, 1995.
14. Ibid., p. 1683.
15. Ibid.
16. Ibid.
17. Tennison, "WIC Policy Analysis," p. 12.
18. Quoted in Ibid.
19. Ibid., p. 13.
20. Quoted in Karen Baar, "Poverty Programs that Work," *Public Health*, 2(4) (Fall 1996), pp. 16–21.
21. Michael Harrington, with the assistance of Robert Greenstein and Eleanor Holmes Norton, *Who Are the Poor?* (Washington, DC: Justice for All National Office, 1987), p. 15.
22. Quoted in Bartlett et al., "Hunger, Poverty and Farming in the 90s."
23. See U.S. House of Representatives, *1992 Green Book*, p. 1688; and Kristin Cotter, "Texas WIC: Strategy for Outreach Policy," unpublished paper, Graduate School of Social Work, University of Houston, Houston, TX, Fall 1996.
24. Children's Defense Fund, *The State of America's Children, 1988* (Washington, DC: Children's Defense Fund, 1988), p. 186.
25. Isaac Shapiro and Robert Greenstein, *Holes in the Safety Nets* (Washington, DC: Center on Budget and Policy Priorities, 1988), pp. 33–34.
26. U.S. House of Representatives, *1992 Green Book*, p. 1628.
27. Shapiro and Greenstein, *Holes in the Safety Nets*, pp. 33–34.
28. Harrington et al., *Who Are the Poor?* p. 26.
29. Quoted in Bartlett et al., "Hunger, Poverty and Farming in the 90s."

30. M. Racine, "Attempts to Feed the Hungry Affected by Budget Reform," *Houston Chronicle* (January 29, 1996), pp. 2D, 10D.
31. Quoted in H. Price, "Stop the Rise of Hunger in America," *New Pittsburgh Courier* (October 29, 1994), p. 6.
32. Ibid.
33. A. A. Skolnick, "More Children Cry as Congress Shakes its Head," *Journal of the American Medical Association* (274)10 (1995), p. 783.
34. C. Aikens, "One in Six Struggle with Chronic Hunger," *Oakland Post* (April 19, 1995), p. 6.
35. Harrington et al., *Who Are the Poor?* p. 26.
36. M. Drabenstott and M. Duncan, "Another Troubled Year for U.S. Agriculture," *Journal of the American Society of Farm Managers and Rural Appraisers* (49)1 (1985), pp. 58–66.
37. Cited in Joanne Mermelstein, "Criteria of Rural Mental Health Directors in Adopting Farm Crisis Programming Innovation," unpublished Ph.D. dissertation, Public Policy Analysis and Administration, St. Louis University, 1986, p. 3.
38. Ibid.
39. "U.S. Farm Sector, In Annual Checkup, Shows Strong Pulse," *Farmline* (December–January 1991), p. 2.
40. Ibid., pp. 4–5; also see Jim Ryan and Ken Erickson, "Balance Sheet Stable in 1992," *Agricultural Outlook* 46 (January–February 1992), pp. 29–30.
41. Ibid., p. 29.
42. G. Kaye Kellogg, "The Crisis of the Family Farm in America Today," unpublished paper, School of Social Work, University of Missouri-Columbia, 1987, p. 3.
43. Howard Jacob Karger, *The Sentinels of Order: A Case Study of the Minneapolis Settlement House Movement, 1915–1950* (Lanham, MD: University Press of America, 1987).
44. Everett E. Luoma, *The Farmer Takes a Holiday: The Story of the National Farmer's Holiday Association and the Farmers' Strike of 1932–33* (New York: Exposition Press, 1967).
45. United States Department of Agriculture, "History of Agricultural Price Support and Adjustment Programs, 1933–84," *Bulletin No. 485* (Washington, DC: Economic Research Service, 1984), pp. 8–9.
46. Kellogg, "The Crisis of the Family Farm," p. 4.
47. Steve Little, "Parity: Survival of the Family Farm." Unpublished paper, School of Social Work, University of Missouri-Columbia, 1986, pp. 8–9.
48. Mary Ahearn, "Financial Well-Being of Farm Operators and Their Households," United States Department of Agriculture, *Report No. 563*, (Washington, DC: Economic Research Service, September 1986), p. iii.
49. Ibid.
50. Mermelstein, "Criteria of Rural Mental Health Directors," pp. 5–6.
51. Ibid., p. 7.
52. Quoted in John M. Herrick, "Farmers' Revolt! Contemporary Farmers' Protests in Historical Perspective: Implications for Social Work Practice," *Human Services in the Rural Environment* (10)1 (April 1986), p. 9.
53. J.M. Rawson, "The 1995 Farm Bill: Overview," Congressional Research Service Issue Brief, Washington, DC: The Library of Congress, 1995.
54. Fred Gale, "What's Behind the Declining Farm Count?" *Agricultural Outlook* (June 1992), p. 26.
55. Little, "Parity," p. 9.
56. Ibid.
57. United States Department of Agriculture, "Economic Indicators of the Farm Sector," *Farm Sector Review, ERS, ECIFS* 4–3 (Washington, DC, 1984), pp. 4, 16.
58. Little, "Parity," pp. 10–11.
59. Osha Gray Davidson, "Rise of America's Rural Ghetto," *San Diego Union Tribune* (January 27, 1993), p. B6.
60. Ibid.
61. Kellogg, "The Crisis of the Family Farm," pp. 9–10.
62. U.S. Government, "Conference Committee Approves Five-year Farm Bill," news release, Washington, DC, October 16, 1990, n.p.
63. American Farmland Trust, "1996 Farm Bill Review," 1996. On-line: http://farm.fic.niu.edu/aft/fbreview.html
64. The Council on Sustainable Development, "Sustainable America: A New Consensus," 1995. On-line: http://www.whitehouse.gov/WH/EOP/pcsd/info/highlite.html
65. Vir Singh, "World Wide Cropland Losses," *Earth Times* (November 20, 1996). On-line: http://www.earthtimes.org/romesummitvirsinghnov13.htm

66. Singh, "World Wide Cropland Losses."
67. American Farm Trust, "Why Save Farmland? 1996" On-line: http://farm.fic.niu.edu/aft/aftwhysave.html
68. American Farm Trust, "What's Happening to America's Agricultural Resources?" 1996. On-line: http://farm.fic.niu.edu/aft/aftwhathap.html
69. Ibid.
70. Richard Estes, "Toward Sustainable Development: From theory to Praxis," *Social Development Issues* (15)3 (1993), pp. 1–22.
71. Katherine van Wormer, *Social Welfare: A World View* (Chicago: Nelson-Hall, 1997).
72. James Midgley, *Social Development: The Development Perspective in Social Welfare* (London: Sage, 1995).
73. See V. A. Wilk, *The Occupational Health of Migrant and Seasonal Farmworkers in the United States* (Washington, DC: Farmworkers Justice Fund, 1985); Juan Ramos and Celia Torres, "Migrant and Seasonal Farm Workers," *Encyclopedia of Social Work*, 18th Ed. (Silver Spring, MD: NASW, 1987), p. 151; and National Center for Farmworker Health, *Facts About America's Farmworkers* (Washington, DC: National Center for Farmworker Health, 1996).
74. See L.M. Ghelfi (Ed.), *Rural Conditions and Trends*, vol. 6, no. 1 Washington, DC: USDA Economic Research Service, Spring 1995; and Kathryn Porter, *Poverty in Rural America: A National Overview* (Washington, DC: Center on Budget and Policy Priorities, April 1989), pp. 3–4.
75. See Ghelfi, *Rural Conditions and Trends;* and Bartlett et al., "Hunger, Poverty and Farming in the 90s."
76. Bartlett et al., "Hunger, Poverty and Farming in the 90s."
77. H.R. Rodgers and G. Weiher, Jr. (Eds.), *Rural Poverty: Special Causes and Policy Reforms* (Westport, CT: Greenwood Press, 1989).
78. Ibid.
79. Porter, *Poverty in Rural America*, pp. 7–11; see also Scott Barancik, *The Rural Disadvantage: Growing Income Disparities Between Rural and Urban Areas* (Washington, DC: Center on Budget and Policy Priorities, April 1990), pp. ix–x.

PART FOUR

◆ ◆ ◆ ◆ ◆ ◆ ◆ ◆ ◆ ◆ ◆

The American Welfare State in Perspective

CHAPTER 18

The American Welfare State in International Perspective

BY JAMES MIDGLEY

As closer links have been forged in communications, travel, trade and international cooperation, the nations of the world have become much more interdependent. All over the world, people are better informed of developments in other countries and they now have a better appreciation of the cultures of other societies. Increased world trade has also resulted in greater global economic integration. Today, many Americans wear clothes, drive cars, consume foods, and use electronic appliances that were produced overseas. This has direct implications for the domestic economy. The export of capital by American businesses and the loss of jobs resulting from cheaper imports has become a major political issue.

As the lives of ordinary people are increasingly affected by international events, they need to be prepared to cope with the demands of globalization. Those who are best equipped to participate in the global economy and adapt to the realities of increased international collaboration are the most likely to be successful in an increasingly interdependent world.

This requirement also applies to those involved in social welfare. Today, social policy and social work are greatly affected by international events. As will be shown in this chapter, economic changes brought about by globalization are having a direct impact on government social programs. International events can no longer be regarded as distant or irrelevant. As global forces impinge increasingly on domestic affairs, social policymakers and social workers will have to cope with the demands of the new world order.

This chapter seeks to provide an introduction to the field of international social welfare by examining the American welfare state in comparative perspective. It takes some of the topics discussed elsewhere in this book and links them to a growing body of international knowledge. In this way, it seeks to illustrate the relevance of an international perspective for the study of social policy in the United States. For example, it compares social welfare in America with other countries and reviews some of the conclusions that have been drawn about the nature of the American welfare state. It also compares explanations about the origins and functions of social welfare in the United States with the experiences of other countries and in this way, tests the validity of these explanations. The chapter is also concerned with the so-called "crisis" of the welfare state. As the federal government has cut social programs and as an antiwelfare ideology has taken root, some social policy writers believe that social welfare is experiencing a crisis of major proportions. By reviewing international trends, the extent of the problem can be better assessed. It is hoped that this chapter issues will illustrate the importance and usefulness of an international perspective in social policy.

THE NATURE OF GLOBALIZATION

While human beings have always been affected by international events, the impact of these events on their daily lives is now unprecedented. Today, Americans watch television reports about natural disasters in remote regions, go out to eat ethnic foods originating in other nations, drive motor cars manufactured abroad and vacation in distant lands. Many now have access to the Internet and can instantly communicate with colleagues many thousands of miles away. The scale of these activities would have amazed earlier generations. Even 50 years ago, very few people traveled abroad, and few were directly affected by international events. Today, international travel and communications with people in other countries is taken for granted. International awareness has also increased as people of different languages and cultures have migrated to the United States. In addition, many more people are now aware of the role of global economic forces in their daily lives. Many recognize that their jobs and livelihoods are no longer only dependent on local economic activities but that global economic forces directly affect their incomes and future well-being.

These changes are the result of a process known as globalization. Globalization involves the international economic, social, and political integration of the world's nations. It derives from increased international contacts, migration, and enhanced collaboration between different countries. It has also come about as a result of increased trade, communications, political cooperation, and social contacts. Globalization not only fosters greater links between the world's peoples but promotes the emergence of an inclusive worldwide culture, a global economy and an awareness of the world as a single place rather than a collection of discreet nation states. The process of globalization also fosters the emergence of a common human identity in which people recognize that they are not only members of separate communities, ethnic groups, and nationalities but that they also belong to a single human family.

Although some people believe that the process of globalization is a positive one, others dislike the changes which are taking place. Those who favor globalization are known as internationalists. They believe that increased economic integration, political cooperation, and social contacts will eventually result in the emergence of an international identity that transcends national loyalties. However, many people are troubled by the possibility that some future world government may replace the nation state or that their locally rooted cultural identity will be subsumed by an allegiance to some international political entity. Some are worried about the immigration of foreign people into their communities. Many are concerned about global economic forces that they believe are destroying jobs and lowering living standards. Others are critical of the role of international banks and multinational corporations, which, they assert, are exploiting poor countries and harming local economies in the industrial nations. There has also been much concern in social policy circles about the impact of the global economy on government social programs. As governments reduce spending in an attempt to make their economies more globally competitive, needy people are suffering. Although globalization may be affecting people everywhere, its impact is not universally welcomed.

Although globalization has many critics, it is unlikely that it can be halted. The revolution in communications technology, the rapid diffusion of culture and a significant increase in global trade have created powerful forces that cannot be controlled, let alone reversed. For this reason, many governments are now integrating their economies into the global system and participating more actively in international activities. Many believe that globalization will bring benefits to those who are best able to adapt to the new world order and most capable of exploiting the opportunities created by globalization. It is for this reason that many countries are today promoting international contacts and investing in programs that will enhance global participation. Throughout the world, communications are being improved, trade agreements are being signed, and efforts are being made to promote greater cultural and political collaboration. In addition, universities and other educational institutions are placing more emphasis on international curriculum content so that students will be better prepared to respond to the challenges of the global age.

THE IMPORTANCE OF INTERNATIONAL SOCIAL WELFARE

There are similar developments in social welfare where greater efforts are being made to enhance international collaboration. Professional associations such as the International Federation of Social Workers and the International Association of Schools of Social Work are encouraging their members to exchange ideas and experiences and it is very likely that social workers will make greater use of practice innovations from other countries in the future.[1] Schools of social work are incorporating more international content into the professional curriculum.[2] Developments in social policy are also being informed by events in other parts of the world. Many governments have entered into international agreements on the provision of health, social security, and other services. In addition, it is likely that attempts to formulate new social policies will rely much more extensively on developments in other countries.

Those working in social welfare in the United States can benefit from knowing more about the welfare systems of other countries. A knowledge of social policy in other societies is not only useful in its own right but also can promote an understanding of the origins, roles, and functioning of social policy in the United States. By comparing recent events in the United States with trends in a other countries, better insights into complex social welfare issues may be gained.

As in other countries, social policy in the United States has been preoccupied with domestic concerns and comparisons between the United States and other countries are seldom made. However, there are a group of American social policy investigators who have studied the human services and welfare policies of other countries. Unfortunately, their work is often regarded as an exotic intellectual exercise which, although interesting, has little relevance to mainstream social welfare research. Today, this attitude is changing and many more social workers and policymakers now recognize the benefits of international collaboration.

There are good reasons why American social welfare investigators should relate their own research to international trends. First, it is useful to know how social policy in the United States compares with other nations. How do other countries administer their social services? Do their social provisions differ significantly from those in America? What historical factors gave rise to the welfare state in other parts of the world, and how do these compare with developments in the United states? Answers to these questions are important and can promote knowledge and understanding.

Second, information about social policy in other nations can help to test theoretical propositions. Often, social scientists reach conclusions about the role and functions of social welfare on the basis of data collected in just one country. While these propositions may indeed explain local events, they can only claim to be truly scientific if they have general validity. This requires that propositions be tested in a wider field and that social welfare in many different societies be analyzed.

Third, comparative research can help to test normative claims about the welfare state.[3] For example, it has often been said that the United States spends too much on social welfare and that high social expenditures are a primary cause of the nation's economic problems. However, comparative research reveals that the United States spends less on social programs than other industrial countries and that many of other industrial countries have a better economic record.[4] By examining claims about welfare policies in the international context, it is possible to muster effective arguments for or against particular normative propositions.

Finally, comparative social policy research can help the process of social policy formulation and evaluation. It is useful for social policymakers to be able to learn from the experiences of other countries when seeking to introduce new social programs. In this way, programs can be more effectively developed and costly mistakes can be avoided. In addition, it is useful to be able to assess the effectiveness of social policies with reference to their performance in other nations. If other countries have found that a particular policy approach does not meet its stated objective, this information can help American social policymakers seeking to evaluate the outcomes of their own social programs.

Methodological Questions

As the benefits of comparing American social welfare policy with developments in other countries are recognized, more social policy investigators will relate their findings to events in other nations. However, the task of linking research about social welfare in the United States with research in other societies is not an easy one. First, it is difficult to obtain accurate data about social needs and social policies in other nations. For example, a major study of poverty and income inequality that was undertaken for the World Bank in the 1970s reached many interesting conclusions, but it was based on research data that was of dubious reliability, out of date, and difficult to compare.[5] Fortunately, as information sources in many parts of the world have become more reliable, this problem may eventually be overcome.

Another problem is how to define the policies or programs to be compared and how to select countries for comparison. In the United States, the term *social security* is used to refer to the federal government's old age retirement, invalidity, disability, and survivor's income maintenance program. In many European countries, however, the term refers to all income maintenance programs including public assistance and family allowances. In Latin America, the term *social security* includes the provision of medical care. Clearly, these different uses need to be understood, and their different meanings standardized before useful comparative research can be undertaken.

It is also difficult to decide which countries should be compared with the United States. Some experts contend that useful comparisons can only be made with countries that have similar social, economic, and political characteristics. There is no point, they claim, in comparing social welfare in the United States with an African or Asian country. Others disagree, arguing out that the purpose of the comparison is more important than the countries selected for comparison. For example, if an investigator wants to compare antipoverty programs in the United States with those of an African country, this is legitimate if the comparison is made within the context of particular research objectives. The investigator may also want to make policy recommendations and show that antipoverty programs that have been effective in the African country can be useful in reducing poverty in America.[6]

These and other methodological problems must be taken into account when comparing the social policies of the United States with those of other countries. However, while methodological problems pose difficulties, they are not insurmountable and do not prevent international studies from reaching useful conclusions. Used with caution, comparative studies can inform research into American social policy and help investigators understand its complex features.

INTERNATIONAL PERSPECTIVES ON THE AMERICAN WELFARE STATE

Like many European countries, the United States is often described as a welfare state. Usually, the core programs of the American welfare state are identified with federal programs such as Social Security, Medicaid and Medicare, Temporary Assistance to Needy Families (TANF), Supplementary Security Income (SSI), the Food Stamps Program, housing assistance, educational grants, Head Start, veteran's benefits, and various jobs training programs.[7] These programs coexist with state and local programs (which are often subsidized by the federal government) such as public education, social services for children, programs for the mentally ill, general assistance, worker's compensation, correctional programs, and services for the elderly and other needy groups.

In addition to these services, a great variety of tax provisions, legislative enactments, and other measures also have an impact on human welfare. These include federal tax incentives that encourage savings for retirement, legislative prohibitions on discrimination against minorities and the physically disabled, and economic policies that foster investment and employment creation. Of course, different experts place more emphasis on some of these programs than others, and often only a few of them are regarded as being a part of the welfare system. However, most agree that Social Security and major income-tested programs, such as TANF, Food Stamps, and housing assistance, form the core components of the American welfare state.

It is these key elements that are most frequently compared with the social provisions of other societies. On the basis of these comparisons, many social policy investigators believe that the American welfare state is not as comprehensive or as generous as European welfare states.[8] They point out that while European countries have public medical insurance programs that cover the whole population, the United States depends largely on a private system of medical care, with government involvement being limited to assisting the elderly and poorest groups. They also contend that the United States lacks a comprehensive system of family allowances. Like medical care, these programs are a major part of European welfare states.

In addition to having less extensive social programs, the authors of comparative studies believe that American welfare programs are more fragmented than those in Europe. They also claim that American social welfare is characterized by an incremental style of policymaking that responds haphazardly to political pressures. In Europe, on the other hand, social policy is said to be the result of systematic social planing. European welfare states are also more activist in that they seek to manage the economy more aggressively and to maintain high levels of employment. In the United States, private initiative and a reliance on the private market with minimal government intervention is believed to be the best method of fostering human well-being.

On the basis of these findings, several social policy analysts have concluded that America is a reluctant welfare state—a laggard in social policy and human service provision. Harold Wilensky, a leading scholar in the field of comparative social welfare, summed up this idea when he wrote:

> The United States is more reluctant than any rich democratic country to make a welfare effort appropriate to its affluence. Our support for national welfare programs is halting; our administration of services for the less privileged is mean. We move toward the welfare state but we do it with ill-grace, carping and complaining all the way.[9]

Typologies of Welfare States

With his colleague, Charles Lebeaux, Wilensky sought to summarize the differences between the European and American welfare states by constructing a typology of social welfare systems. The typology contrasts the *residual* with the *institutional* approaches. The residualist approach is concerned with providing a minimal safety net for the poorest sections of the population rather than catering for the population as a whole. Wilensky and Lebeaux believed that social policy in the United States is essentially residualist in nature. On the other hand, the institutional approach, which typifies European social welfare, seeks to provide a variety of social programs for the whole population and to combine economic and social objectives in an effort to enhance the well-being of all.[10]

These ideas were developed by the British social policy writer, Richard Titmuss. Titmuss agreed that the residual approach typified social welfare in the United States and that in Europe, an institutional approach was dominant. However, Titmuss noted that some countries did not fall into the residual and institutional dichotomy. For this reason, he added a third category to the typology which he called the industrial-performance model. He believed that this approach characterized social policy in the former Soviet Union and communist Eastern European countries.[11]

Several subsequent attempts have been made to construct typologies of welfare states that go beyond Wilensky and Lebeaux's twofold category. One of the first was by Norman Furniss and Timothy Tilton, who provided a threefold classification that encompassed what they called the "positive state," the "social security state," and the "social welfare state." The United States exemplified the first, Britain the second, and Sweden the third.[12]

Canadian writer Ramesh Mishra, who has written extensively about international social welfare, retained the twofold approach developed by Wilensky and Lebeaux, but he stressed the efforts of some countries to forge strong alliances between government, labor, and business in order to reach a consensus on social welfare issues. This approach is known as corporatism. In corporatist societies, social welfare is integrated into the economy and other institutions of society. Countries such as Sweden, Austria, and Australia are typical of the corporatist approach. Mishra used the term *integrated welfare state* to connote the corporatist approach. On the other hand, Britain and the United States were noncorporatist in that they did not integrate social and economic policy or seek to forge a consensus around welfare issues. For this reason, Mishra called them differentiated welfare states. Mishra was one of the first writers to suggest that Britain was not, as Titmuss believed, like the rest of Europe but rather more like the United States in its approach to social welfare.[13]

Gosta Esping-Andersen's typology also recognized the corporatist type when classifying welfare states. However, he grouped countries somewhat differently from Mishra. In addition to the corporatist category, (Italy, Japan, France, and Switzerland), Esping-Andersen identified two other types, the liberal welfare state (Australia, Britain, and the United States), and the social democratic welfare state (Austria, the Netherlands, and the Scandinavian countries).[14] More recently, Norman Ginsburg (1992) constructed a fourfold typology comprising the social democratic welfare state (Sweden), the social market welfare state (Germany), the corporate market welfare state (United States), and the liberal collectivist welfare state (Britain).[15] However, of the various typologies of welfare states that have been developed by social policy investigators, Esping-Andersen's is perhaps the most widely accepted.[16]

Although the typologies differ from each other, they use similar criteria when classifying countries. All place emphasis on *government* social programs and neglect the role of voluntary organizations and other nonstatutory activities in social welfare. The typologies also reveal the normative preferences of the authors. While the typologies are intended to classify countries for analytical purposes, it is clear that they give expression to beliefs about the desirability of the role of government in social welfare. Those who favor extensive government involvement in social welfare have represented countries with extensive public programs more favorably in the typologies than those which do not place as much emphasis on government involvement. For this reason, it is not surprising that most of the typologies depict the United States negatively in comparison to European welfare states.

American Welfare Exceptionalism

America's apparent unwillingness to emphasize government social welfare programs have been described by Edwin Amenta and Theda Skocpol as "welfare exceptionalism."[17] They have also summarized explanations of the country's reluctance to create an institutional European-style welfare state. One of these explanations is that the racial, ethnic, and religious diversity of the United States has prevented the emergence of a comprehensive welfare state. Unlike Europe, where people are more united and have a stronger sense of civic responsibility, the pursuit of self-interest by a great number of different groups in the United States mitigates against the emergence of a single, national system of provision that caters to all citizens.

Another explanation is based on the country's high degree of political decentralization that impedes the emergence of strong central political institutions. Combined with a high degree of diversity, the tradition of decentralization creates cleavages in American society that effectively prevent the emergence of a strong, centralized, and comprehensive welfare state. It has also been noted that the United States does not have a long tradition of bureaucratic government that can support centralized welfare programs. Some have claimed that this is because of the absence of a feudal tradition. Developing this idea, others have pointed to the unique role of the courts in American policymaking, the separation of the executive and legislative branches, and the role of powerful political interest groups all of which impede the emergence of a strong, centralized welfare state.

Another explanation stresses the role of America's unique individualist culture pointing out that the ideology of individualism is far stronger in the United States than in Europe and that it is fundamentally antithetical to state welfare. It has also been argued that trade unions are weaker in the United

States than in Europe and that the political Left, which has played a major role in the emergence of the European welfare states, has not been strong in the United States.

While the notion of welfare exceptionalism offers interesting insights into social policy in the United States, it can be criticized. For example, the idea that the United States is a welfare laggard is based largely on a comparison of social programs such as health insurance and family allowances. The absence of these programs is usually emphasized by those claiming that the United States does not have a comprehensive welfare state. While it is true that government health care and family income maintenance programs are poorly developed in the United States, the role of indirect support for families through tax relief and tax deductions for medical expenses is often ignored, as is the significance of Medicare and state and local health care programs.

In addition, the United States has excelled in other social fields. During the nineteenth century, it led the world in the development of public education, and it still compares favorably with many other countries in terms of access to education, particularly at the tertiary level. The United States is also a pioneer in environmental protection and while this is not always regarded as an integral part of social policy, the impact of the environment on human well-being should not be underestimated.[18] Comparative studies have also shown that when particular social programs such as retirement pensions are compared, the United States fares quite well.[19] In addition, recent historical research reveals that the United States was ahead of other Western countries in the late nineteenth century in developing income maintenance programs for veterans and for women with children. At the turn of the century, no other industrializing country had introduced mother's pensions, and none came as close to creating a "maternal" rather than "paternal" welfare state.[20]

Another problem is that comparisons between Europe and the United States are often characterized by strong personal biases. For example, a strong pro-British bias pervades Titmuss's writings. He has been criticized for presenting his arguments in a way that ensures the moral superiority of the institutional welfare state model.[21] It is also apparent that the European countries have very divergent welfare systems and that not all European welfare states are centralized, comprehensive, or highly activist. Studies of welfare policies in other parts of the world have also shown the American welfare state in more favorable terms. For example, unlike the United States, Australia did not until recently have a universal social security system, and it relied extensively on means-tested social programs.[22]

However, it is difficult to reach the conclusion that the United States is one of the world's welfare leaders. Despite its extensive educational and social security provisions, the country does not compare favorably to the other industrial nations in the extent, comprehensiveness, or coverage of its welfare system. In fact, its position has deteriorated in recent years as social programs were retrenched under the Reagan, Bush, and Clinton administrations. Public expenditure data from the Organization for Economic Cooperation and Development (OECD), which is comprised of the major industrial nations, show that social expenditure in the United States amounted to 20.8 percent of GDP in 1980. This figure was considerably lower than the OECD average of 25.6 percent. In 1985, social expenditure had decreased to 18.2 percent, placing the United States seventeenth out of a ranking of 21 OECD nations.[23]

Although many American social policy writers have complained about their country's comparatively low level of welfare provision, others are not disturbed by these findings. They claim that unfavorable comparisons between the United States and other countries are based on the idea that state involvement in social welfare is a good thing. They reject this assertion and do not believe that social needs should be met primarily by the government. Instead of relying only on the state for social welfare, these *welfare pluralists*, as they are known, argue that people can enhance their well-being through their own efforts, the help of neighbors or their families, by purchasing services on the market, or by obtaining help from voluntary organizations.[24] They point out that in the United States, people make effective use of nongovernmental agencies and that international comparisons should not just cover government social programs. They also point out that although the United States may lag behind in public welfare provision, people enjoy exceptionally high standards of living and unequaled opportunities. This is why the country remains a magnet for immigrants from all over the world who do not come to receive government handouts but to share in the American dream.

DYNAMICS OF THE AMERICAN WELFARE STATE

Most books about social policy in the United States are descriptive, seeking to depict current social policies and programs in factual terms. Few use theoretical concepts to explain the changes that have taken place. Although descriptive accounts are useful, the expansion of government involvement in welfare is the result of complex forces that need to be analyzed in theoretical terms. Although theoretical research into social policy is still underdeveloped, it has generated important propositions and provided useful insights into the dynamics of social welfare. The findings of these studies need to be examined with reference to developments in other countries. Through comparative analysis, it may be possible to uncover the basic processes that account for the origins and functions of social policy in modern societies.

The Origins and Functions of Social Policy

Many historical accounts of the emergence of social welfare in the United States have been published. In an attempt to make the material more manageable, these studies usually identify different chronological periods in the development of social welfare. For example, they often distinguish the colonial phase, the time of the Civil War, the period of rapid industrialization, the Progressive Era, the New Deal, and the expansion of the welfare state. Usually, the periods are linked together to form a longer evolutionary model that shows that over time, government became increasingly responsible for social welfare and that this resulted in the creation of the welfare state. Although many welfare historians regard the process as a slow evolutionary one in which more and more governmental programs are added, others view the creation of the welfare state as a "big bang" coming into existence suddenly as the result of major social upheavals.[25] However, while they may disagree about the timing of the inception of the welfare state, most scholars believe that the modern welfare state represents the culmination of an inevitable and desirable process of social welfare evolution.

There can be no doubt that the development of social welfare in the United States has involved a substantial increase in government intervention. During the last hundred years, many more federal and state programs have been added, and expenditures on the social services have increased significantly. Charles Prigmore and Charles Atherton have shown that public expenditures on the human services only amounted to about 3 percent of GNP at the turn of the century; by 1980, they had reached 17 percent.[26]

Social policy analysts believe that the expansion of government social programs during the last hundred years did not just happen automatically but that it came about a the result of wider social and economic forces. They have proposed different theories to account for this development. They also believe that the welfare state fulfills specific social functions that can be explained in theoretical terms.

One popular explanation of the origins and functions of the American welfare state may be called the *social conscience* or *humanitarian impulse hypothesis*. This explanation contends that the modern welfare state is the result of the inborn altruistic concern that human beings have for other people. Proponents of this explanation believe that human beings are a social species and that they have an instinctive need to help each other. Many social welfare textbooks support the idea that social welfare gives expression to humanitarian feelings. They usually emphasize the charitable activities of the ancient Jews and Greeks, early Christians, medieval communities, and nineteenth-century philanthropic organizations. These accounts show that caring has been an integral part of human society since early times.[27]

However, proponents of social conscience theory point out that the process of industrialization has undermined people's natural humanitarian instincts.

Urbanization, individualism, and competitiveness have all weakened their desire to help others. In addition, industrialization and urbanization have created massive new social problems that cannot be met through mutual help alone. For this reason, the government is compelled to intervene. In industrial society, therefore, the state becomes society's social conscience and represents the collective humanitarian instincts of its citizens. As Prigmore and Atherton argue, the modern welfare state recreates the institutional arrangements that characterized pre-industrial societies.[28]

A second explanation of the origins and functions of the welfare state is the *industrialization-welfare hypothesis*. This theory also stresses the role of industrialization in the development of the welfare state but that humanitarian motives are not believed to be very important. Instead, this approach suggests that industrialization undermines preindustrial welfare institutions and places political pressure on government to intervene. The traditional welfare functions of families and communities are replaced by government welfare programs, not because government has strong humanitarian motives, but rather because government has no option. With the disintegration of traditional welfare institutions, poverty, deprivation, and social need increases; as a result, the government intervenes to establish a variety of social programs designed to substitute for the traditional welfare system. Proponents of this theory also believe that industrialization is more important than political ideologies in the creation of welfare states. Irrespective of their political and ideological characteristics, all societies undergoing industrialization expand their social programs and become welfare states.[29]

A third approach is the *maintenance of capitalism hypothesis*. This approach also contends that industrialization is relevant to the creation of modern welfare states, but it emphasizes the role of capitalist industrialization in the creation of the welfare state. It contends that the welfare state emerges and functions to promote the interests of capitalism. A popular exposition is of this point of view is provided by Frances Piven and Richard Cloward, whose historical study of public welfare programs in the United States concluded that the government creates social programs to control the labor force.[30] During times of economic depression and civic unrest, the government makes these programs generous in order to minimize unrest and to placate the working class. During times of economic growth, on the other hand, it uses welfare punitively to compel workers to seek jobs and to work hard. Those who cannot or do not work and seek welfare instead are given little help and are subjected to harsh treatment in order to deter them from using the welfare system. In this way, the welfare system also serves to discourage those in employment from becoming dependent on government social programs.

A variation of Piven and Cloward's theory is provided by Mimi Abramovitz, who argues that welfare programs are used by government to control women. Examining the history of social policy in the United States, she argues that social programs have been designed to reward women who fulfill roles such as childbearing and homemaking. These roles are defined by men. Similarly, social programs seek to punish women who do not conform to patriarchal values.[31]

A more complicated explanation of the relationship between social welfare and industrial capitalism is provided by James O'Connor, who argues that the American government introduced welfare programs to ensure that capital accumulation takes place and that people accept the capitalist system.[32] These accumulation and legitimation functions, as he calls them, are essential if capitalism is to survive. To help capitalist accumulation, the government introduces social programs that create an efficient labor force and reduce the costs of labor. Public education, health care and similar programs all help to make workers more efficient and productive. Similarly, because governments rather than capitalist businesses are responsible for meeting social needs, they reduce the costs of labor and make businesses more profitable. Governments also try to legitimate the capitalist system by creating social programs that do not necessarily promote capitalism but that enhance social contentment. These "social expenses" include social security, services for the disabled, welfare payments, and other provisions, all of which foster contentment and prevent civic unrest.

O'Connor also argues that the accumulation and legitimation functions of welfare capitalism are contradictory and that sooner or later, the state's ability to provide services that maintain the system will be exhausted. A crisis will then emerge. As will be shown, these ideas have direct implications for studies of the problems that have faced the welfare state in recent years.

The International Evidence

Although several other accounts of the origins and functions of welfare have been formulated, the three theories just discussed are the best developed explanations of the dynamics of welfare in the United States. All have supporters and all have a degree of plausibility. These theories have been subjected to critical analysis by American scholars, and some of the theories' weaknesses have been exposed. They have also been tested internationally to determine whether they apply to other Western countries and offer useful interpretations of the dynamics of welfare.

Unfortunately, the international evidence does not provide a great deal of support for any of these theories. First, despite the claims of the social conscience theorists, there is not much evidence to show that governments around the world give expression to the humanitarian instincts of their citizens. Indeed, many governments are brutal, oppressive, and quite uninterested in welfare. This is true not only of countries that are at an early stage of industrialization when it is claimed that humanitarian tendencies are weak, but also of nations that have achieved a high degree of industrialization. The idea that the former Soviet Union and other communist countries created extensive social programs because of a humanitarian impulse is countered even by sympathetic studies of social policy in these countries.[33] Although there are, of course, examples of governments that have enacted social legislation and introduced social programs that bring real benefits to ordinary people, it is unrealistic to characterize all governments as representing the collective humanitarian impulse of society.

The idea that industrialization has an internal logic that creates social welfare programs has been popular and has been verified by a major statistical study undertaken by Wilensky.[34] Comparing 64 countries, he claimed that industrialization is the primary causative factor in the genesis of welfare and that other factors are of little relevance. However, when the hypothesis is examined with reference to detailed historical trends, problems emerge. For example, government welfare programs were only introduced in Europe long after industrialization was well advanced. Another problem is that countries with similar levels of industrialization differ in the extent to which they create social programs. As was noted earlier, many experts believe that the United States is a welfare laggard, establishing less extensive welfare programs than other industrial countries. If industrialization gives rise to state welfare, why do similar welfare programs not emerge in all societies with a similar degree of industrialization? Ann Orloff and Theda Skocpol have examined this question by comparing welfare and industrialization in Massachusetts and England. While these regions had similar levels of industrialization at the turn of the century, welfare state programs emerged in Britain but not in Massachusetts.[35] Another study by James Midgley compared industrialization and welfare in Korea, Hong Kong, Singapore, and Taiwan (the "'four little tigers," or newly industrializing countries of East Asia).[36] The study was designed to test the relationship between industrialization and welfare. Midgley concluded that there was no clear pattern in the way government welfare programs emerged in these countries and little evidence that they were directly linked to industrial development.

The capitalist maintenance hypothesis also encounters difficulties when examined in the international context. Some scholars claim that international evidence supports this theory, but others disagree. Many have pointed out that the first social insurance programs in the world were introduced in Germany by Chancellor Count Otto von Bismarck specifically to undermine the labor movement and to placate workers. However, they fail to mention that this was achieved after fierce opposition from German aristocrats and business elites who did not share Von Bismarck's political foresight and skill.[37] Capitalist interests in many different countries have frequently opposed the introduction of the welfare state, and this hardly lends support to the idea that welfare programs are introduced to serve capitalist interests. As the Reagan and Thatcher administrations revealed, capitalists will try to abolish government welfare provision if they have the political prospect of doing so.[38]

Research has also showed that welfare programs in many countries are not in fact introduced by capitalists for conspiratorial purposes but instead are the result of the political struggles of working class people and their political representatives. In Britain and Sweden, working class movements, unions, and Left-wing intellectuals were able to forge coalitions with political elites and bureaucrats that resulted in the introduction of extensive social programs.[39] Business interests were generally hostile to the expansion of government social programs. Far from acting as the promoter of capitalist interests, the government functioned autonomously introducing welfare programs either at its own volition or under pressure from working-class organizations.

The international evidence suggests that current theories of the origins and functions of the American welfare state are still of limited explanatory usefulness. Many rely on a single cause interpretation and oversimplify what are very complex historical and political processes. Future research is likely to offer more cautious explanations in which a variety of causal factors are identified. It is also likely that more emphasis will be placed on actual political activities, on the ways different interest groups bring pressure to bear on governments, and on the role of beliefs and ideologies in social welfare. Current explanations are excessively deterministic and tend to reify commonplace events. Although it is true that wider social forces influence social welfare, they need to be examined with reference to actual processes and behaviors that affect the dynamics of welfare.

THE CRISIS OF THE WELFARE STATE

The idea that government should intervene to enhance the welfare of the population was widely accepted in the years after the Second World War. Political leaders, intellectuals, and ordinary citizens alike regarded the welfare state as a positive development. Although government welfare had some detractors, they were in a minority, and the liberal welfare consensus as it became known dominated American life for many years. In addition, many people accepted the idea that government should assume a larger responsibilities for welfare. When the Johnson administration's War on Poverty programs were created, they were generally well received.

However, by the 1970s, it became apparent that the welfare consensus was under strain. During the late 1960s, the negative rather than positive aspects of social programs were emphasized by critics from both the political left and right. These programs were frequently attacked for being punitive, meager, and supportive of the status quo. Piven and Cloward's study of public welfare led many scholars to believe that the welfare state was really a mechanism of capitalist manipulation and oppression. Many agreed with O'Connor that the welfare state could not indefinitely fulfill its twin functions of accumulation and legitimation. Not only is capitalism inherently unstable, experiencing frequent periods of recession and crisis, but the attempt to use welfare as a means of holding the system together is unworkable. As people demand more and more social programs, the accumulation function is impeded, and the state is unable to provide generous legitimation social benefits. This contradiction in the system eventually leads to a major fiscal crisis of the state, and causes the system to break down.

Thinkers on the political Right also attacked the welfare state. Noted economist Milton Friedman, who had been a long-standing opponent of social programs, became a media figure for his frequent assaults on government intervention, and, during the 1970s, the idea that the welfare state was damaging the economy gained currency. This idea was articulated by Harvard economist Martin Feldstein, whose statistical studies concluded that Social Security was having a negative impact on savings and economic investment.[40] In addition, it was argued that as social expenditures continued to rise, the tax burden would reach unacceptable levels. Apart from the negative economic effects of high taxation, it was argued that the continued expansion of government would eventually transform America into a socialist country.

The idea that the continued growth of the welfare state would increase the power of government and foster its unwelcome intrusion into the lives of ordinary people comported with a long-standing aversion to government intervention in American culture. It was fueled by Friedman's claim that the growth of the welfare state posed a greater threat to America's security than the Soviet Union. In an interview in *Newsweek* in 1983, he argued that the United States's huge tax burden, caused by the welfare state, was reducing the country's diplomatic and military effectiveness and would relegate the country to a position of little importance in the modern world.[41]

These ideas echoed Friedman's earlier claim that the welfare state was creating a huge central bureaucracy that would use its powers to curtail individual liberty. A similar argument was made by James Buchanan and other members of the Public Choice School who claimed that the welfare state did not function primarily to serve the needs of ordinary citizens but rather to perpetuate the interests of civil servants and politicians. It was also argued that the welfare state was impeding government's ability to promote the public interest. Highly organized interest groups had become dependent on government and had perpetuated the status quo at the expense of others. The welfare state had not only created an economic crisis but it had become ungovernable.[42]

Critics also claimed that the welfare state was having a negative affect on the attitudes and work habits of ordinary people. The increase in the numbers of people receiving AFDC during the 1960s and 1970s was linked to America's declining economic performance, falling productivity, and labor unrest. Many citizens came to believe that government programs were undermining beliefs about work and ambition. Hardworking taxpayers would have to support a growing multitude of lazy, irresponsible individuals living comfortably on welfare. Unless curtailed, welfare would sap the country's vitality and turn the American dream into a nightmare.

These attitudes were reinforced by severe economic difficulties during the 1970s. Attempts by governments to use the theories of John Maynard Keynes to stimulate the economy were unsuccessful. Although Keynes's ideas seemed to work during the 1930s, they did not have the required effect during the 1970s when inflation emerged as a major problem. Government spending designed to surmount recessionary trends not only failed to stimulate higher economic growth but appeared to fuel inflation. This resulted in *stagflation*, a new economic problem that government policy seemed powerless to counteract. In addition, in 1974 and again in 1979, the world economy experienced major oil shocks that dramatically increased energy costs and had harmful economic effects.

Although the welfare state could not be held responsible for the energy crisis, many attributed economic difficulties, the growth of bureaucracy, social discontent, and other problems to government social programs. The welfare state was widely believed to be in crisis, and instead of looking to government for solutions to the country's economic and social problems, many concluded that government was the cause of these problems. The Watergate scandal, America's weakened international influence, and the low popularity of Presidents Ford and Carter further undermined confidence in government. The stage was set for a new dispensation in which a strong leader would emerge to bring new ideas and policies to solve the nation's problems.

Ronald Reagan fulfilled this role. The president set about reducing government expenditures and retrenching the welfare state, which he blamed for the nation's ills. During his administration, social programs were severely cut. By the end of his first term, unemployment insurance had been reduced by 17 percent, child nutritional programs by 2 percent, food stamp expenditures by 14 percent, AFDC by 14 percent, and the Community Service Block Grant program by 37 percent.[43] Tax concessions to the wealthy and the increase in the federal deficit also weakened the welfare state. David Stockman, the president's budget director, approved of the deficit, claiming that it would put an effective brake on government social spending.

However, apart from reducing means-tested programs, the Reagan administration was not able to destroy the welfare state. In particular, it was not able to abolish the major, universal entitlement programs, such as Social Security, that are its cornerstone. Although the Reagan administration launched an attack on Social Security, it became apparent that this move was unpopular. During the 1984 presidential campaign, when Walter Mondale accused the Reagan administration of trying to abolish Social Security, the President reversed his position and declared his staunch support for the program.

The Reagan attack on the welfare state was also impeded by the rapid rise of unemployment in the early 1980s. Adopting Friedman's monetarist prescriptions to reduce inflation, high interest rates caused a dramatic slump in economic production. In 1982 alone, the growth rate fell by 3.2 percent, causing unemployment to rise by 4.5 million.[44] The perpetuation of high unemployment rates was politically risky, and accordingly, monetarist controls were relaxed. In addition, expenditures on unemployment compensation increased to provide support for the unemployed. The return of a Democratic majority in Congress contributed further to the slowdown in the implementation of the administration's antiwelfare agenda.

Although the welfare state survived the Reagan era, it has not been unscathed. Indeed, as a result of budget cuts, many government programs have been weakened. Staff morale has fallen and the effectiveness of services has been impeded. The budget deficit is sizable and many believe it needs to be significantly reduced if serious long-term economic problems are to be avoided. While many hoped that the election of President Clinton in 1992 would reverse the damage that had been done to the country's social programs, few believe that he has given high priority to social policy. In addition, there is a dearth of new proposals that can reinvigorate social policy and provide a basis for reconstructing the American welfare state. Despite the President's 1992 campaign promises, David Stoesz contends that he failed to provide a new rationale for social welfare.[45] In 1996, to make matters worse, the president signed into law the Personal Responsibility and Work Opportunity Act, which transferred responsibility for the administration of the federal government's AFDC program to the states and ended the entitlement to case assistance that was introduced during the New Deal. This law is widely viewed as an abrogation of the fundamental principles of the New Deal. At the same time, the problems of poverty, homelessness, crime, infant malnutrition, drug use, and inner-city violence continue to present major challenges. Accordingly, many believe that the crisis of the American welfare state has not been resolved.

The Welfare Crisis in International Context

During the 1980s, some social scientists compared the crisis of the American welfare state with developments in other countries, and many concluded that the other welfare states were also in trouble. This was particularly true of Britain. Britain had also encountered serious economic difficulties and widespread social discontent during the 1970s where stagflation, strikes, and popular discontent were also attributed to government social programs. As in the United States, the ideas of Milton Friedman and other radical Right-wing thinkers were widely accepted. The work of O'Connor as well as British Marxists such as Ian Gough were also believed to offer useful explanations of the crisis.[46] Paradoxically, few realized at the time that the writings of O'Connor and Friedman were very similar. Both writers attributed economic problems to the welfare state, and in their different ways, both regarded social programs as inimical to sustained economic growth.

While comparisons between Britain and the United States suggested that the welfare state was in crisis everywhere, more careful comparisons of other countries reached different conclusions. For example, Mishra found that countries such as Austria and Sweden, which had created social-corporatist welfare states, coped reasonably well with economic adversity.[47] Although these countries also faced economic difficulties, resistance to high taxes, and other problems, they kept unemployment low, maintained reasonably good rates of economic growth, and did not experience the high levels of poverty, homelessness, and other social problems that plagued Britain and the United States.

Comparative research has also demonstrated that many of the explanations of the welfare crisis, as well as arguments made against the welfare state by American critics, do not hold up when examined with reference to other societies. As was shown earlier in this chapter, the belief that high social expenditures are responsible for the economic problems facing the United States cannot be sustained when it is realized that the United States spends less on social welfare than most other industrial countries. Many countries which have higher rates of economic growth than the United States also spend more on welfare. Theodor Marmor, Jerry Mashaw, and Philip Harvey showed that Canada, France, Ireland, and Norway all had higher social expenditures and higher rates of economic growth than the United States during the 1970s. Social expenditures in Japan, which had the highest rate of economic growth of all the industrial countries, was only slightly lower than the United States.[48]

Similarly, the idea that the welfare state diminishes individual freedom is hard to support when compared with other countries. Despite its comprehensive welfare state, Sweden is a highly democratic society with strong traditions of local government. As Charles Andrian points out: "Local government in Sweden remains powerful. County and city governments retain fiscal independence [and] locally raised taxes finance health and educational programs."[49]

The finding that other countries have reasonably successful welfare states has important implications for American social policy. If other industrial countries can manage to provide adequate social services to their people without retarding economic development, and if they can improve the quality of life for their citizens, surely the United States, which has abundant human and natural resources, can do the same.

Although countries do not always learn from each other, a better knowledge of social policy in countries that are successful welfare states can help to solve domestic problems. By being more aware of developments in other parts of the world, more effective solutions to local problems may be found. Of course, this is not just a matter of transferring expertise. The introduction of social policies that will make a significant difference to the current crisis in welfare depends on a host of factors, including effective political leadership, popular support for government initiatives, and the ability of the nation's leaders to cooperate and to take a more inclusive view of social welfare. This, in turn, requires changes in the wider social and political ethos and a greater commitment to the common good.

CONCLUSION: PLANNING THE FUTURE OF THE WELFARE STATE

Although many social policy writers previously believed that government involvement in social welfare would continue to expand and that America would eventually become more like a European welfare state, most now accept that future government involvement in social welfare will be limited. As a result of the changes that have taken place since the early 1980s, many believe that the American welfare state has become more fragmented, less generous, and unable to respond to the country's pressing social problems. Others take a different position arguing that despite recent retrenchments, the welfare state has not been significantly altered. They insist that more radical cuts are needed if the economy is to be vigorous and if people are to be self-reliant and responsible. Yet, others believe that the changes that have taken place are appropriate. They claim that social expenditures were excessive and needed to be curtailed. Recent cutbacks do not amount to a crisis in welfare but to a much needed corrective that will ensure that government social programs are appropriate to the country's needs and fiscal abilities.

These very different interpretations reflect different beliefs about the future of the American welfare state. Although some are very pessimistic, believing that poverty and deprivation will increase and that government will be unable to meet the social needs of its citizens, others are more optimistic claiming that social programs will continue to provide appropriate levels of social provision. Others contend that new ideas are needed to enhance the relevance of the American welfare state to current social and economic realities. When the welfare state emerged in the 1930s, social, demographic and economic conditions were very different from today. If social welfare is to remain viable, it must adapt to these changes. As was noted earlier, there is a dearth of new ideas that can invigorate the American welfare state. The Clinton administration and the leadership of the Democratic Party have not formulated proposals that can provide a viable basis for a reconstructed welfare state. Despite the president's earlier promise to revitalize American social policy, no new paradigm has emerged.[50]

If the fundamental principles of the welfare state are to be safeguarded, social policy experts must plan for the future. Instead of being defensive, they need to put forward new ideas that can win the support of political leaders and the electorate. Fortunately, as shown elsewhere in this book, numerous proposals for reconceptualizing the American welfare state have been formulated. In addition to homegrown initiatives, some have been influenced by international developments. All can stimulate new debates about the future of the American welfare state.

One idea that can form the basis for future planning is that the government should not be the primary provider of social services but that it should function as the facilitator and coordinator of welfare activities. As was noted earlier, proponents of this approach are known as welfare pluralists. They believe that social welfare should not depend exclusively on government but on a mix of activities that include personal effort, the family, community support networks, voluntary organization, and the private market. A future welfare state should institutionalize these diverse sources of welfare and ensure that they function effectively.

Of course, the American welfare state is already quite pluralistic in nature. However, the services provided by the informal, voluntary, and commercial sectors are haphazard, and if a reconstructed welfare state based on pluralistic principles is to emerge, a more active planning and coordinating role for government will be required. Advocates of welfare pluralism such as Neil and Barbara Gilbert argue that the government needs to be more effective in fulfilling this *enabling function*.[51] They believe that the government should not provide social services itself but actively assume responsibility for facilitating, coordinating, and planning social programs. It should also ensure that social welfare objectives are met. Some proponents of welfare pluralism such as Richard Rose and Arthur Gould have argued that countries such as Japan, which have effectively institutionalized a pluralist approach, can serve as a model for other industrial nations.[52] They point out that the high standard of welfare that the country enjoys has not come about through extensive government social programs but through the government's ability to facilitate voluntary services, strengthen family and community support systems, and encourage employers to provide for their workers. By using this approach, the Japanese government has not only managed to keep social spending low but ensured that its citizens have a high standard of living.

Another approach to future welfare planning is based on the idea that social policies need to be integrated more positively with economic development. It was noted earlier that social programs have been criticized for being a drain on the economy and for maintaining people in a state of unproductive dependence on government. Although claims about the negative effects of social expenditures have been exaggerated, it is true that few social welfare programs are designed to contribute positively to economic development. Instead, most are concerned with remedial and maintenance oriented functions. Critics argue that millions of people today are beneficiaries of a variety of social programs that transfer resources from the economy to support their consumption needs. It would be better if these resources were used in ways that met social needs and, at the same time, produced a rate of return to the economy. Proponents of this *developmental* or *productivist* approach to social welfare believe that social policies that serve these functions will be more readily supported by the electorate and political leaders who have become increasingly critical of the welfare state. If it can be shown that social programs contribute to the economy instead of detracting from it, they are more likely to garner popular support.

One advocate of this approach is the social worker Michael Sherraden who has proposed that the government encourage the accumulation of assets among low income groups. Poor people should not only be exhorted but assisted to save through the creation of individual development accounts. Payments made into these accounts will be matched with government contributions and the savings accumulated may be used to pay for education, housing and other social needs.[53]

Another example of the developmental approach is the use of skills training and job placement programs for school dropouts, AFDC recipients, and disabled people. A variety of programs have been established to assist these people acquire the education and skills they need to find remunerative employment and become productive citizens. However, employment programs are not widely used and often they are poorly administered. In addition, they often stigmatize the recipients and as recent developments in the United States reveal, they are being cynically used to reduce the numbers of people receiving welfare. This is unfortunate because other countries have used this approach to reintegrate needy people into the economy. In an interesting international study, Desmond King showed how badly American and British job training and placement programs compare with those of Germany and the Scandinavian countries where activist labor market policies are effectively used to promote employment among these groups.[54] The experiences of these countries could be helpful in ensuring that employment training and placement programs are more effectively used in the future.

American social policymakers can also learn from the experiences of many Third World countries, which have long sought to promote developmental social welfare.[55] Because of their overriding need for economic development, the governments of many of these countries have given priority to programs that contribute to economic growth. While many still retain conventional remedial and maintenance oriented programs, priority is given to programs that promote human capital, social capital, and productive employment or self-employment.[56] The value of the developmental approach was emphasized at the United Nations *World Summit on Social Development* that was held in Copenhagen in 1995. The summit, which was attended by many international leaders, reiterated the need for new ideas that can address the world's pressing social problems. The developmental approach may prove to offer a viable basis for planning a future reconstructed welfare state.[57]

◆ ◆ ◆ *Discussion Questions* ◆ ◆ ◆

1. Discuss some of the ways in which international research in social welfare can inform social policy in the United States.

2. Examine the major methodological problems facing social policy investigators who wish to undertake international research.

3. Give some examples of how international evidence can be used to support or refute criticisms of the American welfare state.

4. Describe one or more typologies of welfare states. How useful are these typologies for international social welfare research?

5. What do you understand by the term *American welfare exceptionalism?* Do you think this term accurately describes social welfare in the United States relative to other countries?

6. Discuss theories of the origins and functions of the welfare state. Which of these theories do you think most accurately describes the emergence of social welfare in the United States?

7. Examine the international evidence concerning the "crisis of the welfare state," and tell whether you think the evidence supports the idea of an international welfare crisis.

8. Discuss some of the proposals that have been made for the future planning of the American welfare state. Which of these proposals do you favor?

Notes

1. M. C. Hokenstad, S. K. Khinduka, and James Midgley, *Profiles in International Social Work* (Washington, DC: National Association of Social Workers, 1992) provided accounts of social work from many different countries that show that social work is now well established as a profession in different parts of the world. The book urged social workers to share ideas and experiences and to enhance the international exchange of information.
2. The International Committee of the Council on Social Work Education has actively promoted the inclusion of international content in the curriculum of schools of social work. For a discussion of how this may be achieved, see Lynne M. Healy, *Introducing International Development Content in the Social Work Curriculum* (Washington, DC: National Association of Social Workers, circa 1991).
3. The term *normative* refers to statements that relate to values and beliefs about social policy and that assess policies as being either being "good" or "bad" for society.
4. Organization for Economic Cooperation and Development, (OECD), *Social Expenditures, 1960–1990* (Paris: OECD, 1985).
5. Hollis Chenery, Montek Ahluwahlia, C. L. G. Bell, John H. Duloy, and Richard Jolly, *Redistribution with Growth* (Oxford, England: Oxford University Press, 1974).
6. James Midgley and Peter Simbi, "Promoting a Developmental Focus in the Community Organization Curriculum: Relevance of the African Experience," *Journal of Social Work Education*, 29 (1993), pp. 269–278. The authors argue that African community development can inform social workers trying to organize community-based antipoverty programs in the United States.
7. In 1996, the federal government enacted the Personal Responsibility and Work Opportunity Act which replaced the AFDC program with a program known as Temporary Assistance to Needy Families (TANF).
8. Harold L. Wilensky, "Introduction" to Harold L. Wilensky and Charles M. Lebeaux, *Industrial Society and Social Welfare* (New York: Free Press, 1965), pp. xvi–xvii; Harold L. Wilensky, *The Welfare State and Equality* (Berkeley: University of California Press, 1975); Theodor R. Marmor, Jerry L. Mashaw, and Philip L. Harvey, *America's Misunderstood Welfare State* (New York: Basic Books, 1990); Bruce Janssen, *The Reluctant Welfare State: A History of American Social Welfare Policies* (Pacific Grove, CA: Brookes/Cole Publishing Co., 1993); Theda Skocpol, "America's Incomplete Welfare State: The Limits of New Deal Reforms and Origins of the Present Crisis," in Martin Rein, Gosta Esping-Andersen and Lee Rainwater (Eds.), *Stagnation and Renewal in Social Policy* (Armonk, NY: M. E. Sharpe, 1987), pp. 35–58; Edwin Amenta and Theda Skocpol, "Taking Exception: Explaining the Distinctiveness of American Public Policies During the Last Century," in Francis C. Castles (Ed.), *The Comparative History of Public Policy* (New York: Oxford University Press, 1989), pp. 292–333; Arnold J. Heidenheimer, Hugh Heclo, and Carolyn Teich Adams, *Comparative Public Policy* (New York: St. Martin's Press, 1975).
9. Harold L. Wilensky, "Introduction" to Harold L. Wilensky and Charles M. Lebeaux, *Industrial Society and Social Welfare*, p. xvi–xvii.
10. Ibid.
11. Richard M. Titmuss, *Social Policy: An Introduction* (London: Allen and Unwin, 1971).
12. Norman Furniss and Timothy Tilton, *The Case for the Welfare State* (Bloomington, IN: Indiana University Press, 1977).
13. Ramesh Mishra, *The Welfare State in Crisis* (Brighton, England: Wheatsheaf Books, 1984).
14. Gosta Esping-Andersen, *Three Worlds of Welfare Capitalism* (Cambridge, England: Polity Press, 1990).
15. Norman Ginsburg, *Divisions of Welfare: A Critical Introduction to Comparative Social Policy* (London: Sage, 1992).
16. These typologies seek to classify the social welfare systems of the industrial societies and do not refer to the developing countries of the Third World. Attempts to construct comprehensive typologies that include the developing countries are still preliminary. See James Midgley, "Models of Welfare and Social Planning in Third World Countries," in Brij Mohan (Ed.), *New Horizons in Social Welfare and Policy* (Cambridge, MA: Schenkman, 1985), pp. 89–108; Stewart MacPherson and James

Midgley, *Comparative Social Policy and the Third World* (New York: St. Martin's Press, 1987).

17. Edwin Amenta and Theda Skocpol, "Taking Exception: Explaining the Distinctiveness of American Public Policies During the Last Century," in Francis C. Castles (Ed.), *The Comparative History of Public Policy* (New York: Oxford University Press, 1989), pp. 292–333.
18. Wilensky's comparative analysis of 64 countries rated the United State high in education and environmental protection but stated that this was at the expense of traditional social programs. See Wilensky, *The Welfare State and Equality*. See also Arnold J. Heidenheimer, Hugh Heclo, and Carolyn Teich Adams, *Comparative Public Policy* (New York: St. Martin's Press, 1975), p. 258.
19. In 1975, Wilensky (Ibid p. 105) noted that the United States "allocates a larger fraction of its total welfare spending to pensions that any of the twenty two richest nations [in the world]." However, more recent expenditure data from the OECD show that while pension expenditures remain comparatively high, the United States is by no means a world leader. See Organization for Economic Cooperation and Development (OECD) *Social Expenditure*, 1960–1990.
20. Theda Skocpol, *Protecting Soldiers and Mothers: The Political Origins of Social Policy in the United States* (Cambridge, MA: Harvard University Press, 1992).
21. Robert Pinker, *The Idea of Welfare* (London, Heinemann, 1979).
22. M. A. Jones, The *Australian Welfare State: Growth Crisis and Change* (Sydney, Australia: Allen and Unwin, 1980); Terry Carney and Peter Hanks, *Social Security in Australia* (Melbourne: Oxford University Press, 1994).
23. Organization for Economic Cooperation and Development, (OECD), *Social Expenditure, 1960–1990* (Paris: OECD, 1985).
24. See Martin Rein and Lee Rainwater (Eds.), *Public/Private Interplay in Social Protection* (Armonk, NY: M. E. Sharpe, 1986); Sheila Kamerman, "The Mixed Economy of Welfare." *Social Work*, 29 (1983), pp. 5–11; David Stoesz, "A Theory of Social Welfare" *Social Work*, 34 (1989), pp. 101–107; Neil Gilbert and Barbara Gilbert, *The Enabling State: Modern Welfare Capitalism in America* (New York: Oxford University Press, 1989); Richard Rose, "Common Goals But Different Roles: The State's Contribution to the Welfare Mix," in R. Rose and R. Shiratori (Eds.), *The Welfare State East and West* (New York: Oxford University Press, 1986), pp. 13–39).
25. An example of the former approach is Hugh Heclo, *Modern Social Policies in Britain and Sweden* (New Haven, CT: Yale University Press, 1974), while an example of the latter is Christopher Leman, "Patterns of Policy Development: Social Security in the United States and Canada." *Public Policy*, 25 (1987), pp. 261–291. See also Theda Skocpol, "America's Incomplete Welfare State: The Limits of New Deal Reforms and Origins of the Present Crisis," in Rein, Esping-Andersen, and Rainwater (Eds.), *Stagnation and Renewal in Social Policy*, pp. 35–58.
26. Charles S. Prigmore and Charles R. Atherton, *Social Welfare Policy: Analysis and Formulation* (Lexington, MA: Heath, 1979).
27. See Prigmore and Atherton, Ibid; Robert Morris, *Rethinking Social Welfare* (New York: Longman, 1986); Frank R. Breul and Steven J. Diner (Eds.), *Compassion and Responsibility: Readings in the History of Social Welfare Policy in the United States* (Chicago: University of Chicago Press, 1980); Ralph Dolgoff and Donald Feldstein, *Understanding Social Welfare* (New York: Longman, 1980).
28. Prigmore and Atherton, *Social Welfare Policy*, p. 10–19.
29. Wilensky and Lebeaux, *Industrial Society and Social Welfare*; Wilensky, *The Welfare State and Equality*; and Gaston V. Rimlinger, *Welfare Policy and Industrialization in Europe, America and Russia* (New York: Wiley, 1971).
30. Frances Fox Piven and Richard Cloward, *Regulating the Poor* (New York: Pantheon, 1971).
31. Mimi Abramovitz, *Regulating the Lives of Women* (Boston, MA: South End Press, 1989).
32. James O'Connor, *The Fiscal Crisis of the State* (New York: St. Martin's Press, 1973).
33. Victor George and Nick Manning, *Socialism, Social Welfare and the Soviet Union* (London: Routledge and Kegan Paul, 1980); Bob Deacon, *Social Policy and Socialism: The Struggle for Socialist Relations of Welfare* (London: Pluto Press, 1983); Bob Deacon (Ed.), *The New Eastern Europe: Social Policy Past, Present and Future* (London: Sage Publications, 1992).
34. Wilensky, *The Welfare State and Equality*.
35. Ann Shola Orloff and Theda Skocpol, "Why Not Equal Protection: Explaining the Politics of Public

Social Spending in Britain 1900–1911 and the United States, 1880s–1920," *American Sociological Review,* 49 (1988), pp. 732–744.

36. James Midgley, "Industrialization and Welfare: The Case of the Four Little Tigers," *Social Policy and Administration* 20 (1988), pp. 225–238. A different perspective on the role of industrialization on the development of social programs in the developing countries is provided by Christine Cockburn, "The Role of Social Security in Development," *International Social Security Review,* 33 (1986), pp. 337–358.
37. Rimlinger, *Welfare Policy and Industrialization in Europe, America and Russia.*
38. Howard Glennerster and James Midgley (Eds.), *The Radical Right and the Welfare State: An International Assessment* (Savage, MD: Barnes and Noble, 1991).
39. Walter Korpi, *The Democratic Class Struggle* (London: Routledge, 1983); John Stephens, *The Transition from Capitalism to Socialism* (London: Macmillan, 1979).
40. Martin Feldstein, "Social Security, Induced Retirement and Aggregate Accumulation." Journal of Political Economy 82 (1974), pp. 905–926. However, other studies have questioned Feldstein's conclusions. See Henry Aaron and Lawrence W. Thompson, "Social Security and the Economists," in Edward D. Berkowitz (Ed.), *Social Security After 50: Successes and Failures* (Westport, CT: Greenwood Press, 1987), pp. 79–100.
41. Cited in Charles F. Andrian, *Social Policies in Western Industrial Societies* (Berkeley, CA: Institute for International Studies, 1985), p. 204.
42. James Buchanan and Gordon Tullock, *The Calculus of Consent* (Ann Arbor: University of Michigan Press, 1962); James Buchanan and R. E. Wagner, *Democracy in Deficit* (New York: Academic Press, 1977). See also Marmor, Mashaw, and Harvey, *America's Misunderstood Welfare State.*
43. James Midgley, "Society, Social Policy and the Ideology of Reaganism," *Journal of Sociology and Social Welfare,* 19 (1992), pp. 13–28.
44. Ibid., p. 25.
45. David Stoesz, *Small Change: Domestic Policy Under the Clinton Presidency* (New York: Longman, 1996).
46. Ian Gough, *The Political Economy of the Welfare State* (London: Macmillan, 1979).
47. Mishra, *The Welfare State in Crisis;* Ramesh Mishra, *The Welfare State in Capitalist Society* (Hemel Hempstead, England: Harvester Wheatsheaf, 1990).
48. Marmor, Mashaw, and Harvey, *America's Misunderstood Welfare State,* pp. 62–64.
49. Charles F. Andrian, *Social Policies in Western Industrial Societies* (Berkeley, CA: Institute for International Studies, 1985), p. 24.
50. Stoesz, *Small Change.*
51. Gilbert and Gilbert, *The Enabling State.*
52. Richard Rose, "Common Goals But Different Roles: The State's Contribution to the Welfare Mix," in R. Rose and R. Shiratori (Eds.), *The Welfare State East and West,* pp. 13–39; and Arthur Gould, *Capitalist Welfare Systems: A Comparison of Japan, Britain and Sweden* (New York: Longman, 1993).
53. Michael Sherraden, *Assets and the Poor: A New American Welfare Policy* (Armonk, NY: M. E. Sharpe, 1991).
54. Desmond King, *Actively Seeking Work? The Politics of Unemployment and Welfare Policy in the United States and Great Britain* (Chicago: University of Chicago Press, 1995).
55. James Midgley, "Towards a Developmental Model of Social Policy: Relevance of the Third World Experience," *Journal of Sociology and Social Welfare,* 23(1), pp. 59–74.
56. These three approaches to ensuring that social programs contribute to economic development are explained in more detail in James Midgley, *Social Development: The Developmental Perspective in Social Welfare* (Thousand Oaks, CA: Sage Publications, 1995).
57. These ideas have to some extent been examined by American social policy writers, but they need to be more systematically presented if they are to form the basis for future social welfare planning. See David Stoesz, "The Functional Conception of Social Welfare," *Social Work,* 33 (1988), pp. 58–59; David Stoesz and Howard Karger, *Reconstructing the American Welfare State* (Lanham, MD: Rowan and Littlefield, 1993).

CHAPTER 19

Reconceptualizing the American Welfare State

This chapter examines the need to restructure the American welfare state so that it can better respond to the changing political, economic, and social forces facing the United States. First, we situate the American welfare state within a broad continuum of welfare states. Second, we base restructuring on a public philosophy of "radical pragmatism" and propose five principles necessary for real welfare reform—greater economic productivity, strengthening the family, increased social cohesion, the strengthening of community, and greater social choice. Finally, we present programs designed to make the welfare state more responsive to the real needs of both the working and the nonworking poor and, at the same time, more congruent with the new economic realities of the United States.

Although this chapter includes concrete proposals for restructuring the American welfare state, it does not represent a finished product. Much of the framework presented here is derived from earlier work we have done.[1] Moreover, some of the ideas in this chapter (e.g., the restructuring of public assistance through a work requirement and the establishment of a national service corps) have been enacted during the Clinton presidency. As such, the ideas in this chapter are offered not as a "complete" proposal for welfare reform but rather as a useful starting point for a discussion and debate on the future of the American welfare state.

THE GLOBAL ECONOMY AND THE AMERICAN WELFARE STATE

Welfare states grew steadily during the relatively stable economic period of the 1950s to the early 1970s. By the mid–1970s, however, most industrial economies began to experience high inflation, high rates of unemployment, sluggish economic growth, and unacceptably high levels of taxation. During this difficult period, Western governments were forced to reassess their overall economic strategies, including the resources allocated to welfare activities. Hence, beginning in the early 1970s, most Western governments either cut welfare programs or arrested their growth.[2]

All Western nations are experiencing a crisis rooted in the need to compete in a new global economy.[3] According to conservative policy analysts, national survival in the new economic order can be achieved only if government cuts costs and becomes more efficient. In addition, they argue for the creation of government policies that encourage the accumulation of the capital necessary for investment, industrial modernization, and corporate growth. Conservatives maintain that this precondition for economic survival occurs only when government freezes or lowers personal and corporate tax rates. The subsequent loss of tax revenue, however, often results in heavy governmental debt, cuts in all services (including social services), a deterioration of the infrastructure, and myriad social problems.

The general emphasis on efficiency and profitability also leads to industrial reorganization, which in turn leads to rapidly changing production technologies that displace workers and result in plant closures and downsizing. These policy changes are exacerbated as cuts in governmental services coincide with the increased demand for social services by victims of the global-based economic changes. Hence, Western industrial nations face a two-pronged assault on the welfare state: (1) the impact of the global economy on government spending, and (2) an increase in the use of social services by workers dislocated by global economic changes.

Most Western industrialized nations pursued liberal social policies after World War II.[4] In the United States, most presidents since Franklin D. Roosevelt tolerated—and in some cases even promoted—a liberal social welfare agenda. Although the general belief in the United States was that people should adjust to the market rather than the other way around, the social consensus also dictated that human capital should be strengthened in order to make people more economically competitive.[5] Thus, social welfare programs were developed to increase human capital in education, employment, health, and housing. The belief was that as human capital increased, the dependent person (or at least his or her children) would eventually compete in a free market. For those who could not compete because of serious deficits (handicaps, old age), a system of social insurance or public assistance was developed to ensure a minimum level of subsistence. Thus, the dual focus of the welfare state was (1) to create programs to increase human capital and (2) to create programs to subsidize people unable to participate in the workforce. Even conservative presidents like Richard Nixon acquiesced to this welfare consensus.

A more conservative welfare consensus emerged by the mid–1980s. This new consensus called for: (1) minimal welfare benefits; (2) the abolition of universal social welfare benefits in favor of rigid means-tested programs; (3) a no-growth approach to the welfare state while retaining (albeit curtailed) fundamental programs that affect the elderly and the employed; (4) a retreat from governmental social welfare obligations in the belief that primary welfare functions should revert back to the family; (5) the privatization of social services; (6) a continuation of governmental funding for services combined with contracting out to the private sector the responsibility for delivering those services; and (7) an emphasis on economically rationalizing social services. In effect, New Right ideologues argued that the liberal welfare state was a failed social experiment.[6] This conservative argument was given some credence by the nagging federal debt.

In order to combat the conservative position, it is necessary to develop welfare programs that increase rather than restrict economic productivity (thereby also lowering the federal debt). Despite the difficulty in creating such programs, social policies must be developed that address the new economic realities and the shifting consensus around welfare issues. In order to accomplish these aims, new principles must be developed to guide social policy.

FIVE PRINCIPLES FOR WELFARE REFORM

Since its inception in the 1935 Social Security Act, the American welfare state has been based on a public philosophy of welfare liberalism. This philosophy holds that the state has the obligation to extend rights of economic citizenship through deploying governmental social programs. As has been the case in northern Europe, a full-fledged welfare state assures basic goods and services—employment, income, housing, health care, and personal social services—through universal programs that are funded through progressive taxation.

However ideal this configuration, events of the past two decades demonstrate its increasing irrelevance in the American context. The demise of welfare liberalism was signaled with Ronald Reagan's election to the presidency in 1980 and the subsequent, centrist-conservative administrations of George Bush and Bill Clinton. Programmatically, federal legislation has begun to deconstruct the

American welfare state. Catastrophic health insurance, enacted in 1988, was repealed the following year, the first retraction of a social insurance program in the history of the American welfare state. In 1996, Bill Clinton shocked liberals by signing the Personal Responsibility and Work Opportunity Act, ending the 60-year income entitlement to poor families. Further devolution of public assistance programs to the states and the prospect of restructuring social insurances, particularly Medicare and Social Security, are indications that the American welfare state is being dissembled. Exactly what form it will assume is unknown; however, it seems certain that new social entitlements inaugurated by the federal government are unlikely.

Accompanying federal retreat from poverty, circumstances of the working- and welfare-poor have deteriorated. An underclass has emerged in the United States, a social phenomenon that conservatives have cleverly used to throttle liberals who have advocated extending social entitlements. Finally, the social and economic circumstances of working- and middle-class Americans has become increasingly precarious. As opportunities have stagnated along with wages, more affluent Americans have shown an ugly streak. Punitive initiatives around immigration and affirmative action have been approved by voters in California, and the retraction of welfare assistance to legal immigrants has been lauded by many elected officials. The rapid deterioration of public support for welfare programs compels those concerned about social justice to rethink the traditional philosophical basis of social policy.

Orienting a new social agenda in pragmatism offers two advantages. First, it distinguishes a social policy initiative from earlier forms, particularly the welfare liberalism that has driven the conservative assault on social programs. Second, pragmatism is a peculiarly American philosophy, one that complements the national culture. Approaching the end of the century, American philosophers are reviving pragmatism and applying it to the postindustrial context.[7] In calling for a "prophetic pragmatism," Cornel West notes the relevance of the philosophy to progressive action: "Prophetic pragmatism calls for reinvigoration of a sane, sober, and sophisticated intellectual life in America and for regeneration of social forces empowering the disadvantaged, degraded, and dejected. It rejects the faddish cynicism and fashionable conservatism rampant in the intelligentsia and general populace."[8] Although pragmatism can reawaken moral thought and propel social action, given present circumstances, it must be more "radical" than "prophetic."

Radical pragmatism orients social policy around five themes: (1) increasing economic productivity, (2) strengthening the family, (3) increasing social cohesion, (4) strengthening the community, and (5) greater social choice. By reconstructing social programs around these values, the American welfare state can be made more congruent both with domestic demands and with international developments. By exploiting the capacities of capitalism, the state, and the nonprofit sector—singly and in tandem—radical pragmatism provides opportunities in social progress that are more robust and dynamic than the bureaucratic programs associated with the liberal welfare state at the same time being more responsible and caring than the void that has accompanied conservative prescriptions for welfare reform.

A post-New Deal welfare strategy must demythologize socially held beliefs about human nature and welfare. For example, many liberals believe that if given a chance all poor people will choose to work. Some liberals also argue that the underclass has the same values as the middle class, except that they are poor. These notions are too simplistic to be a sound basis for social policy. Those in poverty differ as much as nonwelfare populations; some of the poor will eagerly exploit opportunities to raise themselves out of poverty, while others will not. Any welfare initiative that establishes a single policy for *all* poor people will inevitably prove unsuccessful. Therefore, welfare policies must be developed that consider the differences in human nature and, where appropriate, provide positive incentives. In short, a post-New Deal welfare philosophy must incorporate a realistic assessment of the capacity of the labor market to provide a sufficient number of high-paying jobs, while at the same time, deal in a more sophisticated manner with the idea of human nature. As part of that reexamination, realistic expectations about the welfare state must be developed, as well as valid benchmarks for measuring the success of social programs.

Increasing Economic Productivity

To reestablish the legitimacy of the welfare state it is necessary to demonstrate how social programs can contribute positively to the nation's productivity. In the early decades of the post–World War II period, the federal government grew dramatically, making it a significant player in the national economy. However, government receipts as a percentage of the gross national product have stagnated during the past two decades.[9] Even more disturbing, continued expansion of unchecked entitlement spending threatens to crowd out discretionary programs. As the Kerrey-Danforth Entitlement Commission reported:

> In 2012, unless appropriate policy changes are made in the interim, projected outlays for entitlements and interest on the national debt will consume all tax revenues collected by the federal government. In 2030, unless appropriate policy changes are made in the interim, projected spending for Medicare, Medicaid, and Federal employee retirement programs alone will consume all tax revenues collected by the Federal Government.[10]

Social advocates have recognized that the expansion of social programs requires a robust economy, but they have yet to integrate these programs fully with the nation's economic requirements. After decades of aversion to reciprocal welfare arrangements, social planners must go well beyond welfare-to-work initiatives in reconstructing social welfare. Although the Family Support Act of 1988 broke new ground by including "transitional benefits"—child care, Medicaid, transportation allowances—for a year after a welfare mother gains employment, the question remained as to why poor women should have to be on AFDC in order to obtain benefits that most people in the workforce take for granted. That welfare recipients would be perceived as advantaged left the public seething about public assistance benefits. Subsequently, the 1996 welfare reform legislation terminated AFDC as an open-ended entitlement for poor families, capping expenditures and devolving the program to the states. Heads of households on public aid have a five-year lifetime limit on receipt of assistance, and the states have the prerogative of instituting time limits of less than two years. Thus, if advocates of the poor were unwilling to relate public welfare to economic productivity by integrating recipients into the labor market, elected officials would do just that—and with a vengeance.

Relating welfare to productivity takes social policy in a new direction. Assuring the working poor of basic benefits should become a priority of social welfare policy. For example, the implementation of a "minimum benefit package" to complement the minimum wage would demonstrate how social programs are value workers' performance. Universalizing benefits such as health care and child care for all those who participate in the labor market is not only justifiable; it also shows middle-income workers that social programs enhance the nation's economic standing.

Although America's high productivity in the 1950s and 1960s allowed it to subsidize a large portion of its workforce, this keen technological edge has been reduced and with it the capacity of the economy to subsidize a large number of nonproductive citizens. To reassert the legitimacy of the welfare state, policymakers must create welfare programs that encourage productivity rather than dependency. The resentment of hardworking and financially strapped citizens toward welfare may eventually be overcome once recipients are seen as contributing to the economy.

Strengthening the Family

The American family is undergoing profound stress as a result of changing economic and social conditions. For example, two incomes are generally necessary to ensure a family middle-class status; yet at the same time, good-quality day care is difficult to find. Fears that their children will fall victim to drug or alcohol abuse or to teenage pregnancy or that they will drop out of school adds to the difficulties experienced by many American families. But when vulnerable families turn to social programs, the essential benefits are absent.

Social welfare policy must support the American family rather than tear it apart; yet welfare programs have sometimes the opposite. Prior to its repeal by the 1996 welfare reform act, the AFDC program had been indicted by liberals and conservatives alike for contributing to family disintegration. The percentage of unmarried teenage mothers had risen so rapidly that as long ago as 1984 it was triple of what it had been 25 years before.[11] Tragically, the relationship between public assistance and family breakup was most evident in minority communities where single-parent households were becoming the norm and welfare was quickly replacing a wage earner as the source of family income.

In the past, liberals had great difficulty establishing a national family policy because of conservatives' fear that it would lead to governmental intrusion in family life.[12] For example, problems in the very definition of *family* plagued liberal attempts to develop a family policy, as evidenced by the political fiasco of President Jimmy Carter's call for a White House Conference on the Family. In a dramatically changing social landscape, an exact configuration of family policy is hard to come by. Richard Louv has provided a useful perspective on this dilemma. For Louv, family policy should seek to support the "web" that keeps families from falling into the safety net of government welfare programs. Some of these family supports would be more generous maternity and sick leave, an increase in high-quality and affordable day care, full medical coverage for all families, an increase in after-school and latchkey programs, and adequate unemployment insurance benefits.[13] By carefully enforcing profamily policies in the workplace, the schools, and lead the community, much can be done for families without relying on onerous welfare programs.[14]

For intact families, basic needs such as shelter can no longer be ignored. Homeownership is becoming a dim prospect for millions of American families as skyrocketing prices outpace income (see Chapter 16). For poor families unable to purchase or rent a home, the prospect is even bleaker. By the late 1980s, the Congressional Budget Office reported that 84 percent of low-income renter families—more than 11 million households—complained of problems of high-cost, substandard, or overcrowded housing.[15] Despite the crisis in affordable housing, in 1996 President Clinton signed a housing bill that, for the first time, added *no* new housing units for the poor.[16] It comes as no surprise, then, that an increasing number of the homeless are not single aberrant men and women but intact families with children. Clearly, basic supports for vulnerable families must be a priority of any social policy.

Increasing Social Cohesion

The interaction between social classes that occurred during the late 1960s has diminished since the ebbing of the Civil Rights movement and the abolition of the military draft. Moreover, the belief in a collective social entity, in which groups accept their interdependence on each other and on society, has also weakened. In effect, the narcissistic pursuit of self-interest that characterized the Reagan and Bush years has come to symbolize the loss of national direction in a highly material, consumer-driven culture. Former Secretary of Labor Robert Reich has gone so far as to suggest that technically well-trained and affluent professionals are "seceding" from their economic, political, and social obligations to American society.[17] The lack of social integration and the increased separation of the classes clearly contributes to the reemergence of racism as a potent force in American political life.

Any new conception of social policy must expand on the idea of social obligation between social classes to include those who are better off. Upper- and middle-income groups should be encouraged, through economic incentives or appeals to altruism, to fulfill their social obligation toward the less fortunate in ways more meaningful than simply paying taxes. Traditionally, the "progressive" part of progressivism has referred to the expectation that the wealthy would be better able to pay for public services than those less well off (hence the origin of progressive taxation). But leaving the obligation at taxes alone is insufficient, particularly when the rich dodge their responsibility to pay their fair share. Even if the wealthy paid a greater portion of their income in taxes, that would address only the economic disparities in society. Public policy must also reinforce social integration. The civic-mindedness of both the poor and the well-to-do is essential for both democratic government and a free society. Recent Congressional approval of a voluntary national service program, Americorps, reflects the concern of many that social obligation is not a responsibility of the poor alone.[18]

Strengthening the Community

The deterioration of America's inner-city communities is obvious even to the casual observer. The decay in physical infrastructures such as schools, roads, housing, and communications has reached crisis proportions in many American cities. This disintegration in the physical infrastructure corresponds with a decay in the human capital of inner-city communities. High crime rates (involving increasingly younger professional criminals), epidemic rates of drug and alcohol abuse, the proliferation of crack houses, the high incidence of teenage pregnancies, and a dramatic growth in the number of long-term unemployables characterize much of America's urban landscape. These problems have resulted in many inner-city areas becoming a no-man's-land, where even the police are afraid to patrol. Not surprisingly, the communities hit hardest by these problems are the ones with the least resources to combat them.

Except for those cities favored by the Clinton administration's Empowerment Zone initiative, many states and cities have been left to compensate for the absence of federal leadership in community development by establishing their own programs, often with the assistance of nonprofit groups.[19] Unfortunately, these preliminary excursions into community development are inadequately supported because of the social and economic characteristics of many disadvantaged communities. The deterioration of poor communities has been so profound that the term *underclass* is employed with increasing frequency by social commentators. A consensus is also emerging around the realization that efforts to combat chronic unemployment, welfare dependency, family disintegration, and social disorganization will be ineffectual without a comprehensive approach that reinforces community institutions.[20] The restoration of social institutions in poor communities must be a priority of future social policy. Moreover, social policy must incorporate nonprofit voluntary agencies to restore the institutional base of poor communities.

Greater Social Choice

Since World War II, there has been a slow progression in the choices available to beneficiaries of social programs in the United States. The GI Bill offered returning veterans a choice of educational providers. Significantly, African Americans used their GI benefits to a greater extent than other groups.[21] Medicaid, enacted during the War on Poverty, provided poor people with access to health care they had previously lacked.[22] By the 1980s, Medicaid recipients were using health services at the same rate as their middle-class counterparts. Section 8 of the 1974 Housing and Community Development Act offered thousands of poor people the opportunity to escape the ghettos of public housing.[23]

Citing benefits such as cost-effectiveness, social integration, and geographic mobility, the President's Commission on Privatization concluded that "vouchers are a workable and preferable means of assisting low-income households to obtain housing."[24] Vouchers have also been advanced as a way of making public education more responsive to the needs of disadvantaged children,[25] with Wisconsin initiating a demonstration program for poor Milwaukee children in 1990. Yet, despite these applications, the promise of vouchers in social services has not been realized, and less than 10 percent of cities and counties have used vouchers for this purpose.[26]

If the nation is to mainstream its poor, it is essential to give them a range of choices similar to those available to better-off citizens. Too often, the poor are given no choice but to rely on a governmental monopoly of services—one that is often characterized by red tape, inferior service, and unresponsiveness to client needs. A scathing indictment of the welfare bureaucracy is offered by former AFDC recipient Theresa Funicello:

> When affluent people decide some service they want for themselves isn't up to snuff, they vote with their feet and their pocketbooks. In that sense, markets work quite well for anyone with the power to participate in them. As long as poor people are prohibited from having a choice—a say in deciding which services they need and which providers are most capable of satisfying them—the competitive element, if there is one, is entirely in the hands of

> Big Brother. Most of the people in every form of this business know this: *There is not accountability in the social service field* [original emphasis]. None demanded, none supplied.[27]

Any government monopoly of service in a democratic-capitalist society operates on the assumption that clients are unable to make wise decisions about their needs. While such paternalism may be warranted in select cases, it is unwarranted when applied to all the poor, many of whom are just as capable of making sound decisions as their fellow middle-income citizens.

Creatively developed, these strategies for promoting productivity, family integration, social cohesion, community infrastructure, and social choice could serve as the basis on which to reorganize the American welfare state. Although some of these ideas may seem conservative—indeed, conservatives have frequently invoked these categories to disavow public policy—there is no reason that they cannot be used to achieve progressive ends. The challenge to advocates of social justice is to integrate these values into public policy so that the public itself can appreciate how social programs contribute to the overall well-being of the United States.

RESTRUCTURING THE AMERICAN WELFARE STATE

Full-time work in the United States does not guarantee a family economic security. Social policy toward families of the working poor has been haphazard at best. Too often, social programs fail to reinforce the integrity of workers and their families. In many states, benefits are denied workers simply because they persist in working, although their wages are so low that they are entitled to public assistance. Until recently, roughly half of all state AFDC programs contributed to family disintegration by requiring one parent to leave home in order for the children to be eligible for benefits. Under the Family Support Act of 1988, states provided AFDC grants to two-parent families, but they could limit benefits to six months a year.[28] The idea that social policy could require a parent to move in and out of the home at six-month intervals so that the children can receive necessary income and health benefits does little to advance the notion that social policy is, in some minimal sense, rational. The 1996 welfare reform initiative is contradictory about supporting the poor who work. Although many states have allowed the welfare poor to keep more of their earnings than had been allowed under AFDC, the imposition of arbitrary time limits on receipt of benefits will subvert the poor who enter the labor market but are unable to achieve economic self-sufficiency quickly. Productivity, family stability, social cohesion, community strength, and social choice are benchmarks around which future thinking about American social welfare can be organized. In tandem with these principles, we propose a welfare state composed of three main programs: (1) a family conservation program, (2) a community revitalization initiative, and (3) a national service program.

A Family Conservation Program

Any social policy initiative that purports to preserve, stabilize, and strengthen the American family must be composed of both preventive and remedial components. The basic axiom for social policy is similar to that for medicine: It is far easier and less costly to *prevent* social dysfunction than to *treat* it. Thus, the preventive component in any family policy must establish social conditions that encourage working families to conduct their lives with a minimal use of income maintenance programs. The preventive approach would consist of eight core programs designed to encourage family conservation: (1) the stabilization of Unemployment Insurance (UI); (2) the establishment of a minimum wage that is annually adjusted in proportion to the regional average wage; (3) the creation of a minimum benefits package; (4) the development of high-quality and affordable day care; (5) the establishment of individual development accounts (IDAs); (6) the creation of progressive individual retirement accounts (IRAs); (7) national health care; and (8) a universal maternal and child health program. The remedial component of a family conservation program would consist of a stable incomes program (SIP), a comprehensive income maintenance program designed to incorporate the principles of reciprocity, productivity, and social choice in a viable and cost-effective income maintenance structure.

Preventive Approaches to Poverty: Firming Up the Income Floor

Any preventive strategy to curb poverty must incorporate a firm income floor for America's poor working families (i.e., those who are poor but not in immediate need of direct governmental welfare). Creating a firm income floor requires a three-pronged approach: stabilizing the unemployment insurance program, stabilizing family income by establishing a minimum wage that is keyed to the average wage, and establishing a national minimum benefits package. This system of minimum income/benefits security must be complemented by an increase in the availability of high-quality and affordable day care.

Stabilizing the Unemployment Insurance Program. Former Secretary of Labor Robert Reich has argued that the global economy is forcing Americans into an increasingly stratified job market, one that is composed of routine production services (traditional production jobs), in-person services (person-to-person service jobs), and symbolic/analytic services (jobs characterized by problem solving, problem identification, and strategic brokering activities). According to Reich, those in the first two job categories will experience difficult economic times as high-paying manufacturing jobs become scarcer and as the competition for in-person jobs become greater and the wage and benefit levels lower. Workers in the third category, by contrast, may experience greater prosperity. Reich argues that the American economy will be characterized by several economic boats, each one growing more economically independent of the other.[29] If Reich's argument is correct, it only reinforces the urgency of protecting vulnerable economic groups from a capricious global marketplace in which they have little economic influence.

Workers facing job losses brought on by changes in the global economy usually turn first to the government's primary line of defense: the Unemployment Insurance program (UI). Initially designed to cushion the effects of employer layoffs for both individual workers and local economies, the UI program contracted sharply in the 1980s because of changes in federal and state laws. Low levels of unemployment coverage contribute to high rates of poverty, especially in a recession. Jobless workers without UI benefits, especially the long-term unemployed, are more likely to fall into poverty. However, Byzantine state and federal eligibility guidelines prevent or discourage many jobless workers from using the UI system. The result is that many poor working-class families are sent spiraling into poverty by the loss of one or two paychecks. In order to inhibit this cycle, straightforward eligibility guidelines for UI should be promulgated on a national level. The UI system should also be administered by the federal government in order to ensure uniformity across all states. The compensation for lost income is too important to be left to the whims of individual state legislatures. Moreover, UI benefits should be linked to regional differences in the cost of living.

A Minimum Wage Program. In 1950, the minimum wage brought a worker to 56 percent of the average wage. Throughout the 1950s and 1960s, the minimum wage hovered between 44 and 56 percent of the average wage. However, by 1991 it had dropped to 41 percent of the average wage, bringing a family of three to about 85 percent of the poverty line. This figure compares unfavorably with the 120 percent of the poverty level reached by the minimum wage in 1968.[30] The most recent minimum wage increase to $5.15 per hour brings a family of three to 83 percent of the poverty level.

In order to stabilize the income floor for working families, the minimum wage should be based on a fixed percentage of the average wage. Specifically, a benchmark year could be chosen by which to calibrate present and future minimum wage increases. For instance, because the minimum wage hovered between 44 and 56 percent of the average wage throughout the 1950s and 1960s, we propose that the minimum wage be 50 percent of the average yearly adjusted wage. Moreover, because the average wage differs regionally (supposedly reflecting differences in regional costs of living), the minimum wage should be adjusted to the regional average wage.

This formula would have several benefits. First, a firm income floor would assure all working-class families of a minimum wage that would not fall below a certain percentage of the average wage of their fellow citizens. Second, this formula would help stem the growing disparity between the income brackets. By having a stable income floor adjusted to the average wage, even if working-class Americans did not do better, they would at least not be doing worse in relative terms. Third, establishing a stable income floor would also prevent a decrease in wages (at least as a percentage of the average wage) from providing a disincentive for labor market participation. Finally, the creation of an automatically adjusted minimum wage would help still the shrill congressional battles that break out every time there is an attempt to raise the minimum wage.

Because the minimum wage fails to pull families out of poverty, government contractors should be encouraged to supplement the minimum wage in order to arrive at a "living wage." In 1994, Baltimore required contractors to supplement the minimum wage for workers on their payrolls. Since then more than a dozen states and localities have considered or adopted a "living wage" as one provision in contracting.[31]

A Minimum Benefits Package. Any progressive minimum wage legislation must also include a minimum benefits package. Many of the poor currently work without benefits in part-time or seasonal jobs. Various service industries (e.g., convenience stores and fast food franchises) avoid paying benefits to employees by limiting their hours of work. Through a minimum benefits package, employees working 20 hours a week or more would be assured of health care benefits, child day care, and family leave through portable benefits accounts that would follow them from one job to another.

Revenues for the minimum benefits package could be derived from several sources. Appropriations for child care under the 1996 welfare reform could establish a fund for the minimum benefits plan, which would be maintained by nominal mandatory contributions from employers and employees. In order to discourage employers from further reducing an employee's hours in order to dodge participation in the program, a "McTax" could be levied against employers who hire workers for less than 20 hours per week. To keep employee and employer payroll tax levels low (so as to avoid interfering with job creation), the minimum benefits fund could be supplemented by modest increases in excise taxes. For example, the Congressional Budget Office calculated that almost $10 billion per year would generated by increasing the cigarette tax to 48 cents per pack, increasing the alcoholic beverage tax to $16 per proof gallon, and indexing these taxes for inflation.[32]

Day Care. Most mothers work because of financial need, and about 25 percent are the primary wage earners for their children. Many two-parent families also require dual incomes to meet their basic necessities. In 1993, 66.9 percent of women with children under age 18 (58 percent with children under age 6) participated in the labor force.[33] Despite increasing numbers of working mothers, the federal government has not been actively involved in setting day care standards, instead leaving this responsibility to the individual states. Even with state regulations (often spotty at best), about 43 percent of all children spend their days in out-of-home child care facilities that are exempt from minimal health and safety standards.[34]

High-quality private day care is unaffordable for most poor working-class families. Moreover, nonpublic institutional child care is also becoming unaffordable for much of the middle class. If the United States is to marshal its productive capacity more effectively, it must ensure that high-quality, affordable, and accessible day care is available for all families. Moreover, if family preservation is a major national goal, then it is critical to ensure that poor working-class families are provided with opportunities to participate fully in the labor force. A minimum wage program and a minimum benefits package must be complemented by universal day care services. Much of the physical and human infrastructure needed to establish a comprehensive day care system can be realized through a community revitalization program, an initiative discussed more fully later in this chapter.

Substantial funding for child care could be derived by reducing the dependent-care credit for upper income families and making the credit refundable for poor families. If the dependent care credit were gradually reduced for families earning more than $30,000 a year, $7.2 billion would have been generated from 1996 through 2000. These revenues that could have been diverted to low-income families by creating a refundable tax expenditure for child care.[35]

Preventive Approaches to Poverty: Building Economic Security

A viable policy for family preservation requires that policymakers take into account the relationship between strong families and economic security. Economically unstable families are at greater risk for dysfunctional behavior and for becoming welfare recipients. In America, assets provide the basis for much of the political, social, and economic power enjoyed by the middle class. To ensure that poor working-class Americans enter the economic mainstream, it is necessary to help them accrue assets.

Individual Development Accounts. The concept of *stakeholding*—the substitution of assets for income transfers through social policy—has now become part of the social policy debate. Pioneered by Michael Sherraden of Washington University's George Warren Brown School of Social Work, stakeholding is advocated in response to the realization that the distribution of assets is even more skewed than is income, and that the poor can gain directly from benefits that encourage "savings, investment, and asset accumulation rather than income, spending, and income." Accordingly, Sherraden has proposed the creation of individual development accounts (IDAs) to bolster assets for the working poor. IDAs would be designated for specific purposes: housing, postsecondary education, self-employment, and retirement. The federal government would simply match IDA deposits made by people in qualifying low-income families.[36] Through IDAs the federal government could reinforce activities that strengthen families. A provision for IDAs was incorporated in the 1996 welfare reform legislation.

There are multiple options for funding IDAs. Immediate funding could be derived from earmarking revenues from gaming for IDAs. This is justified because the poor are more likely to engage in gambling than other economic groups, a function of their limited opportunities through more conventional activities. Long-term funding for IDAs could obtained by levying a national sales tax on *nonessential* goods purchased by the more affluent. For example, a 5 percent national sales tax (which would exempt food, housing, and medical care) could have netted more than $63.4 billion in 1997.[37]

Progressive Individual Retirement Accounts. The IDA concept could also advance retirement security for older Americans. Despite the extensive coverage of Social Security, millions of the nation's elderly remain in poverty. In order to encourage workers to plan ahead for their retirement, younger employees should be given clear incentives to supplement their contributions to Social Security. One way to do this is to calibrate individual retirement accounts (IRAs) so that tax deferments granted to poorer workers are greater than those given to the well-off.

The working poor underutilize IRAs for several reasons. First, the effective income tax on their wages is relatively low, thereby providing little incentive to use the tax-saving feature of IRAs. Second, many workers believe that Social Security will take care of them when they retire. Third, the working poor have little disposable income and have pressing needs for immediate cash. If progressive IRAs are to have an effect, they will need to provide more attractive incentives for the working poor to invest. Moreover, it must be made clear that Social Security alone is not sufficient to provide a comfortable lifestyle after retirement. With an aggressive education campaign directed at low-wage workers combined with a more favorable contribution formula, the working poor can do much more toward planning for their retirement income needs.

The current Social Security program can be enhanced by other relatively minor changes. While an expansion of income security is desirable and should be shared equally among workers, contributions should be assessed by a more progressive method than is currently used. The easiest method to increase Social Security revenues is to remove the present cap on taxable earned income so that the wealthy will contribute their fair share. If the ceiling were lifted so that all income were taxed, more than $18.5 billion would be added to the Social Security coffers.[38] A similar reform would be to make the withholding tax progressive. By way of illustration, designating three rates for individual contributions of 3, 6, and 9 percent related to income, could give minimum-wage earners a substantial tax break, middle-income workers a slight reduction, and upper-income groups a tax hike. Depending on what income levels were determined for each tax level, this system could make the withholding tax "revenue neutral" or "revenue positive."

On the other hand, the Social Security payroll tax cannot be increased indefinitely without risking a decline in economic growth or even intergenerational reprisal. Virtually ignored has been the possibility of increasing the supply of workers who contribute to Social Security. This is particularly significant because the ratio of workers to beneficiaries will have plummeted from 5 to 1 in 1960 to 2 to 1 in the year 2040.[39] Unless the supply of workers is dramatically increased, major adjustments will have to be made to maintain current benefit levels, including a doubling of the payroll tax.

A straightforward approach for increasing the supply of workers is to integrate immigration policy with income security policy. Approximately 7 million undocumented workers are currently in the United States, and every year hundreds of thousands enter the country illegally in search of employment.[40] The Immigration Reform and Control Act of 1986 offered a one-year window during which persons who had been in the United States since January 1, 1982, could apply for "amnesty." Because only 2 to 3 million people took advantage of this provision, the great majority of undocumented workers continue to work illegally without basic wage and workplace protections. Unfortunately, tens of thousands of these workers are contributing to a Social Security program from which they will never collect benefits.[41] Instead of a one-year period during which established workers could apply for legal residency status, immigration policy should incorporate a rolling amnesty date; workers and their families who have been in the United States for five years, say, could apply for legal residency status. In addition, education, health, and social service benefits should be available to qualifying workers to encourage their participation in the labor force. A more humane amnesty provision for undocumented workers would go a long way toward assuring the baby boomers that they will be supported in the manner to which they have become accustomed; and it would also ensure that undocumented workers are not exploited for their contribution to the nation.[42]

Preventive Approaches to Poverty: Health Care

Any meaningful proposal for preserving the American family must include a national health care plan. Despite the massive and uncontrollable infusion of funds, the United States fails to insure health care to more than 40 million citizens. The deregulated and disorganized method of U.S. health care provision is unnecessarily costly, especially when compared to the systems of other industrial nations. While U.S. government-sponsored health care for the poor is being rationed because of government funding rescissions,[43] American health care has come under increasing commercial pressure from large corporate health care providers and insurance companies that continue to profit from skyrocketing health care costs.[44]

National Health Care. Although the demise of the Clinton administration's Health Security Act has dampened enthusiasm for health care reform, continued increases in the number of uninsured Americans virtually assures that it will return to the policy agenda. Three options have been suggested for restructuring American health care: (1) a national health insurance plan modeled after Canada's; (2) a national health service similar to that of the United Kingdom; and (3) a mandatory contribution plan through which employers would insure workers not covered under other plans.[45] The most plausible candidate for a U.S. national health program is a variation of the third option. The Congress would charter a federal health management authority that would be empowered to negotiate with local health care providers for a basic health care package available to all citizens—a National Health Plan.

Financing the National Health Plan would come from several sources. Taxing a portion of employer-paid health insurance would add $58 billion to federal revenues from 1996 through 2000. Taxing Hospital Insurance and Supplemental Medical Insurance benefits, while exempting the low-income elderly, would generate $45.2 billion from 1996 through 2000.[46] Finally, local authorities might assess a tax on commercial health care providers. A modest 5 percent tax on occupied rooms in for-profit hospitals, similar to the hotel tax, could defray some of the health care costs for the poor. When health care becomes a commercial activity, it should be taxed as such. These revenue sources would create a pool from which to pay for the uninsured.

Under a National Health Plan, much of the cost would be met simply by selective, incremental tax increases. Primary health care offered by private providers would be honored, yet all Americans would be assured of basic medical care while entitling them to their choice of providers. Government would be restricted to negotiating care for the uninsured and not otherwise interfere in the medical marketplace. Through such an arrangement, the United States would retain its status as the world's leader in health care, at the same time assuming its moral responsibility to assure health care for the medically indigent.

A *Universal Maternal and Child Health Program.* To make family conservation a primary focus of social policy, a commitment must be made to ensure that all infants receive the best nutritional and health care possible. The absence of a universal maternal and child health program is a national embarrassment whose consequences are predictable. The WIC program provides health and nutritional benefits to poor women, but only about half of those who are eligible participate.[47] The social and psychological costs of fetal alcohol syndrome have been brought to public attention by Michael Dorris's award-winning book *The Broken Cord.*[48] Increasingly, delivery room personnel are confronted with infants who were exposed to illegal drugs in utero. The Department of Health and Human Services predicts that 4 million infants and children who have been exposed to cocaine will require billions of dollars of care during the next 10 years.[49] In California, some 72,000 infants are born each year with prenatal exposure to alcohol and illegal drugs.[50] It follows that a universal maternal and child health program is justifiable not only because of concern for the life opportunities of at-risk infants but also because the nation cannot afford to shoulder the costs of care for long-term disabilities. An American maternal and child health program could be created by consolidating the present Maternal and Child Health Care Block Grant, the WIC program, and relevant components of the Medicaid program. Funding to make the program universal so that all mothers and children are able to participate could be derived from the funding pool of the National Health Plan described above.

Taken together, these preventive programs can protect America's most vulnerable workers from those events most likely to make them poor. Ensuring America's working-class families a stable income floor, the prospects of economic mobility, and basic health care means that the need for governmental income maintenance programs will be reduced. Moreover, these investments in human capital will contribute to a more productive labor force better able to compete in a volatile international economy. By improving the productivity of American workers, social welfare programs thus improve the overall economic well-being of American society. Accordingly, preventing poverty translates into greater social stability. In the absence of such preventive programs, it is only a matter of time before the violence erupting in America's poorest communities will spill over, with a fierceness, into the country's more affluent communities. If, as Robert Reich suggests, we are not all in the same economic boat, we clearly inhabit the same sea.

Combating Poverty: A Stable Incomes Program

The profound economic changes already under way will require that low-income Americans, including many who participate fully in the work force, receive remedial economic help. A stable incomes program (SIP) is intended as a starting point for examining alternatives to the current income maintenance programs.

When people attempt to understand the American welfare system, they are often struck by the redundancy of welfare programs, their lack of integration, gaps in coverage, and the arcane criteria for eligibility. On closer examination, one finds many welfare departments staffed by untrained workers who labor under nearly impossible conditions of low pay, poor supervision, and huge client caseloads. Baffling state and federal manuals outlining eligibility criteria and procedures can occupy a full shelf of office space. It is not surprising, then, that clients often receive different assessments of their eligibility depending on which welfare worker they happen to meet on a given day. This situation is further complicated by the lack of follow-up and client tracking. At best, most welfare departments have become financial dispensaries rather than purveyors of *social* services. Indeed, the public welfare department has disintegrated to such a point that Alvin Schorr, a longtime supporter of public welfare, admits that "many human service departments cannot manage to answer the telephone, let alone conduct a civilized interview."[51]

As symbolized by the 1996 welfare reforms, the American welfare state has run aground. With multiple, overlapping programs replete with complex eligibility criteria, few people —including many welfare administrators—fully understand the tangle of welfare services. This tangle is understood least of all by clients trying to make their way through an incomprehensible maze of programs. Apart from its complexity, welfare programs also include administrative structures that can devour 10 percent or more of the potential benefits earmarked for clients. In that sense, the complexity of the welfare state itself represents a significant expenditure.

Far from reflecting a well-thought-out and integrated series of social programs, the American welfare state is a patchwork nonsystem cobbled together by last-minute negotiations, adroit political maneuvering, and political concessions. Although when viewed separately, most welfare programs embody good intentions, taken as a whole, the welfare state reflects a jumble of redundant social programs. In that sense, the whole is less than the sum of its parts.

To rectify the problem of program duplication and inequitable welfare benefits, redundant welfare programs should be integrated into one administrative unit, and geographically sensitive welfare benefits should be developed. Specifically, to restructure social welfare programs more rationally, TANF, SSI, and EITC could be collapsed into one income maintenance program—a stable incomes program (SIP)—which would necessitate only one administrative unit. In addition, all social programs—including Food Stamps, WIC, LIHEAP, and Section 8[52]—should be scoured for their income support features, which could then be incorporated within the SIP structure. In effect, a single income maintenance program would replace the tangled web of social programs that currently provide income assistance to the poor.

Restructuring social programs would also require reorganizing the delivery of benefits. Instead of collecting piecemeal benefits from TANF, SSI, EITC, food stamps, and other programs, each client would receive a single income/benefits package developed with the assistance of a case manager. This income/benefits package would combine market wages with a supplemental cash grant that would bring the working and nonworking poor to a poverty threshold based on the median family income in a target region.

Increasingly, states are achieving efficiencies in benefit delivery by converting from checks to Electronic Benefit Transfer (EBT). Through EBT, recipients can use Automatic Teller Machines to obtain benefits and Point of Service vending when purchasing goods, such as food stamps. EBT offers significant advantages to clients, particularly in terms of destigmatizing benefits. A logical method for reorganizing the delivery of income maintenance benefits would be to require recipients to identify a community-oriented financial institution, such as a community development credit union or bank, to which their benefits would be direct-deposited. Until benefits were drawn, this would leave significant reserves that could be used to capitalize community development activities. Direct-deposit of SIP benefits could thus serve to not only support the wages of the working poor, but also to generate much needed infrastructure repair and development in poor neighborhoods.

In exchange for direct-deposit privileges, a community-oriented financial institution would be required to offer basic financial services. These would include the services that most affluent Americans take for granted: checking, savings, and financial planning. Additional services would include financial education so that the poor could purchase a home, career planning in order to optimize training and education benefits, and tax preparation so that poor workers can take full advantage of the Earned Income Tax Credit. Logically, the vehicle for long-range financial planning would be the account-holder's IDA.

Operationalizing SIP. The organizational auspices for the SIP program would be a community-oriented financial institution, such as a community development bank or a community development credit union. This agency would be a quasi-governmental entity in the form of a nonprofit agency with a board of directors or a privately held human-service collective. Individualized services would be provided by case managers who are human-service professionals specially trained in personal finance and domestic problems. Social workers would be logical candidates to provide case management services because the SIP program would customize benefits to the social economy of eligible individuals. Eligibility for SIP would require that a client's income fall below 40 percent of the regional median family income, with assets limited to $30,000.

Case managers would classify SIP beneficiaries into four employability categories: (1) clients who cannot realistically be expected to participate in the labor force (e.g., the totally disabled); (2) clients who can participate in the labor force within a protected environment (e.g., handicapped or mentally ill clients requiring sheltered workshops); (3) clients who can participate in the labor force on a part-time basis (e.g., mothers with infants); and (4) clients for whom labor force participation on a full-time basis is possible. Clients who cannot participate in the labor force will be required to substantiate their disability by undergoing thorough medical examinations and periodic case reviews. Firm criteria would be established to rate handicaps in terms of percentage of disability. In addition, state welfare departments would monitor clients judged unemployable by the local agency through the use of intensive case reviews. Any agency found to be consistently classifying employable clients as totally disabled would risk closure.

All SIP clients would work with case managers to develop an individualized plan designed to maximize their welfare benefits, increase their human capital (i.e., through further education or job training), and optimize their personal assets. Clients falling within each of the four employability categories would be provided with a plan to maximize their life opportunities, particularly with reference to IDAs. Totally and partially disabled clients would receive a plan that helped them to maximize welfare and support service benefits. Because employment (either in the private labor market or in a community development agency) would be mandatory for all able-bodied recipients, there would be no incentive to provide lower benefits for those who could not participate in the labor force. In effect, nonemployable people would receive the same benefit levels as those low-wage workers in the labor force. Those people for whom limited or full-time labor force participation was possible would have SIP plans that reflected job training and educational opportunities. Full-time workers whose current earnings placed them below the SIP eligibility threshold would be provided with a package that combined labor market income with supplemental welfare funds, thus allowing them to be at 40 percent of the regional median income. Moreover, those in the workforce would be provided with plans containing incentives that encouraged deriving a greater share of their income from labor market sources. These plans might include job retraining opportunities, career counseling, or further education. Finally, clients who fully met the objectives of their plan, yet still earned less than 40 percent of the regional median family income, would receive a small supplemental benefit. (A mainstay of SIP would be to reward rather than punish initiative.)

Apart from formulating economic plans, case managers would also be responsible for helping clients to budget their money. In instances where clients were judged incapable of managing their resources, the case manager would function as a broker, dispensing income on a monthly basis. Case managers would also function as a constant point of contact for clients during their participation in the SIP program. Social service referrals and client tracking would be a major responsibility of the case manager. Apart from determining eligibility, case managers would also function as client advocates, ensuring that clients received the full benefits to which they were entitled. In effect, the case manager would be responsible for individual clients from their point of entry into the SIP program until their termination.

Redefining Poverty. By allocating benefits indexed to the median family income in a target region, the SIP program would eliminate the current poverty classification. The official poverty line currently provides a set of income cutoffs adjusted for the size of the household, the number of children, and the age of the household head. The poverty threshold is adjusted yearly using the consumer price index (CPI).

The current poverty line contributes little in terms of understanding poverty. For one, the cost of living differs so dramatically from state to state and between cities and rural areas that a single, national poverty line is almost meaningless. A more accurate, fair, and geographically sensitive measure of poverty would be based on a percentage of the median family income (which is influenced by differences in regional price levels) in a specific geographic area. In other words, the country would be divided into target areas based on metropolitan and rural areas. Within each target area, the poverty line would be based on a percentage of the median family income for that region. Benefits would be set nationwide to equal 40 percent of the median family income in a regional area. This benefit level would correspond to 1.5 times the minimum wage; or, put another way, it would equal the wages of 1.5 full-time minimum wage earners. A regionally adjusted poverty line would result in SIP benefits for eligible families fluctuating nationally because they would be keyed to regional rather than national median family incomes.[53]

Because the SIP program would include a mandatory work requirement for *all* recipients judged capable of labor force participation, there would be no incentive to choose welfare over work, thus ending the inherent competition between minimum wage employment and welfare receipt. Looking at benefits on a national level, a welfare family now claiming all its benefits and receiving about $12,000 a year would accrue about the same amount under this formula. However, a single female householder with a four-person family who earns a minimum wage of $5.15 an hour (a yearly salary of $10,300) would now "earn" $12,240 under this formula. Because median family income does not vary widely with the size of the family (most American families have about two children), there will be no incentive to increase family size to gain greater benefits. Finally, eligibility for the SIP program would be capped at 40 percent of the regional median family income. Redefining the poverty threshold in this manner would eliminate the need to readjust the poverty line yearly for inflation and would ensure a fairer and geographically more sensitive measure of poverty. In addition, a work requirement would positively influence the labor supply, thereby increasing the pool of Social Security contributors.

Social Service Vouchers. If independent providers are to supply the bulk of human services in postindustrial America, it is essential to devise a mechanism through which social objectives can be achieved while allowing professionals autonomy and clients the freedom to choose the person or agency they deem best suited to help with their problem. The dispensing of social service vouchers is one method for providing a wide range of services to the poor in a manner that is both responsive and cost-effective. Under the SIP program, eligible clients could choose a Family Resource Center (FRC) from which to seek services. For those seeking social services, vouchers would be provided that allowed them to choose from a range of service providers who would be reimbursed through the FRC. Service providers from the private sector would be required to meet the standards established by the government for reimbursement purposes. While many of the existing private nonprofit agencies would participate, a voucher system would also open participation to the approximately 20,000 social workers in private practice who could also affiliate with the FRCs.[54]

Each FRC would be responsible for maintaining a client information center, which would update a roster of eligible service providers as well as their performance as evaluated by former clients. Jurisdictions would provide those services now assured through Title XX: home-based care, day care for children, protective and emergency services for adults and children, as well as employment, education, and training services. Because the kinds of services needed by the poor vary widely, an inclusive "service provision inventory" would be developed, similar to those already used in the provision of psychiatric and health care.[55] Reimbursement would be related to the type of care provided, and rates would be negotiated annually between providers and the government.

Because the SIP program and the use of vouchers would effectively make the public welfare department a regulatory agency, a substantial reduction in personnel would occur, and direct service employees of the welfare department would be encouraged to affiliate with FRCs. The most desirable outcome would be the formation of FRCs that are privately held, community-based social service collectives.[56] The funding for social service vouchers could be derived from the $2.8 billion appropriated for Title XX, although states and localities would be free to supplement this for special needs. In applying market principles to the delivery of social services, the use of vouchers can be expected not only to replicate successes in other areas of service delivery, but also to provide low-income beneficiaries the same measure of choice enjoyed by their more affluent compatriots.

Released from their role as providers of direct services, welfare departments would function as financial and administrative conduits, regulators, and evaluators. Specifically, welfare departments would certify individual FRCs and their professional affiliates. The welfare department would subsequently be responsible for regulating, monitoring, and investigating the services provided. This would occur in the same way that state agencies are responsible for monitoring the services provided by group homes for the mentally ill or mentally retarded. For example, welfare departments could make unannounced visits in order to evaluate the progress of individual clients and the quality of services provided. Released from the role of being the funder, provider, and monitor of their own social services, welfare departments would be free to concentrate on ensuring that clients received effective income maintenance and social services. Moreover, welfare departments would shield themselves from charges of encouraging client dependency by helping to ensure that recipients moved in the direction of greater economic independence.

Funding SIP and FRCs The initial funding for SIP and FRCs would come from reallocating funds from TANF ($22 billion), SSI ($27 billion), EITC ($25 billion), Food Stamps ($28 billion), WIC ($5 billion), and the income support features contained in other social programs. These funds would then be transferred to a Human Capital Development Fund within the Internal Revenue Service. Through the SIP program, these funds would supplement the wages of those in the workforce and provide benefits for those outside the labor force. Administration of community-oriented financial institutions whose case managers would assist the poor would be derived from the direct-deposit revenues of SIP. Additional revenues could be obtained from encouraging commercial banks to meet their Community Reinvestment Act obligations by making deposits in community-oriented financial institutions as well as nonprofit agencies who could be encouraged to view such accounts as an investment in local development.

FRCs would be reimbursed on a capitation basis. In other words, they would be given a specific sum for each client enrolled in a particular FRC. Seed money for start-up costs and for administering the FRCs would come from the substantial savings realized by collapsing the administrations of SSI, TANF, and the

Food Stamps Program. Part of this money could then be lent to FRCs at low interest for the purposes of establishing the organization. The loan would then be repaid as part of the capitation formula.

The SIP program would offer several advantages over traditional welfare programs. For one thing, the SIP program would target help directly on clients through intensive case management services. By developing individualized plans, clients would be deterred from becoming totally dependent on welfare programs (as currently happens in most welfare departments) and thus have a better chance of getting their real needs met. Furthermore, since help would be linked to work requirements, the SIP program would encourage rather than discourage labor force participation. Because a work requirement is a key component in the SIP program, there would no longer be a need to peg welfare benefits below the minimum wage so as to discourage a preference for welfare receipt over work. As a consequence, tendencies toward intergenerational welfare dependency would be reduced as recipients accumulated job skills in the public sector and translated them into private sector employment.

The SIP program would also address the administrative confusion caused by redundant welfare structures. A streamlined administrative structure with minimal overlap would result in more money being available for client programs, more cost-effective social programs, and more effective client programming. The SIP program would also decentralize welfare services and thus offer clients greater freedom in choosing their service providers. A standardized welfare program coupled with a geographically sensitive poverty threshold could result in less client migration to states with higher welfare benefits.

Perhaps the most important advantage of the SIP program is that it would reestablish the idea of an interdependent society. By building a more solid income floor under poverty, the poor would have a shorter distance to climb to reach the average wage. As the economic distance between the poor and the middle class shortens, those in poverty will experience more hope (and thus more motivation) to raise themselves to middle-class levels of economic security.

Community Revitalization

Any serious proposal for welfare reform must address the social deterioration of American communities. During the past two decades, there has been a marked slowdown in public investment in the nation's infrastructure, including schools, public buildings, highways, bridges, airports, and public utilities. According to Robert Kuttner, nonmilitary public capital expenditures grew at an average annual rate of 4.1 percent from 1948 to 1969 (greater than the rate of economic growth). However, from 1969 to 1977, those same expenditures grew at a rate of only 1.6 percent. During the Reagan years, they plummeted to 0.9 percent per year, or less than half the rate of overall growth.[57] This cut in public spending had a differential impact on communities. While affluent communities built new schools, roads, and public utilities during the 1980s, poor inner-city neighborhoods became more desolate as their infrastructures (both physical and human) rotted from a lack of attention and the quality of life in many American communities dropped precipitously. When Claude Brown returned to Harlem 20 years after the publication of his *Manchild in the Promised Land*, he was shocked by the casual viciousness of gang members toward their victims.[58] Daniel Patrick Moynihan observed that "In many if not most of our major cities, we are facing something very like social regression. . . . It is defined by extraordinary levels of self-destructive behavior, interpersonal violence, and social class separation intensive in some groups, extensive in others."[59] The social pathology attributed to economic dislocation was exacerbated by the policies of the Reagan, Bush, and Clinton administrations. Failing to institute a coherent community development policy, these administrations had to rely on economic growth as a vehicle for benefiting lower-income workers, but the trickle-down effect has been mere seepage.

Community Enterprise Zones. The Clinton administration's Empowerment Zone initiative should be restructured and expanded into a Community Enterprise Zone (CEZ) program that strengthens poor communities. This CEZ would provide technical assistance and time-limited grants for the purpose of generating basic commodities, such as jobs and housing. The geographic basis of a CEZ would be an economic catchment area of from 4,000 to 50,000 people, thereby accommodating both rural and urban environments. Eligibility for community development grants would depend on the social and economic conditions of the catchment area, which are determined by specific socioeconomic indicators such as the incidence of poverty, unemployment, and business closings. Catchment areas would be eligible for benefits when the rates for two of these three indicators exceeded one standard deviation above the national average.

Two types of community aid would be provided. For communities in which the infrastructure had deteriorated substantially, CEZ benefits would consist of technical assistance and development grants. Rather than provide assistance directly, government would contract for services from existing organizations that had established a successful track record in economic development, such as the Enterprise Foundation or the Local Initiatives Support Corporation. For communities experiencing acute dislocation, a system of incentives—including tax credits—would be instituted to retain and promote entrepreneurial activity.

Funding for the CEZ program would be derived from a Community Enterprise Zone Fund created by combining Community Development Block Grants ($4.6 billion for 1996) and Economic Development Administration appropriations ($440 million for 1996), supplemented by nominal limits on mortgage interest deductions in excess of $300,000 (a figure that totaled $3.8 billion in 1996).[60] When combined with the capital generating capacity of private community development ventures, such as the Enterprise Foundation and LISC, the resulting $8.84 billion would a long way toward insuring communities against economic dislocation.

A *Community Revitalization Program.* During the past decade, a series of community work experience programs administered by the Manpower Demonstration Research Corporation (MDRC) have shown that welfare-to-work could prove an effective strategy for reducing welfare costs, depending on the presence of supports for job training and employment. Although initial assessments of the welfare-to-work demonstrations were cautious,[61] later studies revealed an unexpected finding: Although the most dependent AFDC recipients consumed the most program resources, they also represented the greatest program savings once they were participating in welfare-to-work.[62] Studies such as these provided the justification for incorporating welfare-to-work efforts in the Family Support Act of 1988 and the work requirements that featured so prominently in the welfare reform initiative of 1996. Unfortunately, a serious deficiency in these welfare reforms is that aside from supporting job-seeking activity, the legislation says nothing about *which* employment is considered desirable. Charles Moskos argues that "In structuring jobs programs, policy makers have paid insufficient attention to the types of service performed. . . . Only when training programs involve young adults in the delivery of vital services to the community can they hope to inculcate the values that make for good citizenship."[63]

Incorporating civic content into welfare-to-work could be accomplished by connecting the SIP program to a community revitalization program through which public assistance beneficiaries would contribute to the neighborhoods in which they live. Under a community revitalization program, public assistance beneficiaries who were deemed employable but who were not working or engaged in education/training activities would be referred by their case manager to a community development agency to which their benefits would be assigned. In order to collect benefits, those on welfare would have to engage in joblike tasks identified by the community development agency. Community development entities would be nonprofit organizations meeting standards of the state department of social services relating to personnel and benefit management, but would otherwise be free to define community development projects and to assign beneficiaries to them.

Instead of developing the dependency associated with public welfare, beneficiaries would be treated like employees of the community development agency. Although still receiving public assistance, they could develop a track record that would be of use in the private labor market. In effect, this benefit assignment strategy addresses a major flaw in welfare programs. According to William Raspberry, "You cannot get good at welfare. . . . It does no good for a welfare mother to impress her caseworker with her quick grasp of her sense of responsibility or her willingness to take on an extra task. There is no way for a welfare client to distinguish himself, in any economically useful way, from any other welfare client. There are no promotions on welfare."[64]

In order to encourage the responsiveness of community development agencies toward beneficiaries, welfare recipients would choose a community development agency in which to enroll. Once enrolled, beneficiaries could transfer to another community development agency—or to other employment—much as employees change jobs in the labor market. Such an arrangement would ensure a measure of social responsibility on the part of welfare beneficiaries in a way that directly benefits the communities in which they live. Moreover, this arrangement would allow the reciprocity goals of the SIP program to be realized, even for the difficult to employ. In effect, those judged employable by their case manager (but not in other job-related programs) would be referred to a community development agency in which they would be required to contribute their labor in exchange for social welfare benefits.

Apart from helping clients to develop positive work attitudes and job skills, community development agencies could also help to rebuild the decaying physical and social infrastructure of poor communities. In this capacity, work teams under the auspices of community agencies could be used to demolish or renovate abandoned buildings (places often used as crack houses and gang headquarters) and to rebuild roads, bridges, schools, and other public buildings. In addition, such teams could be used to build new community institutions, including day care centers, parks, schools, shopping areas, and industrial parks.

Rebuilding a poor community's physical infrastructure must also include rebuilding its *social* infrastructure. As part of their commitment to community revitalization, community development agencies must develop low-cost day care centers that allow poor families the opportunity to fully participate in the labor force. They must also develop effective preschool and child health and immunization programs. Finally, community development agencies can provide the economic and social leadership that will help communities to compete effectively in a complex economy. This could be done by establishing building-trade cooperatives and personnel agencies and by creating economic incentives that would encourage small and medium-size industries to relocate in inner-city communities. As part of these economic incentives, the community must be able to provide protection from crime to both its inhabitants and the potential industries. This goal could be accomplished by creating local security teams that work in conjunction with the police department to patrol neighborhoods and, where appropriate, to make arrests.

A revitalized community infrastructure can accomplish several goals. Above all, it can lead to a renewed sense of local self-initiative. This goal is particularly important in that a fiscally paralyzed federal government cannot be expected to develop the innovative programs necessary to restore economic and social vibrancy to poor neighborhoods. A revitalized infrastructure may also succeed in attracting back a portion of the black middle class that fled inner-city areas during the past three decades, thus restoring some of the social and economic leadership that has been lost.[65] Finally, vital communities can better capture and exploit the human capital that is wasted by abject poverty, poor education, drug and alcohol abuse, and criminal activities. Recapturing human capital will help not only the poor communities but also the larger society that must effectively marshal its human capital to compete successfully in an expanded economic theater.

Social Intervention Teams. Public confidence in social programs has diminished in proportion to their inability to deal effectively with people identified as being harmful to themselves or capable of doing harm to others. While the individual consequences of self-destructive behavior are often recognized and subject to legal sanction, the aggregate consequences are not. When the number of individuals harmful to themselves and others proliferates and is concentrated in one community, the result is not simply an arithmetical increase in the number of destructive persons; it also destroys the very competence of the community. The community is no longer able to maintain its essential functions, one of which is to ensure the safety of its residents.

Unavoidably, human-service professionals are held responsible by the public when people known to public agencies engage in life-threatening behavior. Two current problems illustrate this: homelessness and child abuse. As a result of deinstitutionalization, thousands of psychiatric patients were discharged from state hospitals in the 1970s and 1980s to often nonexistent community programs. Unable to maintain themselves independently, many ex-patients became homeless street people and are now a prominent part of the urban landscape. The social control issue also contributes to what has become a crisis in the various child protective services (CPS). Douglas Besharov, an attorney and fellow of the American Enterprise Institute, noted that "of the 1,000 children who die under circumstances suggestive of parental maltreatment, between 35 and 50 percent were previously reported to child protective agencies."[66] New York acknowledged that half the deaths in the city due to child abuse and neglect "occurred in families already reported to the public child welfare agency."[67] Larry Brown, author of the American Humane Association's standards for CPS, has observed that "the biggest indictment [of CPS] today is that there are plenty of children in the system whose victimization is not treated appropriately."[68] By the mid–1990s, the CPS situation had degenerated to the point the failure of child welfare professionals to protect abused children had become a national scandal.[69]

A more realistic approach to both these social control issues is simply to consider life-threatening behavior a public safety problem rather than a human service problem. Accordingly, child and adult protective service workers should be reassigned to local police departments, where they would work with police officers in social intervention teams.[70] Social service studies of and field experiments with police street patrols suggest that police/social work teams can be established and that they can effectively manage a wide range of problems that social service departments alone are not prepared to handle.[71] In order to bridge the different orientations to human problems of these two groups, special training programs would be established as part of a national police corps. As part of this program, an undergraduate student aid program could supply public safety departments with officers trained to help communities manage social control problems.[72] Funding for college grants could be derived from targeting Pell grants and consolidating portions of the existing training programs in mental health and social services. Much of the funding for maintaining social intervention teams could come from combining the existing appropriations for police and protective service personnel.

A National Service Program

Postindustrial America has witnessed both the unparalleled success of some of its citizens and a serious deterioration in standard of living for many more. Moreover, many of those who have benefited from the expansion of the service sector have been those very professionals who, despite their pledge to promote the common welfare, have failed to provide services to their fellow citizens. In a development that would have seemed implausible a generation ago, the corporate sector has exploited the rapidly emerging markets in human services such as hospital management, health maintenance, nursing care, and even corrections. These developments speak to the commercialization of compassion and the subordination of goodwill to market forces (the very dynamics that too often generated the need for services in the first place). To the extent that commercialization has dampened the nation's voluntary spirit, it is necessary to bolster America's service ethic.

A National Service Corps. In 1960, John F. Kennedy sparked the idealism of young Americans by giving them the opportunity to help others through a short-term commitment to living and working in disadvantaged countries. The Peace Corps, and later VISTA, provided many poor communities in the United States and abroad with technical assistance they could not otherwise have afforded, and it provided young people with an exposure to people they would otherwise never have encountered. Recently, six states have followed up on this idea by creating conservation services, the best known being the California Conservation Corps.[73] The popular support these programs enjoy indicate that a range of income groups would participate in a national service program. Indeed, the creation of a modest national service program, Americorps, figured prominently in the first term of President Bill Clinton.

According to a proposal fielded by Charles Moskos, a national service corps would allow volunteers to elect one-year stints in a nationwide program for which they would be paid $100 per week plus benefits and would, upon completion of their service, be eligible for "generous postservice educational and job training benefits." Enrolling approximately 600,000 youth (excluding those enlisting in the military), a national service corps could make a substantial contribution toward reconstructing distressed communities. Volunteers could engage in such activities as establishing tutorial programs for schoolchildren, helping residents in slums rehabilitate housing, assisting the frail elderly, and organizing child care services, among others. Approximately half the $7 billion budget of the Moskos proposal could be derived from consolidating current job and training programs,[74] with the remainder coming from CEZ appropriations. In order to reduce duplication, Americorps and VISTA should be combined.

A national service corps is appealing for several reasons. To start with, it would make available to hard-pressed communities personnel they would not otherwise attract. Significantly, national service would expose affluent volunteers to the circumstances of their less well-off fellow citizens, and it would demonstrate to less-advantaged Americans that others are not indifferent to their plight. Perhaps most significantly, a national service corps would perform an essential democratizing function by "increasing the variety of class mixing situations."[75] Moskos noted that "With our tradition of voluntary organizations, coupled with comprehensive national service, we could set our country on an entirely new course of effective yet affordable delivery of human services."[76]

Volunteer Tax Credit. The institutional origins of social welfare in the United States are reflected in the myriad nonprofit agencies of the voluntary sector. Organizations such as the Red Cross, Boys' and Girls' Clubs, Boy Scouts and Girl Scouts, the Ys, and various sectarian agencies have provided incalculable benefits to American communities. More recent innovations of the voluntary sector have found solutions to a variety of new problems besetting the United States: the first sale of a federally subsidized housing project in Washington, D.C., to its tenants, engineered by Kimi Gray; the construction of a model facility for the homeless in San Diego by Father Joe Carroll; the establishment of a school for inner-city African American children in Chicago by Marva Collins; the development of a youth development program for delinquency-prone minority adolescents in Philadelphia by Sister Falakah Fattah; and the organization of an international home ownership program for low-income families—Habitat for Humanity—by Millard Fuller. Nonprofit social agencies embody virtues that strike a chord with most Americans: local control, neighborliness, and community well-being. Yet, these organizations are besieged by increased demands for service while governmental support has ebbed. In order to make up for government cuts in social welfare, current nonprofit expenditures for human services, $11.7 billion in 1995, would have to roughly double. Yet, it is unlikely that traditional supports of the voluntary sector—individual and corporate charitable contributions, private philanthropy and foundations, bequests and gifts—will, even in combination, make up for government rescissions.[77]

An important way of revitalizing the voluntary sector would be to give incentives to people to contribute to their local nonprofit social service agencies. The most immediate way to do this would be to restore the deduction allowed for charitable contributions by nonitemizing taxpayers, which was withdrawn by the Tax Reform Act of 1986. However, if voluntary agencies are to fill the void left by government cuts in social expenditures, it will be necessary to raise more revenues than deducted contributions would produce; thus the individual deductions should be changed to a partial tax credit. Furthermore, the relationship between altruistic citizens and nonprofit social service agencies could be strengthened by rewarding those who committed substantial time as volunteers. For all practical purposes, these volunteers become quasi employees, often assuming a function that cannot be provided by a salaried employee because of inadequate agency funding. Therefore, persons committing more than 30 hours a month to a tax-exempt social service agency should be able to establish volunteer tax credits that would allow them to deduct a portion of the economic equivalent of their volunteering against their tax liability. The amount that this tax expenditure would represent as a loss to the U.S. Treasury would be negligible compared to the value of investment it would encourage in community institutions.

Nondiscrimination in Service Provision. To the extent that the private sector continues to provide a major portion of human services, it is essential to ensure that people have the right of access to these services. In the past, for-profit health and human-service firms have discriminated against people with complex problems who are dependent on government insurance. Instances of preferential selection (when providers skim more treatable, less costly clients for care) and dumping (when indigent clients are capriciously transferred to public facilities without the provision of necessary care) have been documented.[78] Even voluntary sector agencies have been criticized for avoiding multiproblem clients.[79]

Severe penalties should be levied against *all* private sector service providers who discriminate against clients with public sponsorship. This would be a fair price to charge proprietary firms that are profiting from human misfortune. A modest regulation that worked to spread the obligation to serve high-cost clients among all providers could correct market incentives that now tend to disadvantage providers willing to serve a disproportionate number of difficult clients. A nondiscriminatory requirement would also be important for voluntary sector agencies that profess primary concern for community welfare in order to become tax-exempt. In short, nonprofits and for-profits that demonstrate a pattern of discrimination would run the risk of losing their license or tax-exempt status.

Mandate Community Service. As a related measure, mandatory community service should be included in professional licensing standards. The state grants members of professions the exclusive right to practice their particular skills—and thereby to establish a professional monopoly—in exchange for the assurance that service to the community will be a priority in the application of their skills. For some time, the community's welfare has suffered as some professionals have used the freedom to practice as a license for personal aggrandizement. Flagrant disregard of the interests of the broader community are no less than a violation of the social contract between a profession and the state. When human service professions cease to function in the interest of society, the state reserves the authority to oblige them to do so as a condition of their exclusive right to practice. In the same manner that professional licensing authorities require continuing education as a demonstration of professional competence, mandatory community service can certify a professional's altruism.

Accordingly, a state licensing authority can require community service as a condition for licensure. The most forthright way to institute this requirement would be to append it in the form of, say, 100 hours of service in a governmental or nonprofit agency. Professionals already employed in governmental and nonprofit agencies would be exempt. Certification of having volunteered in a governmental or nonprofit agency would be verified through a form completed by an agency's personnel office. Extended beyond human services to include health, legal, and related professions, mandatory community service could assure substantial in-kind contributions to agencies serving the poor.

CONCLUSION

The social policy initiatives described in this chapter—stable incomes, community revitalization, and national service—can serve as the basis for reorganizing welfare programs in a manner that is more consistent with the American experience. These strategies recognize the influence of capitalism on the labor force and on the human-service professions. These proposals also enhance the altruistic capacity of a voluntary sector that has always played a prominent role in American culture, and these proposals acknowledge the deterioration of families and institutions, particularly in poor communities.

Instead of relying on the federal government for redress, these proposals encourage local communities to seek solutions to their own problems. Whenever possible, the revenues for these policy initiatives should be derived from restructuring existing programs and from reasonable and modest taxes on activities that are related to particular objectives. In some instances, social objectives can be achieved without increased revenues, by simply clarifying the social contract among involved parties. The result is an arrangement that is peculiarly American.

Oddly enough, this arrangement for social welfare policy may also serve as a prototype for social policy in the more established welfare states of Europe. In a provocative analysis, Scott Lash and John Urry have proposed that postmodern "disorganized" capitalism, such as that evident in the postindustrial era, requires a different form of social policy than that characteristic of the fully articulated welfare states of Northern Europe. According to Lash and Urry, the nature of future social welfare will be "less bureaucratized, more decentralized and in cases more privatized . . . as the welfare state of organized capitalism makes way for a much more varied and less centrally organized form of welfare provision in disorganized capitalism."[80] If Lash and Urry are right, the American welfare state may not be an institutional laggard but, instead, a model for future social welfare policy among the industrial nations.[81]

◆ ◆ ◆ *Discussion Questions* ◆ ◆ ◆

1. Is the welfare state in harmony with the realities of the changing political, social, and economic forces facing the United States? What is the greatest single problem facing the American welfare state. Why?

2. Describe several broad goals that the American welfare state must move toward to ensure its future viability. What new philosophical approaches, if any, should policymakers adopt in order to make the welfare state more compatible with the current realities facing the United States?

3. Of the five welfare reform principles proposed by the authors—greater productivity, strengthening of the family, increased social cohesion, community revitalization, and social choice—which, if any, are the most important and why? Are the authors' five welfare reform principles congruent with the values and ethics of professional social work practice? If not, why?

4. Which of the general welfare reform programs proposed by the authors is the most viable and why? Is significant welfare reform feasible? Why?

5. In your opinion, what programs, principles, or policies would constitute *real* welfare reform?

Notes

1. See David Stoesz and Howard Jacob Karger, *Reconstructing the American Welfare State* (Savage, MD: Rowman and Littlefield Publishers, Inc., 1992).
2. Howard Glennester and James Midgley (Eds.), *The Radical Right and the Welfare State* (London: Wheatsheaf Books, 1991).
3. See Barry Bluestone and Bennett Harrison, *The Deindustrialization of America* (New York: Basic Books, 1982); Samuel Bowles, David Gordon, and Thomas E. Weisskopf, *Beyond the Wasteland* (Garden City, NY: Anchor Press, 1983); Bennett Harrison and Barry Bluestone, *The Great U-Turn* (New York: Basic Books, 1988); Robert Reich, *Tales of a New America* (New York: Times Books, 1987); and Lester C. Thurow, *The Zero-Sum Solution* (New York: Simon and Schuster, 1985).
4. See Charles Atherton, "The Welfare State: Still on Solid Ground," *Social Service Review*, 63 (Fall 1989), pp. 167–179; and Joel Blau, "Theories of the Welfare State," *Social Service Review*, 63 (March 1989), pp. 226–237.
5. Ibid.
6. Martin Anderson, "Welfare Reform," in Peter Duignan and Alvin Rabushka (Eds.), *The United States in the 1980s* (Stanford: Hoover Institution, 1980), pp. 145–164; George Gilder, *Wealth and Poverty* (New York: Basic Books, 1981); Lawrence

Mead, *Beyond Entitlement* (New York: Free Press, 1986); and Charles Murray, *Losing Ground* (New York: Basic Books, 1984).

7. John Diggins, *The Promise of Pragmatism* (Chicago: University of Chicago Press, 1994).
8. Cornel West, *The American Evasion of Philosophy* (Madison, WI: University of Wisconsin Press, 1989), p. 239.
9. J. Kirlin and D. Marshall, "The New Politics of Entrepreneurship," in L. Lynn (Ed.), *Urban Change and Poverty* (Washington, DC: National Academy Press, 1988).
10. Bipartisan Commission on Entitlement and Tax Reform, *Interim Report to the President* (Washington, DC: Bipartisan Commission on Entitlement and Tax Reform, 1994), p. 6.
11. Lisabeth Schorr, *Within Our Reach* (New York: Anchor Press, 1988).
12. Bridgitte Berger and Peter Berger, *The War Over the Family* (Garden City, NY: Anchor Books, 1983).
13. Richard Louv, *Childhood's Future* (Boston: Houghton Mifflin, 1990).
14. Ibid.
15. Congressional Budget Office, *Current Housing Problems and Possible Federal Responses* (Washington, DC: United States Government Printing Office, 1988).
16. Jason DeParle, "Slamming the Door," *The New York Times Magazine* (October 20, 1996), p. 52.
17. Robert Reich, *The Work of Nations* (New York: Alfred A. Knopf, 1991).
18. See Charles Moskos, *A Call to National Service* (New York: Free Press, 1988); and Timothy Noah, "We Need You: National Service, An Idea Whose Time Has Come," *Washington Monthly* (November 1986), pp. 7–10.
19. David Osborne, *Laboratories of Democracy* (Cambridge, MA: Harvard Business School Press, 1988).
20. John McKnight, "Do No Harm: Policy Options that Meet Human Needs," *Social Policy*, 20 (Summer 1989), pp. 3–10.
21. D. O'Neill, "Voucher Funding of Training Programs: Evidence from the GI Bill," *Journal of Human Resources*, 12 (Fall 1977), pp. 46–51.
22. D. Rogers, R. Blendon, and T. Maloney, "Who Needs Medicaid?" *New England Journal of Medicine*, 24 (July 1, 1982), pp. 106–115.
23. Committee on Ways and Means, U.S. House of Representatives, *Overview of Entitlement Programs, 1992 Green Book* (Washington, DC: U.S. Government Printing Office, 1990).
24. David Linowes, *Privatization: Toward More Effective Government* (Washington, DC: United States Government Printing Office, 1988), p. 15.
25. J. Chubb and T. Moe, "Choice is a Panacea," *The Brookings Review* (Summer 1990), pp. 4–12.
26. E. Morley, "Patterns in the Use of Alternative Service Delivery Approaches," in *Municipal Year Book* (Washington, DC: International City Management Organization, 1989), pp. 23–42.
27. Theresa Funicello, *Tyranny of Kindness: Dismantling the Welfare System to End Poverty in America* (New York: Atlantic Monthly Press, 1993), p. 252.
28. Committee on Ways and Means, U.S. House of Representatives, *Overview of Entitlement Programs, 1990 Green Book* (Washington, DC: U.S. Government Printing Office, 1990), p. 546.
29. Reich, *The Work of Nations*.
30. Isaac Shapiro, *The Minimum Wage and Job Loss* (Washington, DC: Center on Budget and Policy Priorities, 1988), p. 13.
31. Jon Jeter, "A Rise for the Working Poor in Maryland," *Washington Post* (November 11, 1996), p. A1.
32. Congressional Budget Office, *Reducing the Deficit: Spending and Revenue Options* (Washington, DC: U.S. Government Printing Office, 1995), p. 398.
33. House Ways and Means Committee, House of Representatives, *Overview of Entitlement Programs* (Washington, DC: U.S. GPO, 1994), p. 533.
34. *Overview of Entitlement Programs*, 1990, p. 410.
35. Congressional Budget Office, *Reducing the Deficit*, 1995, p. 349.
36. See Michael Sherraden, *Stakeholding: A New Direction in Social Policy* (Washington, DC: Progressive Policy Institute, 1990); and Michael Sherraden, *Assets and the Poor* (Armonk, NY: M. E. Sharpe, 1991), p. 16.
37. Congressional Budget Office, *Reducing the Deficit*, 1995, p. 393.
38. Figures used are from Congressional Budget Office, *Reducing the Deficit*, 1991.
39. Committee on Ways and Means, U.S. House of Representatives, *Background Material and Data on Programs within the Jurisdiction of the Committee on Ways and Means, 1985 Edition* (Washington, DC: U.S. Government Printing Office, 1985), p. 261.
40. Sam Fulwood III, "Uncountable Problem at the Border," *Los Angeles Times* (May 17, 1990), p. A3.

41. Ted Conover, *Coyotes* (New York: Vintage, 1987), p. 207.
42. The need to revise immigration policy to account more adequately for undocumented workers is underlined by two developments: the proliferation of *maquiladora* plants along the U.S.–Mexico border; and the recent interest in a North American trade treaty, among the United States, Canada, and Mexico, in response to the consolidation of the European Economic Community in 1992.
43. See Melinda Beck, "Not Enough for All," *Newsweek* (May 14, 1990), p. 8; and Victor Cohn, "Rationing Our Medical Care," *Washington Post Weekly* (August 13–19, 1990), p. 26.
44. David Stoesz, "Corporate Health Care and Social Welfare," *Health and Social Work*, (Summer 1986), pp. 34–42; Eli Ginzberg, "For-profit Medicine," *New England Journal of Medicine*, (319) 12 (September 22, 1988), p. 92.
45. Alain Enthoven and Richard Kronick, "A Consumer-Choice Health Plan for the 1990s," *New England Journal of Medicine*, (320)1 (January 5, 1989), pp. 56–69.
46. Congressional Budget Office, *Reducing the Deficit*, 1995, pp. 352, 363.
47. Dana Hughes, *The Health of America's Children* (Washington, DC: Children's Defense Fund, 1987), p. 84; *Overview of Entitlement Programs*, 1994, p. 828.
48. Michael Dorris, *The Broken Cord* (New York: Harper and Row, 1989).
49. Denise Hamilton, "Crack's Children Grow Up," *Los Angeles Times* (August 24, 1990), p. D7.
50. "Drug-exposed Births Exceed 72,000 a Year," *San Diego Union* (July 14, 1990), p. A6.
51. Quoted in Howard Jacob Karger and David Stoesz, "Welfare Reform: Maximum Feasible Exaggeration?" *Tikkun*, 4 (March/April 1989), p. 121.
52. Although the Food Stamp Program is generally not considered to be an income maintenance program, it does nevertheless provide income support for working and nonworking poor families.
53. While it would be possible to obtain accurate median incomes in most regions of the United States, we recognize that certain geographical areas will have skewed incomes that will require specific adjustments to be made in the benefit formula.
54. Telephone interview with Donna DeAngeles, National Association of Social Workers, September 27, 1990.
55. The *Diagnostic and Statistical Manual III* (DSM III), used by mental health professionals, and the Diagnosis Related Group system developed by Medicare are prototypes.
56. Privately held, community-based collectives have demonstrated their superiority to governmental and corporate forms of service provision. See David Stoesz, "The Family Life Center," *Social Work*, 26 (September 1981), pp. 166–170; Jonathan Rowe, "Up from the Bedside," *American Prospect*, (Summer 1990), pp. 10–14.
57. Robert Kuttner, *The End of Laissez-faire* (New York: Alfred A. Knopf, 1991), p. 275.
58. Claude Brown, *Manchild in the Promised Land* (New York: Macmillan, 1965); Claude Brown, "Manchild in Harlem," *The New York Times* (September 16, 1984), p. F5.
59. Daniel Patrick Moynihan, *Came the Revolution* (San Diego, CA: Harcourt Brace Jovanovich, 1988), p. 291.
60. Congressional Budget Office, *Reducing the Deficit*, 1995, pp. 154, 156, 342.
61. For instance, Judith Gueron, "Work for People on Welfare," *Public Welfare*, (Winter 1986), pp. 30–41.
62. Daniel Friedlander, *Subgroup Impacts and Performance Indicators for Selected Welfare Employment Programs* (New York: Manpower Demonstration and Research Corporation, 1988).
63. Charles Moskos, *A Call to Civic Service* (New York: Free Press, 1988), p. 90.
64. William Raspberry, "Welfare's Limits," *Washington Post* (April 11, 1988), p. A15.
65. For a discussion of black flight from inner cities, see William Julius Wilson, *The Truly Disadvantaged* (Chicago: University of Chicago Press, 1987).
66. Douglas Besharov, "Contending with Overblown Expectations," *Public Welfare* (Winter 1987), p. 7.
67. Leroy Pelton, "Resolving the Crisis in Child Welfare," *Public Welfare* (Spring 1988), p. 20.
68. Larry Brown, "Questions and Answers," *Public Welfare* (Winter 1987), p. 21.
69. Lela Costin, Howard Karger, and David Stoesz, *The Politics of Child Abuse in America* (New York: Oxford University Press, 1996).
70. Pelton, "Resolving the Crisis," makes this recommendation with regard to child protective services.

71. Harley Treger, *The Police-Social Work Team* (Chicago: Jane Addams School of Social Work, 1975).
72. Progressive Policy Institute, *The Police Corps and Community Policing* (Washington, DC: Progressive Policy Institute, 1990).
73. Moskos, *Call to Civic Service*.
74. Ibid., pp. 155–160.
75. Timothy Noah, "We Need You," p. 38.
76. Moskos, *Call to Civic Service*, p. 154.
77. William Diaz, "Welfare Reform and the Capacity of Private Philanthropy," in Dwight Burlingame et al. (Eds.), *Capacity for Change? The Nonprofit World in the Age of Devolution* (Indianapolis: University of Indiana Press, 1996).
78. Stoesz, "Corporate Health Care and Social Welfare."
79. Richard Cloward and Irwin Epstein, "Private Social Welfare's Disengagement from the Poor." In Meyer Zald (Ed.), *Social Welfare Institutions* (New York: Wiley, 1965).
80. Scott Lash and John Urry, *The End of Organized Capitalism* (Oxford, England: Basil Blackwell, 1987), p. 231.
81. Christopher Pierson, "The 'Exceptional' United States: First New Nation or Last Welfare State?" *Social Policy and Administration*, 23 (November 1990), pp. 15–21.

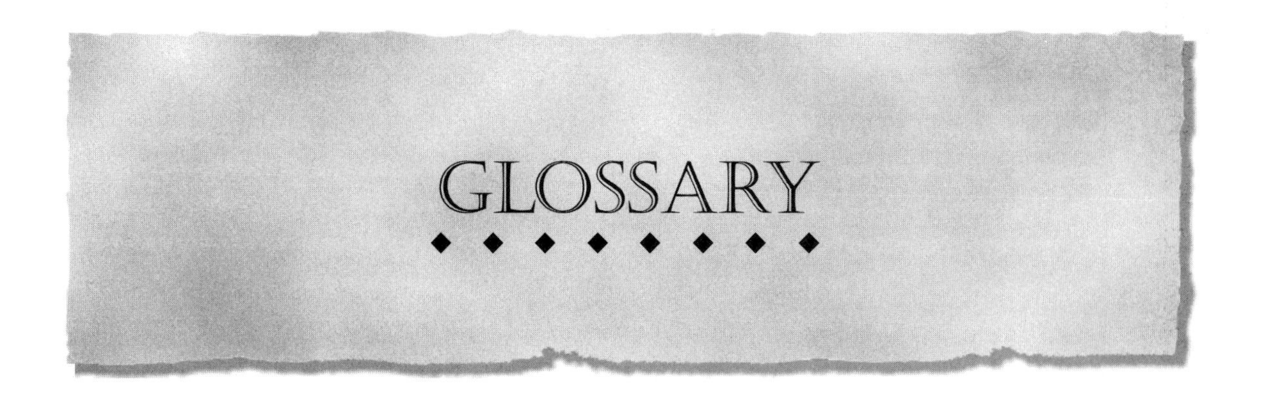

GLOSSARY

Absolute Poverty. A measurement and classification of poverty that is based on the minimal standard of living (including food, shelter, and clothing) necessary for survival.

Acute Care. A pattern of health care in which a patient is treated for an acute (immediate and severe) episode of illness.

Affirmative Action. Programs designed to redress past or present discrimination against minorities (including women) through criteria for employment, promotion, and educational opportunities that give these groups preferential access to such resources or opportunities.

Ageism. Age-based discrimination against elderly persons.

Alleviative Approach to Poverty. Strategies designed to ease the suffering of the poor rather than to eliminate the causes of poverty. Examples include AFDC, SSI, and the Food Stamps Program.

All-Payer System. The imposition of uniform prices on medical services, regardless of the payee.

Almshouse. A historic institution that was used to maintain the poor. Almshouses, or poor houses as they were sometimes called, were in common use in Great Britain and the United States from the seventeenth through the nineteenth centuries.

Ambulatory Care. Health services provided without the patient being admitted. The services of ambulatory care centers, hospital outpatient departments, physicians' offices, and home health care services fall under this heading.

Ancillary Services. Professional charges for X-ray, laboratory tests, and other similar patient services.

Area Poverty. Geographic regions that are economically depressed.

Block Grant. A method of funding social programs by which the federal government makes monies available to states for a wide range of services, including social services. Block grants usually allow states more freedom by diminishing or eliminating federal program regulations. Block grants are usually fixed in terms of the amount available.

Brown v. Board of Education of Topeka, Kansas. A 1954 landmark U.S. Supreme Court decision ruling that "separate but equal" facilities in education were inherently unequal.

Bureaucratic Disentitlement. The denial of benefits to eligible recipients by agents of public agencies.

Bureaucratic Rationality. The ordering of social affairs by governmental agencies.

Capitalism. An economic system in which most of the production and distribution of goods and services occurs under private auspices.

Capitation. The method of payment in which the provider is paid a fixed amount for each person served regardless of the actual number or nature of services delivered.

Case Management. The process by which all related matters of a case are managed by a single professional, often a social worker.

Categorical Grant. A method of funding social services through which the federal government makes available to the states monies that must be spent for very narrowly specified service needs.

Chronic Care. Long-term care of individuals with long standing, persistent diseases or conditions.

Charity Organization Society (COS). A voluntary organization active in the late nineteenth and early twentieth centuries that attempted to coordinate private charities and promote a scientific approach to philanthropy.

Chronic Unemployment. The rate of unemployment attributable to persons who have persistent trouble finding work because of an absence of low-skilled jobs or because they have severe deficiencies in basic social and work skills.

Circuit Breaker Programs. Tax rebate programs designed to relieve the low-income, elderly, or disabled homeowner or renter from the burden of property or utility taxes.

Clinical Entrepreneurs. An interest group within American social welfare that is associated with private practice and the provision of social welfare in the private marketplace.

Clinical or Critical Pathways. A "map" of preferred treatment/intervention activities.

Comprehensive Major Medical Insurance. A policy designed to provide the protection offered by both a basic and major medical health insurance policy.

Commercialization. The consequence of subjecting social welfare to the marketplace, including advertising for services, marketing services, and pricing services.

Commodification. Term describing a governmental policy that takes social needs formerly met in the public sector (e.g., health care, counseling services) and places them within the private market sector.

Commonweal. The general good, or the public welfare.

Communitarianism. The political philosophy that strives to seek a middle ground between conservatism and liberalism. Communitarians are often socially liberal, although they maintain that freedom must have it bounds. They are in favor of moral education.

Comparable Worth. The idea that workers should be paid equally when they do different types of work that require the same level of skill, education, knowledge, training, responsibility, and effort.

Conservatism. An American ideology emphasizing the role of the marketplace and the private sector in meeting both human and social welfare needs.

Corporate Sector. That part of the mixed welfare economy consisting of large, for-profit human-service corporations.

Corporate Social Responsibility. The concept that corporations should be held accountable for practices and decisions that adversely affect those communities in which they do business. In addition, corporate social responsibility refers to the responsibility of corporations to promote the general well-being of society.

Cost-of-Living Adjustments (COLAs). Adjustments designed to keep income maintenance and social insurance benefits in line with inflation. COLAs affect Food Stamps, Social Security, and SSI benefits.

Cost Shifting. Charging one group of patients more in order to make up for underpayment by others.

Culture of Poverty. Term used by a theoretical school that maintains that poverty is transmitted intergenerationally and that certain of its traits are found in diverse cultures and societies.

Curative Approach to Poverty. An approach designed to rehabilitate the poor through attacking the causes of poverty, for example, illiteracy, poor nutrition, or lack of employment.

Cyclical Unemployment. A type of unemployment attributable to swings in economic performance, such as recessions.

Decommodification. A welfare state that, through generous social programs, allows people to opt out of the labor force without a significant loss of income, jobs, or general welfare. Decommodification can also be used to categorize social programs that take needs formerly met through the marketplace (e.g., health care or personal social services) and turn them into public utilities (i.e., needs met by the public sector).

De Facto Segregation. Racial segregation that is not legally mandated by the state but that characterizes school systems and residential housing patterns.

Deinstitutionalization. Term used to describe the removal, in the late 1960s, of many mentally ill or mentally retarded patients from state institutions and their placement in community settings.

Deliberate Misdiagnosis. The intentional distortion of a diagnosis in order to avoid labeling a client or for the purpose of collecting insurance payments.

Democratic Capitalism. The type of political-economy characteristic of the United States, with a democratic polity and a capitalist economy.

Dependency Ratio. The number of workers required to pay into the Social Security system to support one retired worker living on Social Security.

Diagnostic Related Groups (DRGs). A prospective form of payment for Medicare-incurred charges. Specifically, DRGs are a classification scheme whereby hospitals are reimbursed only for the maximum number of days an illness or surgical procedure is designated to take.

Discouraged Workers. Those who have stopped seeking work out of frustration with their poor employment prospects.

Disentitlement. The removal of an entitlement status for a group of people. Specifically, the PRWOA disentitled poor beneficiaries from receiving lifetime benefits.

Donaldson v. O'Connor. The court decision ruling that mental patients could not be confined unless they were dangerous to themselves or others, and also that they should not be confined unless they are being treated and cannot survive without hospitalization.

DRG—Diagnosis Related Groups. A statistical system of classifying any inpatient stay into groups for the provider purpose of payment.

Dual Labor Market. A labor market divided into two classes of workers. See Primary Labor Market and Secondary Labor Market.

Durable Medical Equipment. Items of medical equipment owned or rented that are placed in the home of an insured to facilitate treatment and/or rehabilitation.

Earned Income Tax Credits. A federal program that functions somewhat like a negative income tax. Specifically, qualified working families or single people receive a tax rebate from the federal government that exceeds the taxes they paid.

Electronic Benefit Transfers (EBT). The attempt by the federal government to use technology in the delivery of benefits. This can include automatically depositing public assistance benefits into the savings accounts of recipients, the use of debit cards in food stamp benefits, and so forth.

Emergency Assistance Funds. Special needs payments that can be made under the AFDC program for extraordinary needs such as homelessness prevention, fuel or utility bills, and burial.

Emergency Assistance Program. A program that operates under AFDC and is intended to provide short-term cash assistance to families in crisis.

Employee Assistance Programs. Social services provided by companies for their employees in recognition that many personal problems are either directly related to, or have impact upon, the workplace.

Employee Retirement Income Security Act of 1974—(ERISA). Also called the Pension Reform Act, this act regulates the majority of private pension and welfare group benefit plans in the United States.

Entitlements. Governmental resources (cash or in-kind) to which certain groups are entitled, based on their ability to meet the established criteria. Entitlement programs have open-ended resources in that people cannot be denied benefits because of governmental resource constraints.

Equal Rights Amendment (ERA). An act that if passed would give women the same rights under the law as men.

Establishment of Paternity. Policies that require unwed mothers to identify the fathers of their children in order to aid states in their efforts to collect child support.

Exclusive Provider Organization (EPO). Similar to a Prospective Provider Organization (PPO) in that it often uses primary care physicians as gatekeepers. It is "exclusive" because the member must remain within a limited network to receive benefits.

Family Cap. Usually refers to the policy that recipient mothers will not receive any (or only partial) benefits for any children born while they are on public assistance.

Fee-For-Service. A method of reimbursement based on payment for services rendered. Payment may be made by an insurance company, the patient, or a government program such as Medicare or Medicaid.

Feminization of Poverty. A social trend marked by the increasing frequency of poverty among women. It is thought to be related to the high incidence of women relying on governmental aid, the low wages that characterize traditional female employment, occupational segregation, and family decomposition (divorce, desertion, or death).

Fill-the-Gap. An AFDC benefit method used by some states in which countable income (i.e., labor market income) does not result in a dollar-for-dollar reduction in the AFDC payment a family receives.

Freedmen's Bureau. An agency set up by the U.S. government after the Civil War to ease the transition of African Americans from slavery to freedom. Formally called the Bureau of Refugees, Freedmen, and Abandoned Lands.

Frictional Unemployment. The rate of unemployment, usually about 3 percent, considered inevitable for a viable economy.

Functional Welfare. A social welfare-related concept that holds that social service benefits should be justified in relation to productivity. Usually a standard of conforming conduct is required on the part of recipients in exchange for benefits.

FY (Fiscal Year). A term used by government and social service agencies in reference to a budgetary rather than a normal year. Fiscal years often begin on July 1 rather than January 1.

Gatekeeper. A primary care physician responsible for overseeing and coordinating all aspects of a patient's medical care. In order for a patient to receive a specialty care or hospital admission, the gatekeeper must preauthorize the visit.

General Assistance. State or locally run programs designed to provide basic benefits to low-income people who are ineligible for federally funded public assistance programs.

Gentrification. Resettlement of existing low-income neighborhoods by middle- and upper-class homeowners or investors. This development can result in forcing poor and indigenous residents out of their neighborhoods.

Global Budget. Refers to the institution of a regional or nationwide cap on private and public health care spending.
Governmental Sector. That part of the mixed welfare economy consisting of social programs administered by government, particularly the federal government.
Great Society. Formerly called the War on Poverty, the Great Society comprehended a series of social welfare programs (including community development, training and employment, and health and legal services) enacted between 1963 and 1968 during the administration of President Lyndon Baines Johnson.
Greening/Greens. An environmental orientation to social policy. Greening often incorporates an environmental awareness with a social justice perspective.
Gross Domestic Product (GDP). A measure of the total output of goods and services produced by a country's economy.
Gross National Product (GNP). A measure of the total domestic and foreign output claimed by residents of a country. It is made up of the Gross Domestic Product (GDP) and of incomes accruing to foreign residents.
Halderman v. Pennhurst. The court decision ruling that institutionalized patients were entitled to treatment in the least restrictive environment.
Health Care Access. The patient's ability to obtain medical care. Access is determined by the availability of medical services, the location of health care facilities, transportation, hours of operation cost of care, and so forth.
Health Insurance Purchasing Cooperative (HIPC). A government or quasi-government entity established to purchase bulk health insurance for businesses and individuals.
Health Maintenance Organizations (HMOs). Membership organizations that typically provide comprehensive health care. Members usually pay a regular fee and are thus entitled to free (or minimal-cost) hospital care and physicians' services.
Home Health Care. Full range of medical and other health related services such as physical therapy, nursing, counseling, and social services that are delivered in the home of a patient by a provider.
Homework. An economic system of production in common use during the late nineteenth and early twentieth centuries in which workers were paid on a piecework basis for work done at home. This system was frequently used in the garment trades.
Homophobia. The fear of (and subsequent discrimination against) homosexuals on the basis of their sexual preference.
Housing Starts. Number of new houses begun in a given period.
Housing Stock. The number of currently available houses.
Human Capital. Productive investments that are embodied in humans. These include education, training, skills, experience, knowledge, and health. Increases in human capital result from expenditures on education, job training, and medical care.
Human-Service Executives. An interest group within American social welfare that is associated with human-service corporations and advocates the provision of social welfare through large-scale for-profit programs.
Human Services. A recent concept equivalent to social welfare.
Iatrogenic Diseases. Diseases that are directly caused by medical intervention.
Ideological State Apparatus. The means (i.e., education, the print media, the family, television, and tradition) by which the primary ideology of a society is promulgated and maintained.
Ideology. A set of socially sanctioned assumptions, usually unexamined, explaining how the world works and encompassing a society's general methods for addressing social problems.
Income Distribution. The pattern of how income is distributed among the various socioeconomic classes in a society.
Income Inequality. The unequal distribution of income across socioeconomic classes.
Income Maintenance Programs. Social welfare programs designed to contribute to or supplement the income of an individual or family. These programs are usually means-tested and thus based on need.
Indian Child Welfare Act of 1978. Legislation that restored child-placement decisions to the individual tribes.
Individual Development Accounts. Savings accounts designed and subsidized by individual states which allow low-income people to amass assets that can be used for specific purposes such as home purchase, education, and starting a small business.
Indoor Relief. A historic term used to designate relief services offered in an institutional setting.
In-Kind. Noncash goods or services provided by the government that function as a proxy for cash, for example, Food Stamps, Section 8 housing vouchers, and Medicare.
Inpatient Care. Care given in a hospital, nursing home, or other medical institution.
Institutional Welfare. A conception of welfare holding that governmental social programs that assure citizens of their basic needs (for food, housing, education, income, employment, and health) are essential to an

advanced economy. Such programs are considered a right of citizenship.

Job-Lock. Individuals' inability to change jobs because they would lose crucial health benefits

Job Opportunities and Basic Skills (JOBS). This program was created in the Family Support Act of 1988. The bill required a portion of a state's welfare caseload (usually AFDC mothers) to participate in a work or training program.

Keynesian Economics. An economic school that proposes government intervention in the economy through such activities as social welfare programs to stimulate and regulate economic growth.

Liberalism. A primary American ideology that advocates government intervention in the market in order to ensure the provision of basic goods, services, and rights to disenfranchised populations who are otherwise unable to obtain them.

Liberation Theology. A theological school, most often associated with Roman Catholicism, that argues for a stronger connection between religious dogma and social justice. Liberation theology has been especially successful in developing countries in South and Central America and in Africa.

Libertarians. A small but influential group that advocates more individual responsibility and a very limited role for government in social and economic affairs.

Licensed Certified Social Worker. A social worker holding the Master of Social Work degree who has practiced for two years under supervision and who has passed an examination. Twenty-nine states license social workers.

Managed Care. A loose umbrella term for the organization of networks of health care providers (e.g., doctors, clinics, and hospitals) into a system that is cost-effective. Institutions or individual health care providers who are in managed care systems agree to accept set fees for each service or flat payments per patient. HMOs are one example of managed care.

Managed Competition. A hybrid health care system based on free-market forces and governmental regulation in which health care is organized to encourage competition among health care providers. Specifically, employers and other consumers form large purchasing networks that accept bids for health care from HMOs or other health plans. The competition among health care providers for contracts is intended to foster quality and lower costs.

Manpower Development and Research Corporation (MDRC). The MDRC is a well-known research organization that has done significant studies in various areas of social welfare policy. MDRC is best known for its research and demonstration projects in the area of workfare.

Market Rationality. The ordering of human affairs by corporate institutions within the marketplace.

Means Test. Income and asset tests designed to determine whether an individual or household meets the economic criteria necessary for receiving governmental cash transfers or in-kind services.

Medigap. Private health insurance plans that supplement Medicare benefits by covering some costs not paid for by Medicare

Milford Conference Report. An important report issued in 1923 that addressed professional social work issues.

Milliken v. Brady. A 1974 U.S. Supreme Court decision that ruled that school busing across city-suburban boundaries to achieve integration was not required unless the segregation had resulted from official action.

Mixed Welfare Economy. An economy in which governmental, private nonprofit, and private for-profit providers of social welfare coexist within the same society.

National Association of Social Workers (NASW). The major national organization of professional social workers.

National Health Insurance. Various insurance-based proposals that incorporate comprehensive health coverage for the entire nation.

Neoconservatism. A recent American ideology, based on conservatism, that recognizes the necessity for social welfare but designs social programs so that they are compatible with the requirements of a market economy and traditional values.

Neoliberalism. A recent American ideology, based on liberalism, that assumes that universal social programs, such as those advanced by liberals, are implausible because of current social, political, and economic limitations. Neoliberals opt for more modest changes in social welfare programs.

New Deal. The name given to the massive Depression-era social and economic programs initiated under the presidency of Franklin Delano Roosevelt.

NGO. A nongovernmental organization (private or voluntary) that plans, delivers, or funds social services.

Occupational Segregation. The domination of low-wage sectors of the labor market by a minority group. For example, women are thought to be occupationally segregated in "pink-collar" jobs, as secretaries, receptionists, typists, and so forth.

Office of Economic Opportunity (OEO). The federal agency that was charged with the responsibility for designing and implementing the Great Society programs.

Oligopolization. The process through which a small number of organizations effectively control a market.
Omnibus Budget Acts. Inclusive budgets passed by Congress.
Outdoor Relief. A historic term used to designate relief services offered in the home of a client.
Pay-Go. A system for determining federal budgetary allocations that emerged out of the 1991 Omnibus Budget Reconciliation Act. In short, funding for any new program (or enhanced funding for an existing program) must come from reallocating existing money.
Per Capita Income. A determination of income based on dividing the total household income by the number of family members.
Permanency Planning. A strategy for helping foster children to live in families that offer continuity of relationships and the opportunity to establish lifetime relationships.
Personal Social Services. A term most often used by the British to denote social services that are delivered on a face-to-face basis (e.g., counseling and rehabilitation services).
Personal Responsibility and Work Opportunity Reconciliation Act of 1996 (PRWOA). Passed in 1996, the PRWOA is a comprehensive act that created the TANF program, limited benefits to both legal and illegal immigrants, changed the qualifications for SSI, and established the precedent that government no longer had the responsibility for maintaining the poor indefinitely. In effect, it disentitled the poor from income support programs.
Play-or-Pay. A proposed health insurance plan in which employers would either provide their employees with *private* health insurance or be forced to pay into a government pool whose funds would be used to provide health coverage for otherwise noncovered citizens.
Plessy v. Ferguson. The 1896 U.S. Supreme Court decision that formally established the "separate but equal" doctrine in race relations.
Pluralism. The character, climate, or practices of a heterogeneous society in which many competing interest groups help to shape social policies.
Policy Framework. A systematic process for examining a specific policy or a set of policies.
Political Action Committees (PACs). Organizations, usually associated with special interest groups, that divert campaign contributions to candidates running for public office in order to influence their later decisions on public policy.
Political Economy. The blending of economic analysis with practical politics. In effect, political economy views economic activity within a political context.
Political Practice. A method of social work practice by which social workers advance their priorities either by assisting those in political office or by running for office themselves.
Poverty Line. A yearly cash income threshold (based on family size) set by the federal government to determine if an individual or household can be classified as poor. Sometimes called the poverty threshold or poverty index.
Policy Institute. A private organization, funded by contributions and government contracts, that researches social problems and proposes social policies.
Posttransfer Poor. The individuals or families who remain under the poverty line even after receipt of public assistance.
Preexisting Condition. A physical condition of an insured person that existed prior to the issuance of his/her policy or his/her enrollment in a health plan.
Preferential Selection. The selection of clients for treatment according to the organizational needs of the provider as opposed to the needs of the client; usually used to describe the practice of private providers who prefer insured clients with less severe problems.
Pretransfer Poor. Individuals or households who are under the poverty line *before* receiving public assistance funds.
Preventive Approach to Poverty. Social welfare strategies (e.g., social insurance programs) designed to prevent people from becoming poor.
Preventive Commitment. The institutionalization of persons who do not meet the requirements for involuntary hospitalization but who are likely to deteriorate without inpatient care.
Primary Care. Basic or general health care rendered by general practitioners, family practitioners, internists, obstetricians, and pediatricians.
Primary Labor Market. The full-time jobs that provide workers with an adequate salary, a career track, and benefits.
Primary Prevention. Efforts designed to eliminate the causes of social problems.
Private Practice. The provision of clinical services through the marketplace by individual practitioners or small groups of practitioners.
Privatization. The ownership or management of social services by the private sector, either nonprofit agencies or proprietary corporations. Privatization of public assistance refers to attempts by individual states to have for-profit corporations manage the delivery of their public assistance benefits.
Professional Monopoly. The right to exclusive practice granted an occupational group in exchange for its promise to hold the welfare of the entire community as its ultimate concern.

Progressive Movement. A social movement popular in the United States from the late 1800s to World War I. Progressives stressed the need for morality, ethics, and honesty in all social, political, and economic affairs. This movement advocated numerous progressive reforms. It was also successful in establishing progressive legislation, including the progressive income tax.

Proprietary. A social welfare organization that provides services on a for-profit basis.

Prospective Payment System (PPS). A payment method that establishes rates, prices, or budgets before services are rendered and costs are incurred.

Prospective Provider Organization (PPO). PPOs use primary care physicians as gatekeepers and are often a part of managed care.

Public Choice School. A school of political-economy that suggests that because interest group demands inevitably lead to budget deficits, government should therefore limit concessions to these groups as much as possible.

Public Policy. Policies designed by government that contain a goal, a purpose, and an objective. Public policy may also incorporate a standing plan of action toward a specific goal.

Public Transfer Programs. Programs such as AFDC, SSI, and Social Security that transfer money from the governmental sector to families or individuals who are either entitled to it or who have earned it.

Quangos. Quasi-governmental organizations that have some affiliation with government but that are predominately private.

Race to the Bottom. This refers to the incentives that states have under TANF block grant guidelines to provide the lowest and most restrictive forms of public welfare assistance.

Racism. Discrimination against or prejudicial treatment of a racially different group.

Radical Social Work. Adherents believe that the political-economy is incapable of incremental reform and that the system must be challenged through various means to advance social justice.

Rationalization. Measures designed to make an organization or agency as efficient and cost-effective as possible.

Redlining. In the area of housing, the refusal of mortgage or insurance companies to provide services in selected neighborhoods thought to be high-risk areas for defaults or excessive claims.

Reciprocity. The requirement that a specific activity or standard of conduct be demonstrated in order for a client to obtain welfare benefits.

Relative Poverty. A measurement and classification of poverty that is based on and related to the standard of living enjoyed by other members of a society.

Repressive State Apparatus. The set of societal institutions—the police, courts, jails—that intervene to control dissidents when they threaten social stability.

Residual Welfare. A conception of welfare holding that the family and the market are the individual's primary sources of assistance, but that governmental "safety-net" programs may provide temporary help.

Secondary Labor Market. Jobs that are characterized by irregular, seasonal, or part-time employment and that pay relatively low hourly wages, provide no benefits, and offer no career track.

Secondary Prevention. Early detection and intervention to keep incipient problems from becoming more debilitating.

Self-Reliance School. A relatively new school of political-economy advocating low-technology and local solutions to social problems.

Settlement Houses. Organizations that began in the late nineteenth century as an attempt to bridge the class differences marking American society. Based on the residence of middle-class volunteers in immigrant neighborhoods, settlement houses emphasized the provision of social services as well as reform activities.

Sexism. Discrimination against women based solely on their gender. Sexism can also be directed at men.

Single-Payer System. A centralized system of health care payment in which the government assumes the costs (but not the delivery) for health services. People choose their doctor and hospital, and the government pays the bill according to a fixed-fee schedule. Coverage is often universal and is rights-based rather than employment-based. Canada is the best-known example of a single-payer system.

Single Spigot. Synonymous with a single-payer system in which one governmental authority is responsible for reimbursing health care providers.

Social Darwinism. The application of Charles Darwin's theories on the laws of nature (i.e., the survival of the fittest) to thinking about human society. Two of its main proponents were Herbert Spencer and William Graham Sumner.

Social Gospel Movement. A progressive movement in late nineteenth- and early twentieth-century America that attempted to merge Christianity with a concern for social justice.

Social Insurance. A system that compels individuals to insure themselves against the possibility of indigence.

Similar to private insurance, social insurance programs set aside a sum of money that is held in trust by the government to be used in the event of a worker's death, retirement, disability, or unemployment. Individuals are entitled to social insurance benefits on the basis of their previous contributions to the system.

Socialism. A school of political-economy that attributes the need for social welfare to the social problems caused by capitalism. Socialists advocate restructuring the political-economy—in the American case, capitalism—as the most direct way of promoting social welfare.

Social Justice. Connotes equity and fairness in all areas of social, political, and economic life, as well as the provision of basic necessities to all without regard to their participation in the market, an objective of liberals and progressives.

Social Services. Programs designed to increase human capital by ameliorating problems in psychosocial functioning, providing necessary goods and services outside normal market mechanisms, and providing cash supplements for the lack of market income.

Social Stratification. The vertical segmentation of the population according to income, occupation, and status.

Social Wage. A term used to refer to the additional "wage" a worker receives as part of the universal benefits paid out by a welfare state (e.g., health care coverage or housing loans).

Social Welfare Policy. The regulation of the provision of benefits to people who require assistance in meeting their basic life needs, such as for employment, income, food, health care, and relationships.

Sociopolitical Planning. Methods for anticipating program needs that are interactive, involving groups likely to be affected by a program.

Spells of Poverty. Periods of time (often limited) in which individuals or families fall below the poverty line.

Standardization. The reduction of services to a common denominator in order to lower provider costs.

Structural Unemployment. The rate of unemployment attributable to long-lasting and deep maladjustments in the labor market.

Supply-Side Economics. A school of political-economy that proposes reductions in social programs so that tax dollars can be reinvested in the private sector to capitalize economic growth.

Sustainable Development. A theory that stresses the need to develop an appropriate balance between material needs and future resource availability. It calls for a form of balanced economic development.

Swann v. Charlotte-Mecklenburg Board of Education. A 1971 U.S. Supreme Court ruling that approved court-ordered busing to achieve racial integration in school districts with a history of discrimination.

Tardive Dyskinesia. Permanent damage to the central nervous system, evidenced by involuntary movements, caused by psychotropic medication.

Technomethodological Planning. Methods of anticipating program requirements using data bases from which projections of future program needs can be derived.

Temporary Aid to Needy Families (TANF). TANF was included as part of the Personal Responsibility and Work Opportunity Reconciliation Act (PRWOA) and is a replacement for the AFDC program. It is a block grant program based on workfare, time-limited benefits (a maximum of five years), and strict work participation rates. The TANF program was instituted in 1996.

Tertiary Prevention. Efforts to limit the effects of a disorder after it has become manifest.

Think Tank. Popular name for a policy institute.

Time Limits. The length of time a recipient (or a recipient's family) is allowed to remain on welfare. The federal government has instituted a five-year lifetime cap on benefits; several states have set shorter caps.

Total Quality Management (TQM). An operations management technique of using all employees to define production/service processes and improve output quality and cost effectiveness.

Traditionalism. A social movement that gained increased strength during the 1970s. Traditionalists seek to make social policy conform with their conservative social and religious values.

Traditional Providers. An interest group within American social welfare associated with voluntary nonprofit agencies that promotes local institutions as a preferred method of solving social problems.

Usual, Customary, and Reasonable (UCR). That fee established by a majority of practitioners in a given community for a given procedure. The UCR is defined by insurance companies to determine the proper level of payment for covered procedures.

Underclass. The lowest socioeconomic group in society, characterized by chronic poverty; that is, its members are poor regardless of the economic circumstances in the society at large.

Underemployed. Individuals who are working at jobs in which their skills are far above those required for the position. It may also refer to those who are employed part-time when their desire is to be employed full-time.

Unemployment. The condition of individuals over 16 years of age who are looking for work.

Voluntary Sector. That part of the mixed welfare economy consisting of private, nonprofit agencies.

Vouchers. A system of government-issued coupons that allows lower income consumers to choose freely between various services, often including education, social services, and other benefits.

War on Poverty. See Great Society.

Welfare Behaviorism. Refers to the attempts of public officials to modify the behavioral patterns (through instituting specific social policies) of low-income people, especially beneficiaries.

Welfare Bureaucrats. Interest groups within American social welfare associated with governmental social programs that advocate the provision of social welfare through large-scale public social programs.

Welfare Capitalism. An advanced system of social welfare existing in progressive capitalist countries.

Welfare Dependency. The economic dependence of a family or individual on the provision of governmental welfare services, especially cash grants.

Welfare State. A welfare state is one in which the national government ensures essential goods, services, and opportunities to residents as a right of citizenship.

Welfare State Exceptionalism. A term often used to characterize the U.S. welfare system and the differences between it and other welfare states, especially those of Western Europe.

Workfare. A system begun in the late 1960s whereby AFDC or AFDC-UP recipients were required either to work or to receive work training (sometimes in the form of higher education). The concept of workfare underlies the welfare reform bills passed in 1988 and in 1996.

Work Participation Rates. This refers to the percentage of individuals on public assistance that states are required to have in the workforce under TANF guidelines.

Working Poor. Those families or individuals who are in the work force (full- or part-time) but who are still at or below the poverty line.

Worthy Poor. A term sometimes used in reference to groups of people who are poor through no fault of their own—for instance, the handicapped, children, and widows—and are thus thought deserving of charity. Conversely, the unworthy poor are those people who are able-bodied—vagrants, the idle, drunkards—but who refuse to work. This classification formed part of the basis of the English Poor Laws of 1601 and can still be seen in modern social policies.

Wyatt v. Stickney. The court decision requiring states to provide adequate levels of treatment to hospitalized mental patients.

YAVIS Syndrome. The tendency of clinicians to prefer clients who are Young, Attractive, Verbal, Intelligent, and Successful.

INDEX